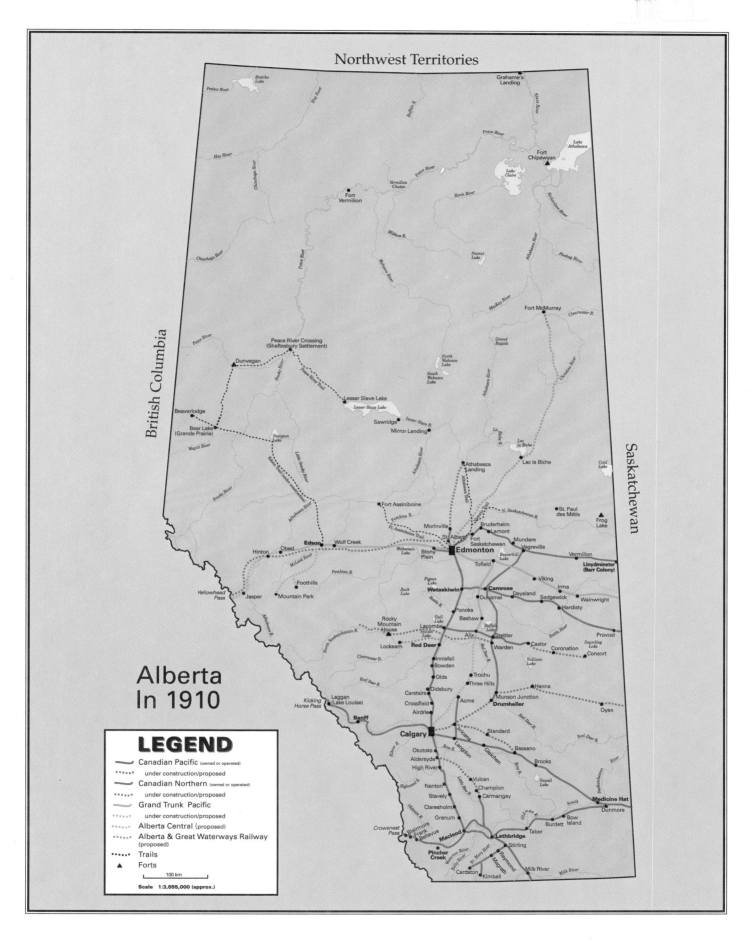

Alberta
In 1910

LEGEND

———	Canadian Pacific (owned or operated)
••••••	under construction/proposed
———	Canadian Northern (owned or operated)
••••••	under construction/proposed
———	Grand Trunk Pacific
••••••	under construction/proposed
••••••	Alberta Central (proposed)
••••••	Alberta & Great Waterways Railway (proposed)
▪▪▪▪▪	Trails
▲	Forts

100 km

Scale   1:3,655,000 (approx.)

Northwest Territories

British Columbia

Saskatchewan

ALBERTA IN THE 20TH CENTURY

A JOURNALISTIC HISTORY OF THE PROVINCE IN TWELVE VOLUMES

VOLUME TWO

THE BIRTH OF THE PROVINCE

United Western Communications Ltd.
Edmonton
1992

Consultative Committee: Donald M. Graves, a Calgary businessman; Hugh A. Dempsey, curator emeritus of the Glenbow-Alberta Institute in Calgary; Brock Silversides, photo archivist, Edmonton; Martin Lynch of Kaslo, BC, former chief of the copy desk of the Globe and Mail; Richard D. McCallum, president of Quality Color Press Inc. of Edmonton; Robert E. Klappstein, former high school principal, New Sarepta, Alberta.

Editor: Ted Byfield
Managing Editor: Richard Dolphin
Designer and photo editor: John Zacharias

Writers
Ted Byfield
Terry Johnson
Robert Collins
Courtney Tower
Larry Collins
Janice Tyrwhitt
Link Byfield
Robert Bott
Hugh A. Dempsey
Carol Dean
Virginia Byfield
Geoffrey Shaw
Stephani Keer
Brian Hutchinson
George Oake
Victoria Maclean
Calvin Demmon
Mary Frances Doucedame
George Koch

Supervisor of Research: Kathleen Wall

Researchers
Joel Witten
Colby Cosh
Greg Amerongen
Rod Frey
Valeri Jobson
Fia Jampolsky

Proofreader: Gillian Neelands

Lithographer: BK Trade Colour Separations Ltd.

Editorial Assistant: Yvonne Chan

Printer: Quality Color Press Inc., Edmonton

The publisher gratefully acknowledges the generous assistance of the Glenbow-Alberta Institute of Calgary, the Provincial Archives of Alberta in Edmonton, the National Archives of Canada and the Library of Parliament in Ottawa.

The Birth of the Province

© Copyright 1992 United Western Communications Ltd.

(Alberta in the 20th Century; v. 2)
Includes bibliographical references and index
ISBN 0-9695718-1-X

Second Printing

1. Northwest, Canadian — History — 1870-1905
2. Alberta, District of (Alta.) — History
3. Alberta — History, 1905-1945. I. Byfield, Ted
II. United Western Communications. III. Series.

FC3672.B57   1991   971.23   C93-091013-3
F1078.B57   1992

Alberta in the 20th Century

Table of Contents

Section Five LIFE IN A NEW PROVINCE

Section Six THE CRISIS AT THE END OF THE DECADE

The Cover Photograph: *The new Alberta Legislature towers above old Fort Edmonton in an Ernest Brown photograph believed to have been taken just outside the range of this volume in about 1912. Courtesy of the Provincial Archives of Alberta, B-6635.*

List of Maps

Foreword

People who write history are something like the time travellers of science fiction. They go back to another age, and immerse themselves inside it so wholly that they begin to live in that period. Its celebrities, its politicians, its problems, its issues, even its humour and pathos, acquire for them a certain eerie immediacy. They find themselves taking sides, favouring some of the characters and opposing others, familiarizing themselves with the people, the towns and the landscapes, much as though they lived there.

Working simultaneously for the last six months as a political columnist and as a writer of popular history, I find I have had two prime ministers — one named Mulroney and the other named Laurier. The fact that both were dependent on their Quebec caucus, and had to somehow reconcile it with their western one, intensifies this schizophrenia. At the same time I have been following the departure of two premiers — Donald Getty and Alexander Cameron Rutherford — each of whose governments made large loans to doubtful business enterprises with disappointing results.

In one respect, however, the two eras differ significantly. In our own, the 1990s, most of us do not seem altogether sure why we're in this world and what we're supposed to do about it. This uncertainty bewilders us and afflicts everything we do. But for the Albertans of the century's first decade there was no doubt at all about such things. They knew why they were here, and what they were supposed to do, and they did it.

This attitude of unquestioning purpose and amazingly steady resolve pervades the whole first decade. Most obviously, of course, it spurs the settlers. It brought them here to begin with, and it drives them through what must have seemed insurmountable difficulties. But it is evident in everything else as well: in medicine, in sports, in the paintings and the music of the time, and in the photography, in the schools, in the labour unions and in every business venture. The preachers have it, and the politicians have it, even the drinkers have it, and the women have it in particular.

For this is pre-eminently the decade of the Alberta woman. Pedants will see the '60s, '70s and '80s as the great era of female emancipation. In fact the real change in public attitude occurred much earlier, in an age when rights and recognition were not bestowed by statute but earned by sacrifice. Woman was the soul of every household and the miracle worker of every farm, and her amazing performance over those ten terrible and triumphant years brought female suffrage to the West before it appeared anywhere else in the country. That she, who had done so much, so well, so consistently, should be denied the vote seemed to almost everyone preposterous.

We would lose this pioneer fervour, of course. No doubt we had to. Only for so long can human societies sustain such a passion to forge, create and develop. It would begin to die in the decade that followed, along with many other things, in the slimy trenches of the Somme and in the casualty lists from Vimy Ridge. More of it would slip away in the years ahead as we confronted the hard realities of economics, finding that we must be traders on the markets of the world, but that most of the factors determining our success or failure were far beyond our reach. We could no more control international markets for grain than we could control the weather, and we were vitally dependent on both.

Yet times of great human accomplishment endure, for they have two functions for a society. First they serve as a trigger, they start things going. And just as important, they serve as a model. They lay down the foundation, set the tone, establish an identity. So much of history, say the sceptics, is mere folklore. What do they mean, "mere?"

When a Galician farmer trudges with his family for four days across a trackless prairie, finds the survey stake he has been looking for, and falls on his knees weeping, and kisses the land because for the first time he owns some, he is telling us what it means to be a farmer.

When a child's arm has been mangled in a binder, and his mother takes needle and thread and coolly and successfully sews it back together again, she is telling us what it means to be a mother.

When a knock comes on the door of a snow-swept cabin, where a woman and her children have seen no one else for weeks, and she opens it in the howling wind and finds an ice-encrusted man standing there, who says, "Mounted Police, ma'am — Everything out here okay? — We're just making the rounds," he is showing us what it means to be a policeman.

When a doctor races his buggy for hours across a prairie to a fly-infested hovel, scrapes the green slime from the slough to find water to boil his instruments, and delivers a healthy baby for a mother who lives, he is telling us what practising medicine is all about.

And when all these and hundreds of other such stories are put together into one comprehensive whole, they are showing us what it means to be an Albertan.

So it's all folklore. Let's hope so, and let's pray that this volume contributes to it in some small way. For without folklore, without a common tradition upon which we all stand, neither this province nor this country has any chance whatever of living through another century.

Ted Byfield,
Nov. 20, 1992

How Volume II Was Produced

Work began on Volume II of the series, *Alberta in the 20th Century,* in May, 1992, and the first printing took place in January of 1993.

Volume II confronted us with certain problems not encountered in the production of Volume I.

For one, we were able in the first volume to use the reporting and editing staff of *Alberta Report* newsmagazine which cancelled every second edition during the summer of 1991 to make possible the history project. This year the editions were not cancelled and we did not have this advantage. As a result other writers were recruited to the task, and we are very pleased with the work they have done.

For another, Volume I covers the period prior to 1900. Since no province of Alberta existed at that time, the volume necessarily concerned the Canadian West as a whole, and the amount of published material available was great. Volume II, however, concentrates almost entirely on Alberta itself where the range of published material is slimmer and we were far more dependent on original documents.

In producing it, however, we became aware of the profound debt all Albertans owe to those who could be called our pioneer popular historians. The work of James G. MacGregor, twenty books in all, gives the province a rich historical storehouse, whose value is only beginning to dawn upon us. Along with MacGregor must be placed the names of three others — Grant MacEwan, James H. Gray and Hugh Dempsey — who have all contributed mightily to the treasury, as have the delightful stories of Tony Cashman and Max Foran.

Behind these stand what could be called our academic historians — Cecil Lingard, the mighty Thomases, Lewis G. and Lewis H. (who are not related), Howard Palmer, David Hall, Ronald C. MacLeod, and many others in our faculties of history, without whose work such a book as this could not be undertaken.

We are indebted, too, to other Albertans. To Richard McCallum and Quality Color Press in Edmonton whose technical advice brought the costs within feasibility, for the art direction of John Zacharias of BK Trade Color, to provincial photo archivist Brock Silversides, to June Honey of the Edmonton City Archives, to the staff of the Glenbow Museum, to George Milner who put the index together, and in particular to Ric Dolphin, whose work for six crucial weeks as managing editor turned the manuscripts into the book you are now holding.

Finally, we must thank Hugh Dempsey, Martin Lynch and Bob Klappstein for the indispensable verification work they contributed, and above all the Glenbow Museum and the Provincial Archives of Alberta who have preserved our past for this and a thousand other projects like it.

To all these and to hundreds of others who helped out, our sincere thanks for a project we hope will have lasting value for all Albertans.

UNITED WESTERN COMMUNICATIONS LTD.

List of Contributors for Volume II

Robert Bott is a Calgary-based writer, editor and communications consultant who specializes in energy, forestry and environmental issues. His published works include *Mileposts*, the history of Interprovincial Pipe Line Ltd., and *A Place of Vision*, a coffee-table book about the University of Calgary.

Link Byfield has been editor of *Alberta Report* since 1990 and publisher since 1985. He grew up in rural Manitoba and joined *Alberta Report* as an agriculture reporter in 1978.

Ted Byfield is the founder of *Alberta Report, Western Report* and *British Columbia Report* news-magazines. After seventeen years on daily newspapers, he helped found the St. John's Boys' Schools in Manitoba and Alberta where he taught history for ten years. He started *St. John's Edmonton Report*, the ancestor of *Alberta Report*, in 1973.

Virginia Byfield is a senior editor of *Alberta Report* newsmagazine who in a twenty-year career has edited its political, educational, cultural and religious departments.

Larry Collins taught high school in Saskatchewan and Alberta before joining the *Edmonton Journal* as a reporter in 1955. Since 1972, he has been a freelance writer.

Robert Collins was raised in rural Saskatchewan and has been staff writer with *Maclean's* and *Reader's Digest*, editor of *Toronto Life* and *Imperial Oil Review*, and has published twelve books including the best-selling *Butter Down The Well*. He is completing another on his forty years in journalism.

Carol Dean is an Edmonton freelance writer who for eighteen years has covered local and provincial politics for weekly newspapers and magazines.

Calvin Demmon, who served as a writer and later as editor for *Edmonton Report* (*Alberta Report's* predecessor) during its first five years, is currently a columnist for the *Monterey Herald* in California.

Hugh Dempsey is a well-known western historian. He is chief curator emeritus of the Glenbow Museum in Calgary and has written several books on Indians and the history of Alberta.

Mary Frances Doucedame is a freelance writer living in Los Angeles who served for five years as a staff writer on *Alberta Report* newsmagazine. Born in Winnipeg, she is a graduate in history from the Sorbonne, Paris.

Brian Hutchinson, a Calgary freelance writer, was a senior editor at *Alberta Report* magazine until December, 1991. He obtained an honours degree in history from Carleton University in 1989.

Terry Johnson is a senior editor for *Alberta Report* newsmagazine. He has also worked as a reporter and editor on weekly newspapers in Alberta and BC and was a host of the Vancouver Co-op Radio show "Union Made."

Stephani Keer was born in Calgary and has lived there most of her life. She is associate editor of the *Calgary Sun*, and writes columns on politics and religion.

George Koch is a graduate in philosophy from the University of Alberta and in journalism from the University of Western Ontario, who covered the Alberta Legislature in Edmonton and parliament in Ottawa for *Alberta Report* newsmagazine and is now a freelance writer in Calgary.

Victoria Maclean made her own epic journey west from Ontario in 1973. She observed the '80s from the vantage point of the *St. Albert Gazette* and the '90s on the *Edmonton Sun*, where she serves as associate editor.

George R. Oake is a born and bred Albertan. He is the *Toronto Star's* western bureau chief and dedicates his chapter on newspapers to the memory of his mother, Alberta Evelyn Oake, who was born in the province and named for it and died Sept. 17, 1992.

Geoffrey Shaw, currently working on a Ph.D in military history at the University of Manitoba, received an M.A. from the University of Victoria in 1992. He is also a qualified firearms technologist.

Courtney Tower has been a reporter for forty years, since leaving the Saskatchewan homestead. He recently ended thirteen years with *Reader's Digest*, and now freelances with foreign and Canadian magazines.

Janice Tyrwhitt, a writer and editor with a particular interest in Canadian social history, is the author of *Bartlett's Canada* and *The Mill*. She lives in Toronto.

The Royal Canadian Regiment at the Battle of Paardeberg, which resulted in the surrender of 4,000 Boers on Feb. 27, 1900.
Canadian War Museum, CN-8511

Prologue
THE WAR AT THE TURN OF THE CENTURY

A new kind of war for a new kind of century

AS THE BOER COMMANDOS SLAUGHTERED BRITAIN'S THIN RED LINES, THE CALL WENT OUT FOR HIT-AND-RUN FIGHTERS — ALBERTA HAD THEM

Canadian War Museum, 91573

Bugler Williams of the Royal Canadian Regiment sounds the cease-fire as Boer General Cronje surrenders at Paardeberg, South Africa, February 1900 in a painting by R. Caton Woodville.

by GEOFFREY SHAW

Alfred Aspinall peered through the morning sun at the band of about eight horsemen trotting toward him. Now this was curious, he thought. Could they actually be Boers, the people he had come about halfway around the world from Innisfail, District of Alberta, to fight? Surely not. They looked like a collection of cowboys.

Thirty minutes later Aspinall had been given grave reason to revise his estimate of these rough farmer-soldiers who spoke a kind of derivative Dutch called Afrikaans. Of the twelve Canadians in his patrol, two were dead, and four were prisoners of the Boers. Nearly all their horses had been shot. Aspinall himself had been hit three times — first through the shoulder, then through the left arm, and then the tip of his left index finger had been blown off.

The action exemplified the hit-and-run fighting in which the Boers were so expert. Their original eight had suddenly materialized into a hard-riding contingent of about 200, whose superb horses rapidly began to overtake the fleeing Canadians. The latter dismounted, a furious fight ensued, and the survivors, Aspinall among them, barely made it back to the Canadian camp. This the Boers shelled at

liberty, and then vanished as mysteriously as they had appeared.

Aspinall was typical of the approximately 5,000 Canadians who had volunteered for this strange war. About 1,000 of them came from the West and about a quarter of these had been co-opted out of the North-West Mounted Police. Aspinall had been born in England, migrated to Canada at 17, ran a store for several years at Innisfail, then joined the Mounties. That Canada should have any interest whatever in the battle of some frontier farmers on another continent and in another hemisphere for independence from the British crown would seem incompre-

(L-r) Thomas Goodrich Wilson, Galvery Bolster and O'Brien Bolster, ranchers from the Livingstone area of southern Alberta, in the uniform of the 2nd Canadian Mounted Rifles (D Squadron).

Politics, ranching, landbreaking and railroad building were all in the news, but the big story was the strange war in South Africa.

hensible to all but those who valued the British crown. That element, however, included most of English-speaking Canada, and in particular most of the rising and thriving settlement of Calgary in Canada's promising but largely unpeopled prairies. As the new century dawned upon the new Canada, therefore, the undoubted valour of Canada's troops provided the top headlines in the newspapers of the future Alberta for more than a year. Politics, ranching, landbreaking, railroad-building, bridge construction, and drinking were all terribly important, but the big story was the Boer War.

The British Empire had been challenged by the Boers and British Canada must therefore heed the Empire's call. Later sceptics would hold, of course, that the reason Albertans found themselves on the veldt in South Africa had more to do with Britain's economics than Britain's moral rectitude. Lucrative diamond resources had been discovered there in 1869. The largest goldfield in the world had also been found. Soon the strength of the British pound greatly depended on South Africa's resources and powerful men like Cecil Rhodes

(Upper left) Canadian gunner at Hart River, South Africa, March 31, 1902.

Lt. Alfred Aspinall, of Innisfail, one of the North-West Mounted Police who eagerly signed up for the Boer War.

Boer commandos at Spion Kop 1902. The Boers were fighting for their homes on home ground among a sympathetic populace.

A cartoon in the 'Canadian Battle Series' depicts Laurier as a reluctant and malingering soldier in the Boer War.

realized that Britain's own economic viability was inextricably tied to its South African interests. But the Dutch farmers who had colonized the lands in the 18th century championed another principle, namely that the local people should own the local resources. Ironically this was the same principle that Albertans would fight for throughout much of the coming century, but none could know the irony at the time.

The war broke out after a Boer named Paul Kruger became president of the Transvaal, and Rhodes financed a force of armed men to whip Kruger and his burghers into line. However, the group surrendered to a unit of Transvaal farmers, now armed by Germans with better equipment than that of the British army. Kruger demanded a formal British apology. When Britain predictably ignored him, Kruger declared war. That was Oct. 12, 1899. Britain dispatched 10,000 troops to the Cape Colony. They were to prove woefully inadequate.

Eighty-five years earlier, the British army had won world renown by defeating Napoleon at Waterloo. Unhappily it had learned little since. British infantrymen, steadfast as robots, would advance in line, pouring regulated volley-fire with a fearsome machine-like precision into the ranks of the enemy. Then, one hundred yards from them, they would fix bayonets and charge, routing the foe in hand-to-hand combat. Thus had they slaughtered countless tribesmen from India to the Sudan who were foolish enough to attack them in open battlefield. But technology had advanced. Now one man, in a properly prepared defensive position and armed with the new magazine rifle and smokeless powder, could hold off twenty of the best trained troops of Napoleon's day. The Boers knew this. The British, though they had had ample opportunity to learn it and the whole American Civil War had evidenced it, did not. Their casualty figures, often fourfold those of the Boers, testify to the result. That the British had 5,774 dead compared with the Boers' 4,000, reflects the British sending in of masses of troops late in the war. Losses would have been worse otherwise. The Canadians accounted for about one per cent of the British force. Canadian casualties numbered 136 dead, 88 in battle and 48 of disease. Canadian wounded totalled 252.

The Boers had other advantages. Though they possessed no orthodox military manuals, Afrikaner boys were taught how to ride a horse and shoot a rifle with deadly accuracy. Except for their German-trained regular state artillery, the Boer army was a citizen force without uniforms, pay, or formal training. It was not, however, without organization. The basic Boer commandos, which had long operated against the native tribesmen in defence of their scattered settlements and independent farming communities, were essentially units of mounted infantrymen, fighting for their homes on home ground, amidst a sympathetic population.[1] Finally, the German government had been quietly arming the Boers with the latest field artillery and with the superbly accurate 7x57 mm Mauser rifle whose rapid stripper-clip fed magazine gave the Boers a devastating firepower.

Thus from the start the war became a succession of British calamities. At the Battle of Lombard's Kop near Ladysmith in October, 1899, the British lost 1,500 men and were forced to retreat. Nothing was learned. In January, 1900, the British lost 1,700 men at Spion Kop, once again because they left themselves exposed to Boer firepower. But the greatest catastrophe occurred the following month. At a place called Colenso, the British suffered 1,127 casualties and saw much of their artillery captured. The Boer losses: six killed, 22 wounded.

To people throughout the empire all this was outrageous and called for decisive retaliatory action. But none sensed this more urgently than the member of parliament for the Ontario

constituency of Victoria North, Samuel Hughes, an outspoken proponent of citizen soldiering whose devotion to the Empire was matched only by his contempt for its professional soldiery. The need for Canadians in South Africa, said Hughes, was pressing. Western Canadians, ranchers, cowboys, Mounted Police, were the perfect match for the Boers. The government must act now, he declared. But the government was that of Wilfrid Laurier whose central strength lay in Quebec.

The Mounties of the day, young adventurers from England and the East, were enthralled by the prospect of fighting the Boers.

Canada's declaring war in some distant interest of the British Crown, said Laurier's Quebec lieutenant, Joseph Israel Tarte, would come to his province as utterly mad. But opinion in the rest of Canada firmly supported Canadian military action. Could Tarte begin to imagine, asked Laurier, the outrage if his government did nothing? Before 1899 ended, Laurier authorized the dispatch of Canadian troops.

But there weren't very many to dispatch, however. Since the North-West Rebellion (Vol. 1, Sect. 4, ch. 2) Canada had little need of a standing army. In the East, however, the Royal Canadian Regiment was brought to full strength and 1,057 men and four nurses crossed the Atlantic as a first contingent. In the West, the ideal source of immediate manpower seemed the North-West Mounted Police. The Mounties at the time consisted mostly of young men from Britain or central Canada who craved adventure and had joined the force to find it. The prospect of service in distant South Africa enthralled them. When a new military unit was created, and entitled the Canadian Mounted Rifles, the NWMP garrisons at Fort Macleod, Lethbridge and Medicine Hat were stripped down to help fill the ranks of its "C Squadron."

Sam Hughes was not alone in discerning an urgent need for Canadians in South Africa. Similarly persuaded was Donald A. Smith, that strange figure who bridges the fur trade and the railway era of western Canadian history (Vol. 1, p. 121-127). Now titled Lord Strathcona and Mount Royal, he was a white-bearded octogenarian of apparently undiminished energy who divided his time between the West, Montreal and London, where for his final eighteen years he served as Canadian high commissioner to Great Britain. Like Hughes, Smith was convinced South African fighting was far better suited to the roughriders he knew from the Canadian prairies than what he called "the sedulously drilled infantrymen of the English pattern." Always more ready to act than talk, Smith telegraphed Laurier on New Year's Eve, 1899, that he would arm, equip and convey to South Africa, at his own expense, a mounted regiment of 400 men, quite apart from the

Number 4 Troop, C Squadron of Strathcona's Horse regiment photographed in Ottawa, March 1900. By the time they reached Cape Town, half their mounts had perished.

I have just finished reading *Esmond*, which I enjoyed very much. One advantage of my forced sojourn in this country is that I may improve my education. Indeed, reading occupies the greater part of our time, though I cannot fix my attention on a book for very long under these miserable circumstances.
- *from the diary of Lt. H. Frankland, Royal Dublin Fusiliers, Feb. 12, 1900, a prisoner of war in Pretoria.*

¹ **To the Boers, war was a community effort. Each burgher supplied his own rifle, ammunition and horses. Service was not compulsory; an individual with farm or family problems could absent himself and return home. Officers were elected and the men were not bound by their orders. Their marksmanship was legendary. Some could hit a target squarely a kilometre away.**

This enigmatic man married the same woman four times

BE HE SCOUNDREL OR NATION-BUILDER, LORD STRATHCONA'S LAST PUBLIC ACT WOULD GIVE ALBERTA A GREAT REGIMENT

Donald Alexander Smith, the fur trader-financier-politician whose chance encounter with another western visionary in a prairie blizzard eventually led to the creation of the Canadian Pacific Railway (Vol. 1, p. 121), left his final imprint on Alberta history in the Boer War. He founded and bankrolled the regiment which for the coming century would bear his name, Lord Strathcona, to the battlefields of the world. Historians, however, paint an unusually contradictory portrait of this man.

His first biographer, Beckles Willson, describes a shrewd but benevolent entrepreneur who by tireless diligence played a pivotal role in the formation of western Canada. The much more sceptical Peter C. Newman, historian of the Hudson's Bay Company, portrays an unscrupulous scoundrel who in later life sought to salve a bad conscience with lavish works of charity and patriotism.

Beyond any doubt, however, Donald Smith, Lord Strathcona, was one thing more — a man obsessed for a lifetime with the Metis woman he had taken up with after her husband had deserted her. Throughout his life he sought to "regularize" this relationship and in fact was formally and legally married to her four times.

Like many other grimly determined men, Smith was powerfully influenced by his mother. He was born in 1820 in a small Scottish trading town, one of the three sons and two daughters of a tippling shopkeeper whose wife imbued her children with the virtues of cleanliness, good manners and the Bible. It was said Smith could recite all 150 psalms from memory. His mother got him a job as a clerk in the town, but her brother was John Stuart, second-in-command to Simon Fraser, the Nor'Wester who descended and named the great river. Uncle John's stories lured Donald into the service of the Hudson's Bay Company.

Here, as related in Volume I, his suspected dalliance at Montreal with Frances Simpson outraged her husband, HBC governor George Simpson. He would have no "upstart, quill-driving apprentice dangling about a parlour reserved to the nobility and the gentry," declared Sir George as he banished the apprentice to the Labrador department. The chief factor there was Richard Hardisty, an Englishman whose family name appears and reappears in HBC history. Hardisty's daughter, Isabella Sophia, was married to one James Grant, another young HBC clerk. When Smith arrived, she was either legally separated from her husband, or he had simply abandoned her. The record is not clear which. By Smith's account Grant had seriously abused her. In any event she became from that time forward his lifetime preoccupation and

only intimate confidant.

Smith's career is probably unparalleled in the history of Canadian commercial enterprise. From humble clerk, he struggled to become governor of the HBC, spending exactly three-quarters of a century in the service of the company. For 42 of those years he was also a director of the Bank of Montreal, and for eighteen years its president. As explained in Volume I, his was a central impetus in the construction

Donald Smith, who became Lord Strathcona. (Opposite page) the Strathconas on parade, Fort Osborne Barracks, Winnipeg, 1910.

of the Canadian Pacific, and he drove home the last spike at Craigellachie, BC, in 1885. He spent fifteen years as president of Royal Trust, and six as chairman of Burmah Oil and Anglo-Persian Oil.

Through much of this time, he was also active in politics. Prime Minister John A. Macdonald used Smith's influence with the Metis to settle the first Riel Rebellion at Red River in 1869-70, out of which emerged the province of Manitoba. Smith served a term in the Manitoba Legislature, then two terms in the House of Commons where he earned the lasting enmity of the Tories by helping bring down their government over the Pacific scandal. He later returned to parliament as member for Montreal West from 1887 to 1896, and spent his last eighteen years as Canadian high commissioner to Great Britain.

His biographer Willson attributes all this to diligence, imagination and a fierce determination for survival, evidenced early on soon after he was banished to Labrador. With so much winter travel over his frozen department, his eyes began to pain him severely, and the Indians warned him that repeated snowblindness would soon cost him his eyesight. Alarmed, he wrote Simpson about it, asking permission to come to Montreal to see a doctor. Hearing no reply, he left his post and took a supply boat into Montreal. Simpson had him examined by a doctor, concluded he was malingering, and ordered him to leave that very night for an even more distant post, this time on foot.

Where others might have quit on the spot, Smith obeyed, and stumbled into his destination snowblind and starving, one of his Indian guides already dead. But he stuck it out regardless and, through such tenacity, eventually rose in the company's service. Newman has a much less flattering explanation for Smith's phenomenal success, namely an overweaning ambition, a ruthless readiness to exploit others, and an insatiable greed. Far from being diligent, says Newman, Smith was in fact appallingly inattentive to detail. He describes Smith's performance in the Labrador department as lacklustre. His true genius, in business as in politics, lay more in his pronounced opportunism, Newman holds. Smith was always to be found in the right place at the right time, and was a superb and vicious corporate politicker.

He actually connived to have his father-in-law replaced as chief factor by himself, though Hardisty had been making glowing reports of Smith to head office. He established a network of informants who spotted rivals for promotion, then set about besmirching their reputations to disqualify them. With the death of Simpson, Smith was transferred back to Montreal. By then he had cleverly enriched himself by setting up an investment scheme for his fellow factors, giving them three percent rather than the usual two percent on their annual savings, while in fact getting his cousin, financier George Stephen, to invest it at rates up to eighteen percent.

Thereafter, writes Newman, Smith proceeded to ingratiate himself with the HBC governors by betraying the interests of his fellow factors. The outpost traders wanted a fairer share of the £300,000 Canadian government payout to the HBC. Smith got them £107,055, but persuaded them to sign away any claim they might have to the future sale of lands the HBC retained throughout the territories. Not realizing they had forfeited a far greater payment and any future claim on the company, the traders threw a feast for Smith in Montreal, presenting him with a £500 set of sterling silver.

Newman says that Smith later compounded this exploitation by replacing the traders' pension fund with another which effectively shrank the pensions of employees already retired and limited the pensions of the others to a one-time payment. When a chief factor discerned Smith's scheme and urged him to do the right thing by his fellow employees, Smith dismissed their claim as merely "an historic concern."

But in Newman's view this conduct was characteristic of Smith. During the days when he ran riverboats on the Red River, Smith had the competition's vessel rammed and sunk. As Macdonald's envoy during the Riel insurrection, he tried to bill the Canadian government for proceeds lost by the HBC as a result of the rebellion. More than most, he used bribery as an accepted *modus* of politics. During the insurrection, he bribed Riel's followers into abandoning him, then billed the government for the bribes. Later he rigged the election in his Manitoba riding. Prime Minister Macdonald, who did not hate men easily, found it within himself to hate Smith. "That man Smith is the biggest liar I ever met," said Macdonald. Smith, too, is remembered for an aphorism. "To rest," he used to say, "is to rust."

So throughout his life, he did little resting. By 1897, however, with the last spike twelve years driven and for reasons known only to God, he turned to philanthropy. He donated $2.5 million to McGill University. Along with Stephen, he financed the building of the Royal Victoria Hospital in Montreal. He provided the seed money for the Boy Scout movement. He donated to various unemployment funds. He donated two ships to Dr. Wilfred Grenfell's mission in Labrador. Always eager for recognition, and distinction, he was created Baron Strathcona and Mount Royal in 1887, and two years later he financed and founded the Alberta-based regiment that still bears his name. Queen Victoria, well aware of his social-climbing propensity, is said to have deflated him once by referring to him as "his Labrador Lordship."

The Queen's favour mattered greatly to him, but not nearly so much as that of the part-native woman, by now Lady Strathcona, to whom every record reflects him as unfailingly loyal and devoted. When she died on Nov. 7, 1913, he was by all accounts devastated. For the first time in his life, he stopped working, and within ten weeks, on Jan. 21, 1914, he followed her to the grave. During these final days he had been possessed with the idea that his marriage might not have been legal or proper, regardless of the fact that he had had it confirmed so many times by religious and civil authorities. Right to the end he had his lawyers working to confirm the legality of the union.

He was buried beside her in Highgate Cemetery. Ironically in the same London graveyard lie the remains of another 19th-century luminary, remembered in a very different way. Highgate is also the burial place of Karl Marx.

— *G.S.*

Foote Collection, Manitoba Archives, 2885

Depiction of soldier, possibly A.H.L. Richardson (inset), returning into enemy fire to rescue an injured comrade. Richardson was awarded the Victoria Cross.

Canadian contingents already raised. They would be recruited in the Canadian north-west, would be unmarried, expert marksmen, at home in the saddle, and efficient as roughriders or rangers. Thus came into being Calgary's Strathcona Horse. In the coming century, it was to exchange its horses for tanks, and would leave its name and its blood on a score or more battlefields throughout the world. Its first commander: Colonel Samuel Benfield Steele, the Mountie veteran who had led Steele's Scouts in the North-West Rebellion (Vol. 1, p. 154).

At 50, the Ontario-born Steele was already something of a folk hero. His military career went back to the Fenian Raids of 1866 and the First Riel Rebellion of 1870. He had come up through

Steele, commander of Strathcona's Horse, once lifted a 300-pound weight then walked with it.

The Boers call us
A dirty ragged crew
And designate our corps
A useless mob.
Which is far from complimentary
To a guy who tries to do
On a dollar, when a
Tommy gets a bob.
- From the 'S.A.C.' by Henry Stelfox, who served in the Boer War under Lord Baden Powell, and who later settled in Wetaskiwin.

the ranks and joined the NWMP as a sergeant major and later been commissioned as a sub-inspector. His physical strength was storied. It was said he once, on a dare, lifted a 300-pound load to his shoulders and walked with it. So were the demands he made on his men. When his soldiers once complained of piles, he ordered them to gallop bareback for five miles to burst "the source of their complaint." Steele personally selected the first Strathconas. They were, he said, "with only a few exceptions, western outdoorsmen who could ride and shoot and fend for themselves without requiring the amenities of civilized life...the very pick of the cowboy, cowpuncher, ranger, policeman, ex-policeman of the Territories and British Columbia." They were "all of them used to long hours in their saddle, experienced men, very few under 25, and the majority over 30...and well used to hard work, range riding, patrolling, surveying, prospecting, freighting and farming."

No mere British horse would beat Billy H.

WHAT SWEET DELIGHT THERE WAS FOR THE CANADIAN BOYS IN BESTING
THEIR IMPERIAL MASTERS — ALL IN GOOD FUN, OF COURSE

Canada's "colonial" troops in the Boer War took certain delight in occasionally besting their British "superiors." The following is reprinted from A.L. Haydon's Riders of the Plains.

A line regiment under General Hutton's command in the Bloemfontein district was boasting one evening of a horse, an Australian waler, which none of their men could mount. The horse was a big, powerful, black brute, full of devil, and the consensus of opinion was that he had better be shot or sent to the Remount department to be broken in. He was of no use for present service. An officer of the CMR happened to hear this, and ventured to dissent.

'I'll bet you,' he said, 'that I've a man in my troop who'll ride him.'

The challenge was taken up, and the following morning fixed upon for the contest. The CMR officer went to his men and said: 'The –th over there have a horse they can't manage. Now I want one of you to show 'em how to ride it.' At this pretty well all the troop stepped forward, but it was explained to them that they couldn't all get on the waler's back, and that one man alone was needed.

'You can settle it among yourselves,' said their officer, 'I just want the best man, that's all.'

The troop decided the question by selecting Billy H—, an ex-cow-puncher of wide reputation as a 'buster.' The horse wasn't born, he declared, that could beat him. So in the morning Billy, dressed in cowboy style, shirt and 'shaps,' and wide-brimmed hat, and armed with a stout quirt, strolled down to the appointed place where the –th were waiting to see the fun.

Walking leisurely up to the Imperial officer, who was resplendent in all his glory of gold lace and plumes, Billy prodded him in the chest with his quirt.

'Whar's this son-of-a-gun you say you kain't ride?' he asked.

For a moment or two the officer had no breath to make a reply with, but, on recovering himself, he ordered the

Members of the 2nd Canadian Mounted Rifles breakfasting at the foot of Majuba Hill, March 1902. The type of man no mere cayuse could stymie.

waler to be brought out. Then Billy H— took the matter in hand. The big black horse having been turned loose was skillfully 'roped' by Billy's friends, and the ex-cow-puncher's own saddle was placed upon it. When the animal struggled to its feet Billy was in his seat, ready for action.

The waler was something of a terror; there was no gainsaying the fact. He bucked and corkscrewed and twisted and bit, and indulged in all the devilments that an outlaw horse could possible devise. But through it all Billy H— sat tight, as if he were part of the animal itself. To his comrades' loud cries of 'Stay with him, Billy! Stay with him!' he spurred and quirted the waler to a pitch of madness, until the frenzied brute tore wildly across the veldt. It came back to give vent to more bucking, but not for long. The cowboy proved the master, and when he threw himself off at last he had succeeded in making the horse do just what he ordered. The buck-jumper was tamed.

The Imperial officer had watched the exhibition with amazement, nor was he alone in this. Very few of those present had seen a better display of riding.

'Wonderful!' he exclaimed, 'wonderful, by Jove! I should never have believed it possible!'

Billy H—, with his saddle on his arm and his quirt trailing on the ground, spat some of the dust out of his mouth.

'Wa'al,' he said, 'I dunno. I guess in my country we'd jest call that hoss a goldarned cayuse.'

Canadian Trooper Bob White. The saddlery and attitude was western.

But all this was little help on the Atlantic crossing. Most had never sailed before. Apart from violent seasickness, a far worse problem beset them. Pneumonia raged among their horses, stabled deep in the hold of the ship. Many became shark feed. "It was a pitiful sight to see so many exceptionally fine animals thrown overboard," lamented Col. Steele. By the time the Strathconas reached Cape Town, half their mounts, 176 horses, were gone. Many more, said one soldier,

One bullet went through Richardson's stetson, two ripped his tunic. Suddenly a fence lay ahead and his horse refused to jump.

"and we would have been the Strathcona Foot." Then came another downer. The replacement animals provided in South Africa were not the equal of the ones lost. It was humiliating.

In action, the Strathconas eventually met Smith's high expectations, but not without some

Horse-playing members of the South African constabulary, and (below) Cpl. Cecil Rice-Jones. The sniping became monotonous.

hard lessons first. The diary of Corporal Cecil Rice-Jones of Elkwater Lake in the Cypress Hills country tersely recalls their first bloodying: "Ran into an outfit of Boers and had a very lively time of it. Boers twelve to our one. Jenkins killed. Captain Howard and Trooper J. Hobson captured. Two horses killed, one wounded, four missing." In fact, the enemy had lured the Strathconas into a trap. The Boers had concealed themselves in an orchard around a house from which they flew a white flag. The Canadians, approaching it unwarily, met a hail of fire. Private A. Jenkins of Red Deer died instantly when a Boer bullet exploded two cartridges in his bandolier.

That was July 1, Dominion Day, 1900. Four days later they stumbled into another trap. Thirty-eight Strathcona horsemen pursued a small Boer party, set out as bait, which led them into an ambush, with about 200 Boers on either side of them. The engagement, however, became memorable in the regiment's history. Wheeling around, the Canadians retreated at a gallop. Corporal Alex McArthur, already wounded twice, fell when his horse was shot from under him. Sergeant A.H.L. Richardson turned back. Bullets screaming around him, he threw the wounded man over his saddle. Richardson made his way back to the camp under heavy fire from the Boers hot behind him. One bullet went through his Stetson, another two ripped his tunic. Suddenly a single-strand wire fence lay before him. His horse, foaming and exhausted, refused to jump it. The Boers yelled at him to surrender. But then a Boer bullet hit his horse in the shoulder. The startled animal leapt forward over the fence, fled furiously to the Canadian camp and died an hour later. Richardson won the Victoria Cross.[2]

The cowboy skill of the Strathconas kept them constantly on patrol, ahead of or beside the main body of the army. This greatly exposed them to the enemy and made entrapment an unremitting hazard. Sent to gather up rifles, said to have been cached in a Boer house, 34 Strathconas found out too late they'd been led into another trap. About 150 Boers lay concealed in the building and around it. More guarded in their approach this time, they were able to take cover as soon as they realized the ruse. Still they advanced on the building. Sgt. E.C. Parker crept within 25 yards of the enemy. The Boers called upon him to surrender. He refused, and a moment later he fell, his body riddled with bullets. Outnumbered more than four to one, the Canadians gave up their attack and retired with relatively few casualties. When the Boer force left the house to pursue them, the Canadian fire proved too hot for them, so they gave up. The Canadians were learning.

They possessed as well a strong element of blind tenacity, known in some circles as cussedness. Because of this, their British commanders gave them some ticklish jobs. Ordered at one point to secure the hills surrounding the army against Boer infiltration, Strathcona Sergeant A.E.H.

[2]The Victoria Cross is the highest British award for valour. Four Canadians won it in the Boer War. Arthur Herbert Lindsey Richardson was the first. He was born in Southport, England, in 1874, came to western Canada at 24, and joined the North-West Mounted Police, eventually becoming a sergeant. The other three won the VC in the same action at Komati River on Nov. 7, 1900. They were Sgt. "Eddy" Holland of Ottawa, Lt. H.Z.C. Cockburn of Toronto, and Lt. R.E.W. Turner of Quebec City. Turner later commanded a brigade in the First World War, was promoted lieutenant-general, and knighted.

(L)Two Boer prisoners in Klerksdorp, March 26, 1902; (r) Boers captured after Paardeberg.

Logan had just posted his three mounted troopers, Privates W. West, H.J. Wiggins and a man identified only as Private Jones, at their positions when the four were suddenly attacked by a contingent of over 100 Boers, who had concealed themselves close by. The Boer commandant called upon them to surrender. The four responded by opening fire. Back upon them came the fusillade of 100 Boer Mausers. Sergeant Logan saw that escape was impossible. Abandoning their horses, the four dashed behind a few nearby boulders, determined to make a stand there until reinforcements came up. They didn't. From this inadequate shelter, the four continued to fire into the enemy now less than 100 yards away. Again the Boer commandant loudly called upon them to surrender, but their rifles spoke the only answer. When the infantry cleared the ground the following day, the four were found together, some with rifle still at shoulder, their bodies riddled with bullets, all their ammunition gone. Before them were the bodies of seventeen Boers.

Only once did the Strathconas find themselves in a textbook setpiece battle where one entrenched army faced another, the Strathconas in the British line. Regimental historian Andrew

The British scorched the earth: they burned the Boers' homes and interned their women and children in disease-ridden camps.

Miller vividly describes what ensued: "In the first grey of the morning dawn, the enemy opened fire from an entrenched position, his rifle discharging, twinkling like firefly flickers from the still darkened hillside. In a few minutes the air was filled with the whistle of flying bullets, as they sped on their way striking to the front of the entrenchment or passing over them forcing up the dust as they hit the ground beyond. The whole of the enemy's position seemed lined with sharpshooters. The Strathconas returned the fire with vigour, until soon every rifle barrel was in a burning heat. Occasionally a few burghers would be observed shifting their positions, and during the instant they exposed themselves the fire would be directed their way.

I am now riding my third horse. The last one I left out on the veldt and packed my saddle into camp. This country is one scene of desolation from one end to the other. Nothing like Canada. Canada with a capital C. It has been a wet summer with you. Oh well never mind, there will be lots of fine summers in Alberta yet.
- *C.E. Kendrew, of Strathcona's Horse, from a letter to his brother in Edwell, Alberta, 1902.*

Burning a Boer farm, from the Illustrated London News. British patriotic zeal turned to moral horror.

"By six o'clock the whole army was moving. The sharpshooters having previously advanced and driven the enemy's pickets, the British artillery came up and 56 guns opened fire all along the extended front of five miles, to which the Boer gunners replied with a tenacity born of determination to succeed in stopping the advance. With over eighty guns booming their angry challenges, scores of pom-poms sharply coughing on every hillside, and 20,000 rifles cracking as they sent forth their spiteful bullets, it seemed that the whole universe had joined in the struggle. The roar of battle was appalling, drowning even the words of command, and obliterating the senses of the combatants to everything except the task before them. Until two o'clock in the afternoon the fighting continued, neither side seeming to have much advantage, although the British continued to move closer to the Boer position. About that hour, however, the Boer fire grew feebler, and steadily diminished as trench after trench was vacated. Before nightfall it had practically ceased, and it became known that the enemy's left flank had been successfully turned and crippled and the Boers forced to vacate the Vogestruispoort hills and fall back." Thus ended the Battle of Belfast, an ominous forewarning of the kind of maelstrom most of Europe and much of the world was to experience in the century's second decade.

Such dazzling action, however, was not the routine. Like all wars, the South African became day by day a grinding attrition of the nerves. Corporal Rice-Jones' diary descends into a recitation of sniper activity: "Aug. 26: Boers sniped heavily all day…Aug. 27: Big guns in action and good deal of sniping…Nov. 10: A lot of sniping…Jan. 3: Sniping all day…Jan. 4: Heavy sniping…Jan. 5: Sniping all day…Jan. 7: Sniping all day…Jan. 8: Sniping all day…" And the war evidenced human rage as well as human heroism. One Strathcona patrol encountered a force of Boers holed up in a farmhouse, flying a white flag. The officer who advanced to receive their surrender was shot dead on the spot. Incensed, his troopers took the farmhouse, captured thirty Boers, and had hanged nine of them before another Strathcona officer put a stop to the executions. In the circumstances, however, the anger of the men was conscionable.[3]

Yet the unpredictable Boers were equally capable of gallantry. "One of our men, an old soldier named Flynn," recalls the military historian J.F.C. Fuller in *The Last of The Gentlemen's Wars,* "was wounded and his horse killed. The horse fell on Flynn and pinned him to the ground. The Boer who had shot him stepped out from behind a rock, pulled him out from under his horse and tied up his wound, making a pretty good job of it."

The last task assigned the Strathconas proved a failure. They were ordered with other British units to capture the elusive Boer guerrilla commander, Christiaan Rudolf de Wet, whose surprise attacks were exacting a frightful toll on the British columns as the Boers retreated north. "The trail taken by both armies was littered with dead and dying horses, abandoned wagons, and the abandoned equipment of men too exhausted to carry it a step further," recalls W.A. Griesbach,[4] an Edmontonian whose reminiscences of the war make the most readable Canadian account. Hunter and hunted came close to the breaking point, but in the end de Wet escaped.

The Canadian Mounted Rifles, meanwhile, had built themselves a reputation for unparalleled ferocity. When their patrols stumbled into overwhelming Boer numbers, they would divide as they galloped away, thus splitting the Boer force. A trooper identified only as Waldy — "Old Man Waldy" to his compatriots — finding himself thus pursued, dropped from his horse to the ground and faced his two pursuers who also dismounted. Neither party could see the other, but the

Drawing of surrender of Cronje at Paardeberg, South Africa.

THE WAR AT THE TURN OF THE CENTURY

Boers had no reason to expose themselves since reinforcements would soon join them. Waldy suddenly rose to his knees. Both Boers fired and missed. He shot both dead, remounted, and ambled back into camp.

When the Boers attacked a group of CMRs on June 22, 1900, says the official record, "a small party of Pincher's Creek men of the 2nd Battalion displayed the greatest gallantry and devotion to duty, holding in check a force of Boers by whom they were largely outnumbered. Corporal Morden and Private Kerr continued fighting until mortally wounded. Lance-Corporal Miles and Private Miles, wounded, continued to fight and held their ground."

By 1902 the British had 300,000 men in South Africa against the Boers' about 70,000. The tide of war had turned, and Boer president Paul Kruger had escaped to Europe. The British response to the Boer hit-and-run war was grim but effective. The British scorched the earth, burning the Boers' homes, and interning children, women and old people in camps so cramped and disease-ridden that 20,000 people perished in them. In May, the Boer army formally surrendered, but the victory was clouded. Opinion in Britain had turned from patriotic zeal to moral horror over the wanton treatment of Boer civilians. The Canadians had already headed for Canada.

Their homecoming was not uniformly glorious. Indeed, the Canadian Mounted Rifles created a trans-Canada scandal. In the process of demobilization their discipline broke down. As the unit traversed the country there were repeated incidents of brawling, firing off guns and terrifying the citizenry. "These men were not criminals," observed Griesbach, "but their idea of a good time was to raise hell and fire off their weapons indiscriminately. Many of them were real cow-punchers, and others were merely the synthetic variety. Men of this type require a rigid discipline and a good deal of casualties to reduce them to a proper state of mind. This we never had." [5] When Griesbach's unit arrived in Winnipeg the police took away their rifles until they were re-entrained for Calgary. There was at least one incident at sea. The Irish brothers, Jack and Andy, from the area of Evarts, Alberta, a community near Sylvan Lake, whose surname does not survive in the records, seized the ship's canteen and distributed free beer to their fellow Canadian passengers, many of whom became dead drunk. Since the army couldn't charge 1,400 victorious soldiers with mutiny, it settled for fining them $8 each when they were demobilized.

The return of the Strathconas was more civilized. They went first to London where each man received the Queen's South African Medal.[6] Lord Strathcona himself gave them a "luncheon," in fact a magnificent banquet, warmly shaking the hand of each officer and man as he arrived. Later he tendered further hospitality for the officers in the great drawing-room of the swank Savoy Hotel. This event was not without untoward incident. Colonel Sam Steele, one of his subalterns Agar Adamson later recalled, "arrived a bit tight and grew tighter." He repeatedly interrupted Lord Strathcona's speech, then loudly demanded to make a speech of his own. "Lord S. pulled him up and said that they would have speeches on other occasions. He insisted upon continuing, in the middle of which [Steele] wanted to jump ship. He left the table...lost his way, and found himself in a kitchen, on the stove where he 'relaxed nature.' He then returned, and wound up being sick on the carpet."

In Canada, the Strathconas were treated as heroes wherever they went. All veterans of the Boer War could acquire a half-section of land or exchange their land allotment for money. However, some Albertans never did return to the prairies, one of them the Victoria Cross winner Sgt. Richardson, who lived out his life in obscurity at Liverpool, England, and died in 1932. Some never could settle back into civilian or police life, one of them a NWMP trooper called Kimbrey who began to drink heavily, and eventually shot himself sitting on his bed in his lodgings at Frank, Alberta, the result, it was said, of being jilted by a prostitute called Mabel Burns. Some remained in South Africa, serving in the South African constabulary which checked the Boer terrorism that persisted for years.

What did the war accomplish for Alberta? It provided a fine regiment, and it provided an omen. The omen was the fervid British patriotism that it spontaneously evoked. The same would be called upon again a dozen years later when the enemy was not a contingent of farmer-soldiers, but a modern army able to deal out death with a technological efficiency the world had never before seen. This would strip every Alberta city, town and village of many of its finest young men and diminish the province for decades to come. But who could have seen that as Albertans cheered their heroes home?

[3] This was somewhat the same activity that the famous Australian lieutenant, Harry Harbord "Breaker" Morant, had been involved in, and later shot for. Having been told by British officers to treat prisoners harshly, he and another lieutenant did so. But public opinion in Britain was turning against the army, so they were "made an example of" by the same officers who had given them the order, thereby providing the Australians with the plot for an award-winning movie, *Breaker Morant*, released in 1981.

[4] Trooper Griesbach was typical of the "young gallants" who volunteered for South Africa. He was the son of NWMP Superintendent A.H. Griesbach whose presence of mind prevented bloodshed when Edmontonians came to arms to save their land titles office (Vol I, p 271). Trained as a lawyer, he returned to practise in Edmonton, became an alderman there in 1905, and mayor of Edmonton in 1907. He served as a colonel in the First World War, was elected to the House of Commons in 1917 and named to the Senate in 1921.

[5] Griesbach would read back into these incidents the symptoms of what he would later conclude was an endemic weakness in the Canadian army, namely the relatively poor quality of the officer cadre. The CMRs had "run amok" because the commissioned officers failed to support the non-commissioned officers. In South Africa, some officers would return from an engagement with only a few men, others with more men than they had started out with. In action, he concluded, the men had simply attached themselves to officers they trusted and abandoned those they didn't.

[6] The evidence suggests that the Strathconas made a very favourable impression upon the British high command. For example, before leaving South Africa, General Sir Redvers Buller made the following declaration about them: "I have never served with a nobler, braver or more serviceable body of men. It shall be my privilege, when I meet my friend Lord Strathcona, to tell him what a magnificent body of men bear his name." The British did not routinely speak in such terms of "colonial" forces.

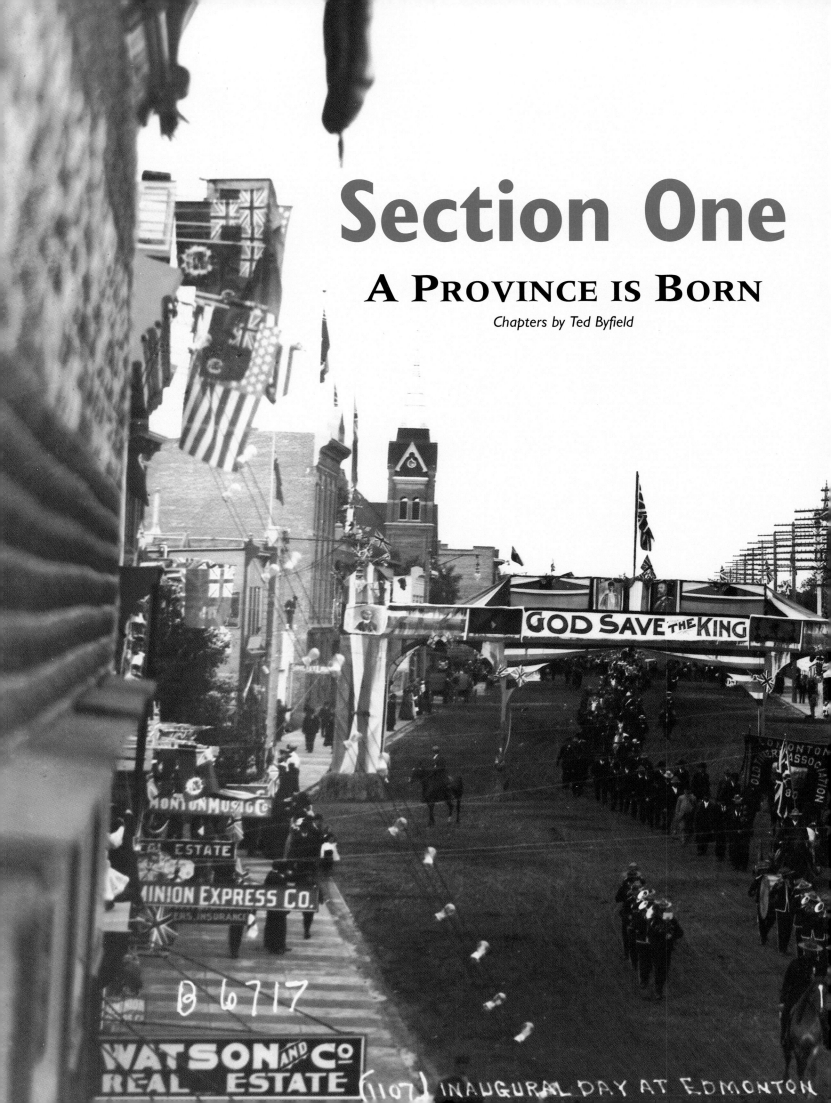

Section One

A Province is Born

Chapters by Ted Byfield

*Inaugural Day parade, Sept. 1, 1905,
Jasper Avenue, Edmonton*
Provincial Archives of Alberta, B-6717

CHAPTER ONE

FREDERICK WILLIAM HAULTAIN

Born: Nov. 25, 1857, in Woolwich, England

Died: Jan. 30, 1942, in Montreal

Knighted: 1916

Career Apex: Premier of the North-West Territories, 1896-1905

Major Accomplishment: Played a large part in gaining responsible government and provincehood for the Canadian prairies.

Quotation: 'What we want in the West, and what we have a right to expect, is to be established as a province with equal rights with the rest of the Dominion. We do not ask more, and we will not be willing to take less.'

The lonely romantic who won provincehood for Alberta

FREDERICK HAULTAIN SAW ONE BIG PROVINCE CONTROLLING ITS RESOURCES. HE
DREAMT, TOO, OF A BEAUTIFUL YOUNG WOMAN CALLED MARION

On the third floor of the Alberta Legislature, on
a pillar facing away from the main rotunda and significantly distanced from the stately portrayals
of the province's premiers and lieutenant-governors, the observant visitor encounters a noncon-
formity. The plaque identifies the portrait as that of the Honourable Sir Frederick Haultain, premier of the North-West Territories before Alberta became a province. But there's something about
its subject that doesn't quite belong in oils. For one thing, Haultain is smoking a cigarette. For
another, he is very faintly grinning, as if relishing some point well
made in argument. There is an indecorous absence of solemnity.
He's enjoying himself, something entirely out of place in this som-
bre assembly.

And in a sense that may be true. Frederick William Alpin
Gordon Haultain always did seem somehow out of place in politics. True, he was a devastating debater who in one celebrated confrontation demolished the plans of Manitoba to take over most of
what is now Saskatchewan. He was an able administrator, a tireless campaigner, a determined promoter, a speaker the crowds
flocked to hear and to cheer because he could make them roar
with laughter. And he was charming; even his foes couldn't sustain enmity for him. At one point he was unquestionably the most
popular politician in the West. Yet in the biggest undertaking of his
political life he considered himself a complete failure. He had four
goals for the terms of the provincehood of Alberta and
Saskatchewan — he gained none of them. And then, in the politics of one of the provinces he brought about, he failed miserably
again.

What can possibly vindicate such a record? Only the history of
western Canada ever since. For in every contention but one, subsequent events would uphold Fred Haultain, and he would live to
see it. So no doubt he *is* enjoying himself there on a pillar in the Legislative Building of the
province his efforts created. He was right, and he knows it.

Perhaps Haultain was doomed to fail. Like most politicians, he began at heart a romantic.

Blow-up of Marion Mackintosh Castellain, taken at a riding party in Regina in 1895.

**There's something about the painting's subject that doesn't quite
belong in oils. For one thing Haultain is smoking a cigarette. For
another, he is very faintly grinning.**

Unlike most, he remained one. There was always a Right Thing to Do, and you did it — whatever
the cost. You did it in politics and you did it in love. And even more disastrous than his political
failures were his failures in love.

These began at the party thrown for the newly arrived lieutenant-governor of the North-West

Territories, at the territorial capital of Regina in 1893. From the start, it was obvious that Charles Herbert Mackintosh would be no prize as vice-regal representative. He was arrogant, pompous, and seemingly oblivious of the fact that the North-West Territories was acquiring, under Haultain's leadership, responsible government. This meant that Haultain, as chairman of the territorial executive council, could properly hold the title of premier, and that Mackintosh's function would be to rubberstamp the decisions of the territorial assembly (Vol. 1, Sect. 7). But Mackintosh had compensating attributes, namely seven daughters, the third and prettiest of whom was Marion. Haultain, though a 36-year-old bachelor about eighteen years her senior, was instantly and irrevocably smitten.

This had never happened before, it seemed. Although Haultain obviously enjoyed the company of women, he was curiously awkward with them. Among men he was a fascinating and witty conversationalist. Among women, says his biographer Grant MacEwan, who knew him personally, he would often fall silent, too shy even to speak.[1] However, at another party two years later in

Glenbow Archives, NA-3668-2

Charles Herbert Mackintosh: Marion's father was no prize as vice-regal representative.

Regina's Windsor Hotel, he gained courage enough to ask Marion to dance. Miss Marion Mackintosh, reported the *Regina Leader*, "looked a poem in a pale blue moiré with sprays of cream verging to pink wrought to pattern. Her tall splendid figure carried the court train with perfect grace. The bodice, pointed and very short, was cut quite low and a fragile ending of chiffon about the throat gave a dainty finish." Thereafter Haultain was lost forever — or at least for the next forty or so years — though the public would not learn of this infatuation until long after he was dead.

Marion, alas, was not smitten at all. Not by Haultain, anyway, though she seems to have regarded him as a fatherly friend. The man who captured her fancy was a young Englishman, Alfred L. Castellain, who came, it was said, from a titled family and actually possessed a coat of arms.[2] Castellain's occupation was not altogether prepossessing. He sold wine and liquor, now legal in the territories although the clergy increasingly regarded it as a sinister trafficking in the means of human misery. But Castellain's liquor ads appeared regularly in the *Leader,* and he gave every evidence of wealth

Marion, reported the *Leader*, 'looked a poem in a pale blue moiré with sprays of cream verging to pink wrought to pattern. Her splendid figure carried the court train with perfect grace.'

and prosperity. Hence, on Feb. 13, 1896, a year after the Windsor Hotel ball, the *Leader* was able to announce that Marion St. Clair Mackintosh had been married in Ottawa to Alfred Louis Castellain of Regina, NWT. The bride had entered the church on her father's arm, preceded by five of her sisters acting as bridesmaids. The newlyweds were to sail from New York five days later for a honeymoon in England. It was an account that must have caused profound sorrow to the premier of the West.

There was much else to occupy his attention, however. That year, 1896, was momentous in Canadian politics. The long Tory regime that had led Canada into Confederation in 1867 and ruled it ever since, apart from a five-year interval, staggered at last to an end. The polished Wilfrid Laurier, soon to become Sir Wilfrid, led the Liberals to a thunderous victory. The most significant consequence in Regina was the institution of full responsible government, which had been Laurier's promise to the territories (Vol. 1, ch. 2). Regina itself was as diminutive as the territorial government it directed. The capital's population in the 1901 census was 2,249, far less than Calgary's 4,091 and less even than Edmonton's 2,626, though both Calgary and Edmonton fell within the territorial jurisdiction. Saskatoon was then a mere hamlet of 113 people. Indeed, by far the biggest city in the territories was Dawson in the Yukon with 9,142, destined to rise to a high of 16,000, all drawn there by the promise of gold, and almost all destined to depart before the century's first decade ended.

Over this vast tract, which extended north to the Arctic Ocean, Haultain functioned as premier. Each year the 35 members of the territorial legislature travelled to Regina for the annual session, where they used to ease the strain of daily debate

Manitoba Premier Rodmond Roblin. Haultain's intentions clashed with Manitoba's ambitions. By 1901 it had devolved to one-on-one combat.

by holding great oyster dinners at the Palmer House, followed by yarn-spinning, whiskey and a lusty singsong, led of course by the premier (who was a church chorister). Party politics did not detract from these raucous festivities because in the territorial legislature there were no party politics. Haultain, a Conservative at the federal level, by 1899 had a cabinet that consisted almost entirely of Liberals. Party affiliations were a necessary evil in federal politics, he said, but the West could not afford them.

This non-partisan ideal was not universally accepted, however. Richard Bedford Bennett, the brash young Conservative lawyer who had been elected from Calgary in 1898, was skilful, energetic and plainly ambitious for national office. One way to achieve this would be to rebuild the Tory party in the West. In the Laurier election of '96 it had barely hung on to one of the four territorial constituencies. In the federal election of 1900 it lost all four. For Bennett the avenue to national politics lay through the territorial assembly, but here he encountered Haultain's non-partisanship, an obstacle to any Tory resurgence.[3] He therefore appointed himself as opposition leader. His strategy did not begin well. He accused the premier of misappropriating $20,000 and the charge was proven spurious. A much more fruitful field for opposition soon emerged, however. Bennett became spokesman for a two-province West, with Calgary the capital of the western province. Haultain favoured one big province. So Bennett didn't join the Palmer House singsongs. He had more important things to do, and he didn't drink.

By 1898, Haultain discovered himself facing a new kind of problem. Frankly, he was bored. Responsible government was achieved, so what was left? He could not forget Marion Mackintosh, whose marriage soon encountered grievous trouble. Castellain had gone broke in Regina. His advertisements stopped appearing in the *Leader*, he was forced to sell his chattels to pay his creditors, and he left for England with his wife. So Marion was gone. Haultain must accept that. But should he return now to the law practice he had established fourteen years earlier in Macleod, which had elected him to the territorial legislature in 1887 and had returned him by acclamation ever since? Or should he stay on and pursue the next and most obvious step for the territories?

That step was provincehood — "autonomy," as the lawyers and politicians called it. The case for it was clear enough. After all, Manitoba had been made a province nearly thirty years earlier with a population of about 12,000. The 1901 census would show the territories with 165,555, and already the aggressive settlement policies of Clifford Sifton, the federal minister of the Interior, were becoming everywhere evident. In 1896, the year Sifton took over the department, a mere

[1]MacEwan's *Frederick Haultain: Frontier Statesman of the Canadian North West* was the only biography of Haultain at the time this history was written, but he is the central figure in C.C. Lingard's *Territorial Government in Canada* and in Lewis H. Thomas's *The Struggle for Responsible Government in the North-West Territories*. All three historians — Thomas, Lingard and MacEwan — became, like most of the people who knew him, captivated by Haultain.

[2]True enough, University of Alberta historian Lewis H. Thomas reported in an article about Haultain. The coat of arms of the Castellains appears in *Fairbairn's Book of Crests and Families of Great Britain and Ireland*. It also appears on correspondence from Castellain preserved in the papers of Charles Herbert Mackintosh.

[3]The clearest exposition of Bennett's strategy against Haultain appeared in Vol. 6 No. 1 of the periodical *Prairie Forum* in 1981, written by Stanley Gordon of the University of Alberta history department.

Walter Scott, the Liberal MP for Assiniboia West, Jan. 3, 1901.

1,857 people had taken up homesteads. The number of homesteaders for 1900 was 7,486. For 1905 it would be 30,819. You could see by the packed colonist cars on the Canadian Pacific that the population was exploding. And provincehood had always been the federal aim for the prairies. As far back as 1881, when the old Tory government's Department of the Interior had divided the territorial prairies into the four districts of Alberta, Assiniboia, Saskatchewan and Athabaska, the plan had been that each should eventually become a province.

Furthermore, the territorial government, though now democratic, was in a fiscal bind. While Ottawa poured people into the area, it expected the Haultain administration to provide what a later generation would call "the infrastructure" — the roads, bridges, ferries, schools and hospitals without which this new agricultural society could not survive. The most obvious source of revenue was the sale of land, but these funds went to Ottawa. The territorial government was expected to apply — meaning beg — for annual grants, none of which ever approached the amount sought. One memorandum to Ottawa showed that where the population had risen 56 per cent in five years to 1896, the grants had risen only sixteen per cent. No formula had been worked out as the basis of these grants, so Haultain's cabinet had no way of knowing how much money would be coming in. Nor could the territories spread payment for these facilities over future years by borrowing, like every other government. They were prohibited from incurring debt. They could issue licences and collect various fees, but this produced little revenue. Another obvious source was a tax on the CPR, but this was prohibited by the CPR charter.

Indeed the railways made another case for provincehood. As the settlers streamed onto the land, Canadian Pacific expansion did not keep up with them; some found themselves thirty or even fifty miles from the tracks. Grain had to move from the farms on wagons, and roads were appalling. Survival itself became doubtful. Plainly there was a need for more lines. One, the Canadian Northern, was beginning to build west from Manitoba. Another was being mooted by Ottawa, but there was a big argument over how it should be financed. Then, too, the CPR was so stingy with boxcars that unmarketable grain was piling up on the farms. About all this, the territories could do nothing. A province might.

The concept of provincehood was by no means new. It had been advocated by the *Calgary Herald* as far back as 1891 when the *Herald* proposed that a province called Alberta be established between British Columbia and a north-south line running somewhere between Swift Current and

Haultain wanted one big province between Manitoba and British Columbia called Buffalo. Those who favoured dividing it, he called 'Little Westerners.'

Medicine Hat. Naturally, Calgary would be the capital. But the idea did not catch on. Four years later, however, from the depth of the 1890s depression, James Reilly, ex-mayor of Calgary and a perpetually unsuccessful candidate for the territorial legislature, wrote a letter to the *Herald* urging Alberta provincehood as the only way to revive the prairie economy. A big public meeting followed that loudly endorsed Reilly's idea, but Haultain cooled some of this ardour. If Alberta acted independently of the rest of the territories, he queried, why should it expect any better success than Manitoba, whose fiscal problems were horrendous? In the end the meeting agreed to publish a pamphlet, *Provincehood for Alberta.*

The Calgary enthusiasm met with a predictably chill reaction northward. "We notice," sneered an editorial in Frank Oliver's *Edmonton Bulletin,* "that the hog-like propensities of Calgary are still to the fore and that Jimmy Reilly and a few other political hacks have been airing themselves on provincial autonomy. Not that they think it is necessary for the welfare of the whole of Alberta, but simply the little patch of about one mile by two miles known as the city of Calgary. Calgary to be the capital; Calgary to be the head of a half-dozen railways running nowhere of any importance to Alberta; Calgary to be the head of a lot of useless schemes as long as it can get plenty of money to spend in and about it; Calgary to have all the appointments for running the proposed provincial autonomy." Getting more seats in the federal parliament, said the *Bulletin*, would be a lot more use than provincial autonomy. Oliver, just incidentally, was planning to run for parliament the following year. He did, and won.[4]

A year later, in 1897, at a meeting of the Fort Saskatchewan Agricultural Society, a committee was established to press for provincial autonomy. Edmonton leaders jumped on the bandwagon, but urged that the new province of Alberta be enlarged to include the District of Athabaska, lying to the north and northeast, because Edmonton was beginning to see its future as the gateway to the North. Official Ottawa scoffed at the proposal.

But by the century's turn, the press all over the West was taking up the cause, typified by an editorial in the *Medicine Hat News*, a city then located in the District of Assiniboia, not the District of Alberta. "We do not wonder," wrote its editor, "that Mr. Haultain's government is getting tired of begging at the federal treasury. We are something like a college boy, smart and with good prospects, and anxious to get along, but the remittance from home is too small, and as his education increases his wants grow, and he is obliged to wait tables and scrub floors to get along financially."

By the legislative session of 1900, Haultain had made up his mind. He would fight for provincehood. But he wanted one big province between Manitoba and British Columbia, and from the US border to the 57th parallel which crossed the territories just north of Fort McMurray. In other words, it embraced the settled part of the area that his government already administered. The territorial government would "evolve" into a provincial government. Those who favoured dividing the territories into two or more provinces he called "Little Westerners." He was for One Big West. He called his province Buffalo, after the animal that had swarmed across its plains. The task was to persuade the Laurier government of this vision.

He accordingly presented a resolution to the territorial House in May 1900, calling for an "inquiry" into territorial autonomy. In a three-and-a-half-hour speech, described by historian C.C. Lingard as the best of his career, he enunciated the case for provincehood. However, he deliberately withheld from the resolution the question of whether there should be one province or two, in order to unite the Legislature behind it. The resolution passed unanimously on July 20, 1900. It was laid before the federal cabinet five days later.

He ventured to call on the Castellains and what he discovered shook him. Marion now had a child and was living in penury. Castellain had simply deserted her.

The territorial ministers waited expectantly for the reply. Days passed, then weeks, then months. None came. Finally, in March 1901, a letter arrived from Clifford Sifton that evinced a qualified enthusiasm. "While financial embarrassments rather than constitutional aspirations have led the North-West government and legislature to discuss the provincial status," it said, "I think that sufficient practical reasons can be given for the early establishment of provincial institutions in the West." He called a conference for October between territorial and federal officials to discuss a procedure. The territorial people celebrated a victory. Sifton was in favour. What else could matter? Provincehood was as good as achieved.

That summer, however,[5] there came another traumatic experience in Haultain's personal life. Queen Victoria had died the previous January; in August representatives of every government in the empire assembled in London for the coronation of her eldest son, the charmingly dissolute and superbly diplomatic Edward VII. While in England, Haultain ventured to call on the Castellains. What he discovered shook him. Marion now had a child, a little girl she called Mimi. But Castellain had simply deserted her. She was living in penury with the child, helped inadequately by her husband's family, not at all by her own. Haultain undertook to support her secretly. She refused his help, but he sent it anyway. He was being a real father to her but that, unhappily, was not the role he had wanted to play.

[4]These newspaper excerpts and other published memorabilia associated with the creation of the province have been usefully gathered in *The Formation of Alberta: A Documentary History*, prepared by U of A professors Douglas Owram and R.C. MacLeod and published in 1979 by the Historical Society of Alberta.

[5]In a letter from Haultain which disclosed his secret marriage, discovered in the Mackintosh papers, he says this trip to England occurred in 1902. This is probably an error, since the coronation was in 1901.

Period photo montage of the members of the Legislative Assembly of the North-West Territories, 1904. By then Haultain was joining Laurier's list of least favourites.

MEMBERS LEGISLATIVE ASSEMBLY, 1904.

A. SMITH, MOOSOMIN.	J. W. WOOLF, CARDSTON.	J. C. CLINKSKILL, SASKATOON.	E. C. McDIARMID, CANNINGTON.	H. GREELEY, MAPLE CREEK.	R. A. WALLACE, HIGH RIVER.	L. J. A. LAMBERT, ST. ALBERT.
J. W. SHERA, VICTORIA.	A. McINTYRE, MITCHELL.	T. McNUTT, SALTCOATS.	C. W. FISHER, BANFF.	R. SECORD, EDMONTON.	J. W. CONNELL, SOURIS.	W. T. FINLAY, MEDICINE HAT.
J. J. YOUNG, EAST CALGARY.	A. C. RUTHERFORD, STRATHCONA.		Hon. A. E. FORGET, (LIEUTENANT-GOVERNOR)		Dr PATRICK, YORKTON.	G. M. ANNABLE, MOOSE JAW.
G. W. BROWN	T. McKAY				A. S. ROSENROLL	Dr DE VEBER

For two good reasons, Haultain took his finance minister, the territorial treasurer, to the October conference. For one, the man was extremely able and could answer instantly any fiscal question the federal officials might raise. For another, the principal federal minister involved, apart from Laurier himself, would be Clifford Sifton. The territorial treasurer was his older brother, Arthur, who nine years later would become the second premier of Alberta. So there would be a Sifton on both sides of the table.

Though the meeting was closed, historian Lingard reconstructs it. Haultain meticulously made the case for provincehood. Arthur Sifton strongly supported him. They then waited for Clifford Sifton's concurrence from the other side of the table, where he sat with Laurier, three other federal cabinet ministers, and Walter Scott, the Liberal MP for Assiniboia who owned the *Regina Leader* and had been Haultain's unfailing ally in the fight for responsible government. Strangely, however, Clifford Sifton's enthusiasm seemed to have waned. Like the others he asked many questions, raised problems, saw difficulties. Would Premier Haultain be good enough to set forth his proposal in the form of a draft bill, embodying provincehood as the territories saw it?

The bachelor Haultain (back row, left) was everybody's family friend. Here he is photographed at afternoon tea with the family of W.H. Hogg, manager of the Bank of Montreal in Regina, on floor with child. Haultain's life-long friend, C.W. Peterson, then of the territorial Department of Agriculture, is in the back row, third from left.

In 1902 when I was in London I found her practically penniless with a sick infant and Isobel on her hands. From that time until she came to Canada in 1904 she was the unwilling recipient of help from me. When she came out to Ottawa in 1904, it was without any knowledge or suggestion on my part and I had nothing to do with her decision to get a divorce. In fact I strongly opposed the idea of an American divorce, but at the time (this most confidentially) she was helped by a man she intended to marry and would not listen to my advice. She went to Sioux Falls

"In 1902 when I was in London I found her practically penniless with a sick infant and Isobel on her hands...I had nothing to do with her decision to get a divorce...But at the time (this most confidentially) she was helped by a man she intended to marry."

Excerpts from Haultain's letter to Marion's father, May 10, 1910.

Saskatchewan Archives Board, Regina

must be attended to. I am getting into good practice and have to attend to it to keep it. Any idle move or unnecessary gossip will only injure me and not help anyone else. Anyway I resent the idea that anyone has to force me or threaten me in order that I should do what is the great hope and happiness of my life. I am devoted to Marion and am looking forward to having her to look after and it will not be my fault if she is not comfortable and happy. I want more than ever to be on good terms with

"I should do what is the great hope and happiness of my life. I am devoted to Marion and am looking forward to having her to look after and it will not be my fault if she is not comfortable and happy."

that and undertook to see that she would not want ordinary comfort as long as I was alive and well. I was, of course, very fond of her but didn't dream of her marrying me at that time, and felt that I couldn't ask her to as long as she was dependent on me. She knew I would marry her at any time and finally made up her mind that she would not allow me to do anything more for her unless we were married. A bald statement of the conditions of that time will not explain how easy it was for me to agree. It was probably weak, but you must make allowances for me. We got married, then, in March 1906, on

"I was, of course, very fond of her but didn't dream of her marrying me at that time."

Premier Haultain would indeed be good enough, and two months later just such a bill was sent to Ottawa, embodying three of his four key principles for autonomy. There should be provincial control of land and natural resources, a provincial right to tax the Canadian Pacific, and full provincial control of education as provided for in the British North America Act. Other proposals dealt with the way a capital could be chosen and special compensatory taxes for lands that had been granted to the CPR. Haultain omitted his fourth key principle — one big province. A few territorial members favoured two.

Meanwhile, Ottawa was under pressure from another quarter. Manitoba at that time was the freak province of Confederation. It had been given provincehood prematurely and out of dire necessity, as the only possible means of settling the first Riel Rebellion. But the central wherewithal of provincial finance, control of crown lands and through them the resources the lands produce — forest products, petroleum, coal or minerals — had been denied. In the case of Manitoba alone, Ottawa retained control of land. Manitoba therefore was denied a fundamental provincial right, which persuaded Haultain that the terms of provincehood for Manitoba must never be repeated in the new province.

Manitoba had begun as a tiny rectangle around Winnipeg and the Red River, known as "the postage stamp province." Its border had been extended in 1881 and again in 1884, at one point stretching east to Lake Superior until a lawsuit brought by Ontario pushed it back to the western limits of Lake of the Woods. In the murmurings for provincehood in the adjoining North-West Territories, Manitoba saw a solution for some of its problems. It sought to persuade Ottawa to extend Manitoba's boundary westward, up to and including Regina. A second province, it proposed, could then be formed between Manitoba and BC.

Manitoba's shrewd and affable Tory premier, Rodmond Roblin, naturally knew that this might not prove too attractive to people in the eastern territories, the ones Manitoba proposed to annex, or at Regina where the proposal created something close to apoplexy. But he knew, too, that elsewhere in the territories his scheme would have definite attractions, notably at Calgary, because the disappearance of Regina into Manitoba would establish Calgary as the prime candidate for capital of the province that remained.

By December 1901 the Manitoba campaign had devolved down to a one-on-one confrontation. A debate was arranged between the premier of Manitoba and the premier of the West, Roblin versus Haultain. They met before a jammed hall at Indian Head, District of Assiniboia, one week before Christmas 1901.[6] Both were viewed as master debaters. It was a clash of giants, though by far the heavier burden lay on Roblin who must somehow persuade his farmer audience that their best fortunes lay with Manitoba. The territories, too, would no doubt one day become a province. But who knew how long that would take? And in the meantime, for schools, roads, bridges, hospitals and everything a province could provide, they must depend on the panhandling government at Regina. From Manitoba these would be available immediately.

In reply Haultain argued that the territorial choice lay not between what they had now and what Manitoba could provide, but between provincehood in Manitoba and provincehood on their own. Because provincehood, he assured them, was definitely on the way. In addition they must consider whether they wanted to assume a share of Manitoba's debt, which had been incurred providing services for other areas. They must consider how much more control over the railway industry one big province would have as compared with several little ones. And they must consider that the larger the province the more diverse could be its economy and therefore the more stable. No winner was declared, of course, but if the applause of the crowd was an indicator, Haultain had won hands down. Moreover, he had so solidified the resistance of local people to annexation by Manitoba that from Indian Head onward the Manitoba plan was doomed.

But a major reversal awaited him on the main front of territorial provincehood. Christmas 1901 came and went, the new year began and very shortly the Ottawa response to his October submission became known. The Laurier government was opposed to provincehood at this time. Haultain and his ministers were thunderstruck. What had gone wrong? The explanation, as they were later to discover, lay in the root problem of Canada, the one that had dogged it for nearly 150 years, the struggle between French and English. The territorial quest for provincehood had raised the issue all over again.

— *T.B.*

[6] Dec. 18, 1901, was to put the little community of Indian Head doubly into history. On the same day in the afternoon, in the same hall, homesteader William R. Motherwell called the meeting that led to the creation of the Territorial Grain Growers Association, which in turn generated the whole political farm movement in western Canada. Whether Motherwell also had a hand in organizing the Roblin-Haultain debate that night is not known.

The six proposals for splitting up western Canada

THE ALBERTA-SASKATCHEWAN SCHEME WAS ONLY ONE OF MANY IDEAS
FOR PARTITIONING THE VAST AREA BETWEEN MANITOBA AND BC

When the Laurier government in 1905 came to decide whether and how it would divide the four districts of the North-West Territories, at least six proposed arrangements of provinces had been advocated. Some were widely supported, others advocated by an individual or a group. The six were:

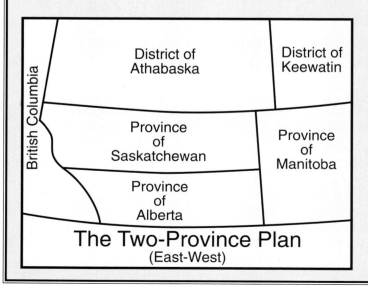

The Haultain Plan

A. The Haultain Plan: endorsed by about three-quarters of the territorial legislature. This would have created one big province — Haultain suggested it be called "Buffalo" — which would extend from Manitoba to BC and from the American border to the 57th parallel. Haultain argued: (a) that this area was already being administered as a unit by the territorial government; (b) that two governments would create useless administrative duplication; (c) that a greater diversity of agri-

The Two-Province Plan
(East-West)

culture and industry would create greater economic stability; and (d) that a big province in the West was essential to counter the power of Ontario and Quebec. Laurier contended that such a province would be too large. Privately he also said he feared it could overwhelm the two central provinces.

B. The Two-Province Plan — North-South: the one ultimately adopted, advocated by a Calgary group headed by R.B. Bennett and supported by Liberal MP Frank Oliver of Edmonton, but by only seven members of the territorial legislature. The western arguments for it were that with one big province the seat of government was too far removed from the people; with two the administration could keep better track of

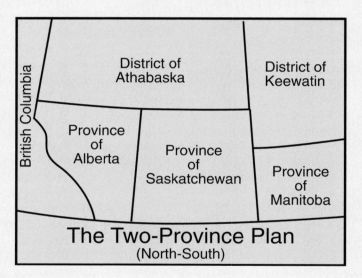

The Two-Province Plan
(North-South)

local needs. Calgary also urged that it, being by far the largest city, would become the capital. Oliver backed the scheme because he felt sure that through his power in Ottawa he could make Edmonton the capital.

C. The Two-Province Plan — East-West: advocated by Thomas McKay, territorial member for Prince Albert West, and supported by T.O. Davis, MP for the District of Saskatchewan. It envisioned two provinces divided by a line running east and west along the southern border of the District of Saskatchewan and slicing the old District of Alberta in two just south of Red Deer. The argument for this scheme was economic. The southern plains country, which was largely pasture, differed greatly from the northern parkland, which was given to grain. It was also pointed out that each would have a railway; the Canadian Pacific in the south and the projected Grand Trunk Pacific in the north.

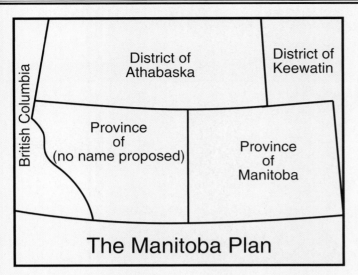

The Manitoba Plan

D. The Manitoba Plan: forcefully put forward by Manitoba's Roblin government. It proposed that the western boundary of Manitoba be moved westward to the third meridian of the Dominion Land Survey (106 degrees west longitude). This would see Regina and Moose Jaw both absorbed by Manitoba. Advancing the plan, Roblin met territorial premier F.W.G. Haultain in their famous debate at Indian Head. It was rejected because of strong resistance from the territorial people involved.

Among less widely publicized ideas were several more imaginative ones, such as:

E. The Three-Province Plan: strongly urged by Thomas H. McGuire, a former judge from Prince Albert. It would have made the three southern districts of the territories — Alberta, Assiniboia and Saskatchewan — into provinces, and left the District of Athabaska in the North-West Territories. It would also have left the eastern boundary of Alberta the same as the district boundary, about 100 miles west of its eventual location.

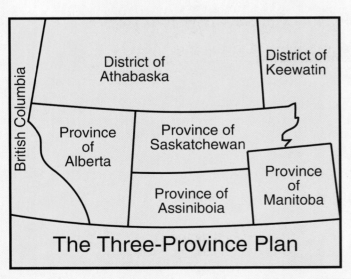

The Three-Province Plan

F. The British Columbia Plan: a scheme mooted by the Calgary *Herald* in 1896, after its campaign for the early provincehood of the District of Alberta fell through, which drew much scorn both in BC and the territories. It would have seen BC annex the whole District of Alberta. The *Herald* dropped the idea quickly. Scoffed the *Regina Leader:* "The question now is whether the *Herald* will advance another fad, or turn in and assist in making of the territories 'the grandest province of the greatest Dominion of the most mighty Empire upon which the sun has ever shone.' " The *Leader* was advocating what became the Haultain plan, though Haultain had not yet adopted it.

Dr. C.C. Lingard, definitive historian of the quest for provincial government in the territories, says in his *Territorial Government in Canada* (University of Toronto Press, 1946) that time has vindicated the Haultain plan. The territorial government was indeed administering the whole area satisfactorily.

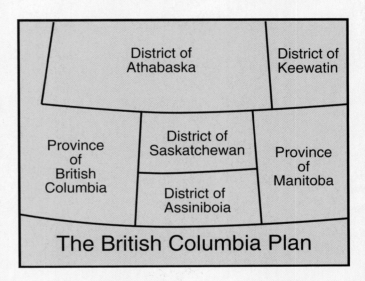

The British Columbia Plan

The argument that one proposed province was primarily cattle country and the other grain was false. A Department of the Interior study showed that both provinces had an almost equal inventory of grain and grazing land. As for the size of the proposed province, it would have been 506,985 square miles. In 1912, the federal government expanded Quebec northward to cover 594,534 square miles and Ontario to cover 412,582. So the "too big" contention was a hollow one.

The real reasons why one big province was rejected, Dr. Lingard concludes, were the petty rivalry among local interests for the capital, the fact that Laurier ignored the territorial assembly in making the decision, and "the fear in the older provinces that one large province would assert a preponderant influence in the dominion of parliament." As the future history of the prairies unfolded, however, Haultain was increasingly vindicated by events, and in the freight rate wars and energy wars with Ottawa one big province could have made a decisive difference.

— *T.B.*

CHAPTER TWO

SIR WILFRID LAURIER

Born: Nov. 20, 1841, at St-Lin (now Laurentides), Canada East, north of Montreal

Died: Feb. 17, 1919, Ottawa

Knighted: 1897

Career Apex: Prime Minister of Canada, July 1896 - October 1911

Major Accomplishment: Balanced the interests of French and English Canada during a period of industrial growth and rapid immigration to the West.

Quotation: 'I am branded in Quebec as a traitor to the French, and in Ontario as a traitor to the English. In Quebec I am branded as a Jingo, and in Ontario as a separatist. In Quebec I am attacked as an imperialist, and in Ontario as an anti-imperialist. I am neither. I am a Canadian.'

Autonomy for Alberta was Laurier's ticking bombshell

BUT THE LIBERAL CHIEF NAVIGATED THE STRAIT BETWEEN CHURCH AND STATE
AND SOLVED A LITTLE PROBLEM CALLED HAULTAIN IN THE PROCESS

Unbeknownst to the West, a proposal for territorial provincehood could easily have ripped the Laurier government down the middle. One aspect of Haultain's draft bill, regarded generally in the territories as obvious and inconsequential, would be regarded in Quebec and Ontario as dynamite enough to bring down the government. This was the question of whether the new province should, or should not, provide publicly supported Catholic schools. Of course it should, said many Quebeckers, being devout Catholics. Certainly not, said many Ontarians, being militant Protestants. To retain power Laurier needed both provinces. Which way would he go?

The Haultain bill took a moderate Protestant position. It simply left the question up to the new province to decide. But this, Quebeckers feared, would automatically mean no Catholic schools because most territorial citizens were English-speaking Protestants. True, the territorial cabinet itself did not quite take this position. There were already eleven denominational schools in the territories, nine Catholic and two Protestant. All eleven were publicly supported, but their curriculums were under the control of the territorial government. Haultain's intention was to maintain this status quo. This satisfied most Catholic laymen. Most Catholic clergy, however, regarded the situation as altogether inadequate.

The bishops in Quebec were particularly opposed. They were still outraged, and with considerable justification, over the way the same question had been handled in Manitoba five years earlier. At the time of the first Riel Rebellion, Manitobans were largely French-speaking Metis, and the Manitoba Act had guaranteed that a French Catholic school system would be permanently preserved when the province came into being. Thereafter, however, tens of thousands of Ontarians, many of them militant Protestants, had poured into the province, taken over the government, and abolished the Catholic schools. Guarantee or no guarantee, they said, the British North America Act made education a provincial responsibility and this was the provincial government decision.

The Manitoba Catholics appealed the case right through the Canadian courts to the Privy Council in London, and lost. Meanwhile it had become a seething political issue. The Tories, anxious to regain the Quebec support they had lost by executing Louis Riel (Vol. 1, p. 158), introduced into parliament a bill to disallow the Manitoba statute, exercising a federal power later removed from the Constitution. Laurier, by now the Liberal leader, opposed the disallowance bill and fought

---

The question of Catholic schools in the new province pitted Ontarians against Quebeckers. Laurier needed both. Which way would he go?

---

the election of 1896 on that issue. His position as a Catholic, however, was anomalous. On the one hand, he crusaded as a defender of provincial rights. If a federal parliament can successfully disallow a Manitoba law, he declared, it could also disallow a Quebec law; the Manitoba School Act could provide the precedent by which the English majority in parliament could gradually take over Quebec. But on the other hand, the effect of his crusade was to sustain the Manitoba School Act that closed the Catholic schools. While the Quebec people flocked to vote for him, their bishops

Msgr. Donatus Sbaretti. His message to Laurier: support for the Catholic schools is expected.

were singularly unsupportive. Many saw him as a closet anti-Catholic. They were reaffirmed in this suspicion by Laurier's final disposition of the Manitoba schools. Religious teaching was permitted in the public schools in the last half-hour of the day by a clergyman of any denomination, and parents must approve of children taking part. French could be the language of instruction in French-speaking communities, and some Catholic teachers must be hired by public school boards. In Manitoba, local French Catholic leaders denounced it as a betrayal of minority rights and in Quebec one archbishop declared: "I tell you there will be a revolt in Quebec that will ring throughout Canada and these men [i.e. Laurier's Liberals] who are today triumphant will be cast down. The settlement is a farce. The fight has only begun."

Laurier's Quebec opponents were given another reason for suspicion when he formed his cabinet. While the controversy over the Manitoba School Act raged throughout the '90s, the man who had distinguished himself as the most formidable foe in the West of both Catholic schools and the official use of the French language was Manitoba's attorney-general. He had worked long and hard in the legislature, on public platforms and in the courts to completely secularize the province's school system. He had prevailed, and was seen by many churchmen as the most dangerous anti-Catholic in the West. His name was Clifford Sifton, and now he reigned as Laurier's senior western minister. Nor was Sifton the only militant Protestant in the Laurier inner circle. Another was William Stevens Fielding, Laurier's minister of finance[1]; still another was William Mulock, his postmaster-general.

No sooner had Laurier taken office, therefore, than the bishops in Quebec began to pressure him about the territories. Catholic schools had been authorized there by the Northwest Territories Act of 1875, but the territorial government had systematically reduced them to a mere adjunct of the public system. What would Laurier do about this, the bishops demanded, in the event the territories became provinces? (Their correspondence with him was confidential, of course, but came to light when his papers were published after his death in 1921.) Moreover, by the turn of the cen-

---

The Tories had a new leader in Robert Borden, Laurier's equal in debate and representative of a rejuvenated party that had distanced itself from the 'old men' of Macdonald's day.

---

tury the bishops had a powerful ally. The papal legate in Ottawa was Monsignor Donatus Sbaretti, Archbishop of Ephesus, a distinguished ecclesiastical diplomat who soon achieved close communication with the Prime Minister's Office. The message Msgr. Sbaretti conveyed was unmistakable. If Laurier did not establish truly Catholic schools in the territories, he could expect to find himself vigorously opposed in the next election by the church in Quebec. On the other hand, if he *did* establish them, where did this leave Clifford Sifton? He would have to publicly defend the same policies he had so passionately condemned when he was attorney-general of Manitoba. Finally, what about Laurier's own integrity? He had been elected as the champion of provincial rights in Manitoba. Was he now, by imposing Catholic schools on a new province rather than letting the province itself decide, to present himself as the foe of provincial rights? It seemed an impossible choice.

None of this Quebec pressure on Laurier was known by Clifford Sifton, when he cheerfully encouraged the territorial ministers in his letter of March 1901. As far as the territorial Catholic schools were concerned, he felt, as did Haultain, that nothing more need be done than to preserve the status quo. Then he discovered Laurier to be mysteriously loath to act on the issue — indeed, adamantly opposed to acting on it in the immediate future. Hence the cabinet's flat rejection of the territorial proposal in January 1902.

In the meantime, what was Haultain to do? He could either abandon the quest for provincehood, despite the confident reassurances he had made to the farmers at Indian Head. Or he could

Why, in the name of patriotism, attempt to resurrect the now-dormant separate school question? Why, when we have profound peace, attempt to prejudge public opinion? The school question will come up again all too soon.
- Sir Wilfrid Laurier in parliament, June 7, 1904.

continue the fight. He decided to fight, and his first task was to be sure he had his electorate behind him. He put a resolution before the territorial legislature "regretting" the rejection by the Laurier government. It carried 21-7, the seven holdouts being those who favoured two provinces. He then called a territorial election for May 21. His platform: one big province with full control of land and resources, full control of education, and an end to the CPR's tax exemption. His supporters were elected by a good margin, but the two-province people took seven seats; the question of how many provinces would continue to divide the House. Among the newcomers was a scholarly lawyer from Strathcona, the city across the North Saskatchewan River from Edmonton, Alexander Cameron Rutherford, the dignified gentleman who was to become the first premier of Alberta.

Further developments complicated the problem. Since Laurier had declared the federal government opposed to provincehood at this time, his MPs in the territories had to assume the same position. This was difficult for Frank Oliver, who with his *Edmonton Bulletin* had by now taken to speaking in favour of it. Walter Scott, the Liberal MP, must make an even more abrupt about-face; he had been an outspoken supporter of provincehood from the beginning. And the federal Tories had a new leader in Robert Laird Borden, a Halifax lawyer who was Laurier's equal in debate and represented a rejuvenated Tory party that had finally distanced itself from the "old men" of Macdonald's day. Borden toured the West in 1902 and quickly discerned a Liberal vulnerability in the conflict between the prime minister and the territorial government. He declared himself and the federal party unequivocally in favour of immediate provincehood for the territories, with full provincial control over land and resources. Hence Haultain, the Tory, and his cabinet of Liberals found themselves opposing the federal Liberal government, while the federal Tories loudly campaigned on their behalf. In the course of the next year this chaotic situation would begin to destroy the non-partisanship that was the foundation of Haultain's provincehood campaign, and with it Haultain's political career.

The government was rejecting provincehood, declared Clifford Sifton, chiefly because the territories couldn't agree on how many provinces there should be. Haultain replied that such a contention was "not worthy of serious consideration." Certainly the people were not unanimously in favour of one province, he acknowledged. "Could you ever get a people to be unanimous on any question? By far the greater number are in favour of one province and I am simply acting on their behalf." He strove at first to sustain his political neutrality, surrounded as he was with Liberal ministers, in particular Arthur Sifton, his treasurer, and George Hedley Vicars Bulyea, a New Brunswick-born school teacher elected to the assembly from South Qu'Appelle, who served as the territorial minister of public works. Thwarted by the Ottawa Liberals, however, Haultain inevitably gravitated towards the Tories, despite the fact that their foremost luminary in Calgary, R.B. Bennett, was entrenched as territorial leader of the opposition.

At some stage in the midst of these developments there came another letter from his secret love Marion. She had returned to her family home in Ottawa and had met a wonderful American, she said, who wanted to take her to his home in Sioux Falls, South Dakota. She was considering a divorce from her husband. What did Haultain think? He advised her against the divorce, and no

Glenbow Archives, NA-1514-2

Opposition leader Robert Borden. Sensing an opportunity, he declared himself in full support of provincial rights over land and resources.

[1] Fielding was from Nova Scotia, a province where many had bitterly opposed confederation with Canada in 1867. Indeed, a Nova Scotia government had been elected in 1867 on the promise that it would keep Nova Scotia out, but could not prevent passage of the BNA Act. Nova Scotia, in other words, did not join Canada; it was shanghaied. Twenty years later, with the province's once-prosperous economy disintegrating, Fielding led Nova Scotia Liberals to victory on a "leave Canada" platform. But he, too, failed to accomplish this. He later ran federally, joined the Laurier cabinet, and was widely viewed as Laurier's logical successor. Events, however, were to turn out differently.

[2] Haultain's correspondence with Marion has never been found. In a subsequent letter to her father, parts of which are reprinted in the last chapter, he discloses that he had opposed the divorce.

Haultain chose to campaign for the Tories in 1904. 'Let us fight for our rights with all the energy we can command,' he urged.

doubt raised questions about the integrity of the American. But as he soon learned, she ignored the advice, obtained the divorce, and left with the American for South Dakota.[2]

The following spring, in March 1903, Haultain's political dilemma reached crisis point. He was invited by the Borden Tories to attend their convention in Moose Jaw, where they intended to found a territorial Conservative association. How could he refuse? He had always insisted he was a Conservative in federal politics and Borden was now the champion of the territorial cause. But if he accepted, would he not imperil the unity of his own cabinet? How could he claim to be a political neutral if he so thoroughly identified with the critics of the Liberal government? He attended the convention and urged the Tories to remain neutral in territorial politics, but accepted the post of honorary president of the association. The Tories cheered. The Laurier Liberals took it as an act of war.

The first backlash came from his old ally, Walter Scott, whose *Regina Leader* demanded he resign as territorial premier. Frank Oliver, the onetime non-partisan independent editorialist but now an unswerving Laurier devotee, began an attack on him through the *Bulletin* that would grow more strident as the next federal election approached. Throughout 1903, Haultain's own language became increasingly anti-government, though his cabinet of Liberals held fast.

For Laurier, Haultain's Tory activism was more than a passing problem. If Laurier were to create one big province out of the territories, Haultain undoubtedly would become its premier. And Haultain, whatever his protestations, was a Tory. So both this new province of "Buffalo," along with Roblin's Manitoba, would be Tory. He would be building a Tory fortress in the West. Clearly something had to be done to get rid of Haultain. But what?

Regina's Walter Scott had a suggestion. Appoint Haultain to the bench. A judgeship was thereupon quietly offered him, and with it, of course, financial security for the rest of his life. But would

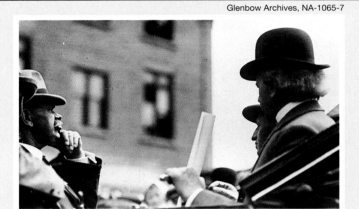

Laurier (right) during a visit to Calgary late in the decade. He'd supported Riel once, but in 1905 he opposed western resource control.

The fear of second-class, second-rate provincehood

THE FOUNDERS OF CONFEDERATION HAD DOMINION OVER THEIR LAND AND RESOURCES. BUT WOULD ALBERTA?

From the Ottawa perspective, the most explosive question to be decided when new provinces were created in the West was the "school issue" — whether they should have state-supported Catholic schools. But in the territories this was not paramount. Of greater concern to westerners was who would own the public lands. Would it be the federal government (then called the dominion government) or the new province or provinces?

They had good reason to worry. Canada at that time had seven provinces. Six of them — Ontario, Quebec, Nova Scotia, New Brunswick, Prince Edward Island and British Columbia —

were what could be called "full provinces." The other, Manitoba, was a kind of "half-province." The difference lay in the control of public lands.

When the six full provinces were formed, all lands that were not privately owned were automatically turned over to their governments. With them went the revenues they produced — from the sale of homesteads, or timber, or from any coal, gold, silver, base metals, gas or oil, or from the power that could be produced from their rivers. This constituted a major source of revenue without which no provincial government could function.

Although Manitoba was the least of the seven provinces, it was not the last — the last to join Canada, that is. It was in fact the fifth. The original Canadian Confederation in 1867 consisted of four: Ontario, Quebec, Nova Scotia and New Brunswick. Three years later the Canadian government acquired the western properties of the Hudson's Bay Company and sent out a governor to rule them as a colony.

But the local people rebelled under Louis Riel, barred the governor at the border, and set up their own government (Vol. I, p. 121). The rebellion was settled when Ottawa agreed to make Manitoba a province in 1870.

Manitoba's population, however, was only about 12,000 people, mostly French Metis. Ottawa feared that if the lands were left in local control the buffalo-hunting Metis would simply close them to cultivation, thereby blocking settlement.

Therefore Ottawa retained control of Manitoba's public lands, compensating the province by means of a per capita annual subsidy that in effect subjugated it in perpetuity to the dominion government. Settlers poured into the province and developed it, but the Manitoba lands nevertheless remained firmly in federal control.

To the people of the North-West Territories, therefore, the question was this: Would they gain full provincehood like the six, or be made another half-province like Manitoba? Long before Feb. 21, 1905, when Laurier brought in Bill 69 creating accepting it be The Right Thing? What about people like the farmers he had reassured at Indian Head? He would be walking out on the cause. Haultain refused the appointment. Scott was furious at what he considered absurd ingratitude. The judgeship went to Arthur Sifton instead, making the Liberal Bulyea Haultain's No.1 lieutenant.

Meanwhile, the Tories warmed to Haultain. Bennett paid unaccustomed tribute to him when the territorial legislature opened in 1903 for what was to be its last session. The Tory press turned up the steam. "'No Surrender!' is the motto," proclaimed the *Calgary Herald*, "and nothing will be left undone until the people of the territories are granted the same rights as their fellow men in the eastern provinces." The "conduct of the administration at Ottawa," it said, "is quite sufficient to raise another rebellion in the North-West Territories." "How different are the views of Sir Wilfrid concerning self-government when the North-West Territories appeal for autonomy," sneered the

---

The Tory press turned up the steam. 'Nothing will be left undone,' said the *Herald*, 'until the territories are granted the same rights as the eastern provinces.'

---

the province of Alberta, and Bill 70 which created Saskatchewan, the argument was already raging. The territorial assembly to a man was insisting on full provincehood. But people in Ottawa were putting up other arguments.

What about immigration, they said. The federal government was laying out vast sums to bring homesteaders to the new territories, and was maintaining generous land-sale policies to make sure these people got farms. How could Ottawa be sure the provinces would maintain these land policies?

Moreover, the dominion government had actually "bought" the region from the Hudson's Bay Company. In the case of the six full provinces, the colonial governments that existed before they joined Confederation already owned the public lands.

Territorial residents considered these arguments both false and self-serving. Was not every town and city using all possible expedients to encourage immigrants to settle there? Why would they not maintain generous land-sale policies?

As for the claim that the dominion government "bought" the lands, that was not what had happened at all. A brilliant Calgary lawyer named Charles A. Stuart, later to become an Alberta Supreme Court judge, explained the case in a speech to the Young Men's Liberal Club of Calgary.

The payment Canada made to the Hudson's Bay Company was not in compensation for the land, he said, but for the investment the company had made in the West. The land itself was ceded from Britain to the dominion government, just as Britain had turned over all crown lands to the other colonies when they had gained independence. "According to all the precedents of British colonial history, and according to the spirit of the Canadian constitutional arrangements, the assembly of the new province will be entitled to assume control of this source of revenue," he declared.

Moreover, as strategists like territorial premier Frederick Haultain were acutely aware, there were other and later precedents than the Manitoba one. These were set when provinces number six and seven joined Confederation.

When British Columbia became a province in 1871, the year after Manitoba, provincial ownership of public lands was instantly assumed — so much so that the dominion government actually compensated the province with an annual cash payment for the extensive Canadian Pacific right-of-way.

When Prince Edward Island became a province, two years after BC, the dominion government not only recognized PEI's right to the lands, but gave the province money to buy back any unoccupied land that the British government had ceded to British peers and other proprietors back in colonial days.

Nevertheless, when Laurier brought in Bills 69 and 70, the Ottawa decision was adverse, and Laurier wouldn't budge on it. The public land of Alberta and Saskatchewan was to remain in the control of the dominion government. They were to be half-provinces like Manitoba.

Since Ottawa's given reasons for doing this didn't make much sense, people naturally wondered what the *real* reasons were. They could only guess at them.

First, Ottawa doubtless coveted the mining and resource revenues which, particularly in the case of Alberta coal, were beginning to look very lucrative indeed.

Second, Ottawa wanted to retain as much political control as it could. The West, it realized, did not share quite the same cultural background as the East. In the East there were two "founding nations." In the West, if you took into account who settled it, there were a score or more "founding nations," one of them the United States.

Third, the purpose of territorial development, as Laurier's senior western minister himself had said, was to bolster the industrial growth of Ontario and Quebec. That's why Canada was settling the West. In other words, provinces number five, eight and nine were to remain semi-colonies.

This issue, in one form or another, would rage for the entire century.

— *T.B.*

Cartoonist Newton McConnell in the Toronto News, March 1905. Provincehood was coming, Laurier promised, but he gave no details on its form.

THE WEST — AUTONOMY — PROVINCIAL RIGHTS — SOFT SOAP

HE WONT BE HAPPY TILL HE GETS IT.

Montreal Star, than when he is in London negotiating further independence for Canada. The Laurier-supporting newspaper *Le Canada* explained to its readers that the demand for autonomy in the West was actually "an invention of the *Montreal Star*." This irked the Tory *Edmonton Journal*, which headlined: "Laurier insults the people of the territories."

To resolve all this, Laurier developed a threefold plan. His first move was fiscal. He increased generously the grant to the territorial government. At the same time the Liberal press, though defensive, endeavoured to pacify passions where before it had sought to arouse them. Scott's *Regina Leader*, hitherto an outspoken supporter of provincehood, now discovered that the need for it had been eased by new railway policies and heftier federal grants. Oliver's *Edmonton Bulletin* assured its readers that the territories were now getting more aid from Ottawa than they would

R.B. Bennett redux

MAYBE THE AMBITIOUS CALGARY LAWYER AND FUTURE PM WASN'T JUST AN OPPORTUNIST AFTER ALL

Richard Bedford Bennett, the Calgary lawyer who enters Canadian history in the territorial legislature and who became Canada's prime minister during the Great Depression, died in Britain in 1947, a man rejected by, and disgusted with, the country he felt he had given his life to. For nearly half a century his image was to remain frozen in history as an arrogant, crafty, unfeeling autocrat of ruthless ambition, boundless energy, and no sympathy whatever for his fellow man. Long after he was gone from office, socialist politicians could still recall to the electors the days of "Iron Heel Bennett."

But in the 1990s, nearly half a century after his death, a different side of this mysterious and reclusive man began to emerge. It was revealed by another Calgarian, the popular historian James H. Gray, who published a book that reassessed the character of Richard Bedford Bennett.[a] By filtering through the 627,000 items in Bennett's personal papers, biographer Gray was able to reconstruct Bennett's childhood in New Brunswick and his career in Calgary up to his election as Conservative national leader in 1927.

R.B. was the brilliant first-born son of an ambitious Methodist mother and a work-weary father preoccupied with a disintegrating family ship-building business. What

Richard Bedford Bennett as a young lawyer. He quickly became known as Calgary's best-dressed citizen.

as provinces. Provincehood, it believed, would be a "detriment" to the West. The Toronto *News*, however, guessed right. Territorial autonomy was not being delayed for fiscal reasons, it said, or because of any uncertainty over the number of provinces, but because Laurier couldn't face the school issue. James Clinkskill, territorial MLA for Saskatoon, went farther still. "The hierarchy," he said, "want a clause in any autonomy act…which would give them absolute control over these schools." His assertion, events would soon prove, was absolutely right.

The prime minister's second move was purely political. Could he not offset the imposing strength of Haultain's legislature, he wondered, with a bigger federal caucus from the territories? If there were eight or ten constituencies between Manitoba and BC, could it not be contended that they represented the views of western people just as effectively as the territorial members? [3] He knew, too, that the tens of thousands of people pouring into the territories, all of them brought there by Clifford Sifton's immigration schemes, were far more likely to vote Liberal than Tory.[4] Accordingly, in 1904 Laurier redistributed the constituencies, increasing territorial representation in the Commons to ten from four. He also called a general election for November 3.

The election intensified Haultain's predicament. Would he stay out of it, or would he campaign for the Tories? He chose the latter, and hurled himself into the Tory cause. He spoke at Regina, Moose Jaw, Edmonton, Medicine Hat, Calgary, Red Deer, Macleod, Okotoks, Lacombe, St. Albert and Strathcona. "Let us fight for our rights with all the energy we can command," he urged. "The only way to show the Liberal government that we are in earnest is to turn them down at the polls. Give them a crushing defeat and we will get the rights we demand."

[3] This same contention — that a federal caucus from a given province can represent the views of the people as reliably as a provincial government — would be made by another Liberal prime minister eighty years later. Pierre Trudeau argued that in approving Canada's "repatriated" constitution his federal Liberal caucus from Quebec represented the approval of the people of Quebec. The provincial government of Rene Levesque had refused to approve it.

[4] Roy Romanow, who nearly nine decades later would become premier of Saskatchewan, once said that when his father arrived in Canada he knew two sentences in English: "Me Canadian. Me Liberal."

---

emerges is a boy passionately devoted to his mother, who schooled him in evangelical Christianity, the Bible, hard work, teetotalism, and the responsibility "to earn all you can, save all you can, and give all you can."

Bennett was a bookish youngster but not a quiet one. In fact, he was what a later generation would call "a smart ass,"

While still teaching Bennett read law, articled with a reputable firm in Chatham, New Brunswick, and eventually attended and excelled at Dalhousie law school. Practising in Chatham, he ran for city council. Aitken, who seems always to have admired and emulated him, was his campaign manager. He won, but did not serve long.

The year of the Laurier triumph, Bennett stepped off the train in Calgary. It was cold. He checked into the Alberta Hotel, where he would live for the next two years and eat for the next thirty.

described by a couplet that fellow students composed in an inventory of his class: First there came Bennett, conceited and young, who never quite knew when to hold his quick tongue.

Conceited though he might be, however, Bennett was in no sense cold. He held his Tory and Methodist convictions passionately, and learned from his youth onward to expound and defend them heatedly on the public platform. He became a country school teacher, prepared his own program of "basics" for his students, and was known for both the high standards he demanded of bright pupils and the patience he showed for slower ones.

He also formed some lifetime friendships, one of them with a brash youngster nine years his junior whom he met on a ferry dock one day. This was Max Aitken, destined to become the British press mogul Lord Beaverbrook. Another friend was Alma Russell, an acquaintance of his youth for whom he developed a strong affection. But it led to nothing further, although after she moved to Vancouver they corresponded for the rest of her life. She never married; neither did he.

Something intervened — namely, a letter from James Lougheed, the most eminent lawyer, Conservative luminary and senator in Calgary. This town 2,625 miles (4,200 km) to the west-north-west, on the bald and dusty prairie, was a terrain and social milieu that Bennett could scarcely have imagined, but Lougheed's real estate enterprises had left little time for a law practice. He wanted a competent partner to run the office; Dalhousie recommended Bennett and Bennett accepted. In 1896, the year of the Laurier triumph, R.B. Bennett stepped off a train at the Calgary station. It was January, and cold.

He checked in at the Alberta Hotel, where he would live for the next two years and take his meals for the next thirty. Next day he toured what there was of this frontier railway

[a] *R.B. Bennett; the Calgary Years*, University of Toronto Press, 1991. Author Gray, a former reporter for the *Winnipeg Free Press*, came to Calgary in the 1950s and specialized in articles on the oil and gas industry. He began writing history with an autobiographical account of Depression Winnipeg called *The Winter Years*, and went on to publish various books on the West. His journalistic style and reporter's eye for intriguing detail put them among the most readable of all western Canadian historical works.

The Liberal press replied harshly. This was non-partisan? Scott's *Leader* again demanded he resign as premier. Haultain was plainly an "enemy of the Grand Trunk Pacific," the new transcontinental railway Laurier was planning for the West, said the Liberals. The *Edmonton Journal* quoted a rumour printed in the *Winnipeg Telegram* that Bulyea would resign from the territorial cabinet.

Clifford Sifton had returned unexpectedly to Ottawa. Surely, thought Haultain, they are not going to act immediately. Then the following day he was summoned by Laurier.

(Bulyea did not.) The *Bulletin*, reporting on Haultain's Edmonton appearance, lavishly quoted Oliver's castigation of him as the villainous agent of the hated CPR monopoly. The *Edmonton Journal* replied that Haultain "tore to shreds the poor defence of Mr. Oliver," and "with quiet, forcible argument and merciless sarcasm" recalled Oliver's "erratic" record on the autonomy question.

Laurier's third and decisive move clinched the outcome. If the Liberals were returned to power, he said, territorial autonomy would be enacted the next year. Beyond that bare promise he did not go; the terms of provincehood were left unstated. But the announcement bollixed both sides in the West. Haultain and the Tories lost the whole basis of their attack, while the entire Liberal pack suddenly had to reverse themselves again, and chorus that immediate autonomy was not such a bad

town in winter, grimly beholding the dust-caked snow, the dirt streets, the brawling bars, the four or six blocks of one- and two-storey buildings that comprised Calgary's downtown area. Over and through it all hung the unmistakable odour of horse manure. Next day he entered Lougheed's offices across the street from the hotel in the Clarence Block, and the firm of Lougheed & Bennett was born.

Bennett came to love Calgary, but not quickly. In that first year or two, he admitted later, he would have left if he could. At one point the *Revelstoke Herald* actually printed a story that he was moving there. But gradually his roots went down. When his younger brother, George, followed him to Calgary the two moved into the rooming house on Reinach Avenue, which R.B. would occupy for the next twenty years. He joined the congregation of First Methodist Church on Second Street West, served on the board, taught Sunday school, arranged for a new church site and handled the legal work,

Glenbow Archives, NA-64-3

The Clarence Block on Stephen Avenue which housed the law offices of Lougheed & Bennett. R.B. turned the legal battle with prosecutor Sifton into an exercise in personal animus.

idea after all. In the consequent confusion, however, the Liberals were returned to power with 139 seats, five more than before. The Tories won 75, five fewer than before. In the West, the results were the same. Of the ten seats, seven went Liberal, three Tory. Across the country, Borden had failed. In the West, so did Bennett. Haultain too lost credibility, and was now recognized as an undisputed foe of the triumphant Liberals.

Christmas came and went, with Haultain as usual the guest in other people's houses, having no family of his own. On New Year's Eve, he and Bulyea, faithful as always, left for Ottawa where they were to discuss with a cabinet committee the terms for provincehood. They arrived in the capital on January 4. Soon other delegations from the West were arriving as well. From Fort Saskatchewan and Prince Albert came requests for bridges over the North Saskatchewan River. Saskatoon (now bursting with growth) wanted a bridge over the South Saskatchewan. Calgary, Edmonton, Lethbridge and Red Deer advanced compelling arguments why they each should be chosen as capital of whatever province might be formed. Dr. R.G. Brett, longtime MLA for Banff, came down to present the case

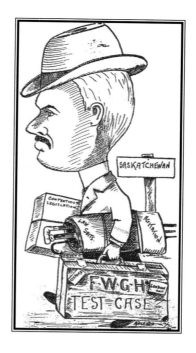

Kaleido cartoon in 1905. Haultain's political life was becoming as much of a disaster as his love life.

and plunged into temperance campaigns. Soon Max Aitken also arrived, appalling his old friend by opening a bowling alley across the street from Bennett's office. The West did not appeal to Aitken, however. He spent a desultory couple of years in Calgary, moved briefly to Edmonton and then went back east.

But Bennett became a fixture. His immaculate attire, altogether out of character with a frontier town, quickly won him recognition as Calgary's best-dressed citizen. His table at the

lour. Sifton represented the prosecution, and Bennett turned the confrontation into an exercise in personal animus. The significance was not, of course, apparent then — Bennett, the future prime minister, versus Sifton, future premier of Alberta.

The grand contest between them occurred in the Harris-Grouin attempted murder case, one of the few criminal trials Bennett ever fought. Calgary farm implement dealer Edward Harris had caught his wife and his business partner, George Grouin, *in flagrante delicto*. He attacked Grouin and in the ensu-

Bennett cited the ancient legal rights accorded cuckolded husbands. He established that Grouin habitually seduced wives. Soon he had the whole courtroom cheering for Harris.

Alberta Hotel, well to the rear but commanding a view of the whole dining room, became a gathering point for the city's Tories — provided they didn't smoke. Bennett eventually tolerated drinking in his presence, but smoking hardly ever.[b]

From this table he would walk each evening across the street to the Clarence Block, and work long into the night beneath the high-powered acetylene gaslights Lougheed had installed. Under their contract, Bennett collected 20% of the firm's net income until his earnings reached $3,750 a year, 30% of any earnings above that. Both percentages rose by 5% annually.

His income in the first year was under $1,000, hardly encouraging. He was gaining profile, however, particularly after his first courtroom clash with a man he singularly disliked. Arthur Sifton was not only a hyperactive Liberal, but a brother of Laurier's Interior minister, Clifford Sifton, the biggest Liberal in the West. Bennett was handling an appeal for a Calgarian convicted of illegally operating a billiard par-

ing scuffle wounded him with a revolver. The case attracted wide attention, though it seemed conclusive enough. Harris was plainly guilty. Sifton appeared for the prosecution.

But Bennett rapidly complicated things. He cited the ancient legal rights accorded cuckolded husbands. He established that Grouin habitually seduced other men's wives. Soon he had the whole courtroom cheering for Harris, while the judge repeatedly pounded for order, eventually clearing out the crowd. Bennett won an acquittal for Harris, and his reputation was made.

Then too, with the new century came boom times. His investments in farm real estate began paying off handsomely,

[b] Historian Gray reports that the only person allowed to smoke in Bennett's presence was his back-slapping and raucous neighbour from the Clarence Block, an insurance and real estate agent named George Robinson, whose cigars Bennett, for some reason, always endured. Doubtless it was because Robinson had warmly befriended Bennett when he first arrived in the city.

SPECTACULAR EXTRAVAGANZA.

AUTONOMY BILL

SEPARATE SCHOOL CLAUSE

N. McCONNELL

A puppet show at Ottawa, supported by the State, controlled by the Church.

The McConnell cartoons in the Toronto News (here and opposite page) hammered Laurier mercilessly on the Alberta school question.

for a mountain capital, while a telegram arrived declaring the case for Medicine Hat. A Manitoba delegation was on hand to be sure than any rights or benefits conferred on the new province or provinces be conferred likewise upon Manitoba. Father Albert Lacombe and Bishop Emile Legal arrived from St. Albert, concerned of course with the school issue. Their presence, and the nature of certain questions asked by the federal ministers, created "an atmosphere of foreboding" on the school question, the *Regina Standard* reported.

The House met on January 11. The Speech from the Throne announced only that legislation instituting provincehood would be introduced at that session. Then began daily meetings between Haultain and Bulyea and a cab-

---

the firm's earnings soared, and Bennett cut a new and better deal with his partner. But their biggest client was to become his worst political liability. Lougheed & Bennett represented the hated Canadian Pacific, whose monopoly was everywhere resented and whose habit of ignoring complainants unless they sued did very little for the popularity of R.B. Bennett.

From this, more than anything else, came the impression of cold indifference to human need. Bennett did not live ostentatiously. True, he owned a huge house in Mount Royal and was worth $1 million before the decade ended, but he continued in his rented room on Reinach Avenue. True also, he was rapidly becoming an authority on the CPR's discriminatory freight rates, which as a politician he would militantly oppose. True also, he had successfully represented the carpenters' union against the city's building contractors, declaring to the horror of his business associates: "I will give my best efforts to any labour organization which endeavours to uphold right causes, make better the homes of the people, and help to build a strong and reliant race." None of this could offset the fact that R.B. was also counsel to the CPR.

The legend of Bennett's supposedly cold, dispassionate nature, historian Gray points out, is utterly at odds with his political record, at least as regards temper. He had a frightful one, frequently loosed upon political foes. When he first ran for the territorial assembly at 28, two years after his move to Calgary, opponents mocked his youth and inexperience. He blew up on the platform at Olds. His opponents were expiring old men, he charged, disappointed in quest for any higher office and bereft of new ideas. Outside the hall he became embroiled with one opponent in a shouting match,

which came so close to blows the police were called. He then threatened to assault the policeman. It was the talk of the town, and Bennett easily won the seat over three other candidates.

In the 1900 federal election, however, he represented the Tories against Edmonton's powerful Frank Oliver and was soundly defeated. A "CPR lawyer" was a phenomenon Oliver delighted to attack and destroy.

In the territorial legislature, Bennett's conflict with Premier Frederick Haultain became similarly vehement. Haultain seemed a study in dullness, he said, with a policy of drift. But what really bothered him was Haultain's rejection of party politics. To Bennett, the passionate Tory, it seemed unnatural. He wrote Conservative leader Robert Borden: "It is idle for us to attempt to understand Mr. Haultain's ways. He is a good Conservative but he appoints Grits...The assurance of fealty to a leader and loyalty to a party count in my judgement for very little when the physical evidence of the fealty and loyalty advances the interest of the opposing party."

Thus it was chiefly R.B. Bennett who lured the territorial premier to the Conservative convention at Moose Jaw that began the process of Haultain's destruction (see main story). However, Bennett never could organize a bloc in the legislature that came anywhere near threatening Haultain's control of it. For all his talent and commitment to party, Bennett was a poor organizer of people to a massive cause. Haultain had this vital skill; Bennett didn't. In the end this deficiency would defeat the diligent young lawyer from Calgary.

— *T.B.*

inet committee consisting of Laurier, Justice Minister Charles Fitzpatrick (a Quebecker), Postmaster-General Mulock and Regina's Walter Scott. The obvious absentee was Clifford Sifton, who was taking treatments in the US for a medical condition. How could anything possibly be decided, Haultain wondered, in Sifton's absence?

Haultain again presented the territorial draft bill as the basis of the discussions, which proceeded each morning, the federal people giving no clue whatever where they agreed and disagreed. He soon learned, however, that Laurier was holding meetings each afternoon with his seven-member western caucus. He also discovered that they seemed to be far better informed about federal thinking than were he or Bulyea.

Ottawa was alive with all sorts of rumours, one of which gained immediate credence — that there would be two provinces, not one. Calgary was jubilant; it would surely become the capital city of the westerly one. Another clue to the progress of negotiation was even more ominous. Walter Scott's *Regina Leader,* hitherto the strongest possible advocate of provincial resource control, ran an editorial that discovered great merit in the idea that the federal government should retain jurisdiction over the land.

On February 20 came a startling development. Clifford Sifton had returned unexpectedly to Ottawa and had gone directly to the prime minister's residence that night. Surely, thought Haultain, they are not going to act immediately. He was confident that he, as territorial premier, would at least be shown a draft of the bill before it was made public. But the following day he was called to the prime minister's office and handed a sheaf of papers, the drafts of two bills, one called the Alberta Act, the other the Saskatchewan Act. These were to be introduced in the House immediately. A quick glance disclosed their content.

Haultain wanted one province; there were to be two. He wanted crown lands turned over to provincial jurisdiction; they would remain under Ottawa's control. He wanted the province to decide education policy, in particular whether there should be Catholic schools; publicly supported schools would be mandated, under church, not state, control. He wanted the Canadian Pacific tax exemption removed; it was to remain. His political life was becoming as much of a disaster as his love life. He had failed to win for his beloved territories as surely as he had failed to win his beloved Marion.

For more bad news had come from Marion. Her American suitor had abandoned her and her daughter. She was alone and ill and desperately needed to enter hospital. Her family would not help her. Finally, Haultain no doubt took thought for his own finances. "I had nothing," he would later write, "when I went out of office in 1905." All his savings had been sent to Marion.

And what, he wondered, would Clifford Sifton do?

— *T.B.*

MGR. SBARRETTI—" Now Wilfrid, you see that the goods are delivered."

" HIS MASTER'S VOICE."

CHAPTER THREE

CLIFFORD SIFTON

Born: March 10, 1861, near London, Ontario

Died: April 17, 1929, New York City

Knighted: 1915

Career Apex: Minister of the Interior, 1896-1905

Major Accomplishment: Aggressive immigration policy resulting in the large-scale settlement of the West.

Quotation: 'I think a stalwart peasant in a sheepskin coat, born on the soil, whose forefathers have been farmers for ten generations, with a stout wife and half a dozen children, is good quality.'

The Laurier-Sifton showdown in which Alberta was born

PRESSURED BY THE PAPAL ENVOY, LAURIER HUMILIATED HIS INTERIOR MINISTER AND DESTROYED HAULTAIN, BUT SIFTON'S WILL PREVAILED

As Frederick Haultain looked for the first time on Bills 69 and 70, the federal legislation that would create the provinces of Alberta and Saskatchewan, one intriguing question doubtless surpassed even his bitter disappointment. All Ottawa was soon asking the same question. How could Clifford Sifton possibly countenance these bills? They established a system of government-supported, church-run schools, repudiating everything Sifton had stood for and fought for throughout most of his political career. Clifford Sifton could not possibly have approved them.

Then, too, there were the strange circumstances surrounding their introduction. No one outside the cabinet's most intimate inner circle had been allowed to see them, it was supposed, until three hours before Laurier brought them into the Commons. And Sifton hadn't even been in Ottawa for nearly two months. Surely Laurier wouldn't act without Sifton? Was critical western legislation being brought in behind the back of the senior western minister? Was this Laurier's way of dumping him? That seemed preposterous, yet how else could you explain what was happening?

No one would ever know the full explanation for this mystery, but with the publication years later of Laurier's correspondence certain key facts came out. The Laurier papers disclose that in March 1904, seven months before he called the general election, the papal legate in Ottawa, Archbishop Donatus Sbaretti, asked Laurier for a guarantee, "signed by you as chief of the government and leader of the Liberal Party," that Catholics would be given their own schools when autonomy was granted in the North-West Territories. Laurier replied six days later that "in any province where a system of separate schools exists, the Legislature shall not have the power to do anything which may prejudicially affect those schools." Since separate schools already existed in the territories, said Laurier, their survival "cannot be a matter of doubt."

This assurance persuaded the Catholic church to support Laurier in the October election, but Sbaretti remained insistent and vigilant. On December 30 he wrote Laurier: "I would be grateful to you, if the draft of the bill for the admission of the territories as a province of the dominion would be given me at least by the first of January." (In other words, forthwith.) Laurier replied the next day that the draft wasn't ready. However, on February 11 a draft of the section dealing with the separate schools was provided to Sbaretti and he wrote to Laurier: "I am glad to say we have succeeded in agreeing on a clause." At this point, Haultain, premier of the territories, had seen no part of the bills, nor had he been given the least hint of what was in them. Laurier had provided a state paper to a church envoy before revealing it to the elected Canadian officials most immediately concerned.

The bills had been drawn by Sifton's sharpest adversary within the cabinet, the minister of Justice, Charles Fitzpatrick, a devout Irish Catholic from Quebec who had first distinguished himself twenty years earlier as the chief counsel for Louis Riel (Vol. 1, p. 158), and who would shortly become chief justice of Canada. Fitzpatrick had reported to a five-man cabinet committee consisting of four Catholics—himself; Laurier; R.W. Scott, who was minister of state and government leader in the Senate; and Henri Bourassa, MP for Labelle and a leading Catholic intellectual[1] — and one Protestant, William Mulock, the postmaster-general. Why had Mulock supported the school section? Because, he later said, he regarded it as doing nothing more than reaffirming the existing government-controlled Catholic schools in the territories.

It was exactly here that the misunderstanding lay. In 1875 parliament had conferred upon the French Catholic minority in the territories the unequivocal right to their own schools. But the territorial legislature by 1901 had passed a series of ordinances that in effect brought these separate schools under the state system, which controlled their teacher training and curriculum and inspected them. Sifton was prepared to sustain the territorial separate schools as they now existed; Laurier was restoring the rights they possessed in 1875 before they had been compromised. He wanted the separate schools to have their own textbooks, their own inspectors, freedom to teach religion however they chose, and the right to teach in French. It was this that Sbaretti had approved.

William Fielding, minister of Finance, photographed and in caricature as a member of the 'By-Town Coons' orchestra by Henri Juliens.

But Fitzpatrick's bill went further still. It also conferred upon the separate schools a fixed proportion of the land revenues of the territories, amounting to a permanent and generous endowment. This had escaped Mulock's notice. It did not escape Sifton's.

Surely Laurier wouldn't act without Sifton? Was this Laurier's way of dumping him? That seemed preposterous, yet how else to explain it?

Historians largely agree that Laurier's dissimulation with Sifton that winter amounted to bald deceit. At the end of December Sifton had gone to Indiana for a month to take treatments in the mud baths there for a nervous disorder.[2] During his absence Laurier wrote him detailed letters about those sections of the autonomy bills that dealt with the land issue. Sifton noticed there was no mention of the school section. He wrote to inquire whether Laurier had "discerned any serious difficulty in dealing with it." Laurier answered: "I am slowly working it out. I am satisfied with the progress we have made on it, though everybody dreads it."

Sifton found the baths so beneficial that he wrote Laurier he would remain until February 15. Then he extended his stay yet another week, assuming Bills 69 and 70 would not be introduced until he returned. Suddenly, on February 20, he received a telegram from Laurier. They were being brought in the next day. Alerted and alarmed, Sifton hastened back to Ottawa. He arrived three days later, read the bill appalled, and then read the speech Laurier had given in introducing it. The speech particularly outraged him. Laurier had said:

> I never could understand what objection there could be to a system of schools wherein, after secular matters have been attended to, the tenets of the religion of Christ, even with the divisions which exist among His followers, are allowed to be taught...We live by the side of a nation, a great nation, a nation for which I have the greatest admiration, but whose example I would not take in everything, in whose schools Christian morals are not taught. When I compare these two countries...when I observe in this country of ours a total

absence of lynchings and an almost total absence of divorces and murders, I thank heaven that we are living in a country where the young children of the land are taught Christian morals and Christian dogmas.

It was an attack on the American concept of "national schools" for which Sifton, himself a devout Methodist, was a militant advocate.

Sifton immediately began to foment a caucus revolt against Laurier. He first met with the sev-

The press in Protestant Ontario, including the Liberal press, opened a wild attack on the government as the agents of Rome. The Quebec newspapers, on the other hand, calmly approved.

en Liberal MPs from the territories and assured himself of their support. That night he confronted the prime minister, declared that he could not support the bill, and resigned from cabinet. One of Sifton's biographers, J.W. Dafoe, editor of the Sifton-owned *Manitoba Free Press*, later reconstructed their meeting on the basis of Sifton's recollection of it. The resignation implied that Protestant Liberals were no longer loyal to him, Laurier had responded, so perhaps he should quit instead. (Laurier later confirmed he said this, but added that he had no intention whatever of actually doing it.) Sifton remained unmoved. Each, he said, "must decide his course." Then, Dafoe adds: "The feeling, that in time became almost an obsession with Laurier, that he must not be asked to do anything that would affect his prestige with his own people, was already taking possession of him." Nevertheless, Laurier made a key concession. He agreed to consider any amendment to the school clause Sifton might propose.

This meeting was on a Friday evening, February 24. The following Wednesday, March 1, Laurier announced to a hushed House Sifton's resignation as minister of the Interior. It was startling news in the West. The *Calgary Herald* carried the biggest headline in its history. A subsequent speech by Laurier's finance minister, W.S. Fielding, who had also been away from Ottawa when the bill was introduced, threw him on the Sifton side, prompting justifiable rumours that his resignation was also imminent. Mulock's resignation was also touted, but incorrectly. How could Mulock quit? He had approved the legislation he would now be resigning over. Meanwhile, the press in Protestant Ontario, including the Liberal press, opened a wild attack on the government as the agents of Rome, while the Quebec newspapers calmly approved.

By mid-March Sifton had recruited so much support in the caucus that Laurier capitulated. The Sifton amendment in effect established separate schools that were not separate. They could be operated by Catholic school boards, but their teachers must be certificated by the public system,

Saskatchewan Archives Board, R-B11485 p.2

Charles Fitzpatrick, minister of Justice. Part of the Catholic brick wall Sifton found himself up against.

National Archives of Canada, 25955

William Mulock, Postmaster General. How could he resign over the bill he'd approved?

[1] Bourassa was the grandson of Louis-Joseph Papineau who led a rebellion in Lower Canada in 1837 against the British colonial government. A journalist, he would found in 1910 the newspaper *Le Devoir*, which would remain small in circulation but a highly influential voice of French-Canadian culture and intellect for the century. He was also a committed Catholic and the Laurier papers later revealed he had agreed to run in the 1904 election specifically to help Laurier with the territorial school question.

[2] These water and lithia baths were at a place called Mudlavia. They were excellent, said the advertisements, "for all forms of Rheumatism, Gout, and all Diseases of the Kidneys, Blood, Skin and Nerves." Edwards in the muck-raking Calgary *Eye Opener*, however, claimed that Sifton had not been there at all (see sidebar).

their curriculum controlled by it, and their schools inspected by government agents. "The church," Sifton wrote to Dafoe, "is absolutely eliminated." Peter Talbot, the new Liberal MP from Lacombe, wrote to his friend A.C. Rutherford, the Liberal territorial MLA from Strathcona: "It was necessary to prove to Quebec that their province was not the whole dominion."

In effect, the Sifton amendment simply sustained the territorial separate schools in the compromised form legislated by the Haultain government in 1901. Laurier himself introduced the amendment on March 25. Moderates on both sides accepted it. The militants did not. Ontario

---

Without hesitation Sifton recommended Oliver as his successor. Laurier agreed. Edmonton cheered. It knew that Frank Oliver would give it great influence in Ottawa at this critical time.

Protestants wanted no separate schools at all. Laurier's biographer, O.D. Skelton, inventories their reaction. The Orange Order declared the amended bill "reactionary, inquisitous, insidious, vicious." The general superintendent of the Methodist church called it "mad, monstrous, hideous and oppressive." Conventions of the Presbyterian and Baptist churches demanded its withdrawal. The celebrated journalist and lecturer Goldwin Smith declared that the new provinces would be

Was it sex that killed Clifford Sifton's political career?

THAT'S CERTAINLY HOW BOB EDWARDS LURIDLY DESCRIBED IT, BUT THERE MIGHT HAVE BEEN OTHER REASONS FOR THE INTERIOR MINISTER'S RESIGNATION

Why Clifford Sifton resigned from the Laurier cabinet in February 1905 is no mystery. To have supported the school clauses in the Alberta Act as Laurier originally presented it would have rendered him an unprincipled hypocrite. But why he stayed out after Laurier amended the legislation to his satisfaction has remained one of the unresolved puzzles of Canadian history.

"To those who disliked Sifton or disagreed with him, to many who could not distinguish the subtleties of the education issue," writes his biographer D.J. Hall, "there had to be some dark and hidden secret, a source of dubious profit or a seamy scandal, that would account for the abrupt departure of so powerful a politician."[a]

Among possible "dark and hidden secrets," Hall offers two and then dismisses them both. The first, circulated by the Tories, saw Sifton as caught red-handed in some scandal-ridden scheme of profit that was about to be exposed. No detail was ever published, although years later one clue to its nature was offered by Henri Bourassa, the MP and Catholic intellectual who resolutely opposed Sifton on the school question. Sifton, Bourassa speculated, may have been in league with the railroad promoters Mackenzie and Mann to wreck the Laurier government and thereby destroy Laurier's Grand Trunk Pacific scheme. Observes J.W. Dafoe, an earlier Sifton biographer: "Mr. Bourassa is perhaps as poor an authority as there is in the world" on such a subject.

The other possibility was a sex scandal, a supposed affair between Sifton and the wife of an Ottawa lumberman named Mackey. This found its way luridly into print in the *Calgary Eye Opener* which on March 4, 1905, began its sensationalist lead article by paraphrasing the language of the Book of Common Prayer:

Endue our ministers with righteousness, O Lord, and make thy chosen people less bughouse.

* * *

Clifford Sifton has resigned, ostensibly over the school question. This implies a conscience on the part of Clifford. The idea of Clifford resigning on the ground of conscientious principle is laughable in the extreme. What has really made him resign is the trouble he has gotten himself into over a married woman in Ottawa. It is the Charles Dilke case over again.[b]

Now then take a long breath and prepare for a little telegraphic dispatch, announcing that Clifford is about to take a trip to Europe for his health.

The story of Sifton's escapade wherein he seems to have been ministering to the Interior in great shape, reads like some of the spicier cantos in Don Juan. The outraged husband is Walter Mackay, son of the late millionaire, William Mackay, the old lumber king of Ottawa. [Edwards either deliberately or carelessly misspells the Mackey name.] It appears that Mackay started for Montreal one night, but for some reason turned back and spent the evening at the club instead. Returning to his residence about two o'clock in the morning, he tried to open the front door with his latchkey, but the latch was fixed on the inside so that he could not get in.

bound forever to propagate the Roman Catholic faith.[3] And in Quebec, for precisely opposite reasons, many Catholics considered the amendment a treasonous compromise. Sbaretti wrote bitterly to Laurier:

> First by the Hon. R.W. Scott, the Secretary of State, in person, and afterwards by you in your letter of March 7th, 1904, confirmed by another on the 12th of the same month, I was solemnly promised that the right of the minority to separate schools in the North-West Territories would be guaranteed in the Constitution of the provinces to be erected therein, as in the provinces of Ontario and Quebec.

> In the elections of last November on the strength of your promise, I exercised my influence with the Prelates and Catholics of this country that no excitement or agitation would be created on the question of schools in the North-West Territories, and I promised that the same questions would not be discussed in the Catholic papers. And my efforts were successful, as you are well aware.

> I am extremely sorry to say that the clause read to me last evening does not fulfil the promised security...Moreover in the present clause the very existence of separate schools is not legally secure against an act of a hostile legislature...

> I beg of you therefore to reconsider this matter and not to force upon us the conscientious

[3] The English-born Goldwin Smith was an early libertarian and disciple of Adam Smith. He migrated to Canada and became a zealous supporter of the Canada First movement, which aspired to develop the country as an Anglo-Saxon bastion that restricted immigration to people from the British Isles. The movement gradually came to centre exclusively in Ontario, then collapsed entirely. Disillusioned, Smith gave up on Canada, advocated its annexation to the United States, and became a lecturer at Cornell University. His articles continued to draw much attention in Canada, however, until his death in 1910. While his Protestantism was gradually stripped of all belief in God, Dafoe notes, it retained a militant hatred of clergymen, especially Catholic ones.

So away he went round to the back door of the house to see if he could get in that way.

Approaching his back door, what was his surprise to see it cautiously opened from the inside and a big, tall man issuing therefrom. "Burglar!" thought Mackay, and quickly seized hold of the mysterious unknown. It was pretty dark at the time, and the two of them tugged and rolled all over the backyard. Finally, to Mackay's surprise, a ray from the moon revealed the sinister features of the minister of the Interior.

"Hello, Sifton! What are you doing here at this hour of the night?"

"Oh," quoth Clifford, puffing, "your wife was in trouble over some legal matters and sent for me to discuss them."

"Well that's strange," said the husband scratching his nose dubiously. "I suppose it's all right, though."

Next day, however, Mackay put on his thinking cap, and rather foolishly aired the story downtown, telling his friends about it. Their ill-concealed amusement showed him

Clifford Sifton with his family in 1910. Why he stayed out of the cabinet after Laurier's concessions, remains a mystery.

[a] David J. Hall, an associate professor of history at the University of Alberta, published a two-volume biography on Sifton (University of British Columbia Press). Volume 1, entitled *The Young Napoleon*, appeared in 1981, *The Lonely Eminence* in 1985. Sifton's first biographer was the man who edited his *Manitoba Free Press*, John W. Dafoe, who published *Clifford Sifton in Relation to his Times* (Macmillan Canada) in 1931, two years after Sifton's death.

[b] Sir Charles Wentworth Dilke, a powerful minister in Gladstone's government in Britain and Gladstone's presumed successor, was destroyed at the height of his career in 1885 when he was named as co-respondent in the divorce of 22-year-old Virginia Crawford from her husband, a Scottish lawyer. The evidence against Dilke was discredited, but the media continued to pursue the case. Finally Dilke persuaded Queen Victoria to reopen the matter for further hearings. Ironically, these established that while there was no evidence of an affair between Dilke and Virginia, he had for some time been the lover of her mother. So his career was finished anyway.

necessity of taking open opposition to a clause unacceptable to us and detrimental to our present rights.

But Laurier would reconsider nothing. He now knew the Sifton amendment was the best he could get, and already the controversy was provoking stormy sessions in the Commons. Indeed, the debate over the Alberta Act would turn out to be the longest yet recorded in Canadian history. (The debate centred on Bill 69; any changes were automatically applied to Bill 70 as well.) Night after night, week after week, month after month, the House sat past midnight, once until 3 a.m. The Tories were fighting to bring down the Liberal government on the question of separate schools in the territories — as the Liberals had brought down the Tory government on the question of separate schools in Manitoba (Vol. 1, p. 278).

The conflict was further exacerbated at the end of March when Archbishop Sbaretti, a determined man, announced that Laurier was considering wiping out the proposed province of Saskatchewan entirely, and extending Manitoba westward instead, on condition that Manitoba re-establish its Catholic schools. Laurier instantly denied it, and Sbaretti conceded there had been a "misunderstanding." But the fury in the Quebec and Ontario media exploded again. Laurier had hoped to hold the inauguration ceremonies for the new provinces on July 1. He had to postpone them to September.

but too plainly that they had for some time been alive to what he, husbandlike, was blind. Then the row began.

A private conference was held at the Mackay home, among those present as conciliators being Father Whalen, Archbishop Duhamel and Sir Wilfrid Laurier. Father Whalen next day took the lady to his former home in Quebec. Sifton just about this juncture left for the West, this stirring incident having taken place just before the elections. Ye Gods, and we didn't know about it!

By the time he returned the scandal had become the property of the politicians and of the inner circles of society, though no newspaper dared breathe a word.

What between the uproar in his own family and the demands for reparation on the part of the husband, Clifford thought it as up to him to duck his nut. He left for parts unknown, and remained away from his seat in parliament, neglecting his duties and pretending he was in a sanatorium somewhere for his health. His health must have been all right at this juncture, if we know anything about this line of business.

* * *

Sifton returned to Ottawa a discredited man and handed in his resignation. That is the whole story. For the benefit of his dupes, the public, it was arranged that he should retire with dignity under the benign wing of the school question.

The story of the incident was noised about Ottawa and references to it appeared years later in the private papers of various high-ranking Liberals, Tories and civil servants. Sifton himself never denied it, which proved nothing since he consistently made no comment on unpublished rumours.

Historian Hall, however, offers far more probable reasons for Sifton's remaining out of office. For one, Laurier had humiliated him. By introducing the Alberta Act with clauses utterly incompatible with Sifton's thoroughly established views, Laurier had signalled he wanted Sifton out. He had done the same thing in 1904 to his Railways minister, A.G. Blair, by announcing the construction of the government-supported Grand Trunk Pacific, which Blair had publicly opposed. Blair was left with no option but to resign, and then took part in an unsuccessful campaign to unseat Laurier as leader.

Again, says Hall, after more than eight years as Interior minister Sifton was bored with, and exhausted by, that portfolio. He had asked Laurier to make him minister of Justice. Laurier had appointed militant Catholic Quebecker Charles Fitzpatrick instead, and Fitzpatrick was more than a rival candidate for the post. An Irish Catholic, he represented everything Sifton regarded as unfortunate in the Liberal party — its growing Quebec orientation, its implicit Catholicism, its two-nation view of Canada. In private correspondence later made public he referred to the unamended Bill 69 originally presented by Laurier as "the handiwork of that fellow, Lucifer Fitzpatrick." The appellation was coined by a Toronto lawyer, but Sifton did not adopt such terms loosely.

A combination of these factors, Hall concludes, probably accounts for Sifton's permanent departure when the Laurier government was at the pinnacle of its power and popularity. But the accomplishment Sifton left behind is beyond question. Hundreds of thousands of immigrants were by now flooding into western Canada. "I shall be content," Sifton later reflected, "when the history of this country shall be written, to have the history of the last eight or nine years, so far as western administration is concerned, entered opposite my name.

— *T.B.*

It was assumed that Sifton, his amendment accepted, would return to the government. He did not. This set off wide speculation that there was more to his resignation than just the school question (see sidebar). His departure was to have permanent significance for Alberta. As Interior minister, he had frequently collided with Edmonton's Frank Oliver, whose habit of independence and unconcealed doubts about the eastern European immigration program had established him in Sifton's mind as a rebel. Without hesitation, however, Sifton recommended Oliver as his successor. Laurier agreed. Edmonton cheered. It knew that Frank Oliver would give it great influence in the federal cabinet at a critical time. In the House the Tories sniped nastily at Oliver. But in Calgary the *Herald* wishfully speculated that he would now become pro-Alberta, rather than simply pro-Edmonton, so that his appointment would be good news for Calgary too. It definitely was not, however, as subsequent events would conclusively demonstrate.

Meanwhile, in the territories, the ostensible subject of all this eastern religious fervour, interest in the school question ran very close to zero. The *Calgary Herald* looked eastward at all the uproar and scoffed:

> Rival gangs of politicians are shouting themselves hoarse in Ontario over the educational affairs of Alberta...Ontario is being inflamed by orators who display amazing zeal in the affairs of the country 2,000 miles removed. Is it just possible that Alberta would be more thankful to these enthusiasts if they would urge more even-handed justice for the West in the way of distribution of the natural resources of the country, a more equitable boundary division, capital location, and other features of substantial value in the new provinces?

John Ewan, a reporter for the *Globe*, wrote in amazement to Laurier that "the average western man is not much worked up" about the education question.

What the average western man was worked up about did him little good. Edmonton was made the interim capital until the Alberta legislature chose a permanent one. This alarmed Calgary. The eastern boundary of Alberta had been moved east eighty miles to the 110th meridian, taking Medicine Hat out of Assiniboia and putting it into Alberta. This alarmed Medicine Hat. The 110th meridian divided the grassland prairie. This alarmed the Western Stockgrowers Association, which wanted the line moved east to the 107th. Finally, the 110th was discovered to run smack through the middle of the Barr colony headquarters town of Lloydminster. This very much alarmed the Barr colony. Its founder, the Rev. G.E. Lloyd, wrote in dismay to Laurier: "This

George Hedley Vicars Bulyea, after he became lieutenant-governor of Alberta. Even he felt that his old friend Haultain had gone too far.

The western boundary of Saskatchewan, following the 110th meridian, ran smack through the middle of Lloydminster. Founder Lloyd considered this 'a very serious matter.'

would be a very serious matter for us, practically ruining our new town just as it has begun to grow."

To all these concerns Laurier turned a deaf ear. Already the West was discovering the minus side of the party system. Western Liberals couldn't speak out because of party discipline. Western Conservatives could speak out all they pleased, but they were disregarded since they were in opposition. Who could and did speak for their concerns was Haultain, but he was now premier of a government that was about to disappear. His office had become irrelevant. Nevertheless, for the record, he wrote to Laurier, formally declaring the opposition of the dying territorial government to what was being done to the territories.

Haultain believed there was no case for two provinces. Two administrations would greatly inflate the cost of provincial government; the area was now one political unit; an administrative structure to cover it already existed; the line that divided it was purely arbitrary. So why split it? He vehemently objected to Ottawa's continuing control of land and resources. Though the federal financial compensation was generous[4], there ought not to be first-class provinces (i.e. Ontario,

[4]Federal subsidies took two forms — those paid to all the provinces in lieu of customs and excise revenues, and those paid to the new provinces in lieu of land revenues. Ottawa estimated the inventory of public lands in each at 25 million acres and appraised them at $1.50 an acre, or $37.5 million. It promised to pay one percent of this value per annum — or $375,000. This would increase to one and a half per cent per annum when their populations reached 400,000, two per cent when they hit 800,000, and three per cent when they exceeded 1,200,000. For the first five years, a further one-quarter per cent was to be paid to construct public buildings, or $93,750, and $50,000 more to compensate for customs revenue, the same amount then paid to New Brunswick. The *Calgary Herald* warned its readers not to be dazzled by the big numbers. In 1902 alone the federal government had taken in one million dollars in public land and resource revenues from the West.

Famous oversized Herald headline. Laurier had said to Sifton that perhaps the PM should quit instead — though he had no such intention.

Quebec, Nova Scotia, New Brunswick, Prince Edward Island and BC, which controlled their own lands) and second-class (Manitoba, Saskatchewan and Alberta, which did not). In a federal system, this was unjust. Finally, to dictate to the provinces a key school policy was a clear violation of provincial rights. Whether and how there could be separate schools should be a provincial

Night after night, month after month, the debate in the House lasted past midnight. Laurier had hoped to inaugurate the new provinces on July 1, but the bills didn't pass until July 5.

decision. Laurier's contention that the separate schools "pre-existed" in the territories, as they did in Ontario and Quebec, was not true, he said. Ontario and Quebec had decided this for themselves before they entered Confederation. The territories had not. Territorial separate schools had been laid down by an Ottawa statute in 1875.

But apart from writing a letter, what more could Haultain do? He remained in Ottawa throughout March and April, pleading a hopeless cause. In May he thought he saw an opportunity to strike back. By an old parliamentary rule, later to be scrapped, cabinet appointees had to resign their seats and run again in a by-election. This meant a by-election in Edmonton for Frank Oliver, and another in London, Ontario, whose Liberal member, Charles S. Hyman, had become minister of Public Works. A third was necessary in nearby North Oxford to fill a vacancy. The Tories would naturally try to use the Ontario by-elections to arouse a Protestant vote against the autonomy bills. There was no similar opportunity in the West. Defeating Oliver in Edmonton was quickly dismissed as hopeless. His appointment promised tremendous advantage to Edmonton. Were Edmontonians likely to reject him now? The Tories didn't nominate. Oliver was acclaimed.

But Haultain and R.B. Bennett campaigned hard in Ontario, urging electors to vote against "Laurier, Hyman, Sbaretti and the Pope." They adopted the extreme Protestant position, demanding the complete abolition of separate schools in the territories. (Dafoe observed drily: "The high appeal to principle was vigorously seconded by the low appeal to prejudice.") The *Calgary Herald* enthusiastically predicted a Tory victory in both constituencies and consequent reconsideration of the autonomy bills. But the Liberals handily won both by-elections. And Haultain, the supposed territorial "non-partisan," now appeared one hundred per cent Tory and a bigot to boot.

Even Bulyea, Haultain's ever-loyal Liberal colleague, finally decided Haultain had gone too far. Haultain might demand the right of the provinces to decide for themselves. But after all, did the legislation with the Sifton amendment not reaffirm the separate schools exactly as Haultain's

This new province of Alberta, by virtue of its extent and varied character, is destined to become the brightest gem in the crown of the great empire that encircles the world. It is a delightsome land that lies on the sunny slopes of the eastern side of the Great Rockies where Alberta's sparkling mountains roll down their golden sands. With its prairies and its mountains, its forests and fertile fields and a healthy invigorating climate with perennial youth in the very air, there is avenue and opportunity for every kind of effort and enterprise.

- from "The Province and People of Destiny," an inauguration souvenir pamphlet.

own administration had established them? Bulyea decided to resign from the territorial administration, but Laurier dissuaded him. Until the new provinces took over, he said, Bulyea was needed where he was.

On May 4, Bills 69 and 70 made it through second reading with a majority of 81. Borden freed the Tories to vote their consciences and thirteen supported the legislation. The *Calgary Herald* headline announced: "A Crime of Coercion Perpetrated Today." On July 5, four days after the date originally slated to inaugurate the new provinces, they received third reading and were passed. They were signed into law July 20. Inauguration ceremonies were set for September 1 in Edmonton and September 4 in Regina. So Haultain must now, once again, decide his future. Would he run in Alberta, continuing to represent Macleod? Or would he run in Saskatchewan where support for his views was much stronger? Would he run as a Tory, thereby renouncing his contention that partisan politics do not belong in provincial government? Or would he somehow run as a non-partisan, opposed by both the Conservatives and the Liberals? Or would he retire from public life and not run at all? Could he perhaps marry his secret love, Marion, who was now back in England, supported by him? Marrying a divorced woman would not help his political career, but he could probably survive it. Anyhow, was it not perhaps time to terminate his public life?

All through July Haultain pondered, hopelessly complicating the politics of both provinces and both parties. He was widely regarded as unbeatable anywhere in the West. Even the Liberal *Edmonton Bulletin*, which had nipped at his heels for years, said as much: "Premier Haultain is placed in the unique position of being able to choose from two future provinces. He has the opportunity to continue his political career in either — a very rare position for a politician."

Very soon, however, Haultain's indecision created resentment everywhere. The Tories could hardly nominate a leader in either province until he disclosed what he would do. The Liberal case was not much better, since an election against Haultain posed a much more formidable challenge than one against, say, R.B. Bennett. The only person who could assuredly beat Haultain in Alberta was Frank Oliver, and as far back as March Oliver had made it clear he wasn't interested in becoming premier. "It seems to me," wrote Talbot to Rutherford, "that if Haultain remains in Alberta it would be difficult to get rid of him."

By August impatience with Haultain became public. Said the *Medicine Hat News*: "The continued silence of Premier Haultain affords, designedly or otherwise, an opportunity to his newspaper friends to engage in a campaign of systematically and persistently 'booming' him, an opportunity

---

Haultain's future was uncertain. Could he perhaps marry Marion, who was now in England? Marrying a divorced woman wouldn't help his political career. But perhaps it was time to terminate that.

---

which they are by no means slow to embrace. We are daily told in glowing terms of his integrity and his ability, and admonished as to the great desirability of having him cast his lot with Alberta. It is not necessary at this moment to question either the integrity or the ability of the honourable gentleman...But if his integrity is what it is claimed to be, he will lose no time in giving fair notice to the province which is to be deprived of his ability."

In July Laurier made a key decision. He nominated George Bulyea as lieutenant-governor of Alberta, and Amedee E. Forget, lieutenant-governor of the territories, to fulfil that function in Saskatchewan. The vice-regal office entailed a delicate political task. In order to establish the machinery of government, the lieutenant-governor must designate an interim premier. This premier would call an election in the 25 constituencies into which the federal legislation had divided each province. The leader of the winning party would then form the government in the usual way. But with the interim premiership would come not only the great credibility the office bestowed, but also control of the patronage appointments in the initial government. So who would these interim premiers be? The obvious choice in one province or the other was Haultain, the only western leader known to command an electoral majority (and an enormous one at that). But Haultain was a Tory.

Edmonton's day of triumph

IT'S OUR BIG CHANCE TO SHOW WE'RE A CAPITAL, SAID THE BULLETIN, SO DO NOT GLOAT OR RAZZ

Programme

After the First Page of this Programme had been printed
Several Changes and Additions were made by the Inaugural Committee. The following is a correct Time Table
of the entire proceedings:—

TUESDAY EVENING. Smoker for the R. N. W. M. P.
at the Exhibition grounds.

WEDNESDAY EVENING. Military Parade 6.30
Push Ball, Exhibition Grounds, 7.00

THURSDAY EVENING. Meeting Governor - General
and party. Reception and Concert in Thistle Rink

FRIDAY MORNING. 9.30 to 10.30, Parade
11.00 to 11.45, Review on Exhibition
Grounds

12.00 to 1.00, Swearing in of the Lt.-
Governor and Salute

FRIDAY AFTERNOON, 1 to 2.30, Baseball, Wetaskiwin vs. Edmonton

INNINGS	1	2	3	4	5	6	7	8	9	10	Runs
WETASKIWIN —											
EDMONTON —											

2.30 to 3. Musical Ride

3 to 4.30. Lacrosse, Calgary vs. Edmonton

CALGARY —	Goals
EDMONTON —	

4.30 to 6. Polo. Score

That Edmonton should be chosen even as the interim capital of the new province of Alberta came to the northern city that spring of 1905 as a delightful shock. They'd campaigned for it all right. And because they were in the midst of the parkland prairie rather than grassland prairie, they were surrounded by far better grain land. So they were receiving most of the new tide of immigration. They voted right, too, and their Frank Oliver had taken over the most powerful western portfolio in the Laurier government as minister of the Interior. But notwithstanding all this, they knew — little as they might want to acknowledge it — that Calgary was the big centre.

Calgary had the big railway, the Canadian Pacific. In September 1905 Edmonton still had no direct railway connections east or west. You had to go through Calgary. Calgary had the cattle money. Edmonton was on the northern fringe of settlement.

The capital, of course, was only "provisional." The Legislature, once it was elected, would make the permanent decision. But provisional or not, Edmonton resolved to look like a capital when the great day arrived, September 1, on which the leading dignitaries of Canada would be there to see the lieutenant-governor sworn in, and proclaim the existence of the province of Alberta. How big a crowd could Edmonton turn out? Its population, together with Strathcona, had been recorded in the 1901 census as 4,176, but it had grown significantly since. Even so, could they assemble 10,000? Some said 20,000, but that seemed wildly optimistic.

For months before the big day, while in Ottawa the Commons continued to argue late into the night over Bill 69, the Alberta Act, the plans were formulated. There must be a great concert the night before, then on the day itself a massive parade along Jasper Avenue and down McDougall Hill to the Rossdale Flats and the fair grounds which would one day become the John Ducey Park baseball stadium. Here a pavilion must be set up for the governor-general and the prime minister to address the new province.

These preparations were observed coldly from Calgary which continued to assume that the whole Edmonton exercise

The inauguration parade, and program from the day. Could Edmonton get even 10,000 people to come?

was, like the phenomenon of the provisional capital, faintly ridiculous. It remained for Bob Edwards and the *Eye Opener* to voice this sentiment. "They are getting very toney up in Edmonton," said the *Eye Opener* on June 24, "with their fair and inauguration festivities in sight. Many of the smart young ladies have taken to wearing open-work shoes to display pretty hosiery, a charming idea. It is now in order for the men of Edmonton to start wearing open-work hats for the purpose of displaying the wheels revolving in their heads."

One thing that would really make things festive, it was decided, was lights. The city power plant announced that electricity would be free for the week. Strings of coloured lights were draped over Alberta College which was to be the centre for the event. The fire hall and the Alberta Hotel were similarly adorned. Arches with sheaves of grain and spruce boughs were erected over Jasper Avenue.

Alderman William A. Griesbach, the Boer War veteran and historian, advanced an idea that at first offended his fellow council members. They should wear top hats and frock coats, he said. "Some of the aldermen bucked," he recalls in his memoirs, *I Remember*, "and declared with oaths and curses they would not wear such a contraption. However, a certain amount of pressure was applied and J.J. Mills, the clothier, came up to the next council meeting and measured everybody for top hats and frock coats."

On Thursday, the day before the event, the *Bulletin* pub-

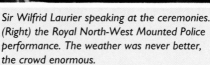

Sir Wilfrid Laurier speaking at the ceremonies. (Right) the Royal North-West Mounted Police performance. The weather was never better, the crowd enormous.

lished a special issue admonishing Edmontonians not to razz their visitors and gloat over them. "It is in every way fitting that the event should be marked by a demonstration that is thoroughly provincial in nature, scope and attendance. Nothing savouring of localism should be permitted at this time to offend the susceptibilities of those who honour Edmonton with their presence. Tomorrow and to her guests the city must not be one of the main rivals for western supremacy in politics or in commerce but the capital of the province of Alberta in spirit as in fact."

The weather could not have looked more promising — day after day of bright blue skies with memorable prairie sunsets and gentle evening breezes, perfect summer weather. (The *Herald* in Calgary forecast snow for Edmonton on September 1, but admitted the following day this was an error.) Then, barely on time for the concert, the official party arrived by special train at the Strathcona station on the Thursday night. Foremost among them was the Governor-General, Albert Henry George, 4th Earl Grey and Lady Grey,[a] followed by Sir Wilfrid and Lady Laurier. The Calgary dignitaries included Senator James Lougheed, Chief Justice Arthur Sifton, and several members of the territorial legislature including R.B. Bennett. Frederick Haultain, premier of the territories and an MLA for Macleod, was apparently not invited.

The party arrived at the Thistle Rink at what would become 102 Street and 102 Avenue, just in time to hear Vernon Barford, organist of All Saints Church, lead the 41-voice choir (29 men and twelve women) and fifteen-piece orchestra in a resounding "God Prosper Him Our King," the first of twelve numbers on the program.[b]

The official party returned to Strathcona to sleep on the train, and the following morning they were to see a sight that even Edmontonians could scarcely believe. The crowd that

surged into the city for the day's events exceeded everything foreseen. There was, of course, no official count. The estimates ran from 12,000 to 20,000. The parade was the highlight. There were three bands, led by the Canadian Mounted Rifles Band of Calgary. Then came the official party, then the Old Timers Association, the Imperial Medallists Association, the Edmonton Fire Department Band, then 1,800 school children (1,500 on foot and 300 little ones riding in wagons), then the farm organizations, the labour organizations, the Fort Saskatchewan Rough Riders Band, the St. Jean Baptiste Society, the German Society, the Lacrosse Club, the Hockey Club, the Baseball Club, the Polo Club, the St. Albert Citizens' Band and other citizens in carriages and on foot.

Greisbach's description of this procession remains the best:

There were bands, floats from patriotic societies, and contingents from various sporting clubs marching in the procession. This part of the procession was concluded by a very excellent float advertising Ochsner's beer. Bottles of cold beer were handed out to any thirsty individual who held up his hand in the crowd...

The citizens (in the parade) in a few cases were citizens of Edmonton but for the most part they were farmers who came in for the day and joined the tail-end of

[a]Earl Grey would pay but one visit to Edmonton. However, the cup that bears his name, and denotes supremacy in Canadian football, would return to it three times in the 1950s, three in the 1970s and four in the 1980s.

[b]Barford was one of Edmonton's prized possessions. An Oxford man, highly trained in the English cathedral tradition, he had arrived in Edmonton in 1900, and would be the centre of much of its musical life for the next sixty years, directing choirs, choruses, operatic companies and orchestras. A delightful word portrait of him appears in Tony Cashman's *Best Edmonton Stories.*

the procession as it moved along. The horses were taken out of the plough and the vehicles were democrat wagons or ordinary farm wagons. The farmer and his wife sat in the front seat and the horses with their bewhiskered fetlocks trotted along, occasionally becoming sufficiently interested to shy at a banner or some unusual sight.

The farmer's wife held the last child in her arms; the remainder were in the wagon box to the rear. Little girls wore starched pinnies and hats which had by this time come off and were hanging on their backs by the elastic chin-strap which was around the little girls' necks. In the wagon were sheaves of greenfeed for the horses, half a sack of oats, several pails of feed for the family, while behind the wagon rode the half-grown sons of the family on half-broken horses, some with saddles and some without.

Between the hind wheels of the wagon trotted the family dog. The farmer is said to have a fear of city slickers, and the farm dog, who is largely a vegetarian, fears town dogs, who have a habit of ganging up on him, so he places himself between the hind wheels of the wagon, his rear to some extent covered by the boys on horseback immediately behind, and supported by the love and loyalty which he has for the family in his charge.

The Governor-General took his position in front of the Edmonton Club. As the mayor and council passed they raised their new silk hats with a flourish, and when the citizens in carriages began to pass they did not recognize the Governor-General, never having seen him before and not knowing that he was there. A few flourished their whips and the odd half-breed raised his hat.

Down to the fair grounds trooped the procession where beneath the pavilion at exactly noon Earl Grey made George Henry Vickers Bulyea lieutenant-governor of Alberta, and Sir Wilfrid in a five-minute talk marvelled at the astounding changes that had occurred to the prairies since he had last visited Edmonton in 1894.

Then with a trumpet's blast C Squadron of the North-West Mounted Police galloped like a cavalry charge down upon the pavilion and stopped dead before it while the NWMP cannons from above Fort Edmonton where the Legislative Building was soon to arise boomed forth the birth of Alberta.

There followed a "patriotic rally" at McDougall Methodist Church and after that the great ball at the Thistle Rink with everyone in his finery and the city blazing with light as it had never blazed before. For one desperate moment, notes Tony Cashman in his *Best Edmonton Stories*, the lights dimmed in the Thistle and the nervous citizenry wondered if the generators could handle it all. They did. The lights brightened, and the band played on.

Even the *Calgary Herald* had to admit grudgingly in its headline the next Monday: "Inaugural Ceremonies at Edmonton Celebrated Under Circumstances Very Favourable to the Occasion." Deep in the story, however, a certain niggling became evident. "There was regret expressed," it said, "that the Fire Brigade Band of Calgary had not also been invited." It added: "It was a noticeable fact that not one of the gentlemen from Calgary occupied seats in the pavilion and their absence therefrom was noticeable."

Glenbow Archives, NA-1711-1

But the day had been glorious, some few of those little children in the parade would carry the memory of it to the century's end, and that evening in a blaze of gold the sun set for the first time on the province of Alberta.

— *T.B.*

Edmonton in its finery parading down McDougall Hill to the Exhibition Grounds. Beer was handed out freely.

Laurier himself would, of course, make the decision as to who was to be interim premier, but his orders must be carried out by Bulyea in Alberta and there could be a major controversy over it. On July 25, Laurier wrote to Bulyea offering the position and adding:

> When you and Haultain came to Ottawa, in the early part of January last, I thought, and indeed everyone thought, that as soon as the two provinces came into existence, the then existing government of the territories would naturally become the government of Saskatchewan.
>
> The attitude of Haultain has made this, in my judgement, an impossibility. When, in the early part of the struggle which followed the introduction of the bills Haultain went out of his way to openly take side with the opposition, I am free to admit that I was keenly disappointed, but even then I did not come to the conclusion that the breach was irreparable.
>
> When however he threw himself into the contests of London and North Oxford, and especially when he announced his intention of carrying on the provincial elections on the avowed policy of destroying the school system of which some weeks before he had said that if he were a dictator, he would not change a single disposition of it, he left us no alternative but to accept the declaration of war.
>
> I realize that such a disposition of things must be particularly painful and embarrassing to you. On the one hand I know full well that you never approved of Haultain's course. On the other hand the ties of friendship which have grown between you and him, resulting from long association in the same administration, would make it a most invidious task to have to oppose him and fight, with all the firmness which a political contest means in this country, and especially such a contest as is involved in the policy of which he has declared himself the champion.

Bulyea, who sat for South Qu'Appelle and who lived in Regina, doubtless immediately got the message. Laurier did not want him to lead the party in his home province. He had another man in mind for that — Walter Scott, the Regina MP and newspaper publisher. Scott easily won the provincial Liberal convention and became party leader.

With Oliver in the federal cabinet, the most obvious choice for Liberal leader in Alberta was Peter Talbot, who came west from Ontario to teach school in Macleod in 1890, moved to Lacombe as a teacher and farmer, and took the federal constituency of Strathcona for Laurier in 1904. His chatty letters to his friend Rutherford, MLA for Strathcona, would provide historians with an inside glimpse of Alberta's Liberal establishment. A letter from Laurier to Bulyea made it clear that the federal cabinet favoured Talbot, but Talbot did not want to run. He threw his support behind his friend Rutherford, over the misgivings of many Liberals who doubted Rutherford's capabilities and were urging he be compensated instead with one of the new Alberta seats in the Senate. On August 7, Talbot wrote Laurier trying to assuage these concerns:

> There is no doubt that owing to the fact I am better known in the southern part of the province than is Mr. Rutherford, my selection would be the more popular. But our friends are quite reasonable and I firmly believe will work faithfully for our cause no matter who may be called upon to lead us.
>
> In Calgary I also found a feeling in my favour. The Liberals there look upon Mr. Rutherford as almost an Edmonton man and would prefer me principally on that account.
>
> From Calgary to Leduc there is really no difference to speak of. I think either of us would have as large a following as the other. From Leduc north I think Mr. Rutherford would prove the stronger. The great question in the north is the location of the permanent capital and I think that Mr. Rutherford would be preferred.
>
> Rutherford and I are the best of friends and I had a confidential talk with him. I spoke to him of the senatorship, but I think he is too fully committed to his own constituents for the position of premier of the province to now think of withdrawing. At least he did not give any indication of a desire to take anything but the premiership. When I found this to be the case I thought it best to induce my warmest friends to give him their loyal support. This I think they will do...

It is not yet known what Mr. Haultain will do. I am inclined to think he will run for a constituency in Alberta, although some of his political friends say he will remain in Sask...

So Rutherford was chosen "president" of the provincial Liberal association. The Alberta Tories, though still uncertain what Haultain might do, meanwhile chose R.B. Bennett as leader. Frank Oliver remained plainly unhappy with the Rutherford choice and even tried to persuade him to resign in favour of Talbot. Oliver wrote to Laurier:

Rutherford was the choice, although Talbot would have been preferred and would have been chosen had he not definitely given way to Rutherford. He was influenced in this action, I think, by the belief that Rutherford had already tacitly been chosen for and had accepted the position, and that to have turned him down would have dissatisfied Rutherford and his friends and thereby promoted a split.

On my return in company with Talbot I suggested cautiously a change, but Rutherford would not accept the suggestion, although it was made as favourable to him as possible. Talbot will largely and earnestly support Rutherford. So I think the only thing to do is have Rutherford called.

In mid-August Haultain finally announced his decision. He would run in Saskatchewan as the

The real winner in the school controversy

Neither Laurier nor Sifton but educator John Dewey would prevail in Alberta

The argument that divided the House of Commons and the Laurier government over the Alberta Act was essentially an argument among Christians — the same argument that had been raging among them for nearly 400 years, that of Protestant versus Catholic. Each must control schooling if it was to pass on its beliefs from one generation to the next. The legislators finally reached a compromise that became the basis of education in Alberta. Separate schools could exist, but only under state control. Public schools would be allowed limited religious observance or instruction, if local school boards agreed. But at the close of the 20th century, historians with the advantage of nine decades of hindsight would pose the question: Who really won that debate?

Was it Henri Bourassa, the saintly member of parliament from Labelle, who was viewed at the time as a radical francophone nationalist but who was in fact far more interested in preserving and propagating the teachings of Christ than he was in preserving the use of the French language?

Or was it men like D.D. McKenzie, lawyer and Liberal member for the Cape Breton North-Victoria constituency in Nova Scotia, a Presbyterian who saw, as did Bourassa, that all education must rest on some kind of philosophical or

John Dewey, the founder of child-centred learning. In the end, neither the Catholics nor the Protestants won. He did.

leader, not of the Conservatives, but of what he and his supporters called the Provincial Rights Party. "Premier Haultain," sneered the *Edmonton Bulletin*, "has at last condescended to inform the people of the territories that he has decided to confer his distinguished services upon the province of Saskatchewan." The *Bulletin* went on to observe that by now Haultain was probably unelectable in Alberta. In any event, Haultain's "provincial rights" concept was highly impractical. The Liberals were running as a party, so he could count on little support from them. Neither could he count on such Tory organization as there was, nor the money that the Tories could have offered. But it was

At neither the Edmonton nor the Regina inauguration was Haultain, the man who more than any other had brought the provinces about, included among the guests. It was a deliberate and spiteful snub.

consistent with what he had always advocated. It was not allied to a national party. Again, it was the Right Thing to Do.

Following the inauguration ceremonies in Regina, Lieutenant-Governor Forget designated Liberal leader Walter Scott as interim premier to form the Saskatchewan government. At neither the Edmonton nor the Regina ceremony was Haultain, the man who more than any other had brought the provinces about, included among the honoured guests, though most members of the

religious assumptions, but felt this could be accomplished through the public schools?

Which side really prevailed?

The answer: Neither side. It was neither Clifford Sifton nor Wilfrid Laurier who would largely decide the philosophical direction of Alberta schools, both separate and public. Nor was it Frederick Haultain, nor Archbishop Sbaretti, the papal legate who lobbied and agonized over the Alberta Act, nor Dr. T.S. Sproule, member for Grey East and head of the Orange Order in Ontario. Rather, it was a professor of psychology and philosophy at the University of Chicago, soon to move to Columbia in New York. He, more than anyone in Canada, determined the philosophical basis of education in Alberta and therefore the real outcome of the debate.

In 1899, two years before the territorial executive passed the ordinance that brought the separate school curriculum under virtually complete government control, John Dewey published *The School and Society*, proposing a radical change in education. Rather than a place where children are taught skills and values, a school should become a workshop for democracy, where the teacher ceases to be an "authority figure" but is rather a fellow worker, at most a counsellor, and the children themselves decide what they should study and do.

Three years later Dewey published *The Child and the Curriculum*. This was a treatise on "child-centred" education that "liberated" children from the "directional" and "dictated" influence of adults. Therefore such things as "standards of performance," or "marks," or pass-or-fail examinations must have no place in a proper school.

As the century unfolded, variations of Dewey's philosophy became the orthodoxy of North American education. Educators from all over the continent, including Alberta, flocked to Chicago and Columbia to imbibe it.

Philosophically Dewey was what is called a pragmatist, holding that nothing beyond the natural can be known to human beings. Education therefore should confine itself to what can be seen and concluded from nature. Concepts of God could not be drawn from nature and could therefore have no part in education. Neither for that matter could concepts of morality. Nothing in nature could make one form of conduct any more "right" than another. The schools therefore should leave right and wrong for the pupils to decide for themselves. Each one, as a generation six decades later would learn to say, was to "do his own thing."

Acceptance of this philosophy would be impeded by two world wars, because a society in wartime becomes exceedingly performance-oriented. But by the 1960s such inhibitions were gone and departments of education everywhere embraced in varying degrees the Dewey concept.

The very powers that Haultain and Sifton had bestowed upon the state system were then, of course, used to hasten its conversion. Teachers were trained in the Dewey approach and nothing else. Whole faculties of education proliferated its assumptions. Curriculums were radically altered to conform to it. Departmental examinations were eliminated. Report cards ceased to provide "marks." Inculcating "self-esteem" in the pupil, rather than imparting knowledge and skills, became the goal of the educator.

If the leaders of the great debate on the Alberta Act had lived to see the schools their efforts eventually produced, what would they have thought? Probably they would all have been horrified, none more so than Henri Bourassa or D.D. McKenzie. But Bourassa could at least claim to have foreseen such an outcome.

— *T.B.*

THE PROTEST OF THE WEST.

AUTONOMY
(ALKALI
WATER)

THE, BULL:—"You may coerce me into it, but it's another thing to make me drink."

WONDERFUL FEAT.

MANAGER SIR WILFRID :—" Bravo ! Sifton ; best swallowing act I ever witnessed."

The West as the coerced bull, and Sifton being coerced by Laurier, as seen through the eyes of Toronto News cartoonist McConnell, in 1905.

territorial legislature were. It was a deliberate snub. Grant MacEwan, Haultain's biographer and himself once leader of the Alberta Liberal Party, called it "a demonstration of political spite." The influential Toronto weekly *Saturday Night* declared:

> This strong, able man who has locally directed nearly every good thing that has been done for the territories, is to be ousted from any share of the government of either of the two provinces. No device known to politics has been unused to keep him from having any share in the new administration. No trick of party conventions, political intrigue or private pull or push has been neglected to put this able, honest man out of business.

In the ensuing Saskatchewan election in December 1905, Haultain's Provincial Rights Party took eight seats, Premier Scott's Liberals seventeen. Haultain became leader of the opposition, a post for which he was singularly unsuited. "As opposition leader, he was a distinct failure," wrote his friend and longtime associate, C.W. Peterson, editor of the *Farm and Ranch Review*. "His was a constructive mind. He devoted most of his time to helping and advising the new government and very little to creating obstacles for them, all of which is precisely what his friends expected him to do." He remained opposition leader through two more elections that did not improve the standing of the Provincial Rights Party. After the second Haultain had to relent in his long-held views and it became the Conservative Party of Saskatchewan.

In the course of all this, his chief adversary, Premier Walter Scott, became his warm admirer and comrade, as he had been back in the old territorial days. And Scott somehow discerned a mysterious undisclosed factor in Haultain's life. In 1918, Scott wrote to a friend:

> Doubtless every man has his handicaps which seem the worst to him in the world. I often puzzle and wonder over Haultain. Good health, trained in political atmosphere, thoroughly educated, strong intellect, lightning perception; what I required a long day to do Haultain could do in an hour, in my view the best parliamentary debater I have ever heard excepting Sir Richard Cartwright [5]—what can have been Haultain's singular handicap? He was surely hobbled by some handicap, because I know that from the moment in 1904 when I first was challenged to meet him in that campaign, I was wholly confident that I could successfully do it—and I never lost that confidence—although it seemed like putting the plough horse on the race track against the thoroughbred. Haultain certainly had me in a hostile mood

towards him in 1905, but long ago I got over that; and there are few men even amongst my political friends that I like as well as him.

The 'handicap' in Haultain that Scott had discerned was almost certainly Marion. She came back to Canada in 1905, still on his money. Then she suddenly decided she should accept no further help from him unless he were her husband. On what he later said was "a few hours' notice" they were secretly married in Ontario in March 1906, three months after the Saskatchewan elec-

'Democracy,' Haultain said, 'is not perfect; it is just the best arrangement that mankind has put together.'

tion. She was 29, he 48. He wanted her to return with him to Regina. She refused. She could recover her health, she said, only if she returned to England. Here she was admitted to an expensive hospital whose monthly bills left the leader of the opposition, now embarking on a Regina law practice, almost unable to pay for his own upkeep. Gradually she stopped writing to him. In 1910 he received a letter from her father, who knew of the marriage, upbraiding him for not taking better care of her.

Haultain's reply, parts of which are reprinted on page 36 discloses his secret life. It lay for many years in the unexamined papers of his father-in-law, Charles Herbert Mackintosh, until University of Alberta historian Lewis H. Thomas discovered it and published it in an academic paper in 1970.

But Haultain did not live miserably ever after. In 1912 he was made chief justice of Saskatchewan. In 1917 he was knighted and became Sir Frederick. Also that year he became chancellor of the University of Saskatchewan, the institution whose foundation he had long envisioned. Generally regarded as the founder of the university, he was re-elected chancellor for seven more three-year terms.

Marion, the wife with whom he never lived, died in 1938 at Guelph, Ontario, probably in the sanatorium there, aged 62, and was buried in Beechwood Cemetery, Ottawa, as Marion St. Clair Castellain. Her marriage to Haultain was not recorded in the *Parliamentary Guide* or in *Who's Who in Canada*. A few months after her death, Haultain married a childhood friend, a widow named Mrs. W.B. Gilmour, and went to Montreal to live. He died there on January 30,1942. His ashes are interred at the University of Saskatchewan.

He remained to his death a critic of party politics in provincial government. "Democracy," he once told the Saskatoon Club, "is not perfect; it is just the best arrangement that mankind has been able to put together so far—and it would be better if politicians gave more thought and attention to principles and less to their respective parties. When personal gain is the deciding force in the individual's choice of party, the political conscience will suffer blemish and democracy will feel the hurt. Issues will then be distorted and the voting results will not be a true reflection of the public will."

Party politics destroyed the political career of Frederick Haultain. But western distrust of established political machines was not erased. It was by now etched so deeply in the collective psyche of the prairies that it would rise boiling to the surface again and again in the century that lay ahead. And none would become a more convinced foe of the party system than the man who now rose to the centre of the political stage in Alberta, Alexander Cameron Rutherford.

- T.B.

[5]Sir Richard Cartwright, a Kingston businessman and politician, was a Macdonald Tory who broke with the party two years after Confederation, and later joined the Liberals, becoming minister of Finance in the Mackenzie government. Under Laurier he led the Ontario wing of the party and as minister of trade fought for reciprocity with the United States. He died in 1912.

CHAPTER FOUR

FRANK OLIVER

Born: Sept. 14, 1842, in Peel County, west of Toronto

Died: March 31, 1933, in Ottawa

Career Apex: Minister of the Interior and superintendent of Indian Affairs, 1905-11; founder of the Edmonton *Bulletin*, 1880

Major Accomplishment: Securing capital status for Edmonton, thus ensuring the northern city's future as a rival to Calgary.

Quotation: 'We did not go out to the North-West simply to produce wheat. We went to build up a nation, a civilization, a social system that we could enjoy, be proud of, and transmit to our children...'

Oliver's awesome gerrymander that buried Calgary as capital

HIS CONTRIVED CONSTITUENCY MAP CREATED THE FIRST LEGISLATURE AND ENSURED THE NEW PROVINCE WOULD HAVE TWO BATTLING CITIES

What most interested Albertans, as legislation creating their province was prepared in Ottawa during that January of 1905, was not whether it would be required to have government-financed Catholic schools, or whether it would be allowed to control its own land and resources, or even whether there would be two provinces or one. Riding high above all these questions was another, in which interest ran fierce and all-consuming: Which city would be the capital? Or, if there were two provinces, where would the two capitals be?

The question was pivotal. It would shape Alberta's politics for all time. It would play a decisive role in the first election. And it would help destroy the political career of the Liberal stalwart who became Alberta's first premier, and turn him into a Tory.

It is not quite true that Calgarians did not care whether there were two provinces or one. They cared very much. For if there were one, the capital would probably remain in Regina, seat of the territorial administration. But if there were two provinces divided by a north-south line, they rea-

> **The *Herald* prepared a map showing how Calgary centred the prairies and the Kootenays. The map depicted Edmonton centring almost nothing.**

soned, then plainly the capital of the western one would have to be Calgary.

Calgarians exuded confidence on that score. Back in the 1880s they had brashly tried to unseat Regina as the territorial capital. In 1901 the Calgary Board of Trade sponsored an official visit by the territorial legislature, including a tour of the city, a visit to the brewery, a fine banquet, and speeches that extolled Calgary's potential as a provincial capital when one was needed. One guest, T.G. Rothwell, the law clerk of the Department of the Interior, told the *Herald* he had to admit that Calgary's main streets were as impressive as Ottawa's. The *Herald* prepared a map, with rings at fifty-mile intervals around the city, showing that Calgary centred the prairies and the Kootenays. The map had fifty-mile rings around Edmonton as well, showing that it centred almost nothing. "Business and Bustle on the Bow" was Calgary's slogan.

Rival centres remained disdainfully unimpressed, particularly with the *Herald*, which, said the Regina *Leader*, "belittles all other places and makes invidious comparisons between them and Calgary." It added: "When facts and figures fail to substantiate Calgary's claim, then the figures affecting other centres are falsified and made to do duty." Such a charge, replied the *Herald*, "is false, absolutely, and must have been dictated in a spirit of deliberate malice or inexcusable ignorance. The *Herald* has never spoken disparagingly of any town or city in Canada."

If two north-south provinces were created, however, Calgary's rival would not be Regina but Edmonton, the old fur trading centre on the northern fringe of settlement. In January 1905 Edmonton was still eleven months away from direct rail connections with any major centre but Calgary. The 1901 census showed its population as 2,626 against Calgary's 4,091. Need more be said?

A great deal more need be said, as a matter of fact, and Edmontonians persistently said it. Add

Strathcona across the river (which Edmontonians insisted on calling South Edmonton), with a population of 1,550, and the total population of the northern centre exceeded Calgary's. Take into account that the new immigration was more rapidly expanding the North than the South, because the rainfall was more dependable. Take into account the Peace River and the far north. Soon Edmonton becomes the centre of everything. The lack of a transcontinental railway was offset by promise. Not one but two transcontinental railways, the Canadian Northern and the Grand Trunk-Pacific, were headed towards it, and the former was due to arrive that very fall. The *Edmonton Bulletin* reprinted the *Herald* map, accompanying it with a set of facts that made Edmonton the obvious capital. "If the province was extended to the North Pole," retorted the *Herald* "and if every member of the remote Indian tribes were added to those of the white settlers, Edmonton would not yet be in the centre of Alberta's population."

So raged the controversy, but not equally. Calgary's decided disadvantage was one of overconfidence. So declares Alexander Bruce Kilpatrick, whose 1980 paper at the University of Victoria was entitled *A Lesson in Boosterism: the Contest for the Alberta Provincial Capital, 1904-1906.* "Edmonton's victory was achieved, not because it held any locational advantage over its opponents," writes Kilpatrick, "but rather because its boosters were more aggressive, more energetic and more adept at promoting their city than were their counterparts in rival communities."

Not that the capital competition was restricted to Calgary and Edmonton. Smaller centres like Okotoks, Wetaskiwin, Cochrane and Lacombe all made submissions to Ottawa, extolling their potential. Medicine Hat considered itself a serious contender if there were an east-west split between the provinces rather than a north-south one, because Medicine Hat was closer to the middle of the grasslands. Even Vegreville, population 78, made its case: abundance of ozone in the atmosphere, it explained, made Vegreville's climate particularly salubrious for people with tuberculosis, asthma, rheumatism and malaria. Moreover, Vegreville didn't have chinooks, so sleigh traffic didn't get bogged down by unexpected thaws.

The rivalry between Calgary and Edmonton made a case for Red Deer as a compromise. "Nature has provided a site for a beautiful city on a splendid river," wrote the railway promoter and industrialist John T. Moore, then living in Red Deer. "Already it is a town of many handsome homes with modern conveniences of electric lights and power, telephones, waterworks, good drainage, and being the geographical centre is the most convenient for all concerned. Dear Sir Wilfrid, please give it a place in your warm consideration."

An especially compelling case was made for a "mountain capital" at Banff; among other advantages, it could be "easily fortified in time of war." One centre distinguished itself in this competition by not joining it, notably Lethbridge. Explained the *Lethbridge Herald:* "Lethbridge is the only sane place in Alberta. All the rest are capital crazy. Anybody knows Lethbridge would be the capital by snapping its fingers, but we don't want it. We are going to be the commercial capital, not the political capital."

Even Vegreville made a case for being chosen capital: abundance of ozone made its climate particularly salubrious to the tubercular, the asthmatic, the rheumatoid and the malarial.

Until the early fall of 1904, when Laurier abruptly declared he would institute autonomy on the prairies (meaning provincehood) if his government were returned in the November election, the question of the capital was largely hypothetical. This election, the *Herald* assured Calgarians, would have no bearing on the selection of the capital. It was a sad miscalculation. The election, in fact, set in motion a chain of events that doomed Calgary's chances.

Before the election, a redistribution of the Commons had increased territorial representation to ten from four, and the representation of the District of Alberta to four from one. A constituency called Alberta lay from roughly Macleod south to the US border, one called Calgary from there north to a line running across the province at the latitude of Innisfail. The constituency called Strathcona ran from there north to Edmonton, and the one called Edmonton took in everything from there to the northern boundary of the territorial district. In the old House, the sole representative had been Frank Oliver, a Liberal and a passionate Edmontonian, constantly deplored by the

OPENING OF ALBERTA'S

FIRST LEGISLATURE

EDMONTON MAR. 15. 1906

ERNEST BROWN.

Conservative *Herald* for his pro-Edmonton bias. In the new House, said the *Herald,* Calgary could have its own member, and this would make all the difference.

And indeed it did, though not, unhappily, as the *Herald* expected. Tories were returned in Alberta and Calgary, Liberals in Strathcona and Edmonton. The Edmonton member was Oliver, of course. Strathcona's MP was Peter Talbot of Lacombe. He had no interest whatever in Red Deer's aspirations, though Red Deer was in his constituency, which doomed any hope Red Deer may

The opening of the first Legislature of Alberta, Thistle Rink, March 15, 1906. Something close to panic seized Calgary.

Alberta's first cabinet: centre left,
Premier A.C. Rutherford; centre
right, G.H. Bulyea (lieutenant-
governor); top left, W.T. Finlay
(Agriculture); bottom left, W.H.
Cushing (Public Works); top right,
Charles Cross (attorney-general);
bottom right, L.G. De Veber
(minister without portfolio).

have had. Talbot's main support came from the town of Strathcona. Therefore, like Oliver, he backed the Edmonton cause, and both sat in the government caucus because Laurier was returned by a landslide.

The same election also finished any hope Medicine Hat may have had. Located in the District of Assiniboia, it had assumed that its MP, Walter Scott, would advance its case. But Scott naturally espoused the aspirations of Regina, where he lived and had most of his support, to continue in that role.

The Calgarians got to Ottawa before Oliver, but Oliver got to Laurier first. Laurier said the Calgary case would be considered, then quietly ordered Edmonton be made provisional capital.

The first clue to the government's course came shortly after New Year's when Frederick Haultain and a delegation from the expiring territorial legislature arrived in Ottawa. Laurier polite-ly met them daily, but talked also to his seven-man Liberal caucus from the territories. It became evident that he would follow the advice of the seven, not of the territorial members. The second clue came in mid-January when the *Edmonton Journal* "scooped" two stories in a row, reporting both as well-founded rumours: first, that there would be two provinces, not one; and second, that Edmonton would be the "provisional" capital of the westernmost province, with the final decision

A PROVINCE IS BORN

being left to the provincial legislature. "Edmonton Dreams Dreams and Locates the Capital," sneered a *Herald* headline. The third clue got off the train in Calgary on January 30. The territorial MLA, R.B. Bennett, returned from Ottawa to warn Calgary that the *Journal* stories were true and that Edmonton was definitely winning the first round.

Something close to panic seized Calgary. The Calgary Board of Trade called an emergency meeting that very day, and persuaded Mayor John Emerson to organize a public rally three days hence. By then the Calgarians concocted what they considered a splendid scheme. They would

---

Oliver and Talbot simply sat down together and drew Alberta's constituency map, a masterpiece of gerrymandering. The other five Liberals were appalled, but Oliver rode down all opposition.

---

advance the cause of Banff as permanent capital, rather than Edmonton. Since Banff had nothing like adequate facilities for housing a government, the actual administration would accrue to Calgary anyway, and the new legislature might eventually move the capital itself into Calgary as well. But in the meantime Calgary would be advancing an objective interest, not a selfish one. A cry for "fair play," they assumed, could easily win the support of other southern centres to the cause.

To carry this proposal to Ottawa, Calgary named what it considered a powerhouse delegation: Mayor Emerson; Saddlery Store owner R.J. Hutchings; the longtime city promoter, lumberman and ex-Mountie James Walker; the medical doctor Edward H. Rouleau; and prominent Liberals W.M. Davidson, editor of the *Albertan*, gifted lawyer Charles A. Stuart, the defeated Liberal candidate Dr. C.J. Stewart, and former mayor W.H. Cushing. Bob Edwards in the *Calgary Eye Opener* saw the weakness. These were representatives of southern Alberta, all right, but they all came from Calgary. They were supposed to be advancing Banff, but there wasn't a Banff man among them, he observed. Nonsense, was the reply. Who could resist such a formidable array?

Edmonton had an answer: Frank Oliver. When the Edmonton MP heard of the Calgary delegation, he too left immediately for Ottawa. Mayor Kenneth W. MacKenzie called a public meeting. Calgary's altruism on behalf of Banff was publicly jeered at, and Edmonton assembled its own powerhouse delegation to send to Ottawa: Mayor MacKenzie; J.H. Morris, president of the Board of Trade; and the prominent Liberal lawyer, C.W. Cross.

Southern Liberals leapt into the fray. Party associations in ten towns from Bowden south telegraphed Ottawa supporting the Calgary case. Wetaskiwin and St. Albert backed Edmonton. Not to be outdone, Red Deer also sent a delegation to Ottawa where it was joined by businessman Moore, and enthusiastically endorsed in a letter to Laurier from John J. Gaetz, a clergyman and a Liberal. The spectacle of these hordes of Albertans all descending on Ottawa bemused Toronto's *Saturday Night*, which urged they be housed in separate hotels to prevent rioting.

The Calgarians got to Ottawa before Oliver, but Oliver got to Laurier before the Calgarians. He appealed to the prime minister with the argument he knew Laurier would find most convincing. Whatever the composition of the delegations, he said, the election clearly demonstrated that Calgary was a Tory town and Edmonton was Grit. "I submit," he told Laurier in a letter, "that your government is still in honour bound to give the preference to where your friends are in the large majority, as compared with the place where your opponents are in the majority." Laurier told the Calgarians that their case would be given "full consideration," then quietly ordered that the provisional capital be established at Edmonton. Calgary's Tory MP, the lawyer Maitland S. McCarthy, a member of a leading Ontario legal family, could do little to help; he was sitting on the wrong side of the house.

For the first three weeks of February Laurier's decision was not known, however. Strathcona MP Peter Talbot, by no means confident of an Edmonton victory, wrote to his friend A.C. Rutherford, Strathcona's territorial MLA:

> Things are getting hot. The delegates from Calgary, Edmonton and Red Deer are all here and have been heard. I have just returned with the Red Deer contingent from an interview with Sir Wilfrid. Moore put up a pretty strong argument for his town. It turns out that the actual vote south of the Red Deer River at the last election was over 1,000 more than north

of that river. Of course that takes in Medicine Hat and also part of the Battleford district west of the 4th Meridian, so I fear we may lose.

I will fight for the finish on having the temporary capital at Edmonton or Strathcona. I fear Bulyea and Scott are in league with Haultain. J.A. Reid was the one who prepared the figures on the last election. Neither Oliver or I have been able to detect any material errors yet. We have a meeting of NW members with Haultain and Bulyea this PM.

I expect a big fight. I may fall in the fray. Red Deer and south will put the knife into me when they get the chance, but I will try to stay with the parts of my constituency that gave me a big majority. We will do the best we can in the matter of redistribution, but I have fears.

In Calgary, meanwhile, Edwards kept up a running vilification of Edmonton in the *Eye Opener*, which had wide readership in Ottawa. Two examples from his February 4 edition:

> Once Edmonton got the provisional capital it would take all hell and a whole lot of policemen to make her give it up. Let Edmonton be content with her new $14,000 jail. She needs that more than the capital.

*   *   *

> Edmonton now estimates that it has a population of over 4,000. Estimates are easy to make. Calgary with her bona fide population of 11,000 is seriously thinking of estimating her population at 25,000 just to prove that its imagination is not inferior to Edmonton's.

*   *   *

On the afternoon of February 21, when Laurier appeared in the Commons to introduce Bill 69, the Alberta Act, the speculation came to an abrupt end. Edmonton would be the capital until the Alberta Legislature voted to move it.[1] The *Calgary Herald* responded to the news with hysteria, discerning behind the decision a mysterious conspiracy by the Bishop of St. Albert and the Grand Trunk Pacific Railway to accomplish the *Herald* did not say what. Even the fury of the Liberal *Albertan* seemed unbounded. It called the decision "unfair...unpatriotic...cowardly...traitorous." In Edmonton, the *Bulletin* contemptuously responded: "Few passions are more desperate or vociferous than baffled greed, and to expect that the organs which had devoted themselves solely to the business of preventing Edmonton being made the temporary capital would accept defeat either in silence or good nature...was to expect the hopeless." The *Bulletin*, by contrast, "has no desire nor intention to emulate the mud-slinging propensities" of the *Herald*. The *Edmonton Journal* was content merely to observe that Calgary was acting "like a spoiled child."

When tempers cooled, however, Calgarians rapidly regained their confidence. After all, Bill 69 designated a capital only temporarily. The permanent capital would be decided by the Legislature, and the Legislature would be controlled by southern Alberta because the total population of the south was more than double that of the north. All that need be done, therefore, was to elect the Legislature and let it pass the requisite resolution. Historian Kilpatrick observes that Calgary's vigilance thereupon relaxed again. At the suggestion of the Board of Trade, the city formed a committee to pursue the capital, but the committee never met. The *Herald* continued to scoff at the thought of a capital on the "fringes" of settlement where, it noted on April 19, property values were already skyrocketing due to the unwarranted expectation that the capital would become permanent. On April 27 it carried a land agent's ad seeking prospective sites for the new Legislative Building in Calgary. But once again, Calgary had underestimated the political factor. Clifford Sifton had resigned as minister of the Interior, the most powerful western portfolio in the government. His successor: Frank Oliver.

In order to elect a Legislature, constituencies had to be established in advance. Bill 69 provided for 25 seats in an initial Alberta legislature, which could later add to or subtract from that number. The boundaries of these 25 constituencies would be set in legislation to be introduced later in that Commons session. Calgary assumed that at least thirteen of the seats, and probably more, would be located from Innisfail south — providing enough strength to move the capital out of Edmonton. Laurier could not directly concern himself with such details as constituency boundaries, of course. He delegated the task to the obvious man, his new minister of the Interior.

Laurier plainly expected Oliver to follow established practice — that is, appoint a bipartisan committee to draw the constituency map. The committee's membership was equally obvious: the four Alberta MPs, the two Conservatives from the south (McCarthy from Calgary and John Herron, a Pincher Creek rancher, who was elected for the constituency called Alberta) along with Oliver and Talbot from the north. Or Oliver might turn the job over to a judicial commission. The astonishing fact is that Oliver did neither. He and Talbot simply sat down together and drew the map themselves. Oliver told Laurier he could not gain the assistance of McCarthy and Herron. Both later told the Commons they had never been asked. The other five Liberal members from the territories were appalled and said so privately, but Oliver rode down all opposition and persuaded Laurier to present his constituency map to the House. With it died any hope of Calgary's ever becoming the capital of Alberta.

Strathcona MP Peter Talbot. In cahoots with Oliver et al.

[1] **This provision remains in effect. That is, the Alberta Legislature can, by the passage of a resolution, move the capital away from Edmonton.**

[2] **Alberta and Saskatchewan, both defined by politics more than economics, are the only Canadian provinces not dominated by one large urban centre. Instead, each has two. The closest parallel is New Brunswick, but Fredericton, the capital, has only half the population of Saint John.**

The map, which would shape the political and economic structure of the province for the whole 20th century by guaranteeing it two major centres rather than one,[2] was a masterpiece of gerrymandering — engineering the boundaries of a political constituency to produce a desired electoral result. It effectively gave Edmonton and Strathcona six seats while Calgary got one. This was achieved on the "pie" formula. The core of Edmonton was given one member. Five triangular surrounding constituencies came into the Edmonton outskirts from the outside, however, and the city portion of each had sufficient population to dominate the geographically larger rural section. Calgary was given no such advantage. In addition, Oliver's and Talbot's two federal constituencies had thirteen provincial members, where McCarthy's and Herron's southern constituencies had only twelve. This was accomplished in part by conferring two seats on the far north, called Peace River and Athabasca, although a voting population scarcely existed there.

Calgarians remained blissfully unaware of these machinations throughout April. The *Herald* had assured them the Oliver appointment was good news for Calgary. As Interior minister he would look beyond Edmonton, and thus be far more amenable to a capital at Calgary. Late in April Calgary put on a civic banquet to honour the new minister, doubtless to encourage his newly acquired broader view. Afterwards, however, some suspicious Liberals besought his assurance that the constituency boundaries would be determined by a judicial commission. They didn't get it, and on May 1, the Liberal lawyer, Charles Stuart, wrote to Rutherford asking the northern Liberals to support the southern in their quest for a judicial commission because "if there is any belief in further favour...it will simply put the Liberal Party out of business in this district for all time to come."

Oliver meanwhile acknowledged to the *Edmonton Journal* that, yes, he did retain "a warm corner in my heart for Edmonton." On May 5, Calgarians discovered exactly how warm that corner was. Oliver unveiled his map to the Commons and Calgary went into apoplexy. The *Herald* called it "the crowning infamy of a nefarious deal" and saw it as the conspiracy of Wilfrid Laurier and

'See the Mighty Hosts Advancing' — the Saskatoon Phoenix spoofs the western siege of Ottawa in the war over the capitals, March 3, 1905.

Monseigneur Sbaretti, the papal legate at Ottawa, "to do a brazen injustice to the whole of central and southern Alberta." It was the work of "conspirators." It was "a violation of every rule of British fair play." It was "an unscrupulous deal...a treacherous affair" and Frank Oliver was the central culprit behind it. He was plotting with "foreigners" to make Alberta a Catholic, French-speaking province. The Liberal *Albertan,* though appalled by the map, observed that the hysterical reaction of the *Herald* posed the greatest obstacle to persuading Laurier to change it. The *Lethbridge News,* the *Macleod Gazette,* the *Pincher Creek Rocky Mountain Echo* and the *Raymond Chronicle* poured forth demands that Laurier cancel the Oliver constituency map and name a judicial commission. Both the lawyer Charles Stuart and the former Liberal candidate Dr. C.J. Stewart telegraphed to Laurier:

> Great indignation among Liberals, not only in Calgary city but in surrounding districts, over proposed constituencies and ask reference to independent commission. The division is grossly unfair to the country south of Red Deer and cannot be defended. We warn the government that unless changed, long continued soreness and ill feeling between north and south will be endangered and party interests in this region totally destroyed.

Laurier, now alarmed, summoned Oliver and Talbot. The latter spent the entire morning of May 19 reassuring the prime minister that the population claims of the south were erroneous. Talbot that day wrote to Rutherford:

> We are having a tangle here over the distribution schedule of the Autonomy bill. The Calgary Libs. are putting up a big kick. I spent all forenoon today with Sir Wilfrid convincing him that the distribution was a fair and just one. He showed me a statement made by Dr. Stewart of Calgary which would indicate that Calgary was the centre of population, etc, etc, etc.
>
> It was the most absurd statement I ever saw. Our friends in Calgary are no good. The schedule will come up for discussion in a few days. The Cons. will fight it to the finish. It is possible they will obstruct proceedings for months. Calgary and the CPR are backing them up. Sir Wilfrid thinks when the facts that I placed before him are put before the House even the Tories may be convinced. He is of the opinion that when our case is put before the country, it would do no harm to have it settled by a Comm. of Judges. To this I don't think Oliver will agree...
>
> I suppose you are in touch with the Lib. candidates. You will find lots of trouble but I think you are the man to smooth matters out.

Historian Kilpatrick describes Laurier as still not fully convinced, and it took another half-day session with Talbot to reassure him. Even then he still favoured the judicial commission, but Oliver apparently talked him out of it. Meanwhile, as Talbot foresaw, the Tories exploded in the House over the issue and Conservative leader R.L. Borden advanced a motion to hand over the Alberta constituencies to a judicial commission. Calgary confined its efforts to pushing its MP, McCarthy, to make protests in the House. McCarthy contended the southern population was 120,834, the northern 69,021, so that the south should have about fifteen seats, the north ten. But no one was really listening.

Kilpatrick is persuaded that if Calgary had done more, such as send another delegation to Ottawa, it could have pressured the wavering Laurier into insisting on the commission. This would probably have changed the constituencies and with them the location of the capital and the whole history of Alberta. But that did not happen. The Borden motion was defeated, a similar motion by James Lougheed was beaten in the Senate, and the constituencies remained as Oliver and Talbot had drawn them. Oliver concluded the debate by chiding McCarthy for not better protecting the interests of his constituents, and the *Albertan* deplored the failure of the Calgary Board of Trade to do its job as well as the Edmonton board had done.

For the next month, the *Herald* screamed abuse at the government. On May 13 it portrayed Edmontonians as "gloating" over Calgary's defeat, and threatened to waylay northbound immigrants with warnings that wheat wouldn't grow in the Edmonton area. On May 20 the *Herald* checked what it considered a typical voters' list in Oliver's constituency and found it crowded with Galician (i.e. Ukrainian) names. "These are recent arrivals in Canada," said the *Herald*, "and there are many more thousands of them on whose judgement the Canadians of the West are to be deprived of self-government." On May 22 it quoted Talbot as conceding that the proposed province's northern region was "unfit for settlement," yet it was to have two seats in the Legislature. On June 7 it attacked the Edmonton Board of Trade for defending the "shameful ger-

---

In its pre-election issue the *Herald* presented an array of front-page headlines: 'Sir Wilfrid a Traitor to the West,' 'Crime Against the West' and 'Very Shady Politics.'

---

rymander." On June 24 it was back at Oliver again for "one of the most shameful jobs Dominion politics has ever produced," while noting that the bill "is apparently going through with the hurrah of the coercion forces." And so, in July, it did.

In August the province's Liberals met in their first provincial convention at Alexander Hall on Calgary's 1st Street W near 8th Avenue, and chose Alexander Cameron Rutherford (see sidebar) as party leader because the favourite, Peter Talbot, didn't want the job. The *Herald* ran a generous front-page welcome, appealing to the citizenry not to abuse the northerners. "Calgary is honoured by their presence," it said, "and everything should be done to make their visit pleasant. The Calgary district has no politics when a question of acting the host is concerned."

It was advice that the *Herald* itself discernibly failed to heed, however. An accompanying story razzed the Liberals for taking over the province before it was even started. "With a somewhat amusing assurance the delegates around the hotel lobbies are settling everything connected with the government of the new province," it said. "They are appointing cabinet ministers, selecting sites for capital buildings and deciding on the distribution of the plums of office (among them-selves) on a most generous scale. They are even deciding the salaries of the ministers and they are to be nice fat salaries. The only part the public is expected to play in all this is to obediently salaam to the eminent statesmen from the polar regions, vote as they are told, and ask no questions."

On the matter of "plums" the *Herald* knew whereof it wrote. Politics at the turn of the century meant patronage. The whole upper echelon of the civil service was politically appointed, as were many of the jobs down to the lowest levels. Thus Talbot unabashedly writes Rutherford to ask for help getting a sheriff's position if he fails to get a senatorship. He writes again eleven days after Rutherford became leader:

> I enclose a letter to you from my son-in-law Benj. Lawton. He is strictly temperate, a first-class book-keeper, accurate at figures, perfectly honest and knows how to keep his mouth shut. I have had him in view for the Ag. Dept. He would be a good hand in charge of statistics etc.

By forming the initial administration, the Liberals were able to establish a whole system of patronage, handing out government jobs to people entirely sympathetic with them, whose survival in those jobs depended on the survival of the government. Thus George J. Bryan, applying for the post of deputy commissioner of education, writes Rutherford with what he considers a key qualifi-cation: "I am and always have been an ardent Grit. There is no one, in northern Alberta at least, who will deny the truth of this statement."

Tories, too, accepted the consequences. A civil servant named A.C. Murphy from the old terri-torial administration writes to Rutherford:

> I herewith tender you my resignation as Inspector of Stock under your government. I could not consistently hold any office which would put me under any obligation to you or your government. I consider that the people of Alberta, and in fact the people of the whole of Canada, have been sold by Laurier and his tools. I do not consider this a province at all in the sense that are the other provinces of Canada. I voted, talked and took an active part in trying to defeat you. I consider this my duty.

Lewis H. Thomas, the University of Alberta historian, in his book *The Liberal Party in Alberta* reaches this conclusion: "The basis of the Liberal Party's success in Alberta elections was its control of the machinery of government." This was the advantage it inherited from Ottawa when the province was born.

The day after he was sworn in, Lieutenant-Governor Bulyea formally called upon Rutherford to form a government and seek a mandate. Rutherford chose a five-man cabinet. Taking the education and treasury portfolios himself, he named the former mayor and Calgary Board of Trade president William Henry Cushing as minister of public works, and a 32-year-old Edmonton lawyer, Charles Wilson Cross, as attorney-general. A Medicine Hat lumberman and rancher named William Thomas Finlay became agriculture minister, and a former Mountie and Lethbridge doctor, George DeVeber, minister without portfolio. DeVeber, Finlay and Rutherford himself were members of the territorial assembly. It was to be a short-lived cabinet. On the surface, southern Alberta had three members, northern Alberta two. In practical fact, however, it was a three-man cabinet. DeVeber went to the Senate within a year and Finlay retired because of ill health. No sooner were these departments established than Rutherford called an election for November 9.

It was a strange campaign. The Tories had all the disadvantages of opposition and none of the advantages. That is, they had no access to patronage and none of the fund-raising capability that tends to accrue to the government in office. But neither could they criticize the government's record, because it didn't have one. They must content themselves, therefore, with attacks on the Autonomy bill itself, most of whose implications the average elector could not yet understand. He didn't like the idea that other provinces could control their own lands and resources where Alberta could not, but then again there was a generous federal payment instead — or at least it looked generous. If he were Protestant he might resent the fact that separate schools had been "imposed" upon Alberta, but then there were separate schools already; it was a familiar situation. If he lived in southern Alberta, he might easily object that his region had been shorted some ten or more Legislature seats, but this had happened principally because he had voted Tory in the federal election. So why vote Tory again? Moreover, leading this hopeless cause was R.B. Bennett, the territorial MLA best known as counsel for the Canadian Pacific Railway.

'The citizens of Calgary are not a unit, the same as they are in Edmonton. Up there, there is a constant evidence of union and community of interest. There are no inter-knocking societies.'

The Liberals meanwhile, if they could not run against the Tory record because they didn't have one either, could at least run against the CPR. So they described its counsel as determined to wreck the plans of the Liberally-endorsed Grand Trunk Pacific to bring a transcontinental railway into Edmonton. And in Edmonton, they had a superb line: A vote for the Tories is a vote to move the capital to Calgary.

Both sides published platforms. The Liberal manifesto sounded like a treatise on democracy. The Liberals believed the "intelligent opinion of the people is the true source of power." They believed in "provincial rights" in education, that public ownership of utilities should be "kept steadily in view," in a "strong economy," in bridges, in taxing lands held by the CPR and Hudson's Bay Company, in working for the establishment of a university, in spreading provincial spending across the whole province — and in staying out of debt. The Tory platform, since the Tories were not in office, could be more specific. They wanted all aid to Catholic schools cut off, land and resources put under provincial jurisdiction, more wagon roads and bridges, and government ownership of utilities, particularly telephones.

However hopeless his cause, the Tory candidate in Edmonton plunged into his task with fierce vigour. Lawyer William A. Griesbach, of Boer War fame, would in less than two years become mayor of Edmonton. In his autobiography, *I Remember,* Griesbach recalls the provincial campaign fondly. He began it by leading a contingent of "Young Conservatives" into an otherwise somnolent Tory nomination meeting for Edmonton. The Young Conservatives moved that the convention adjourn and reassemble as a convention of "independents." The other party members looked on bewildered as both these motions were carried. Griesbach's "independents" then adopted a

What? Calgary fully represented at the inauguration of Edmonton as the capital of Alberta? Has the millennium really come? Will St. Peter dine with Satan?
- Bob Edwards, the Calgary Eye Opener, Sept. 3, 1905.

　　A PROVINCE IS BORN

platform of their own — de-funding Catholic schools and demanding Alberta be given its resources. As Catholics stalked out of the meeting, Griesbach was declared the candidate.

Having no money, he took over an empty building at Ninth Street and Jasper Avenue and recruited two socialist friends to help him, one of them an enormous man named Jackson who was gifted as a brawler. The first friend would plant a chair on the sidewalk, and harangue passers-by to hear a fine speech by the independent Conservative candidate. If anybody heckled, Jackson would sidle up to him as a disincentive. When Griesbach's noon crowds began to approach 200 people, the Liberals sent in their own large men to break them up. Fights recurrently erupted between Jackson's people and the Liberals, which in turn drew bigger crowds than ever. Griesbach lost the election, of course, but respectably, and he obviously enjoyed every minute of it.

The Tories were nowhere ascendant in the province. Bennett, doubtless weary of being pictured as the sinister servant of the detested CPR, decided to counterattack. He told a crowd of 1,500 in Calgary's Lyric Theatre that Liberal candidates were canvassing the province, offering grants of $1,000 to build roads provided the town voted Liberal. "They're bribing the people with public funds!" shouted Bennett. Amid roars and cheers from the crowd (the Liberals yelling "Names!" "Withdraw!" "Retract!" "Take it back!"), Works Minister Cushing strode white-faced across the stage. Glaring at Bennett, he shouted, "That's a lie!"

"It's true and I can prove it!" retorted Bennett. He thereupon charged that candidate William Franklin Puffer of Lacombe had told a Mr. Earley he had $1,000 for "road money" immediately available. Francis Austin Walker, of Fort Saskatchewan, Liberal candidate for Victoria, had made the same statement. "Why are these men entrusted by the minister of public works with money that should be expended by the county authorities?" He had affidavits from the people involved, Bennett claimed.

Like most other election charges, nothing ever seems to have come of these. By now voting day was only two weeks away, weeks chiefly absorbed in a newspaper war that was dominated by the *Herald*'s increasingly fevered histrionics. "Deep Resentment of People of Alberta Against Methods of Ottawa Machine Makes Coercionists' Defeat Probable," an October 23 headline proclaimed. A subhead spoke of the "Shameful Plot by Which the Ottawa Machine Hopes to Delude the Province into Accepting a Dishonest Deal." On October 31 the top-of-the-front-page headline declared: "This Is the Last Straw! Threat Made Through the Leading Coercion Organ That Unless Alberta Goes Liberal the Grand Trunk-Pacific Will Shut Down — Conservatives Charged With Attempted Murder." On November 3 the *Herald* summed up the election issue: "Choose on November 9 Between Freedom and Slavery." And on its last pre-vote issue it presented readers with an array of front-page headlines: "Sir Wilfrid a Traitor to the West," "Crime Against the West!" "Very Shady Politics," and "An Insult to Labour."

The bust of Frank Oliver which once resided at the Edmonton exhibition grounds. The Herald *spoke of the 'infamous Oliver gerrymander.'*

In Edmonton the *Bulletin* was more businesslike. On election eve it carried the following "Instructions to Voters":

> An elector desiring to vote presents himself at the poll, and is handed two pencils, a blue and a RED, and a ballot. He then retires to the compartment used for marking ballots and selects a pencil of the colour assigned to the candidate for whom he desires to vote, which in this election should be red, and makes a cross on the blank side of the ballot. He will then fold the ballot, wet the gummed edges, and hand the same to the deputy returning officer.
>
> Vote for Cross and use the red pencil.

The result was a phenomenon that would be repeated often in Alberta throughout the coming century — an almost total sweep. The Liberals immediately took 21 of the 25 seats. When final results trickled in it became 23 out of 25. They narrowly lost High River after a series of bitterly contested recounts, and lost Rosebud due to the disaffection with the government of the local Mennonite community. In Calgary Cushing defeated Bennett by 25 votes, resulting in an acrimonious fight over the recounts made worse when the *Herald* discovered the presiding judge had been a Liberal campaign manager. Cushing's victory was confirmed.

The *Herald* called it "the worst exhibition of Ottawa interference ever displayed in a provincial election," and later added that "Alberta was dishonoured when it was forced by a venal Ottawa machine to accept the infamous Oliver gerrymander...A horde of Polacks and Galicians and innumerable imported pug uglies has inflicted the province with a form of government that is contrary to British traditions of law and fair play." The *Bulletin* proclaimed: "The Capital Is Here to Stay." At Strathcona on election night, in the Odd Fellows Hall over the Douglas Bros. store, Rutherford's admirers cheered lustily when the returns showed he had won Edmonton, then went wild when they heard he had swept the province and that Cushing had defeated Bennett.

The premier and other leading Liberals, surrounded by torchlights and riding in a carriage pulled by the admiring throng, processed down Whyte Avenue to Main Street (104 St.) where the Rutherfords lived at the time, and on to the field opposite the Baptist Church for an enormous bonfire. Placards read: "Our Premier: A Strathcona Man," "The People Have Spoken," "Alberta United," and "Rutherford is All Right." The "Liberals shouted themselves hoarse at their first great victory in Alberta," reported the *Bulletin*. However, the Tories were swift to observe that 12,741 votes had been cast in the south against 10,403 in the north, clear evidence of a gerrymander. They noted also that the government did not have a clear majority in the south. The Tory vote, combined with that of the fledgling Labour Party (see Section IV, Chapter 1), exceeded the Liberal vote.

It remained then for the Legislature to decide on the capital. Rutherford magnanimously agreed to an open vote on the question. Cushing announced a major effort over the winter to sway the new MLAs to the Calgary cause, although he knew it was hopeless. He would not only have to hold all the southern members, but win some from the north as well. Before the house even met, therefore, Calgary had given up.

This finally ended any hope for Red Deer, which all the while had been counting on a deadlock between the two major cities for which it might provide a compromise solution. Now no compromise would be required. It was also discovered that John T. Moore, the Red Deer businessman elected MLA because of his undoubted influence in the capital question, wasn't even going to be in Alberta in the weeks preceding the first legislative session. "Where is our vaunted champion?" demanded the *Red Deer News*. "When we learn that he is away in eastern Canada and is not likely to return until a few days before the meeting of the House, we feel we have been deceived as a people. Our member is about to become a laughing stock of the province and is about to drag us down in undergoing his own humiliation." In vain the Red Deer council put on a dinner for the legislature members, demonstrating to the MLAs the magnificent potential of their town as a capital. They already knew the chances of an even split were just about nil.

Edmonton prepared for the opening of the Legislature on March 15 with the same vitality it had mustered for the inauguration of the province the previous September. Frank Oliver sold his house on the southeast corner of what would become 100 Avenue and 103 Street,[3] so that it could become the official residence of the Lieutenant-Governor. The Thistle Rink was lavishly prepared for the opening session, and some 5,000 jammed in to hear Bulyea read the throne speech. A reception followed in the new McKay School[4] where the regular sittings of the house would be held. Several evenings later a dress ball was held at the Thistle, stunting even Bob Edwards' capacity for sarcasm. He described it in the *Eye Opener:*

> The Lieutenant-Governor and Mrs. Bulyea were present, as well as the editor of this paper. Indeed everyone of any distinction was there, except Donald Ross, Jack Coleman and Fraser Tims, all of whom had to stay down town and saw off on a game of pedro.
> At this function we met many charming ladies prominent in Edmonton society, and they certainly were most attentive and cordial to the visitors. We shall always think kindly of them for this.
> The rest of the stay in Edmonton was made up of private luncheons and dinners, the

intervals being taken up refusing drinks. The opportunity for getting on a glorious drunk was probably the most brilliant that has ever been placed at our disposal and it seems a pity that considerations of bi-chloride of gold should have interfered with the evident desire of our friends. Believe us they are a whole-souled people. Of course their motto is, "What we have, we hold," but that is their business.

They take it for granted up in Edmonton that they are going to get the capital. This is not to be wondered at, since Calgary has not made the slightest effort in that direction. The citizens of Calgary are not a unit, the same as they are in Edmonton. Up there, there is constant evidence of union and community of interest. There are no inter-knocking societies. The business and professional men seem to be on excellent terms of camaraderie and the women are all on speaking terms and seldom snub each other. This is a wonderful showing.

On April 25, Cushing brought in the motion that would terminate the debate, formally moving that the capital be moved from Edmonton to Calgary. His motion was defeated 16-8, with three southern MLAs voting for Edmonton. (One of them, J.A. Simpson, member for Innisfail, later explained that he favoured Edmonton because they treated him so well when he attended curling bonspiels there.) The debate was brief and unemotional, a mere recognition of the inevitable, and the *Bulletin* congratulated the southern members for not using it as an opportunity to launch "internecine warfare" within Alberta.

But though none would have guessed it at the time, the sufferings of Calgary were not yet over. This time the whip would be held not by the ferocious Frank Oliver but by the courteously dignified "Sandy" Rutherford himself. Before the session ended he introduced a bill, which at first attracted little attention, authorizing establishment of a university. Most people no doubt assumed that the actual development lay years ahead. British Columbia, after all, had been a province for 35 years and still had no university. As Rutherford spoke to the bill, however, it became alarmingly evident he planned something immediately. Resistance swiftly emerged. Even the *Edmonton Bulletin* urged Rutherford to "hold off," at least until sufficient primary schools had been established. The *Calgary Herald* called it "premature." Rutherford, benign as always, simply ignored the criticism, won second reading for the bill on April 22, and soon afterward saw it passed and assented to. The University of Alberta had come into legal existence.

Carefully omitted so far was any mention of where it might be located. Calgary, confident as always, assumed that since Edmonton had the capital, Calgary would become the site of the university. Rutherford had other ideas. After Laurier refused him any federal funding for the site, he personally negotiated the purchase in his own name of a full river lot, the Simpson property, on the south bank of the river about a mile west of his home. Then, after he was safely through the legislative session of 1907, he announced as minister of education that the university would be located in Strathcona on property whose acquisition had already been arranged. (For the story of the first years of the University of Alberta (see Sect. 5, ch. 2).

Again unbridled anger broke out in Calgary. But this time there was a major difference. The reaction of the Tory *Herald* was one of resignation. It called Rutherford "a parish autocrat" and said this was the sort of treatment Calgarians had come to expect. Edwards in the *Eye Opener* blamed southern MLAs who, he said, "are not loyal to their constituents, only to their party superiors." The *Bulletin* defended the decision on the grounds that Edmonton got the capital, Calgary got the normal school, and now it was Strathcona's turn. Calgarians, of course, already regarded Edmonton and Strathcona as simply Edmonton.

But Calgary bitterness ran deep and long. That most powerful of the city's Liberals, *Albertan* editor W.M. Davidson, took personal umbrage at Rutherford's action. It was "the despotic act of a small dictator," he wrote. "That one selfish act not only aroused the bitterest disappointment to Calgarians, but it turned out to be a disastrous blow to the government." Alberta "learned the stature of the premier who had stepped down from his pinnacle and revealed himself in his real parochialism."

The significance is that Davidson wrote that assessment in 1941. Thirty-four years after the event it still rankled. Cushing too was severely embittered, although he was not ready to say so then. It was plain that Rutherford now had major trouble in Calgary, trouble that at the decade's end would explode and terminate his political career.

[3]By the 1900s the site would be occupied by a small federal building named for Frank Oliver, one of the few monuments left to the man who, by fair means or foul, ensured that Edmonton would be one of Alberta's two major cities.

[4]The school is a misspelled memorial to Dr. William MacKay, surgeon for the Hudson's Bay Company, who came to Edmonton in 1898. It was located on McKay Avenue, later 99th, which was also misspelled.

An Ottawa miscalculation put Rutherford in office

'UNCLE SANDY' WORKED HARD TO BECOME PREMIER,
BUT HIS INDEPENDENT INCLINATIONS WOULD DO HIM IN

Alexander Cameron Rutherford descends through about a half century of Alberta history as a man of tireless energy, unflappable patience, flawless goodwill and, says his biographer, a popularity in the South Edmonton area "approaching veneration."

These virtues made him the first premier of the province and founder of the University of Alberta. But with them came an uncompromising insistence upon justice, fair play and democracy that had characterized the old Reform movement in Ontario out of which he had emerged and in whose tradition he stood, and that eventually led to his political downfall.

His demise was hastened, too, by a certain political naivety. He had neither the "killer instinct" so essential to the consummate politician nor the warning antenna that signals trouble before it happens. He tended to blunder into things. They might eventually work, but they cost him dearly. Thus the great university that would rise atop the bank of the North Saskatchewan stands as his monument. But for his political career it was a death trap.

This same impracticality dogged Rutherford from childhood. The son of Scottish immigrants who settled near Ottawa in 1855, he was raised on a farm and decided to become a dairy farmer himself, yet never learned to milk a cow or drive a team. His father went into local Liberal politics and served on the township council of Osgoode in Ontario's Carleton County. There Rutherford attended high school and was afterwards sent to a Baptist college near Hamilton. Upon graduating, he taught school for a year in Osgoode, then was enrolled in the McGill law school at Montreal. He graduated in 1881 and was articled to the Ottawa firm of Scott McTavish & McCracken where he became the protege and affectionate admirer of Sir Richard Scott.[a]

Rutherford was called to the bar in 1885, the year of the North-West Rebellion, when he was 28. Over most of the next decade he ran the Kemptville, Ontario, office of an Ottawa law firm, and married Mattie Birkett, daughter of a prominent

Ottawa family and niece of a member of parliament. By 1895, they had two children, Cecil Alexander Cameron Rutherford, and Hazel Elizabeth. Then in the summer of 1894 Rutherford took the journey that would lead to his life's work. Out of curiosity, he travelled to Calgary on the Canadian Pacific, then north to Strathcona on the C & E. The whole Edmonton area captivated him, but in particular Strathcona, population 200, that had established itself at the railhead. Here, he concluded, a man could raise a family, develop a law practice and grow with the community.

He moved his family west the next year and plunged into the life of little Strathcona with an energy that seemed boundless. He became honorary president of the South Edmonton Football Club, secretary-treasurer of the school board, president of the Edmonton Athletic Association, vice-president of the South Edmonton Literary Institute, auditor of the South Edmonton Agricultural Society, worthy master of the Acacia Masonic Lodge, and secretary of the Edmonton District Butter and Cheese Manufacturing Association. When the Royal Templars of Temperance staged an elocution contest, Rutherford was the judge. When the community held hearings to decide if Strathcona should become a town, Rutherford was chairman. When the town held an election for its first council, Rutherford chaired the nomination meeting and acted as returning officer. When a public debate was called on a resolution to abolish capital punishment, Rutherford took the affirmative — and lost.

Meanwhile, he opened a law office in the old Parrish Block at Main Street (later 104th) and Whyte Avenue, became secretary-treasurer and legal officer for the town of Strathcona, gained a wide reputation successfully defending the Indian Crazy Calf in a celebrated murder trial, and became solicitor for the Imperial Bank.

The town grew rapidly and Rutherford sank his capital into real estate. Across the street from the Parrish Block, he built the Rutherford Block. A few doors north on Main Street, he bought a small one-storey house. A second storey was added

'Sandy' Rutherford and family, circa 1900. Strathcona, he concluded, was a place a man could raise a family, develop a law practice, and grow with the community.

in 1899 and yet another three rooms in 1905. Meanwhile, his eyes were fixed a mile to the west upon the Simpson property, a full river lot undeveloped, upon which he secretly envisioned that a university would one day appear. So he bought land near it.

Contemporary with all of this, he dove into politics. He had scarcely arrived in town in 1896 when Strathconites nominated him to contest the Edmonton seat in a by-election for the territorial Legislature. He was defeated by the veteran Matt McCauley. Two years later, he tackled McCauley again, this time in a general election, and was again defeated, but only narrowly. In the 1902 general election McCauley didn't run and Rutherford was swept to victory. A keen supporter of Frederick Haultain's non-partisan government, he was elected deputy speaker of the territorial legislature.

Otherwise he was a straight party man, became president of the Strathcona Liberal Association in 1900, and was a delegate to the convention that nominated Frank Oliver to contest the constituency called Alberta in the 1900 general election. Oliver won. In the following federal election, three new seats were added to the District of Alberta, one extending from Edmonton south to and including Red Deer and called Strathcona. For Rutherford, it seemed a natural. But he declined in favour of the school teacher-farmer from Lacombe, Peter Talbot, who won the seat and became a confidant of Rutherford's.

Staggering as it may seem, Rutherford's political career did not cause him to cut back on his community role. In 1902 he became with Lord Strathcona a patron of the Strathcona Curling Club. He served as honorary president of the Strathcona Baseball, Curling and Football Clubs. He was a member of the council of the Strathcona Board of Trade, a delegate to the Alberta Baptist Association in its convention at Wetaskiwin, and a deacon, trustee and auditor of First Baptist Church.

In January of 1905, while the West waited anxiously for Laurier's autonomy legislation, he went to Ottawa with a Strathcona delegation sent to discover the local plans of the Canadian Northern and Grand Trunk Pacific railways. But he had to hurry home when a third child, Marjorie, born in the fall of 1903, died suddenly of pneumonia. In Ottawa, he discovered something else. There were to be two provinces, and the party favoured him to take the Liberal leadership in the western one, to be known as Alberta.

Rutherford, says his biographer Douglas R. Babcock, was probably taken aback by this.[b] Despite the amazing spectrum of his community activities he was nowhere recognized as an ambitious man. The *Strathcona Plain Dealer* speaks of "his modesty and retiring disposition." The Edmonton historian Tony Cashman says he was greeted on the street as "Uncle Sandy." He was "no orator," the Tory press agreed, but the *Medicine Hat News* saw other compensations: "If not an orator, Mr. Rutherford has a way of throwing a very clear light on any subject, and after a conversation with him it is easy to understand how an opponent would hesitate before attempting to gloss over

facts with eloquence when in the presence of a man possessing his analytical acumen." The historian Lewis G. Thomas in *The Liberal Party in Alberta* described Rutherford as "precise in speech and manner, a book collector, deeply interested in the problems of higher education and the Baptist Church."

The question uppermost in the minds of the party hierarchy at Ottawa, however, was his loyalty to the federal Liberal organization. Ernest Watkins, a Calgary lawyer and author of a brief history of Alberta's premiers entitled *The Golden Province*, sets out what he considers the qualifications Liberal Ottawa sought in a provincial premier: "Ottawa has never wanted, nor tolerated, any display of independence by a provincial leader. The provincial leader is a divisional commander in an army led from Ottawa, required to have an accurate appreciation and control of the local situation, expected to use his initiative in his moves on his own political battlefield without too much help from the outside, but always under compulsion to obey without question any directions given from above. He must accept the fact that, politically, he is expendable and that when he has been expended his rewards may not be very handsome.

"A Liberal administration in Alberta would therefore always be under close scrutiny by Ottawa...It was necessary for those in Ottawa to be ready to step in at once if that administration faltered and federal interests were in danger of damage...Rutherford was never a man to show real independence in his actions, but he could blunder."

But Rutherford's biographer Babcock is more charitable. He does not believe Rutherford "blundered" into independence of action, but rather inherited an attitude of independence from his Ontario forebears and brought it west with him. In his administration as premier, therefore, he would not be content to see Alberta treated as the colony of Ottawa. "While owing something to his personal vulnerability as a politician, his fall from power is attributable in part to the conflict between Rutherford's Ontarian aspirations for Alberta and Ottawa's colonialist outlook on the West. In this rapid and early disaffection from the Liberal party and the federal establishment, his political career both exemplified and nurtured the process of alienation in Alberta. Rutherford may well be considered the Alberta archetype of western alienation."

Just how all that happened is described in Section 6 of this volume.
— *T.B.*

[a]There was an irony here. As a key minister in the Laurier cabinet, Rutherford's legal mentor, the Roman Catholic Sir Richard Scott, would play a central role in drawing up the original Catholic school section in the Alberta Act. Rutherford, the Baptist Liberal from the West, would help Clifford Sifton defeat Scott and remove all direct church control of the Catholic schools, as described in the previous chapter.

[b]Douglas Babcock of Edmonton, a Toronto-born anthropologist who took a master's degree from the University of British Columbia, was a researcher for the Historical Resources Division of the Alberta Department of Culture for eighteen years. His book, *A Gentleman of Strathcona: Alexander Cameron Rutherford* was produced as an occasional paper for the Historic Sites Service in 1980 and later published by the University of Calgary.

Passengers boarding the train for the inaugural crossing of the North Saskatchewan River by the Edmonton Yukon and Pacific Railway, on Oct. 20, 1902.

Provincial Archives of Alberta, E. Brown Collection

Section Two

THE RESURGENCE OF EDMONTON

Chapters by Terry Johnson, Ted Byfield & George Koch

The rude patch of mud and dust that suddenly became a city

AS THE CAPITAL-DESIGNATE, EDMONTON HAD SOME GROWING UP TO DO, STARTING WITH THE WORST EMBARRASSMENT OF ALL — CITY COUNCIL

by TERRY JOHNSON

In 1905 Edmonton's commercial core, which stretched along Jasper Avenue from Syndicate Avenue (now 95th St.) to Sixth Street (106th) and from the riverbank to Peace Avenue (103rd), was a ramshackle collection of wood-frame hotels, livery stables, realty offices and retail outlets. The muddy streets were lined with wooden sidewalks complete with hitching posts. And that embarrassing reminder of its fur-trading past, Fort Edmonton, still squatted in disrepair and neglect above the river valley. Only four years earlier, the *New York Times* had dismissed the town as "a city of broken dreams, a run-down elephant's graveyard for failed prospectors."

To be sure, even by 1905 Edmonton didn't look like a capital city. "Depending upon whether the previous week had enjoyed a dearth or a downpour of rain," writes James G. MacGregor in *A History of Edmonton,* the packhorses and surreys that tramped along Jasper Avenue "raised a cloud of dust or splattered pedestrians with mud or slush."

Jasper Avenue as it looked in 1904 (this page) and 1909 (facing page). Edmonton boomed in a manner exceeding all optimism. In eight years its population multiplied tenfold.

Provincial Archives of Alberta, B-5033

1904

JASPER AVE. LOOKING EAST FROM HEIMINCK BLOCK 1904

But the beginnings were there. In 1902 the first bridge over the North Saskatchewan, later known as the Low Level, was finally completed. Mackenzie and Mann's Canadian Northern Railway was due to reach the city in November, 1905. The government-bankrolled Grand Trunk Pacific had just started building from Winnipeg and was said to have chosen Edmonton as its prime divisional point between Winnipeg and Vancouver (see next chapter). The Canadian Pacific,

---

There was far more booze than was needed as evidence to convict the bootlegger, the city fathers agreed. So they poured themselves a round. Still far too much. No harm in another.

---

alarmed by the actions of its competitors, had revived its long-delayed plan of building a high-level bridge over the river from its fourteen-year-old terminus across the river in the town of Strathcona.

All this and the continuing influx of settlers into northern Alberta had sparked a long-anticipated boom. In the first five years of the decade Edmonton's population almost tripled, rising from 2,626 in 1901 to more than 7,000 by 1905. The city's residents were sure people would come even faster now it was the capital. "Every Edmontonian could rejoice that at last the city was to take its rightful place in Canadian affairs," writes MacGregor. "All the members of the Board of Trade could pat themselves on the back that their hopes were being confirmed, that their efforts were being rewarded and that Edmonton was indeed destined to be a great city. All the real estate vendors ran around rejoicing, unrolling maps of new building lots."

Indeed, Edmonton did verge on a boom that would probably exceed the wildest optimism of its boosters. In the next eight years its population would multiply tenfold, reaching 70,000 by 1914. Between 1905 and 1914, its assessment would soar from $6 million to $190 million as the wood-frame stores and stables in its commercial core were replaced by banks, office buildings and

1909

Mayors William Griesbach (left) and John McDougall. Griesbach was well-meaning but out of his depth; McDougall, reluctantly, came to the fore.

You say you did not think I worshipped money so much as to deprive myself of civilized society and the pleasures of such. But I ask you to believe me when I tell you that it is true that I have always had one object in view ever since leaving home and that was to make money, not for the sake of the money for I don't worship money at all, very far from it — many is the dollar I have given away to those in want — but for what it would bring. It would be the means of bringing me home and then I would ask my first and only love to share it with me, that and only that is what brought me and is keeping me out here and in the pursuit of it. I have suffered hardships and disappointments that you would not believe. This is true every word of it and now will you doubt that I love you Lovisa.
- taken verbatim from a letter written by future Edmonton tycoon and mayor John McDougall from the fur-trading post of Victoria Mission, northeast of Fort Edmonton, to his future wife, living in Cannington, Ontario, Feb. 12, 1877.

apartment blocks built of brick.

As new buildings went up, old ones had to come down, one of them the old Edmonton Hotel, Donald Ross's establishment on the flats that bore his name that had been there since 1876. The *Journal,* lamenting the loss in a 1906 editorial, argued that some effort should be made to preserve the city's "historic structures."[1] That same summer the old Hardisty house, part of the Fort Edmonton establishment that was being used to isolate smallpox victims, was burned down.

As the new century began unfolding and the prospect of capital status grew brighter, municipal politics failed to keep pace. The town's government was something of an embarrassment. All services were provided out of a single building, the original Number One Fire Hall, built in 1893. The town council met there. It housed the police station and town office. And town employees were given a free bunk in return for volunteering for the fire brigade.

Moreover, many felt council's deliberations (some would say, carryings on) frequently did not befit a promising metropolis, nor did the decorum. Anecdotalist Tony Cashman tells how, after one council meeting, the aldermen paused to examine the evidence seized by a police raid on a local bootlegger. There was far more than the quantity needed to get a conviction, the town fathers agreed. So they poured themselves a round. Still far too much. No harm in another. And another. By morning, the town clerk was alarmed to discover all the evidence gone. The town fathers hurried to another bootlegger, and bought enough to refill the bottles. The first bootlegger was convicted. Law and order was preserved.

Even the efforts of the town dogcatcher, hired in 1900 to round up the packs of yapping mongrels roaming the streets, did little to enhance the town's image. The dogcatcher, a man named Bruchel, built a pound on the Rossdale flats and went to work with stick and slip-noose. He succeeded eminently and soon had accumulated such an enormous collection of curs that complaints began appearing in the *Bulletin.* Nights had become "hideous" and sleep impossible in Rossdale due to the "impromptu solos, quartets and choruses" at Bruchel's pound. Finally one sleepless citizen opened the pound's gate and set them all free. Bruchel rounded them all up a second time, and with them a pair of Russian wolfhounds owned by an English remittance man. The latter, enraged, marched to the pound, pushed Bruchel aside, kicked open the gate and left — followed by all the dogs.

Very amusing, said the town's more sober boosters, but hardly propitious for a centre with serious ambitions for capital status. Hence in November 1904, the Town of Edmonton was declared the City of Edmonton and vast plans for municipal improvement were advanced. (Its neighbour over the river, Strathcona, became a city in 1907.) Streets must be paved, schools built, and sewer and water mains run to new subdivisions. The city needed a take-charge captain at its helm. And, voters reasoned, who better than that dashing young hero of the Boer War, William A. Griesbach, the young Tory whose street corner election meetings in the 1905 provincial election had attracted such notice? (See Prologue, and Sect. I, chpt. 4.) So in the December 1906 mayoral election, they opted for the bemedalled W.A. Griesbach who defeated R.J. Manson by 536 votes to 477. But the 27-year-old "boy mayor," writes MacGregor, found himself "a bit beyond his depth."

Griesbach, to be fair, was immediately confronted with a plateful of problems he had inherited from his predecessor, Mayor Gus May. There was, for one, the long-promised street railway. In 1904 the town had awarded the franchise for the railway to a Montreal businessman, W.G. Trethaway, who paid the city $10,000 for the contract and guaranteed service by 1905. The move was controversial. "Council, in giving immediate consideration to Mr. Trethaway's proposal and in taking no steps to ascertain if there could be found someone who could take the franchise on better terms, have been entirely blind to the true interests of the town," wrote one aggrieved citizen

THE RESURGENCE OF EDMONTON

in the *Bulletin*. The deadline was past, and there was still no sign of Trethaway's promised streetcars.

Meanwhile, Strathcona had moved ahead of Edmonton and had signed an agreement with the locally owned Strathcona Radial Tramway Company, authorizing it to begin work immediately on a line that would run along Whyte Avenue, down Cameron Street (99th Street) to Scona Road and the Low Level bridge, and across it into Edmonton where it would stop. The agreement was subject to the approval of the Strathcona ratepayers in a vote that September.

Then there was the telephone system. In 1905 the city had bought Alex Taylor's Edmonton District Telephone Company for $17,000. With 500 customers, it reported a $4,150 profit in 1906. But the exchange, with its "hello girls" who placed each call, was no longer suited to the city's needs. People were demanding something that modern cities already possessed, dial telephones.

To make matters worse, voters were still smarting over the previous council's decision to buy the 140-acre Kirkness property for use as an exhibition grounds in the northeast, and 100 acres of land for Coronation Park in the northwest. Led by Mayor May, the council had met in secret in January 1906 to complete the deal, agreeing to buy the land in their own names until the purchase could be approved by plebiscite. The result was a public outcry, particularly against the east end location for the exhibition grounds — a property, declared the critics, which is in fact a swamp.

A happy real estate dealer, about 1903. In a couple of years he would be happier still.

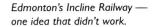

Edmonton's Incline Railway — one idea that didn't work.

[The Edmonton Hotel was historic for at least one thing. Remittance man Reginald Crowder arrived in 1901 and became a social celebrity. Stranded the following year when his remittance cheques failed to arrive, he took a job as bartender. Horrified society matrons cut him off the invitation list for the prestigious Bankers' Ball. Tony Cashman in *Best Edmonton Stories* tells how he showed up anyway, partnered with an Indian girl who was a vivacious dancer. Women were scandalized as their husbands strove to dance with the girl. The ball, says Cashman, "was a disaster." When his cheques resumed, Crowder moved to Calgary.

Taken aback by the angry response, council members postponed a vote on the matter until sentiment turned. But controversy dogged them. In March, for example, there was the suffrage question. After the legislature offered to discuss amendments to city and town charters on request, Alderman Tom Bellamy (for whose family Bellamy Hill would be named) suggested the municipal franchise be extended to women on the same basis as men. That is, any woman 21 or older who

Part of the tent city about 1907. The housing shortage was such that by the fall of the year 5,000 were living this way.

I think this is the dirtiest city in Canada, the streets are a disgrace to any place and the sidewalks in many places are made of plank put down I should judge about twenty years ago and now are all rotten and decayed...

* * *

The city is full of pickpockets and hold-up men. Every paper that one picks up has three or four new cases to report, and accounts of several bodies floating in the river.

* * *

In all my travels I did not see a drunken man on the street in London or on the continent, but here you can see them quite often and the police pass them by.

- John McDougall writing to partner Richard Secord from Montreal, Aug. 1, 1907.

owned $500 in property would be entitled to the vote in municipal elections. It can't be done, interjected the city solicitor. Married women could not own property. Anything they owned belonged automatically to their husbands. But, with May's support, aldermen did agree to give the vote to properly-qualified spinsters and widows.

For a moment it looked like a tremendous gain for women's suffrage. But then Alderman John Boyle spoke up. The city, he said, was asking the legislature to pass socialist legislation. May was so moved by the speech that he switched sides and forced a vote, narrowly saving Edmonton from "petticoat government," as the *Bulletin* reported. But given the passions raised by the debate, council decided to postpone the park plebiscite.

The vote was postponed again after yet another kerfuffle, this one over the fire brigade. May, reasoning that the city needed a new, more experienced fire chief in keeping with its greater size and importance, demoted the current chief to make room for his future replacement. That prompted the entire 35-man brigade to walk out in solidarity with their boss. The city was left

McDougall was a hard man to love, according to MacGregor, 'gruff and perhaps intolerant of moral weakness and stupidity.' But no one could quibble with what the mayor had accomplished.

without fire protection until, in an emergency meeting, council agreed to bring back the old chief, and raise the pay of the brigade members.

In December 1906, at the end of May's term, the park question was finally put to a vote. Fortunately for mayor and aldermen, who had no desire to continue as permanent owners of the two plots of land, voters approved the measure. By then it was becoming clear that the city would indeed grow into the Exhibition and Coronation Park sites.

Mindful of his predecessor's mistakes, the newly elected Griesbach wasted no time in demonstrating his take-charge manner. One of his first acts was to order police to clean up the streets and shut down the brothels. Then he started a horse-run garbage department to bring a bit of military spit-and-polish to the town. But problems crept up faster than he could solve them.

For one, people were arriving too fast for the city's builders to keep up. By June 1907, 2,000 Edmontonians were living in tents. By the fall, an estimated 5,000 were camping out, almost a

THE RESURGENCE OF EDMONTON

third of the city's total population. Canvas communities sprang up on the river flats, beyond the Canadian Northern tracks in the east end, and all along the as-yet undeveloped view lots above the river valley. Some even perched their tents on the steep cliff below what would soon become the site of the Macdonald Hotel. The precipitous slope was treacherous at times, but the cliff yielded a free supply of coal to its tenants.

These unusual living conditions created further problems. Disease. The rapid spread of typhoid fever and other illnesses in the tent towns contributed to the summer's isolation hospital scandal, writes MacGregor. Local newspapers reported that doctors charged with looking after patients at the overburdened facility were rarely found there, the attendants were usually drunk, and the nurses, unable to use the sanitary trenches, had to resort to the nearby creek. Griesbach was forced to commit $19,000 to build a new hospital.

The spread of disease added to the city's relief burden. At the time, welfare was a municipal responsibility. To a later generation the welfare budget would

A political store display in the window of McDougall & Secord, Sept. 1, 1905. Boosterism hit new heights of ridiculousness.

seem preposterous, even allowing for a fifteen- or twenty-fold increase in living costs. In 1905 Edmonton spent only $493 on relief, compared to $50,000 for capital expenditures. But, lacking armies of social workers, the city had to improvise its response to need. Thus the plumbing department found itself caring for a baby whose father had died of typhoid and whose mother remained seriously ill. "If the boy turns out to be dull, he might do for council," suggested the *Journal*. "But if he is bright we can make a commissioner of him."

It was a fiscal crisis that finally undid Griesbach. As new residents flooded in and new subdivisions opened, the city had to furiously build roads, schools and other infrastructure to keep pace.

In an ad, the Board of Trade offered an Edmonton superiority for every letter of the alphabet. 'X-rays,' it said, 'cannot find a more prosperous location.'

Between 1904 and 1914 the public school board alone built sixteen schools at a cost of $1.9 million. Residents bristled when the work wasn't done. In the fall of 1907, for example, parents living north of Sutherland Street (106th Ave.) refused to send their children to Rat Creek School because there were no sidewalks. They also complained that their children "had to pass several houses of ill fame" on their way to and from school.[2]

The city's tax base was growing with the population. In 1907, the assessment rolls climbed from $17.5 million to $23 million. But taxes weren't being collected quickly enough to meet commitments. By July 1907 the municipal treasurer reported that the city was out of money, and that the Imperial Bank would not lend it any more. In September Griesbach tried to solve the problem by issuing $697,000 in debentures. But the 5% debentures traded at only 93 cents on the dollar. Taxpayers were outraged.

[2]Rat Creek flowed across what was then the northern section of the city from Norwood, through the future site of Clark Stadium, and eastward into the North Saskatchewan. A more refined generation would later name it Kinnaird Ravine.

As Griesbach's one-year term drew to a close, businessmen feared the city's financial problems might jeopardize its continued growth. The school boards were not receiving money from the city council. The line of credit was exhausted. The telephone problems remained. There was no sign of a high-level bridge. And the street railway problem, if anything, was worse. Griesbach had intervened in Strathcona's September ballot on its tramway contract, urging Strathcona's voters to reject it so that a joint system could be worked out with Edmonton. Instead they approved it 781 to 186. Work began immediately on the Strathcona system. Edmonton still didn't have one.

Sensing that all was in confusion at Edmonton city hall, the Board of Trade searched for a saviour. It drafted, wisely as it turned out, long-time Edmonton merchant and former mayor John A. McDougall. McDougall at first declined. He wanted to make money in the currently booming real estate market. He had made a great deal already. After arriving in Edmonton in 1883, he had successfully competed with the Hudson's Bay Company as a fur trader. That proved even more profitable after he hired ex-teacher Richard Secord as a fur buyer. The two became partners, and expanded into the retail trade as McDougall & Secord with a store at Jasper and First Street (101st) that became one of early Edmonton's landmarks.

At the turn of the century, the dominion government had begun issuing land scrip to the Metis living in the Peace River district. Each piece of scrip entitled its bearer to a quarter-section of

Alberta wanted a Legislature like Minnesota's

THE AIM WAS NOT ORIGINALITY BUT EQUIVALENCE WITH STATE CAPITOLS SO THE BUILDING EMULATED THE WORK OF A GREAT AMERICAN ARCHITECT

It's no accident that the Alberta Legislative Building resembles the state legislative building of Minnesota. The structure at St. Paul, designed by American architect Cass Gilbert, had just been completed when Edmonton was named Alberta's capital. Mindful of Gilbert's high reputation, Public Works Minister W.H. Cushing visited the Minnesota house.[a] He liked it. Then Premier Alexander Rutherford visited it. He liked it too. So when the provincial government hired Allan Merrick Jeffers to design the Alberta Legislature, the American-born architect was given straightforward instructions: Give us a legislative building like the one in St. Paul.

There was no talk at all of coming up with a distinctively Albertan or Canadian design. The new province didn't want to set itself apart from the metropolitan centres of the US and Europe. It wanted to join them, explains Diana Bodnar in *The Prairie Legislative Buildings of Canada,* her 1979 University of British Columbia Master of Arts thesis. "Geographically isolated communities attempted to link their prairie environment, architecturally at least, with American and European centres for cultural, economic and political activity," she wrote. "They wanted to prove that they were respectable, that they were progressive and equal."

Neither did Rutherford have any trouble settling on a site for the new building. It had to be on the spot where Fort Edmonton still stood. The province bought the 21-acre property from the Hudson's Bay Company for $84,000, shortly after Edmonton was confirmed as capital. The *Edmonton Journal* didn't think much of the decision. Noting that the CPR was planning to bring a high-level bridge over at adjacent Ninth Street (now 109th Street), the paper worried that the smoke and noise from the trains would interfere with the legislators' deliberations. The choice of site also shifted Edmonton's development westward. But by building the Legislature above the fort, the province symbolically demonstrated how far it had come since the fur trade had given it birth.[b]

The five-storey, $4-million, T-shaped structure "was a mammoth undertaking for those days," said Brian Woolfenden, the consulting architect on the 1987 renovations to the legislative chamber and rotunda. Except for its granite base and six entrance colonnades, also built of granite, a

Glenbow Archives, NA-1042-9

Architect Allan Merrick Jeffers (front row, far right) with some of the workers who carved the columns for the Legislature, 1911.

unclaimed land. Many Metis were willing to part with the pieces of paper for a few dollars or a bottle of whiskey. "Everyone who had money traded in scrip," writes MacGregor in *Edmonton Trader: the Story of John A. McDougall*. "It was the thing to do. And McDougall had lots of dollars and Secord knew lots of Metis."

Secord began taking two suitcases on his trips north, one for his clothes, the other crammed with $5 and $10 bills with which to buy scrip. Upon his return, the scrip could be sold to homesteaders eager for a plot of land. In 1902 the pair advertised that they had scrip to 150,000 acres of land for sale, at $2 an acre. Both men became fabulously wealthy, at least by Edmonton standards. In 1905 they built the Empire Block next to their Jasper Avenue store. In 1907 they sold their fur and retail business to Revillon Brothers, the Canadian arm of the French fur-trading house of Revillon, and established a mortgage-lending operation.

Still, McDougall felt indebted to the city. He agreed to return to city politics, defeated candidate J.H. Picard by 1,217 votes to 737 in the election of 1907, and succeeded Griesbach. At his first council meeting, in January 1908, one alderman pointed out there were 500 phones in Edmonton, and 600 more people had applied for them, but the Lorimer Company in Toronto which had contracted to supply the essential automatic dialling system had done nothing. McDougall went to Toronto, found that Lorimer hadn't even begun building the switchboard

yellowish-brown sandstone mined from the Glenbow Quarry near Calgary provided the exterior finish.[c] Its interior was completed using 22,000 square feet of white marble, weighing 1,950 tons, quarried in Quebec and Pennsylvania. Like the Minnesota building that served as a model, it was topped with a dome built of 200 tons of reinforced steel.

The legislature's design is a style architects call Beaux Arts Classicism. Developed at the Ecole des Beaux Arts in France in the late 19th century, it is based on "an eclectic mixture of historic classical elements," writes Jac MacDonald in *Historic Edmonton: an Architectural and Pictorial Guide*. The symmetrical plan, the fluted columns and the combination of round and flat-arched windows are all common Beaux Arts features.[d]

Excavation began in 1907. By Oct. 1, 1909, when Governor-General Earl Grey used a silver trowel to symbolically turn the soil on the future legislature grounds and set the keystone of the building in place, Alberta's capital was ready to celebrate. The city decorated itself with more than two miles of bunting, 11,000 flags and 5,000 incandescent lights. A parade including Boer war vets and 2,500 school children marched along Jasper Avenue to the grounds. The day finished with a ball at the Thistle Rink. Actually, wrote the *Edmonton Bulletin*, "the rink had vanished. And in its place stood a fairy castle, a drama of decorative devices."

In late 1911, Alberta's MLAs were able to hold their first sitting in their new home. Until then, the legislators had made do with makeshift quarters at the Thistle Rink and McKay Avenue School. The building was formally opened in 1912 by the Duke

Legislature under construction. By late 1911, the MLAs were able to move in.

of Connaught, then Canada's governor-general. Since then it has undergone several renovations. But in 1987 David Carter, then speaker of the legislature, said it remained "the number one building in the province in its combined importance—its political, architectural and historic focus."

— *T.J.*

[a]Gilbert is best known for designing New York City's Woolworth Building. The 66-storey Manhattan skyscraper, finished in 1913, would remain one of New York's major landmarks throughout the century.

[b]Fort Edmonton, long-since abandoned, stood in disrepair until 1915 when it was torn down because it spoiled the view of the river valley from the Legislative Building.

[c]The soft sandstone chosen has given trouble to the building's modern-day custodians. Much of the exterior detailing is being lost through weather-induced erosion and decay.

[d]The Bowker Building, completed in 1931 at 109th Street and 98th Avenue, is another Edmonton example of the Beaux Arts style.

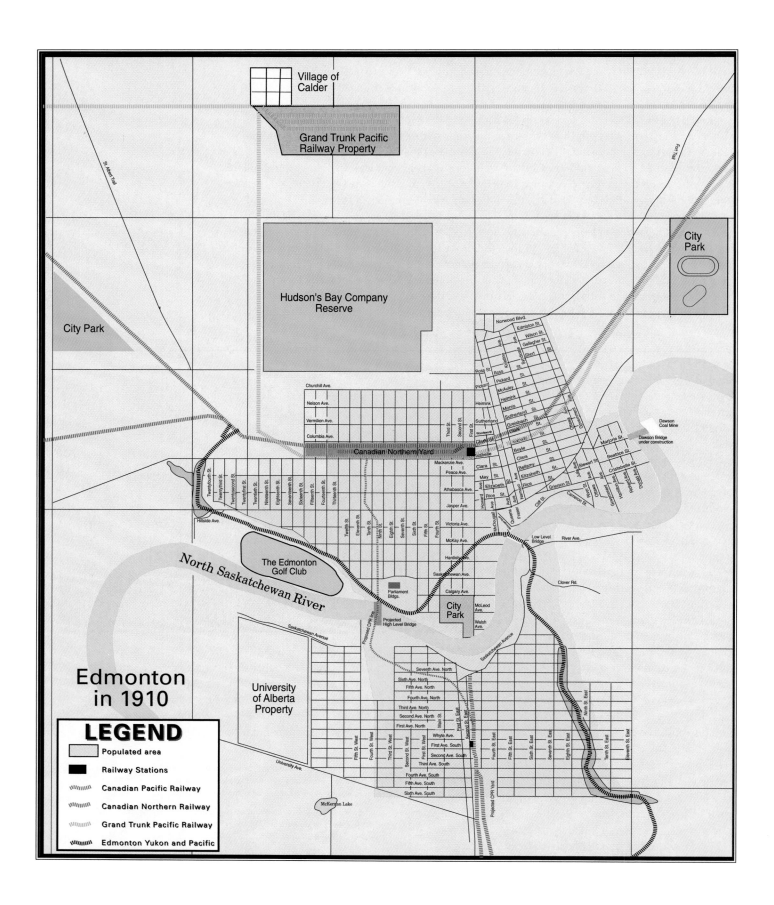

Edmonton in 1910

LEGEND

Populated area

Railway Stations

Canadian Pacific Railway

Canadian Northern Railway

Grand Trunk Pacific Railway

Edmonton Yukon and Pacific

because the company was still trying to sell enough shares to finance the work. The mayor gave Lorimer sixty days to produce, or the contract would be cancelled.

Lorimer threatened to sue but McDougall, unperturbed, went on to Chicago to visit Strowger Automatic. The US company offered to do the job for $56,000, promised to forfeit $10,000 if it didn't ship the equipment that very month, agreed to forfeit another $25,000 if the lines weren't installed by April 1, and offered to throw in $100,000 to cover legal fees if Lorimer took

Laying the streetcar tracks along Jasper Avenue, May 4, 1908. The boom could not last forever, however much it seemed it would.

The exchange, with its 'hello girls' who placed each call, was no longer suited to the city's needs. People were demanding what modern cities already had, dial telephones.

Edmonton to court. Strowger got the contract, and on April 20 the automatic dialling system went into service.

As for the streetcars, McDougall recommended Edmonton make a deal with Strathcona Radial Tramway and develop both systems together. He put forward a money bylaw under which Edmonton would buy out Strathcona Tramway and form a new company that the city would run. The company agreed to the terms and Edmonton voters approved the deal by a resounding vote of 710-7. Mayor McDougall appointed Charles Taylor as the street railway's first superintendent, and

The first throes of elegance in a city yearning for it

BY THE TURN OF THE CENTURY, EDMONTON WAS ABANDONING CLAPBOARD AND WOODFRAME FOR SOMETHING WITH A BIT MORE CLASS

Edmonton's new Canadian Bank of Commerce at Jasper and 1st Street. Designed to reflect wealth and stability.

Edmonton has never grown so quickly or changed so much as it did in the first decade of the century. Within that ten years it discarded its clapboard and wood-frame past for office blocks, so-called luxury apartments and other modern buildings that befitted the city's commercial optimism. Much of that architectural record remained till the century's end, and there is no better example of Edmonton's emergence as a major centre than its turn-of-the-century banks.

At the beginning of the decade, Canada's financiers were hardly interested in Edmonton, then little more than a frontier outpost. By the end of 1903 it boasted only three banks housed in simple brick structures, and two others in false-fronted, wood-frame buildings. But as the boom took off, the banks were among the first to reflect the city's growing importance.

In 1904 the Bank of Commerce erected a three-storey stone building at the northwest corner of Jasper Avenue and First Street (now 101st St.). Neo-classical in design, its high entranceway was flanked by four, two-storey-high stone columns. The Bank of Montreal and Merchants Bank built similar structures the following year on the two northside corners of Jasper and Howard Street (100A St.). Each had richly detailed interiors to convince clients of the bank's wealth and stability, and each included upper-floor suites for staff. The residences, common in banks of that era, deterred thieves and enabled bank managers "to control the lifestyle of their single male employees," writes David Spector in "Edmonton Bank Architecture: The Neo-Classical Age 1904-1914," an article in *Alberta History* magazine.

As Edmonton continued to grow, its financial institutions erected ever more opulent structures. The Imperial Bank, built in 1907 on the northeast corner of Jasper and McDougall Avenue (100th St.), was the most impressive. It was the first in the city to make use of exterior building materials from outside the province. Its base, stepped entranceway and giant columns were built of Tyndall stone quarried near

Winnipeg. The manager's room was finished in antique oak. The banking hall boasted marble floors, columns and a tiled ceiling.

But banks weren't the only buildings to reflect the city's confidence. The Arlington Apartments at Victoria Avenue and Fifth Street (100th Ave. and 105th St.) by the 1990s had lost much of their original elegance. But when the five-storey, red-bricked structure was completed in 1909, at a cost of $130,000, its 49 high-ceilinged apartments were, by the standards of the day and the city, accorded luxury status. Because the developer wanted to take advantage of the real estate boom that was under way, construction proceeded at a frantic pace: a team of 25 bricklayers and fifty carpenters managed to complete a storey a week.

The apartments themselves were all elegantly finished. "Each suite featured a built-in reversible Murphy bed and oak buffet, inset with a mirror and flanked with oak spindles," writes Jac MacDonald in *Historic Edmonton: an Architectural and Pictorial Guide.* "Oak closet doors were faced with a small china cabinet, built-in writing desk and shelving." Tenants included Richard Hardisty, son of a former Fort Edmonton factor, and John Blue, Alberta's first provincial librarian.

The MacLean Block on the northwest corner of Jasper Avenue and Seventh Street (107th) was to survive as another reminder of the city's commercial growth. Built in 1909 for $35,000 by city real estate developer Dr. James D. MacLean, the three-storey, 25,000-square-foot block was then further west than any other Edmonton commercial structure. Its first major tenant was the Imperial Bank of Canada. Saved from the wrecker's ball in 1977 and restored, its main floor became a retail area, its second storey housed offices.

The city's rapid expansion was also demonstrated by the era's surviving schools. Two of them — Norwood School and Old Scona High School, both designed by local architect Roland Lines — were still in use as the century drew to a close. Norwood, built in 1909 at Norwood Boulevard and Kirkness Street (111th Ave. and 95th St.)[a] to serve the new subdivision of Norwood, was then Edmonton's largest school. On opening day its ten classrooms were packed with 400 students. One, Eleanor Palmer, who later became Mrs. J.L. Cleary, remembers that the drinking fountains in its hallways were a special attraction. The school later gained a

gymnasium, while its top floor, once an assembly hall, was converted into a library.

Old Scona High School, built the same year for $100,000 at Strathcona's Second Avenue North and First Street West (84th Avenue and 105th Street)[b], also survived late into the century. When opened, the 400-student school boasted such modern conveniences as indoor plumbing and central heating. It was narrowly saved from demolition in the 1980s when plans for a new 105th Street bridge and connecting freeway were shelved, and was thereafter protected by Alberta Culture as a historic site.

The boom would create much more architectural wealth, particularly in the form of large fashionable homes, but nearly all of these appeared in the century's second decade.

— *T.J.*

[a]95th Street was called Kirkness Street, north of Norwood Boulevard (111th Ave.), and Syndicate Avenue south of Norwood Boulevard.

[b]Strathcona's original system numbered its east-west thoroughfares as avenues north or south from an axis, Whyte Avenue. Roads running north and south were numbered streets, east or west from an axis, Main Street, which later became 104th. The system was changed to accord with Edmonton's after the cities were merged in 1912.

The Arlington Apartments under construction in 1909. The city was moving in the direction of luxury.

ordered him to get the streetcars running on the Edmonton Radial Railway Tramway before the end of the year. Taylor produced. By November 1908 he had an elaborate system in operation that served the four population clusters of the two cities:

• The most densely populated was the Norwood section which lay east of First Street (101st), north as far as Alberta Avenue (118th Ave.), east to Government Avenue (92nd St.), and south to Jasper. This area included the main business district that lay along Jasper in the vicinity of Namayo Avenue (97th St.).

• The second lay north and south of Jasper from First Street (101st St.) west to Sixteenth Street (116th St.).

• The third lay in Rossdale on the river flats.

• The fourth was Strathcona which had developed spottily from the river to its southern city limits on what would become 72nd Avenue west to the future 112th Street, and east just beyond Mill Creek Ravine.

With money funded by the borrowing bylaw, Edmonton Radial began with seven streetcars and in November 1908 launched a system that ran from northern Norwood, down to Jasper Avenue, west to Ninth, south to Saskatchewan (97th) Avenue, east to the bridge and across it, up Scona Hill to Whyte Avenue and west on Whyte to Strathcona's Sixth Street (110th St.). The next year, six more cars were acquired, bigger ones whose pay-as-you-enter facilities were the last word in urban transit.[3]

That all this was due to the impetus of John McDougall, none doubted. But McDougall was a hard man to love. He was, writes a sympathetic MacGregor, "gruff and perhaps even intolerant of moral weakness or stupidity." But no one could quibble with his accomplishments in office. By the time his one-year term expired, Edmonton was beginning to look like a modern city. Telephone and electric lines were being snaked along the streets. One mile of Jasper Avenue had been paved, much to the delight of the city's pioneer motorists. At a public meeting in the mayor's honour, city residents presented him with a chest of sterling silver in recognition of his work on their behalf. In Saskatchewan river gold, the chest was inlaid with the figures of a buffalo, a Red River cart and Jasper Avenue.

Notwithstanding McDougall's spectacular success, the city was still faced with a myriad of problems. For one, there was the dreadful condition of the North Saskatchewan, Edmonton's only source of water. "The rise of the river brings down an accumulation of filth and decayed vegetable matter, rendering the water absolutely unfit for drinking," observed the *Journal* in June 1908. The following year it fretted that, if something wasn't done soon about the river's poor state, cholera and typhoid would kill everyone along its banks. Everyone, that is, who didn't buy the Noxall germ-proof filters that Ross's Hardware stocked up with and heavily advertised.

Negotiations with the CPR on completion of a high-level bridge dragged on inconclusively. Edmonton and Strathcona both wanted it, but they balked at the additional $1 million it would cost to add a traffic deck to the railway structure. A deal was eventually reached in June 1909, with the two cities and the province each contributing to the cost of building the bridge. But construction would not begin until the following year, and it would not be completed until 1913.

An electric power problem was also developing. The coal-fired generating plant on the Ross Flats could not satisfy the needs of the rapidly growing city. The *Journal* reported in January 1909 that the new street railway would have to cease operations at certain times because of a lack of available power. While the city hosted the International Council of Women that summer, in fact, a trolley carrying almost 100 of the council delegates ground to an embarrassing halt on the Saskatchewan Avenue hill (97th Ave.) where the new Legislative Building was about to go under construction. The women had to be carried uphill in two trips. Perhaps, the *Journal* suggested, it was time the city investigated the "practically unlimited" power of hydro-electricity.

And, though everyone agreed that natural gas was a more suitable fuel than coal for heating the city's homes and businesses, no one agreed on what to do about it. "On the gas question, Edmonton's burghers voted themselves into a corner," says historian MacGregor in his *A History of Alberta*. "They wanted gas but on the one hand they were afraid that someone might make money at supplying it; on the other, if the city supplied it, it might lose money. That left everyone sitting on the fence."[4]

These, however, were just minor irritants. For Edmonton, everyone knew by the end of 1908, was bound for greatness. And there was vast wealth to be made during the voyage. The real estate market alone gave first-class evidence of it. A land boom gripped the city that year and continued almost until the outbreak of the First World War. Edmonton's rail connections, its capital status, the prospect of amalgamation with Strathcona and the continued influx of settlers into north-central Alberta all guaranteed the city's future growth.

The Board of Trade fuelled the fire, boosting Edmonton's "ideal" business potential. A fevered campaign was launched to dispel the Calgary-sponsored thesis that Alberta's capital was in "northern Alberta." The board published map after map to prove it was in "central" Alberta, and showing webs of rail lines and major roads fanning from it to the country and the continent. Sometimes the boosterism reached into the ludicrous. In a 1906 *Bulletin* advertisement, the board offered an Edmonton superiority for an activity that matched every letter in the alphabet. "X-rays," it said, "cannot find a more prosperous location."

The boundless optimism and speculative spirit that accompanied the land boom, however, were hardly rooted in common sense. The city expanded in all directions, often needlessly. Street railway lines were run into undeveloped neighbourhoods, sometimes attracting charges of outright graft because of the buoyant effect it had on land values. And almost everyone in town with a few dollars in hand was plunking it down in the real estate market. Of 200 businesses in operation in 1907, eighty were real estate agencies. However even as late as 1910 the boom was only beginning and the next three years were to see it explode.

Not everything Edmontonians touched turned to gold. The Incline Railway, built by hotelier Donald Ross in 1908 at the foot of First Street to hoist passengers and freight up from the river valley, at first did a thriving business. Described as a cross between an outdoor escalator and a San

---

Almost everyone in town with a few dollars was plunking it down in the real estate market. Of the 200 businesses in 1907, eighty were realtors. And the boom was just beginning.

Francisco cable car, the hoist operated from 7 a.m. to 7 p.m. during the summer months, with extra trips added for baseball matches. By June 16, 1910, it had carried a total of 144,760 foot passengers at five cents a trip, and 76,099 vehicles at 15 cents. But the novelty wore off and the hoist ceased operation in 1912.

Neither had the boom destroyed all traces of Edmonton's not-so-distant fur trading past, as labourer Billy Lund abruptly learned. In 1908 workers had uncovered ten 25-pound kegs of black powder in a Fort Edmonton building being used, ignominiously enough, as a poultry station. They decided to dump the kegs in the river. But Lund, who was tenting on the flats, fished a couple out of the water, carried them to his makeshift home, and tested a bit of the powder on his stove. "It was good," writes MacGregor. "When it exploded it flashed over to the keg, which wreaked a deafening detonation shaking buildings for blocks. Lund was badly burned and battered. His dog was in the tent at the time and was neither seen nor heard of again."

Still, by 1910, Edmonton had landed solidly in the 20th century. Residents could take in a moving picture for a dime at the Bijou Theatre, built in 1908 on McDougall Street (100th), just across from Market Square. Thousands of Edmontonians trooped to the Bijou later that year to catch a newsreel of the funeral of King Edward VII, shipped from England and shown in the same month it occurred. They could head downtown to shop on one of the city's fleet of electric trams, but they might have to dodge a car racing along the paved streets. In March 1910 Dr. Whitelaw, the city's medical officer, was fined $10 for travelling seventeen mph along Jasper Avenue. At his trial, the doctor insisted that his automobile couldn't possibly have reached that high rate of speed. "If this goes on," he added, "we will all have to get speedometers installed." They could even marvel at the Legislative Building under construction at the foot of Ninth Street, just above what was left of Fort Edmonton.

The boom could not last forever. Theoretically people knew it. But when it came to an abrupt end in 1913, on the eve of the First World War, many would lose their shirts and the city would lose almost a third of its then-70,000 residents. But in the spring and summer of 1910, fortune's smile seemed as certain and as eternal as the old North Saskatchewan itself.

[3] Edmonton's *Saturday Evening News* spoofed the rampaging transit explosion with a front-page cartoon map showing Edmonton and "that part of Canada which is not within the city limits." A heavy black line showed the route of the proposed electric railway, "some 200,000 miles in length, of which about 1/4 mile of track has already been laid." The black splotch at the map's centre, the caption continued, "is not an accident—it used to be known as the Great Slave Lake, but has now been boarded in and is used as a skating rink for children." The map also showed a few transfer points on the radial tramway. One said, "Change here for Pacific Ocean—ten minutes walk." Another said, "Change here for Halifax—three feet away."

[4] In 1909 the Nova Scotia-born American boy-wonder utility industrialist Cyrus Eaton suggested he could provide gas out of straw, but the price of straw soared at the news and the scheme collapsed.

CHAPTER TWO

How a feud among tycoons led to a ruinous railway war

DELIGHTED EDMONTONIANS SAW THEIR CITY BECOME A BIG RAIL CENTRE
BUT AS THE ROADS RACED EACH OTHER WESTWARD, DOOM WAS ASSURED

The Canadian Northern arrives in Edmonton, on November 24, 1905. It was the most important day in his career, said Donald Mann.

by TED BYFIELD

To those in northern Alberta who beheld that strange spectacle in the spring of 1910, it seemed utterly insane. Here was their new railway headed across to the Rockies, the Grand Trunk Pacific, to be built with no sharp curves, no grade rising more than 26 feet to the mile, plainly one of the most expensive rail thoroughfares in the world, running straight out of Edmonton towards Yellowhead Pass at Jasper and slated to continue on to the Pacific at Prince Rupert. But now, right alongside it, in fact sometimes less than fifty feet away from it, surveys were proceeding for another railway, the Canadian Northern. It was about to parallel the GTP westward from Edmonton across the prairies and then over the Rockies — nearly 250 miles of side-by-side track, much of it through mountains. Something was plainly wrong. But could big government and big business err so wildly? Surely not.

The answer, they would discover during the next decade, was definitely yes. Indeed, they were seeing only one aspect of the greatest calamity in Canadian transportation history. Looking eastward they could have seen other aspects. Canada, a country scarcely able to support one transcontinental railroad, was to have three. One would run through more than a thousand miles of northern Quebec and northern Ontario muskeg, at nearly triple the cost of railroad building in the Rockies, touching nothing more than fur-trading hamlets, and with practically no potential for agricultural development.

The eventual outcome was inevitable. Within the next ten years, before 1920, four of Canada's five major railways would be utterly bankrupt, so that the government would either have to take them over or leave most of the country with no rail service at all. There was an ironic justice in this, however, for the catastrophe had occurred in the first place through the destructive workings of the French-English schism in Canadian government that had beset the country since its birth.

But none of this had been evident to most Albertans until about 1910. Indeed, to Edmontonians in particular, the Canadian Northern and the Grand Trunk Pacific seemed to confer inestimable economic benefit. For 27 years their city had yearned for a transcontinental line. Now it was to be a major divisional point on two of them. Only when the Grand Trunk Pacific and the Canadian Northern began a clearly suicidal contest between Edmonton and the coast, both using

(L-r) William Mackenzie, Donald Mann, and Charles Melville Hays. Hays had the ear of the prime minister; Mackenzie and Mann had Sifton on their side.

The American Hays, himself described as a 'cold-blooded raider of the treasury,' considered competitors Mackenzie and Mann to be uncouth products of the Canadian backwoods.

the same Rocky Mountain pass, did Albertans begin to see that the two were intent on driving each other out of business. Something must have gone gravely wrong with Canadian railroad policy. Something in fact had started going wrong ten years earlier, at the turn of the century, when three railroaders of fierce determination and disparate personality appeared on the Ottawa scene. Prime Minister Sir Wilfrid Laurier, riding an economic boom and approaching the zenith of his career, proved to be as inept at business as he was skilled at politics, and hopelessly unable to contend with railroad promoters.

Two of the three, William Mackenzie and Donald Mann, were partners. Their rise from construction bosses to tycoon promoters of the amazing Canadian Northern Railway has been related in an earlier volume (Vol. 1, Sect. 4, ch. 4). The third was their competitor and adversary, the American Charles Melville Hays. He would later be described by Interior Minister Clifford Sifton as a "cold-blooded raider of the treasury." But in 1900 he was known as the president and saviour of the chronically insolvent Grand Trunk, central Canada's mainline railway between Montreal and Toronto, which had been stretched west to Chicago and southeast from Montreal to Portland, Maine, giving it access to the Atlantic and to Europe.

Hays was an American corporate bigtimer, the kind of "substantial" man Laurier trusted. Both Laurier and Hays saw Mackenzie and Mann as the uncouth products of the Canadian backwoods, mere opportunists and fly-by-nighters who would sell out their Canadian Northern and abandon their commitments in the West as soon as the price was right. The feeling was mutual. Mann in

Railway Branchline Construction in Alberta

particular saw Hays as an American pirate, ruthless even by the standards of the US railroad industry, who had ingratiated himself with Sir Wilfrid Laurier through exaggeration, deception and outright lies.

But there was far more to Hays than mere ambition. He was a performer. He had taken over the Grand Trunk in 1895, and in two years rendered it profitable. Though it represented the biggest British overseas investment at the time, it had not previously turned a profit in all its 45 years. By 1897, thanks to Hays, it was doing so, and its British owners felt that at last they could relax and earn dividends. But Hays had other ideas for the Grand Trunk. The immediate future might be bright, he said, but in the long run the Grand Trunk would find itself in deep trouble.

The biggest opportunity in Canadian railroading, said Hays, lay in the West, which Sifton's aggressive immigration policies would soon see teeming with people, most of them grain farmers. Hundreds of thousands of tons of grain must move east each year, and more thousands of tons of freight move west from the factories of southern Ontario and Quebec to supply the settlers. Nearly all of this traffic was cornered by the Canadian Pacific which, after it had built its western main line, had invaded Grand Trunk territory in central Canada, taken over a collection of small railroads, and was directly competing with the Grand Trunk. It had an immeasurable advantage. Everything headed west must use its lines, as must all the grain coming east. It would merely be a matter of time, therefore, until the CPR forced the Grand Trunk out of business.

However, continued Hays, all was not hopeless. Sifton's immigrants were taking up farms on the northern prairie rather than the southern. The CPR mainline ran through the south and the company was being woefully slow to respond to opportunity in the north. It had only two northern spur lines, both leased from private companies: one from Calgary to Edmonton, the other from Regina to Prince Albert. Service on both was awful. The time had therefore come for a second transcontinental, in effect a huge western extension of the Grand Trunk that would traverse the northern passes of the Rockies — the Yellowhead west of Edmonton perhaps, or the Pine or Peace passes in the Peace River country — and reach the Pacific on the northern coast of British Columbia at Port Simpson. This development of the northern prairie would do for the Grand Trunk what the southern development

David B. Hanna. He was regarded as the most competent railway superintendent in the country.

Just as the CPR had been the crowning achievement of Sir John A.'s Tories, so too could the extension of the Grand Trunk to the Pacific be the jewel in Sir Wilfrid's crown.

had done for the CPR. Government guarantees would, of course, be necessary, as they had been with the CPR. But just as the CPR had been the crowning achievement of John A. Macdonald's Tories, so too could the extension of the Grand Trunk be the jewel in the crown of the Laurier Liberals.

To Laurier this plan seemed irresistible. But, as Clifford Sifton was quick to point out, there was a major flaw. It was not true that the northern prairies entirely lacked railroad service. Mackenzie and Mann had taken it upon themselves to acquire a whole cluster of fragmentary lines in Manitoba, the North-West Territories and northwestern Ontario. By 1901 they had assembled them as the Canadian Northern and were connecting them to the Great Lakes. They were building a line southeast from Winnipeg, across a corner of Minnesota, then back into Canada and across northwestern Ontario to Port Arthur (later part of the city of Thunder Bay). With their bonds guaranteed by the government of Manitoba, they had become a formidable and aggressive company and were already planning to push westward to Prince Albert and Edmonton. Just how would they fit into the Grand Trunk's scheme?

To Sifton the answer was obvious. The government should back the Grand Trunk in building a line from Ontario to Winnipeg, and back Mackenzie and Mann's Canadian Northern in building a line from Manitoba through Prince Albert and Edmonton to the coast. Together they would constitute one trans-continental system, the one road handing off traffic to the other. Obvious, perhaps, to all but Charles Melville Hays, who flatly refused to see the Grand Trunk "reduced" to a partnership with the two fly-by-nights. Their whole operation could easily be bought out, he said. When the Grand Trunk's directors demurred, Hays promptly quit and accepted the presidency of the Southern Pacific. He was back in the United States less than a year, however, before the Grand Trunk directors were pleading with him to return. He could, they said, formally approach the

I was destined for the tracklayer or the "pioneer" as we called it, whose fireman had fallen sick. This machine was an ingenious aggregation of cunning devices for the handling of heavy ties and half-ton rails with as little human effort as possible. It has no boiler power of its own but was pushed by two locomotives. The front locomotive furnished steam to the pioneer, while the second — which was requiring my services — pushed/pulled the train. The train consisted of cars carrying enough material to lay a mile of track, followed by the commissary, cooking, dining and bunk cars of the tracklaying gang so that in case of any breakdown or delay they had their home and chuck close at hand.
- *from* Getting the Knowhow by Frank Gilbert Roe.

Saved by the lonesome barking of a dog

MALCOLM MACLEOD'S PERILOUS JOURNEY THROUGH THE PRAIRIE COLD
RISKED AN ICY DEATH BUT RESULTED IN AN IMPORTANT BRIDGE

Malcolm H. MacLeod. Nearby a CPR man froze to death.

After the Edmonton-bound motorist leaves North Battleford, Saskatchewan, Highway 16 takes him deep into the North Saskatchewan valley. As he ascends the other bank, far to his right he can catch a view of a long railway bridge that carries the Canadian National across the same river. The man who discovered the site for this bridge was Malcolm H. MacLeod, consulting engineer to the Canadian Northern. The following story of how he discovered it is told by David B. Hanna, operating chief of the Canadian Northern.

MacLeod left his fur coat with Stovel, and taking a couple of bannocks for lunch he travelled in moccasins and a heavy pea jacket. The day was intensely cold. Speed was doubly of the essence of the programme — to cover the ground in the time allotted, and to keep from freezing. In the Battleford latitude, daylight is done about four o'clock.

Once more, the day's work seemed commonplace enough to the men who did it. From fireside and radio, twenty years afterwards, it looks what it was — a daring adventure, in an empty country, with a temperature that made lonely human travel more hazardous than most people ever know, and the possibility of a blizzard starting without warning, to the extremest risk of life and limb. Indeed, only a few days after MacLeod all alone, with a walking suit, two bannocks, a box of matches, a compass and a jack-knife his only exterior defenses against disaster, hurried down the valley looking where to place an imagined bridge, a CPR engineer named Bass, who was making a trial line for the CPR below Battleford, was frozen to death quite near his camp.

MacLeod strode over the ice till noon, seeing no place where a railroad might advantageously be brought down the north bank, a bridge built over the wide current, and conducted up the southern escarpment. He ate his bannocks, resting long enough to be warned by thirty below that further repose was impermissible. He trudged again till three o'clock, and then, tired enough, he sat on the ice for a smoke. Seeing Stovel and the team, on a bare knoll overlooking the vale, about three miles behind him, he assumed that all would be well.

He resumed his walking, and as dusk was falling began to leave the river bed. But a wolf's bark, which seemed to give notice to a pack, warned him to keep somewhat longer on the ice. When he did climb up a partially wooded ravine, and reached the top, the seeing was not good. Evidently he and Stovel must each be searching for the other's tracks.

MacLeod found nothing, and being very weary, and among bluffs where dry wood was, he tried to light a fire. The wind, which was moving the snow in the wreathing gusts which every driver and walker over the uncharted wintry plain knows so well, prevented any such consolation, and the cold prohibited a stop in one spot for more than two or three minutes. So MacLeod walked for warmth in the darkness, searching as well as he could for a sleigh track, and finding nothing, and bearing eastward towards Bresaylor. At last he came to a fence, and vainly tried again to make a fire.

The night before, Stovel and he had been saved by a dog. Providence was again to use the friend of man — for, as the isolated engineer was in motion to avoid being frozen stiff, and was longing for the moon to rise so that he could read his compass, a dog barked, an indubitable dog. In a little while MacLeod was inside a house, the good lady of which set food before him.

Stovel had been there about two hours before, very much excited, and saying that he had lost sight of his friend, and failed to find him. Afraid something was amiss, he had gone to Bresaylor[a] for a fresh team, and human help.

An hour later there was a knock at the door — it was Stovel and the postmaster's son — and all was clear for another night alongside Her Majesty's mails.

Next morning the examination of the riversides was continued, the team again following the Saskatchewan's southern skirt. About nine miles above Battleford, in the afternoon, MacLeod reached the mouth of a wide and wooded ravine, which seemed to offer prospect of the only good crossing he had seen in a tramp of nearly fifty miles. [At that site, above Battleford, the bridge was built.]

While he was exploring the ground, he saw Stovel above him, making all sorts of frantic appeals for company. Thinking that some calamity had befallen, MacLeod abandoned his job, to render aid to his distressed and distressing colleague. Nothing was the matter, except that the solicitous Stovel was determined to run no risk of recent history repeating itself with a dog's bark.

[a]Long before the railway arrived, three would-be settlers named Bremner, Sayers and Taylor, trekked all the way from southern Manitoba in search of land. They selected a site near Battleford, and named the town with the first syllables of Bremner and Sayers' names and the last syllable of Taylor's. Result: Bresaylor, Saskatchewan.

dominion government with his plan for a second Pacific railway, but he must in no sense commit the Grand Trunk to carrying it out. Hays heard exactly half of this instruction.

His first move, of course, was to approach the loathed Mackenzie and Mann and propose they sell out to the Grand Trunk. They turned him down flat. For one thing, it was 1901 and they discerned that the West was on the verge of a boom. Why sell now? For another, their branchline system already rivalled the CPR's. Finally, they had assembled a great team. On the operational side, there were men like David B. Hanna, whom they regarded as the most competent railway superintendent in the country. In Ottawa they had the redoubtable William Henry "Billy" Moore, whose connections and exploits made him the town's top lobbyist. Their chief engineer was Malcolm Hugh MacLeod, whose intuition for the best spot to cross a river or the best path around a muskeg amazed the whole industry. And in London, they had the crotchety but ingenious Robert M. Horne-Payne, a paraplegic who worked from a wheelchair but reputedly could adduce on sight exactly how many Canadian railway securities could be sold in any given British community in any given year.

Charles Rivers Wilson. If he had met Mackenzie in London, the whole railway history of Canada may have been different.

But they had no transcontinental ambitions. Although in moments of exuberance Donald Mann might talk wildly of a sea-to-sea Canadian Northern[1], his sober assessment was that the company needed 5,000 miles of prairie branch lines before it could afford a connection to either ocean. In 1901 it had less than 2,000. Still, it was boxed in in the West, and must make some sort of deal with the CPR, or with the government, or with an American road, to move grain eastward and goods westward. So it wanted to talk to the Grand Trunk, not to sell out but to do business.

Mackenzie went to London in March, 1902, to arrange to sell Canadian Northern bonds,

Railroad luminaries immortalized themselves, their relatives and their girlfriends in the place names of the West.

guaranteed by the Manitoba government. He called on the seventy-year-old Charles Rivers Wilson, the retired British civil servant who was president of the Grand Trunk, to whom Hays as general manager ostensibly reported. Mackenzie repeated the proposal of Clifford Sifton, that the Grand Trunk operate an eastern system in conjunction with the Canadian Northern's western system, the government financing or backing a connecting line between them through northern Ontario. To Rivers Wilson the plan made eminent sense. Since it involved nothing like the risks of Hays' transcontinental ambitions, it would recommend itself to the Grand Trunk's nervous stockholders, and would save the cost of developing a Grand Trunk subsidiary in the West. He therefore wrote to Hays urging him to make such a deal with Mackenzie and Mann.

Hays responded explosively. Doubtless furious that Mackenzie had gone above his head, he told Rivers Wilson that the pair were bluffing, and the way to force them to come to terms was simply to announce a magnificent scheme in which the Grand Trunk would create a subsidiary that would serve the West and be known as the Grand Trunk Pacific. Since its lines would parallel those of the Canadian Northern, the mere announcement would arrest the sale of Canadian Northern bonds and frighten Mackenzie and Mann into selling out. If they wouldn't sell out, the

[1] On New Year's Day, 1902, a silver spike was driven home to mark the opening of service on the Canadian Northern between Winnipeg and Port Arthur. Mackenzie and Mann gave $2 to every workman on the line, $5 to every gang foreman, and $25 to every general foreman. Mann waxed eloquent and foresaw the Canadian Northern connecting Atlantic and Pacific within seven years. Many years later, after the Canadian railway collapse, he described such talk as "crazy."

A railway construction crew laying track, 1909. Flatter and smoother than any other North American road.

GTP could "starve them out." To cap his plan, Hays invited George A. Cox to serve as president of the GTP. Cox just happened to be president of the Bank of Commerce, banker to Mackenzie and Mann.

But Hays had reasoned without taking into account Clifford Sifton, who by now could see a major crisis shaping up, caused principally by Charles Melville Hays and the GTR. Since Hays wouldn't deal with Mackenzie and Mann, Sifton agreed to strengthen their hand. By 1901 their lines extended west as far as Dauphin, Manitoba. They wanted to move westward to Prince Albert and Edmonton. Sifton promised a federal bond guarantee of up to $13,000 a mile on the extension. The rumour caused rejoicing in Edmonton. At last the "northern" city would have a railroad "of its own."

By the fall of 1902 negotiations reached a crisis point. Laurier, captivated by the vision of a transcontinental "Laurier Liberal" railway, called Hays, Rivers Wilson, the banker Cox, Mackenzie and Mann into his office and tried to coerce an agreement. He failed. The five met again the following week in Hays' office in Montreal. It was said that Mann weakened and finally agreed to sell out, but Mackenzie would have none of it, so no deal was reached. However, the negotiations did work one great change. Cox, watching in particular what he considered the ineptitude of the aging Rivers Wilson, became persuaded of two things. First, the future of Canada lay in the West. Second, the future of western railroading lay with Mackenzie and Mann. He turned down the GTP presidency, ordered a major expansion for the Bank of Commerce in the West, and threw himself and his bank into the cause of the Canadian Northern.[2] With its Manitoba lines guaranteed by that province and its transit of the prairies assured by Sifton's commitment of a federal bond guarantee, Mackenzie and Mann could afford to wait on events.

Hays could not. He was impelled, said Sifton later, "by a sentimental ambition to own a transcontinental line." G.R. Stevens, historian of Canadian National Railways, is much harder on him. "Out of these wrangles," he writes, "there emerged in many minds an image of the [Grand Trunk] company as an arrogant and impersonal organization, contemptuous of its customers and arbitrary in its behaviour. To this unfortunate impression Hays contributed. He was hard and stubborn in his dealing with the public, and he was much too prone to denounce his critics." Stevens pins the blame on Hays for the eventual destruction of the whole Grand Trunk system.[3]

On Oct. 21, 1902, Hays formally advanced the Grand Trunk's proposal in a letter to Laurier. It was also signed by William Wainwright, comptroller of the GTR, a Lancashireman who'd been with the railway since 1862 and after whom the GTP's first divisional point in Alberta would be named. (The village of Irma, two stops down the road, was named for Wainwright's daughter.) The Grand Trunk Pacific would run from the little town of Callander, Ontario, on the southern outskirts of North Bay[4], where it would connect the northernmost Grand Trunk line in Ontario to Winnipeg, Edmonton, and the Pacific at Port Simpson. (When the line was built the Pacific destination was moved 25 miles south to Prince Rupert.) The line must receive, said Hays, a $6,400-a-mile cash subsidy, a 5,000-acre-a-mile land grant, a contract for its own construction, tax exemption for twenty years, and the right to import all construction materials tariff-free. Laurier turned down the proposal as too generous, but asked Hays to submit another one.

As Laurier expected, Hays went to work on a revised proposal immediately. What Laurier did not expect, however, was the deep rupture the Grand Trunk Pacific plan would create in his cabinet. His railways minister was a New Brunswicker, Andrew G. Blair, who was distinguished in Canadian politics as the only man prepared to defend the government-owned Intercolonial Railway. The Intercolonial, running eventually from Montreal to Halifax, had opened in 1858 as Canada's commitment that helped bring Nova Scotia into Confederation. Owned and operated by the federal government, it was so renowned for chaotic administration, for indifference to customers, and for patronage, nepotism, undependability and gargantuan losses that it had poisoned both the public and most politicians against any more government-owned railways.

None of this scepticism was shared by Andrew Blair. Since the Intercolonial could not be sold because nobody would buy it, said Blair, the solution was obviously to expand it. It rather than the Grand Trunk should build and operate the second transcontinental line to the Pacific because — and here was his main point — this would direct Canadian grain shipments through Moncton, rather than through Portland, Maine, the Grand Trunk's Atlantic terminus.

Laurier's Quebec members had an even better idea. Look at the way Sifton had used the CPR to funnel immigrants and homesteaders into western Canada, they said, thus making it an extension of English Canada. Surely it was now Quebec's turn. For years Quebeckers had had a dream called the Trans-Canada Railway. It would run from Quebec City to Moosonee on James Bay, thence to Norway House in northern Manitoba, thence to Lesser Slave Lake, and finally through the Rockies to Port Simpson on the Pacific. The effect would be to provide a shortcut from the West to Quebec City, without a dodge into southern Ontario. As the line built west, French-speak-

As the Canadian Northern crews pressed on, the CPR had awakened and was criss-crossing the prairie, while the GTP surveyed what was promised to be the finest railroad in the world.

ing settlement would do for northern Quebec and northern Ontario what English-speaking settlement had done for the West.

Finally, there was the Sifton plan for the two-company operation — the Canadian Northern in the West, the Grand Trunk in the East, and a government-sponsored road in between. Its weakness was the Grand Trunk's eastern terminus at Portland, however, which would mean the entire traffic of the northern prairie would be channelled through a US Atlantic port.

Throughout the spring of 1903 the Laurier cabinet wrestled with these competing schemes. What emerged was a compromise proposal: that the government finance a line from Moncton to Quebec City that would then bridge the St. Lawrence and carry on across northern Quebec and northern Ontario to Winnipeg. It would be known as the National Transcontinental, built by the government and leased to the Grand Trunk Pacific. The GTP lines would run from Winnipeg through Edmonton to Port Simpson. There would be no land grants to the GTP, though the government would guarantee its construction bonds up to $13,000 a mile, much more in the mountains. The Grand Trunk must put up $5 million cash before the job could proceed.

[2] One consequence of George Cox's "conversion" to the Canadian Northern was the fine Bank of Commerce branch that appeared soon after at Jasper Avenue and First Street in downtown Edmonton and would remain there for the rest of the century. Cox had begun as a telegraph operator and became one of Canada's foremost financiers. Besides heading the Bank of Commerce, he was president of Canada Life, and president, vice-president or director of over forty companies. Laurier made him a senator. An active Methodist and temperance leader, he gave much of his money away. However, Cox's commitment to the Canadian Northern did not entirely remove him from the orbit of the GTP. He continued to sit on the GTP board, clearly working both sides of the street. His associate, E.R. Wood, sat on the GTP board with him until Cox's death in 1914, after which Wood's name disappears from the GTP directorate and turns up on the Canadian Northern's.

[3] Stevens' two-volume work, Canadian National Railways, Clarke Irwin, Toronto, 1962, is one of four excellent sources for the story of the struggle between the Canadian Northern and the Grand Trunk. The others are: The Canadian Northern Railway: Pioneer Road of the Northern Prairies, 1895-1918 by T.D. Regehr, Macmillan Canada, 1976; The Railway King of Canada: Sir William Mackenzie by R.B. Fleming, UBC Press, Vancouver, 1991; and the anecdotal history, Trains of Recollection, by the Canadian Northern's own David B. Hanna, Macmillan Canada, 1926, which for the sheer delight of reading exceeds them all.

[4] Apart from its railway distinction, Callander would attract national attention again, 32 years later, as the birthplace of the Dionne quintuplets.

Life in a private car wasn't all that cosy, says Hanna

THE TALE OF THE 'PAMPERED' TYCOON, TRAVELLING IN LUXURY, TOLD THE EMBITTERED FARMER TO COUNT HIS BLESSINGS

Grand Trunk Pacific officials on their private railcar in Edmonton, 1904.

The following is excerpted from Trains of Recollection, *the memoirs of David B. Hanna:*

One chilly evening, just after sundown, a Saskatchewan farmer was crossing, with his yoke of oxen, a siding where stood a car, well lighted and blinds undrawn. He saw a short-bearded, middle-aged man sitting, with three other prosperous-looking persons, at the table, which was well-appointed with spotless linen, and the sort of ware without which a meal is nowhere. He watched a white-coated man enter; and he halted his cattle to see this man hand around a dish, and stand respectfully while the other people took from it what they required.

Fascinated, the farmer stayed there till the meal was concluded, cigars were burning, and the blinds were drawn. He was abroad later than he had expected, and had not reckoned on so chilly an evening. He shivered as he commanded Buck and Bright to proceed — and he talked to himself — as he has told the story since.

The lazy luxury of these railway magnates! Lolling over the country in private cars, waited on hand and foot, out of the money which poor devils like himself, shaking with cold, and working their bodies to skin and bone, paid to the railway for dividends and luxuries like the cars that made these men

feel like kings and act like tyrants. The farmer would soon show these oppressors where they got off at. They'd begin by getting off the private car — and so on and so forth, in human nature's human way.

One story is good till another is told. The rolling-in-luxury side of this episode of a siding on a chilly October night is this: The man at the table head was the railway president. Two of his guests were representing financial houses. The fourth man was his secretary. The car had been dropped at the siding because, next morning, teams would be there to drive the party forty miles north to inspect the country through which it was intended to build a branch line — and in which it had been reported that there were many farmers to whom getting out their grain was a burdensome operation, depriving them of the chance to prosper by their season's work.

The financial men were from London, and could facilitate or hinder the flow of millions of dollars to Canada for the development of agriculture. They were touring the country to see what sort of conditions their clients were being invited to back. They wanted to visit a typical piece of country without railway facilities — and to get an idea of the courage and capacity of pioneers who would start farms in the wilderness ahead of means of economically getting their produce to market.

The president was on his annual inspection trip — just as

necessary to efficient discharge of his duty as a farmer's Sunday walk around his fields is to his knowledge of his crops. He did not want to drive for whole days across new country. His trusted engineers and locators were in the habit of doing that, and time was valuable. But it was good policy to go personally with the men who were extremely influential in the money market that was as important to the Saskatchewan farmer as the wheat market is. All day he had been with his guests, telling them about the country, and observing the condition of the track and stations through which the train passed, and receiving messages off the telegraph wire.

Long after the farmer had gone to bed, and his oxen had exchanged cud-chewing for slumber, the railway president, having said "Good-night" to his guests, was dictating replies to the messages he had received during the day, and working as hard as if he had been in his office fifteen hundred miles away. It is true that the car looked like self-indulgent wealth to the farmer sitting in the wagon outside — to whom it seemed the height of luxury to be waited upon by a man in a white coat. But it was all in a hard day's work to the man who was getting the money to build railways into the prairie country, without which the owner of a yoke of cattle would be forlorn indeed. The president, who came from the farm, would regard it as the height of luxury to have nothing more to worry about than to sit on a binder for a few hours, and see the nodding heads of wheat fall onto the carrier, to be delivered in rows of sheaves to the stooker.

Any businessman who has worked his heart out to establish something out of nothing, and has overcome difficulties that had a knack of springing up out of nowhere, and spoiling the best-laid calculations, knows that most capital has to be wrung out of trouble.

The farmer too, knows this — for sitting on a binder isn't all golden grain — and chores have their own worries. But he is apt to associate difficulties only with manual labour. Never having travelled in a car that is also an office he doesn't apprehend what working on wheels really is.

The proposal satisfied all the political needs. It served, if not Nova Scotia, at least New Brunswick. It rejoiced the heart of Catholic Quebec, whose clergy immediately began laying plans for church-sponsored colonization through northern Quebec and Ontario. And it relieved the Grand Trunk of the inordinate cost of building through some 1,000 miles of bush and muskeg. The only drawback, of course, was the fact it was economically indefensible. Nothing but fur trade posts lay along nearly its entire length. In short, it was a disaster, but in July 1903 the prime minister offered it to his caucus as the government's compromise response to the Grand Trunk plan. Blair quit the cabinet in disgust and sat as an independent. Quebec Liberals said he was in the pay of Mackenzie and Mann. Laurier made him chairman of the new Board of Railway Commissioners and told him to keep his criticisms of government railway policy to himself.

Hays accepted the plan with private misgivings. He confidently assured the government that the Grand Trunk would certainly funnel its western traffic over the new line to Moncton, rather than over its present lines to Portland, though the latter were shorter and cheaper. Meanwhile he told Rivers Wilson confidentially that the government's all-Canada route was "the veriest claptrap" and made it clear the Grand Trunk would continue to use Portland, whatever promises had been made to the government.

Rivers Wilson became increasingly apprehensive as Laurier persisted in amending the contract up to the moment of signing. "I am greatly vexed at the turn events have taken," Rivers Wilson cabled to Hays. "The idea that the Grand Trunk should enter on such a vast liability was never entertained for a moment while I was in Canada...It would have a disastrous effect on our credit." Hays replied that if the Grand Trunk didn't accept the government's terms, Mackenzie and Mann would. Thus threatened, Rivers Wilson endorsed the contract and carried it through a Grand Trunk directors' meeting. It was signed on July 29, 1903, with the proviso that it must be approved by the Grand Trunk's stockholders' meeting in London in February 1904.

At that shareholders' meeting, Rivers Wilson and Hays faced what amounted to an angry mob. One director had already quit over the GTP scheme and his resignation letter was

Provincial Archives of Alberta, A-1984

The Canadian Northern Railway track-laying crew entering Fort Saskatchewan, Nov. 8, 1905. All of a sudden, Edmonton had a feast of railways.

Provincial Archives of Alberta, A-11,355

The town of Wolf Creek in 1909. When the division point was moved to Edson, it vanished.

read to the stockholders. It prophesied the complete destruction of both the Grand Trunk and the Grand Trunk Pacific if the scheme went ahead. But Rivers Wilson quelled the revolt. He read last-minute concessions made by Laurier — an increase in the bond guarantee for the mountain region, the completion deadline extended to eight years from five, the Grand Trunk allowed to market some GTP stock to raise more capital.

These disclosures seemed to reassure the shareholders. Then Hays took over and with a rousing speech painted a picture of all the fine things the GTP made possible, including a foreseeable steamship trade with the Orient. The mood of the meeting began changing. Then Alfred Smithers, hitherto a determined critic, pronounced himself persuaded and welcomed the scheme, a service that would see his name immortalized on the map of Canada as a GTP divisional point in west-central BC. So the contract passed. Conservative leader Robert Borden had a stenographic record kept of the London meeting, and later read it contemptuously to the Canadian Commons where the Tories razzed and deplored the Laurier "concessions." This was one of the rare occasions, notes CNR historian Stevens, when Laurier blew up on the floor of the House.

The uncertainty over the outcome of the February meeting had forced him to postpone the 1904 election from spring to fall. By then, however, the GTP scheme was being heralded as the greatest possible boon to western Canada. Even CPR executives said they welcomed it, and in the

---

GTP surveyors chose the Yellowhead route through the Rockies. Here they encountered unanticipated problems such as beavers and rock that shattered into gravel.

United States the Northern Pacific confidently announced that it, too, was considering building a line through the Canadian prairies, with a spur running north to Edmonton. Undoubtedly the GTP venture helped the Liberals win in 1904.

But it was not good news for the Canadian Northern, or (as events would eventually show) for anybody else in the Canadian railroad industry. It meant that the Canadian Northern, to avoid being cornered in the West, must now also become a transcontinental railway. The government guarantee on its line to Prince Albert and Edmonton had passed into law. But even before the bill had been made public, in February 1903, Mackenzie had again called on Rivers Wilson in London, a copy of it in his pocket. Mackenzie knew the bill meant that, whatever its commitments to the Grand Trunk, the Laurier government would not allow the Canadian Northern to vanish. Such an assurance would almost certainly have moved Rivers Wilson to overrule Hays and work out a compromise plan with the Canadian Northern. But Rivers Wilson was holidaying on the continent and the meeting did not take place. So both projects went ahead. Some historians say that missed opportunity probably sealed the fate of four major Canadian railroads.

Now, in 1904, Mackenzie and Mann had no choice. If Hays was not to "starve them out" they must spread their operations into eastern Canada. By now they knew how to do it. Just as they had in the West, they took over a number of faltering lines and connected them all into an eastern division of the Canadian Northern.[5] In 1906 they scored another coup. One of the two north-south lines of the CPR was the Qu'appelle, Long Lake and Saskatchewan which ran from Regina to Prince Albert, crossing the South Saskatchewan at a religious colony called, hopefully, Temperance. Fearing business would not do well in Temperance, the QLL&S had built its station across the river at what was then a lesser establishment, named for the prolific western berry, Saskatoon. The QLL&S, owned by unhappy British bondholders, was leased to the CPR. When the lease expired, Mackenzie and Mann took it over. Suddenly, they had gained access to the heart of CPR country on the southern prairie. Canadian Northern service on the line began inauspiciously, however, in the terrible winter of 1906-07. The first Canadian Northern locomotive over the line was buried dead in the snow for two weeks.[6]

In 1904 also the Canadian Northern began building west from Dauphin, Manitoba. It changed its plan to run through Prince Albert, ran a spur there instead, and struck straight for Edmonton, crossing the South Saskatchewan just north of Saskatoon, and the North Saskatchewan at its south elbow twenty miles northwest of that city. It then recrossed the same river just upstream from the old territorial capital of Battleford, enraging Battleford's citizenry by creating a new town, North Battleford. From there it headed directly west to Edmonton, abandoning an earlier plan to circle northwest along the south bank of the North Saskatchewan. The crews were cheered lustily as they crossed the future boundary line of Alberta and brought rail service to the Barr colonists at Lloydminster, the people pitching in to help with the work.

By the construction season of 1905 Canadian Northern crews approached Edmonton.[7] Vermilion station came into being. Settlers to the west were so delighted to see the railway arrive

[5]Even by Canadian Northern standards some of these acquisitions were dubious. In *Trains of Recollection* Hanna tells how the engineer of one of them, the Quebec and Lake St. John, sometimes had to borrow money from the passengers to buy coal before the train could leave the station. Such incidents, he notes, "look romantic to hindsight, but were grievous to be borne when they occurred."

[6]Hanna tells how a steam locomotive could "die." In exceedingly cold weather, when the fireman opened the door to throw in more coal, the blast of cold air entering the firebox could suddenly chill and crack the water pipes from the boiler, causing water to pour down and put the fire out, thereby stopping the engine. The engine could be refired only when the water pipes were repaired in a roundhouse. Another engine had to be sent out to bring in its "dead" companion. Such an event would only occur in the coldest of weather. Hanna, when Canadian Northern general superintendent, spent a whole night wandering lost in the bush after an engine died on him on the prairies and he tried to get to a farmhouse.

[7]The original Canadian Northern line into Edmonton would generally be followed many years later by the Saskatchewan and Alberta highways numbered 16 that would share the name "the Yellowhead Highway." The rail and highway routes separate, however, where the latter runs straight west from Vegreville to Edmonton. The Canadian Northern line continued northwest from Vegreville, passing through Mundare, Hilliard, Chipman, Lamont and Bruderheim, then crossing the North Saskatchewan at Fort Saskatchewan and striking southwest into the city.

It took a mob to do it, but Edmonton got its railway

THE CURIOUS VICTORY AT THE SWITCH ULTIMATELY MADE IT POSSIBLE FOR EDMONTON TO BECOME ONE OF CANADA'S GREAT RAILWAY TOWNS

If any spoken word could be calculated to boil the red blood of the solid Edmonton citizen at the turn of the 20th century, it was "railway." Edmonton didn't have one. It had been promised the Canadian Pacific mainline seventeen years before, in 1883, and then lost it to Calgary. Again, in 1891, it had been promised a line north from Calgary, but that line had been stopped across the North Saskatchewan in Strathcona and the Canadian Pacific refused to bridge the river.

Finally, in October 1902, came the third promise, this one a seeming certainty. But at the last moment, the Canadian Pacific deliberately obstructed it again. So Edmontonians rose in a kind of civic insurrection, and in a cheering mob defied the CPR and brought the first train down Mill Creek Ravine, across the newly completed Low Level Bridge, and onto Ross Flats where the track came to a dead end. A three-mile line wasn't much. But it was a railroad. And it was in Edmonton.

This curious victory was, in fact, the forerunner of a decade that would see Edmonton become one of the great railway centres in Canada. But who in his wildest imagination could have seen any of this on that morning of Oct. 20, 1902, when something called the Edmonton Yukon and Pacific huffed over the Low Level Bridge, a cheering band of citizens crowded onto a flatcar and into several boxcars behind the locomotive?

The Edmonton Yukon and Pacific was one among thousands of such corporate entities created in the North American railway era. Characteristically, they began with the names of the two towns they intended to connect, appending the words "and Pacific" to augur some vague transcontinental aspiration. But the EY&P had begun much less pretentiously. It had been the Edmonton District Railway, the promotion of a syndicate of Edmonton businessmen.[a] In 1895 they sought a charter to connect a line with the CPR in Strathcona, bring it down Mill Creek Ravine, and build the first bridge over the North Saskatchewan with assistance from the town of Edmonton and the dominion government. It would then ascend the bank into Groat Ravine, and cross the prairie along the old portage to the Athabasca River.

The city concurred, but the dominion government balked, as did the Hudson's Bay Company, the grounds of whose fort the railway must traverse. As a joke, one of the backers ran this "obituary" in the *Edmonton Bulletin*:

DIED

At Edmonton, Saturday, 10th
instant, after a useless and uneventful life,
'The Edmonton and District Railroad,'
aged nine months.

The first train into Edmonton, having just crossed the Low Level Bridge, Oct. 20, 1902. James Entwistle, who gave his name to the town to the west, was the engineer.

> Our little railroad scheme is dead
> And yet no teardrop splashes,
> Because we hope our little bridge
> will rise up from the ashes.[b]

However, the little scheme was not dead. The following year, the Yukon gold rush exploded upon the West. The EDR charter was sold to eastern promoters who advanced grandiose plans for a $30-million line from Edmonton to the Klondike. The plan collapsed, but at least by now the bridge was built and opened for wagon traffic.

Moreover the EY&P charter to cross the Rockies gave it value to Canadian Northern Railway promoters William Mackenzie and Donald Mann who acquired the EDR, changed the name to the Edmonton Yukon and Pacific, and in July 1901 ordered an uncertain zig-zag track laid down the mud-sliding slopes of Strathcona's Mill Creek Ravine. The fact it rained day after day didn't help with the construction; three times the completed roadbed slid into the ravine.

By the following spring, 1902, it was finished, but now there were new troubles. The CPR refused to connect it to its line in Strathcona. In April, the federal government authorized the connection. The CPR appealed. The order stood. Finally, on October 6, a Canadian Northern construction boss named W.J. Pace, armed with the federal order, appeared with a crew at the authorized connection point, and began ripping out CPR track to install the switch that would connect the EY&P.

CPR officials appeared, along with a Town of Strathcona policeman, and presented Pace with an order to cease and desist. Pace read the order, handed it back the constable, and his men kept right on working. Whereupon the policeman pulled out a warrant for the arrest of W.J. Pace. Still Pace ignored it. His men, however, were by now thoroughly frightened and withdrew. A conference ensued when out of the CPR roundhouse to the south came a yard engine. It advanced to the spot where the switch was to be installed and hissed to a stop, panting defiantly. Since it was impossible to install a switch with a locomotive on it, Pace ordered his men back to the Low Level bridge to work on it instead.

Word of the incident rapidly spread through Edmonton. A crowd assembled and by that afternoon purposefully ascended the EY&P line to the scene of the proposed switch, where the locomotive still stood guard. Pace was there but no workmen were to be seen. It was getting late. At about five o'clock a whistle from the south announced the arrival of the day's train from Calgary. The guardian yard engine rolled south to the roundhouse to clear the way for the northbound passenger train.

On a signal from Pace, his crew suddenly appeared, tools in hand, from the nearby bushes. While the Edmonton crowd protected the workmen and flagged down the approaching train, the tracks were torn out and the switch was installed. By now, cooler heads had prevailed and the CPR management decided they must do business with the EY&P. A few days later a Canadian Northern locomotive with some rolling stock arrived from the south and was switched onto the EY&P line. On October 20, a great day for Edmonton, the crowd thronged aboard the flatcars and into the boxcars and locomotive engineer James D. Entwistle delicately negotiated the grade down Mill Creek, crossed the Low Level Bridge, and arrived at Ross's Hotel on the Edmonton side.

For the next three years Entwistle and a fireman provided service on the three-mile line, digging coal out of the adjacent river bank to fire the locomotive. The EY&P station stood at what would later become 98th Avenue and 102nd Street. But by now much bigger railway events preoccupied Edmontonians.

The year 1905 would be doubly momentous for the northern city. On September 1, as the interim capital, it hosted the inaugural ceremonies for the new province (see Sect. I, ch. 3 sidebar). On Nov. 24, 1905, another event occasioned a second special holiday. The Canadian Northern line from Winnipeg arrived in the city, affording for the first time direct access to the outside world without going through Calgary.

The Canadian Northern line crossed the river at Fort Saskatchewan, then ran southwest into the city, along what would one day become the route of its first Light Rail Transit line. By the night of Thursday, Nov. 23, the steel was laid as far as Clark Street, south of the future stadium, and on the morning of the 24th, the work locomotive pushed the track-laying rig down as far as the intersection of First Street and Mackenzie Avenue (101st Street and 104th Avenue). On the northwest corner was the new Canadian Northern station.

A crowd of some 2,000 roared its approval as Lieutenant-Governor George Bulyea hammered home a solid silver last spike.

There were speeches from Interior Minister Frank Oliver, Mayor Kenneth W. MacKenzie, former mayor William Short and a big formal banquet that night in the Queen's Hotel. The Canadian Northern's Donald Mann promised the immediate inauguration of passenger service direct to Winnipeg with the most modern of sleeping cars, diners and day coaches, lighted throughout with acetylene gas.

"Twenty-six years ago," said Mann, "I was present at the celebration in Winnipeg when the first engine crossed the Red River on the ice bridge. I was also present at the beginning and at the finish of nearly all the railways in this western country. But the completion of this road into Edmonton today is the most important event in my railway career." Few could doubt that he meant it.

— *T.B.*

[a]Herbert Nelson, William Edmiston, John Kelly, Colin Strang, John Cameron, Thomas Bellamy and Joseph Picard were principal shareholders in the EDR.

[b]Olive L. Batchelor, a librarian and history student at the University of Lethbridge, dug this tidbit out and included it in an article she wrote about the EY&P in a 1991 edition of *Alberta History*.

that they named their town for one of its founders, and Mannville appeared on the Alberta map.[8] On October 14, exactly 44 days after Alberta had become a province, they reached New Vegreville, bypassing Old Vegreville a few miles to the southwest. Almost the whole town — stores, houses and other buildings — was rapidly moved to the new site.

In the next eight weeks, the Canadian Northern crews pressed across the prairie to the already prepared railway bridge at Fort Saskatchewan, then swept southwest into Edmonton (see sidebar). The following year one spur was run north to Morinville and another west to Stony Plain, connecting at the head of the Groat Ravine with the old Edmonton Yukon and Pacific, which only three years earlier had provided the city's first railway connection to the outside.[9]

To the south, the Canadian Pacific had awakened from its lethargy. Countering the Canadian Northern, it built a parallel line northwest across the prairies from Portage la Prairie to Saskatoon. At the same time, it built east from Wetaskiwin on the Calgary and Edmonton to Camrose, then on to Hardisty, and eventually linked up with its Portage line at Saskatoon. Thus the CPR was able to provide a direct Winnipeg-Strathcona service, though it still did not cross the river into Edmonton.

Meanwhile, the surveyors of the Grand Trunk Pacific carefully prepared what Charles Melville Hays promised would be the finest railroad in the world, from Winnipeg through Edmonton to the coast. It would lie between the Canadian Northern and the Canadian Pacific, and its most severe grade, all the way to the Pacific, was to be no more than one-half of one per cent. That is, nowhere on the entire line would the grade rise more than six inches for every one hundred feet, or 26 feet to the mile. By contrast the Big Hill, then still in use on the CPR between Lake Louise, Alberta and Field, BC, required a grade of 4.5 per cent, nine times as steep as the GTP (Vol. 1, p. 138). The GTP's gradual grade required deeper cuts through hills, more backfilling through ravines, more trestles and bridges, a much higher construction cost, and much slower progress. But the consequent operating cost would be far less.[10] In addition Hays demanded 85-pound rail (per yard of track) rather than the usual 65-pound.

Work started on the GTP line in Manitoba on Aug. 29, 1905, just three months before the Canadian Northern actually arrived in Edmonton. Compared with the lightning construction speeds of the Canadian Northern and Canadian Pacific, progress was painfully slow; controversy tracked along with it. The railway bypassed Saskatoon to the south, then further infuriated the populace by setting up a monopoly taxi service to run people back and forth from the station. In the end the GTP built a loop line into the city and out again. As the boom spread through the West, and workmen could find better paying jobs in the cities, the GTP faced a severe labour shortage, then came under investigation for hiring Asian workers. The Laurier government placed a tariff on imported steel rails, creating a bonanza for Canadian manufacturers. But they could not meet demand, and GTP roadbed construction consequently far preceded the actual track. In 1908 the *Calgary Herald* deplored the "endless delays" in construction, and said they were deliberately planned so completion of the line could help the Liberals in the 1908 election.

Not until July 1909 did the GTP track reach Edmonton, but it did this, as it did everything else, in grand style. A magnificent bridge carried it high over the North Saskatchewan at Clover Bar.

Once their main lines were in, both systems ran branch lines south into CPR country. The Canadian Northern paralleled the CPR's Calgary and Edmonton with a north-south line to the east, striking south from Vegreville to Camrose, thence to Stettler and then on to Drumheller. There it connected with the Canadian Northern's Goose Lake line which ran from Saskatoon to Calgary, crossing the Bow in east Calgary, and creating a station at around Centre Street and 17th Avenue. The GTP started at Tofield, came down between the CPR's Calgary and Edmonton and the Canadian Northern, bridging the Battle with a spectacular bridge at Duhamel southwest of Camrose, then proceeding south. At the same time the CPR built east from Lacombe on the C&E to Stettler, then went on to Coronation and Consort.

Mainline construction of the Grand Trunk Pacific did not stop at Edmonton. It plodded on due west, backfilling the big bog on the city's western outskirts so it could take a first-class track through Spruce Grove, Stony Plain, Evansburg and Wildwood to a designated terminus at Wolf Creek, just east of its projected crossing of the McLeod River. Here its prairie region was to end and its mountain region begin. A town of 2,000 rose overnight at Wolf Creek, with banks, hotels, restaurants, boarding houses, dirt streets and rough dwellings. But rampant property speculation caused a sudden change in management plans. The divisional point was moved twelve miles west and named for Edson J. Chamberlain, the GTP's vice-president and general manager. Wolf Creek virtually vanished.

From 1905 to 1908 a recession in the bond market tamed the ambitions of Mackenzie and Mann. If they couldn't borrow, they couldn't build. Of necessity the Canadian Northern consisted of two unconnected railway empires, the one lying between the Rockies and the Great Lakes, the other between the Great Lakes and the Atlantic, the vast wilderness of northern Ontario separating them. In addition, the wall of the BC mountain systems divorced the western system from the Pacific coast, from the promise of trade with the Orient, and from the water connection to Europe that the Panama Canal, now abuilding, would supply by 1914.

Fortified by federal grants and guarantees, however, the Grand Trunk Pacific laboured under no such inhibition. Since 1905 its surveyors had been testing three passes through the Rockies. By 1908, they had decided on the Yellowhead. Mackenzie and Mann had a prior claim to it, which they had acquired with the Edmonton, Yukon and Pacific, but the BC government repudiated this. Therefore, even before GTP steel reached Wolf Creek, work began in August 1910 on the roadbed west.

First the contractors must pick their way through the Rockies' foothills to the Athabasca River, naming the station there for GTP general passenger agent W.P. Hinton. They crossed the Athabasca, skirted Brule Lake, and here encountered problems of a kind railroad builders had not seen before. Near the mouth of the Miette River, which flows in from the Yellowhead Pass, the material they were using to fill up depressions began fracturing into fine gravel and blowing into the cuts they had just made through the flanking mountains. They had to erect screens to keep the gravel in place until the roadbed was put down. At Jasper they encountered beavers whose dams they would remove, only to find the beavers had restored them overnight. To cross through the pass and descend its western portal down the defile of the Fraser River, they had to build a tote road, now mattressing it with corduroy logs to cross the muskeg, now blasting it out of solid rock. Mica shales in the throat of the pass kept sliding in on them. Finally they came beneath the shadow of Mount Robson and thence to Tête Jaune. The Rockies were behind them, but by now it was 1912.

Meanwhile the bond market had recovered, and Mackenzie and Mann leapt into action. In the East they persuaded the dominion government to guarantee bonds for yet another line through northern Ontario, running east from Port Arthur (Thunder Bay). This, with the Canadian Pacific and the National Transcontinental, made three. In BC they persuaded the provincial government to guarantee bonds for a line from the Yellowhead Pass to Vancouver, using the North Thompson Valley and the opposite bank of the Fraser Canyon not already occupied by the CPR. In Alberta, they won special federal subsidies to run a line from Edmonton to the Yellowhead and then south-east into the Bighorn Range of the Rockies. They took the money, built the coal railroad west from Red Deer instead, then converted the supposed Yellowhead coal railroad into a western extension of their main line.

This meant paralleling the GTP. But by now all caution was thrown to the winds. Two years behind the Grand Trunk Pacific, Canadian Northern construction crews headed west from Edmonton. Perhaps to conceal the blatant waste, they built first through St. Albert, then north-west to Villeneuve, Calahoo and Onoway, then along the shores of Lac Ste. Anne to cross the Pembina River right beside the Grand Trunk Pacific at Entwistle. From there to beyond the Yellowhead the two lines lay side by side, the Canadian Northern hacking out yet another passage from the shifting walls and muskegs of Yellowhead Pass, its rock sometimes falling on the GTP line below.[11] Historian Stevens calls it "perhaps the most foolish trackage ever built in Canada," all of it constructed with government subsidies or guarantees. The Canadian Northern line would not be opened until 1915. Then, in 1917, four-fifths of it was torn up because the steel rails were needed for the war effort.

These and other calamitous decisions would create what in the next decade would become known as "the Canadian Railway Problem" that would see the Grand Trunk, the Grand Trunk Pacific, the Canadian Northern and the Intercolonial all go bankrupt together and spell the ruin of Mackenzie and Mann. But that story must be left for another volume.

— *T.B.*

[8] The luminaries of the Canadian Northern left their names across the country: Port Mann outside Vancouver; Hanna in Alberta; Atikokan, Ontario, after William Mackenzie's official car; Erwood, Saskatchewan, after E.R. Wood, a Canadian Northern director; Davidson, Saskatchewan, after Col. A.D. Davidson, Canadian Northern land agent; Kindersley, Saskatchewan, after Sir Robert Kindersley who assisted in Canadian Northern financing. Canora, Saskatchewan, is taken from CAnadian NOrthern RAilway. According to Eric and Patricia Holmgren's *2,000 Place Names in Alberta*, Mundare was named for the Canadian Northern station agent; Minburn for Mina Burns, said to be the Ottawa girlfriend of a Canadian Northern executive; Munson for either a Canadian Northern locomotive engineer or a Canadian Northern lawyer; and Prevo as the phonetic rendering of Francois J.B. Prevost, Canadian Northern lawyer in Montreal. The town of Donalda honoured Donalda Crossway, Donald Mann's niece in Cobourg, Ontario.

[9] The Canadian Northern's Stony Plain line was later abandoned, though traces of it can still be found crossing fields south of Highway 16 immediately west of Edmonton.

[10] Stevens points out that a locomotive in that day could haul 495 tons on a 1.2% grade, 576 tons on a 1% grade, 1,058 tons on a .4% grade, and 2,183 tons on level track. Canadian National notes that, by 1990, an EF-640 diesel-electric locomotive, regularly in service on its western lines, could haul 3,272 tons on a 1.2% grade, 3,875 tons on a 1% grade, 8,314 tons on a .4% grade, and 31,005 tons (or nearly fifteen times the turn-of-the-century load) on level ground.

[11] Fragments of the old Canadian Northern line could still be seen on the Yellowhead Highway at the end of the century. For instance, at Fraser Crossing, immediately west of the BC border where the Fraser River plunges out of the mountains to the south, the highway comes alongside the piers of an old railway bridge which once carried Mackenzie and Mann's ill-fated line. The Canadian Northern roadbed could be discerned approaching the bridge from either direction.

CHAPTER THREE

The interior of Calgary's first streetcar, 1909, with (l-r, front) Commissioner S.J. Clarke, Commissioner A.G. Graves, Mayor R.R. Jamieson, and Superintendent T.H. McCauley. Pork barrel or no pork barrel, Calgary was moving into the future at a rapid pace.

The angry young metropolis on a fast track to prosperity

ROBBED OF CAPITAL STATUS, CALGARY SEETHED, BUT THE RESENTMENT FUELLED A BOOM IN THE INDEFATIGABLE CITY THAT BEAT ITS RIVAL BY A THUMBED NOSE

by GEORGE KOCH

Spurred by its key location on Canada's first transcontinental railway and on its burgeoning cattle industry, Calgary entered the 20th century firmly convinced it would become the great metropolis of the Canadian West. Its loss of both the provincial capital and the provincial university to Edmonton (the "Frozen City of the North," as Calgarians would have it) scarcely diminished that dream. Neither did the taunts of Edmonton editorialists who dubbed the southern city "Cow Camp." What these reversals did do, however, was establish an inter-city rivalry as a given fact in the politics and economics of the province for years to come.

And during the century's first decade, Calgarians discovered one thing more. Politics was not decisive. Provincial capital or no provincial capital, university or no university, Calgary boomed as it never had before, and never would again until the 1970s. What mattered far more was the enthusiasm and determination of the citizenry. Fanning both the boom and the fury against Liberals and Edmonton was the *Calgary Herald*, until 1908 a locally owned newspaper.[1]

"Calgary's prospects," said the *Herald* in 1902, "were never brighter than they are today. The country around us in all directions is filling up rapidly. Between four and five thousand new settlers came into central and north Alberta during the month of April alone. Our local industries are all in a flourishing condition, and our businessmen, both wholesale and retail, have no cause for

The frontier began to lose its dominance. Buses and streetcars appeared. The bowler was almost as popular as the Stetson.

complaint in the volume of business that is coming to them. The principal industry of the country — ranching — is constantly improving and extending...Both in Calgary and the surrounding district, building operations are extremely active, and there is plenty of employment."

The city in 1902 covered only about one square mile, the distance between the North-West Mounted Police barracks on 6th Street SE and the courthouse on Ross Street (now 4th St. SW). But its downtown district already boasted fine sandstone buildings, telephones, a fire department, law offices, three newspapers and eight churches. In the next eight years the frontier, though still present, began to lose its dominance. Street and building construction was everywhere evident and everywhere complained about.[2] The bowler hat, observes W.B. Fraser in his history called

[1] The *Herald*, founded as a weekly in 1883 when the Canadian Pacific reached Calgary, was acquired by the Southam interests of Hamilton, Ontario, in 1908. Its strident advocacy of the city, the province, and the Conservative cause thereafter gradually tamed. It acquired a more "national" perspective. The Southams took over the *Edmonton Journal* in 1912.

[2] Explosive growth had its messy aspects; downtown construction in 1904 provoked a typical *Eye Opener* joke. "I'm glad I am a child," says the infant prodigy from his baby carriage. "Why, my darling skookum-wookums?" asks the fond mother. "Because I stand a show of living for 75 years longer and seeing the day when Stephen Avenue will be free from...excavations, gravel heaps, sand mounds, mortar beds, pipes, barricades and street-corner loafers." Says the mother: "Oh, you dear sanguine child!"

Glenbow Archives, NA-3496-23

Joint meeting of the Board of Trade and city officials in 1910. Calgary's chronic optimism sometimes descended into arrogance or blind confidence, but it could get things done.

Calgary, was becoming almost as common as the Stetson. Buses and streetcars appeared. The 1908 Dominion Exhibition made all Canada pay attention (see sidebar).

Moreover, the city acquired tycoons. Among the best-known were the so-called "Big Four" — George Lane of the Bar U Ranch, meat-packer Pat Burns (see Sect. 4, ch. 4), cattle breeder and brewer A.E. Cross, and politician and rancher A.J. McLean. Most came from humble origins. All got their start in the cattle business. All became wealthy and influential. And along with many

---

'Calgary,' gloated the *Edmonton Journal*, 'is still a good deal worked up over the selection of Strathcona for the university.'

---

others they all contributed mightily to Calgary's economic development and emerging urban character.

Some fine and functional buildings, both wood and stone, edified the cityscape. There was the imposing sandstone James Short School, put up in 1904. There was the Grain Exchange Building. James Lougheed built the Lyric Theatre on Stephen Avenue in 1905 and the big Sherman Rink at Notre Dame Avenue and McTavish Street (17th Ave. and Centre St.) was available after 1907 for roller skating, ice skating, and big gatherings and shows.[3] Alex and Archie McKenzie opened the Orpheum at McIntyre Avenue and McTavish (7th Ave. and Centre) in 1908.

Then, too, the "prestigious" neighbourhoods appeared — Mount Royal, Elbow Park, Elboya

'Mr. Boom' and his fellow opportunists

IN A CITY WHERE THE POPULATION WOULD GROW TENFOLD IN A DECADE, THE BIG LAND SCANDAL WOULD PRECEDE THE BIG LAND BOOM

The "Great Calgary Land Boom" was driven by a combination of bullish civic confidence, a severe mid-decade housing shortage caused by increased immigration, and frenzied speculation surrounding two more expected railway lines. It was furthered by ready supplies of timber, sandstone and clay for brick-making. Although it exhibited many of the unsavoury aspects that accompany unrestrained growth, the period marked the transition from large town to genuine city. In fact during that single decade Calgary grew more than tenfold — from 4,000 to over 40,000 (the 1911 census put the population at 43,704).

The Great Land Boom should not be confused with the earlier Great Land Scandal, notes W.B. Fraser in his history, called simply *Calgary*. The scandal was a kind of precursor. One evening in March 1904, city council abruptly decided to sell 500 city-owned lots. At a subsequent evening meeting, councillors agreed on valuations for them all in just half an hour, then put them up for sale. Although they failed to inform the public, the lots were all sold by noon next day. One hapless citizen offered $100 for one of them, only to be told it was being held for someone "in the know" who was paying $35.

An uproar ensued. Irate townsmen jammed the council chambers, petitions circulated, heated editorials erupted, and a law firm declared the sale illegal. A year later Mayor Silas Ramsay was finally forced to order an investigation, although

by this time most of the guilt-ridden (or fear-ridden) buyers had returned the land to the city. Chief Justice Arthur Sifton concluded that Ramsay and the council had exhibited "gross carelessness." Two aldermen were disqualified from holding office; the city clerk and city solicitor resigned.

Meanwhile the Great Land Boom was gathering momentum. By 1908 real estate investment was seen as safer than money in the bank. For the clever, and the lucky, it was. E.H. Riley, who won the provincial constituency of Gleichen for the Liberals in 1909, bought what would become the Hillhurst subdivision in 1904 at $40 a lot, and sold it six years later at up to $1,200 per lot. As the fever increased men began flipping land in weeks, days, even hours. Some were said to make profits of $1,000 or more on a deal, with barely time to fill out the necessary paperwork on the purchase before reselling.

Eighth Avenue downtown property went from around $3,000 a lot in 1905 to $1,800 per frontage foot in 1909. Real estate agents stirred the action by arranging financing so that anybody could get in on the game for as little as $1 down and $1 a week. There were an estimated 2,000 agents operating in the city, writes Max Foran in *Illustrated History of Calgary* — ten per cent of the city's adult males.

Foreign buyers were ideal clients. Many "neighbourhoods" they bought into — with names like Manitou Park, Balaclava and Pasadena — were far from downtown or right

[3] In 1975 *Calgary Herald* columnist Leishman McNeill recalled hearing the noted Nellie Melba sing at the Sherman Rink about 1908, as part of the old Orpheum vaudeville circuit. "Frank Wrigley, who was organist of Knox Church, underwrote the $6,000 guarantee..." he writes, "and I remember top price was $5, an unheard-of price for Calgary, but the rink was packed."

Panorama of Calgary, looking south across the Bow, about 1910. Calgary's city council was bullishly pro-development.

outside the city, and some were so remote they were never developed at all. Newspaperman Bob Edwards wrote of the farmer who had approached a real estate agent for a home in the city. The agent drove the farmer for miles, then pointed to a field and asked, "Wouldn't that be a lovely place for you and your wife to build your city home?" The agent then asked, "By the way, where is the farm you want to sell?"

"My farm?" said the farmer. "Why, we passed it a couple of miles back, nearer Calgary."

The boom turned into outright frenzy when speculation began at the end of the decade over the coming branch lines of the Grand Trunk Pacific and the Canadian Northern Railway, and over news of CPR plans to build a major maintenance facility in Calgary. Where, the speculators wondered, would the stations and shop buildings be located?

Fortunes were made and lost. Names like Peter Prince, I.S.G. Van Wart and William Cushing (notwithstanding the fact he was provincial Public Works minister) were inextricably linked with the proceedings. But no speculator was more flamboyant, writes Grant MacEwan in *Calgary Cavalcade*, than F.C. Lowes, the real estate trader and developer who by the age of thirty would become the city's first millionaire and earn the nickname of "Mr. Boom."

An Ontario insurance agent and an amateur boxer, Lowes came to Calgary in 1902 and switched to real estate in 1906. For him, too much was never enough. He employed 400 people in Calgary, owned four cars (at $5,000 or so apiece, at a time when there were only a few dozen in all of Calgary), kept several dozen horses (jumpers), and spread his operations to Edmonton, British Columbia, Washington state, New York and London.

This was the first great flare of boosterism, Max Foran observes, and virtually all elements in the city were caught up in pro-growth enthusiasm. Both the *Calgary Optimist* and the *New Telegram* were unabashed promoters. "Calgary has most cities faded to a whisper even now and it will have them all lashed to the mast when the warm weather comes," declared one editorial.

The city, which had begun with only one square mile of land, began annexing surrounding sections, encompassing forty square miles by 1912. Total building for 1903 was officially valued at $371,025. By 1910, the figure was $5.5 million. During the decade, about 25% of Calgary's labour force worked in the construction trade. Buildings of five storeys were erected in the business district. Stephen Avenue, the main business street, was now complemented by Scarth (1st Street West). Wholesalers spread along the CPR line immediately south and west of downtown, especially on Pacific Avenue (10th).

Action in residential real estate was even faster. The city spread from inside the Bow River valley up and out onto the surrounding prairie. This was the era when Calgary acquired a suburban element — a word that was already in use. The number of houses grew from less than 1,700 in 1901 to more than 11,000 by 1911, and still there was a shortage.

The Great Land Boom would peak and crash in the decade to come, but it wasn't all just hucksterism and hustle. It carried the city to a level of economic activity that would not be matched until the 1950s, and whatever imagery might attend the future Calgary Stampede, it spelled the end of the frontier town.

— *G.K.*

and Windsor Park. Pat Burns' sumptuous sandstone house went up in 1901, and R.B. Bennett's mansion in 1909. Real estate developers not only opened up Crescent Heights, but built a bridge over the Bow River to make it a convenient place to live. Most residential expansion was southwestward, however. Industry concentrated in the east, along with some residential developments aimed specifically at the working man. Schools followed the spreading population.

Although primary industries and the construction trades were still dominant, it was now that

'Edmonton is a lively place, all right,' sniped the *Herald*. 'The editorial in one of the dailies was about the dog catcher capturing a farmer's pups. That's the place to have capital.'

many of the city's secondary industries began. By 1910 nine industrial plants employed nearly 1,000 men. But the CPR remained the city's major job-provider, and it opened a large switching yards that employed 300 more men.

Calgary's city council was bullishly pro-development. Many aldermen were themselves in the real estate or construction industries, notes Grant MacEwan in *Calgary Cavalcade*, and the council's top priority was facilitating economic expansion. Aside from regrettable interludes like the Great Land Scandal (see sidebar) the main concerns were planning and financing local improvements and practising boosterism.

Glenbow Archives, NA-3544-28

The Calgary Power Company generating station on the Bow River, about 1912. Its existence persuaded the CPR to build the Ogden repair shops, providing 1,200 jobs.

Running water and electric power were no longer considered luxuries, but essential services. A private company had installed the first water mains in 1899 along Reinach Avenue (4th Ave. W), then south on Scarth Street (1st St. W) and east on Stephen. The water came from the Bow not far from the site of the future Louise Bridge, writes Tom Ward in *Cowtown*, and steam-driven pumps supplied pressure.

Not enough pressure, however. Later city commissioner A.G. Graves would remember that the

City Hall under construction, 1909. The value of building starts increased fifteen-fold in about seven years.

whole system was in "a demoralized condition" by 1899. "The mains were nearly all four-inch pipe," he recalled, "and when a fire occurred and a good pressure was required it invariably happened that the pumps would break down."[4] So the city bought out the Calgary Gas and Waterworks in 1900 for $90,000, making the waterworks the first city-owned utility. But not until

The winner of the Hundred Thousand Club's essay contest was Ernie Richardson who got $50 in gold for an entry entitled, 'Calgary, Alberta, commercial metropolis of western Canada.'

1905 was the council able to replace the faltering steam pump with an electric one that could handle 2.5 million gallons a day. New mains were urgently needed, and more of them. So was some sort of filtration system, and a reservoir. Besides, a gravity system would clearly be better; even electric pumps break down.

In 1907, after much discussion, the councillors allotted $340,000 for a gravity system that was

[4]Fire Chief Cappy Smart described his city's pre-1900 waterworks system as supplying four hydrants, several watering troughs and two drinking fountains that he considered "more ornamental than useful." When his men tried to test the pressure in 1891 it suddenly dropped to zero; somebody back at the pumphouse had inadvertently turned off the water in mid-exercise.

The Greatest Show in the West

CALGARY'S 1908 DOMINION EXHIBITION BROUGHT BLIMPS, STEER-BITING AND A SENSE OF HAVING ARRIVED

The 1908 Dominion Exhibition was one of Calgary's great triumphs of the decade, and a none too likely one considering how tough things had been for the city's Agricultural Society. Back in 1897 it lost its land by defaulting on the payments. However, early in the new century the city fathers bought back the 94-acre fair ground from its current owner, Tory politician R.B. Bennett, for the then-considerable sum of $7,000. They leased it to the Agricultural Society, now reorganized as a no-dividend joint-stock operation called the Inter-Western Pacific Exposition Company. Under organizer Ernie Richardson, Calgary went from having no fair at all to staging a wildly successful national exhibition.

Richardson was one of the many young men who ventured West to make his name. He went to work for Charles W. Peterson, a former deputy commissioner of agriculture for the North-West Territories, and became joint secretary of the Calgary Board of Trade. He would go on to make a career of organizing public spectacles throughout western Canada.

Just winning the right to put on the Dominion Exhibition, the sixth held in Canada, was an achievement.[a] The *Calgary Herald* lavished praise on its chief promoters: on Richardson, on exhibition president I.S.G. Van Wart, and on Colonel James Walker, for doing so. With municipal and federal grants of $85,000 and a year to prepare, Richardson put on a spectacle such as had never yet been seen in the West.

It began with a mile-long parade through downtown Calgary (the forerunner, of course, of the Stampede Parade), led by Grand Marshal James "Cappy" Smart, the fire chief.[b] Every conceivable element of society was represented: farmers, cowboys, Mounties, Indians, merchants and railroaders. Notables like Senator James Lougheed, Chief Justice Arthur Sifton, Lieutenant-Governor George Bulyea and president Van Wart sought to lend decorum to the event. But Calgarians, ever the party animals, were also able to imbibe freely in various ways, including one illicit booth selling "strong cider."

Besides the usual horse-racing and rodeo events, there were Indian races, fireworks, the Oklahoma-based Miller Brothers' Wild West Show, polo matches between Calgary and outlying towns, and brass bands like the Highlanders from Hamilton and the Iowa State Band. (The city's own Fire Brigade Band, with 35 uniformed members, had won the Northwest Band Competition in 1902.) Despite the physical danger of many events, the one fatal accident occurred when sheep rancher W.D. Kerfoot of Cochrane was thrown from his horse and killed in front of the grandstand.

A display that turned out to be literally inflammatory was "Strobel's balloon-motor combination," a type of airship consisting of an oblong, fabric-covered frame filled with a lighter-than-air gas, steered by fins, and with propellers powered by a gasoline engine. Unlike later blimps, it was filled with explosive hydrogen rather than inert helium. The balloon-motor airship rated a major photograph in the *Herald* — but it caught fire July 4 and was destroyed, severely burning its pilot. He survived, however.

Public response to the exhibition was tremendous. First-day attendance, which featured a flight by the not-yet destroyed Strobel airship, was 25,000, at 25 cents per head. By contrast, Calgary's first fair, held in 1886 and grandiosely billed as "The Greatest Outdoor Show on Earth," attracted a total of 500.

On the more earthly level, interest in livestock displays was strong at a time when most Albertans faced the practical reality of carving a living out of the often inhospitable prairie. Fairs served an important practical function, keeping people abreast of developments in farm equipment and improvements

Glenbow Archives, NA-1473-1

Sifting through the remains of Strobel's balloon, July 1908. The pilot was severely burned, but survived.

in livestock breeding. There was also strong interest in 1908 in displays from across the West. Kelowna, for example, brought samples of fruit, while Medicine Hat touted the benefits of natural gas lighting.

Although most people revelled in the physically rougher events, even before 1908 a few voices were already calling for rodeo reform. In a 1905 editorial, the *Herald* decried a notorious local practice "in which a huge cowboy grabs a steer by the nose with his teeth and throws the animal to the ground...in the presence of women and children, the finer sensibilities are outraged."

Another editorial decried a bucking contest in Blairmore "in which three horses were cruelly punished to make them do something mean," namely, to buck. "The day for this alleged form of entertainment has gone and the practice should be stopped both by public disapproval and where necessary by legal action," and the contest "furnished striking evidence of the necessity of the organization of a society for the prevention of cruelty to animals."

Although total attendance at the Dominion Exhibition came in at just under 90,000, it actually lost money. No matter — the organizers and the citizens were satisfied. Even Edmontonians were impressed; the *Edmonton Bulletin* built an entire issue around it. Though less well-remembered today

than the first Stampede (held in 1912), the 1908 exhibition launched Calgary into a great tradition of successful and lucrative public events, one that would give the city a reputation for hospitality and enthusiasm.

Historian James Gray has argued that the Exhibition and the Stampede, which would merge in the 1920s, were fundamental in shaping Calgary's urban identity. When Ernie Richardson retired in 1940, attendance at the Calgary Exhibition and Stampede had reached a quarter-million. As Richardson put it, prophetically: "We're only starting. Give us time and we'll show the world something in exhibitions."

— *G.K.*

[a]At the time, writes Grant MacEwan in *Calgary Cavalcade*, Ernie Richardson was also lobbying to make **Calgary** the site of the University of Alberta, and to become home to the government's recently acquired herd of bison. Although he and his allies lost on both those counts, with the university going to Strathcona, which would soon become part of Edmonton, and the bison to a reserve near Wainwright, Interior Minister Frank Oliver may have backed their bid for the Dominion Exhibition as a kind of consolation prize.

[b]Cappy Smart, fire chief for 35 years, missed very few civic undertakings, according to Leishman McNeill, longtime *Herald* columnist and president of the Calgary Oldtimers' Association. At a 1901 Calgary reception for the Duke of York (later King George V), for example, all the Indian chiefs in their blue coats with brass buttons were introduced. Then, so the story goes, the royal visitor and his duchess turned to Cappy, who was also in navy blue uniform. "And this, Your Royal Highnesses, is Chief Smart." "My word," remarked the duke, "what a splendid looking savage!"

Stephen Avenue during the Dominion Day parade in 1908. Calgary was developing a confidence that belied its years.

The peculiar attraction of the parade was that it was real and there was no play-acting about it at all. The Indians were alive and most of the 2,000 in the parade had taken part in many bloody battlefields. The early missionaries were there in person, as were the early traders, the cowboys and all the other early settlers...The rear of the parade was made up of the very modern Calgary, the city of champions, the gaudy automobile parade, gaily decorated horses and the interesting floats of the merchants.
- from the souvenir booklet of the Dominion Day parade, July 1, 1908.

fed from the Elbow about five miles west, thus achieving a 300-foot drop. This required installation of eleven miles of thirty-inch wooden stave pipe, and was supposed to supply eight million gallons a day. In very short order the new system became inadequate, unable in particular to satisfy the needs of the new southwest districts. But for two more decades the city kept adding to it and patching it. Not until 1933 would the Glenmore Reservoir and a whole new complex solve the problem. In the meantime, however, most of Calgary did have running water most of the time.

The supply of electricity was just as erratic. It had been developing in piecemeal fashion since 1887, a process described in Ward's *Cowtown*. This began with a fight between the Electric Light Company, which operated two steam-driven dynamos in the lane behind the Bank of Montreal, and Peter Prince of the Eau Claire Company, who installed the necessary machinery beside his sawmill and fired it with sawdust or coal. The Electric Light Company faded out, however, although not before two of its linemen were apprehended pulling Prince transformer fuses — thus putting out the lights in most of the hotels on Atlantic Avenue (9th Ave. SW).

Later Prince built two dams to harness and regulate the varied flow of the Bow River, but even so could not maintain a steady supply. When his contract with the city ended in 1904, council decided to install a municipal system based on a steam plant at Atlantic Avenue and 5th St. SW). It was later moved to Victoria Park. This was quite successful, and the city kept adding to it. The real solution, however, was provided by the new Calgary Power Company, formed in 1909, which immediately began work on the first big hydro-electric powerhouse at Horseshoe Falls on the Bow.[5] It would produce fourteen megawatts, and proved an important factor in persuading the CPR to build the huge Ogden repair shops in Calgary, providing 1,200 jobs. It would also go on to provide much of the province with electricity for the rest of the century.[6]

City council also began paving roads, eventually setting up its own paving operation and making street railways feasible. During the 19-year tenure of Chief Thomas English, the police

force grew from two constables in 1890 to 26 in 1909. The wage for a constable was raised to $65 a month in 1904. As the decade ended the force was about to be completely reorganized, and to double again, and in 1911 would get a motorized Black Maria.

Council bought the fire department its first motorized truck in 1909 (see sidebar). The firemen in this period were important for other functions. In 1901 they began sponsoring a May 24 sports day that became an annual civic event. Under the direction of Chief Cappy Smart they built a bandstand in the CPR Gardens near the later site of the Palliser Hotel, and they also provided the music. That year the 35-piece Fire Brigade Band got a new leader. Lawyer Crispin Smith had refused to hand over evidence in a court case and had been jailed, says historian Ward. It was an unpopular decision. His release was greeted by a cheering crowd and a fanfare by the firemen's band. Smith was so impressed he became its conductor, always performing in a bearskin hat, Prince Albert coat and white belt.

Along with big-city services came the beginnings of big-city bureaucracy. In the winter of 1905 the *Herald* indignantly recounted the experience of a resident whose frozen water pipes had burst. He reportedly had to stand by helplessly watching them spout for 24 hours because only city employees were authorized to turn off municipally owned pipes, and none was available to perform this minor (fifty-cent) operation. Snarled the *Herald*: "The inscrutable wisdom of the system responsible...may have a reason, but it has never been supplied the water consumers of the city."

The city was becoming quite cosmopolitan. Japan's Prince Fushimi paid a visit in the summer of 1907, greeted by thousands of citizens and a great display of municipal hospitality. Goodwill towards Asians did not necessarily extend, however, to the resident Chinese. There was considerable anti-Chinese feeling among the city's predominantly Anglo-Saxon population. A

The lobby of the Alberta Hotel, about 1900, with Edward Shelley at the desk. The city was acquiring tycoons.

[5] The Horseshoe dam, the first hydro project upstream on the Bow, was built by 200 men with picks, shovels and wheelbarrows. It took them two years, says historian Tom Ward, and they completed it less than two months behind schedule.

[6] Early electric power companies faced a number of pioneering problems. One was public fear and ignorance. "This room is equipped with Edison electric light. Do not attempt to light with match," said a sign in one Calgary hotel. "Simply turn key on wall by the door. The use of electricity for light is in no way harmful to health, nor does it affect the soundness of sleep."

1904 city council resolution to confine Chinese laundries to non-residential parts of town was probably more an attempt at racial rather than commercial segregation. The pretext: the Chinese worked all night, lighting up neighbourhoods and making noise. But in any case the Chinese community clustered around Pacific Avenue (10th Ave. SE). The first Chinese-Canadian Calgarian, incidentally, was born in 1906.

Other ethnic groups were also getting established in larger numbers. Some 2,500 German immigrants, for instance, attended a social gathering on the Bow River in 1910. Many of these likely came from out of town for the occasion, but the Riverside district, popularly known as Germantown and noted for its free-roaming cows, had a considerable population of Germans and eastern Europeans. By 1910 they had built the first German and Moravian churches. Italian and French-speaking communities also appeared.

This was the decade when civic boosterism went wild, historian Max Foran observes in his *Calgary: An Illustrated History.* The city's board of trade expended enormous energy clamouring for another railway to break the CPR monopoly and drive down its freight rates. Edmonton, which up to 1905 had no railroad, by the end of the decade had two with a third just across the river in

Twenty passengers at eighteen mph
THE FIRST BUS ARRIVED IN 1907, THE FIRST STREETCAR TWO YEARS LATER

Very early, it seems, Calgarians became addicted to mobility. Maybe it was the vastness of the vistas. Maybe it was the staggering size of the early landholdings. Maybe it was the same love of freedom that brought people there in the first place. Maybe it was an economy dependent on moving things around: cattle up from Texas, logs down the Bow River, grain to the Lakehead. Whatever it was, the place that called itself the "City of Horsemen" well into the 20th century was also quick to adopt leading-edge transportation technology.

The first car appeared on Calgary streets in 1903 (see Sect. 3, chpt. 4), and as the city's affluent acquired the latest in private automobiles, the *Herald* reported in 1907 a city purchase of three "large motor omnibuses" from Halley Industrial Motors, Glasgow, Scotland. The covered-in vehicles, which had solid rubber tires and 40-horsepower gasoline engines, could carry twenty passengers at eighteen miles an hour.

Glenbow Archives, NA-1009-18

First Street streetcar (southbound) emerging from subway under CPR tracks, about 1910. The first cars began travelling between downtown and the Exhibition Grounds in 1909.

Strathcona and now finally planning to cross. Calgary must have the same, local boosters urged. "Competition would mean not only better freight rates but the opening of new districts from which a vast amount of trade could be expected," declared the *Herald*.

But Edmonton's advantages lay in other spheres besides railroads. Its acquisition of the university for neighbouring Strathcona was a particularly bitter blow. "Calgary," gloated the *Edmonton Journal*, "is still a good deal worked up over the selection of Strathcona for the university city of the province." It certainly was. "In southern Alberta," raged the *Herald*, "one united feeling of disgust was prevalent at the selfish policy of 'grab,' exhibited by the Rutherford government in this last instance." Calgarians began pushing for what the *Albertan* called "a great university for western Canada." It would transcend provincial boundaries and thereby leap to academic prominence. The scheme would come to be in the next decade, but its life was to prove very short.

There seemed to be no end to what the city's rambunctious newspapers would do to score a few points against their resented northern rival. Early in 1906 a *Herald* staffer in the capital, trying to file a late story and finding Edmonton's telegraph and telephone offices shut down,

Glenbow Archives, NA-5061-24

Preparing Stephen Avenue for automobiles, streetcars and omnibuses, 1908. The fire department motorized too, but with regrets.

The buses were considered ideal for a far-flung, rapidly expanding city and outlying towns, requiring less capital investment than electrically driven railways. "It is expected that the introduction of these new and powerful omnibuses into western Canada will be the beginning of a revolution in methods of travel near the towns," predicted the *Herald*. And so they were, too. The Halley buses would look quaint 85 years later, but their front-engined, extended-coach design would change little in principle for years to come.

Then the fire department motorized, though not without regrets. Its horse-drawn reels had been a matter of great civic pride. The horses (Jimmy and Squibby, Dick and Frank, Bob and Brownie and Old White Wings) lived in stalls behind the reels. When an alarm sounded, writes Leishman McNeill in *Tales of the Old Town*, the stall doors opened automatically and the trained horses hurried out to stand under their harnesses, which were suspended from the ceiling. Harnessing could take as little as ten seconds, McNeill says, a feat the firemen

demonstrated at the Dominion Exhibition in 1908 with a team they called the Jack Rabbits.

Nevertheless, in 1909, after a municipal plebiscite, Calgary purchased the first motorized fire squad wagon in Canada. This vehicle could carry eight men plus a sixty-gallon chemical tank. Aside from its snappy whitewall tires, its main benefits were said to be much reduced maintenance costs compared to horse-drawn vehicles. One report pegged the maintenance cost of a motorized pump truck at $58 for a five-month period, compared to $196 for the horse-drawn equivalent. Moreover, the motorized vehicles could handle a wider area.

In 1907 the city approved expenditure of $250,000 to begin construction of a street railway. After it spent a further $226,000 to install an electric generator, the first two cars began running passengers between downtown and the Exhibition Grounds in July 1909. The cars, which had flip-down windows and could be heated in winter, were considered a marvel of comfort compared to cold, bumpy coaches.

The single line carried 35,000 passengers in its first week, returning a $7,000 profit in its first six months. By the end of the year Alberta Electric, run by T.A. McCullough, had twelve cars running on thirteen miles of track within downtown Calgary, and to such neighbourhoods as Shoulder Terrace and Bowness Park Estates. The street railway would grow a lot more in the decade that followed — so much so that some would berate it as a white elephant with too few riders, too many lines and too much rolling stock serving in some cases non-existent suburbs. But in 1910 it was state-of-the-art transportation, and was appreciated as such. — *G.K.*

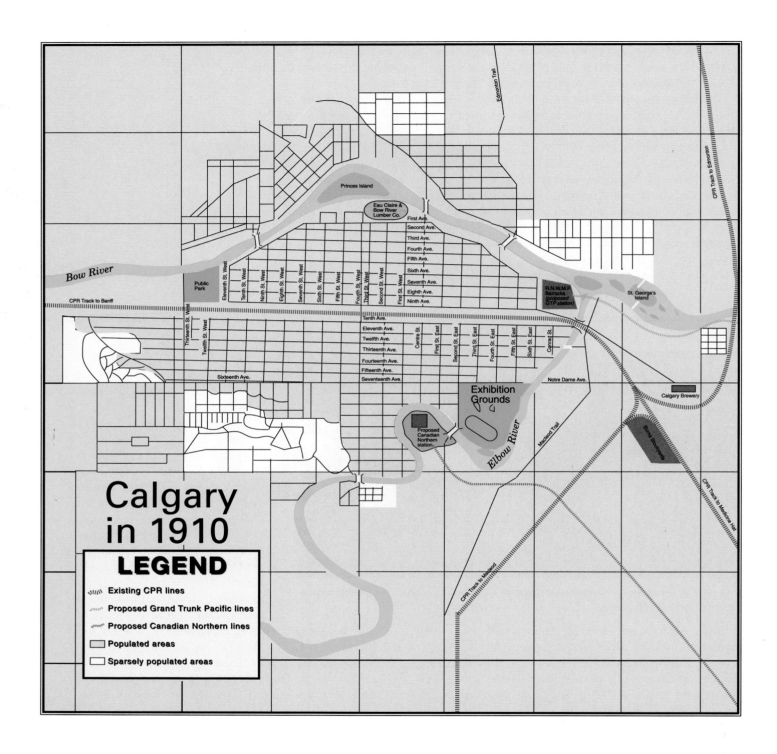

Calgary
in 1910

LEGEND

Existing CPR lines
Proposed Grand Trunk Pacific lines
Proposed Canadian Northern lines
Populated areas
Sparsely populated areas

harrumphed that "the city of Edmonton is dead to the outside world early in the evening." On another occasion, as the Russo-Japanese War raged, the *Herald* sniped: "Edmonton is a lively place, all right...The leading editorial in one of the dailies last week was on the question of the dog catcher capturing a farmer's pups. That's the place to have a capital." On the other hand, Edmonton's supposed stodginess and insularity did not deter the *Albertan* from publishing a local ministerial diatribe describing the capital as a city of "depravity and impurity, with the most appalling vice in high places."

Nor did Calgary gracefully surrender its pre-Laurier near-monopoly on federal political connections. In 1907 the *Herald* denounced a pamphlet issued by Interior Minister Frank Oliver for extolling the economic strengths and promise of Edmonton at the expense of Calgary. Edmonton, for its part, became equally sensitive. When a meeting was held in Calgary to establish the first association of Alberta municipalities, noted the Edmonton newspapers, the capital city wasn't even invited.

At times the rivalry could get downright personal. In the winter of 1907 the newspapers reported that an Edmonton man, displeased with the modest cuisine offered at a Calgary hostel, was heard cursing the waitress. As he left the establishment, a friend of the woman's punched him in the nose, the eye, and the "epiglottis." The assailant was not charged by the Calgary police. But the Edmonton man, William Boyd, was charged with using insulting language and fined $5, not an inconsiderable sum in those days, leaving him with just enough money, as a local newspaper sarcastically reported it, for "two drinks."

Nor was Edmonton above revelling in Calgary's reversals. During the bitter winter of 1906-07, Calgary ran out of coal and many people were said to be in danger of being frozen out of their homes. Edmonton helped out, shipping trainloads of local coal south, but not without a few jibes. The *Edmonton Bulletin* ran a rambling, sarcastic account of the relief effort, at one point insinuating that Calgarians would make up any story to get a few lumps of coal: "By actual count at the coal office there were over three hundred newborn babes in Calgary families on that eventful Sabbath morn, who had to have coal at once, and the number of frail and suffering mothers-in-law who were pinched and reached by the biting cold, was stupendous beyond all the dreams of the census taker." Concluded the *Bulletin*, "...It is better to have a nice coal seam underlying the town than to depend on a chinook which don't always work."

However, magnanimity could creep in at times. "Cheery optimism, unwavering faith in its great future, walking around, so to speak, with a chip on its shoulder and yet hospitable almost to ostentation to the stranger within its gates, Edmonton is a city to be imitated, both in regard to its institutions and its citizenship," wrote one Calgary correspondent in an "on-the-scene" account of the capital. "Their breezy optimism under all circumstances makes the Edmonton people surmount with ease difficulties which would dishearten others."

Meanwhile the *Herald*, the Board of Trade, City Council and the "Hundred Thousand Club" all assiduously extolled the virtues of their city which, the *Herald* repeatedly assured its readers, was still by far the largest.[7] The Hundred Thousand Club, a group of local boosters dedicated to seeing Calgary reach that level of population by 1915, held an essay contest to see who could best sing Calgary's praises. The winner was none other than Dominion Exhibition organizer Ernie Richardson, who received $50 in gold for his entry entitled, "Calgary, Alberta, Commercial Metropolis of Western Canada."

What made it all work? Despite Edmonton's rise, Calgary's assets were undeniable: its CPR connections; favourable climate; ready access to basic resources like water, stone and timber; its proximity to the mountains; its business connections in Montreal, Toronto and Great Britain. And there was another element, which was rooted in the 19th century and would outlast the 20th: a kind of collective confidence. Historian Foran describes Calgary's boosterism as an institutionalized phenomenon, in which all the city's pro-business elements, whoever the individuals themselves might be, work together to push their city forward.

True enough, Calgary's chronic optimism was an attitude that could descend into arrogance or sometimes blind confidence. But at its best, it emerged as what Calgary lawyer and future prime minster R.B. Bennett once called a determination to "make things happen." It was the kind of spirit that in 1912 would prompt the Hundred Thousand Club, as the city's population neared 50,000, to change its name. It became the Quarter Million Club.

[7]Largest, in fact, by far. The 1911 dominion census (which, unlike the special census of Saskatchewan and Alberta taken in 1906, did not become a political issue) would show Calgary city at 43,704, Edmonton city at 24,900, and Strathcona city at 5,579. By comparison, Montreal in 1910 had a population of 470,460; Toronto, 376,539; and Vancouver, 100,401.

American settlers on their way to Alberta.
Provincial Archives of Manitoba, N-7933

Section Three
THE INRUSH OF SETTLERS
Chapters by Bob Collins, Courtney Tower, Larry Collins, Hugh Dempsey & Janice Tyrwhitt

CHAPTER ONE

The biggest ad campaign ever lured one and all westward

THE GOVERNMENT OFFERED FREE LAND FOR MILLIONS. THE DISPOSSESSED, THE ADVENTUROUS AND THE NAIVE POURED FORTH ONTO CANADA'S PRAIRIES

One of the biggest sources of new Albertans was the US. These American covered wagons were among thousands pouring over the border in 1906.

by ROBERT COLLINS

For farmer John Maurer of Gresham, Nebraska, the 1904 newspaper advertisement was the answer to his prayers — an invitation to Paradise. At 35, with a wife and four young daughters, he was getting nowhere working his fingers to the bone on rented land. Yet what tenant could afford to *own* a farm at $100 an acre?

Then he spotted the beguiling ad:

WESTERN CANADA
Has Free Homes for Millions
Upwards of 10,000 Americans have settled
in western Canada during the past five years.
They are **Contented, Happy and Prosperous**
and there is room still for **Millions**.
Wonderful yields of wheat and other grains. The best grazing lands
on the Continent. Magnificent climate, plenty of water and fuel.
Good schools, excellent church, splendid railway facilities...
FREE HOMESTEADS
OF 160 ACRES
The only charge being $10 for entry...

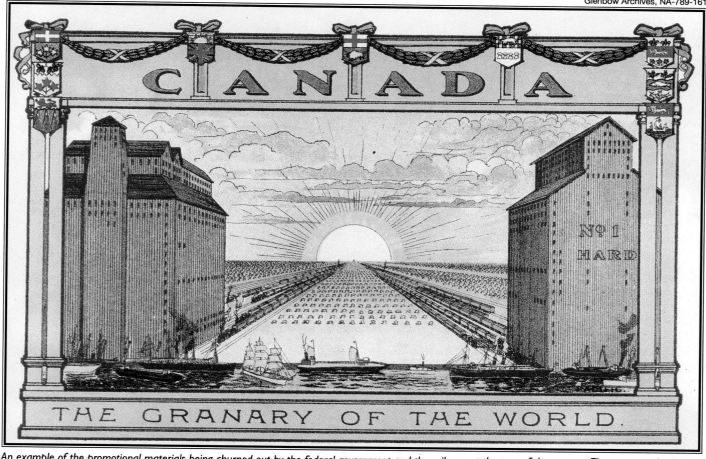

CANADA

THE GRANARY OF THE WORLD.

An example of the promotional materials being churned out by the federal government and the railways at the turn of the century. They suggested soil that merely had to be tickled and images of gold coins being harvested. For some it was nearly true, for most the beginning of an ordeal.

Maurer hopped a train, got a quarter-section eighteen miles from Lacombe and returned the next year with his family and a freight car full of implements, household furniture, cows, chickens, a span of mules and two pigs. He stayed "contented, happy and prosperous" until his death in 1939.

The six Maurers were mere drops in an astonishing human tide of settlement in the century's first decade, raising Canada's population from five million to more than 6,250,000, and swelling Alberta's by a phenomenal 550 per cent to nearly 375,000. The immigrants came from all corners of the earth: the United States, Austria-Hungary, the Balkans, China, England, France, Germany, Holland, Ireland, Romania, Russia, Scandinavia, Scotland, Ukraine and Wales. They came in sheepskin coats, fur leggings, cossack boots, corduroy jackets, tweed caps, lambskin hats, babushkas, sashes and shawls. They enriched Alberta with a multitude of new tongues, tastes and traditions.

And they were tempted, tricked and bowled along by gusts of rhetoric spewed forth from governments, land companies and railways (Canadian Pacific, Canadian Northern, Grand Trunk Pacific, Hudson's Bay and Northwest) — up to then the biggest advertising campaign in history. Much of it was sheer "propaganda," as one federal immigration official acknowledged in a rare lapse into honesty, and it took awful liberties with truth.

Immigrant families on board ship. Sometimes they were packed into steerage like sardines.

German settler August Sorge was enticed to Fort Macleod by an ad showing Johnny Canuck in Stetson hat and highlaced boots, turning up gold coins in the furrow. John Leech left Birmingham for Lacombe after reading that Alberta soil, merely "tickled with a hoe," would burst forth with growth, and the "mean temperature was a balmy 65 degrees." Later, Leech often said he wished he'd known just how mean the temperature could get.

Quebecker Ed Bigelow was drawn to Crossfield by promises of work at $7 a day (he got only $1.75). In France, Georges Bugnet read that a strong intelligent young man could make $25,000

Would-be settlers were tempted, tricked and bowled along by gusts of rhetoric from governments, land companies and railways. Much of it was sheer propaganda.

---

in five or ten years on an Alberta farm. Long afterwards he said ruefully, "We have still to see the $25,000!"

Once in a while the literature was accurate. One ad guaranteed that Canada was "free of malaria." Nobody could argue with that. And the Chalmers family from Scotland — charmed by a poster of a woman on horseback, waist-high in an Alberta oat field — emigrated to Langdon, where they actually met the poster woman and bought Topsy, the horse.

The immigrants were not all naive, but they all desperately wanted to believe. Most were fleeing from military service, grinding poverty or near-slavery. Romanian peasants had worked

A CPR colonist car, circa 1908. Passengers were asked to supply their own bedding. Kettles were boiled on a stove at the end of the car.

Saskatchewan Archives Board, R-B3275-2

160 ACRES
FRITT LAND
200 MILLIONER ACRES
i VESTRA
CANADA
TILL
HVARJE
LANDTBRUKARE

Paikallislait Manitobassa ja Luoteisissa territorioissa oikeuttavat jokaisen

200 milj. acresta viljeltävää maata
WESTERN CANADA,
18 vuotta täyttäneen siirtolaisen saamaan 160 acrea vapaata maata.

160 акрів · 130 моргів австр.
※ ВІЛЬНОЇ
ЗЕМЛІ ※
200 мільйонів акрів під управу
в західній
КАНАДЇ ДЛЯ
КОЖДОГО
ОСЕЛЕНЦЯ

for landowners at starvation wages and sometimes had to borrow money at 100% interest. Ukrainian serfs had been forced to doff their hats within 300 feet of the feudal mansion, couldn't marry without the

Emigrants on board Empress of Ireland, *circa 1910, and advertisements in (from top to bottom) Ukrainian, Swedish and Finnish. Translated, the ads are variations on the theme, '160 acres of free land for each immigrant. Two hundred million acres for management in western Canada.'*

Canada's West had free land, an early maturing wheat and a railway to haul people and grain.

lord's permission and could be inducted into the army at the age of twelve. Estonians came because the Czar's government and the Orthodox church were threatening further russification of their homeland, a Russian possession since 1721. Bernhard Roth came to Bow Island to escape Russia's rampant crime and corruption: "A bottle of whiskey could very often get you off if you murdered a man," he said.

Most had owned little or no land. William Rendell came to Lloydminster from Devonshire where he'd paid rent of $10 an acre plus tithes, taxes and wages: "I determined to throw up the life of slavery for others and strike for independence in Canada for good or ill." Other settlers from eastern Canada and the United States came west to find land for a growing brood of sons.[1]

Canada wanted immigrants as badly as they wanted Canada. In the ten years prior to 1900, its population had inched ahead by a mere half-million. Now the country was emerging from a depression. Urbanization and industrialization in Europe had created new markets, particularly for wheat. Choice farmland was getting scarce

[1]A few adventurers — such as Martin Nordegg, 38, director of Germany's largest printing plant but yearning for Canada — had wealthy backers. One morning in 1906 his boss, George Buexenstein, called Nordegg in and proffered his best cigars. "That country Canada is just now in great fashion," announced Buexenstein, as though he had just invented Truth. He and his rich pals had formed a syndicate and raised $60,000 for Nordegg to take abroad and make them all richer. "Be off to your promised land and good luck to you," Buexenstein cried through the cigar smoke. Just like that, Martin went to Canada where, eventually, he founded Nordegg, Alberta.

'Just Landed' Russion immigrants.

and expensive in the US — up to $100 an acre in Kansas, $200 in Illinois. Canada's West had free land, an early maturing wheat and a railway to haul people and grain. All it needed was the people, and not just any people. "None but agriculturalists," ruled Clifford Sifton, until 1905 the federal minister of the Interior (which embraced immigration). "We do not recognize labourers at all." He favoured "a stalwart peasant born on the soil, whose forefathers have been farmers for ten generations."

But Sifton, like a great many federal politicians after him, was concerned not with western Canada's welfare but with a payoff for the East. "We desire, every patriotic Canadian desires, that the great trade of the prairie shall go to enrich our own people in the East," he told a Winnipeg audience in 1904, "to build up the factories and the workshops of eastern Canada, and to contribute in every legitimate way to its prosperity."

To that end, he persuaded the railways to open up 22.5 million acres of valuable untaxed prairie land and simplified the process of acquiring homesteads: each settler could get a quarter-section of land (160 acres) in any area declared open for settlement. For a $10 fee he had three years to "prove up," meaning live there at least six months of every year, cultivate land, put up

Homesteaders on the trail in 1910. 'What are you doing in this godforsaken place?' asked the wild stranger.

By wagon to a lush, green land of promise

THE DROUGHT-STRICKEN FOSTER FAMILY DREAMED OF SOUNDING LAKE, SO THEY MADE A 160-MILE TRIP ACROSS THE TRACKLESS PRAIRIES

At noon on June 14, 1909, William Foster, wife Hester, their six children aged six weeks to twelve years, and two neighbours loaded wagons and headed north from Irvine to Sounding Lake, between present-day Consort and Provost. It is about 160 miles (255 km) on today's roads — an easy afternoon's trip. It took the Fosters three weeks.

That was in no way extraordinary, given the weather, awful trails and predictable mishaps of 1909. Which is why their journey, as eloquently recorded later by oldest daughter Margaret, is a prime example of what all immigrant settlers endured when entering Alberta by trail.

Foster and family had settled in Irvine, east of Medicine Hat, in 1904. By 1908 drought had brought him to his knees. Sounding Lake sounded like heaven on earth: hay meadows as far as the eye could see, ample water, timber for building, wild fruit and game. Scottish newcomers James Watt and William Morgan, whom the Fosters had befriended, were looking for land too.

There was an alternative route: by train from The Hat to Calgary, train again to Lacombe, then 75 miles by wagon. The Fosters opted for the long trail, and planned it months in advance. Hester sewed heavy factory cotton into a tent, twelve feet square. They packed a month's food: sacks of sugar, flour, rolled oats, a side of pork, 100 pounds of beans, a huge baking

YOU NEED CANADA NEEDS YOU

A London bus, 1907. Initially, Britain was Canada's primary advertising target.

of bread. Into crocks went butter, matches, soap, lard, salt, coffee, tea, yeast cakes, canned milk and dried fruit. They'd have a hot meal morning and night and sandwiches for lunch.

To fit everything into one wagon and a democrat, the men packed only basics: a dismantled disc and sulky plough, garden and carpenter's tools, several axes, three saws. They pushed off down a faint trail through tall grass, blazed by Mounties and surveyors in years past. Watt drove the lead wagon with Frolic, a colt, tethered behind. Minnie the miniature collie trotted beside him in the other wheel-mark. The Fosters followed in their best democrat, towing a second dilapidated democrat with sewing machine, cookstove and the daily lunch.

The air was fresh after a heavy rain (which Foster could have used in other years). During a thunderstorm that afternoon, Frolic broke loose and ran away. There were no fences. Was he lost forever? But after sampling freedom and tender grass, he obediently fell back into place behind his wagon.

That night, as every night, they camped near water, raised the tent, unloaded the stove, put up four feet of stove pipe and lit a fire of buffalo chips. A pot of beans for the next night was set to simmering. Hester made biscuits and spooned out hot pork and beans, with stewed dried fruit for dessert. Older daughters Marion and Margaret washed dishes and tucked young Harry, Rose and Julia into their bedrolls. By dark everyone was asleep. At dawn after porridge and pancakes they were off again.

''This will all be settled some day,'' William sometimes said, sweeping an arm toward the empty horizon. It was hard to believe. Not until four days later did they see a living soul: at Montgomery's Landing beside the South Saskatchewan River. Ferryman Montgomery, his wife and four children lived in a cabin with a sign, "Meals, 50¢": one of the West's many "stopping-houses."

It poured rain that night and the next morning. Everything in and around the tent was soaked. Montgomery lent them an unused log shack. The grateful Fosters stayed three days while the skies cleared, the trail dried and industrious Hester washed and ironed clothes, baked more bread and cooked fresh fruit.

Then, back on the trail, "two slender black lines drawn in the living green of the plain, merging at length into a tiny spear joining earth to heaven," Margaret wrote. Occasionally, bachelors or little families waved from lonely sod shacks with lambs' quarters growing two feet high from the roofs.

One afternoon, halfway through the trek, they rolled down a long slope into Buffalo Coulee, an old riverbed. The loose whitish soil grew steadily softer. The men stopped, pondered, and pressed on. Both wagons sank to the hubcaps.

The men stepped down; the ground held them. Another fifteen feet and they'd be in the clear. They unhitched both teams, drove them to dry land, hitched them to a heavy logging chain hooked to the wagon pole. With much heaving and cajoling, they dragged out wagon and democrats. It took most of the afternoon. They camped early that night, counting their blessings.

Suddenly a wild-eyed stranger lunged over a hill: tall, thin, blue smock and overalls, grey hair and bushy beard topped with a battered hat. He strode into their midst shrilling, "What in the world are you doing in this godforsaken place? A woman and children too! What are you doing here? Where are you going?" They began to explain but with a wave he stomped out of sight. The travellers laughed uneasily, but next day found nothing more godforsaken than they'd already seen.

Finally the landscape changed: meadows, clumps of trees, running streams. Clouds of mosquitoes descended; the travellers ate and slept around smudges. On their twentieth day they rounded upon a small pretty lake. Poplars, willows, reeds and bulrushes lined its shore; countless waterfowl skimmed its surface. Around lay oceans of grass and, on a far horizon, the Neutral Hills. A mile away stood a few buildings and a corral, the only sign of humanity.

The Fosters were still a few miles from their permanent home, but the journey was over. The next morning they began their new life in hospitable pioneer fashion: by inviting their neighbours over for breakfast.   — *R.C.*

English immigrants picnicking in the Ranfurly area, early 1900s. Carefully edited letters from British settlers were used in the campaign to bring more.

buildings and fences. If he lived up to the bargain, the land was his, and he could buy a second quarter-section, called a pre-emption. Canadian veterans of the Boer War were issued a "scrip," entitling each to a half-section of any unclaimed land open for settlement in the West.

On Sifton's signal, the mighty publicity mill began to roll. Pamphlets, maps, atlases and ads poured from the Department of the Interior, railways, private land companies and from the Western Canadian Immigration Association (founded by major land dealers). Their titles sang bewitching songs: *The Wondrous West; Great Growth of Western Canada; Prosperity Follows Settlement in Western Canada; The Western Plains of Canada Rediscovered; Western Canada, the Greatest Wheat Growing Country in the World; The Canadian West, Strides that Have Been Made in Recent Years; Western Canada, Land of Unequalled Opportunity;* and *Canada, the Granary of the World.*[2]

Over six months in 1900 the Immigration branch sent out more than a million pieces of literature; by 1906 it was shipping three million pieces in nine months. Initially, the heaviest concentration was on Britain, for political and sentimental reasons. The 1902-03 promotion budget was: Britain, $205,000; the US, $161,000; continental Europe, $69,000. The durable farmers of rural Scotland and northern England were prime targets. The Scots came, but England sent a disappointing mix of mostly inexperienced urban folk.

Sifton then turned his attention to American farmers. "The first great demand," said his 1901 *Atlas of Western Canada*, "is for persons with some capital." Men with less than $250 were urged to first gain money and experience as hired hands. A $500 stake was better; $1,000 to $5,000 better still. The Americans usually qualified. By 1902 advertisements ran in 7,000 American rural and agricultural newspapers.

Part of the admen's art was persuading Americans that Canada had a potential wheat-growing area four times bigger than the American one, and was not one gigantic iceberg. Thus the bitter western winter became "bracing," the weather so salubrious that "the soft maple tree has been known to grow more than five feet in a single season." Western Canada could support fifty

Glenbow Archives, NA-1328-64437

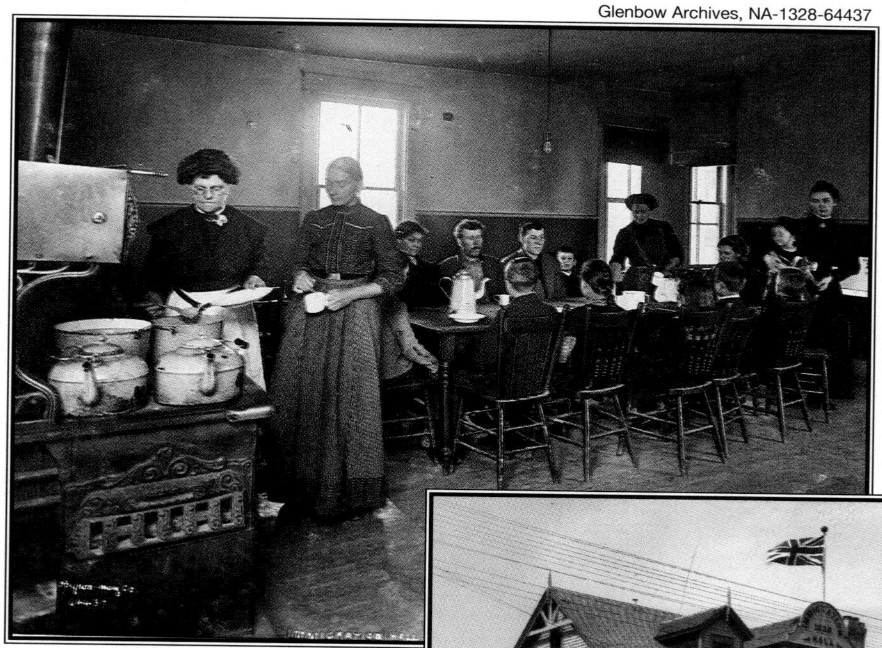

Provincial Archives of Alberta, B4478

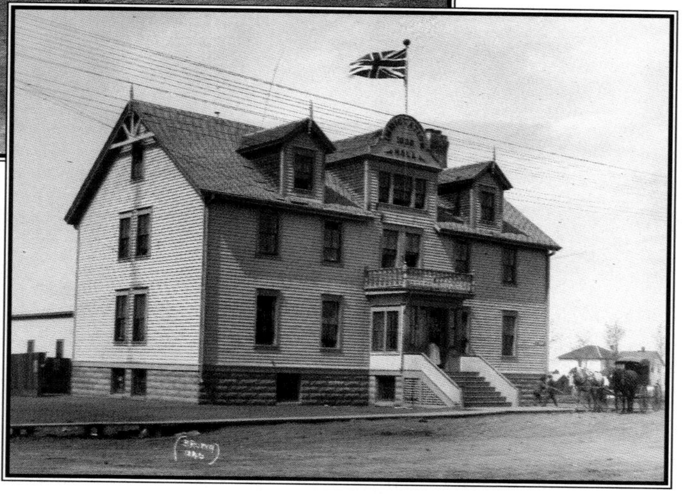

Interior and exterior of the immigration hall in Edmonton; (below) conciliatory cartoon that appeared in a brochure of the day. The Department of the Interior also took its show on the road.

million people and was "the largest continuous wheatfield in the world." The North-West Mounted Police figured prominently as symbols of Canadian law, order and historical romance. In one advertisement, a Mountie's horse had red-stained hooves from trotting through endless prairie vistas of wild strawberries.

Published advertising was only a part of the campaign. The Department of the Interior took its travelling road show to major American fairs, handing out pamphlets by the thousands. It ran western tours for the international press, with food and drink galore. Newsmen were urged to stress the fertile soil, the fine crops and the laughing, prosperous settlers which, as luck would have it, had been shown them. The journalistic freeloaders, Sifton told parliament, would "go back to their homes and give favourable reports about what they have seen...It does not cost much and it is the very best kind of advertising we can get."

Immigration also established eighteen salaried agents in the US.[3] During 1904-05 alone, they fielded 70,948 letters asking about the Canadian West.[4] For a while, agents employed sub-agents who, rather like bounty hunters, were paid by the head: $3 for each male settler lured to Canada, $2 a woman, $1 a child. Agents helped ease immigrants into Canada with a Settlers' Certificate that let them travel from border to debarkation point for one cent a mile. The CPR went one better, offering settlers free transport *within* the United States, through arrangement with American railways.

In 1905, as 55,000 Americans poured in, supporters of the Empire began fretting over

Glenbow Archives

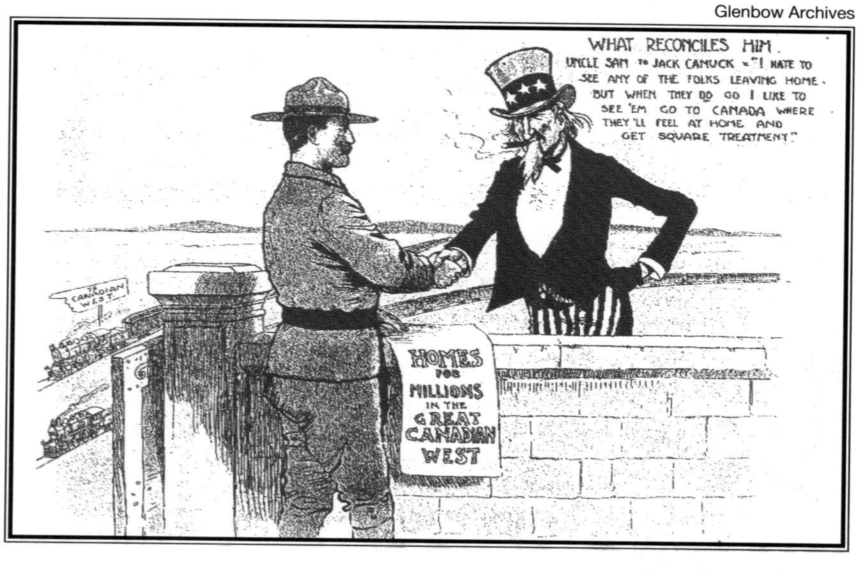

[2]Perhaps the most seductive and oft-quoted propaganda piece was the Immigration Branch's first magazine-style brochure. Its cover shouted:

CANADA WEST
THE LAST BEST WEST
HOMES FOR MILLIONS

A garland of golden maple leaves embraced an idyllic scene: farmer driving a binder through wheat higher than a horse's belly, perfect stooks, handsome farmstead with windmill and tree belt. And down in the corner as a little teaser: "Ranching, Dairying, Grain Raising, Fruit Raising, Mixed Farming."

[3]Sifton also set up agents in Europe, with incentive bonuses. The heads of families had to be farmers, have at least $100 on arrival, and meet all other immigration requirements. Between 1899 and 1906 when the contract was cancelled, these special agents sent close to 71,000 immigrants to Canada and were paid $367,245, averaging about $5 a head.

[4]The shrewd Sifton printed an annual western Canada "Harvest Edition" at his Manitoba Free Press and shipped it in bulk for distribution among US farmers in the winter when they had time to read, and dream.

Englishmen newly arrived, 1906. Jokes about Blighty's unprepared sons abounded.

Of king, country and severe incompetence

THE SONS OF BRITAIN NEVER FALTERED IN THEIR LOVE OF THE MOTHERLAND. IT WAS THE LAND THEY'D COME TO THEY COULDN'T MUCH ABIDE

So bad was their reputation for arrogance and ineptness that by mid-decade "No English Need Apply" signs blossomed across the West. Jokes abounded: one prairie settler swore his English neighbour sowed three bags of oatmeal in the fields so he could grow his own porridge. Another settler hired an English cattle herder who "had a positive talent for sleeping" on the job. A Rocky Mountain guide remembered, "Wherever you went you found some damfool Englishman looking for the outer rim of beyond the beyond." He recalled four English ditchdiggers talking to each other in Latin. "The foreman thought they were plotting against the government!"

In London, even *The Times* turned on them in 1903: "If one in four of these young Englishmen have any substantial balance of capital to show in half a dozen years, it would surprise those who best know their type; and in too many cases it is their own fault. Drink, idleness and restlessness are the most fertile causes of failure, while the lack of experience without sometimes the sense or modesty to recognize it, and take advice, has been too often the bane of others..."

A visitor from Leeds in 1906 confirmed for his countrymen that English were unpopular in Canada; indeed, employers preferred Swedes, Russians, Germans, "even Galicians" because they worked harder. Clifford Sifton, who in the beginning ardently courted all Britons, finally grumbled, "An Englishman out of a job in Canada generally, on examination, is discovered to be addicted to drink."

Yet it was Canada's fault as much as theirs. Most experienced English farmers were content to stay home. Many of the well-meaning novices who came — shopkeepers, coal miners, druggists, ordinary labourers, at least one gymnast and one jockey — couldn't cope with pioneer life.[a] Most recruiting literature had played down western Canada's hardships. As the *Edmonton Journal* summed up, "One cannot look at these hundreds of town-bred people without feeling that their presence is a mistake."

Immigration officials tried to head off misfits, but they often slipped through via such organizations as the Salvation Army, East End Immigration Fund or Self Help Emigration

Society. An English magistrate reportedly scolded a young criminal: "You have broken your mother's heart, you have brought down your father's grey hairs in sorrow to the grave. You are a disgrace to your country. Why don't you go to Canada?" The *Calgary Herald* was more specific: Alfred Smith, 15, charged with theft in Birmingham, was ordered shipped to

sion. Their cocksure attitude and veneration of all things English didn't help. A London journalist travelling among them in 1907 reported, "They talk of 'the flag' and 'the old country' with an effusive affection that startles the mere Englishman."

Many settled in the foothills from Priddis to Pincher Creek,

A remittance man named Buck came to Alberta with $10,000 cash and a quarterly stipend of $250. He lost his ranch to his foreman and ended up as the cook.

Canada as "the only course which suggests itself."

Remittance men, those ne'er-do-well sons of the rich and titled, became symbols of English failure (Vol. I, p. 196). Many were from private schools and comfortable estates. Elder brothers had taken over the family professions, so the younger ones came to Canada to seek fortunes or just to get out of pater's hair. Nicknamed from the occasional money gifts from home that kept them alive, they were objects of endless deri-

playing at ranching and clinging to such upper-crust pursuits as polo, cricket, the fox hunt (with coyote substitutes) and horseracing. Dressing for dinner meant, to most settlers, putting on a clean shirt; the young Brits donned dinner jackets.

Farmer Frank Gilbert Roe knew a remittance man named Buck who'd been such a consummate drunk and layabout in Lincolnshire that his family shipped him to Alberta with $10,000 cash plus a quarterly stipend of $250. Buck bought a ranch, diddled it away until his foreman took over, and ended up as cook on his erstwhile property.

All of this was a bitter pill back home. The breed that built the Empire was being scorned in a mere dominion! When Canada tightened its immigration laws in 1906 — providing in part for deportation of any who became a public charge, the English were the losers.[b] An aggrieved *Yorkshire Post* complained that the law might have been enacted in some quite alien country "instead of a part of the Empire." Canada had a right to bar undesirable aliens, sniffed the *Post*, but how dare it bar people from the country "which bears the naval expenses of the Empire?" Another amendment in 1910 requiring "aided" immigrants to get farm employment or go home enraged London's immigration societies. They demanded, in vain, that the British parliament intervene.

In time the English regained esteem, particularly when they marched away to fight for King and Empire in the First World War. Many persevered to become fine farmers. And if their temporary fall from grace taught a modicum of humility to turn-of-the-century Colonel Blimps, it was a tiny but useful step in Canada's growing-up.

— *R.C.*

[a]Sifton's successor, Frank Oliver, abandoned this restriction of immigrants to farmers only, a move Sifton considered disastrous. By bringing in "the mechanic, the artisan and the drifter," Sifton said, Oliver "flooded Canada, and would have precipitated a crisis in labour if it had not been for the war...They are hopelessly incapable of going on farms and succeeding..."

[b]In the first year of its enactment, 833 British and only 43 Americans were deported.

National Archives of Canada, 1122-5

Hunters and dogs at the Rawlinson Brothers' Ranch west of Calgary in the early 1900s. The re-creation of home included recreating the recreations.

A family of black settlers at Vulcan, 1903. Herbert Darby, Mrs. Darby, her sister and the three Darby children. Herbert Darby was the first cook in the Imperial Hotel when it was moved to Vulcan from Frank after the Frank slide (see Sect. 5, ch. 8).

The people seemed to be mostly from the States, some having resided there about eight or nine years and they all seemed happy and prosperous and they speak well of the country...The grass was in abundance. I saw a trainload of cattle that was being shipped to British Columbia which they said had not been fed a bit of grain and which was equal to our corn fed cattle...I fetched potatoes which made our potato raisers to wonder at their size; parsnips that were nearly two feet long; carrots that were sixteen inches long and thirteen inches in circumference...
- R. Roper, of Iowa, who visited the Lacombe area in 1901, in a letter published in The Hard Wheat Belt.

Americanization.[5] When an American theatre company visiting Edmonton "gave over-prominence to the flag of the Republic," the audience hissed. Conversely, the playing of *God Save the King* brought "a storm of applause," the *Edmonton Journal* noted approvingly, confirming that hearts in the Canadian West still "beat strongly for the British connection."

A report from England reflected the Old Country's concern: Canada, Britain's colonial gem, and especially Alberta, "the pick of the basket among Canadian provinces," was becoming disgustingly American. The news, clothes, hotels, twang of speech, even the humour was American. "Baseball and trotting races are prominent among popular sports while cricket and rugby football, the ball games of the Empire, find little favour. Drinks, from ice water to the complex cocktail, are American. So are the universal domestic cigar and the interminable chewing of peanuts." How to rescue the colony from this Yankee plague? "The only salvation of Canada...rests upon her cultivation of imperialism."

Reporters from all over the globe were wined and dined and encouraged to spread the word. So inspired, a visiting newsman compared Medicine Hat favourably with Chicago.

The masterminds at the Department of the Interior thrived on the controversy. It was perhaps no accident that in 1907 the London *Star* interviewed an expatriate Briton who had "made a fortune in thirteen years in Calgary" as a lumber dealer. He told readers that "Americans and foreigners are fast piling up fortunes in Alberta because the Englishman won't come to his own colony." It was a lovely touch: if avarice wouldn't lure good farmers out of Yorkshire and Lancashire, then maybe patriotism would.

Canada also sent successful immigrant farmers back home to praise the promised land. Immigration produced a pamphlet of carefully edited letters from British farmers exalting western Canada's wonders. Sometimes the propaganda shone through, as in one expatriate's breathless account: "Canada cannot be spelt in letters large enough. It is the beauty spot of the world. It will give employment to all who honestly want it the moment the emigrant arrives."

Newspapers got on the bandwagon. In Toronto *The News* did a Lewis Carroll parody:

> You are rich, Father William, the young man said
> Yet in youth you had never a nickel.
> Since you came to the West Dame Fortune you've wed.
> Now how won you a woman so fickle?
> In the bush in the East, the old man replied,
> I chopped out a homestead for Mary.
> But in the journey toward Wealth we've made better speed
> Since we took up a farm on the prairie...

The *Edmonton Bulletin* published scores of tips for settlers: "How much money will it take to build a small shack and stable? Labour performed by self, $40 to $75"..."What are the market prices for produce? Eggs, 20¢. Butter, 20¢."

Individual communities trumpeted their wonders. A Wetaskiwin brochure revealed that it was "picturesque...very rich soil...well-to-do and energetic settlers...hotel accommodation second to none." Was any place on earth a more congenial spot?

Yes. Medicine Hat proclaimed itself "city of eternal light"; "best mixed farming district in the world"; "climate is the finest on the continent." The Hat claimed its natural gas ("finest, purest ever found in British North America") made it immune to "thunderstorms and other elements

---

Visible minorities were not encouraged. 'Negroes not wanted in the province of Alberta,' cried the *Albertan*. The IODE ladies lived in fear of ravishment.

---

which interfere with electric light." A visiting newsman — perhaps fed, watered and curried by local boosters — compared Medicine Hat favourably with Chicago and Hanchow, China.

Competing cities were not above skulduggery. When Ontario widow Elizabeth Moon reached Calgary with her eight children in 1905, local land developers warned her to stay away from that wilderness, Edmonton. It was dangerous and would never be good for anything but hunting and trapping. Widow Moon went anyway, started a boarding house and was not eaten by bears.

From the beginning, all immigrants were not created equal. Italians, Greeks and Jews were deemed unsuitable farmers. Central Europeans for a while were known as "Sifton's dirty Slavs"

A Ukrainian By Any Other Name

Confusion about the names of the various groups of ethnic Ukrainians who emigrated to Canada in the early years of the century can be clarified a little by looking at a map of pre-1914 eastern Europe. People who spoke Ukrainian were divided among the pre-war Austro-Hungarian and Russian empires. In the Austro-Hungarian empire the name "Ukrainian" was just taking hold around 1900 and the traditional "Ruthenian" (Rusyn) was still widespread. In Canada, immigrants from Austria-Hungary were often called "Austrian" from the state they came from, or "Galician" or "Bukovinian" from the province they came from. Some were called "Russians" or "Little Russians," as were the Ukrainian immigrants from the Russian empire. The general derogatory terms "Hunky" (Hungarian) or "Bohunk" (Bohemian and Hungarian) were at times applied to Ukrainians. The term "Ukrainian" gained ascendancy in western Canada just before and after the First World War. It was popularized by the Ukrainian intelligentsia in Canada and by identification with the Ukrainians' struggle for independence in 1917-1921. In 1921, the Canadian census reflected these developments and gave the option to declare "Ukrainian" as a national origin.

- *Frank Sisyn, acting director, Canadian Institute of Ukrainian Studies, Edmonton.*

[5]America, alarmed at the haemorrhage of its farmers, fought back. Montana opened large tracts of vacant land with irrigation, begging American farmers to try it first. Florida ran ads extolling its fruit groves and golden climate. New England advised its locals to stay home and turn their stony fields into profitable sheep farms. In South Dakota a booklet, *Saved From the Clutches of the King*, described a fictional American rescued from imperialist Canada in the nick of time. An anonymous poet in North Dakota retaliated in doggerel:

> If Medicine Hat were blown away,
> Clear down to the equator, say,
> Then all the beastly cold would flit
> To some place where they've need of it.

Immigrants aboard the SS Empress of Britain, circa 1910.

and his "grand 'roundup' of European freaks and hoboes." The *Calgary Herald* in 1901 argued strongly against Galicians (from the Austro-Hungarian Empire) and Doukhobors; these former serfs could not "assume the same political position as their English-speaking neighbours." (Five years later the same paper accepted the province's 45,000 Galicians with equanimity.)

Blacks and Orientals were treated as creatures from an alien planet. In Banff, the *Crag and Canyon* reflected a common view in a 1903 article. A local "Chinaman" had said something "objectionable" to a white man "who in his wrath struck the heathen in the face" giving him a black eye and a nosebleed. The assailant was fined $5 and costs but the *Crag and Canyon* blamed the victim: "The young man who committed the assault cannot suffer much discredit in public opinion...whether or not the heathen was to blame for the breach of the peace it is a reasonable conclusion that had not the dozen or more Chinamen been imported here the court records would yet be clean. Chinamen and white men do not mix any better than glue and perfume."

A similarly racist *Lethbridge Herald* in 1907 urged the Alberta government to deny Japanese or "a Chinaman" the vote: "Make these yellow men understand we are not going to allow them to secure any influence in our affairs. They have no right to compete with white labour and neither have they any right to compete with white votes..." Later that year a mob attacked a Lethbridge Chinese restaurant because a "celestial" had allegedly killed someone with a hammer.

Public Archives of Canada, 1C-9660

When blacks showed an interest in Canada, the invitation to Paradise was abruptly cancelled. The Department of the Interior tried hard to persuade them the climate was too cold. In 1910 Alberta went berserk when facing possible immigration of Oklahoma's Creek-Negroes (blacks who had intermarried with Indians and were now fleeing racism at home). "Negroes Not Wanted in Province of Alberta," cried the *Albertan*. Around Edmonton where blacks had already taken farms, boards of trade, women's organizations, press and local trades and labour councils sounded the alarm. A petition with more than 3,000 signatures warned the federal government of "the serious menace to the future welfare of a large portion of western Canada, by reason of the alarming influx of negro settlers." The "menace" seemed to be fear of racial violence and, in a separate petition from the Imperial Order Daughters of the Empire, that black men would ravage white women.

Frank Oliver, Sifton's successor

Chinese immigrants — many had laboured on the CPR, and set up laundries and restaurants all over the prairies.

as Minister of the Interior, sent an emissary to Oklahoma. He conveniently reported that Creek-Negroes carried "all the evil traits of a life of rapine and murder." Oliver drafted an order-in-council to bar for one year "any immigrant belonging to the Negro race, which race is deemed unsuitable to the climate and requirements of Canada." The order was never passed, but an informal program of Interior Department foot-dragging and discouragement slowed black arrivals to a trickle. By 1911 there were only 1,524 blacks in the western provinces. About 1,000 settled in Alberta, primarily around what are now Wildwood, Breton and Barrhead and the community of Amber Valley east of Athabasca.[6]

Those lucky American whites who got into Canada by accident of racial acceptability came in covered wagons, railway colonist coaches or boxcars (sometimes stowing away to save money, until they reached the welcoming border). Many left behind prosperous but small properties to find space for their growing families. George Starke, for one, sold an excellent wheat farm and eleven-room house near Spokane in 1909 and took his wife and seven children to more land and a one-room shack seventy miles from Stettler.

Most American immigrants were comparatively better off than Europeans,[7] who were often hard-pressed to scratch together the required minimum money, find their way to a port and endure a horrible ocean journey. Most of the bewildered Europeans had never left their villages before, much less gone abroad.

Getting there from abroad meant cheap ocean travel, sleeping in tiers of crude bunks, and enduring fierce gales, vomiting passengers and incipient mutinies.

Fares varied with season and the travel company. One family went from Liverpool to Winnipeg for $15 ocean fare (steerage) and $18 railway (tourist car) per person.[8] Cheap ocean travel meant sleeping in tiers of crude bunks with a mattress (if any) of straw, amid fierce gales and vomiting passengers. In 1903, aboard the SS *Lake Manitoba*, a converted Boer War troop ship, 2,684 men, women and children were packed into communal cabins and steerage like sardines.[9] It was recorded as a peaceable journey: "Only eleven fights, seven incipient mutinies and three riots..."

Sometimes the stench below decks was so foul that a whiff made stewards sick too. Edward and John Roberts from Wales booked $15 passages to Canada on a harvest excursion. "I became so sick I thought I was going to die," John remembered. "Then I got worse and was afraid I

[6]By the 1930s Amber Valley had 350 black residents, a famous baseball team and lively community spirit but, like so many other small prairie places, it disappeared after the Second World War.

[7]There were exceptions. After thirty years of marriage and six children, university-educated Sarah Ellen Roberts and her husband, an Illinois doctor, had a $1,200 house bearing a $200 mortgage, and a cemetery plot, as total assets. In 1906, in their fifties, they started over as Alberta homesteaders. Railway berths at $7 each were too expensive so the coach travellers "slept little at night for we had to sit bolt upright." They subsisted on a lunch Mrs. Roberts had packed.

[8]Some European immigrants were sponsored by charitable organizations, or the Salvation Army which in 1907 booked as many as 500 passages at a time. The London Daily Telegraph raised £15,000 in subscriptions of one shilling each, to send 250 poor families to Canada. Sponsored immigrants were supposed to repay the debt on a monthly basis.

[9]Authorities advised emigrants to pack everything in trunk-size wicker baskets — light, capacious, inexpensive and strong enough to withstand rough handling.

Preaching the gospel of racial exclusion

SOCIALIST J.S. WOODSWORTH OPPOSED THE IMMIGRATION SCHEME BECAUSE IT DILUTED THE PURITY OF THE ANGLO-SAXON STOCK

Western Canada Pictorial Index, 031-921

"The very qualities of intelligence and manliness which are essential for citizenship in a democracy were systematically expunged from the Negro race through two hundred years of slavery..."

These inflammatory words were not uttered by some redneck Dixie sheriff or imperial wizard of the Ku Klux Klan. They appeared in a 1909 book assembled by the patron saint of Canadian socialism: Rev. James Shaver Woodsworth, Methodist minister, superintendent of Winnipeg's All Peoples' Mission for the needy, and first leader of the Co-operative Commonwealth Federation (now the New Democratic Party).

True, those particular words were not his own. Woodsworth's *Strangers Within Our Gates* was a pastiche of his

Rev. J.S. Woodsworth and his book. His and other contributors' opinions ranged from the politically incorrect to the blatantly racist.

and other writers' thoughts about immigrants. The indictment of Negroes came from an American magazine, *Chautauquan*. But after citing it, Woodsworth commented, "Whether we agree with that conclusion or not, we may be thankful that we have no 'Negro problem' in Canada." He let these and other statements — ranging from politically incorrect to blatantly racist by today's standards — travel under his byline.

Woodsworth tried hard to reconcile his basic decency with the mores of his time and the mission of his church: turning immigrants into worthy Canadians and Christians. He wrote *Strangers Within Our Gates* to "introduce the motley crowd of immigrants to our Canadian people." His concern for their welfare shone through. But he also catalogued them by race, nationality or religion: who was or wasn't desirable, reflecting contemporary fears and bigotry, if not his own.

The tone was set by J.W. Sparling, principal of Winnipeg's Methodist Wesley College. His introduction commended the book to all "who are desirous of understanding and grappling with this great national danger. For there is a danger and it is national! Either we must educate and elevate the incoming multitudes or they will drag us and our children down to a lower level..."

The compassionate Woodsworth told heart-rending tales of immigrants' poverty and hardship. Then he labelled them. The Bohemians (or Czechs) were "the most intelligent and

progressive of the Slavic races." Germans were "among our best immigrants...Even those who detest 'foreigners' make an exception of Germans, whom they classify as 'white people like ourselves.'" The Scots, Irish and Welsh got passing grades; the English less so "due partly to a national characteristic, which is at once a strength and a weakness — lack of adaptability." Most Americans received a thumbs-up for energy, know-how and adaptability. But the Mormons caused the reverend gentleman's gorge to rise.

"Though Americans, they are in no true sense American," he wrote, "and their presence is a serious menace to our western civilization...The practice of polygamy will subvert our most cherished institutions. But more dangerous even than polygamy is the utter surrender of personal liberty, and the acknowledgement of the absolute authority of the priesthood...Can we as Canadians remain inactive while this 'politico-ecclesiastical' system is fastening itself upon our western territory?"

He was easier on Mennonites: "The Mennonite vote is now not to be despised; indeed, in Alberta a Mennonite sits in the legislature." Although "they are actually some seven hundred years behind the times" he found in them the makings of good citizens, "a strong race physically — far from degenerates — they are sober, industrious, and thrifty."

Woodsworth's chosen contributor, Arthur R. Ford of the *Winnipeg Telegram,* was rough on central Europeans. He found it "difficult for us to think of [Poles] other than in that vague class of undesirable citizens," although acknowledging their contributions to the world's science, literature, music and art.

Galicians, from the Austro-Hungarian empire, were rated illiterate, ignorant and in such low esteem "that the word is almost a term of reproach. Their unpronounceable names appear so often in police court news, they figure so frequently in crimes of violence that they have created anything but a favourable impression." Centuries of poverty and oppression had "to some extent animalized" the Galician, Ford wrote. "Drunk he is quarrelsome and dangerous...But he is patient and industrious...He is eager to become Canadianized..."

Ford dismissed Turks, Albanians, Greeks, Macedonians and Bulgarians as "a simple sluggish people who have been oppressed and down-trodden for ages; therefore it can scarcely be expected that they can land in this country, and at once fall in with our peculiar ways, and understand or appreciate our institutions."

Woodsworth himself contributed the appraisal of Orientals. They "cannot be assimilated," he said. "Whether it is in the best interests of Canada to allow them to enter in large numbers is a most important question, not only for the people of British Columbia but for all Canadians." The problem: they took low-wage labouring jobs that white men might (more likely might not) do. "Should they be excluded — if so, on what grounds?...There is, no doubt, a national prejudice that should be overcome. On the other hand, the expression, 'This is a white man's country,' has deeper significance than we sometimes imagine."

The Christian minister even had problems with the thou-sands of wretched waifs shipped over from English slums and orphanages: "Children from such surroundings with inherited tendencies to evil are a very doubtful acquisition to Canada...We would not refuse to help the needy. But we must express fear that any large immigration of this class must lead to degeneration of our Canadian people."

How to "assimilate" the newcomers? That was Woodsworth's and Canada's burning concern. "Peoples emerging from serfdom, accustomed to despotism, untrained in the principles of representative government, without patriotism — such peoples are utterly unfit to be trusted with the ballot," he wrote. Granted, "we must divest ourselves of a certain arrogant superiority and exclusiveness, perhaps characteristic of the English race...We must in many ways meet these people half way — seek to sympathize with their difficulties, and to encourage them in every forward movement. Only those who in time can take their place as worthy fellow citizens should be admitted to our Canadian heritage."

Woodsworth, in later life a champion of the working man,[a] was in 1909 simply a product of his time. For him and his contemporaries, newcomers ought to behave like white Anglo-Saxon Protestants if they wanted to get ahead. Far more horrific: six years later the saintly Woodsworth recommended a western school of eugenics (improvement of the race by breeding those with desirable genes)[b] and ultimately favoured sterilization of "mental defectives."

— *R.C.*

[a]Woodsworth was arrested as one of the leaders of the Winnipeg general strike of 1919. For eighteen years he was a federal MP for the Manitoba Independent Labour Party and became first leader of the CCF in 1933.

[b]University of Alberta PhD student Terry Chapman wrote in her dissertation, "Woodsworth's eventual support of a sterilization program appeared to be the result of a deep-seated frustration in coping with the complexity of the immigration problem. Thus, a simple prejudice against the foreigner was transformed into an acceptance of a eugenics program." Woodsworth was a dominant member of the Bureau of Social Research convened by the three prairie governments. It reported, in part, "Mental defectives are here in hundreds; they are multiplying rapidly; more are coming in every ship-load of immigrants." This culminated in Alberta's Act of Sexual Sterilization of 1928.

Provincial Archives of Alberta, B-5584

The Galician Hay Market in Edmonton, 1903. Among Woodsworth's least favourite.

The photographer captioned this 'Necessity Has No Law,' referring to the horse teamed with an ox. The photo was taken near Edmonton about 1900.

Passed MacGregor, also Carberry. Just saw four teams, four horse each, loaded with settlers' effects. I have just been talking to a western farmer. He says the crops are all burned up with the dry weather. I now see farmers ploughing down their crops, not worth harvesting. What I have seen of Canada so far is very discouraging...The general impression all along the line is that the people are staying in this country for a living or perhaps for money; comforts are not considered.
- from among the complaints in a diary written aboard the CPR by a turn-of-the-century English settler travelling tourist class between Montreal and Calgary.

wouldn't." Often the staple diet, in those days before refrigeration, was bad fish and worse pork. Thirty years after, one immigrant couldn't "face the warm smell of pork without sweat starting on my forehead."

Even a cabin on a relatively comfortable vessel, the *Lake Simcoe*, was no picnic. "The waves were breaking right over the ship," recalled Englishwoman Alice Rendell. "The climate was bitterly cold. The captain had to proceed very cautiously owing to fog and icebergs. Tuesday we were surprised to see snow on the decks. It was impossible to keep your footing...A gentleman slipped over the stairs and broke his leg...a foreigner in the steerage cut his throat and is not expected to live..."

On arrival in Halifax or Saint John, immigrants were prodded, poked and interrogated. Immigration officers wanted to know if they were "strong, vigorous, delicate, ruddy or pale." The medical form asked, "Is applicant honest? Sober? Industrious? Thrifty? Of good morals? Is wife good housekeeper and tidy?"

Canada wanted no "idiots, imbeciles, feeble-minded persons, epileptics, insane persons; persons dumb, blind or otherwise physically defective; persons over 15 years of age who are unable to read; persons guilty of any crime involving moral turpitude; beggars, vagrants and persons liable to become a public charge; persons suffering from chronic alcoholism or the drug habit; persons of physical inferiority whose defect is likely to prevent them making their way in Canada; anarchists, agitators..."[10]

The cross-Canada train trip was an endurance test. In 1904 Englishmen George and Alex Salmon safely crossed the Atlantic in six days, a record for a small vessel at that time. What could go wrong now? Plenty. Between Lake Superior and Winnipeg their railway car, insulated with sawdust, caught fire. The brothers finally made it to Calgary, smoky but intact.

For the John Stephensons and their four children, who'd had a comfortable life in England, with servants, the week-long trip in a colonist car was an eye-opener. The seats were wooden slats; travellers slept on them with bedding, if any. They boiled tea and coffee on a stove at one end of the car.

"Our food was kept in a tin box, only the bare essentials, which were replenished at longer stops," wrote daughter Gladys Rowell, long after. "Mostly of bread and very oily butter made into sandwiches with corned beef or other tinned meats, and oranges and apples. At night none of us really undressed. There was not enough privacy."

At Calgary they bedded down in the free immigration hall, across the tracks from where the Palliser Hotel now stands. The hall was a large communal room with a rough table and chairs and a stove for cooking. The government provided light, heat and cooking utensils for a week; settlers supplied their own bedding and food. The upper floor was divided into cubicles with straw mattresses on the floor. "Mother had our fortune, less than $200, tucked into a small pouch pinned to the top of her corset." A kindly station agent and wife invited the Stephensons for supper that first night and warned them to saturate their clothing with evil-smelling sabadilla powder, to ward off "American bedbugs."

Plain though they were, there were worse places than the immigration halls. Captain Charles McCune and family from Missouri lived two weeks in a CPR boxcar on a Red Deer siding and — when the railway claimed it, and with rain pouring — camped in the railway roundhouse until they finally got homesteads.[11]

"The Canadian boom is on," exulted the *Edmonton Journal* in April 1910 (about five years late in discovering the obvious). "Immigration is flowing at flood tide right into the heart of the western prairies and Canada is commencing to reap the harvest of the millions sown in advertising." But exactly what was that "harvest"?

Earlier the *Edmonton Bulletin* had assessed it in dollars and cents. Canada had spent $600,000 in 1907 on advertising, salaries for officers at points of entry, maintaining immigration halls and paying agents. In the previous seven months, 211,859 immigrants arrived in Canada, of whom 39,000 were Americans. Roughly 5,000 of them were well-to-do farmers, bringing an estimated $8,000 cash apiece: $40 million. Others, mostly tradesmen, mechanics and artisans, brought an estimated total of $1,900,000. The 103,000 from the British Isles brought an average of $100 a head: $10,300,000. All told, the *Bulletin* calculated, immigrants had brought at least $55 million cash into Canada in those seven months. Not a bad return for a $600,000 investment.

In Alberta, by decade's end, the largest proportion of immigrants was American (nearly 22 per cent, bestowing on the province some of its distinctive open-handed, entrepreneurial character) and British (nearly 19 per cent). But there were also 41,000 Germans, 29,000 Scandinavians, 20,000 French, 17,000 Ukrainians — from five to 27 times as many of each ethnic group as in 1900. There were also significantly more Dutch, Russian, Italian and other European immigrants. In ten years Alberta had become infinitely more varied, vigorous and ethnically interesting.

Most important, it was stocked with the indomitable kind of pioneer who would form its backbone in the years ahead. People like Charles Malcher who left Sweden in January 1903 on a cattle boat destined for England. He slept on sawdust in the hold. At Liverpool he boarded a steamer carrying 600 passengers and slept with fourteen others in steerage. He ate standing up, from tables slung by ropes. During the trip a four-day storm blew them 400 miles off course.

Nineteen-year-old Malcher reached Wetaskiwin in March with $12 in his pocket. He hitched a ride 25 miles east and walked the last mile and a half to his Uncle Hedlund's homestead, in light clothing through three feet of snow at 25 below zero F.

Welcome to Paradise, Charles Malcher! The hard times have just begun.

[10] In one nine-month period, 1906-1907, the Interior Department rejected at ports of entry 440 immigrants, including 90 deemed "likely to become a public charge," 29 of "bad character," nine as "criminals," eight prostitutes, seven stowaways, four "feeble-minded," three "opium fiends," and one who "ran away from wife."

[11] The Brodies of Massachusetts were more impressed: "The car is well equipped with ice water, wash bowls, clean toilets, plenty of linens, soap, matches, combs, brushes, cuspidors, good cooking stove and portable dining tables..." Once they splurged on breakfast in the diner: boiled eggs, toast, rolled oats, cream, tea, butter, "everything strictly first class" for $1.10 to $2.

Dominion Lands offices, like this one in Prince Albert in 1909, were inundated throughout the first decade with settlers ready to put up the $10 homesteading fee for a quarter-section of land. Alberta's population quintupled.

The mad and frantic rush for land to call your own

FILLING THE WEST WITH PEOPLE AND FAST — THAT WAS OTTAWA'S PLAN.
WHAT THE PEOPLE DID ONCE THEY ARRIVED WAS LARGELY THEIR PROBLEM

by COURTNEY TOWER

Well, John Hawkes, how do you think we've turned out, nine or so decades later?

In February 1901 the *Calgary Herald* featured a long article by this western journalist, a writer who delights sometimes in his own inventive imagery. Hawkes describes the North-West Territories exuberantly, as "a very respectable Babel...a land of many peoples and tongues." Just

so. Early in Alberta's most tumultuous decade of growth, the fluid decade that set her nature, Hawkes is seeing the ingredients pouring in generously.

"We once met a man on horseback on a prairie trail who proved to be a Syrian from Damascus, the oldest city in the world, wherein is the street called Straight," he writes, unable to link the raw new trail to the ancient city's street. "In the unsurveyed lands of the Beaver Hills, we partook of the hospitality of a Frenchman who had farmed sixteen years in Algeria," he says, now ploughing more likely ground. "Recently we met a man not long arrived from India. French scouts we have met in plenty, while the young sprigs of the British aristocracy who 'haw haw' so languidly...are almost too numerous to mention."

With the attitude of the day, Hawkes writes of finding a few *Japs* at Medicine Hat ("little Orientals" who were "quiet, handy, clean and civil"). He found Chinese ("a small ranche was once pointed out to us in Alberta as being run by two Celestials"). Far more numerous were the northern Europeans of whom he approves, and a medley of "Mormons, Mennonites, Ruthenians, Galicians and Doukhobors."

With such a profusion of races, tongues and creeds, with peoples of "very varying...temperament and moral fibre," Hawkes in 1901 is driven to wonder: "Will the blood mixture produce an improved breed of Britisher or an ethnological mongrel, without any reliable characteristic? This question is one of the first importance to Canada: only time can supply the answer."

Well now, John Hawkes...what do you say?

If great phenomena could talk, what Hawkes was witnessing in 1901 could have told him, earthily, "You ain't seen nothin' yet!" For as he wrote, *real* land fever was transforming Alberta into something he would scarcely have been able to recognize.

Her peoples quintupled from 73,000 then to 374,000 at decade's end. In the ten years, scores of towns and villages emerged. Dominion Lands offices were besieged by crushes of claimants lining the boardwalks through bitter nights of waiting, sometimes to be thumped and shoved out of line by hired thugs called "bullrushers." Sixty-foot-wide lots scarcely yet pegged out on raw land would be bid up overnight to $1,000, $2,000 and more, at the whisper that here, at this special spot in open or wooded wilderness, the magic railroad would be pushing through.

Alberta's population quintupled to 374,000 in the decade. Towns bubbled out of the soil. Impatience and endurance worked in tandem.

Where the trains did stop, at Edmonton, Calgary, Lethbridge, Medicine Hat and lesser points, they dropped off working-class Englishmen in cloth caps (there were far more of them, actually, than toffs in jodhpurs). The trains deposited Ukrainian families with their carved wooden trunks, gaily printed scarves and flaring pants tucked into high boots; Swedes from Sweden and Swedes from South Dakota; Germans from Germany but also from Galicia and Russia and Pennsylvania. Farm settlements were born, or extended, by blacks from Oklahoma, French-speaking farm families from Canada and moneyed folk from France. New languages, foods, religions, lifestyles, arrived and, though begun in mutual isolation and incomprehension, were imprinted upon Alberta. Among the settlers, impatience and endurance worked in tandem, to improve and to prevail.

Terence M'Keone, a lad of twenty (but a veteran of the Boer War where he broke horses for

George Pocaterra doing the laundry outside his cabin in the Highwood River area.

Not very much expense need be gone to in preparing an ice house. Simply put some coal slack or cinders or small poles or brush to provide drainage, then make the cheapest kind of walls and roof, just so the material used to protect the ice, whether it is cut straw or sawdust, can be kept in place. Pack the ice in a solid block in cold weather, cover about a foot deep on sides and top and the job is completed...A pile of ice about ten feet square and five or six feet high will supply the average family, or less, if no dairying is done.
- Farm and Ranch Review.

the English troops), sailed to Canada on the SS *Lake Manitoba* in 1903 with £100 in his pocket and his beloved dog, Biddy, in his arms. On the same ship were 2,000 others from England, the storied, fractured, fractious Barr colonists who dumped the Rev. Isaac Barr as their leader, appointed his deputy in his stead, and left his name on the map of the territories, Lloydminster. By the Vermilion River, young M'Keone built a ten-foot by eight-foot log shack, seven logs high. To provide cash for the breaking, cultivating and fencing of his 160 acres, he trapped, worked out and, when he raised the money to buy a team, hauled mail. He founded a family and paved the way for relatives and friends to come out too: their descendants are scattered through Alberta and beyond.[1]

Mr. and Mrs. Dave Simmons, of Partridge Hill in what was to become Strathcona County east of Edmonton, had been part of a large colony that had come out from Parry Sound, Ontario, in the early 1890s. They were persuaded with free CPR passes to go home and recruit more settlers. They took with them fifty pounds of home-grown wheat, ground into flour, which Mrs. Simmons baked into bread and took to a Christmas 1899 concert to show the bounty of the North-West Territories. In the new century, the Simmons returned with their recruits, in fact the forerunners of the 53,000 Ontarians who by 1910 had joined the 4,500 already there.

Canadians, indeed, were by far the largest group of arrivals in Alberta during the decade, including more than 15,000 French-speaking Quebeckers and former Quebeckers from New England. They found fellow francophones, many of them Metis, already settled in Vegreville and Edmonton, Leduc, Legal and St. Paul. They were almost as isolated by tongue as the Galicians or the Poles, although they were the fourth-largest group in Alberta.

About 80,000 Americans came during the decade, the largest immigrant group entering Canada. By 1911 they accounted for 22 per cent of Alberta's population, although many were returning Canadians and a third were European-born. They included religious groups such as Mormons from Utah, who in 1901 bought 30,000 acres and then a further 226,000 on which to grow sugar beets, put up a sugar beet factory and start the town of Raymond. There were Utopians, such as the French aristocrat who built the settlement of Trochu, and the St. Ann Ranch Trading Company, by the bubbling springs of a quiet, untouched valley of the Red Deer River, on both homestead and Hudson's Bay Company land.

There were feverish speculators, corporate and individual. A British syndicate bought 64,000 southern dryland acres (after a predecessor British scheme had acquired 250,000 acres and failed), and poured the vast sum of $11 million into developing 25,000 acres to begin with. In one year, it had turned the whistlestop of Suffield into a town pulsating with business blocks, banks, homes, stores, livery barns and a famous forty-foot-long bar of solid mahogany in the swank Alamo Hotel. A very few years later, almost all had returned to dust. Some years before, in 1902, the *Calgary Herald* had opposed allowing settlement in arid and

semi-arid areas without sure-fire irrigation plans, rather than the kind that never come into being and leave the settler dry and destitute. Said the *Herald:* "His crops will be so poor that he will have to move out and leave the tombstones behind him."

And there were nervy individuals such as Lou Cavanaugh, who came to Canada with his wife,

(Above) panoramic view of Wainwright in 1909; (below) the first steam threshing machine in Woolford, Alberta, 1903 or 1904. Threshing was done cooperatively, the grain carted to the towns that sprang up around elevators on rail lines.

About 80,000 Americans came during the decade. By 1911 they accounted for 22 per cent of the population.

Anna, and brother, Ed, in a covered wagon from Lansford, North Dakota. Lou and Anna each took out quarter-section homesteads. They also bought six quarters, one and a half sections, of "soldiers' scrip" land, granted to veterans of the Boer War but not taken up. They bought a massive Reeves Steamer and plough that turned over the southern Alberta sod, at Hilda, in long, wide strips. To finance his large ambitions, Lou Cavanaugh brought in new colonists to this Medicine Hat area and set up a general store for them on his farm. He broke scores of miles of sod for others, the old Reeves keeping steam up and two crews busy around the clock. He threshed for others, his big Rumely separator with 44-inch cylinder keeping the teams fetching sheaves on the trot, and the spike pitchers in the fields hopping. Cavanaugh later got up to farming 3,500 acres, it is written, seeding and harvesting with twelve-horse teams.

But by far the greatest number of settlers were single men or individual families who took up the 160-acre free claims, and who sometimes but rarely bought additional land going cheap. Occasionally they squatted on land not yet opened up for settlement, hoping their "squatters' rights" would prevail when it was.

One of these was Charles Christian Jorgenson who drew his all, $400, from the bank at home in Minneapolis and squatted on the north-west quarter of Section 25, Township 59, Range 1, west of the 5th meridian (that is, at Hazel Bluff, later Westlock, north-west of Edmonton). On that $400 he transported himself, wife and seven children from the United States, built a house fourteen feet by twenty feet, with walls of a single ply of siding lumber, and, says son Robert, "in order to really establish himself in this new land [placed]

[1] When the dog Biddy died, she was buried on a sunny slope, a broken wagon tongue plunged into the ground as her marker with the words carved on it, "Biddy M'Keone," her age and date of death. Some years later, when a grown-up Lloydminster was looking for a cemetery location, someone recalled that site, saying "a child is already buried there, by some early settler." The place was chosen, and Biddy may be the only dog in Canada buried in consecrated ground. This is recounted by M'Keone's niece, Theodora C. Reeves.

Illustrated calendar issued by
McCormick Harvesting Machines,
1905.

A number of spectators
assembled and sided imme-
diately with Llewelyn, with
the result that a sort of
Donnybrook fair scene was
enacted. Someone ran for
the police and Constable
Taylor arrived and later
Sgt. Lamb. They stopped
the fighting but their
powers ceased. Agent
Strafford, who had wit-
nessed the whole affair,
however, came out and
asked them to eject off the
premises the whole crowd
with the exception of
young Llewelyn which was
done amid the cheers and
applause of the spectators.
- Account of what happened
when some men attempted
to steal William Llewelyn's
place in the queue at the
Lands office; Lethbridge
Herald, June 6, 1910.

$100 to the credit of his account at the country store."

The process of settling meant following a certain formula. First, the would-be homesteader had to make it somehow to one of the larger towns, such as Calgary, Lethbridge or Edmonton, even if he intended to settle far away in the bush or plains. There, in the Dominion Lands office, he would make what amounted to a $10 bet, that he could prove himself as a farmer within three years.

Europeans arrived in railway colonist cars from Europe by way of Halifax and Montreal, usually with few effects and little money. Canadians too came by rail, or sometimes in wagons drawn by oxen at fifteen miles a day, or sometimes a little faster by horses. Some few came substantially, like the individual whose cows followed the pas-senger coaches in the cattle cars, and twice a day he walked back the jolting, rattling crocodile of cars to milk them. From the US they came often by covered wagon. Enola Gray arrived on horseback, driving thirty head of range horses from Montana to Millet, thirty miles or so south of Edmonton. She would later take her infant chil-dren with her to the fields as she helped her husband clear the land.

At the Dominion Lands office, applicants had to prove very little more than that they were who they claimed to be, and were in the country legally. They needed no stipulated amount of money or effects, barring the $10 for the "entry," the bureaucratic term mean-ing an accepted application for a quarter section, 160 acres. Homestead regulations said "any person who is the sole head of a family" could apply, and "any male over eighteen years of age." Single females were not mentioned.

The free land, for most of the decade, meant any even-numbered section in Manitoba and the North-West Territories that had not already been taken (see sidebar). As the decade ended, odd-numbered sections were opened up.

The homesteader had to clear at least thirty acres, or have twenty head of stock. He had to live on his land at least six months of each year, and cultivate it. He had to put up a dwelling and buildings for the animals, and to fence at least eighty acres. He had to fulfil these requirements within three years to win his "patent," or clear title, his $10 bet with the government. Everyone called it "proving up," and for previously landless thousands that is just what it was: after long voyages over oceans and a continent, after enormous hardship, isolation and labour, you had "proved up" your own land and, not incidentally, yourself.

There were other ways to acquire land. From 1872 through 1894, at the time of taking out his

---

The homesteader had to clear thirty acres, live on the land six months a year, cultivate, build and fence in three years, or lose his $10 bet with the government.

---

homestead a person could "pre-empt" or claim in advance the adjoining quarter-section. He could pay $2.50 an acre for it three years later, after proving up his first lot. Vestiges of this policy remained in the century's first decade.

Land could be bought that had been allotted for veterans of the Boer War. A returned soldier was granted scrip for the land at $2.50 an acre. Most sold their scrip at deep discounts. Purchasers, many of them land speculators, bought and resold that land. Scrip land in Alberta was also avail-able from Metis, awarded it in the settlement of the Riel Rebellion of 1869. Vast tracts were also purchased for resale from the CPR's enormous holdings. Finally, in earlier years of slow immigra-tion the Dominion government had sold large blocks to speculators to encourage new arrivals, and these lands also now came on the market.

The result was probably the biggest land boom Canada would ever know. The newspapers talked it up, the merchants, lawyers and doctors got into it. Prices rose and fell on the plans and

whims of the railroad-builders. Just where, through what district, along what routes settled or unsettled, would they push the steel? A change of plans could make or destroy a community's future, overnight.

Thus Carl Stettler from Switzerland founded the little Swiss and German colony of Blumenau early in 1905, becoming postmaster of a tiny village of eight establishments. But by year's end, only a few lusty months old, Blumenau picked itself up and moved holus bolus two miles west to a new townsite where a rail branchline from Lacombe was coming. They named the new site Stettler. In the mild winter of 1905-06, buildings were slapped up from dawn to dark: seven instant lumber yards strained to meet demand. A local history has it that one lumber merchant took in $13,000 in a day, and carpenters were arrested for working on Sundays. By July 1906 Stettler had 600 residents. A great celebration drew 3,000 people. Flags flew, streamers crossed the streets. There were parades, a band from Red Deer 90-odd miles away, games and photo booths at the fairgrounds. Stettler was going places, for dang sure!

Stettler bustled and grew at the end of steel for just under three years when the Canadian Pacific announced it would push on forty miles farther east, to a one-store location called Williston. On Sunday, May 12, 1909, Stettler businessmen hustled in buggies to Williston, by Monday they were operating the Merchants' Bank in a tent, by Tuesday the Traders' Bank in a

Child by chicken coop, Camrose area, early 1900s. Children worked beside their mothers in the fields.

Certificate of recommendation for a homestead patent, 1908.

FORM K.

This Certificate is not valid unless countersigned by the Commissioner of Dominion Lands, or a Member of the Dominion Lands Board.

Certificate of Recommendation for Homestead Patent.

Department of the Interior,

Dominion Lands Office,

RED DEER 20th March 1908

I Certify that *William Berrington,* who is the holder of a **Homestead Entry** for *the South East quarter* of Section Number ——— *14* ——— Township ——— *35* ——— Range ——— *25* ——— *West* of the *Fourth* Meridian, has complied with the provisions of the law required to be conformed to, in order to entitle him to receive a patent for such Homestead, and that I have recommended the issue of such patent.

Countersigned at Ottawa, this ——— *7th* day of ——— APRIL ——— 190*8*

F. Roy Dixon. Commissioner of Dominion Lands.

E. W. Cottingham Local Agent.

Alberta's first lottery fever

TO PREPARE FOR THE CLAMOUR OF A LAND OFFERING, A FEDERAL EMPLOYEE NEEDED TO TAKE A FEW SENSIBLE PRECAUTIONS IN CROWD CONTROL

K.W. McKenzie's wooden railing was hammered up by 3 p.m. on August 31, 1908. It was his little idea to keep the waiting land claimers in orderly line outside his Dominion Lands office at Sixth Street and Victoria Avenue in Edmonton.[a]

There had been some nasty land-fever scenes at this and other Lands offices. Men in queue for choice quarter-sec-

and resumed her place in the morning. "There was the tall lanky Dakota man with his heavy coat and upturned collar and pea straw hat...[and] the bright active young fellow from eastern Canada," the *Bulletin* reported. "There was the unmistakable Londoner, the fair-haired Norwegian and the swarthy native of southern Europe. For the most part, however, they were British subjects of exceptionally high class."

At 9 a.m. the would-be home-steaders were let in, ten at a time, the process kept orderly by a lone Royal North-West Mounted Police corporal and agent McKenzie's railing. About 100 applications were handled the first day. The others, given numbers for their place in the line, returned as called over the next two days. Telegrams and letters of application were dealt with after them.

Widow Conklin got her quarter section, adjacent to that taken by an F. Reed, number 12. The Pembina squatters most surely got theirs. Mr. McKenzie, walking the queue patiently to answer ques-

Glenbow Archives, NA-2182-4

Hays Bros. land office, Carstairs, c. 1908. Sheaves of wheat were displayed to attract settlers.

tions had been manhandled by gangs and shoved aside. The *Lethbridge Herald* called these incidents "brutal, demoralizing and disgusting," suggesting the drawing of lots instead.

Promptly at 3, Steele Murdoch, an Edmonton tinsmith, took first place in line behind the railing. It would, he knew, be an all-night wait until the office opened at 9 a.m. the next day. As the *Edmonton Bulletin* put it, "All the odd-numbered sections of land in the last great West" would be open

tions and keep anxieties down, told a pretend homesteader (the *Bulletin* reporter standing in line) that, although trespassers, if they had built and had cleared land they would succeed.

An "old man" who waited third in line for eighteen hours was told the 160 acres he wanted was in a pre-emption area near the lands being opened up, to be dealt with in two weeks.

Steele Murdoch, an Edmonton tinsmith, took his place in line. It would, he knew, be an all-night wait until the office opened at nine.

---

to claim. Understandably, sidewalk generals laughed at the notion of a constraining railing.

By 7 p.m. there were thirty applicants in the line, by 10 p.m. seventy, and by 8 a.m. the next day about 250. Thirty young men had trekked in sixty miles from the Pembina River where they had their homesteads picked out and in some cases had squatted for over a year.

Widow Margaret Conklin, from Chicago, was number 13. A selfless young man offered to wait for her: she rested

Other Dominion Lands applications were held in Alberta that day and many thousands of acres of land given away. Order prevailed here because of one police corporal on watch, a land agent who walked the line to answer questions and show authority, and the helpful, constraining wooden rail.
— *C.T.*

[a]The building, on the southeast corner of what would become 106th Street and 100th Avenue, was the occasion of a near riot in 1892 when the Dominion government threatened to move it to Strathcona (Vol. I, p. 271). It was preserved on this site for the rest of the century.

shack,[2] by week's end a general store and a hardware. In a few days a druggist, a jeweller, doctor, butcher, furniture store, livery stable, well-drillers and H.K. Fielding, who sold real estate, had all taken up residence — all of them squatters. No townsite had been surveyed, and certainly there was no railroad as yet. Curtis Rathwell's concrete bake oven, built on Jack Campbell's homestead, produced land-rush amounts of bread, cakes and pies for the Williston store. The oven in front of Campbell's sod shack, according to a local history, "was there long after the soddy was a pile of earth and weeds."

The Dominion Day celebration in Stettler, Alberta, July 1, 1907. Towns like Stettler practically sprang up overnight and sometimes moved the next day in anticipation of railway branch lines.

However, the surveyors picked a beautiful meadow a short distance from Williston, hard by Beaver Dam Creek, with picturesque badlands at the back. On July 23, the CPR land office put up lots for public auction. In madhouse scenes, they sold for from $75 to $1,775 and the first day's receipts were $40,000. Carl Stettler bought a triple lot.

Williston repeated Blumenau. It was instantly torn down, lumber and contents taken to build the new town, Castor (beaver, in French). The sod church in Bob Travers' pasture beside the beaver dam, in which Nettie White married J.I. Bryant, was deserted to become a cattle shelter and eventually to tumble down. By December 1, Stettler opened his three-storey National Hotel, containing a bank, 56 bedrooms and a gleaming mahogany bar with bevelled plate-glass mirror behind and polished brass rail in front. Whiskey was ten cents a shot or $1.25 for the whole 26-ounce bottle. Castor was the place to be, until the First World War banked the fires of enthusiasm.

Land Scrip, issued Dec. 13, 1900.

So it was throughout Alberta. In the south, Pincher Creek folk were considered "old Alberta" (pre-1890) and had come to substantial station (1,027 souls at decade's end). They agreed, by ballot circulated by their paper, the *Echo*, that Pincher Creek was no longer a seemly name — like Rat Portage (Kenora, Ontario) and Pile o'Bones (Regina). In the end, better sense prevailed and Pincher Creek stayed Pincher Creek. Wainwright, the first Grand Trunk Pacific divisional point east of Edmonton, "bids fair to be one of the best towns in the West," reported the *Calgary Herald* in 1908. Wainwright would have "Canada's greatest national park" nearby, giving it world renown "as Canada's greatest buffalo reserve." Camrose, described at fulsome length by the *Herald* over a full illustrated page in 1910, was "the lucky city of the West," destined for greatness because of three railways going through it and a rich farming hinterland.

[2] **Banks were considered primary necessities in prairie towns, but never enjoyed unreserved popularity. Bob Edwards observed caustically in his Calgary Eye Opener in 1908: "From the Monetary Times we discover that the banks of Canada have loaned $14,000,000 to their directors and their firms, but give practically no assistance to the Canadian farmer."**

Glenbow Archives, NA-5025-13

The page one story in the *Herald*'s March 12, 1902 edition was entitled "The Impressions of a Wandering Scribe." He was wandering in what was then called "the north country," roughly from Red Deer to Edmonton. In Wetaskiwin, talk of another railroad, this one running east-west, had sent property prices soaring. One man who had been unable to sell a forty-foot by ninety-foot main street lot for $1,000 now was receiving offers, "but $4,000 is all he wants today and he is not anxious, either." Lacombe district was bustling. Olds was "having a building boom." Didsbury's 300 people were doing well but could do better if the Calgary & Edmonton Railway would put seats in the station, "as it is beastly uncomfortable standing around when your feet are wet and you have corns."

As the decade began to close, all the newspapers reported that east and north-east of Edmonton the Germans, Ukrainians, French Canadians and Ontarians were working wonders. Whether they were producing wonders might be debated, though there was no doubt whatever they were working. Work never ceased for the rural settlers on whom all this enthusiasm was based.

Making a house a home (top to bottom): John Holsworth and his cabin in the Benalto area, 1906-07; soddies abuilding and completed near Coronation, 1907-08.

Experiences vastly differed after the homesteader left the Dominion Lands office, half-proudly and half-anxiously clutching his entry. His fate might depend on whether he had open prairie or woodland to clear, and whether he had money for oxen or horses, for breaking-ploughs, for seeders and binders, for two or three cows and some chickens. Many had almost no money at all.

Glenbow Archives, NA-474-2

Ronald and John Scott, 21- and 23-year-old sons of a pottery owner in Sunderland, England, were granted separate homesteads at Mannville on the new Canadian Northern line by the Edmonton Lands office in April 1906. For the eight-hour train ride back, $4.15 per ticket, they were accompanied by potatoes they had bought at forty cents a bushel and three horses; one horse cost them $65 and the others $52 each. They bought harness ($36.50), a stove ($21.65) and for the trip two bales of timothy hay at 75 cents a bale and three bushels of oats at thirty cents a bushel.

Glenbow Archives, NA-474-3

Glenbow Archives, NA-474-7

Back at Mannville, the brothers batched (from bachelor, meaning a single man or men keeping house), until marriage some time later. A descendant's account of how it went for them is a laconic but true shorthand for the Alberta settler: "They plugged along and broke more land, got more cattle and more buildings. In the meantime they had some good times as well. Dances, picnics and get-togethers were common as more settlers arrived."

Two other brothers, Rod and Scott McLennan, built a substantial two-storey log home in the Battle River valley. The one large room on the first floor was for their two horses. The second floor conformed to Homestead regulations that a homesteader had to live on his own quarter. The house straddled the boundary line between their farms. Rod's bedroom was over his southwest quarter and Scott's bedroom was opposite, over his land.

Sod houses were commonly built by the arriving settler, on the prairie and where the bush was scrub. A settler near Carstairs recalls building a fairly large one for the times, 24 feet square, with walls 24 inches thick. "We ploughed in a place where the sod was tough, with the walking plough, about three or four inches deep. Then with a spade we would cut the sod, 24 inches long, and haul them [the strips] to the house on a stoneboat.[3] Then place them as you would [in building] a brick house and drive pegs in to help keep them in place."

Leta Richardson (later Leta Porter), at the age of thirteen in 1906 helped dig the cellar for their

house while her father, James, 42, went to Stettler for supplies. She and James' bachelor brother, Joe, who "was fat, bald and considered himself old at 52," dug with shovel and pick into hard clay. They managed a cellar hardly deep enough for an adult to stand erect in, but sufficient "for our many jars of canned fruit, vegetables, jams and pickles, as well as the potatoes which Father had planted in the spring." Then the sod house was built, eighteen feet by 24 feet, the 24-inch sod strips "laid as one would build up bricks, one layer crosswise, the next lengthwise, two sods deep, breaking joints by starting one of the two with a twelve-inch sod."

Richardson, a skilled carpenter, framed the windows and door, put in a board floor and a roof of shingles and building paper over widely spaced boards. Between the boards, shingle nails protruded through what was simply shingles and building paper: "In winter each point became a ball of frost. When spring finally came we had a shower indoors."

Sometimes settlers would dig their first home into the earth and put over the dugout pitched roofs of poplar poles covered with sod. Very often, homes were made of logs. These were not usually the squared timbers made of large logs found in Ontario homes that survive today, but trees of lesser diameter. They were notched and laid, most often, one storey high, and roofed with poles and sod. Wet plasters of clay and straw filled the chinks in the logs.

Some original settler homes housed their families for some years, others more quickly became

Unidentified homesteaders in the Edmonton area, 1900. (Left) Bert Thomlinson hauling ice from a small lake near Edmonton, 1910. Stored in icehouses it kept butter and cream fresh in the summer before refrigeration.

[3] **A stoneboat was a rudimentary sledge of the simplest construction, pulled by horses or oxen, used to cart away stones, manure and dead livestock.**

The shaky visionary whose star fizzled

ISAAC BARR BROUGHT OUT THE 1,962 ENGLISH COLONISTS,
BUT A DOUR CLERIC CALLED LLOYD LEFT HIS NAME ON THE TOWN

The Barr colony which established Lloydminster in 1903 astride what soon became the Alberta-Saskatchewan border is doubly conspicuous in the history of Alberta settlement. It was personally planned, promoted and organized by the Rev. Isaac Montgomery Barr, an Anglican clergyman, yet was not a church-sponsored venture. Stranger still, though it successfully settled in the space of two months nearly 2,000 middle-class Britons on empty prairie far beyond the end of the railway, Barr himself was almost immediately repudiated, and has been vilified ever since as an incompetent and a crook. Thus a history of Saskatoon concludes: "...the rascality of Barr is history, and need not be recounted here."

This historical convention would later come under review. Was Barr that bad? While no paragon of virtue and no pastor, the Ontario-born cleric was certainly a visionary. He was a persuasive speaker. His colonization plan, though over-ambitious, nevertheless worked. His great interest, writes his biographer Helen Evans Reid in *All Silent, All Damned: The Search for Isaac Barr*, was in "the panoply of empire" (British, of course). Cecil Rhodes of South Africa and Rhodesia was his major inspiration.

In the summer of 1902, while priest in charge of St. Saviour's, Tollington Park, London, Barr began making speeches and giving newspaper interviews about a "British colony for the Saskatchewan Valley." He issued two pamphlets lavishly describing the potential of the country between Battleford and Edmonton for sturdy British settlers unafraid of work and hardship.[a]

Inquiries poured in. Another Anglican priest, the Rev. George Exton Lloyd, who had been writing to the newspapers about Canadian opportunities, turned hundreds more over to Barr. Lloyd would provide the colony's only overt religious element. He persuaded the Colonial and Continental Church Society to provide the colony with a chaplain who had "Canadian experience." Lloyd, who was born in London and

Rev. Isaac M. Barr: flawed but no crook.

steamship and railway fares, with unlimited baggage. The Canadian government would help with tents and fodder after the settlers reached Saskatoon, then a village of a few hundred at the end of steel. An Edmonton firm (McDougall & Secord) would float lumber for houses down the North Saskatchewan River to within twenty miles of the site.

The pamphlet carefully detailed what settlers must bring, and described the voyage and (pretty accurately) the CPR colonist cars. Barr opened a London office to deal with the accumulating paper work. There was to be a twelve-bed hospital tent with a trained nurse. Settlers could buy hospital-medical insurance for a maximum five dollars a year. They could invest in a "settlement stores syndicate" and a transport company.

In all likelihood Barr was already over his head financially before the contingent sailed. His only personal income was a commission from the steamship company, although the Canadian Northern made him an agent for the sale of adjoining railway lands and he hoped to get a "capitation fee" from the dominion government. (He never did.) Meanwhile advertising and office expenses were heavy, as were expenditures on Canadian agents and supplies.

Things began going wrong immediately. The colonists, 1,962 of them, were to sail March 25 on three Beaver Line ships. Despite Barr's protests, the company changed the depar-

---

Was Barr that bad? While no paragon of virtue, the Ontario-born priest was certainly a visionary. His colonization plan, though over-ambitious, nevertheless worked.

---

had come to Canada as a teacher, had taken his theology in Toronto, offered himself for the job and got it.

Barr made a fast trip to the North-West that fall, and reported to his growing list of prospects in a 28-page pamphlet dated Christmas 1902. Canadian government officials would reserve an ample block of land, but only for six months. Vice-president D.B. Hanna had assured him the Canadian Northern would reach that point in 1903. He had arranged special

ture to March 31 and crammed most of them into one, the SS *Lake Manitoba*. Since this ship's normal capacity was 550, passengers retained vivid memories of dreadful crowding and scarcely edible food. Almost everyone was seasick — as were many of their several hundred dogs.

Barr reportedly kept to his cabin, doing "paperwork," while chaplain Lloyd reassured distraught passengers, mediated fights, gave lectures on Canada, and held church services.

Actually the *Lake Manitoba* had a fairly smooth passage, reaching Saint John, New Brunswick, on Good Friday. But dock authorities refused to land her until Saturday, and further frustration attended money exchange, vaccinations and — primarily — lost, misplaced and damaged baggage.

Barr was not to be found during most of these proceedings, according to Lloyd's memoirs, *The Trail of 1903*. He implies Barr was drunk. He did drink, although he is nowhere else described as drunken. Lloyd by contrast abhorred all drinking, almost as much as he abhorred "I.M. Barr," as he persistently calls the expedition leader.

By then the colonists too were blaming Barr for every problem, from the transport arrangements to the weather. He was caricatured in graffiti, lampooned in songs, and a hardtack biscuit was thrown at him over the food. Lloyd on the other hand was so popular that the colonists gave him $300 to buy a wagon and horses.[b]

The train trip began Sunday and was, as Barr had described, uncomfortable. Conditions in the tent city at Saskatoon were worse. The camp doctor (there *was* a doctor) warned against drinking the water unboiled. Some got sick. Provisions and transport were short. Stoves had been ordered but not delivered. Jack Barr, Isaac's brother and a western horse trader, had brought in far too few horses. The settlers suspected they were being overcharged by the Barrs and the local merchants. When enterprising T. Eaton agents distributed catalogues with much lower prices — but needing two months' delivery — they were sure of it.

Rev. George Exton Lloyd: 'Very reluctantly' he took over.

Barr was making exorbitant profits, charged the *Saskatchewan Herald* and the Saskatoon *Phenix*.[c] He had failed the colonists, and they should settle around Saskatoon or Battleford, they said. A furious mass meeting was held; some colonists turned back. But within a week most of them were on the open trail in overloaded wagons bound to the colony, 160 miles west (260 km), via Battleford. Many found the journey ghastly. Keith Foster provides a typical example in a 1982 article in *Saskatchewan History*: A settler, his wagon in a mudhole, curses as he offloads his marble clock. "My husband never swore in his life until he came to Canada," laments his weeping wife.[d]

Although the April weather treated the Barr settlers kindly, it didn't seem so to them. They had one snowstorm and a terrifying prairie fire, but no casualties. No lumber had reached the colony site yet — the North Saskatchewan was still ice-blocked. There was more acrimony on site. Colonists who arrived before Barr got there May 9 wanted to get onto their homesteads. Others rejected sections chosen from a map back in England. Barr sorted out the homestead disputes. He sent to the Onion Lake settlement, about thirty miles (50 km) north, to buy lumber and provisions. Some angry settlers demanded investment money back, and got it. Then Barr returned to the main body at Battleford, and real trouble began. Chaplain Lloyd had called a meeting there of 142 colonists, who voted to oust Barr. Very reluctantly, writes memoirist Lloyd, he was persuaded to take over himself. Confronted with this ultimatum, Barr signed over everything including his own homestead. Two months later Lloyd announced the repudiation of his name — "a unanimous vote in three places" had designated the colony's town as Lloydminster.

By then, the lumber and supplies had come from Edmonton, settlers were working on their homesteads and the colony was up and running. That fall, according to *The Story of Saskatchewan and its People* (1924) by John Hawkes, Lloydminster had two large stores, post office and telegraph

A formal photo with the NWMP as work gets under way: that Christmas, a 100-voice choir.

office, drugstore, saddlery, butcher shop, blacksmith, livery stable, restaurant and 75 houses. The North-West Mounted Police reported providing direct relief to seventeen of the poorer families that winter. At the same time, however, colonist Alice Rendell was writing her family in England of a big community Christmas party, New Year's dance and 100-voice choir.

But Isaac M. Barr died poor in 1937, a participant in an Australian colonization scheme very like his own (and similarly plagued by snafus). Flawed though he undoubtedly was, says his biographer, he was no crook and not really a failure. She ended by agreeing with colonist Harry Messum: "As you gather the true facts you cannot have any other thing to say but that Mr. Barr did not get a square deal. The

---

The colonists were blaming everything on Barr, from the transport arrangements to the weather. He was caricatured in graffiti, lampooned in songs.

Why had Barr meekly abdicated on the eve of success? "He was a peace-loving man who backed away from confrontation," colonist Frank H. Thorne later suggested. "He could not take criticism." This certainly fits his behaviour pattern throughout, but was he nonetheless a swindler? At a 1905 government policy investigation into "Agricultural Settlements in the British Colonies," deputy minister of the Interior James Smart was asked that question. His reply: "There is no deception as far as we know."

"I have tried without success to find a colonist who himself lost money to Barr or knew someone who did," writes biographer Reid.[e] The syndicate store had a sizeable inventory. The dominion government still had a credit balance for paid-in-advance homestead fees. The British Colony prospered, especially after the Canadian Northern came through in 1904. George Exton Lloyd became bishop of Saskatchewan in 1922 and died, much revered by some, in 1940.

largest group ever to leave the British Isles in one company was established as a success. And the credit and the kudos belong to Mr. Barr."   — V.B.

[a]Eager readers of Barr's pamphlets doubtless missed the caveats buried in the boosterism., such as: "Hard work and plenty of it lies before you, more or less of hardship and not a few privations...If you are afraid, stay at home — don't come to Canada."

[b]Chaplain Lloyd in his memoirs accuses Barr of swindling him out of this money, the only specific personal charge she could discover, writes Barr biographer Reid.

[c]The *Saskatoon Phenix* in its early years spelled the word in this way. The "o" came later.

[d]Other Barr colony histories include: *Lloydminster, or 5,000 Miles with the Barr Colonists* (1924) by J. Hanna McCormick; *My Life and Experiences with the Barr Colony* (1968) by F. Ivan Crossley; *The Promised Land* (1955) by C. Wetton; and *The Rendell Letters* in the Glenbow Archives.

[e]Helen Reid, enthralled in childhood by the reminiscences of Barr colonist Ivan Crossley, wrote an article on the colony for *Maclean's* magazine in 1963. The editors headed it "The Clerical Con Man Who Helped to Settle the West," which she says shocked her into the realization that her thesis did not fit the facts. She subsequently spent four years tracing Barr's life (and very chequered it turned out to be), even tracking down and interviewing his two sons in Australia.

Provincial Archives of Alberta, B.5625

Barr colonists unloading on arrival at Lloydminster Landing, north of the future town. 'My husband never swore before,' said one weeping wife.

The 'Hornet's Nest Tent,' Saskatoon, 1907. Women were in short supply and advertising was needed.

henhouses or pig barns when lumber could be bought or sawn. Eleven young German families from Kulm, North Dakota, put their belongings on ten railway cars and travelled to southern Alberta, where they bought horses and wagons for the long caravan to the Richdale area near Sullivan Lake and Castor. Emanuel and Freda Patzer lived in a tent that summer of 1909 while freighting lumber from Stettler.

The homesteader, not always experienced in farming, started small and worked very hard. A settler in Innisfail in 1902 wrote that he began with "six cows, two horses, a wagon, a few crude implements, a sound physique, abundant optimism and unbounded ambition, but only a modicum of farming knowledge." His world included "no habitation, no telephone, no ploughed or cleared land, no roads, no bridges, no banks...[however] the primary essentials of existence — food, fuel and shelter — although simple, were never absent."

Well, John Hawkes, how do you think we have turned out, nine or so decades later?

Open land could be broken with ease only in relation to bush land. In 1910 around the Nose Hills-Veteran area, two oxen would be hitched to a sixteen-inch sulky (riding) plough and they might break two acres a day. Without bush to impede them, they would make six rounds the full half-mile length or width of a quarter-section, rest two hours and make six more. For settlers with money and other things more pressing or lucrative to do, custom breaking could be hired at $4 an acre.

In a treed area, clearing was by hand, with axes. The stumps and roots would be grubbed out with axe and oxen or horses. Oxen, being patient pullers, were often thought best. Roots and stones had to be picked, the soil disc harrowed to break up lumps and smooth it for seeding. The settler didn't always have the equipment. In 1905, according to one local history, a team of work

Bob MacTavish receiving a haircut from Bruce Hunter outside a shack south-west of Didsbury, c. 1905.

horses cost $250 to $350, a gang plough $75, a riding plough $55, a walking plough $20. The farmer needed $40 for a disc harrow. Many had no seed drill with which to put their first crops in, and broadcast the seed by hand.

After seeding, he would harrow if he had harrows. If not, there were many like William Pfahl who, near Olds in 1902, dragged a tree over his field to help embed the seeds. That country was too dry for the colonists and the Pfahls and other German immigrants headed for the Hand Hills in 1909. Mrs. Pfahl made the three-day trip in a covered wagon with a broken leg, which Mr. Pfahl had set for her.

Through the summer, the farmer would clear and break more land, repair and extend fences, build another barn or shed, cut and stack mountains of hay. He might take the opportunity to work out for a bit. A man and his team could earn $2.50 a day, sometimes more, building roads. Existing roads had to be brushed out from time to time, a hot, dirty, sticky job plagued by mosquitoes. Many a settler worked off his property taxes by putting in a few weeks on the roads and road allowances.

In autumn there was grain to cut, sheaves to stook, cooperative threshing to be done by farmers going to each other's fields in turn. Wagon loads of grain had to be hauled to elevators that, with the train station, were the nucleus of villages springing up through the province. The little towns and villages were only ten or so miles apart, so that a farmer hauling grain could reasonably get to town and back in a day. There were many hours of work to do bucksawing firewood, and piling it for the winter.

When the snow came, there were trees to cut and haul to the yard to dry, for next year's woodpile. The farmer and his sons would saw heavy ice blocks from frozen lakes for the ice house. That was a small building over a pit filled with ice packed in sawdust or straw. It kept butter, milk, cream and eggs cool in summer before being eaten or sold in town. And, oh heavenly memory, it provided ice chips to pack into the ice cream freezer to churn up the best ice cream, for picnics at the river or Sunday dinners, ever known to any farm child.

Although the farm provided food, shelter and even home-sewn clothes, there always was a desperate need for cash. Many settlers trapped for furs or left home for the long winters, hiring out. They cut and hauled logs to sawmills, or sawed lumber at the mills. They made timber props for coal mines, and worked down in the seams. The enterprising settlers of the Pakan district cut and sold ice, at $4 a ton. The settlers freighted goods long distances on hire. In summers they built bridges, dug culverts, improved roads.

When the men went away, and when they did not, the women worked unceasingly. Wives, and children, milked cows, made cream, fed the livestock and the farmyard gabble of chickens, turkeys, ducks and geese. They cleaned barns of their manure. They planted, and harvested extensive vegetable gardens. They sewed clothes, knit clothes, patched and darned clothes. They picked wild raspberries, saskatoons, high bush and low bush cranberries. They filled cellars with preserves — vegetables, fruits, jams, pickles, chicken, beef, fish. Hilda Mohr of Josephburg recalled in a local history, *Cherished Memories,* putting up 400 quarts in one summer.

All you really needed to buy from the store, in food, was spices, salt, sugar, tea, yeast, baking powder. Farmers took their grain to the grist mill to make flour, or sold the grain and bought flour.

In the early days, until settlers built up stocks of cattle, pigs and poultry, many living in the woods, lakes, sloughs and meadows of central Alberta relied on abundant partridges and rabbits for meat. Rabbit often was the only meat families would have. They shot rabbits but bullets cost money, so they snared them and trapped them in pits lightly covered with twigs and grass. They ate so much rabbit that they developed some doggerel about it:

About in 1896 news were heard in the village of Toporonitz that there was a country across big ocean where there is a plenty of land and not so many people — not crowded. The news passed from person to person and soon people started to gather in groups to talk about it. Population in the village was increasing and it began to worry so many people with big families. Or to where a father is going to locate his son when he gets married, for it was up to the father to find and provide a home for his son as soon as he finishes his service in the army.
- Taken verbatim from the diary account of Rev. Demetrius Metro Povich, who moved to the Edmonton area as a child at the turn of the century.

Cowan Ranch, on Dog Pound Creek, 1905

"Rabbits young, rabbits old,
  Rabbits hot, rabbits cold,
  Rabbits tender, rabbits tough,
  Thank you, sir, I've had enough."

Why did the Jorgensons of Minneapolis, the Barr colonists from England, the Ontarians, Quebeckers, Swedes and Germans, even the poorer Ukrainian villagers of Galicia and Bukovina, leave at least relative and settled comfort to pioneer in raw, harsh, isolation? The reason, common to them all, was explained 62 years later for his parents by Bob Jorgenson who said: "To have a piece of land that they could call their own and to build upon it a home."

To build homes, hundreds of thousands of homes, that was the goal wherein dominion government policy and western interests coincided. The big spreads, the great schemes, were all right, to a point. But to draw the large numbers required for a great world granary, to populate the West so the US would keep acquisitive hands off, the essential was an agricultural West full of people who would produce grain and other natural resources, and consume the processed goods, machinery, vehicles, stoves, lamps, utensils, tools and gew-gaws manufactured in central Canada. The great trains, owned in the East and in England, could then thunder back and forth, full of goods and travellers both ways.

The enticement was free land, that, 160 acres, ten and more times as much as European farmers could ever have hoped for, and a new start. Land incarnated a vague thing called freedom that few could define but all understood.

CHAPTER THREE

The misapprehension and mismanagement of the unhappy Indians

FOR EVERY PROUD WARRIOR TROTTED OUT AT AN OFFICIAL FUNCTION, HUNDREDS SUFFERED SQUALOR AND DEATH

by HUGH DEMPSEY

When Canada's governor-general, Lord Minto, visited the Blackfoot and Sarcee Indians in 1900, the townspeople of Calgary were surprised by the splendour of the Indian costumes, and the skill and pride the Indians displayed as they rode in an armed escort for the vice-regal party. "They were as varied as the wild flowers of the prairies," extolled a reporter from the *Calgary Herald.* "Some wore immense headdresses of many coloured plumes and the tails of animals. Several had most beautiful shields attached to the tails of their steeds. Many were entirely naked except for a narrow sash around their loins. Every warrior's face was fantastically daubed with war paint. It is impossible to give an adequate idea of the brilliance of this group of galloping, yelling, gesticulating Blackfeet."

The reporter then explained why Calgarians were surprised. Most had seen only "the dusky natives of these prairies, scavenging around the towns and villages, arrayed in squalid garments, engaged in disgusting occupations, and sunk in stolid misery."

By 1900, both images were true. The misery of two decades of reserve life had reduced many Indians to abject poverty and disillusionment, with diseases like tuberculosis, measles, and influenza killing dozens every year. On the other hand, the isolation of their reserves provided a haven where language, religion, and tribal

Entertainments during Lord and Lady Minto's visit in 1900. Calgarians were surprised at the splendour of costume and pride of bearing.

Glenbow Archives, NA-1075-12

customs could be maintained and preserved, far from the avarice and materialism of white society. Hidden away in old trunks were the costumes of their ancestors, while in their minds was the knowledge of religious rites, legends, and a long tradition of tribal successes in their wars against their enemies.

By the first decade of the 20th century, three treaties affecting virtually all the Alberta Indians had been signed and ratified. Treaties Six and Seven, covering most of the area south of the Athabasca River, had been concluded in the 1870s and the Indians had long since been confined to their reserves (Vol. 1, ch. 2). In the northern part of the province, the Woods Cree, Chipewyans, Slaveys, and Beaver Indians had continued to live by trapping, hunting and fishing, unaffected by the massive land settlement taking place in the south. But the discovery of gold in 1897 in the Klondike soon brought hundreds of prospectors through northern Alberta, following the "backdoor route" to the Yukon (Vol. 1, p. 28). Some made it, most gave up, but a few miners decided to stay on in the Peace River district and along the northern waterways.

Concerned about this intrusion and threats of confrontation, the Canadian government in 1899 asked the Indians to sign Treaty Eight to extinguish their ancestral rights to the region, the terms being virtually the same as those offered in the southern treaties. Travelling along the Peace, Slave and Athabasca rivers, the commissioners gained the adherence of thirteen bands in 1899 and a further seven in 1900. Many of the Indians were suspicious, concerned that the treaty would erode their rights to hunt and fish. Others had heard about the Boer War and were afraid they might be conscripted into military service. The Chipewyans, in particular, thought the terms were niggardly and demanded that the government promise to look after the aged and infirm when they could no longer trap. In the end, however, all accepted the terms and signed.[1]

Perhaps one of the factors that overcame their doubts was the man who was advising the treaty commissioners. He was their old and trusted friend, Father Albert Lacombe, the famous Oblate missionary (Vol. 1, p. 74]. "I urge you to accept the words of the Big Chief who comes here

Anglican Mission school on the Blackfoot Reserve, circa 1900.

[1] Charles Mair, a famous Canadian poet and author, accompanied the treaty-making party as a secretary. His book, *Through the Mackenzie Basin* (William Briggs, Toronto) provides a personal glimpse into the negotiations and the difficult journey along the Peace and Athabasca rivers.

Treaty-making near Fort McMurray early in the decade. In the North, all went well until the coming of the airplane.

in the name of the Queen," he told them. "Your forest and river life will not be changed by the treaty. I finish my speaking by saying, Accept!"

For the next generation, Father Lacombe's predictions came true. Not only did the northern Alberta Indians maintain their old lifestyle, but the prices for muskrat, lynx, mink, beaver and other animals increased steadily. Their hunting grounds were flooded with free traders who com-

---

Many Indians were suspicious of Treaty Eight, but Father Lacombe urged them to accept the words of the 'Big Chief' and all would be well. It was — for a while.

> It suffices us to know, however, that of a total of 1,537 pupils reported upon nearly 25 per cent are dead, of one school with an absolutely accurate statement, 69 per cent of ex-pupils are dead, and that everywhere the almost invariable cause of death given is tuberculosis. Wherever an answer is given to the question 'Condition of the child on entry?' it is either not answered or given as 'good'; so that we have during a fifteen-year period of school history a study full of information from the medical standpoint.
> - from the report on Indian schools by chief medical officer Peter H. Bryce, June 1907.

peted with the Hudson's Bay Company, offering top prices for their catch. Moreover, the free traders paid in cash, as opposed to the credit system used by the Bay. Not until the introduction of the airplane in the 1920s did the situation of Treaty Eight Indians materially change.

But for the south country events proved otherwise. As the Laurier government's massive immigration campaign reached its stride, Frank Pedley, deputy superintendent-general of Indian Affairs, saw what he considered an inevitability. The immigration would "speedily bring outlying bands into close contact with settlement, and face to face with the necessity for making a radical change in their mode of life." He prophesied in error. Instead of being changed by the new settlers, the Indians withdrew more and more to the isolation of their own lands.

When the Indians had first settled on their reserves in the 1880s, the Conservative government estimated it could make them self-supporting within ten years. That unrealistic goal failed, so instead the bureaucrats devoted most of the 1890s to devising and imposing restrictive legislation intended to divorce the natives from their own past. These measures were to plague them through the early 20th century. Sun Dances, or any ceremonies that involved

Glenbow Archives, NC-33-2

Blackfoot man and wife, he a 'progressive' Indian graduated from a residential school, she not. Circa 1901.

giveaways, were discouraged. School attendance became mandatory. Laws against polygamy were enforced. Permits were required for an Indian to leave his reserve. And Indians suspected of gambling or being drunk could be arrested on their reserves without a warrant.

Meanwhile, the government became convinced that farming was the best livelihood for Indians living in agricultural regions. However, Indians did not have access to bank credit, for their chattels on the reserve could not be offered as security. At the same time, imbued with the new sociological theory of the "peasant farmer," the government seemed reluctant to provide machinery that would permit the Indians to farm efficiently. They must do it in the old way (Vol. 1, ch. 3).

Big Sorrel Horse, a Blood Indian, described the result. "My father, Left Hand, was one of the few farmers among the Bloods," he said. "Oxen from the agency were used for breaking and ploughing. Then my father harrowed the ground with pieces of brush from the valley. When the

---

When it appeared the Indians would not be self-sufficient in the allotted ten years, the government took stringent measures to divorce them from their past. School attendance became mandatory.

---

oats had matured, he cut them with a scythe." He threshed the grain by placing it on a tepee canvas in a corral and having the horses run over it. "Five or six sacks of oats were piled on a travois until it was bowed under their weight. It took us three days to go to Fort Macleod and back."

Cattle ranching was introduced in the 1890s, but only at the insistence of the Indians. The Bloods, for example, traded their horses for the first fifteen cows on their reserve, and by 1903 they had increased their cattle herds to 3,500 head. As well they owned 2,500 horses. For their ranching operations they had 37 individually owned hay rakes and 51 mowers.

The Indian Department constantly wrote optimistic reports on the progress their wards were making, yet their own statistics would seem to indicate otherwise. In 1903, for example, there were only 3,500 Blackfoot, Blood, Peigan, Sarcee and Stoney Indians left in the Treaty Seven area of southern Alberta, a decrease of fifty per cent since they had settled on their reserves in 1880. Their land totalled more than 900,000 acres but less than 2,000 acres was cultivated and in 1903 the Indians planted only 600 acres of oats, and no wheat or barley. They also had small plots for potatoes, turnips, corn, and other vegetables.

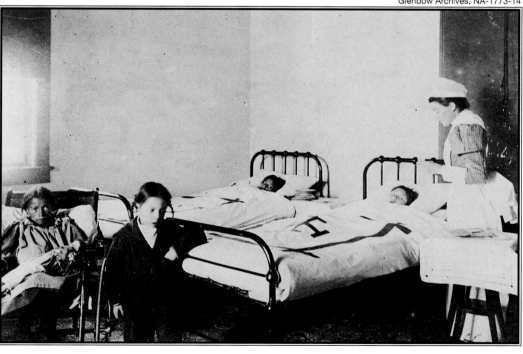

Turn-of-the-century ward in first Indian hospital, Gleichen. Almost invariably, the cause of death was tuberculosis.

Blake's crusade to save the children

THE RETIRED ANGLICAN JUDGE WAS HORRIFIED BY CONDITIONS IN HIS OWN CHURCH'S RESIDENTIAL SCHOOLS AND BLEW THE WHISTLE

In 1908, Samuel Hume Blake, a retired Ontario judge, brother to the former Ontario premier Edward Blake, and a founder of Wycliffe College in Toronto, launched a frontal attack on the Indian residential schools of western Canada. A staunch Anglican, he was appalled when he read a 1907 report by Dr. Peter Bryce, Indian Department medical officer, on the rampant spread of tuberculosis through Indian schools.

Blake conducted an investigation of his own among the Anglican institutions in the West. He found that Indians could not be induced to attend the Calgary Indian Industrial School. It had an enrolment of only seven students, though it was equipped and staffed to handle a hundred. Why, he wondered.

The explanation shocked him. Of the 32 students who had been through the school, ten were dead, mostly from tuberculosis. One of them, Jack White Goose Flying, had died in a tiny building at the school that had been set aside for tubercular patients. The school was closed permanently later in the year.

Blake also learned that Old Sun residential school on the Blackfoot Reserve was down to a record low of twelve students while the total enrolment at all five Anglican schools in southern Alberta was only 121 pupils. These were being supervised by a staff of 25, which included five principals.

Blake was so incensed that he published a pamphlet, *Don't You Hear the Red Man Calling?*, which attacked the missionary work of his church. "It is an outrage," he said, "to talk of compelling the Indians to send their children to school when these schools are conducted in such a way as that they are the means of conveying disease from the one to the other."

Indian advocate Samuel Hume Blake.

families, rather than shutting them up in tubercular-infested dormitories.

Flying to the defence of the residential schools was the Rev. John W. Tims, an Anglican clergyman who had come to the Blackfoot Reserve in 1883. He responded with his own pamphlet, *The Call of the Red Man for Truth, Honesty, and Fair Play*. He stoutly defended the Old Sun school and blamed most of the problems on the Canadian government. However, in a second pamphlet, *Calgary's Appeal on Behalf of Calgary's Children of the Prairies*, Tims nonchalantly admitted that forty per cent of the Indians who had gone to Old Sun school had died, 27 per cent within the first year of leaving. Of the total, forty per cent had died of tuberculosis. His reason for providing these shocking statistics was to prove that the students hadn't been killed by contaminated water at Old Sun school as some had claimed.

The argument rapidly expanded from the ecclesiastical sphere to the political. Early in 1909 Frank Oliver, minister of the Interior, admitted that some of the schools in the West

---

'It is an outrage to talk of compelling the Indians to send their children to school when these schools are the means of conveying disease.'

He demanded that Old Sun residential school be closed because of unsanitary conditions and railed against missionaries who lured children, "no matter what their state may be," into the schools in order to get the annual government grant. He believed that the answer was to revive day schools, and to let Indian children return each night to their homes and

were in poor condition. Perhaps the educational burden was becoming too heavy for the churches to handle, he said, adding that "other arrangements to lighten the burden and achieve better results have to be made."

Then Bishop W. Cyprian Pinkham of Calgary joined the fray. The mission schools in southern Alberta were running a deficit, he said, and the government refused to help them unless Old Sun school was closed. If this happened, day schools such as those proposed by layman Blake would be the only alternative. There, the children would be exposed to the "terrible sensuality, and the general absence of moral restraints, in speech and action" that existed on the reserve. His missions were grievously suffering, declared the bishop, from "the injurious attacks made by the Hon. Mr. Blake upon the Indian school work."

But the conditions at Old Sun residential school were too terrible to be ignored. In the summer of 1909, Blake and the government succeeded in seeing the school closed down and replaced with a day school.

From his office in Toronto, Blake had worked a change. But it didn't last. Two years later, in 1911, Duncan Campbell Scott, superintendent of Indian education in Ottawa, reported: "The attendance at the Old Sun's day school has been so poor that it has been decided to re-open the boarding school. With that object in view, a building fully equipped and modern in every respect will be erected during the coming summer."

Interestingly enough, throughout the whole controversy,

neither Blake, nor Tims, nor Oliver, nor the government seemed to have asked the Blackfoot what they wanted.

— *H.D.*

Girls from the Old Sun Blackfoot school who met the royal party in 1901. (Below) pupils and instructors from the Calgary Indian Industrial School, 1907.

Sir: It is frequently
necessary, especially in the
southern part of the
province, to call Indians living on the Reserves as witnesses for the Crown in
criminal cases. It has not
been the practice of the
Department to pay these
Indians fees for attendance
and maintenance as in the
case of other witnesses.
This practice was adopted
in accordance with the idea
that your Department
would not wish sums of
ready money to be placed
in the hands of Indians, and
also with the idea that the
Indians being put to only
very slight expense in connection with their visit to
town were hardly entitled
to the same treatment
- *Part of the letter from the
Alberta deputy attorney-
general to the superintendent of Indian Affairs,
Ottawa, Dec. 18, 1909,
seeking approval for the
payment policy to Indian
witnesses.*

This department has
no objection to the prac-
tice being continued so
long as the Indians interested do not claim payment of
fees which would be made
to Whites under similar
circumstances. The time of
progressive Indians is worth
as much to them as to
white men and the number
of such Indians is rapidly
increasing in Alberta as
well as elsewhere. It is
thought that it is unlikely
that the Indians will long be
satisfied with anything less
than payment of fees such
as are made to Whites who
are called under similar circumstances to act as wit-
nesses.
- *Part of the letter from the
secretary to the super-
intendent of Indian Affairs
in reply to the Alberta
deputy attorney-general's
request for approval of the
province's Indian witness
payment policy.*

Behind these statistics lay a story of human misery. Only a handful of Indians were successfully engaged in agriculture, or in working for the Indian Department, or for nearby farmers. Most collected their weekly allotments of beef and flour at the local ration house, stood by helpless when their children were forcibly taken away to mission boarding schools, and discovered themselves rapidly becoming strangers in their own land.

Meanwhile an even more formidable enemy began to assail them. This was disease. The major killer was tuberculosis which reached epidemic proportions on some reserves. Poor sanitation, small smoke-filled cabins, malnutrition, and a lack of treatment contributed to its rampage. Inextricably linked to disease was the system of education which herded their children into schools and exposed them to infection.

Dr. Peter Bryce, chief medical officer for the Indian Department, documented the result. His *Report on the Indian Schools of Manitoba and the North-West Territories* paints a devastating horror of poor classroom ventilation, lack of exercise, and the mixing of healthy students with those afflicted. Bryce estimated that a quarter of the students either died in the schools or succumbed soon after their discharge. "Of one school with an absolutely accurate statement," he wrote, "69 per cent of the ex-pupils are dead, and…the almost invariable cause of death given is tuberculosis."

Because the churches received government payments on the basis of *per capita* enrolments, Bryce found that they would accept almost any child, even one with virulent tuberculosis or scrofula. "Such cases," he said, "under the defective sanitary condition of many schools, especially in the matter of ventilation, have been the foci from which disease, especially tubercular, has

---

Bucking the trend, the Bloods traded their horses for fifteen cows and by 1903 had increased their cattle herd to 3,500 head and also owned 2,500 horses.

---

spread, whether through direct infection from person to person, or indirectly through the infected dust of floors, school-rooms and dormitories." He found that many dormitories had no ventilation and for seven months of the year double sashes were used on the windows to save the cost of fuel. "For some ten continuous hours," he said, "children are confined in dormitories, the air of which, if pure to start with, had within fifteen minutes become polluted."

Unsurprisingly, therefore, many parents considered a school term a death sentence for their children. Earlier, in 1895, a Blackfoot Indian named Scraping High had killed the farm instructor on his reserve after his boy contracted tuberculosis in the boarding school and died. When parents refused to release their children, the Mounted Police came to apprehend them.

By 1907 there were three types of schools for Alberta Indians — industrial, residential, and day schools. There were three industrial schools in the province — a Methodist school at Red Deer, an Anglican at Calgary, and a Catholic at High River. The idea of these schools was to take older children away from their reserves and teach them such trades as carpentry and blacksmithing. Men who later became the native political leaders of Alberta, such as Lieutenant-Governor Ralph Steinhauer, Senator James Gladstone, John Callihoo, and Ben Calf Robe, were graduates of these industrial schools.

There also were eighteen residential schools, located on or near reserves and run by missionaries. These schools were preferred by the churches, as they offered complete control over the student from the age of six to sixteen. In addition, the missionary was able to proselytize adult Indians through the children.

Chiefs of the day (l to r), John Drunken Chief (Blackfoot), Mountain Horse (Blood), Yellow Horse (head chief, Blackfoot), and Walking Buffalo (Stoney).

Hence the day schools began to vanish. These were small one-roomed buildings where the students attended classes but went home every night. The missionaries disfavoured them because the pupils remained vulnerable to what the missionaries considered the immoral and pagan influences of reserve and family life. By 1907, only eight remained in Alberta.[2]

Apart from farming and ranching other sources of income were few. In 1901, the Peigans surrendered land for a railway right-of-way. With the funds they bought a sawmill that operated in the Porcupine Hills. The Blackfoot and Blood reserves both opened coal mines, while some of the reserves in the Edmonton, Hobbema, and Saddle Lake areas had small sawmills and grist mills to serve their own people. Individuals from most reserves sold berries, firewood, and Christmas trees to nearby towns and cities.

[2]All eight day schools were north of Calgary. At Hobbema, the Methodists had schools on the Samson and Louis Bull reserves while in northeastern Alberta they were at Whitefish Lake, Goodfish Lake and Saddle Lake. The Anglicans had day schools farther north at Atikameg and at Shaftesbury mission west of Peace River. The Roman Catholics had St. Anthony's day school at Lesser Slave Lake.

Some individuals adapted successfully to the new order. At Hobbema, Little Cattleman had arrived from Montana in the late 1890s with nothing but the clothes on his back. For the first winter he built a shack for his family. In the spring he got a cow and garden seeds from the Indian agent and was able to borrow government implements to break the land and to cut hay. By 1906, according to the Indian agent, Little Cattleman had "eleven head of horses, thirteen head of cattle, a wagon, two sets of harness, a mower and rake." Similarly, Louis Callihoo, at Michel's Reserve near Edmonton, had a large field in crop as well as chickens, sheep, pigs and cattle. In 1905 he also had "implements for all farming uses in an open shed, a cream separator in the dairy, and an organ in the living-room of the house."[3] And in the same year, a Blackfoot named Old Woman at War owned a herd of more than a hundred cattle.

Walter McClintock and the chief. War stories were told.

Chief Brings-Down-the-Sun and the photographer

IN THE IDYLL OF AN INDIAN VILLAGE, McCLINTOCK WAS TOLD A TALE THAT HAS FASCINATED THE EXPERTS EVER SINCE

When Walter McClintock, a photographer with the US National Park Service, visited the Peigan Reserve near Pincher Creek in 1905, he saw a land that was as unspoiled as in the days of the buffalo. A true romantic, he ignored the railway line that cut through the reserve, the village of Brocket, the two residential schools, and the few acres of cultivated land. What he saw were 500 Indians living in a beautiful area of undulating hillsides and "nestled among the groves of green trees in the valley...white Indian tepees, with blue smoke rising from their tops."

He recorded his impressions in a book, *Old Indian Trails*, reprinted 87 years later by Houghton Mifflin Company of Boston. It provides an intimate glimpse of Peigan life at the turn of the 20th century.

McClintock rode to the camp of Brings-Down-the-Sun, a chief of the tribe, and stayed there for several days. As he approached the chief's lodge, he described the scene:

"Gathered round the fire were women and girls dressed in bright colours, busily at work, cooking, making moccasins and clothes; groups of children were at play — all were merry and light-hearted."

The chief was suspicious of McClintock at first because of the trouble he had been having with the government. He complained that the rations for his family had been cut off when he vowed to put on a Sun Dance. "I have to give the ceremony to save the life of a dying child," he said. "Its mother had already made her vow to the Sun." He said that white men had cheated his people and lied to them. "They have taken away our freedom, our country, and our means of support," he said. "Now they try to take away our religion."

The chief became more friendly when he learned that McClintock had been adopted by the Blackfeet in Montana. The visitor was allowed to witness a medicine pipe ceremony, watched children playing arrow games, and noted the rivalry between the two leading medicine men of the tribe.

During the next few days, the chief told of his war experiences, cautioned McClintock not to cut down the trees and berry bushes, and to protect the land's nature. He told several stories, but perhaps his most famous — one that has fascinated archaeologists and historians for years — was about a route taken by ancient peoples.

"There is a trail we call the Old North Trail," said Brings-Down-the-Sun. "It runs along the Rocky Mountains outside the foothills. It is so old no one knows how long it was used. The horse trail and travois tracks were worn deep into the ground by many generations of Indians. My father told me that this old trail was started ages ago by an Indian tribe coming down from the north, and other tribes followed in their tracks. I have followed the Old North Trail so often I know every mountain, stream, and river of its course. It ran from the Barren Lands in the north to the south country, where people have dark skins and long hair over their faces [Mexico]."

Was it an ancient migration route of the Indian peoples? Historians and archaeologists will probably never know.

During his last night with the Peigans, McClintock marvelled at the tranquil life of the tribe. "In the peace and quiet of that wilderness camp," he wrote, "my home in civilization seemed like another world." — **H.D.**

These were exceptions. Most Indians had been unable to make an easy transition from buffalo hunting and trapping to ranching and farming. They resisted change, clinging to their old ways even if doing so contributed little to their livelihood. Indian Department officials became angry, frustrated, and often dictatorial in trying to coerce them into another lifestyle. Speaking of the Crees on the Winterburn Reserve, just west of Edmonton, Indian agent James Gibbons in 1900 referred to them as "a very spoiled lot of lazy Indians...If they would only settle down and work, and keep away from town, they might soon be independent."

Like others, however, he mistook for laziness what was more probably a tenacity for the past, and a resistance to bureaucratic restriction. As hunters and wanderers, many Indians were simply not prepared to be chained to farms or ranches. And those who tried it soon became frustrated or disillusioned by government regulations that dictated when and what to plant so that the government could sell it for them. Neither did they receive the proceeds. Cheques coming in went into an Indian agency account, and the funds were released only when the agent was convinced the money would be put to "good use."

The result was anger and despair that manifested itself in a number of ways. Some Indians, particularly in the south, found their escape in the cheap whiskey offered by bootleggers. Others placed their traditional tribal laws above the Canadian penal code, provoking a direct confrontation with the Indian agent or the Mounted Police. In fact, however, incidents of murder, rape, or other serious crimes were rare, and far below the provincial average. The Indians were basically a law-abiding people, but the laws they abided by did not necessarily conform to those of the new regime.

Hence in 1903 two Peigans named Tail Feathers Chief and Joe Smith were arrested for holding a religious ceremony in that horses, blankets, and other gifts were given away. As this contravened the Indian Act, both men were found guilty by Chief Justice Arthur L. Sifton (later to become premier of Alberta) but were given suspended sentences. "This was the first case of the kind to come before him," said the police report. Sifton warned them not to have any more "give-

Blood farmers with a steam tractor. Not all Indians were victims. The Bloods successfully raised cattle; various individuals became quite prosperous by white standards.

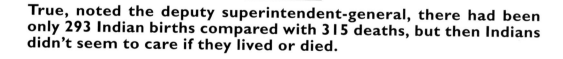

True, noted the deputy superintendent-general, there had been only 293 Indian births compared with 315 deaths, but then Indians didn't seem to care if they lived or died.

away" dances because "he would be very severe with any that came before him again."

Other offences, even attempted murder, derived from a belief in the spirit world and the hereafter. In 1902, Red Crane knew he was dying of tuberculosis. During the Blood Sun Dance, he vowed that he would kill his wife so that their spirits could travel together to the land of the dead in the eastern sand hills. After he made his pronouncement, he slashed and wounded his wife, but he was too weak to strike the mortal blow.

Showing considerable sympathy and understanding, the Mounted Police placed Red Crane under arrest but let him stay in his lodge at the Sun Dance, guarded by an Indian scout until he died a few days later. His widow recovered.

The same was true of horse stealing. This was an age-old custom, but after the turn of the

[3] The Callihoo family are descendants of Louis Calihue, an Iroquois trapper who was brought from Quebec by the North West Company about 1800. His son signed Treaty Six and took a reserve at Riviere Qui Barre, north-west of Edmonton. The descendants were an independent group who had trouble following the dictates of the Department of Indian Affairs. Finally, in 1958, the entire population gave up their Indian status and the reserve was disbanded.

The werewolf of the prairie

IT WAS BELIEVED THE WOODS WERE INHABITED BY HUGE HAIRY WETIGOS WHO FEASTED ON HUMAN FLESH

In 1901 the *Calgary Herald* reported that a Cree Indian near Wabasco had been hacked to death when the villagers feared he had turned into a cannibal monster. A belief had existed for generations that the woods were inhabited by huge hairy creatures known as Wetigos which fed on human flesh. These spirits could also enter a person's body, turn the heart into ice, and transform the person into a cannibal.

According to the *Herald*, the incident at Wabasca began when a medicine man had a vision in which he was told that a Wetigo would enter the village during the winter by a certain trail. A young hunter with his wife and two children left for his trapline shortly thereafter. They were on their way home when the wife mentioned that they were on the trail that the Wetigo was supposed to follow.

That night, the young man became morose and withdrawn. When a coyote howled, he suddenly shouted that he was a wolf and grabbed one of his children to devour it. But before he could harm the child — which in his demented state he thought was a moose — his wife snatched it away.

Next morning the man returned to normal, but he confessed to his wife his dread fear he was turning into a Wetigo. He urged her to leave with the children before he did them any harm. She remained faithfully with him, however, until they reached the village. By day he was normal. At night he prowled about like an animal.

When the villagers learned about the man's condition, they became terrified. A council was called and the medicine man was given the task of killing the Wetigo. He struck the man with an axe while he lay sleeping but only wounded him. The man begged for mercy, but he was dragged outside and killed.

This was not an isolated instance of a Wetigo appearing in northern Alberta. In 1879, a Cree named Swift Runner ate his wife and children near Sturgeon Creek. Explanation: He became a Wetigo. He was hanged by the Mounted Police. In 1885, an old woman from Frog Lake was clubbed and shot to death. She too was believed to have become a Wetigo. In 1887, a woman from Lesser Slave Lake named Marie Courtereille was killed with an axe when she threatened to eat her family. In 1896, a man accused of being a Wetigo was killed at Trout Lake. And in 1899, Moostoos was murdered near

Smoky River after people believed he had become a Wetigo.

Sentences for killings ranged from hanging to two months in jail for manslaughter.

— H.D.

Glenbow Archives

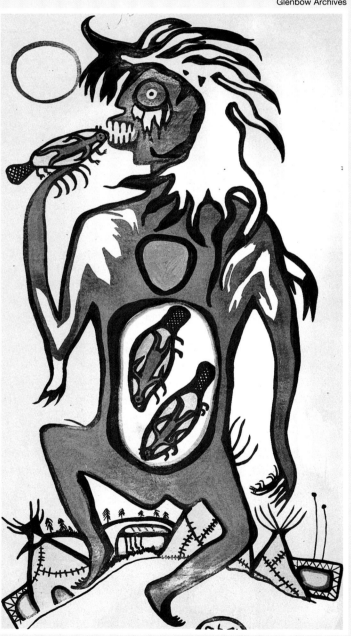

Depiction of the Wetigo, painted in the woodland style by Norval Morrisseau, an Ontario Ojibwa, in 1963

century it took on a new dimension. Instead of raiding enemy tribes, young Indians began to steal from ranchers and sell the animals to settlers and homesteaders. In 1904, a Blackfoot Indian named Dog Child descended upon the ranch of Julius Fornfiest, on the Milk River, and ran off his horses. The police tried to follow his tracks but lost them in the snow. Not until several months later was the Indian apprehended when he sold one of the horses to a man at Medicine Hat.

Such offences were common, but one became celebrated. In 1905 seven Bloods were arrested for stealing dozens of horses in southern Alberta, then running them through the Crowsnest Pass and selling them to a rancher named V.S. Chaput, who was obviously privy to their origins. Among the raiders were two residential school graduates, Tom Daly and Percy Steel. When the ring was broken, fifty horses were recovered in British Columbia and the Indians got sentences ranging up to five years.[4]

The stiff jail sentences were supposed to discourage other Indians from stealing horses. This proved a mistake. Among Indians, Daly and Steel became dashing heroes. The next year four young men, emulating them, embarked upon a similar mission. Hollering in the Night, Yellow Creek, Philip Hoof and Willie Crow Shoe raided ranches near the Blood Reserve then drove the horses about thirty miles north where they sold them to new settlers. All four were convicted and given sentences up to three years in the Edmonton penitentiary. Again they gained a valuable notoriety. An accomplice of the four, Shot Both Sides, did six months in jail and went on to become head chief of the Bloods in 1913. Hollering in the Night became a minor chief.[5]

In the foothills came another kind of confrontation, this time over land ownership. In 1894, a number of Indians had settled on the Kootenay Plains, west of Rocky Mountain House, on the understanding that the area had been given to them at the time of treaty. The Stoneys were therefore upset when two settlers located on a piece of land within their camping area and built a cabin. In response, an educated Stoney wrote a polite note advising them that they were trespassing and attached it to their shutter.

The settlers immediately went to the Mounted Police and expressed their anger at "being ordered out of the country by Indians." Sgt. H.A. Wilson was sent to investigate. When he arrived at the isolated location, he found that the Stoneys had built seven houses, planted gardens, and were raising cattle. Wilson ordered them back to their reserve and told them to abandon their cabins. They complied under protest. Then in 1909 the Stoneys made a formal application for ownership of the land. The government flatly rejected them. In 1945, however, their case was deemed well founded, and the Bighorn Reserve was finally established on the Kootenay Plains.

Most Indians had no trouble with the law. They adhered to the dictates of their Indian agent, knowing they would have their family's rations curtailed if they didn't. At the same time, they retained their language, passed their traditions, culture and values on to their children, and adapted to the seclusion and poverty of their reserves.

As for the government, it ended the first decade of the 20th century on a note of profound self-satisfaction. "It seldom happens that all essentials to the well-being of the aboriginal race prove so uniformly favourable as has been the case during the year now ended," deputy superintendent-general Pedley reported to his superiors in 1910. True, he noted, in Alberta there had been only 293 births compared to 315 deaths, with the total population standing at around 9,000. But then Indians didn't seem to care much whether they lived or died. Possibly, he said, this was because they have "comparatively few interests and enjoyments." Indeed they "lived mainly for the supply of the arising necessities of the day." Only the enlightenment that came with Christianity would change their situation, he was sure.

In the meantime, speculators began to covet under-cultivated Indian lands. Government officials shared this view, seeing the Indians and their reserves as obstructions to the nation's progress. In 1908, the Indian Department announced a new policy, declaring that many bands held lands "beyond their possible requirements" and this was "seriously impeding the growth of settlement." Hence a new policy was called for. The government would take the lead in persuading the Indians to dispose of their lands "in the best interests of all concerned."

Thus, by the end of the decade, the Bobtail, Samson, Louis Bull and Peigan bands had all been persuaded to sell off parts of their reserves, some willingly and others under protest. But these sales were the mere harbingers of the political pressures that awaited Alberta's Indians in the province's next decade.

[4]Although the Indians were jailed, Chaput hired a lawyer and got off scot free, claiming he didn't know the horses were stolen. Said the disgusted Mountie, "I could not understand how any intelligent white man could buy a big, strong horse for $10 or $15 and not suspect something to be wrong, particularly as some of these horses were brought to them early in the morning and showed signs of having been driven many miles."

[5]Hollering in the Night's official name was Charlie Davis. He was a son of D.W. Davis, first member of parliament for Alberta, and a half-brother of G. Rider Davis, longtime mayor of Macleod. Hollering in the Night was raised with his mother's people, spoke no English, and became one of the most respected men on the Blood Reserve.

Mrs. Blenner-Hasset and Clark Allan in an oat field at Hight River, 1909-10.

As the tracks spread overland the towns sprang into being

BUT TRANSPORTATION WAS AT BEST AN ADVENTURE, AT WORST A GRUELLING NIGHTMARE OF POTHOLES, SNOWDRIFTS AND GLACIAL-PACED TRAINS

by LARRY COLLINS

In the summer of 1901 a correspondent for Toronto's *Mail and Empire* travelled the Calgary and Edmonton railway, a line completed ten years earlier. "The daily train is the link with existence," he wrote in the *Calgary Herald.* "In the evening the people come down to the platform to see it come in."

That statement captured the railroad's importance to the early West. For years to come, residents of small towns would gather to watch the train puff in, bringing mail, freight and passengers from the beyond. But the railways not only linked Alberta to the country, the continent and the world. The network they spread throughout the province in the century's first decade provided Alberta's first comprehensive system of transportation within the province itself, when the horse was too slow and too limited for distance travel, and the age of the automobile and truck had not yet arrived.

The *Mail and Empire* man had left Calgary at 1:30 p.m. Saturday and alighted in Strathcona,

Grand Trunk Pacific workers at Stony Plain station, c. 1910. The West was hungering for railways and the settlement that went with them. By 1902 the Calgary-Edmonton run was a mere nine hours.

then the end of the line, at 3 a.m. Sunday. From there he careered down the dusty riverbank roadway (later to be known as Fortway Road) and across the North Saskatchewan to Edmonton "behind a team of the gamest horses any man might want to handle."

By 1902 the service had decidedly improved. A regular passenger train left Calgary at 8 a.m. Monday, Wednesday and Friday and arrived in Edmonton at 5 p.m., nine hours against the *Mail and Empire* man's more than thirteen. On Tuesdays, Thursdays and Saturdays it left the northern city at 8:30 a.m. and got to Calgary at 5:30 p.m. The rails also extended south to Macleod with a mixed train making the round trip from Calgary on Tuesdays, Thursdays and Saturdays. It left Calgary at 7:30 a.m., arriving in Macleod at 12:45 p.m., then returned between 3 p.m. and 9 p.m.

In 1900, the 200-mile Calgary-Edmonton line and the main CPR east-west line made up most of what Alberta had in the way of rails. In 1897 the CPR had brought the old narrow-gauge Turkey Track, running from Lethbridge to Dunmore, a point near Medicine Hat on its main line, and converted it to standard gauge. The web of branch lines that already covered Manitoba would not be duplicated in Alberta until the last half of the decade or later.

But the West was hungering for railways and the settlement that went with them. The Calgary and Edmonton had shown what could happen. Carstairs, 25 miles north of Calgary, came alive as

---

The newspaperman left Calgary on the train at 1:30 p.m. Saturday and alighted in Strathcona, 200 miles north and then the end of the line, at 3 a.m. Sunday.

---

settlers streamed in. By 1906 its institutions included a newspaper, two hotels, two hardware stores, three general stores, five implement dealers, two lumber yards, two real estate firms and two doctors. The *Mail and Empire* writer noted that as the train went north from Calgary the countryside improved, the bare prairie giving way to some trees and water. "In places it looks very much like England."

He was not the only one to be drawn by that central Alberta parkland. Thomas Grant Wolf arrived in Calgary from Gibbon, Nebraska, in 1905. Something of an inventor, Wolf brought a bicycle and fitted it with wheels that would run in the railway tracks, then set off for Edmonton

Bridge

Glenbow Archives, NC-2-267

Glenbow Archives, NC-2-255

Fabulous bridges. (Top) the Duhamel bridge on the GTP Tofield-Calgary line near Camrose; (bottom) construction of the CPR viaduct near Lethbridge. At Duhamel, 62 tons of nuts and bolts had to be tightened by hand.

and a ground-level view of the countryside. At Millet, 20 miles south of Edmonton, he liked what he saw and bought two parcels of good farm land at $4.50 to $6.50 an acre. He fetched his family and belongings by train the next year.

A.G. Anderson came from the US in 1907 with two freight cars loaded with ten horses, ten head of cattle, 300 bushels of corn and machinery that included a binder, drill, mower and wagon. It was a twelve-day trip from Minneapolis to Moose Jaw, on to Calgary, and finally to Carstairs. Anderson was terrified by the train's speed of 35 miles an hour, fearing his machinery would be shaken to bits and his livestock spooked. He almost spoke to the engineer about it.

Rail travel was cheap — in 1901 the CPR offered an excursion rate from Calgary to Vancouver for $25 — but it could still be a worry to cash-strapped settlers. In 1902 six members of the George Calvert family came west from Perth, Ont. The railway allowed one free passage for a man to look after stock. Since one son bore a strong resemblance to his uncle, they took turns hiding when the inspector came around, and arrived in the Calder district on one ticket.

The CPR, which leased the Calgary and Edmonton line in 1903 for 99 years, had dropped many a settler off at Wetaskiwin, Ponoka and Lacombe near the head of the fertile Battle River valley, and wanted to exploit more of that popular area. Its surveyors suggested a route east from Wetaskiwin, with Saskatoon as its eventual terminus. By 1905 the CPR was serving Sparling (now Camrose) which had already blossomed as entrepreneurs got word of where the rails would run.

Not content with just one line, the CPR began building east from Lacombe to serve the area south of the Battle valley. By the spring of 1906 Stettler was established. In 1909 it was announced the rails would go east to a point near Beaver Dam Creek. Three businessmen drove to

Williston to stake out locations, and the next day the Merchant Bank was in business in a tent. The day after that the Traders Bank was operating in a shack and within two weeks 25 businesses had set up, waiting for the rails. Unfortunately, they had guessed wrong. The surveyors chose Castor for a railway stop and the Willistonites had to move. Generally speaking, the rails followed the old wagon trails. Some hamlets, however, which had served the pioneers faithfully, were bypassed and died.

The coal railways moved 150 cars a day, coal one way, grain the other, making them one of Canadian Northern's best ventures. Remarked a farmer: 'They've got you coming and going.'

Anticipating the development of northern Alberta, the Canadian Northern, which reached Edmonton in 1905, built a 21-mile branch line from there to Morinville in 1906. In 1911-12, they would push it a further 74 miles to Athabasca Landing, laying rails on the route once covered by the old portage trail that had made Edmonton a key point in the fur trade (Vol. I, p. 116).

The astute promoters of the Canadian Northern realized early that the settlers would need coal to keep them warm, just as the trains would need it to keep running. There was plenty of it along the lower eastern slopes of the Rockies and in the Red Deer Valley around Drumheller. By 1910 the Canadian Northern was committed to building 700 miles of what would be called "the coal railways." A 173-mile line (275 km) from Drumheller to Vegreville would link up to Edmonton; a line 85 miles long (135 km) would connect Drumheller and Calgary; and a line from Munson Junction near Drumheller would stretch to Alsask on the Saskatchewan border and eventually to Saskatoon, a distance of 222 miles (355 km).

With the Drumheller area in hand, the Canadian Northern turned its attention to the Brazeau

---

God did not fail them

WITH THEIR ODD LITTLE STREETCAR THE ROGUE METHODISTS MADE IT TO THE PROMISED BEAVERLODGE

In 1908, the Christian Association, a group expelled from the Methodist church in Toronto sixteen years earlier for heresy, decided God had called them to western Canada. The next spring five families headed for Edmonton on the hard, slatted seats of a CPR colonist car, carrying their own bedding and food they could cook on a stove set up in one corner.

Finding no block of land suitable for the group, they decided to head for the Peace, specifically the Beaverlodge River Valley, close to the BC border. Told that oxen were better than horses for such a trip, they scoured the countryside and bought eighteen teams plus wagons.

To be included in the entourage was The Car, a kind of small streetcar on wheels built in Ontario by Amos Shark, one of their number, with seats for about ten grownups. It was to carry the women and children. On April 20, 1909, the "Bull Outfit" as it had been nicknamed, consisting of fourteen wagons and The Car, wove majestically through the streets of Edmonton to the acclaim of all.

Some of the young men had never driven a team before but they were paired off with experienced farmers. They made Athabasca Landing in a week and sold The Car to a local man. It was too low for the mudholes and stumps. They also arranged to ship freight ahead by boat, cutting wood to pay the charges.

The ox train slogged on by land but the settlers soon learned the horrors of the northern trails. On the long, still-icy hills they locked the wagon wheels and slid down, the oxen slipping to their haunches. On the climbs as many as three teams had to be hitched to a wagon. Eventually it was decided to ship women, children and older men by boat to Grouard on the west end of Lesser Slave Lake.

Forging on around the harder, rockier north shore, the men cut trail through forest, streams and over boulders that lacerated the oxen's feet, but they reached Grouard. Reunited at last, they pushed on into South Peace country. This, they discovered, harboured the mightiest, meanest mosquitoes on earth.

On July 14, three months after they had left Edmonton, the Bull Outfit reached the Beaverlodge valley, with the Rocky Mountains only fifty miles south. The oxen feasted on the abundant hay. The men fanned out to pick their choice of the land, not yet surveyed, and built homes from the many fire-killed spruce. With two mowers they had brought with them, they put up 250 tons of hay for winter. God had not misled them.

— L.C.

The only women graders of the Grand Trunk Pacific working near Viking in 1907. The railways brought growth and growth brought the railways.

coal country, 150 miles (240 km) southwest of Edmonton, which it eventually linked to the Drumheller-Vegreville line. The coal railways came to move an average of 150 cars of coal a day, making them one of Canadian Northern's best ventures. As a farmer remarked, observing the empty coal cars waiting to load with grain, "They've got you coming and going."

In 1909 the Grand Trunk Pacific followed its arch rival, the Canadian Northern, into Edmonton and was ready for its own branch line program. There had been practically no co-operation between the railroads in branch building. They knew it would be years before the West could provide enough traffic for everyone, but they counted on the generosity of the taxpayers to pull them through. As for the politicians, they knew that branch lines were the road to votes.

By 1913, the Grand Trunk had a branch from Tofield, on its main line, southwest to Calgary. It involved the building in 1909-10 of what some erroneously claimed to be the largest wooden trestle in the world. Situated at Old Duhamel near Camrose, it was 3,972 feet long and 120 feet high at its highest point, and eighty feet wide at the base. Built entirely of wood except for bolts, it featured timbers 32 feet long and a foot square. Deck planking was a foot wide and four inches thick. Sixty-two tons of nuts and bolts, all tightened by hand, held it together.

Alberta saw other great feats of railway bridge building. When the Canadian Northern marched into the province on the way to Edmonton in 1905 it required five major structures from

R.B. Bennett, MLA and owner of a new automobile, was out for a ride in it last night with Mr. Edgar of the Hudson's Bay Company. Their outing was tinged with incident. Mr. Bennett, who was acting as his own chauffeur, had been spinning along Stephen Avenue and had turned down Centre Street. A youth on a wheel loomed up immediately in front and was in some danger of being overtaken and injured. Mr. Bennett both thought and acted quickly. He steered the automobile to one side; it mounted the pavement and bumped with violence into the wall of the bank. The bank and the bicyclist were both uninjured, but the machine itself is at present out for repairs.
— from the Calgary Herald, April 19, 1905.

Alberta's horses were of mixed ancestry, ranging from purebred Percherons to the Indian cayuse which could serve as either saddle pony or draught horse, strong and enduring.

1,500 feet to 2,450 feet long. All were ready by the time the work trains arrived. In 1907 the CPR started work on the largest railway bridge in the world over the Oldman River at Lethbridge. Some 12,500 tons of steel were assembled into 33 steel towers more than 300 feet high. It was 314 feet above the river bed at its maximum height. It cost $1,400,000 and took two years to build, opening on Oct. 23, 1909.

At Red Deer in August, 1910, Prime Minister Sir Wilfrid Laurier drove the first spike for the Alberta Central Railway, a line that had been incorporated nine years earlier. As the crowd cheered, a platform over the railway ditch broke, dumping half a dozen people two or three feet to the ground. It was an omen, for the ACR was typical of some of the follies that beset railway building in the West.

The man behind the ACR was John T. Moore, an Ontario-born businessman who now had his finger in several western pies. Originally, it was to run from Lethbridge through Red Deer to Rocky Mountain House, but as time passed, its promoters saw it as another transcontinental line from Vancouver to Hudson Bay. Following the 1901 incorporation nothing much had happened. Moore had political ambitions (he would become a Liberal MLA in the first legislature) and kept talking up the ACR at election time, but by 1909 the people were getting fed up.

At that point Moore got a promise of federal subsidy which along with some British capital enabled construction to begin. But by 1911 the ACR was running out of money and encountering

Proud was the housewife who might travel to town in a democrat with a team of greys. The woman seated on a box on a stoneboat drawn by a lumbering ox suffered grievously by comparison.

some ridiculous competition with the Canadian Northern on the way to the Nordegg coal fields. In 1912 the CPR took over the ACR, which never did go west of Rocky Mountain House or east of Red Deer.

However, the ACR did build bridges across the North Saskatchewan at Rocky Mountain House and the Red Deer River at Shady Nook. It gave employment to the local people and bought their goods.

From 1901 to 1911 Alberta's population grew from 73,000 to almost 375,000. The railways were mainly responsible for that growth. But if the locomotive was king of the rails, the horse was very much king of the road — or what passed for roads. Thousands of oxen still toiled with wagons and ploughs, but in the century's first decade their numbers were fast decreasing while the horse population grew.

The "iron horse" might bring the settlers to the territory, but they still had many miles to go to reach their homesteads, and for that they depended on horse-drawn transport. The upstart automobile, slated to arrive in 1903, would not seriously challenge the horse during the century's first decade nor even for the next decade to come. Between cities, the railway had taken over. But for the transportation of goods within them, and the conveyance of both people and goods between farm and town, motive power meant horse power.

Streets therefore were principally meant for horse-drawn vehicles and horses, and in places like Lethbridge and Medicine Hat, in the midst of the ranching country, streets also meant dust. Visiting cowboys, in town to celebrate, often raised clouds of it, and in their exuberance these gentlemen sometimes rode right into a store or saloon. They also fell afoul of the law. On June 30, 1906, for instance, the *Albertan* reported that Pat Butlin, "in an intoxicated condition," put on an exhibition of bareback riding in front of the Calgary post office. He was pursued by one Constable Fraser to Seventh Avenue, where he jumped off his horse, "doffed his

(Top) F. Gertrude Diehl transporting milk in her democrat, near Bowden, 1906; (bottom) ox-drawn wagon en route to Lacombe, 1900. The democrat was the sedan, the ox-cart the scruffy pickup of the day.

Glenbow Archives, NA-3648-3

Glenbow Archives, NA-1583-9

185

Automobile stuck in the mud on the Pigeon Lake trail near Wetaskiwin, 1910. Roads were so bad it was said some immigrants had left in disgust because of them.

First automobile in Alberta (a Locomobile steam car), owned by W.E. Cochrane, 1903.

Mrs. Fred Ross with bicycle and dog, Edmonton.

Pioneer wagon that upset on the trail into the Beaverlodge valley, 1909.

THE INRUSH OF SETTLERS

The Battle of Olds

TROUBLE IN HAY CITY STARTED WITH THE CLOSING OF THE CROSSING

The pleasant town of Olds on the Calgary and Edmonton Railway was known as the "Hay City of the West" in 1907. The citizenry were proud of it and were working hard to improve the shopping area. They had properly elevated and gravelled the approaches to the level crossing over the Calgary and Edmonton Railway tracks, for instance. Wagon wheels wouldn't jam on it. It wasn't a big thing, but it was the sort of local improvement that made the difference between a progressive town and an unprogressive one.

That's why they were peeved when the C & E announced that the railway was closing the crossing off. Rail traffic was increasing. They needed a siding there; also a platform. They were so peeved that when the section crew arrived to do the job, it was met by an angry crowd and the town police. Leave the siding alone, said the crowd. The workmen complied.

The result was the Battle of Olds, best established as taking place on June 3, 1907. The Canadian Pacific operated the C & E, and CPR superintendent John Niblock, chief of western lines, was not a man to be trifled with. He huffed in by special train from Calgary with sixty navvies and fourteen members of the North-West Mounted Police, including two officers. The navvies were there to close the siding and the Mounties were there to deal with anyone who tried to stop them.

It was just before noon when the invaders arrived, so they adjourned for lunch before starting work. Word of their presence quickly spread and about 100 townsfolk assembled for battle.

Like other famous generals before him, Niblock made a simple but strategic error. He divided his forces. His men got their usual hour for the noon meal and prepared to rip out the approaches to the crossing. But the Mounties took their usual hour and a half.

Niblock ordered the work to begin anyway and was promptly arrested by town police. The Mounties arrived with Mayor William Dean, who was trying to be peacemaker, and Niblock was released, but the Olds police nabbed another railway official and the foreman of the work crew.

At this point both sides began arresting each other with the Mounties taking some of the local police into custody, using a car on the special train as a temporary jail. It was rumoured no one would be released without $2,000 bail.

But the issue was never in doubt. Under the persuasion of Mayor Dean and their own sense of futility, the residents capitulated and the crossing was eliminated. Prisoners were freed and everyone adjourned to the bar.

Today, a loading platform, three lines of track and an elevator are the only monuments to the Battle of Olds.

— L.C.

---

hat saucily," and started to run. The race was neither swift nor strong and Fraser soon had him, placing both rider and steed under arrest.

Alberta's horses were of mixed ancestry, ranging from purebred Percherons to the Indian cayuse which could serve as either saddle pony or draught horse, strong and enduring. Many horses came off the open range and had little in the way of pedigree or manners.

E. J. (Bud) Cotton landed in Medicine Hat in 1906, young and green from Quebec, and sought out the livery barn as the best place to look for work. There he met a cowhand named Jim Finch who had brought in a bunch of horses for sale. "He would lead in a scary-eyed bronc," recalled Cotton, "then the auctioneer would go to work extolling the bronc's good points, always stressing the fact that here was a 'plumb gentle hoss, saddle and harness broke.' I was doubtful just what he termed 'plumb gentle,' as I witnessed some of the new owners trying to saddle or harness their purchases. Some of these horses simply disappeared out of town in a cloud of dust, not even stopping to let their new owners pick up coats or the miscellaneous groceries and gear that had bounced out of the wagon box!"

Records left from the century's first decade rarely give prices for horses. A man who won one in a raffle had it snapped up for $25. Many were simply bartered. A team (i.e., two animals trained to work together) might change hands for a range cow, two pigs, a second-hand buggy, a crate of chickens, and $50 in cash.

The man who couldn't afford a horse had to walk and the early West boasted some prodigious walkers.[1] In 1905, William Rhyason was one of three owners of a horse on their homesteads near Strome. With pioneer ingenuity they contrived to make the 60-mile trip (95 km) west to Wetaskiwin in one day. All three would start at once, two walking, one riding ahead on the horse. After a couple of miles, the rider would dismount, tether the animal to the nearest tree, and start

[1] Harvey Switzer, who did a lot of walking in Peace country and once walked 240 miles (385 km) from Grande Prairie to Edson, has written: "We were in top-notch physical condition and could walk four miles an hour for hour after hour." An Ontarian of Scottish descent named Johnny MacFadden once walked the 200 miles (320 km) from Calgary to Edmonton in four days.

Airship at Dominion Exhibition, Calgary, 1908. Such craft provided a platform for parachutists.

Crowds on Eighth Avenue watching balloon in flight, Calgary, 1908.

walking himself. When the first two pedestrians caught up with the horse, one would mount and ride another two miles, then leave the horse to graze and rest while he walked on. Eventually the third walker would overtake the horse and climb on for his two miles of riding, which with a bit of luck and timing would catch him up to the first rider. Thus the three, each walking forty miles and riding twenty, could reach Wetaskiwin by nightfall. After a night in town, probably at the Alberta Hotel (25 cents for a bed, 25 cents for a meal), the three would return home to work the land with their faithful friend.

The vehicles the horses drew were as varied as the animals themselves. Probably most common was the heavy wagon, capable of carrying a load of grain or a new settler's effects, perhaps with a seat in front for the driver. More comfortable and smarter was the smaller democrat, with two spring seats but still with room at the back for purchases. Then there was the buggy, lightest burden of all for the horses, but sometimes too light for the mudholes the settlers encountered. In mid-decade, settlers from the US were still coming in by covered wagon to the southern Alberta prairie around Lethbridge.

Many pioneers still stood by the ox, slow and stubborn but incredibly strong. Oxen could pull a load up a hill or out of a mudhole when horses could not. Besides they didn't need oats.

Although often hard to move, the ox was sometimes impossible to stop, as Mr. and Mrs. Sam Pyatt learned. The Pyatts stepped off the train at Hardisty in June of 1908 and after a night in a bug-ridden hotel started off for their homestead in a wagon behind an ox team, the first Mrs. Pyatt had ever seen. All went well until the oxen, probably maddened by heel flies, bolted for the nearest pond and stood there in a snarl of harness. Sam got them untangled but they rested until evening when the insects would be less bothersome.

The ox, of course, had not the social cachet of the horse. Proud was the housewife who on her quarter-yearly trip to town might travel in a democrat with a team of greys. The woman seated on

Horseless carriages in a roadless province

ALBERTA'S FIRST AUTOMOBILES REQUIRED A TASTE FOR ADVENTURE

First automobile in Edmonton. Automobile being driven by Malcolm Groat in the Edmonton estate named for him.

"Billy Cochrane of our town has brought Alberta its first automobile," reported the *Eye Opener*, then publishing from High River. "High River is the pioneer of progress. Okotoks still clings to the Red River cart."

That was Aug. 3, 1903. Cochrane's auto was a steam-powered Locomobile with pressure of 160 pounds, good for twelve horsepower and capable of forty miles an hour on a good road. It seated four and carried a tool box, a picnic basket and a longer wicker accessory for stowing parasols.

The following year Joe Morris of Edmonton saw an ad for a car in a Winnipeg newspaper. Rushing paper in hand to the CPR express office he asked the agent what it would cost to bring the contraption to Edmonton by express. "It will cost exactly $775 delivered to South Edmonton," the agent declared. Morris stipulated he would meet his new purchase in Calgary to drive through the streets there, then pay for reshipping it to Edmonton.

It seemed all the residents of Edmonton and Strathcona were on hand for its arrival. Powered by a gasoline engine, it was painted bright red and mounted with two enormous brass headlamps. A crank stuck out half-way between the front and rear wheels.

Morris jumped in and persuaded an onlooker to turn the crank. One man did but jumped back immediately lest, as he said later, it should blow up. Cranked again, the auto thundered forward. On Jasper Avenue, hundreds lined the sidewalks as the red monster, steam pouring from its hood, sped down the street at ten miles an hour. A few horses tore loose from their tetherings and fled in terror.

The first Edmonton to Calgary automobile trip was recorded in March of 1906. H.W. White of Calgary had bought a 29-horsepower Ford from Georges Corriveau in Edmonton and the two set off at 10 a.m. one Saturday with Corriveau's son and G.T. Lundy of Innisfail for the 200-mile trip down the Calgary Trail. They arrived at 7 p.m. Sunday, having stopped in Red Deer overnight.

Reported the *Herald*: "The roads in many places were very rough and in one place the car ploughed through nearly twenty miles of snow. The stretch from Lacombe to Red Deer was the best of the trip, the car hitting a clip of about forty miles an hour. When the party arrived in Calgary the car was uninjured and not the smallest part of its intricate make-up was missing." It had used twenty gallons of gasoline and a gallon of lubricating oil.[a]

At this time, motoring was more of a sport than a means of transportation. But when Alberta became a province, one of the first tasks of the legislators was to regulate its use and, incidentally, make a little money from it. The Automobile Act of 1906 set the speed limit at ten miles an hour in towns and twenty in the country — except when passing a horse-drawn vehicle when it had to slow to ten. Meeting a rig, the car was limited to five miles an hour and if the horses seemed frightened it must stop altogether. Cost of a driver's licence was $3. Each car was given a licence number that had to be displayed, Alberta No. 1 being given to Joe Morris. Alberta had 41 cars. By 1910, 699 permits were issued.

In Edmonton, Mr. and Mrs. J. C. Tipton were out for a leisurely buggy ride when they heard a motor fast gaining on them. The car veered just in time to miss the rear buggy wheel but cut in so quickly it caught the bit ring of the horse, breaking it and tearing the line out of Tipton's hand. The driver, who turned out to be Mayor Charles May of Edmonton, did not stop to help but "put on steam and was soon out of sight," according to the *Edmonton Bulletin*. Tipton got his rig under control with the help of another motorist and returned home to bring suit against the mayor.

The automobile soon gave notice of its importance to western Canada's economy. By 1906, an estimated 125 cars were scattered west of Winnipeg, worth an average of $2,500 each. Demand was outrunning supply. The upkeep of a car was about the same as for a team of horses, with gasoline in Calgary worth 35 to 40 cents a gallon (roughly seven to nine cents a litre), one gallon taking the driver fifteen to 22 miles (24 to 29 km). In 1907 it was announced that Lethbridge would soon have the West's first auto factory, importing parts but turning out a vehicle particularly adapted to western conditions.[b]

—L.C.

[a]There were, of course, no service stations. Petroleum products in the early 1900s were sold in hardware stores.

[b]A full-page ad in the *Calgary Herald* in 1910 offered the Everitt car for $1,450, same price as in the US, with extra tire and special equipment and a two-year guarantee. The Everitt motor had "152 less parts than our nearest competitor." The 34-inch wheels were usually found only in a $3,000 model. The rear seat would accommodate three people.

a box on a stoneboat drawn by a lumbering ox suffered grievously by comparison. Lillian Fisher and her brother once drove to a dance in Sedgewick with an ox team, tethering them outside town to escape notice. But word leaked out and the two endured much teasing from those who came to watch them wake their reluctant team and start home.

Just as important as the quality of the horse and the quality of the wagon was, of course, the quality of the road. In 1901, Clifford Sifton, minister of the Interior, issued an *Atlas of Western Canada* designed to lure settlers to the Canadian West. Such literature was never given to understatement and the atlas's comment on western roads was typical: "During winter the snow and ice make the most perfect and direct sleigh roads over which enormous loads are drawn with ease to market...These winter roads are the best imaginable, whether for traffic or pleasure. One driving behind a good Canadian trotter, with his merry sleigh bells, wrapped in warm, comfortable furs, in the bright and brilliant atmosphere of Alberta, has an exhilarating experience alone worth coming to Canada to enjoy..."

Sifton did concede that things weren't quite that comfortable in the summer when the farmers, to protect their crops, closed the gates they had left open all winter. However, lied the atlas, "on the whole the summer roads are good; in most places exceptionally good." Well, they weren't. In fact, they were exceptionally awful. That which people later in the century would come to expect of a road simply didn't exist.

In 1902 the *Calgary Herald* declared that the roads in what was then the District of Alberta

---

Probably Alberta's first auto club was organized by Peter Lougheed's uncle Norman in 1908. Norman and his friends completed the trip from Calgary to Banff in eight hours.

---

were so bad that some immigrants had left in disgust. "It is impossible to travel any considerable distance on a straight road in this country," said the newspaper, "without running up against a deep slough or an impassable coulee."

The problem was not so severe on the old trails that followed the best natural path. But the new ones tried to follow the road allowances along the section lines that divided the prairie like a checkerboard, disregarding topography. This meant they were running into hills, ravines, muskeg, creeks, sloughs, small lakes and gorges. With a western bitterness that would echo down through the years, the *Herald* concluded: "So long as we are governed from Ottawa there is no hope for change, and the longer provincial government is withheld from us the greater the expense of altering the course of many of the present roads." Most farmers took their grain to market after freezeup. In summer, some were even reduced to carrying grain by the sackful.

In the early 1900s there were really no main roads in Alberta, only trails. The Calgary-Edmonton Trail, which had flourished after the CPR reached Calgary in 1883, had fallen into disuse with the opening of the C & E in 1891. It would not come to life again until the motor car revived it. Therefore if you wanted to travel between Alberta's two major centres you took the train.

The daring, however, might challenge this. An Edmonton motorist named Mills, for instance, set off for Calgary in 1906, arriving 2 1/2 days later. He became mired in three mudholes and it took him four hours to get out of the last one. On the last 25 miles he lost the trail altogether, arriving in Calgary from the east.

A few city streets were paved in the early 1900s but settlers were still finding their way to their homesteads over wagon trails or open prairie. Bridges might be broken down or non-existent and in fording rivers a wagon box was sometimes in danger of floating away.

Missionaries Robert and Jessie Holmes left Edmonton for Athabasca Landing in 1902 and hit a hole so deep that Mrs. Holmes and the grub box had to be lifted out before the horses could pull the rig through. The bridge over the Vermilion River was broken so the driver had to ford it. "Now sit still, Mrs.," he warned, "and put your feet up on the seat or else you will be swept off."

Thomas Thirsk ran a store at Ferry Point, forty miles (65 km) southeast of Wetaskiwin, and journeyed to that town every two weeks to deposit his money and bring back goods. It took him a day to go and two to come back, using four horses. The road didn't follow the section lines but ran along ridges or high points. The low spots were usually built up with corduroy. Most streams had to be forded.

When Alberta's first government met in 1906, roads, bridges and railways were its top priorities. But its road budget was only half a million dollars, sixty per cent of it for bridges. The government's goal was to make bridges strong enough for threshing machines and steam tractors. Roads were of lesser importance and it would be seven years before a highways branch was organized under the Department of Public Works. Meanwhile, Works Minister W.H. Cushing admitted that any road work done that year would be temporary because it was not certain where the roads would go.

It was the motorists who really established roads. An auto club, probably the first in Alberta, was organized in Calgary in 1908. In August of the following year, Norman Lougheed, whose nephew Peter would later become premier, organized the first Calgary-Banff drive. Operating the touring car belonging to his father, Senator James Lougheed, Norman and his friends completed the 150-mile (240 km) trip in eight hours. By the summer of 1910 a dozen such motorcades had made the trip and the Banff Trail was taking shape.

In 1906 two men made an automobile tour of southwestern Alberta, driving from Calgary to Macleod, then southwest to Cowley. Returning, they had a good run from Cowley to Lethbridge over 85 miles of what the *Herald* called "first class road." The travellers continued east to Medicine Hat but the going there was a little less than first class. A few miles out of Lethbridge they ran into an impassable slough. However, the driver ran the car up a railway embankment and by straddling the rails was able to get around the obstacle. They then followed the 130-mile trail (210 km) to Medicine Hat, returning by train.

The year 1909 saw the first Alberta Good Roads convention, held in Leduc. Those in attendance were mainly interested in improving roads for farm purposes, but they also noted that good roads were important to the development of a community. They asked that municipalities be allowed to borrow money to build streets, with location and construction free from political manipulation.

Meanwhile, travellers to the Peace were still taking the horse and ox north from Edmonton to Athabasca Landing, then around the south shore of Lesser Slave Lake to Grande Prairie. When the Grand Trunk Pacific reached Edson in 1910, that point became the logical jumping-off spot for a 240-mile (385 km) short-cut to Grande Prairie. The Edson Trail as it became known was a nightmare of hills, streams and muskeg. In summer, horses and oxen would flounder in mud up to their bellies while black flies and mosquitoes attacked without mercy.[2]

All in all, 1900 to 1910 was not a good decade for travellers by road. Even with the establishment of a highways branch in 1913, road building was skimped. The main materials used were gumbo and sand, the former impassable when wet, the latter when dry. So the day when the traveller could whisk himself by road from Calgary to Edmonton in an easy three hours was still many decades ahead.

[2]Some forty miles (65 km) north of Edson travellers encountered a particularly vicious incline called Break Neck Hill. Walker Harvey Switzer recalls descending it in winter: "In order to negotiate this in safety we wrapped several log chains around the runners of our sleigh. We then chopped down a jackpine tree about thirty feet tall, cut off all the branches about fifteen inches from the trunk so that they would dig in well, and chained the top of it to the rear of our loaded sleigh so as to hold it back from overrunning the oxen."

City license for 'Double Teams,' Calgary, 1910.

Dreams of flight and fancy

WITH AIR CIRCUSES AND ZANY INVENTIONS AVIATION ARRIVES IN ALBERTA

Glenbow Archives, NA-463-30

Framework of Underwood aircraft at Stettler, 1907. It was first flown as a kite, remaining aloft for fifteen minutes.

by HUGH DEMPSEY **B**arnstormers, amateur inventors, cranks, and mystery men have flown, glided, and talked their way into the early history of aviation in Alberta. The first years were romantic, hair-raising and crazy. As pilots offered death-defying thrills, the crowds waited below for the frail craft to crumble and plunge to earth. Watching too were the wide-eyed boys who pored over every magazine or newspaper article about the Wrights, the Curtisses, and the Bleriots. Many were destined later to win their own wings when Canada became caught up in the Great War of 1914–18.

But the years before the war were ones for dreaming. A fortune awaited the inventor of a successful aircraft. Attention and fame was showered upon the reckless few who would take their machines aloft. And death awaited the incautious and the unlucky.

The first reference to an aircraft in relationship to Alberta appeared in 1876, and even then it was only in the imagina-

While his dates may have been conservative, his ideas were sound.

The only other reference to aviation in Alberta during the 19th century also was based more on imagination than fact. In 1897, during the height of the Klondike gold rush, some Ottawa promoters concocted the idea of using freight balloons to carry passengers and goods between Edmonton and Dawson City. They claimed their balloon would be tested in Ottawa and shipped west. They proclaimed that they would form a joint stock company and sell shares, and that $10,000 had already been subscribed. However, nothing appears to have come of the scheme.

The Wright brothers flew their heavier-than-air machine at Kitty Hawk, North Carolina, on Dec. 17, 1903, but several years passed before anyone disturbed the peaceful clouds high above the Alberta landscape. And when history was made, it was with the old-fashioned hot air balloon.

Balloons were the first aerial craft known to man. The first flights were made in Paris in 1783 and over the years they became a popular form of entertainment throughout Europe and larger centres in the United States.

---

tion of an unknown artist. The man was a member of a survey party searching for a route for a railway through the Rockies west of Jasper. While in the Yellowhead Pass, he made a sketch showing their camp in 1876, a railway crossing the region in 1976, and a dirigible and balloon in the year 2076.

Noting the interest in aviation caused by the Wright brothers' flight, two promoters from Sturgis, Michigan, named Williams and Wright took a hot air balloon on a tour of the West as part of McPhee's Circus. On July 1, 1906, they arrived in Edmonton at the annual fair and that evening, according to a witness, "scores of willing hands were found to assist in holding the great bag in place, while it was being filled with gas from the furnace below."

As the crowds watched excitedly, the signal was given and the great balloon "darted like an arrow up into the air" with "aeronaut" R. Cross hanging from a trapeze. The viewers rushed from the grandstand for a better view and gazed in amazement as the daredevil performed his stunts. The plan was for Cross to reach a safe altitude from which he would make a simple parachute jump to the ground, but his release mechanism failed to work, and the balloon gradually dropped to earth, drifting towards Government House and eventually coming safely to a landing near McKay Avenue School.

Four days later the performance was repeated, but this time everything went without a hitch and the parachute jump became the fitting climax to Alberta's first aerial performance. The stunt was supposed to have been repeated on the last day of the fair but high winds made the flight impossible.

From Edmonton, McPhee's Circus proceeded south to Calgary for further performances at that city's exhibition. On the afternoon of July 11, the balloon was again filled with air as a small army of volunteers held it down. Then, on a signal from "Professor" Williams, the lines were released and the balloon shot aloft, with Williams dangling from a basket below. As the balloon went straight up, WIlliams performed various stunts, to the delight and astonishment of the crowds. When he was only a speck in the clear summer sky, the professor released the rope from the catch hole, opened his parachute and floated gracefully downward — into the middle of the Bow River. On the following day the stunt was repeated, but as winds were light the professor made a perfect parachute landing in front of the grandstand.

In the following year, a trio of Alberta farm boys came close — but how close we'll never know — to achieving Canada's first heavier-than-air flight. The boys, Elmer, George and John Underwood, lived on a farm at Krugerville, a few miles from Stettler. Their father, John K. Underwood, had invented the Underwood disc plough in 1872, so the field of science was not new to the family.

In May 1907, the boys started their experiments with tailless kites propelled by elastic band-powered propellers. The successful kites flew up to 150 yards, proving to the young inventors that they were on the right track.

After these initial experiments, the boys made a flying machine that was a cross between a flying wing and a flying saucer. The main structure consisted of an elliptical wing, 42 feet wide and 26 feet long, surmounted by a vertical fin running its length and extending ten feet above it. This height was later reduced to four feet. At the centre of the wing was a vertical post that extended underneath to a platform for the pilot and motor. Beneath this were two motorcycle wheels, while another two wheels extended down from the outer rim of the wing on either side to provide the necessary stability in

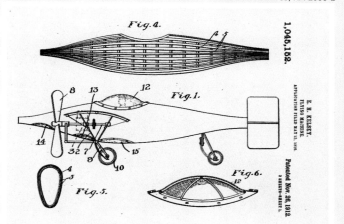

Drawings for a flying machine — invented by Earl H. Kelsey of Bawlf, Alta.

landing or taking off. The entire machine, without pilot, weighed some 450 pounds.

As part of their experiments, the Underwood brothers flew the machine as a kite, the first test taking place in August of 1907. Five sacks of wheat were placed on the platform and were lifted without difficulty. A short time later, John Underwood mounted the platform and the machine was successfully raised to about ten feet in the air where it remained for fifteen minutes, swaying gently at the end of a rope. This was the first manned kite to be flown in Canada.

Encouraged by their success, the boys arranged to obtain a suitable motor from the United States and agreed to install it in time to fly their machine at Stettler's first fair on Oct. 1 and 2, 1907. However, they encountered trouble with the custom's office in Calgary and the engine was never received. As a result, the boys simply placed their invention on display at the fair and did not attempt to send it aloft. Even then the aircraft was the centre of considerable interest.

After the fair, the boys bought a seven-horsepower motorcycle engine which they installed and attached to a four-bladed bamboo and canvas propeller. The motor proved to be grossly underpowered and the aircraft succeeded only in taxiing around the open farmyard. The inventors then removed the motor and continued to use the machine as a kite. However, during 1908 a strong wind tore the craft loose from its anchor and destroyed it.

The obvious question is whether a more powerful motor would have lifted the aircraft from the ground and achieved heavier-than-air flight in Canada a full two years before John McCurdy made his historic flight in the Silver Dart.

Except for the Underwood experiment, the skies over Alberta were reserved for birds and balloons during the first decade of the 20th century. While the newspapers proclaimed the breathtaking flights occurring in the eastern United States, Britain and Europe, aviation was still a form of entertainment and curiosity in the eyes of most viewers.

The Fireguard *by Inglis Sheldon-Williams, showing a man and his team ploughing a barrier against the approaching prairie fire. The tenacity of the settler was astonishing.*

The laments and the hymns of those who made it happen

Life was tough, brutal, but, finally, satisfying in that strange place called Alberta. Here's what the settlers themselves said about it

Edited by JANICE TYRWHITT

T*he following accounts of adversity and triumph have been picked mainly from the local histories of Alberta. It is in these mixed recollections that one finds the tens of thousands of stories of pioneer hardship, horror and absolute pluck that formed the social bedrock of the province. The histories — about 800 of which were published in the 1980s, often with money from the Heritage Trust Fund — vary greatly in accuracy, length, style and literary competence. Yet they share certain things. There's always an astonishment, even awe, on the part of the author for the tenacity of the settler. And there are always those occasions of pure joy detectable in the accounts of the old-timers. One can imagine them, their long days done, the latest crisis managed, standing outside of their rude shacks and looking upon their land, realizing that every square inch of it was theirs, that they had cleared and broken it, transformed it into a home, and that all this had been done not just for themselves but for the children and the grandchildren yet to come.*

Flowers for a Ceiling, Mud for a Floor

David Butler's family lived for two years in a sod house after they moved to the Castor district in 1907, and his daughter Reta remembers, "In the spring the sun melted the snow off the roof and warmed the sod, so green grass, buttercups, crocus and shooting stars appeared, making the roof a flower garden. In time the roof leaked so we had pails and pans sitting around to catch the water each time it rained."

A.B. Reynolds writes in *Siding 16: Wetaskiwin to 1930,* "An early thaw in February caused the roof of the J.W. Bailey log cabin to disintegrate. The family and furniture were overwhelmed by a downpour of muck and black water that left them ankle-deep in mud—and a blue sky over their heads. Mrs. Bailey said she'd very gladly give up a roof of green grass and spring flowers for something that would stay where it belonged."

"As the women enlarged the clearing for a garden, the pile of logs grew. Then Veronia's mother saw the possibility of a log house. She resented living like an animal in a lair and had cried bitterly over it. She longed for the clean white-washed home she had left behind. From then on she worked with the vision of a log house uppermost in her mind. Before the men returned in the fall, the house had been built.

"Veronia recalls how hard her mother worked. Before she was finished building the house, both her shoulders were a mass of raw bleeding flesh. But she refused to give up and in time all four walls were standing...Thus, without spending a penny and improvising as she went, Veronia's mother built them a home in which they lived for many years."

Children in the Days Before 'I'm Bored'

At eleven, John Nyman of High River went to work on the Bar U ranch. *Along the Burnt Lake Trail* records, "Being a slim lad of eleven years, too young to fork hay or handle cows, he was put on the wolfing crew. His job was to crawl into the den with his six-shooter and kill the wolves in there. They seldom caught an old wolf at home, but when they did, John would shoot it and crawl and wiggle backwards out of the den coughing and choking from the dust and gunpowder fumes."

Wesley Maxfield was fifteen when he agreed to help three ranchers herd 500 sheep east through the Neutral Hills. As his sister Minnie says in *Chatter Chips from Beaver Dam Creek,* the men were overtaken by the cruel November of 1906. "They asked our mother if one of our boys could help for the rest of the trip, and as soon as the herd was delivered, one of the men would see that the boy got safely home. Wesley wanted to go so Mother agreed. The winter set in so severe and quick and the ranch was so short of help that they could not spare the man [to see Wesley home], so Wesley stayed on. There was no way of hearing from him, and when a rumour reached us that a boy was missing on Sounding Lake, hope of his return began to fade. All the sheep perished and the ranchers were so busy trying to save the cattle that everyone was busy at the main ranch. Eight miles away was a smaller herd being fed by a man who lived in a little shack. About February 1, the man died of pneumonia, and Wesley was asked if he could do the job. He wasn't very anxious to be away out there, all alone for weeks on end, but he consented. He managed very well all winter, though, and one day in May rode home, safe and sound, and much more grown up."

(From top) Mary Cross and hay wagon, A7 Ranch, Willow Creek, 1910; digging a water well in southern Alberta, date unknown; horses fording the Red Deer River, early 1900s.

Glenbow Archives, NA-2612-25

Building a shack in the Drumheller area, early 1900s.

Home Veterinary Work

American settlers were quicker at learning the ropes. R.W. Elmer, who moved from Oregon to Didsbury in 1907, survived a "harrowing experience" in which four unruly broncs clobbered him with hooves and harrow teeth, breaking his collarbone, after one horse stepped into a badger hole. But an equine injury he took more seriously: "In the fall my best horse ran into the barbed wire fence and the wire girdled a front leg just above the knee. There remained only two inches of skin intact at the back of the knee. I threw him down in the stall, tied him well and with common darning needle and white thread, put in 32 stitches. Quite a mess. He brought a big price next spring."

Slow, Effective and Largely Inedible

Those durable beasts the oxen figure as minor heroes in Sarah Roberts' classic account of homesteading, *Of Us and the Oxen*. From Stettler, on July 16, 1906, "we started for our claims, 65 miles to the east, behind the slowest animals that ever made twenty miles a day — oxen." No more unlikely pioneers could be imagined than the Roberts family. Papa was 58, a doctor who had practised medicine for twenty years in Towanda, Illinois. Sarah was 54, mother of six. Three older children had married and settled down, but how could they afford to put their three younger sons through college? A friend brought back glowing accounts of opportunities in the new province of Alberta. So the spring of 1906 found the Roberts, with their sons Frank, Lathrop and Brockway, lumbering along to their newly filed claims halfway between Stettler and the Saskatchewan border. Two years later, having survived the terrible winter of 1906-07, Papa was still relying on a team of four oxen to break a hundred acres of virgin sod. Since one walks approximately eight

---

The hard choice that made Whitford an Indian

DESTITUTE, WIDOWED AND HUNGRY, A FARMER WAS FACED WITH THE DECISION OF GIVING UP A SON TO SAVE A FAMILY

(From *Salt and Braided Bread: Ukrainian Life in Canada* by Jars Balan. Toronto: Oxford University Press, 1984.)

In the spring of 1905, a Ukrainian farmer near Andrew lost his wife when she was bearing their sixth child, a boy. The blow was especially severe because the winter had been long and difficult, and the family was reduced to eating a thin gruel made of wheat.

A week after the woman's death, the husband was working outside, putting in a garden, when he heard gunshots from a remote corner of his land. Investigating, he came across a hunting party of Cree Indians, one of whom spoke Ukrainian.

The two men began talking, and the farmer explained the unfortunate situation that he and his children found themselves in. When the Indian asked him why he did not hunt to supplement their meagre diet, since game was plentiful in the area, the farmer replied that he was so poor that he did not even own a gun.

They continued talking, and after a while the farmer made a desperate proposition. Realizing that the newborn would probably die without a mother, he suggested that the Indians take the baby with them in exchange for one of their guns. The oldest children would remain with their father, as they could look after each other and also be of help to him.

Sympathetic to the man's plight, the hunters agreed and took the week-old child with them to be raised by the women on the Goodfish Lake Reserve northeast of Vilna. By the time the father tried to persuade him to rejoin the family near Andrew, the boy — now named Steve Whitford — had become so accustomed to his adopted lifestyle that he refused to go. He answered in Cree, "I'm an Indian." [a]

[a] **Whitford eventually became one of the most respected members of the Goodfish Lake community in which he married, living just outside the perimeter of the reserve (since he was never legally recognized as an Indian).**

miles in ploughing each acre, he walked this summer, behind the plough, about 800 miles, which was a pretty strenuous undertaking for a man sixty years of age. And this ploughing was all done during the hot months of June and July."

Being ordinary cattle, oxen were considered acceptable to eat. However, according to Grant MacEwan in *Power for Prairie Ploughs*, after all those years of work the carcass was hardly choice. A man sat down hungry, it was said, and got up tired.

Charles Russell's At Close Quarters, *painted in 1912. Bears and homesteaders were often equally startled when they met.*

Winged and Slithery Pests

From spring to fall, man and beast were plagued by swarms of insects. Verna Burkholder, whose family left Stouffville, Ontario, to join a Mennonite colony east of Stettler in 1906, remembers: "The mosquitoes were so vicious that we were forced to wear net veils on our wide-brimmed straw hats, and to line our long, black cotton stockings with portions of the *Stouffville News*! The heel flies bothered the oxen a great deal. They would often stampede to the nearest slough. One day, one ox blunderingly ran right into the tent, knocking over and wrecking a barrel of Mother's best china."

The Battle River Valley quotes John J. Ruste, a homesteader near Mannville, who got used to snakes in his woodbox but drew the line at sharing his bath. "One Sunday I took my clean clothes and walked half a mile to a good big slough to have a bath. Something was tugging at my shoe and of course I moved and so did the snake—into the water. I walked a little further and there was another snake running into the water, so I walked to the other side. I was just getting my shoes off when I noticed something coming my way—a big snake with a lizard in his mouth—so I went home and had my bath for I did not like that kind of company."

(From top) Preparing an outdoor meal in the Edson area, 1910; John Bolten breaking sod near Ranfurly, 1906; man with mosquito netting, early 1900, location unknown.

Bears and Other Beasts

In *Along the Burnt Lake Trail* a homesteader's daughter remembers, "One day while picking blueberries and dryland cranberries, a wolf attacked me, and if it had not been for our mongrel dog Bengy I would have been carried off. The dog jumped on the wolf and while the two were fighting, I was able to get away and join the rest of the children, who had found sticks and clubs to defend themselves. Our dog came home half an hour after we did, badly chewed up, but fortunately he did survive. The same year, Mother had left baby William right in front of the house. She had gone in for a few minutes, when she heard his cry and went to investigate. She saw a wolf trying to carry him away. But William's hand-me-down clothes were too worn to support his weight and Mother, with broom in hand, managed to get the baby."

On May 18, 1905 a bear raided the poultry yard of a settler west of Leduc. While Mrs. Dixon and her children fled to safety, "one little Miss Dixon was less fortunate in her escape, receiving on one of her arms a grab from bruin's powerful jaws. However, Providence apparently came to the rescue and the little one escaped scatheless, the dress receiving bruin's grinders instead."

Bears and homesteaders were often equally startled when they met. As Olive Woodman's *Hills of Hope* records, Harry Tyrrell and his wife Margaret had just put up the walls of a log cabin in Highvale and spread a tent for a makeshift roof at one end, when came a three-day siege of heavy rain. "During this storm, a big black bear climbed up the wall and rolled the top log which was holding the end of the tent in place. The bear landed in the house, bringing down one end of the tent with him. The bear was obviously as surprised as they were because he just stood up and looked at them. Mrs. Tyrrell and the boys started to yell at the bear while hammering on a tin dishpan. The surprised bear scurried back over the wall and away into the woods.

The Trials of the Unprepared

In *Pioneers and Progress*, Clarissa Wyse remembers hapless neighbours in the Alix district. "They lived in a house dug into a hill like a root cellar, boarded up in the front with one little window and door, and they nearly starved. The mother came over to our house one day, crying, saying they were out of food. Dad went to the granary and cut off about 25 pounds of frozen meat. Mom gave her a quarter of a sack of flour, baking powder and vegetables. Dad took it over on the stone boat. Pretty soon we could see smoke coming out of the chimney and we knew they were probably making mulligan stew."

Worse was in store for this pathetic family: "They didn't have a well. They carried water from our place, and when it was too cold to carry it, they used water from a slough near their house. Some of them got typhoid fever from the slough water, and the mother and one boy died."

Perils in Transit

Arthur Miller was working as a cowhand and coal miner when he slipped while trying to jump aboard a wagon. In *Chatter Chips from Beaver Dam Creek* he says, "I fell under, the rear wheel going over my leg and breaking it above the knee. Fred helped me onto the load. I lay on my stomach and drove the team eight miles to the ranch...The next morning I was loaded in a lum-

ber wagon on a mattress and as they had to walk the horses it took all day to get me to Stettler." There he lodged with an English nurse who took in patients. "The doctor came and they had to cut my overalls off as my leg was so badly swollen. The doctor told me to take hold of the bed and hang on while he set the leg. He pulled it out and put tape on my leg and fastened a twenty-pound iron to keep it in place. He wrapped a two-by-four with cloth and fastened it to my ankle and below and above the break and around my chest. I had to lie flat on my back for eight weeks. When the swelling went down he put a cast on."

In *Chaps and Chinooks* Mrs. Robinson described a trip with her mother and her husband, Joe. "Mother was holding the baby in the back of the democrat. Fording the river, one wheel dropped into some loose gravel. Losing her balance, mother let the baby drop into the river—luckily upstream, and as Kathleen floated under the democrat she washed up against one wheel. Still maintaining control of the colts, Joe grasped Kathleen's long clothes. I calmed myself with half a glass of brandy, then nursed the baby and she slept for twelve hours!"

A.B. Adshead writes in *Pioneer Tales*, "Bridges were few and miles apart; the fords were shifty and not always safe." Every spring, someone died trying to cross a river. Ray Long drowned in high water fording Bragg Creek in a wagon. Mrs. Josh Bond and Mrs. Mike Lamarche and her 14-year-old stepdaughter were lost when they disregarded advice to use Innisfail Bridge, and tried to ford the Red Deer River west of Penhold.

Alberta Homemaker: Four Years' Effort, painted by F. de Forrest Schook in 1909 and shown at the CPR exhibition in New York, 1911. There were always the occasions of pure joy.

199

Wagon stuck in mud hole, Beynon area, Alberta, c. 1910.

THE PRAIRIE WIFE
Far from Medical Aid

'The Prairie Wife — Far from Medical Aid,' *an illustration from the Calgary* Eye Opener.

Snow, Ice and Cold

In the district south of Calgary, an Icelander named Sigurdson stayed guarding his flock of sheep through a storm so fierce that he could keep from freezing only by slaughtering a sheep and wrapping himself in the skin to keep warm.

In *Prairie Reminiscences* Rosebud pioneer John Martin describes the ordeal of Jim Wishart, whose only shelter from a three-day blizzard was a snowdrift where he lived on flour and snow. "At times he thought someone was talking to him and he was not alone while slowly freezing to death. When the storm was over, he started for home. His feet were badly frozen and he rested them by crawling over the snowdrifts. He could see the banks of Rosebud Creek near his home at setting sun, but he was now so weak that he couldn't even crawl. He lay down to die, but in his slumber he heard a voice telling him to get up. He got to the top of the hill in sight of his home. His wife Eliza from the kitchen window saw the dark object in the snow, and soon her son Dave carried Jim home. Eliza tried to save her husband's frozen toes but when they started to decay, she and Dave cut them off with a hammer and butcher knife. Eliza held the knife while Dave struck the back of it. Jim never could wear boots any more."

Of Us and the Oxen describes the Roberts' delight in the summer of 1908 as they watched their first 45 acres of wheat grow shoulder high. Only two weeks before harvest, the air grew sultry. "There was suddenly a mighty rushing and roaring, and the storm in all its fury was upon us. In a few seconds the windows on the east side of the house were shivered to atoms, and hailstones and flying glass filled the air. The hail did not last more than ten minutes, but the havoc was complete. When Papa came in the first thing he said was, 'The crop is gone.'"

A.D. Adshead describes the aftermath of the most severe hailstorm he ever saw: "The poor little chicks in the coop were all drowned, or chilled to death. In the garden, upon which we depended for our winter vegetables, not a potato to be seen, of the cabbages, only a few torn pieces of leaves driven into the ground, and what of the flourishing grainfield that but an hour since had proudly lifted its leaves to the sun? Only a black field of earth was left, with nothing on it except a surface indented all over with holes like huge smallpox marks, where the lashing hail had been driven deep into the soil after having cut to pieces the grain so that not a vestige was visible. And what of the luxuriant prairie grass? Nothing left but the top of the sod, not a pound of hay could we cut there now for winter use for our cattle. We counted dozens of dead ducklings floating on the creek, and the horses came up to the barn with lumps on their backs as big as walnuts."

The Payoff

Jean Bruce in *The Last Best West* writes of a man who took possession of his quarter-section in 1908: "I started to break with four horses tandem and a short handled wooden beam John Deere walking plough. The land was heavy and sticky and hard to break and at times you would have to clean the mouldboard three times on the half mile. Nothing seemed a burden to me that summer. My boots hurt my feet walking in the furrow and one day at noon after I got hitched up I thought I would try it in my bare feet and the cool ground felt so good that I never had my boots on again that summer when I was ploughing. If I wasn't out in the field at 6 o'clock in the morning I thought the day was lost, and at night I went to bed, not tired, but wishing that it was morning so that I could get up again. That year I got eighty acres ready for crop."

The eastern Europeans, though harder pressed by poverty, seemed generally more appreciative of the new land. Kost Zaharichuk, of Smoky Lake, came from Bukovina with only $10, and that autumn earned ten sacks of potatoes by working for a German farmer in Fort Saskatchewan. He said, "My wife couldn't believe it and came fifty miles on foot to see for herself. She knelt over those potatoes and prayed for an hour. She thanked God for not letting us starve to death in Canada."

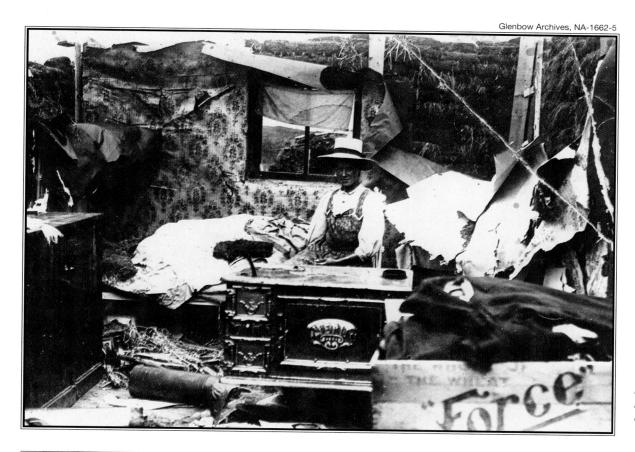

Mrs. C. Bull's home, McLaughlin, Alberta, after tornado, early 1900s.

A comedy of errors in the British style

FATHER WAS A GENTLEMAN FARMER WHO COULDN'T MAKE IT AT HOME.
IT CERTAINLY DIDN'T APPEAR HE'D DO ANY BETTER IN THE COLONIES

In Treasure of Memories, *Jack Timm fondly remembers his father's mixture of British pluck and pioneer incompetence.*

My parents were tenant farmers in England; they called themselves "gentleman farmers." As they were getting middle-aged, and it got harder and harder to make a living, they could either go and break stone on the road until it was time to go to the poor house, or they could emigrate to the colonies; the latter being considered the less disgraceful. Kids used to whisper, "The Timms have got to go to the colonies!"

My parents had read glowing accounts of the wonderful farming land in Canada. The brochures described it as a land flowing with milk and honey. My mother said, "It will be a good experience for Jack." If only she had left out the "good," it would have been more true.

Now it was in 1909 when it all started for me. At breakfast one morning my mother said to Father, "Since we have decided to emigrate to Canada we had better have Jack circumcized as I understand it's all very unsanitary out in those wild places." I couldn't quite see the connection myself, but I remember my good experiences were about to start.

I was sent to the telegraph office to send a cable to my uncle to acquaint him of our impending arrival. The girl said, "Oh dear! Has it come to that? Aren't you afraid? All those red Indians! You could be scalped, or eaten by wild animals."

We stayed that first winter with my uncle in Erskine. We were snowbound and father said he would ride to Stettler and see the land agent to select a farm. I got the horse ready while father was getting into his foxhunting regalia, scarlet, blue and yellow. I remember my mother saying, "You know, Walter is a fine figure of a man on a horse."

Father mounted in the English style, somewhat hampered by the Mexican saddle. "Well, I'm off now," he said, and gave the horse a smart smack with his crop. The horse put his head between his legs and sure enough, father was off! He nose-dived into a big snowdrift.

Father then said he would walk to Stettler, and Uncle said, "Take the shortcut across the frozen lake." It was about forty degrees below zero. We got halfway across and there was a muskrat's house built up through the ice. Father said, "That's a jolly queer thing. I'll just have a closer look," and he disappeared under the ice. I managed to grab him when he popped up and hauled him out. Father spent the rest of the winter in bed with pneumonia.

Towards spring we went to the land agent to select a farm. The agent brought out the map of Alberta and said, "What type of a farm would you be looking for?" My father said,

Montreal Daily Star cartoon depicting the fatuous English immigrant en route. 'The men out here are a jolly lot; they seem to be amused at something all the time.'

"Oh, I'm used to mixed farming," and they picked a homestead on the Saskatchewan border. It said on the map it was level and well watered. Father said that would do nicely.

All the things he had gathered up such as one wagon, a walking plough, three horses, bales of hay, and the boxes of useless stuff they had brought from England were put in a boxcar. I was put in with it and the car was sealed up. After about four days my father opened the door and I looked out on the promised land. We were at the end of steel at Provost.

We finally got two of the broncos hitched to the wagon. The third refused to take any part of it so we led him behind. Someone said, "You may make it to the big ravine the first day and camp on the creek." We got there about dark and before father realized it we had plunged down the bank and into the creek. The broncos all broke loose and disappeared. Father said, "We'll have to stay here until daylight."

I saw a light in the distance and we went to get help.

Three families of Russians came out. They held the lantern first in front of father and then me. I had my sailor suit on, and father had his "gentleman farmer" outfit, complete with starched dicky down the front. I think they thought we had landed from outer space. When daylight came they gave me a good wash and some crushed meal. They had one cow, hitched to a wooden plough with six of the women. I was much impressed. By then the men had got the wagon out and found our horses, so we made another start.

In the course of time we found the main peg at the corner of what should have been the farm. I said to father, "It's level all right," and looking down the huge cracks, I said, "It's well watered too." It turned out to be a dried-up salt pan.

We found our way back to Provost. We went to the land agent and he said, "Too bad, but you can't file again for six months," and that was when I first became aware of corruption in high places. Father said, "That puts me in a terrible fix. It will be winter before we can settle."

The chap said, "I might be able to help you, for a consideration, you understand. Would it be worth ten dollars if I could arrange something?" Father said, "That would be fine."

So the agent said, "Well, just suppose from now on you could be Harry instead of Walter." We again set off, armed with plots showing vacant homesteads all the way south to the CNR. On the "tin can trail," marked with empty food tins, we met up with an old Polish joker called Sasky. He said, "You'd better let me locate you. I'm an expert."

Father thought after his experiences it would be best to employ him. Sasky said the hilly land was best because "you get more acres to the square mile." So that is how we came to Section 17, Township 33, Range 5. Sasky said, "I'm an expert at building shacks, so it would be best to let me do yours." Sasky couldn't read or write but he made sure he would have plenty of lumber. He made the shack half the size and finished up with what he said was enough to build a shed for the cow.

Next time out, mother said she would like to go and see the farm and residence, so we all set off again. The trail had lots of settlers going each way and they told us one day we might make it to McNalty's stopping house by nightfall.

disintegrated in mid-stream. We were all flying into the icy water. We scrambled up the opposite bank. I didn't think it was possible for a person to shiver like I did that day.

Father had to go to Castor for new wheels, so for the next ten days mother and I ate pigweed. I remember she said it was so good for the blood. The mosquitoes sure thought so too.

When father returned he said it would be all right now. When we got to the homestead we could feast on the potatoes and salt pork we had left there, but that was not to be. Bill Doel's bullocks had eaten the potatoes and the coyotes had cleaned up the bacon.

We stayed on the "tin can trail," and one nightfall we passed an empty shack where we stayed the night. The next morning father said, "I'll take Jack and find the homestead." In the afternoon we had travelled some miles. He said, "I'll walk up that big hill and see if I can recognize any landmarks." I tied the horses round the wagon and it got dark, but he didn't show up. A pack of coyotes surrounded the wagon and set up a ghastly howling. The horses were scared and so was I.

Next afternoon a man rode up on horseback. He said, "I found your father wandering about. He's at my place and I will take you there." Later, father said to mother, "The men out here are a jolly lot. They seem to be amused at something all the time." Of course, one look at his turn-out would make a cat laugh.

Father was anxious to make a start at breaking so we hitched the broncos to the walking plough. I led them while father guided the plough. At first he had difficulty getting it to penetrate the hard soil. Finally it went into the ground and he shouted, "Whip them up, it's going fine!" But the share struck a huge rock and the plough shot up and the handle caught him under the chin. He was knocked out cold.

Some time afterward he went to get a cow. An awful storm came up, great chunks of ice with a terrific wind. Mother and I went into the shack just as it lifted into the air. It sailed along into the slough and fell to pieces. We had a lucky escape that time. Father came back, but he had lost the cow. He had his thumb dislocated by one of the stones.

We were getting hungry and we saw the CPR construction

Father said he'd ride to Stettler. I got the horse ready while he was getting into his foxhunting regalia. Said Mother, 'Walter is a fine figure of a man on a horse.'

Mother said, "Oh, that would be nice. I could do with a bed and bath." Mr. McNalty gave us a warm welcome. I went down to the stable. Men were sleeping under their wagons, so we too slept under our wagon all night.

Crossing Sounding Creek was a hazard in spring. Our host said the crossing near the house was all right if you kept clear of the rocks. The last thing I heard as we plunged down the steep bank was Mr. McNalty yelling, "Keep clear of the rocks," but we couldn't see them. The wagon smashed into them and

camp where the cook set us down to a good feed of fresh bread, New Zealand butter and Danish cheese. We thought that a bit odd in the land that flowed with milk and honey.

Coming back we could see a big smoke and found that a prairie fire had burned from the CPR line to the CNR in the south. Our homestead was in the middle of it and everythig was burned black. I met two chaps that had been located in the Butte Hills area and they said, "We are getting out of this Godforsaken place and heading back to the good old USA."

Section Four

THE EMERGING ECONOMY

Chapters by Terry Johnson, Link Byfield, Bob Bott & Carol Dean

The Little Bow Trading Company store, High River, around the turn of the century
Glenbow Archives, NA-370-26

CHAPTER ONE

Into the seeming holes of hell Frank Sherman shone a light

CONDITIONS IN THE CROWSNEST MINES WERE A UNION WAITING TO HAPPEN.
AN ENGLISHMAN ON A MARXIST MISSION MADE SURE IT DID

Crowsnest Museum

Workers at the Bellevue mine entrance 1905. There was a vast gulf between the men who dug the coal and those in central Canada who financed the operations.

by TERRY JOHNSON

By the time Frank Henry Sherman landed in the Crowsnest Pass in May 1900 he was desperate for work. Born in Gloucester, England, in 1869, he had been nurtured as a youth on the social gospel of Methodism. He had sworn off liquor for life and been a preacher. Then, working in the coal pits of Wales' famous Rhondda Valley, he had become a fervent trade unionist which, after a failed strike in 1898, got him blacklisted by management.

He fled to America, only to find that his reputation had preceded him. Mine owners in the Pennsylvania coalfields told him to pack up his family and move on. But where? He had heard of the Crowsnest up in Canada where mine operators, it was said, weren't so particular about whom they hired. They needed as many experienced men as they could find. So Frank Sherman, his wife and young children headed for Canada and the Crowsnest.

He arrived with the boom. Coal had been noted in the Crowsnest in 1845 by the Belgian missionary Father Pierre-Jean De Smet. "We could find nothing but coal, and coal everywhere," Michael Phillipps, a Hudson's Bay Company clerk, reported in disgust in 1874. He wanted gold. However abundant coal was, there was no market for it. Then came the 1897 Crow's Nest Pass Agreement (Vol. 1, Sect. 4, ch. 3) and the CPR pushed a line through the pass to Kootenay Lake,

---

sparking a wild rush to exploit the hard, high-quality bituminous that lay in thick seams along the railway's path. The coal was ideal for stoking the boilers of the CPR's engines and, processed into coke, for fuelling the big smelter built at Trail, BC in 1895. The first Crowsnest mine opened at Blairmore in 1898. Ten other mining towns were established in the pass in the next fourteen months. The $3-a-day wages attracted miners by the hundreds from the US, England, Wales, France, Italy and Bohemia, and from the coal pits of Romania and Hungary.

All of which made an admirable stamping ground for Sherman. Getting a job was easy. The bearded, dark-haired Englishman needed only to present himself to the foreman of the mine in Morrissey on the BC side of the pass, to find himself working underground again. His sober, even-handedness so impressed his fellow workers they elected him the Morrissey mine's first check weighman.[1]

Glenbow Archives, NA-4567-1

Frank Henry Sherman, taken in 1911. He emigrated with his wife and children to a place where he could set about righting wrongs.

But Sherman was not there to mine coal, but to hasten the revolution. In 1903 he was elected president of the newly organized 3,293-member District 18 of the United Mine Workers of America (UMWA), covering an area embracing the Crowsnest Pass and Lethbridge. In the next six years he would lead his miners on the most pivotal Canadian strike of the decade, discard his Methodist beliefs for the class-against-class politics of Karl Marx, and eventually build a radical coalition of union men and unskilled immigrant labourers that would, in 1909, elect Alberta's first socialist MLA.

Times were turning good in Alberta in 1900. After a twelve-year recession, the West was re-establishing itself as a land of opportunity. Wages for skilled tradesmen were relatively high and, for the English-speaking at least, there were few class-based barriers to advancement. "The rich and successful had no reason to go West," writes Calgary historian Paul Voisey. "The very poor

Sherman was not there to mine coal, but to hasten the revolution. He would lead his miners on the most pivotal Canadian strike of the decade.

could not afford it. There was a significant degree of social equality on the frontier and when an elite did emerge it was *nouveau riche.*" In the West's growing cities, businessman and brick mason mingled socially to an extent unheard of in Europe or central Canada. After all, many a successful businessman had been a brick mason short years before.

Yet as Sherman well knew, opportunity was no safeguard against labour strife. He saw that a vast gulf separated the central Canadian industrialists who financed the West's development from the men who laid the track, dug the coal and brought in the harvest. The former were men like Elliott Torrance Galt, whose Alberta Railway and Irrigation Company (AR&I Co.) built the city of Lethbridge and settled the southern prairie.[2] They spoke glowingly of their work in bringing the northwest "under Christian civilization," writes A.A. den Otter in his *Civilizing the West.* But they were also members of "a business world that had divorced its religious convictions from the marketplace." For them, workers were nothing more than cogs in the machinery of business, factors of production to be obtained at the lowest possible cost.[3]

The workers, on the other hand, writes den Otter, formed a "restless, cosmopolitan labour force of young immigrants" who carried amidst their cultural baggage "encounters with the broad sweep of radicalism on two continents." Lured west by labour contractors who promised high wages and

[1] The check weighman, paid by the contract miners themselves, ensured that the company properly weighed the coal cars as they were unloaded. It was a position of great trust—a man not above taking a company bribe could easily short-change his fellow miners, who were paid by the coal they produced.

[2] The AR&I Co. was the off-spring of the North Western Coal and Navigation Co., formed in April 1882 by Galt's father, Sir Alexander Galt, a father of Confederation and Canadian high commissioner in London. The elder Galt used his government connections to wrangle a grant of more than one million acres of land and mining rights, representing virtually all southern Alberta's coalfields, in return for a promise to build a railway into the region. He raised the capital needed for the venture from the British financiers he met through his work in London.

[3] To the miners, Galt evidenced a cold indifference to the effect his business decisions had upon them. In 1894, when the Anaconda smelter in Montana closed, costing his colliery a major customer, he promptly fired all 500 members of his mine crew. Then, in a gesture that infuriated them, he posted the names of the 130 married men he considered suitable for employment. They could come back to their jobs, but only if they accepted a 17% cut in wages.

comfortable accommodation, they were instead crowded into damp, unheated and disease-ridden tents and bunkhouses. Then, after weeks of work, they often found that the contractor's charges exceeded the wages they had earned. There were deductions for everything from meals and transportation to the rough blankets they slept on and the meagre medical care they received. If they dared quit, they could be charged under the Masters and Servants Act for breaking the terms of their contract.

Even the North-West Mounted Police were sympathetic to the men's plight. In 1897, during the first year of construction of the Crowsnest Pass railway, the Mounties arrested and jailed six men for desertion under the Masters and Servants Act. But Fort Macleod police inspector G.E. Sanders attacked the "disgraceful" conditions of their employment. He was particularly angered by the plight of those left penniless after their terms of service finished. They wander "without blankets or even boots in some cases," Insp. Sanders complained. "No provision has been made by the company to return these men to their homes. Winter is coming on and there is likelihood of much hardship and destitution. Some pressure ought to be brought to bear for fairer treatment of the men."

Already, Sherman noted, public outrage at such conditions, and the deaths of two men in a Crowsnest camp in 1899, had prompted Ottawa to pass the Public Works Health Act of 1900, which set health standards in railway and logging camps. But Sherman saw that the law had little effect. Government inspectors, feted during their visits to the camps, turned a blind eye to the squalid accommodations, complained a navvie working on the Grand Trunk Pacific Railway, west of Edmonton. "These inspectors are all the same," he wrote to a Winnipeg newspaper. "What have they amounted to? Nothing. Conditions are worse than ever." Men stricken with disease — even typhoid fever was a problem — were charged for room and board and the medical care they received while unable to work. Those injured on the job were simply let go. One GTP navvy, fired after his fingers were crushed while laying track, begged to be hired back at a softer job. He was finally given work, ironically enough, tending the camp's sick mules.

Spontaneous revolts were common. In 1907, for example, a group of forty Italian navvies

---

Government inspectors, feted during their visits to the camps, turned a blind eye to the squalid accommodation.

---

struck a CPR camp near Nanton, threatening to kill their foremen if the company didn't provide the wages, hot meals and heated quarters they said had been promised them. The CPR, after yielding to some of their demands, transferred the men to other parts of the division "so as not to have them all together in case of further trouble."

But generally the navvies were no match for their powerful corporate opponents. There was no shortage of men willing to take their jobs, however miserable the conditions. Newly-arrived homesteaders were desperate for any kind of temporary paid work to support their farms. Employers used this vast pool of seasonal labour to keep wages low and workers in line.[4] "The navvies had little choice but to accept their fate," notes labour historian Warren Caragata. "No outside organizations were willing to come to their aid and they had almost no bargaining power."

But the railway camps were transitory. The coal mines were not, and it was in the coalfields that radical ideas like those of Frank Sherman could have the biggest impact. Coal, more than anything else, fuelled the West's economic boom. Without it, the prairie farmers would have frozen in their homes, and the trains that carried their grain to markets ground to a halt. To find the skilled men needed to dig it out of the earth, the coal companies recruited from around the globe. But whatever language they spoke or religion they embraced, the miners held one conviction in common: they were never paid enough for spending ten hours a day, six days a week, underground.

Coal mining was deadly work, especially in the Crowsnest Pass. The mines there were rich in methane, highly combustible gas. A stray spark could ignite it and the explosive, ever-present coal dust. Between 1900 and 1945, more than 1,000 Alberta coal miners lost their lives in accidents and explosions, most in the fourteen-mile-long strip of mines between Blairmore and the BC border. Until the 1950s the federal department of mines kept statistics on how many tons of coal were produced per mine fatality.

That work is pretty hard on a boy. I have seen them spitting up coal dust from one end of the week to the other. They hardly ever get a breath of air during the whole ten hours they are there and I don't care if he's made of iron, it will tell on him after years.
- *Alexander McLeod, a Crowsnest Pass miner, in an interview with a 1907 Alberta commission studying the coal industry.*

Even before the explosions at Bellevue in 1910 that killed 29 men and at Hillcrest in 1914 that claimed 146 lives, the danger proved too much for some. Italian immigrant John Marconi was delighted to land a good-paying job as a chute loader at the coal mine in Lille in 1906. Only eighteen, he was earning twice the money he'd made in the construction camps and CPR work gangs that had financed his long journey across the continent. But he didn't last long. One day a dead miner tumbled down the chute and into the mine car he was loading. "It upset him so much," remembered his son, "he quit the mine and got a job as porter at the Lille Hotel."

The miners' home life was little safer. "Some of Alberta's coal towns were as bad as any in the world," writes University of Calgary historian David Jay Bercuson in the academic journal Labour/*Le Travailleur.* Housing was generally poor, with families living in small frame shacks. Few mines had bathhouses so the men, black with coal dust, had to wash up at home. In the evenings, coal oil lamps provided light. Single men were crowded into unventilated bunkhouses that bred disease.

In Lille, a typical Crowsnest mining town, all the houses were company-owned. A wood-frame duplex rented for $9.50 a month, plus $1.50 extra for running water and fifty cents for a chicken pen. The family of Edward Ledieu, one of a contingent of French miners recruited after the 1906 mine explosion at Courriere that killed 1,000 men, was hardly prepared for the spartan accommodations when they arrived ten months later. "I will never forget the expression on my mother's face when she entered the house," remembered Ledieu's son. Curtains divided the

Elliot Torrance Galt (below), whose family built Lethbridge, and the Galt mine (above). It was said his ideas of civilized Christian behaviour didn't extend into his mines.

[4]Few, however, were willing to work at the rock-bottom, $15-a-month wages paid farmhands. To solve the problem, the Salvation Army and other agencies brought in thousands of immigrants on contracts that confined them to their on-farm jobs. It made for a sullen and uncooperative workforce. Complained one Alberta farmer in a 1907 letter to his MP: "The government is trying to bring settlers or farmers into the West all the time. What is needed is men to work for the farmers that are already here or those who are here will have to go out of business. I hired a man from the Salvation Army. He is with me yet but he knows he could get $3 a day if he were free and reminds me of that fact quite often."

Cleaning the coal at the surface of the Entwistle mine, around 1910. Women and children were often used at this stage of operations.

kitchen and dining room from the bedroom. The kitchen stove, bereft of its original legs, sat on four blocks of wood. A packing case served as a kitchen table, and stacked orange crates as a cupboard for pots and dishes. It was all very clean, but Mrs. Ledieu was having none of it. "If this is Canada," she exclaimed, "I am going back home."

The coal operators had hoped that, by recruiting an ethnically mixed workforce, they could resist unionization. Despite the grim living conditions the miners shared, British subjects would not find common ground with Slavs or Italians or Frenchmen, the owners expected. Indeed, in 1899, Galt played on the differences between his Hungarian and English miners to break an organizing drive by a union that called itself the Western Federation of Miners. That fall, in compliance

Sherman strove to turn the mining camps into closely-knit communities. The UMWA organized sports days, picnics and dances and built a miners' hospital in Coleman in 1906.

with a territorial ordinance from the Haultain government, Galt had reduced the mine's workday from ten to eight hours, raising hourly wages accordingly. The contract miners wanted a similar adjustment in their rates of pay.

But the WFM badly mishandled the resulting dispute. With the harvest complete, the community was filling with homesteaders looking for winter jobs. And the men were split — the hourly workers, predominantly Hungarians and Slavs, saw no reason to strike for the benefit of the better-paid contract miners. When Galt threatened a lockout, the divided union had to back down. In the Winnipeg labour newspaper *The Voice*, the WFM correspondent made a laconic admission of defeat. "The silk dresses and diamonds which some of us were so rash as to promise our wives and sweethearts will have to be abandoned until the coming of the new time," he wrote. Sherman, no doubt, carefully studied the mistakes made by the WFM, predecessor of the UMWA.

Soon less than half the miners in the Crowsnest spoke English, but by then Sherman had moved decisively against racial disunity. After taking over the UMWA's District 18, he hired organizers who spoke Italian, Ukrainian or Hungarian. He had union literature translated into the languages of the miners. The press might despise these "foreign elements." He didn't, and he won their respect. In 1909, despite the strong public prejudice against Asians, the UMWA opened its ranks to Chinese and Japanese miners.

He also strove to turn the mining camps into closely knit communities. The UMWA organized sports days, picnics and dances. It established a fund to help injured miners or widows left without husbands.[5] And, to ensure that the men and their families were given medical care, the union built a seventeen-bed miners' hospital in Coleman in 1906, paying the salary of the doctor on staff.

All this helped Sherman batter out agreements with most Crowsnest mine operators on both sides of the Alberta-BC border. But Galt's colliery near Lethbridge, largest in the province, was another matter. Galt had broken strikes in 1894, 1897 and 1899. He was sure he could do it again. So in February 1906, when 363 of his 524 miners met at Oliver's Hall to found UMWA Local 574, the company carefully ignored the event. When Sherman himself showed up in town on March 7, mine manager P.L. Naismith refused to meet him, instead threatening to fire any union member making demands on the company. Two days later, the most pivotal Canadian strike of the decade began.

The company, keenly aware of the riots and armed confrontations that had marked the WFM's organizing drives in Colorado and Montana, expected the worst. Naismith appealed to the Royal North-West Mounted Police to protect the company's property and any men who chose to work during the strike. "A large majority of our men are foreign," he wrote the RNWMP commissioner, "and with a little urging on the part of their leaders, are capable of doing anything."

On March 18 the violence began. A bundle of dynamite was set off as a warning at the vacant home of a non-union mine worker. RNWMP Inspector J.O. Wilson pleaded for reinforcements. "My small force would not be much against 500 men, especially if crazed by drink," he warned. In response, one of every ten members of the entire RNWMP were committed to the dispute: 58 officers and men patrolled the streets of Staffordville, the mining town across the railroad tracks from the city of Lethbridge. A further 21 were held ready for action in Regina. Wilson also deputized eleven company employees as special constables, and planted a plainclothes policeman amongst

In March the violence began. Dynamite was set off at the vacant home of a non-union mine worker. The RNWMP inspector feared for his men's chances against 500 drink-crazed miners.

the eastern European miners.

At first, these preparations seemed excessive. The strikers repeatedly voiced their displeasure at the handful of men who continued to work. The police intervened. And in the first sixty days of the strike, there were two so-called riots, at least one case of arson and thirteen separate explosions. Yet the deceptively high level of violence did not cause a single serious injury. This was probably Sherman strategy. The last thing he wanted was a decisive confrontation with the police. It could only result in the defeat of the strikers and, very probably, the destruction of District 18 itself. So he struggled to rein in the high temper of his membership and to turn circumstances to the union's favour.

The UMWA leader's most important move was to provide transportation out of town to the single, transient men who were the most likely to provoke the police. The Galt colliery's workforce was unusually well established. More than half the miners had settled in the city, bought town lots, and begun raising families. Many had also acquired homesteads and worked their farms in the summer when the mines usually closed. Sherman himself had a small farm at Taber. Men with families and a proven commitment to their community could be counted on to act in a prudent fashion, Sherman reasoned.

In the first weeks of the strike the union turned to the charivari, or rough music (also called a shivaree), to taunt the thirty or forty men who broke ranks and continued to work. Groups of as many as 200 men, women and children tailed the strikebreakers to and from the mine gates, banging on pots and pans, blowing tin horns, and waving banners. The custom had developed in medieval England as a means of expressing community disapproval of such immoral conduct as adultery or wife beating. It was readily adopted by coal miners in the 1800s. And, though the police made it clear in mid-March that they would not allow the charivaris to continue, the parades had by then accomplished their purpose: censured by their neighbours, the non-union men moved with their families into makeshift housing on the mine property.

The first real test for Sherman and the union came at the end of March when a blacksmith decided to quit the union and return to work. The strikers had to warn others that this was an

[5]The same concerns prompted the various ethnic communities to create their own social welfare organizations. In 1906, for example, 72 Italian miners in Lille founded a chapter of the Italian Benevolent Society. Members paid $4 a year in dues. If they were injured or sick, they could draw $10 a week in benefits. All were obliged to attend the funeral of any member who died, or face a $2 fine.

Royal North-West Mounted Police at the Galt coal mine, date unknown. Galt had broken strikes before and was sure he could do it again.

unacceptable or even dangerous decision. So when the man went home to remove his belongings, a group of about fifty union men assembled in the street and began to hoot, yell and beat cans with sticks. Amidst the din, an RNWMP constable pulled his pistol and threatened a member of the crowd.

The incident, though it ended peacefully, could well have prompted Wilson to instruct his men to press charges for illegal assembly against strikers who acted in similar fashion. Instead, Sherman seized the initiative. He phoned the RNWMP commander to complain. And he telegraphed Alphonse Verville, a Labour MP from Montreal, to raise the issue in the House of Commons. Wilson, put on the defensive, removed the offending constable from duty and ordered his men to keep their pistols holstered.

Sherman kept in regular contact with Wilson after the incident, and even helped police prosecute UMWA members who did break the law. In the process, he gained Wilson's respect and helped temper the policeman's initial fears of a massive confrontation. So in late April, when rumours began circulating that Sherman was on his way to Taber to pick up a cache of rifles and ammunition for the strikers, Wilson simply dismissed them. In fact, the UMWA leader had merely left to work his homestead.

Wilson strove, too, to evade possible opportunities for confrontation. For instance, on April 3 a crowd of women threw snow at a strikebreaker trying to remove furniture from his home. The

---

As summer became fall, it looked like the company could outlast the union. With the harvest completed it increased its non-union workforce to almost 250 men.

---

women then pummelled the two Mounties who intervened. "We have a Slav woman who went out and whipped one of the police to a standstill," the UMWA journal boasted. The bruised constable wanted to press charges. Wilson discouraged him. He "thought it better not to bother with women."

Even so the violence escalated. That same day, a crowd of 300 men, women and children jeered at another group of three men who had also come to cart off their possessions to the mine camp. When one of the men swung a hatchet at a boy who was taunting him, the crowd began hurling stones and bottles. The man with the hatchet was cut and knocked to the ground, and a Mountie winded by a blow to his stomach before the crowd dispersed. That night the houses belonging to the three men were burnt to the ground in retaliation. On April 4, a mine gate confrontation between a group of strikebreakers and two drunken miners developed into another full-fledged brawl between 200 stone-throwing union men and a handful of police.

THE EMERGING ECONOMY

By then, however, the union had made its point: despite the heavy police presence, it could still punish men who broke ranks. At the same time, while the violence hurt the UMWA's image, it did not break Sherman's hold on the miners. Running as a Labour candidate in an April 12 provincial by-election in Lethbridge, the UMWA leader lost by only eighty votes to his Liberal opponent and took 95% of

'I recognize only two classes,' said R.C. Owens, 'the workers and the idlers. I represent the workers.'

the votes in Staffordville. The AR&I Co, impressed by the workers' discipline and solidarity, switched tactics. It decided to wait the union out. Tension subsided as the strike wore on into the summer.[6]

The long summer calm broke on August 18 when a charge of dynamite was set off at a working miner's home. The explosion, the first at an occupied building, tore off the front porch and terrified the miner's wife. Sherman promptly accused the company of setting the charge itself to discredit the union. That led the *Lethbridge Herald* to challenge the UMWA leader to produce evidence for his charge. But the flare-up proved temporary.

Throughout the strike, a diplomatic Sherman had met regularly with Wilson to help identify UMWA members who broke the law. As historian William Baker writes, this relationship helped miners and police carve out a *modus vivendi:* the police accepted the union's need to demonstrate its opposition to strikebreaking, while the miners for the most part refrained from physical violence. Wilson, in turn, only half-heartedly investigated the occasional use of dynamite by strikers. Repeatedly assured that UMWA members would not physically harm their opponents, the police grudgingly accepted the blasts as part of the UMWA's arsenal.

As summer turned into fall, it began to look as though the company could outlast the union. With the harvest completed, it was able to increase its non-union workforce to almost 250 men and resume operation of the mine. But many of the strikebreakers were novice miners. Production continued at a fraction of its customary pace. And the very importance of the company's product conspired against it. The Galt colliery was then the principal prairie supplier of domestic coal. A cold fall increased the demand for fuel. A rich harvest reduced the number of cars available for moving what coal supplies were available. Thus, even as UMWA's resolve began to waver, the weather and the grain economy threatened a severe coal famine. The dispute rapidly assumed a political dimension.

Saskatchewan Agriculture Minister W.R. Motherwell, alarmed that both union and company were "thoroughly confident of ultimate success," urged federal intervention. "I fear very much for the safety of our own settlers on the open plains with draughty dwellings and no fuel in sight," he cabled Ottawa. "The situation is so serious that farmers are taking up their fence posts for fuel. You can't afford to deal with negotiations for the sake of diplomacy when the people are perishing without coal." Motherwell's deputy minister was more brusque. He urged the federal department of labour to either order the miners back to work or send in the army to do their jobs. As alarming stories of the crisis reached Europe, politicians worried that the flow of immigrants to the prairies would begin to dry up. Labour Minister Rodolphe Lemieux sent his deputy out to Lethbridge to settle the dispute. This young man's name was William Lyon Mackenzie King, destined to become prime minister of Canada (see sidebar).

King's arrival distressed AR&I Co. manager Naismith. "We are the pioneers in the coal mining industry in this country and operated our mines until a few years ago — covering a period of at least fifteen years — without one cent of profit to our operators," he told the federal mediator. He'd hire back strikers, he said, but "if they do not want to work for us at the wages paid at the time they left us we are satisfied and will continue to give employment to others." Sherman stubbornly insisted that his UMWA members would stay out until they won an agreement recognizing their union.

But King, a superb mediator, played the growing public concern over the strike to the hilt.

Alberta's first socialist MLA Charles O'Brien in 1910. He so upset his colleagues, they threw inkwells at him.

[6] The strike had a depressing effect on local businesses. But the city's Southard department store turned to the now-familiar "everything must go" sale to lure back its cash-poor customers. The store had ordered a large selection of men's and women's clothing for the spring season, it explained in a full-page April 4 ad. "Owing to the depression in business caused by the strike," the store explained, "we have decided to literally slaughter this gigantic stock!" It did not, of course, mean literally.

213

Neither Naismith nor the union dared risk being painted as the villain in the breakdown of the talks. King eventually wrung a 10% wage hike out of the company. Sherman finally capitulated on his demand for union recognition and the dues checkoff, instead suggesting that King's proposed non-discrimination clause be taken to John Mitchell, the UMWA's international president.

That concession made an agreement all but certain, King confided in his memoirs. "I have the men now in a position where it can be positively shown that unless this strike is settled it is because one man in the United States has it in his power to allow people to freeze to death throughout the Dominion." On November 28 King and Sherman boarded a train for Indianapolis. On the way they were joined by Saskatchewan Premier Walter Scott. On December 1 this improbable trio landed in Mitchell's offices in Indianapolis.[7] Mitchell quickly saw what King had seen, namely that allowing people to freeze in the prairie winter would certainly terminate the existence of District 18. So he

The disaster at Bellevue that claimed 29 miners

THE MEN HAD FELT THE METHANE BUILDING IN THE MINE FOR WEEKS, THEN FINALLY IT HAPPENED

It was the fall of 1910 and the 300 men who were working the West Canadian Collieries mine at Bellevue had been on edge for weeks. They couldn't see or smell the methane gas building up underground. But they could hear the faint humming sound it made as it worked through the coal seam. And they knew just how dangerous it could be.

In March in a letter to John Stirling, the province's chief mines inspector, the secretary of the United Mine Workers of America's Crowsnest Pass local, James Burke, complained that the mine was poorly ventilated and full of gas, a fact confirmed by local inspector Elijah Heathcote.

Then on October 31 the fears proved well founded. A stray spark set off the explosion the miners had expected. Fortunately, it was the Thanksgiving holiday. The mine was empty. In the resulting investigation, Stirling learned two days earlier the colliery had kept the men at their jobs though the mine's fans had broken down for two hours. He angrily ordered Western Canadian to keep the mine well ventilated.

On December 3 came yet another warning. The UMWA's Burke dashed off an urgent telegram that gas was building up again. Heathcote, in a quick inspection the following day, could find no evidence for the union's claim, and gave the colliery a clean

Glenbow Archives, NA-3381-2

Draegermen rushed to Bellevue Mine in 1910. Disasters like this one emphasized the need for well-equipped rescuers.

bill of health. Events would prove he shouldn't have.

Finally, at 6:30 p.m. on December 9, luck ran out. With many of the forty men on the night shift still walking to their workplaces, the gas ignited again. No one was hurt in the explosion itself, which was two miles inside the mine. But then came the afterdamp — the deadly mixture of carbon monoxide and carbon dioxide created by the blast.

One group of miners raced towards the nearest entrance and the hope of fresh air. They didn't make it. The rest, panicking, tried to escape the afterdamp by running deeper into the mine. "They felt the shock, were overcome by the gas almost immediately after a few abortive steps, and then all was oblivion," reported the *Lethbridge Herald*.

When pit boss Joseph Oliphant saw the first puff of smoke curl from the pit entrance, he sounded the alarm. Explosion in the mine! Miners raced from their homes to the mine entrance to prepare a rescue. A specially equipped rescue team from Hosmer, BC, rushed to the scene. But the first party to descend met disaster. Few had the Draeger breathing apparatus needed to survive the still-poisoned air agreed and after a ten-month strike the miners returned to their jobs.

However, for the UMWA, it was an incomplete victory. The union had capitulated on at least two key demands. But it had established the union's presence in Alberta, and it set Sherman's star on the rise politically. The *Lethbridge Herald* praised him as "a fighter from way back, a doughty campaigner and able to meet the best of them on the platform." The Liberals, anxious to bolster their pro-labour reputation, wooed the popular union leader as a candidate for MP. Interior Minister Frank Oliver, Laurier's senior lieutenant in the West, even suggested that "the stormy petrel of the political scene in southern Alberta" be given a seat in the Senate. After all, Sherman had already campaigned on a moderate platform of support for "home industries," public ownership of utilities and opposition to the trusts. All that, comments labour historian Allen Seager in Labour/*Le Travailleur*, "was

[7]Told that American labour boss Mitchell was sick, the Canadians were kept waiting until the following day for their meeting. In fact, the UMWA's international president had been drunk. King realized as much. But he told Sherman several months later, "My interests in the labour movement would have prevented me from ever disclosing this fact and putting a weapon so undeserved into the hands of labour's enemies." Mitchell, his health ruined by alcohol, resigned his position in 1908. He was replaced by John L. Lewis, who would head the UMWA for almost half a century.

below. Inspector Heathcote, the local doctor and a dozen other members of the party were brought back to the surface, unconscious. "It takes hold of your legs first and gradually numbs your body all the way up," said one of the rescuers who had to be revived. "You lose all power of locomotion, then you aren't even able to stand and over you go."

Still, the men struggled courageously to reach the others trapped below. Slav miner John Bulavich personally saved the lives of four miners. One of the men walked out unassisted — in his initial flight, he had collapsed near an air shaft and had recovered consciousness there. But rescue team member Fred Alderson joined the growing number of bodies stacked on tables in the impromptu morgue established in the mine's bathhouse. Noticing that the supply of oxygen in one of his fellow team member's tank was running low, he had given up some from his own but had then succumbed himself.

As the night wore on, hope for those left below began to fade. "Dead bodies are piled in heaps," reported the *Calgary Herald*. At the surface, "big, strong miners stalk about, talking of the explosion in whispers." And in the bathhouse, the wives and mothers of men still unaccounted for "ran from body to body, throwing off the covering to see if their loved ones lay beneath. They moaned and sobbed and cried out in their for-

Alberta side of the pass, and if the Bellevue mine had been equipped with the Draeger breathing apparatus, none of the men would have died.

A provincial inquest early in 1911 found that, just as O'Brien had charged, the negligence of West Canadian Collieries was the cause of the accident. But the provincial government chose not to levy any penalties on the company. And the families of the men who died discovered that, despite the inquest ruling, the company's insurers refused to pay out any benefits.

Their plight angered the union. "We 7,000 United Mine Workers in District 18, one and all of us, must make it our business to find out the names of the insurance companies that these coal operators do business with so that we may be in the position to denounce them on the street, in the platform, in the press and if possible in the courts for their cruel, heartless cheating of the poor widows and orphans, especially of our foreign brothers," resolved the union at its 1911 convention.

The UMWA paid for lawyers to help the widows and their families pursue the matter in the courts. Eventually, after appeals that reached all the way to the Privy Council, the Krzus family won a judgement against the company. That success — and the fear of similar lawsuits in future[a] — broke

---

'It takes hold of your legs first and numbs your body all the way up,' said a revived rescuer. 'You lose all power of locomotion, then you aren't even able to stand and over you go.'

---

eign tongues and finally had to be hurried from the room." In all, 29 men, aged nineteen to 50, died in the disaster. They left behind nineteen widows and 31 fatherless children.

The deaths dropped a pall across the Crowsnest. At the funeral procession in Bellevue the following week, almost 1,000 miners marched solemnly behind the coffins. Grief turned to anger as news of the union's unheeded warnings spread. In the legislature, socialist MLA Charlie O'Brien launched "one of the fiercest tirades ever heard in the House," wrote the *Lethbridge Herald*, condemning the company and the local mines inspector for negligence. Lethbridge MLA W.A. Buchanan added that if there had been a rescue station on the

employer opposition to demands for a no-fault, employer-funded insurance scheme for workers killed or injured on the job. In 1918 Alberta followed Ontario's lead and the Workers Compensation Board came into being.

— *T. J.*

[a]As the 1907 coal commission noted, few injured workers could afford to hire a lawyer and sue their employer, even when the case seemed self-evident. But unions proved willing to foot the legal expenses for their members who took their claims to the courts. And the damage awards in successful lawsuits could be substantial. Grand Trunk Pacific engineer George White, for example, broke his leg in an accident at Pembina. His injury was incompetently treated by a company doctor who was not properly certified. In 1909 he won a $5,000 judgement from the railway.

The name Mackenzie King makes its debut in history

AS THE FIRST FEDERAL MEDIATOR, THE FUTURE PM SERVED LABOUR
AND HIS OWN CAREER QUITE WELL

National Archives of Canada, PA-25990

*William Lyon Mackenzie King as a young
labour negotiator.*

For a brash, young bureaucrat as ambitious as William Lyon Mackenzie King, the settlement of the Lethbridge strike must have been intensely satisfying. He'd taken risks. The *Edmonton Journal* deplored the spectacle of the Canadian deputy minister of labour and the premier of Saskatchewan having to travel 2,000 miles to plead in Indianapolis offices with an American labour leader to settle an Alberta labour dispute. But the agreement gave the previously obscure government official a national reputation.

King is "one of the most advanced and best informed students of labour problems in the world," effused the *Lethbridge Herald.* "He is bound, sooner or later, to figure in the public life of Canada to a greater extent than he does now." It was an understatement. He was to become Canada's longest-serving prime minister in the 20th century.[a]

In 1900, when King was appointed deputy minister in the newly created Department of Labour, labour disputes were considered, at best, a private matter between employer and employees. But strikes often had public consequences. King believed the state had a duty to intervene.

That required legislative change. The 1900 Conciliation Act, which offered voluntary federal mediation of labour disputes, proved ineffective. King spent much of his time in the West, a roving peacemaker flitting from strike-bound town to strike-bound town. But employers were loath to accept his services. They had no legal compulsion to bargain. After trainmen struck the western division of the Canadian Pacific in 1903, halting rail movement throughout the prairies and British Columbia, King convinced federal Labour Minister Rodolphe Lemieux that the department needed a stick to encourage the two sides to talk softly. The Railway Labour Disputes Act that Lemieux introduced required federal mediation before a strike or lockout could take place. That didn't sit well with the railways, who felt it gave implicit recognition to the unions their employees had formed. They used their influence in parliament to gut the legislation of its compulsory character.

The coal famine that followed the Lethbridge strike bolstered King's position, however. Given the public outcry, the state could not stand back and let events run their course. But neither should it act as a strictly impartial umpire, interested only in bringing the two sides together, King believed. Instead, the federal mediator saw himself as an active participant in the dispute, a representative of the public with objectives separate from those of either capital or labour. Indeed, King maintained, the strike would not have taken place at all if the positions taken by the UMWA and AR&I Co. had been subject to public scrutiny.

Those beliefs were embodied in the 1907 Industrial Disputes Investigation Act, passed as a direct result of the Lethbridge strike. The act made federal intervention compulsory in all labour disputes in public utilities, railways and coal mines, upon application by either employer or union. Before a strike or lockout could take place, a three-man board with representatives of capital, labour and the public would investigate the issues and recommend terms of settlement.

The act passed its first test. In the spring of 1907, after Frank Sherman, president of District 18 of the UMWA, began bargaining with the newly created Western Coal Operators Association, an employers group representing the Galt and Crowsnest Pass mines, both sides accepted the conciliation board's report. That prompted King to predict that the legislation would "make the strike or lock-out a thing of the past."

That was overly optimistic. Although conciliation boards would be appointed in more than 100 disputes by the end of the decade, many would continue to end in walkouts. Labour came to resent the restrictions the act placed on the right to strike, and its failure to prevent employers from blacklisting union members or signing "yellow dog" contracts (in which workers agreed not to join a union). Sherman, after giving the IDI Act his initial support, called for its repeal in 1907, a demand echoed by the Canadian Trades and Labour Congress in 1916. But, in bringing labour and capital under the jurisdiction of state bodies representing the community's interest, King's legislation became the blueprint for 20th century Canadian labour policy. 		— *T.J.*

[a]Mackenzie King served three terms as prime minister: from Dec. 29, 1921, to June 28, 1926; then from Sept. 25, 1926, to Aug. 7, 1930; then from Oct. 23, 1935, to Nov. 15, 1948, when he retired.

scarcely distinguishable from any red-blooded Liberal platform." But the old check weighman wasn't about to be bought off.

Strikes, wrote Lenin, are "schools of communism." The Galt experience seemed to have schooled Sherman. He had begun the struggle so deeply distrustful of the radicals in his union and so alarmed at the readiness of the Hungarian miners to battle the police that he declared at a public meeting no more miners should be brought from central Europe. They "are the most revolutionary socialists and would make demands undreamed of by English labourers," he said. But by the summer's end he'd begun to see merit in radicalism. By fall, writes Laurier's biographer Joseph Scholl, he was advocating the "uncompromising Marxian orthodoxy" of the Socialist Party of Canada. "Socialism, which is the cause of the people, is the only cause today that stirs the souls of men and women," Sherman declared.

Other less lofty possibilities, however, continued to nag his own soul. He wrote King to discuss the possibility of his running federally as a pro-labour Liberal candidate. He no doubt expected the provincial coal commission, struck by the Liberal Rutherford government after the strike, would bring about reforms in the industry. He expected that King, whom he had befriended, would introduce legislation favourable to the labour movement. Was there not a role for him in all these eventualities?

As it happened, no. Both expectations were disappointed. The 1907 commission, which toured the province, gathered evidence from miners and mine owners, and it recommended the establishment of a workers' compensation fund, beefed-up inspection of mines, and further restrictions on child labour. But none of this was approved by the provincial legislature. As for King, he went the other way. The Industrial Disputes Investigation Act, which King drafted, restricted the right to strike. Sherman took this as an almost personal affront, supported it conditionally, and later demanded its repeal.

So the practical side of Sherman fell before the idealistic side and he turned left. But the SPC, the Socialist Party of Canada, was a strange vehicle for Sherman's aspirations. Formed in BC in 1905, it was led by a core of ascetic intellectuals preaching a "dogmatic, arid, blighting creed of

---

As the first socialist MLA, Charles O'Brien wasted no time in distinguishing himself from fellow lawmakers. Four months after election he was jailed in Regina for causing a disturbance.

---

withering materialism," according to British Labour Party leader Keir Hardie. The party's terse platform called for the immediate nationalization of the country's factories, mills, railways and mines, and the abolition of "the wage system." It damned trade unions — especially the craft unions belonging to the American Federation of Labor — as "reformist" institutions that "divert working men from the true cause of revolution." The party's newspaper, the *Western Clarion,* even called the use of strikes "a stench in the nostrils of decency" that only succeeded in pitting "wage slave against wage slave."

With James Simpson, a Toronto typographer who was vice-president of the Trades and Labour Congress, a Canadian organization, and R. Parm Pettipiece, the fiery editor of the BC Federation of Labour's newspaper,[8] Sherman fought to temper the SPC's anti-union sentiments and simultaneously to win over Canada's organized workers to the socialist cause. His political conversion came at a crucial moment in Canadian labour history. In October 1906, inspired by the electoral success of the Labour Party in Great Britain,[9] the Canadian Trades and Labour Congress met in Victoria to discuss forming a political arm for labour similar to the British model.

Conditions in Canada then were ripe "for Socialism and Labour," noted Ramsay MacDonald, one of the new British Labour MPs and a delegate to the Victoria convention.[10] But Canadian attempts to follow the lead of British workers were stymied by the bitter differences between the "straight labour" men in the TLC and the trade union socialists led by Sherman, Simpson and Pettipiece. The socialist "gang of three" argued that, instead of forming a new party, the umbrella labour body should simply endorse the SPC as its political arm. The bulk of the delegates held out for the more moderate platform already endorsed by the TLC. The split hobbled labour's attempts to field federal and provincial candidates for decades to come. Not until 1961, when the Canadian

[8] Pettipiece, the SPC's western organizer, was no stranger to Alberta. In the early 1890s he had edited the *Strathcona Plaindealer,* (Vol. I, p. 32), sparring regularly with future Liberal cabinet minister Frank Oliver and his *Edmonton Bulletin.* He moved to BC, bought the *Lardeau Eagle,* in the mining boomtown of Ferguson, and for a time churned out the same booster-ish copy as did every other small town paper. But, moved by the plight of the local miners, he turned the *Eagle* into a radical mouthpiece for the Western Federation of Miners and later for the Socialist Party of Canada.

[9] In 1874 two miners won election as Britain's first labour MPs, but their Labour Representation League soon died out. The Trades Union Congress instead decided in 1886 to work in alliance with the Liberals. Keir Hardie, in protest, formed the Independent Labour Party in 1893. In 1900, he was successful in convincing the TUC to support his campaign for independent labour representation. In the 1906 election Hardie's party shocked the British establishment by winning 29 seats in parliament.

[10] MacDonald had toured Canada and become distressed at the inability of Canadian socialists and trade unionists to come to terms. Were it not for this, he saw great opportunity for labour here. British Columbia especially was ready to throw off the capitalist yoke, he wrote. "Miners compose the bulk of its electors. Its lands have been pilfered by corrupt legislators, and its resources are in the hands of one or two monopolists. Within ten years the legislature could be dominated by our people." Without a change in the attitude of the SPC, however, "only a wild, seething strife will be kept up."

Back when union was king of a labouring province

ONCE UPON A TIME IN ALBERTA JUST ABOUT EVERYONE WAS ORGANIZING

As with almost everything else in Alberta, it was the railway that gave birth to the province's trade-union movement. The engineers, machinists, brakemen, firemen and boilermakers who ran and tended the trains formed the elite of the West's workforce. They were proud of their skills, which they jealously protected through a strong apprenticeship system and rigid jurisdictional rules. They carried with them well established traditions of acceptable wages and workloads. And they bristled at any incursions on these accepted practices.

The railwaymen knew it was only their mastery of their separate crafts that stood between them and the rough treat-

That the railway brotherhoods were able to win grudging but swift recognition from the ostensibly stony-hearted Canadian Pacific Railway stands as an astonishing fact in Alberta history. The explanation has much to do with a pioneer American trade union leader named Samuel Gompers. For the CPR, "Gomperism" was plainly preferable to the radical revolutionary movements that at the turn of the century seemed the probable alternative.

This was not a groundless fear. In 1903 the CPR enlisted the help of its existing trade unions to smash the United Brotherhood of Railway Employees, a sister union of the mili-

Labour Day procession in Edmonton, 1906. From Gompers to radicalism.

ment faced by navvies, loggers and farmhands. And they banded together to preserve their privileged positions. In 1886, Canadian Pacific trainmen at Medicine Hat chartered a local of the Brotherhood of Railway Engineers, the first trade union in what would become Alberta. The other running trades soon followed. Until 1900 they were the only organized workmen in the West. As late as 1910 railwaymen made up more than a quarter of all unionized workers in Canada.

tant Western Federation of Miners. The UBRE, which sought to bring all railway employees into a single industrial union, had struck the western region of the CPR in March of that year. The railway launched an all-out counter-assault, with the full cooperation of the trade unions. Days after the strike began the company circulated a pamphlet, pulled from the newspaper of the Brotherhood of Railroad Trainmen, that labelled the UBRE a "dishonest and traitorous organization" run by "a set of revolutionists." The strike was quickly smashed. Even the UBRE conceded that its members lost everything "but the right to hunt for work again."

Radicalism was represented in the American union movement by the Knights of Labor, born in 1869 in Philadelphia's textile mills. The Knights organized on an industrial basis, uniting all workmen, regardless of skill or craft, in single unions. They opened their ranks to women and blacks. And they had explicitly political goals, preaching that "industrial and moral worth," not wealth, should be "the true standard of individual and national greatness."

At their height, the Knights claimed 12,000 members in Canada. A local was formed in Calgary in 1887 and published the *Northwest Call*, the first labour paper in Alberta. Soon it was trying to organize the navvies who were building the CPR and the cowboys on area ranches.

Bricklayers and Masons Union, Local 2, at the Calgary Labour Day parade, 1906. Originally construction trades had joined with railway brotherhoods.

For Gompers, however, the Knights were everything a union should not be. Their anti-capitalist rhetoric only inflamed employers, he argued. And by ignoring craft distinctions, they weakened labour's greatest bargaining point — the indispensability of its most highly skilled members.

Gompers, a cigar-maker by trade, had once been a socialist himself. But in 1886, he began creating the American Federation of Labor (AFL), which confined itself to the organization of skilled workmen. To attempt to organize transient and unskilled workers was simply too great a risk, Gompers contended. The AFL also campaigned for pro-labour political reforms, but it did not challenge the free market system.

The same year the AFL was founded, the more idealistic Knights were dealt a terrible blow by the Haymarket riots in Chicago. On May 1, 1886 (a date later commemorated as May Day), the union led 38,000 Chicago workers on strike for the eight-hour day. Police shot and killed four of the men. A protest meeting in Haymarket Square that followed ended in disaster. Someone in the crowd threw a bomb into police ranks. The officers, firing pistols and wielding clubs, charged

Ontario, the Canadian Trades and Labour Congress formally ended the contest between the two competing labour bodies by expelling all non-AFL unions which sought to organize any workers AFL unions laid claim to.

The triumph of Gomperism in Canada coincided with the boom in the West. The rapid growth of Calgary and Edmonton in the century's first decade created fertile ground for union organizers, especially among the urban construction trades where the demand for the skilled workers needed to build houses, offices and roads exceeded the supply. As a consequence wages were relatively high. Journeymen stonemasons could earn as much as $4.50 a day. Nevertheless, though they were far better off than the navvies and bunkhousemen, the tradesmen had no shortage of grievances. At the beginning of the decade the ten-hour day was standard. Inflation was eating away their pay packets. And the influx of eastern European immigrants, they feared, would bring down wages even further.

In 1901 Calgary's construction trades joined the railway brotherhoods in forming the city's first labour council. Four

As early as 1903 the Calgary Labour Council claimed 1,500 members at a time the city had a population of only 9,000 men, women and children.

through the square, killing several men and injuring hundreds of others. Later, in an atmosphere of public hysteria, four strike leaders were hanged for conspiracy to commit murder.

The incident branded the Knights a dangerous, anarchistic organization. Conservative workers fled to the more businesslike AFL unions. In 1902, at its convention in Berlin,

years later Edmonton followed. In both cities new unions were rapidly chartered. As early as 1903 the Calgary Labour Council claimed 1,500 members — at the time, the city had a total population of only 9,000 men, women and children.

Robert Robinson, the western organizer for the United Brotherhood of Carpenters and Joiners, was particularly effective. On a bitterly cold February night in 1902, he showed up in Frank, the bustling mining community in the Crowsnest almost destroyed the following year in the Turtle Mountain slide, and called a meeting in the main saloon. He signed up every carpenter in town. Two days after his arrival in Calgary the next month, he had added a 90-member Calgary local to the UBCJ's ranks. Edmonton carpenters were wearing union badges a week after a Robinson visit that November. By the end of the decade even tailors, barbers, laundry workers and restaurant waitresses had formed unions.

The development distressed Senator James Lougheed who argued that the unions were an unwanted import from the United States. Noting that most were affiliated to the AFL, he

curtly answered, "That's because there are none." Bennett's blessing doubtless helped the carpenters, after a month-long strike, win their demands for union recognition and the nine-hour day.

But Bennett perhaps had reason. He knew that the mainly British-born members of the carpenters and other trade unions were a strong bulwark against the more radical notions taking hold in the non-English-speaking immigrant communities. The Ukrainians, Hungarians, Czechs and Romanians who fled the Austro-Hungarian Empire were familiar with socialist ideas. Their homeland was a constitutional monarchy with an elected parliament, a lively opposition, trade unions, and strong socialist parties. Many immigrants were not illiterate peasants, but experienced unionists and political activists. In 1891, when Galt recruited a large group of Hungarian miners for his Lethbridge colliery, the local newspaper protested that these "half-civilized men" were "ignorant, vicious and imbued with socialistic and communistic ideas."

City of Edmonton Archives, EA-122-121

Constructing a brick building in Edmonton, 1907. In the days before cranes, it sometimes took the whole crew to hoist a beam into position. The canine member of the team appears to be taking a break.

The Edmonton and Calgary labour councils talked socialism as well. At times their bluster reached alarming volume. Thus, after the brass bands, actors and comics had cleared the stage at a labour rally on April 5 at Hull's Opera House in Calgary, and after the president of the city's building trades had explained the Christian roots of the trade-union movement, another speaker launched into a bitter tirade against the "ruling classes" and their political servants. "The peo-

proposed Canada pass a law making it a crime for any non-British subject to tour Canada and counsel workers to ask for wage hikes. Canada didn't. Nevertheless, some employers vigorously fought all attempts to sign up their workers. In Calgary, for example, the Great West Saddlery Company used lockouts and blacklists to defeat a 1906 organizing drive by its teamsters.

Such harsh methods were not universally admired in the Calgary business community, however. When Calgary's carpenters went out in 1903, their lawyer was R.B. Bennett, a leading light of the Conservative party who spoke out boldly on their behalf. It was a courageous move. He also acted for the CPR. But Bennett was never as stern as he looked. Once, when a reporter complained during an interview that it was "impossible to get any human interest stories about you," he

ple are sending men to parliament today who are the paid agents of the corporations and if they are not bought before they are sent, they are shortly afterwards," he protested. But he was more bark than bite, suggested the *Calgary Herald* the next day. "If speeches had been blows and sarcasm were smokeless powder," the paper jokingly interjected, "the legislature, the large manufacturing industries of Alberta and the newspapers of Calgary would have fallen last night in one promiscuous heap."

Some union men, however, were out-and-out revolutionaries. In 1903 James Worsley, a British metalworker and ex-president of the Calgary Labour Council, joined CPR clerk Alfred Palmer in publishing the province's first socialist newspaper, the *Bond of Brotherhood*. As well as drumming up support for the city's unions, the paper tried to introduce Calgary workers to the teachings of Karl Marx and the progress of the socialist parties in Europe. "The class war existing here is as naked and unashamed as in the old cities most of us have so recently left," wrote editor Worsley. But the paper's intended audience identified itself more easily with William Davidson, the Liberal editor of the *Albertan* and a friend of labour, than with Worsley's talk of Marx. Less than a year later, the *Bond of Brotherhood* folded for lack of subscribers, and its editor returned to England.

For the most part, workers in Calgary and Edmonton had little enthusiasm for all-out class war. They had succeeded in winning recognition of their unions. They supported the Rutherford government, which with its fair wage and anti-child-labour laws had tempered the worst excesses of employers, and which had also eagerly courted the trade union vote. Moreover, in the bustling frontier cities, working men were finding a comfortable place in polite society.

Richard Brocklebank, president of the carpenter's union in Calgary, even won election to city council, until then a businessman's preserve. The Ontario-born unionist had been acclaimed to a council seat in 1902, but was forced out in the next election "by the combined force of property owners and employers who had not yet forgotten the role he had played in the 1903 carpenters' strike," writes Calgary historian Henry Klassen. By 1906, however, Brocklebank had joined management and become boss of construction operations for his old enemy Thomas Underwood. This made him a safe prospect for city government. Hence Brocklebank's program — he campaigned for municipal ownership of utilities and abolition of the $1,000 property qualification for civic elective office — was given a respectful ear.

This Brocklebank brand of socialism even the capitalist press could endorse. In 1904, after an Edmonton businessman assailed the "socialist views" of the city's trade unionists, the

out. "The practical part of socialism will soon become incorporated into the social existence of the Anglo-Saxon race, but there is very little sign that theoretical socialism is making any real advance. We should pick the plums we want out of the socialist pudding but we shall leave it to the less energetic Slav races to digest the rest if it tickles their fancy."

This tenuous acceptance of the politics of the craft unions turned to dismay, however, as "foreigners" joined the union rolls. When the 400 members of Edmonton's newly formed Hod Carriers and Building Labourers Union walked out in September 1906, for example, the *Edmonton Journal* at first opted for neutrality. "The main streets presented an unusual appearance this morning as, clad in their working clothes but wearing the badges of their union, men swarmed in from all parts of the city and marched along Jasper Avenue," the paper reported. One contractor broke ranks and expressed support for the union's demand for an eight-hour day and a $2.50 minimum daily wage. But later at a mass union meeting on the river flats, he found himself embroiled in a heated argument with the head of the city's master builders' exchange.

Soon, however, the neutral *Journal* became edgy. It observed that "a large number of the labouring classes in the city are Galicians. They are becoming conscious of their individuality and power and active leaders are sprouting up amongst them." When a settlement was slow in coming, the *Journal* relapsed into management conservatism. "High wages look good to the foreigners and they are showing no disposition to submit the questions in dispute to arbitration, or amend their initial demands, as the friends of the union advise. The strikers who welcomed the cooperation of foreign elements may find a white elephant on their hands."

Meanwhile, the disdain of the trade unions for the unskilled left vast numbers of workers outside the labour movement entirely. By 1910 the West's navvies and loggers,

---

Some union members were out-and-out revolutionaries. 'The class war existing here,' wrote a Marxist editor in 1903, 'is as naked and unashamed as in the old cities most of us have so recently left.'

Edmonton Bulletin sprang to the workers' defence. "That the present capitalistic system is one of exploitation is scientifically set forth in the declaration of the socialist doctrine," explained the editor of the otherwise decidedly Liberal paper. Carried away with the spirit of the moment, he urged one critic of labour "to study socialism, abandon his defence of capitalism and come over and work for the cooperative commonwealth."

The Conservative *Journal*, likewise taken with labour's calls for public ownership of utilities, suggested reformers adopt this and other "reasonable" elements of the socialist program. "In the new West there is full scope for working out these new ideas," commented the paper in a 1906 year-end editorial. Still, it quickly added, not all these new ideas deserved to be worked

rejected by the mainstream unions, had begun flocking instead to the radical Industrial Workers of the World, nicknamed "the Wobblies." Only the IWW, as leader Big Bill Haywood explained in something less than flattery, would go "down into the gutter to get at the mass of workers and bring them up to a decent plane of living." But the IWW was virtually destroyed in the anti-Bolshevik fever that followed the First World War. Not until the 1930s, when the Congress of Industrial Organizations began organizing the automobile factories of Ontario and logging camps of Alberta and BC, would the country's most vulnerable workers again sport union badges.   — *T. J.*

Labour Congress joined with the Cooperative Commonwealth Federation to form the New Democratic Party, would Canadian labour act in concert at election time.

Even in Alberta Sherman found it difficult to persuade other unions to support the SPC. The Calgary and Edmonton labour councils chose to ignore his invitation to establish a provincial labour party under the SPC's aegis, and continued to campaign for the Liberals. At a meeting in Lethbridge, delegates from the area's construction and railway unions outvoted Sherman and opted to present a labour rather than socialist candidate in the 1909 provincial election. "Socialism will elect no candidate here," declared labour candidate Donald McNabb, a miner. "If we want to win the city, we have to put a candidate on the platform to win." (That candidate, as it turned out, was not McNabb. He polled less than 20% of the vote.)

Farmers were even more reluctant to assemble under Sherman's socialist banner. In 1905 Edmonton area farmers had formed a branch of the left-leaning Canadian Society of Equity. The Society was anxious to join labour in an electoral alliance. Its leader, R.C. Owens, and four other delegates attended the convention called by Sherman in December 1907 to form a provincial labour party. "The labourer and farmer constitute nine-tenths of the people of this dominion and if we worked solidly together how could the other tenth oppress us?" said Owens. "I recognize only two classes, the workers and the idlers. I represent the workers."

But the farmers balked at the convention's adoption of the SPC platform. One noted that his neighbours would laugh at him if he tried to explain the SPC's contention that profit was evil. "It's a profit that farmers want," he said. Two years later, having given up on the cause of farmer-labour cooperation, Owens led his group into the United Farmers of Alberta. All that proves, muttered the SPC's Pettipiece, is that farmers "are colossally ignorant of the labour question."

The rebuffs did little to quash Sherman's enthusiasm for revolution. His miners were happy with his militant class-against-class rhetoric, and he found a ready audience for his ideas among the unorganized immigrant labourers in Calgary and Edmonton. In the 1908 federal election campaign, the *Lethbridge Herald* reported that the quick-tongued union leader had even humbled the city's chief of police. It described the incident.

Sherman, the SPC candidate in Calgary, was campaigning in Lethbridge. He had taken to holding regular, open-air public meetings outside the Queen's Hotel. One evening, as the SPC's Slavic organizer Alex Susnar was haranguing the crowd in his native language, the police chief happened to stroll by. After asking Susnar whether he was a British subject, he pushed him off the box he was standing on and arrested him. Sherman took his place. When the chief ordered the crowd to disperse, Sherman refused. "Men of Canada, I know the duty of an officer of the law and I say he can't arrest me," Sherman shouted to loud cheers. Then he turned to the policeman. "You're a poor specimen of an officer," he continued. "We have a right to speak on the streets if we choose to do so." The police chief, deciding it was wiser to move off than risk a fight, quickly departed.

But all this enthusiasm was not enough to win the UMWA leader a seat in parliament. He polled 743 votes, well back of the Conservative winner (4,105) and the Liberal candidate (3,418). The following year, however, Charles M. O'Brien proved that at least some Alberta voters were ready to consider socialism.

In the *Parliamentary Guide*, O'Brien would proudly confess that he had "picked up his education in logging, mining and railroad camps." The self-taught, Ontario-born Marxist evangelist had come west in 1899 as a navvy on the Crowsnest Pass line, read the *Communist Manifesto*, and went on to become an SPC organizer. A brilliant orator, he developed a rough-hewn brand of class-war politics that had enormous appeal in the coal mining towns and railroad camps of the sprawling provincial constituency called Rocky Mountain. "He would not lay claim to the charm of Laurier, but he is a sagacious old dog at that," commented one comrade. In the 1909 Alberta election, the riding's working class electors rejected the reform-minded Liberals and made O'Brien their representative in the legislature.

The province's first socialist MLA wasted no time in setting himself apart from his fellow lawmakers. Four months after his election he was arrested in Regina for speaking on the sidewalk and causing a disturbance. For that, the soapbox proselytizer was sentenced to seven days in jail. Then in 1910, when the legislature tried to move a routine resolution of sympathy after the death of King Edward VII, O'Brien suggested that, with everyone in a mourning mood, the house also send condolences to the widows and children of 300 miners killed in a recent British mine disaster. "The

Dear Sir, It having come to our knowledge that after the Coroners' Jury exonerated Bro. Decouse from all blame in connection with the accident at Frank, and that in direct opposition of this finding, the Public Prosecutor has acted in a high handed manner in this particular case by having said Bro. Decouse incarcerated on the capital charge of murder, thereby debarring him the privilege of bail until the court of assizes meets...We, by a unanimous vote go on record strongly condemning the stringent action of said official and call upon the members of the provincial government of Alberta to take this matter up. Thereby giving all law-abiding citizens an assurance that there will be no miscarriage of justice in this particular case.

- *taken verbatim from a letter written in September 1906 by the Lethbridge branch of the UMWA to the provincial attorney-general regarding a union member's innocence in relation to the Frank Slide.*

old-line politicians were so upset that anyone would dare link the death of royalty with the deaths of coal miners that they threw books and inkwells at their socialist colleague," writes Warren Caragata in *Alberta Labour: A Heritage Untold*.[11]

Sherman must have been delighted. O'Brien's election, after all, was due in large part to the UMWA leader's role in fashioning the Crowsnest miners into a militant, unified body. But amazingly in April 1909 the man who'd turned down a probable seat in parliament to campaign for the SPC was expelled from the party. The SPC's leaders had always distrusted Sherman's popularity and his union background. So when Alberta cabinet minister W.H. Cushing trumpeted a flattering letter from Sherman during the 1909 election as proof that he had labour support, the SPC used this as an excuse to dump him. The move angered Calgary socialists, who said Sherman had written to Cushing only in an attempt to have him hire a union man who was a friend of Sherman's as a mine inspector. O'Brien called the expulsion "a cowardly and treacherous act."

The ouster disappointed Sherman, but cost him none of his customary spark. He had other things on his mind. Early in April he again led District 18 on strike. This time he was up against the Western Coal Operators Association, an employer group representing every major coal mine in the Pass and southern Alberta. Ottawa threatened to fine Sherman and the union for breaking the Industrial Disputes Investigation Act. The mine owners enlisted UMWA international president John L. Lewis against the illegal strike. Sherman, refusing to back down, threatened to pull his 7,000 members out of the UMWA and establish in its place an autonomous Canadian Miners' Federation. "If Lewis or any of his servants but knock this business up here, it will be the last of the international in Canada," he declared.

He wouldn't live to see his plans through. Shortly after reaching a settlement with the operators that ended the three-month strike, he was stricken by Bright's Disease, a painful and debilitating kidney ailment. On Oct. 12, 1909, he died in the hospital at Fernie.[12] But his idea was not forgotten. A decade later, inspired by the revolution in Russia, the miners would follow their old leader's suggestion, quit the UMWA, and, in the One Big Union, launch a general strike designed to bring down the Canadian government. It didn't, but the spirit of Frank Sherman was doubtless marching with them in the attempt.

[11] O'Brien lasted only one term as an MLA. Although he drew more than 1,000 votes in the 1913 election, the highest total ever by an SPC candidate in a provincial election in western Canada, he fell 81 votes short of his Conservative opponent. The following year, shaken by the onset of the First World War, he fled to the US and faded from history. But in 1921 the riding's miners again succeeded in sending one of their own to the legislature, electing one of the three Labour MLAs who joined the new United Farmers of Alberta government.

[12] Sherman's children carried on in their father's tradition. His son William became president of District 18 in 1922. And his daughter, Annie Balderston, became a prominent leader of New Zealand's coal miners in the 1920s and 1930s. But William Sherman, curiously enough, found himself fighting his father's ideological followers in the 1920s when the Communist Party of Canada took up the elder Sherman's call to break from the UMWA whose international leadership the Communists considered too conservative. The younger Sherman defeated the Communists, but the internal feud, complete with expulsions and assorted fisticuffs, seriously weakened the miners' union.

Rosedale Mines, Drumheller, 1910.

CHAPTER TWO

The end of big-time ranching: Riches to ruin in a decade

THE HUGE SPREADS AND THE SMALL HOMESTEADERS COLLIDED HEAD ON. THE FEDS FAVOURED HOMESTEADING AND THE FARMERS WON — FOR NOW

Glenbow Archives, NA-862-6

A cowboy on a saddle horse in the Cypress Hills in the early 1900s. The wide-open prairie was becoming a patchwork of fenced-in interests.

by LINK BYFIELD

Four years of government by Liberals — the party of sodbusters and "progress" — had by 1900 produced chaos across the length and breadth of the shortgrass cattle country south of the Battle River. Stream bottoms all through the massive closed leases of the southwest were suffering an invasion of squatters holding out for homestead entry, and it was no longer considered politic to burn them down and drive them off as in the old

A characteristic western farmyard, probably in the Edmonton area, at the turn of the century. Pressure for more homesteads was mounting within the Department of the Interior.

days. Making matters worse, Montana cattlemen were now drifting their herds north across the Milk River to steal grass, and long, illegal fences were being strung hither and thither. Rustling was epidemic. And in the desolate drylands north of the Cypress Hills, a second grassland invasion was developing as American cattlemen, increasingly hemmed by settlement for the past fifty years, headed for the last unoccupied prairie on the continent.

There were perhaps 1,000 stockmen operating in the North-West Territories at the turn of the century, of whom some 250 owned commercial herds of several hundred head or more. Tories almost to a man, the larger operators had long understood that their continued prosperity rested on two essentials: secure access to cheap grass, and the production of healthy export cattle for Britain and Chicago. In late 1896 they had formed themselves into the Western Stock Growers Association (still extant a century later). Its first job was to lobby Ottawa and the territorial council in Regina, its second to enforce branding and roundup law (see sidebar), wolf bounties and disease control in the range country.

As David H. Breen points out in his authoritative *The Canadian Prairie West and the Ranching Frontier*, the WSGA's incorporating signatures read like a Who's Who of the old British and eastern

The new Laurier government made no secret that it favoured settlers over ranchers. In 1900 ranchers didn't realize how disastrous this Liberal policy would be.

Canadian closed-lease system: Duncan McEachren, part-owner and manager of the 120,000-acre Walrond; Alexander Staveley Hill, part-owner of the 100,000-acre Oxley and holder of 80,000 acres under his own name; Oxley manager A.R. Springett; Frederick S. Stimson of the 158,000-acre Northwest Cattle Company, and independent leaseholders F.W. Godsal, with 20,000 acres in the upper Oldman River, and E.H. Maunsell with 6,500 acres near Fort Macleod. Voting membership in each of the WSGA's eleven stock districts, spread out from Maple Creek in Assiniboia to the eastern slopes of the Rockies, was open to any cattle raiser for an annual levy of three cents per head of stock; but membership was subject to approval by the directors, to prevent infiltration by settlers, homestead speculators and "progress" minded troublemakers.

The new Laurier government had taken office in 1896 and made it no secret that it favoured settlers over ranchers. But by 1900, it was still unclear to the WSGA how disastrous Liberal policy

Cattle round-up, Milk River Valley, around 1912. More cattle were coming in as less land became available.

would be. Interior Minister Clifford Sifton seemed genuinely sympathetic, and their old ally, land bureaucrat William Pearce, was still in place in Calgary, having barely escaped a departmental purge inspired by the pro-settler Liberal MP Frank Oliver of Edmonton in 1897. Pearce's office budget had been cancelled, but he fought on, hiring a personal secretary to type his reports and refusing to be sidelined. Sifton relented, and Oliver chose to bide his time.

Even under the friendly Tories after 1892, the politically embarrassing phenomenon of massive closed leases had given way to "water reserves" (Vol. 1, Sect. 5, ch. 4). Rather than bar whole townships to homestead entry, Dominion Lands officials would simply assign ranchers much smaller closed leases along streams and sloughs, rendering agriculture in the dry surrounding plains impossible. This way, eastern newspapers weren't continually running maps of the

---

Over-grazing had become a problem. American cattlemen, their ranges severely overstocked, would rail thousands of head to near the Canadian border and let them go.

West showing and deploring land-lease blocks the size of whole counties in Ontario, although the effect of the water reserve policy was almost identical. Despite Oliver's vehement pressure, Sifton and Pearce awarded many new water reserves in 1897, the minister using the occasion to reassure the WSGA that he had no intention of dismantling the lease system.

Nonetheless, pressure for more homesteads in the grasslands was mounting within the Department of the Interior and in the territorial legislature, and between 1900 and 1905 the struggle approximated a bureaucratic civil war. On one side were those, led by Oliver, who envisioned the entire dryland prairie put to the plough. By 1903 this faction was describing southern Alberta as a "mixed farming" country in official reports. On the other were ranching sympathizers, led by veterans like Pearce, who insisted that the shortgrass prairie remain a "special region" of closed leases, water reserves and limited homesteading because it was too dry for sustainable

mixed farming. Pearce was actually very interested in promoting agriculture through expedients like irrigation. But irrigation had barely begun, and from the mid-'80s to the mid-'90s, average precipitation in southern Alberta was ten inches, too little for successful conventional farming.

Sifton, whose own experience was limited to the relatively lush environs of Brandon, waffled a great deal, but seems to have appreciated the ranchers' case, even to the point of resurrecting the old lease policy (not least, of course, because it afforded opportunities for patronage on a grand scale). He became increasingly generous after 1898. In 1902, for example, he assigned 46,000 rangeland acres (equivalent to two townships, or 72 square miles) to Liberal cronies James D. McGregor of Brandon and James H. Ross of Moose Jaw on terms at least as generous as the original Macdonald Tory leases.[1]

One ill result of the water reserve system was that while it did keep out most homesteaders, it led in effect to free or "public" grazing, the tradition of the western United States. Land that wasn't off limits often went to the first herd to arrive in the summer. By 1900 over-grazing had become a serious problem through much of the southern range outside the closed leases: at Pincher Creek, along the Highwood and around Maple Creek. It was soon aggravated by the delib-

A herd of 1,000 cattle, requiring fifty square miles, could support one family and a few cowboys; the same amount of land tilled would support up to 100 farm families.

erate summer drifting of American cattle north of the Milk after 1900. It fell to the Mounted Police to patrol the border. US cattlemen, whose ranges were seriously overstocked in the 1890s, would rail thousands of head to within a few miles of the border and let them go, on the presumption they would be returned after the Canadian roundup. The WSGA complained in 1901 there were an estimated 16,000 head with only six riders to keep them south of the line in the Marias hills.[2]

[1] James Hamilton Ross represented Moose Jaw on the territorial council and later in the territorial assembly from 1883 to 1903. He was Premier Frederick Haultain's principal ally, serving as treasurer, territorial secretary and commissioner of public works. He became commissioner of the Yukon Territory in 1901 after the Yukon was separated from the North-West Territories, and was appointed by Laurier to the Senate in 1904. His son, J. Gordon Ross, was Liberal MP for Moose Jaw between 1925 and 1930, and between 1935 and 1945.

[2] Two Canadian cowboys that year were fired upon in the Sweetgrass Hills southeast of Lethbridge by Montana cattleman Sam Larson. They fired back and he rode off. The next day he rode into their hay camp and apologized, saying he had mistaken them for a Mountie patrol. He stayed for supper.

Cattle swimming through a dipping vat at the Milk River Cattle Company ranch around 1912.

Sifton crony Ross, who was also territorial public works commissioner, proposed an end to closed leases, a grazing permit system to limit cattle to sustainable levels, and the deep-drilling of strategic stock-watering wells in the driest areas to expand the available range and ease the pressure along streams. But the Oliver faction adamantly resisted anything extending ranchers' rights and influence, so the government did nothing.

At the core of all this argument was a simple question: what was the productive value of prairie land? The old ranching rule of thumb was that one cow and calf, or one steer, required ten acres in the foothills, and up to thirty or more acres in the shortgrass drylands. The large dryland operations of over 1,000 head needed at least fifty square miles of land, meaning more than a township (36 square miles). Even mid-sized ranches of 300 head or so, which had become numerous in the 1890s, needed up to fifteen square miles of grass. With minimal fencing, buildings and hay, a herd of 1,000 could support one family and a few cowboys, where the same amount of land would support up to 100 farm families, all of whom would need supplies, equipment, schools and roads.[3] It required up to ninety acres of grass (over three years) to bring a steer to market weight, and during the good years of 1895 to 1905 the steer was worth about $50. As long as grassland was almost free (the standard lease price was four cents per acre annually), and barring excessive loss from mange, blackleg, wolves, rustling, prairie fires and bad winters, the return could be excellent. Given such considerable hazards, however, many a rancher went broke.

Crop-raising economics were entirely different. The most that any single sodbuster family could hope to farm in the early days was half a square mile. If the settler produced twenty bushels an acre, he could afford to pay far more than any cattleman for land. Warnings about drought were routinely dismissed as the self-serving, anti-progress rationalizations of the ranching industry, and all the more so because in the decade after 1905 average precipitation increased fifty per cent to fifteen inches. Unbroken farmland typically traded for $5 to $10 an acre. This forced the wealthier and more astute cattlemen to pay the going farmland rate for strategic lands beside water after 1900. Arthur E. Cross who ranched west of Nanton, for example, spent the entire decade buying select sites, often in co-operation with other ranchers.

Animosity between the two interests was bitter and personal. Rancher H.M. Hatfield expressed its depth when he described an unwelcome new homestead neighbour in 1908: "Birds of this [squatter's] feather flock together, and if he does not bring them he may breed them."[4] "It does nothing but rain here," wrote disgruntled rancher William Cochrane, son of early ranching tycoon Senator Matthew Cochrane, to A.E. Cross in 1902. "There are five [settlers'] shacks below

---

In February 1905, Clifford Sifton resigned from cabinet and was replaced with the ranchers' mortal enemy, Frank Oliver. Their fate was sealed.

---

me on the creek and two just above me, all with dogs. We must pray for a drought."[5] He later reported with apparent satisfaction, "My farmers in Squaw Coulee are sick, two have pulled out and one is left with his woman and seven months old kid. It is dry and their cattle have skinned out with the range cattle — his heart is on the ground." But by 1906, with the southwest settlement invasion permanent and complete, Cochrane wrote, "These blasted sodbusters have driven me to drink."

After 1900, homesteaders flooded into the western range along the Calgary and Edmonton Railway north to Red Deer and south to Fort Macleod. Towns sprang up in a few weeks, and barbed wire was suddenly running everywhere. Ranchers would in short order be assessed municipal taxes of $16 a square mile, whether they owned the land or leased it, for schools and roads they neither needed nor wanted. By 1903 the foothills ranchers found themselves cut off from their summer ranges by the settlement corridor, and by 1905 the old free range days were gone. Cattlemen along the eastern slopes of the Rockies were scaling back and selling surplus land to homesteaders. Some retired in handsomely recompensed disgust, others pastured smaller herds deeper in the foothills, and others re-established themselves in the unbroken shortgrass range of the open prairie.

By 1905 fencing had covered the whole countryside within a 25-mile radius of Lethbridge, and cattlemen were moving north and east into the Little Bow country and towards the Cypress Hills and Swift Current. The last big roundup in the southwest occurred in the fall of 1907 (see sidebar).

Wheat had become king. Lamented one rancher, 'It is heart-breaking to see these awful wounds appearing in this beautiful prairie.'

Meanwhile the Americans continued to flood Alberta with cattle. In 1903 at least three big herds came north. British Lord Delaval Beresford, a member of a noted Anglo-Irish family who had a large ranch in Mexico, railed 30,000 head from El Paso to Medicine Hat, then up the Red Deer River to a range north of Brooks. Charlie Brownfield trailed 5,000 Longhorns for the Connor Ranch in Wyoming from Medicine Hat to the Neutral Hills east of Red Deer. New Mexican Bud McCord railed 3,500 head from Canyon City, Texas, to Billings, Montana, and then drove them north to the Neutrals (see sidebar). Others followed. Old-west Texan Lem Pruitt brought 6,000 head into the Cypress Hills country in

1905. The famous Matador Ranch of Texas tried and failed to establish a large herd of Longhorns in Saskatchewan. It was soon discovered at catastrophic cost that Texas Longhorns couldn't withstand constant winter exposure on the northern range; the British-bred Herefords and Shorthorns could.[6]

Fencing was increasingly a problem, even in the supposedly open range. To protect their grass and the health and breeding quality of their herds as more and more scrub Longhorn stock came north from the US, ranchers were stringing wire illegally. In 1903 the Interior Department reported that various cattlemen had illegally fenced the entire north bank of the South Saskatchewan from Bow Forks to Medicine Hat. Further north, Beresford had fenced across a huge bend in the Red Deer River, enclosing almost four townships. Snowstorms in February and March of 1904 caused some 12,000 cattle to drift upriver from the southeast, and hundreds perished in huddles of a dozen or more when the wind held them against the Beresford fence.

Besides all these problems, Oliver continued to press the settlers' case. In 1901 Pearce was demoted to inspector of surveys and thereafter

Glenbow Archives, NA-1741-1

Texas Longhorns in Union stockyards, Chicago, 1896. American cowboys drove thousands of the breed into Alberta in the early century. Most would succumb to the devilish cold. (Below) branding at the MacDonald Ranch west of Cochrane.

Provincial Archives of Alberta, P-227

[3] Such hay as ranchers did use they normally contracted neighbouring farmers to put up. Some Indian bands were particularly good at it. In 1901, for example, the Bloods near Cardston supplied 800 tons of hay to the Cochrane ranch, 400 tons to the Brown ranch, and numerous smaller contracts.

[4] Such ill will crops up frequently in local histories such as *Prairie Sod and Goldenrod*. In 1903 Minnesota homesteader Charley Keil, filing north of Calgary near Carstairs, was warned by a small-scale local rancher, "You will be hailed, frozen and burnt out and then you will get out. We will take your fences down and turn our horses and cattle out again." The prophesy proved right in all respects but the last; they stayed.

[5] The settler used dogs to drive range cattle away from the wild grass around his farmstead, which he wanted for his own stock. Once enough settlers lined a watercourse, cattle would be driven from place to place, unable to drink, eat or rest. Ranchers, on the other hand, were constantly accused of grazing the nearby lands deliberately to force the settlers out.

[6] By the end of the decade, Longhorns had almost vanished from Alberta. Shell Gillespie, an Arizona cowboy working for George Lane's Bar U herd in the Little Bow country, had two favourites, Baldy and Lobby, who reminded him of home. He found them lying together dead after the terrible winter of 1906-07. While his companion politely studied the horizon, Gillespie hugged one steer and burst into tears. "Well, Lobby," he mourned, "you had to come away up here to freeze to death. I'm leaving this damn country or I'll be with you next winter." He hit the trail that fall, and died many years later in Colorado.

The killing winter of aught-six aught-seven

APPROXIMATELY HALF OF THE ANIMALS ROUNDED UP IN THE FALL OF 1906 WOULD NOT SEE THE SPRING AS ONE BLIZZARD AFTER ANOTHER BURIED THE PROVINCE

The Blizzard *by Inglis Sheldon-Williams; 1870-1940.*

Old-time beef buyer, cattle drover and price manipulator Pat Burns was always one to head off a stampede. "There is not the slightest foundation for any of these stories of thousands of carcasses strewing the ranges," he expostulated in the Jan. 17, 1907, edition of the *Calgary Herald*. "There will be no rise in the price of beef." But the wily Irish meatpacker was dead wrong. The winter of "aught-six aught-seven" would go down as the worst in western ranching history. More than any other event, the Winter of the Blue Snow, as it would later be romantically dubbed, marked the turning point of the cattle industry from free-range to fenced-and-fed. Approximately half the animals rounded up in the fall of 1906 did not see spring. Literally hundreds of tales, most of them tragic, came out of that terrible winter.

After the spring calving of 1906, Wilbur Leroy "Lee" Brainard left the Gallatin hills of southwest Montana with over 600 head of cattle and calves, 100 horses, a camp wagon and a wagon of stripped-down haying equipment.[a] Brainard had heard that there was empty grass up in Alberta, inside the chinook belt, where cattle could forage all winter and needed little or no hay. So off he went with his teenaged son, Albert, an old friend and helper named Dad White, and seven cowboys.

They followed the Missouri through Helena, Great Falls and Fort Benton, and then struck north across the Milk to the Alberta border at Wildhorse. When they reached the South Saskatchewan at Medicine Hat the RNWMP inspected their brands, YN and YO.

The Mounties advised Brainard to find a nearby wintering ground because it was late in the summer, and the only remaining unclaimed land lay farther north where the chinook often failed to penetrate. But Brainard pressed on, north through the great sand hills and across the Red Deer north of Brooks. Keeping Albert and Dad White to help him, he paid off his men at a hay flat on upper Berry Creek near present-day Hanna, ploughed some turf to bank his tent, and cut enough hay for his bulls and horses. His nearest neighbours were forty miles (64 km) to the northwest. The Hunt brothers, ranching near present-day Endiang, were astonished that he had put up so little hay, and offered to winter his cow herd. But the newcomer said he'd take his chances with the chinook.

The first snow fell in mid-October and stayed. The temperature rapidly plunged to –30 and then –40, and the snow kept blowing in, one blizzard after another, deeper and deeper.

on January 29. By noon they were half-way there. They stopped to rest the lathered horses and boil some fresh beef. Then disaster struck.

A towering wall of grey cloud came sweeping down upon them from the northwest. It overwhelmed them in minutes, blotting out the sun, blotting out their fire and leaving them in a dark land of blinding snow and plunging temperatures. All their stock scattered instantly except for Brainard's stallion. They were pinned in their wagon, and as night came on and the cold seeped into them Brainard forced them to march around the wagon to stay awake. Dad White slumped down dead at dawn. Young Albert lost hope. His father pleaded with him and pummelled him, but he couldn't revive his spirit. In a

They shot all the stock too weak to move and began smashing a trail north through the snow. By noon they were half-way there; then disaster struck.

By Christmas time his cattle were starving, eating bits of willow where they could get to it. At New Year he loaded his wagon and drove them west to the hills around Dowling Lake. There they found better shelter from the cutting wind and a little pasture, but more were dying and trying to drift. So when the temperature suddenly lifted in late January, the Brainards made a break for the Hunt place west of Sullivan Lake. Working in their shirtsleeves, they hitched Brainard's stallion and another horse to their camp wagon, shot all the stock too weak to move, gathered the rest and began smashing a trail north through the heavy, chinook-dampened snow

panic the father hoisted him on his back and struck out northward through the storm. But he hadn't gone far before he realized the lad was dead. He returned, laid him with their old friend White, cut his stallion loose and began walking north through the white, shapeless blizzard. At one point he stretched out his hand to greet a long-dead acquaintance, then realized he was delirious. After many hours he bumped into something solid, and collapsed. He came to just long enough to see that it was a rail fence. He had reached the Hunt place. He crawled to the Hunts' shack and collapsed against the door. "Get out of here!" yelled Jack Hunt, thinking it was a steer. "I

Victim of the big freeze photographed by a Beynon-area rancher in the spring of 1907. Cows were found frozen solid standing up.

Ahead of a Blue Norther, *by E.F. Hagell.*

won't get out," came the weak reply. The three Hunt boys hauled him inside and thawed him.

When the weather lifted they got him out to Stettler thirty miles (48 km) to the northwest, where a doctor amputated most of his toes and it took him a year to recover. Undaunted, he brought his wife and three children from Bozeman in 1909. They homesteaded northeast of present-day Hanna, and in 1918 moved to a homestead near Hythe in the western Alberta Peace River country.

Other good men died that winter. In eastern Alberta a rider for the Wilkinson-McCord ranch was lost in the first blizzards of November, as was a teenager named Albert LaRoche. Cowboy C.J. Christianson tells of a Beresford rider whose horse came back trailing the rope that its owner, Nat Scofield,

Lake. The successful Connor ranch, a new American operation in the Battle River country, lost two-thirds of its cattle and was effectively wiped out. Even feed supplies didn't always help; the snow was often too deep for cattle to reach the stacks, and without adequate yards they simply drifted south. That happened to the Code brothers from Ontario, Jack, Duncan and Elias; despite ample hay most of their small herd drifted from their place in the Hand Hills north of Drumheller and perished.

Even many fed cattle simply died of cold. George A. Salmon recalled in *Trails of Tail Creek Country* how as a boy he hauled hay every day to the cattle of Walter Parlby (Red Deer MLA Irene Parlby's husband). Many were too weak to stand and had to be shot. One neighbour found a cow frozen solid standing up. The Dickie ranch at Donalda discovered several standing dead in the bush. The Bush-Fulsher ranch on the Battle River found cattle standing frozen solid in snow over their backs.

Further south and east the story was much the same. Blizzard after blizzard dumped snow two feet deep over the plains and blew the coulees full. "Dad" Gaff was a Kansas buffalo hunter turned Wyoming rancher who had brought his son, six daughters, a box of gold coins and 1,000 head of white-face cattle to the Cypress Hills on the Alberta-Saskatchewan border in '98. He went into the Winter of Blue Snow with 1,300 head and came out with 400. Some had wallowed blindly into the snowbound coulees and were found after the massive drifts receded in May hanging over cotton-

People stared unbelievingly as the softly moaning herd, hair and hide frozen off in large patches, limped through Macleod. Town workers hauled 48 carcasses from the street the next day.

had been holding as he slept. They found the man's body with his saddle where he had been left afoot thirty miles (48 km) north of the Red Deer River.

But if it was dangerous for men, it was frozen, fatal agony for their exposed and unfenced cattle. Tens of thousands drifted south before the wind. Christianson recalls rounding up a number of HUT-brand Wilkinson-McCord steers on the Milk River in Montana, 200 miles (320 km) south of Sounding

wood limbs a dozen feet above the ground. Others drifted south 100 miles (160 km) to the rail line at Chinook, Mont.

The foothills country was cold too, but escaped the worst effects of the wind, and the losses there were lightest. But by January thousands of cattle were drifting from the open northern range beyond the Bow. On January 10 the *Lethbridge Herald* quoted a local rancher as reporting 7,000 strays looking vainly for bare grass on his land. It also printed a Medicine Hat dispatch that thousands of cattle were lying dead along railway snow fences between Medicine Hat and Calgary. On February 14 it reported that so many cattle were milling on the tracks between Medicine Hat and Lethbridge that the train could hardly get through. Skinned and bleeding up to their knees from snow crust, they refused to leave the windswept roadbed to wallow in snowbound ditches.

In January, according to Leroy Victor (Roy) Kelly, author before the snow was gone, exposing tens of thousands of dead animals. The Walrond in the foothills had lost 5,000 head of 20,000. Gordon, Ironside & Fares on the Blackfoot prairie near Gleichen had lost 11,000 of 13,000. "Coulees were piled deep with cattle," wrote cowhand C.J. Christianson. "The few that remained were nothing but skin and bone." The carcasses were so wasted of muscle that they didn't even stink, he observed. "It takes flesh to make what the Indians call 'the big

Winters That Taught Men Something About Haying Machinery, *by E.F. Hagell.*

of *The Range Men*, the citizens of Macleod witnessed a horrifying sight. Thousands of emaciated Bar U range cattle, hair and hide frozen off in large patches, skinned from the knees, slowly tottered through the town, eight or so abreast, taking over half an hour to pass. People stared in helpless disbelief as the doomed herd, moaning softly and piteously rather than bawling, limped southward past hotels, stores and livery stables to certain death in the cold prairie beyond. Town workers hauled 48 carcasses off the street the next day.

Although the weather finally broke in March, it was May smell.' You could ride through acres of carcasses without holding your nose."

Pat Burns, as it turned out, was right about one thing: the price of beef didn't rise. Foreign markets were soft, and domestic demand was more than sated by the number of cattlemen selling their surviving breeding stock. For many, the Winter of the Blue Snow was their last.   — *L.B.*

ᵃThe Brainard story has come down in various shapes. The version recounted by his niece and granddaughter appeared in the local history *Prairie Rose Country.*

had no influence in the debate. While the WSGA complained about the ever-greater numbers of squatters, the department sent out its new deputy, James Smart, to assess the situation (Vol. 1, p. 277). Later that year the department opted to auction off water reserve lands, but Oliver, fearing that the better-capitalized ranchers would dominate the sales and discourage settlers from bidding, successfully lobbied for dispersal by sealed tender. On this basis some small sales were made, but neither settlers nor ranchers liked it because they had no idea what others were bidding.

With the water reserve system in retreat and overstocking a manifest problem, pressure arose for more closed leases. After Sifton handed out a half-dozen large awards in 1902, there were 2.3 million acres (or about 3,600 square miles) of leased land and three million acres applied for.[7] The department again reviewed its grazing policy in 1904, and this time decided that leasing was superior to water reserves and free grazing. In December, Sifton approved a new policy of awarding individual leases of up to 150 square miles in areas unsuited to agriculture, with tenure secured for 21 years at two cents per acre per annum and one cow per twenty acres.

The cattlemen rejoiced, thinking that their hold on the drylands would now be secure. Although they had already lost the wide swath of country running from Pincher Creek to Lethbridge, and up the old cattle trail from Fort Macleod to Calgary, the vast, largely unbroken buffalo grass range between Moose Jaw and Calgary would be their own. Or so it seemed in December, 1904. Their celebrations were to prove short-lived. On February 28, 1905, Clifford Sifton resigned from the Laurier cabinet and was replaced by their mortal enemy, Frank Oliver. Their fate was thereupon sealed.

Oliver hit hard. He completely reversed policies of the past quarter-century. He told the department to dispose of all remaining water reserves without inspection for agricultural suitability, the sole caveat being to preserve the interests of any squatters who had illegally occupied them. As far as "suitability" went, all land was to be considered suitable for agriculture except that which was too stony to break; climate was to be deemed irrelevant. Grazing lease privileges henceforth would be revoked upon two years' notice.

With Sifton gone and Oliver in charge, the WSGA was beaten. After their May general meeting, they proposed that the boundary between the two new provinces run east and west, just south of Red Deer, incorporating the whole cattle country. That proposal was ignored. They petitioned that the new provinces not dispense with the Royal North-West Mounted Police. That one succeeded, but only because the new provinces found provincial policing too costly. They lobbied for ten-year security on lease land rather than two. That was refused. Their sole consolation was that the provinces, which were even more frantic for settlers than Ottawa was, did not win jurisdiction over crown land.

The year 1906 marked the beginning of the end. News of the first successful dryland harvest of fall wheat (wheat seeded in the fall and harvested a year later in mid-summer to gain maximum benefit of snow melt) had emerged in 1905, and in 1906 the Alberta government pointed the first wave of farmers into the remaining ranch country. Many cattlemen simply quit. In 1906 the 63,000-acre Cochrane ranch went to the Mormons at Cardston for $6 per acre, followed a year later by the Walrond. The big Medicine Hat Ranch dispersed its land holdings in 1906, its cattle in 1907. Cattle export numbers increased as stockmen began selling breeding animals, a trend that would climax at the end of the decade.[8]

There was worse to come, much worse. The mercury plunged in November, 1906, and by Christmas range cattle had to be driven out of the coulees to feed on the prairie above. As the wind blew colder and the snow drifted deeper, this became less and less possible. In January the temperature plunged to -50 and worse across the range country. Limited feed supplies were running out, hay was getting harder to haul through deepening drifts, and the exposed cattle were starting to drift, starve, freeze and die — first by the dozen and in February by the thousand. When the chinooks finally returned and the receding snows revealed the losses, it was estimated that about half the northwest ranch herd had been wiped out (see sidebar).

The winter of what was called "aught-six aught-seven" marked the end of the old ranching industry, which had always kept cattle on open winter range, with little resort to hay and even less to grain. Cowboys, it was always said, would not work on foot, meaning that they wouldn't farm. Yet after such a devastating winter, and given the massive pressure for settlement, it was

There is no part of the cow puncher's costume not designed for use. The broad-brimmed felt hat is far more efficient in protecting the eyes from the sun than is a straw hat. The black silk handkerchief protects the neck from sunburn, and the chaps (pronounced shaps) are comfortable for riding and keep the legs warm in a way which nothing else would. The heels of the top boots are made very high in order to prevent the feet from slipping through the large western stirrups, for the cow punchers do not ride with merely the toe in the stirrup, and if by any chance they should be thrown it is a matter of life or death to have the feet free, as otherwise they might be dragged for miles.
– Ibid

(Right) A.E. Cross, his son Jim on saddle horse, and coyote hounds, winter 1910-11. (Left) rancher Billy Cochrane, of Mosquito Creek, in his study with beer paraphernalia, around 1906. 'We must pray for a drought.'

clear that if the cattle industry was to survive at all it would be grain-based on smaller, more developed and more intensively harvested land holdings.[9]

It had always been the ambition of the farming lobby to see the export cattle industry evolve from a ranching base to a farm base. The bad winter and Liberal land policy had jointly decimated the export beef industry, and the farm herd was still woefully unable to compensate. L.V. Kelly closed his seminal work, *The Range Men*, written in 1912, with a speech by George Lane at that year's annual meeting of the National Live Stock Association in Ottawa. A self-made man and part owner of the old Bar U (Northwest Cattle Co.) at High River, Lane had come west to punch cattle 29 years earlier and had seen it all.

The problem with the so-called mixed farming of Alberta, he opined, was that it wasn't mixed at all, it was simply grain farming. That was why cattle shipments out of Alberta had dropped from 75,000 head in 1906, when the collapse began, to 12,000 in 1911. "Now I am sure I am not exaggerating when I say there are over 8,000 real estate men selling land in the western provinces, and it is safe to say that at least 95% of them talk wheat and nothing else...After the land agent has done his part, along comes the steam plough agent, and the gasoline agent, and half a dozen other clever machinery salesmen, and in turn each of these men advises, 'Raise wheat!' Nobody advises the landowner to carry on mixed farming." The result, said Lane, was that Alberta produced only a third of the mutton it consumed, and one-quarter of the hogs. The West imported 25,000 horses in the previous year. If things continued it would soon be importing beef.

But wheat, by the end of the decade, was indisputably king, and would remain so for a long time. Even in the driest reaches of eastern Alberta, towns were springing up and homesteaders were dotted two to the square mile to turn the brown prairie soil upside down.

The cow men hated it but they had lost the argument. Lachlin McKinnon recorded the lament of one old-timer who saw the sod being turned in 1904: "It is heart-breaking to see these awful wounds appearing in this beautiful prairie."

The Glenbow Archives contains the 1919 last will and testament of Swift Current cowboy J.B. Henson. The whole of his real estate, he wrote drily, should be sold to create a fund "to be used for the extermination of that class of Vermin, commonly known as farmers, who are at present polluting by their presence the country adjacent to the South Saskatchewan River...I give to George Windsor my Navajo saddle blanket, to William Vincent Smith my rope, and to Pete LaPlante my rifle...Finally, I leave to every *Mossback* my perpetual curse as some reward for their labours in destroying the Open Range by means of that most pernicious of all implements, the plough."

"We must pray for a drought," William Cochrane had said. The answer to that prayer would take two more decades to arrive, but arrive it eventually did, borne on walls of blowing dust a mile high, a terrifying vindication of what the ranchers knew all along was inevitable.

[7] Typical of the leases of this period was the 1903 award of 10,000 acres to James Russell near what would soon become Drumheller, whose story is recorded in *The Hills of Home*. He built the area's first dipping-tank for mange, an infectious skin disease killed only by swimming cattle through a long, deep tank containing a solution of water, creosote and sulphur. The Russells helped numerous settler families when they began moving into the country late in the decade. In the fall of 1910, however, when Russell left a large supply of wire on a quarter he intended fencing and filing upon the following spring, some of his new neighbours prevented him by hiding it in the river, and fishing it out later to fence their own claims.

[8] The lawyer who handled the Cochrane ranch sale was William C. Ives, later chief justice of the Supreme Court of Alberta. Son of a Quebec-born Mountie, he left home at Pincher Creek to work on the Cochrane ranch at fouteen. He later observed that he made more money handling the one legal job than he did over four years punching Cochrane cattle for $40 a month and beans.

[9] Early ranch wives also were not expected to perform farm chores, although some did just to get useful luxuries such as fresh butter, milk, eggs and vegetables. The ranching culture relied heavily on tins and salt. Otherwise, women were busy enough keeping clothing, bedding and dishes clean, schooling their own children, and nursing the household's sick and injured.

A 500-mile odyssey for some unfenced country

THAT WILKINSON-MCCORD CREW DROVE 3,680 LONGHORNS AND 200 PONIES FROM SOUTH OF THE MISSOURI TO NORTH OF THE RED DEER BACK IN '03

In April, 1902, three men travelling the unfenced plains with light camping gear and a horse-drawn democrat stood atop a hill and took turns looking northward through field glasses at horseshoe-shaped Sounding Lake in eastern Alberta. They were on the north side of the Neutral Hills, so named since Indian days as the border between the shortgrass prairie of the Blackfoot and the parkland country of the Cree. It was a perfect site: sheltered on the north by a low ridge, plenty of small creeks and potholes, waist-high grass in the huge meadow between the arms of Sounding Lake, timber nearby, and no one around for miles.

One of the trio was a local Indian guide. The others were rancher William J. "Bud" Wilkinson of Roswell, New Mexico, and roving Texas cowboy Bill Greathouse, lately of Medicine Hat. Like many American cattlemen, Wilkinson was fed up with homesteaders and sheep, and was looking northward. And like all his kind he was decisive.

Greathouse returned with his old friend and former employer and bossed a roundup that fall and winter, gathering and sorting cattle from all over southwest Texas and eastern New Mexico. The following spring, Wilkinson and his brother-in-law partner, Tom McCord, hired eight trains, loaded all their worldly goods upon them, and headed north to Billings,

Billings, which lies in southern Montana, some 500 miles (800 km) south and slightly east of Sounding Lake. Oddly, no record survives of what route they took, but Mrs. Watt points out that they had to cross the broad Missouri, South

Courtesy of Ron & Sonia Dumaresq

McCord haying crew, 1907.

Saskatchewan and Red Deer rivers. They probably made around fifteen miles a day, and would have had to skirt spreading areas of agricultural settlement in Montana.

Neutral Hills cowboy Ivan Inman recorded the seasoned advice of one of the twelve trail riders, Harvey Lockwood. The trick, he said, was to start early (most cowboys rolled out at 4 or 5 a.m.), to keep the cattle bunched fairly tightly and keep them moving steadily, and to find good grass and water early enough in the afternoon to settle them for the night. All that is known of the trip is that on the Canadian side they were

---

The trick was to start around 5 a.m., keep the cattle bunched tightly and moving steadily, and to find good grass and water early enough to settle the cattle for the night.

Montana. According to local Sounding Lake historian Margaret Watt[a], who arrived in the country at the age of twelve in 1908, the Wilkinson-McCord outfit comprised 3,680 Longhorn cattle branded HUT on the right hip, 200 saddle ponies and draft horses, a massive cast-iron stove and all the tack, wagons, implements and supplies they would need in Canada. Wilkinson, McCord, Greathouse, twelve Texas cowboys and a Mexican cook named Juan set out in May from

hampered by heavy rain, and the basin of Sounding Creek had become a vast bog: they had to bridge the creek itself with piles of willows and haul the wagons across with long chains.

Though he had left before Mrs. Watt arrived in 1908, Wilkinson was remembered as a formidable range boss. The herd arrived in "high summer," and before the winter set in the small crew had built an L-shaped four-room cabin, a workshop, a barn, a storehouse and corrals, all of rough-hewn logs, and had put up enough hay behind fences to get them through until spring.

According to Mrs. Watt, Wilkinson could do anything with rope, cow pony, bronco or camp skillet. Once, when he and some men were driving sixty cattle across Sounding Lake in winter, the ice broke. "Turn them back," cried one drover. But Bud Wilkinson roared, "Never turn back if you want success!" They drove and hauled the animals forward to safety.

There were two women on the ranch: Tom McCord's sister, married to Bud Wilkinson, and the wife of a cowhand named Dick Ellis, who owned two or three dozen of the Wilkinson-McCord herd. Their names come down to us simply as Mrs. Wilkinson and Mrs. Ellis, but they commanded a devotion illustrated by an event of the terrible Winter of the Blue Snow (see sidebar) in early 1907.

One morning Mrs. Wilkinson told the men at breakfast that Mrs. Ellis was deathly sick, and that without a doctor's advice and prescription she might not recover. The men stared at each other. It was about -50 below outside, with a biting northwest wind, and Stettler lay 100 miles (160 km) to the west. It was so cold that they were blackened with frostbite and had to wrap themselves in stinking old raw cowhides just to do chores. Out on the plains the snow was three feet deep

turn back, Wilkinson took his family and their aged black helper Josh home to New Mexico. McCord abandoned a large part of the spread with hopes of gradually re-establishing it. Within a few years, however, the country was filling with sodbusters.

In 1910 a newcomer named Connor managed to steal — legally — the greater part of McCord's winter hay supply under provisions of the Homestead Act. McCord sold out in disgust and returned to New Mexico. The ranch and buildings were bought by William Poynter, who ran it with his wife and three sons.

But men like Dick Ellis stayed on after the last Neutral Hills roundup in 1909, and operated small ranches alongside their more recently arrived farm neighbours. Glen Ellis finished the Neutral Hills grade school later on. Of all of them, though, Bill Greathouse was widest-known, best-loved and probably the longest-lived.

He was born in western Texas in 1866, and grew up in the dying days of buffalo hunts, gunfights and Indian wars. He wore a Colt revolver well into the 20th century, although he never in later years resorted to it. But one time, a bunch of cowboys came by his cabin and fell to playing poker. Greathouse had relieved them of $300 before they called it

Greathouse had grown up in the dying days of buffalo hunts, gunfights and Indian wars. He wore a revolver well into the 20th century.

with a cutting icy crust. Men had died that winter on the open prairie.

Cow-boss Bill Greathouse left the table without a word and saddled his horse. In the barn, Dick Ellis quietly warned him, "You'll never make it." Greathouse just tightened his cinch strap and returned to ask Mrs. Wilkinson what else she might need. She wrote a note to the doctor, wrapped it in a bit of oilskin, and pinned it into his shirt pocket.

Greathouse rode westward into the snowswept prairie toward the next ranch fifty miles (80 km) away, pushing his horse as hard as he dared, and walking before it to break trail through the snow-plugged coulees that lay in his way. When he got there he refused to stop and rest; he simply switched to the best mount the rancher could give him and headed for the next house westward. Nearer Stettler there were more people, and in due course he reached the doctor. While the physician prepared the medicine Greathouse ate a big meal at the Stettler Hotel.

With medicine and instructions safely stored near his body he then rode home, returning each rancher's horse as he went. Dazed with cold and exhaustion, he walked back into the Wilkinson-McCord ranch house 36 hours after leaving it. Mrs. Ellis recovered.

That gruelling winter wiped out three-quarters of the Wilkinson-McCord herd. Ignoring his own advice never to

quits and flopped for the night on his floor. When he pulled on his trousers the next morning his $300 was gone. Out came his Colt as he shouted, "Okay, you sons of bitches, no one's leaving until I get my money back!" A few tense minutes elapsed before his sleepy comrades observed that he had put on the wrong pair of pants.

After the McCord ranch broke up he worked on other large operations farther south, and in the 1920s tried ranching beyond the North Saskatchewan near Meadow Lake. His southern stock began to die, however, because of the weak nutritional value of northern grass, and he had to return to the hard grass south of the Battle River. He never succeeded as a rancher, but he always paid his debts. He had a good baritone voice and a famous skill with his beloved Texas fiddle.

In 1912, newly arrived pioneers put on a basket social and dance to reward Bill Greathouse for his legendary winter ride. The old trail boss insisted that the money be devoted to the new Neutral Hills school, and instead claimed every dance of the evening with the teacher.

He lived on in the cattle country for many years, and was still a Calgary Stampede judge when he died in 1962 at 96.

— L.B.

[a]Mrs. Watt's recollection and research, and that of many others, were incorporated in the local Neutral Hills history, *Treasure of Memories*.

CHAPTER THREE

The spectacular playground of tourist and adventurer

BANFF, THE TOWN THE CPR BUILT, BECAME THE CRADLE OF WESTERN CANADIAN TOURISM ALL BECAUSE OF ITS PEAKS AND ITS SMELLY WATER

Glenbow Archives, NC-53-52

by ROBERT BOTT

The year is 1900. It's a sunny summer day in the foothills west of Calgary. The first-class car of a CPR passenger train is clickety-clacking westward through the Stoney Indian Reserve. During the long journey across the prairies, carloads of immigrants and pedlars have been left behind. Now, as the engine strains to gain the 1,097 feet of elevation from Calgary to Banff, elegantly attired ladies and gentlemen peer through soot-grimed windows to catch glimpses of the snow-capped "alps" ahead.

The long-awaited mountain vistas seem to reach out and embrace the passengers, perhaps reminding some of previous visits to the Dolomites in northern Italy. Excitement grows as the speeding panorama finally slows. The train pulls into Banff Station. Amid a flurry of trunks and boxes, the parched and dusty adventurers alight.

High-rigged, six-seat tallyho coaches, each pulled by a four-horse hitch, head the queue of hacks and drays waiting to carry customers to the CPR's elegant Banff Springs Hotel or various lesser accommodations. Wherever the posh pilgrims are staying, their first priority will be a good soak in the egg-smelly waters that bubble up through faults in Sulphur Mountain.

So arrived most of the 8,000 or so visitors in 1900 to Canada's first national park, then known as Rocky Mountains National Park — birthplace of the national parks movement in Canada and cradle of Alberta's tourism industry.[1] As the new century dawned, Banff had already become a Mecca for wealthy tourists and adventurers from around the world, the jet-setters of the steam age. They flocked in each summer from eastern Canada, the United States, Europe, Australia and even Japan.

One reason they came was to restore health. Dr. R.G. Brett, a medical supervisor for the CPR, did a brilliant job of marketing the supposed benefits of the springs. The Brett Sanitarium (on the site later occupied by the park headquarters building in Banff) and his two hotels were among the most popular destinations. Crutches and canes festooned the buildings, testaments to cures of sundry ailments. Air conditioning and antibiotics had not yet been invented, of course, and in the Edwardian era large cities could be fetid warm-weather breeding grounds for disease. Clear mountain air may have effected more cures than hot smelly water. But whatever the reason, people felt better, and some stayed for weeks or even months.

At the time of its construction in 1888, the 250-room Banff Springs Hotel had been advertised as the largest hotel in the world. Room rates started at the then-princely sum of $3.50 a night and hot water was piped more than a mile to the hotel from the Upper Hot Springs. Other attractions, developed mainly to entertain visitors between their baths and their meals, came to include a museum, zoo, bison paddock, curio shops, carriage and horseback tours, golf course, and boating on Lake Minnewanka.

These activities helped provide income for a permanent population of several hundred. The CPR, local businesses and the government became more eager than ever to attract tourists to "the most beautiful place in the world." A six-page advertising supplement for Banff in the *Calgary Herald* in 1906 calls the resort "The Mecca of all

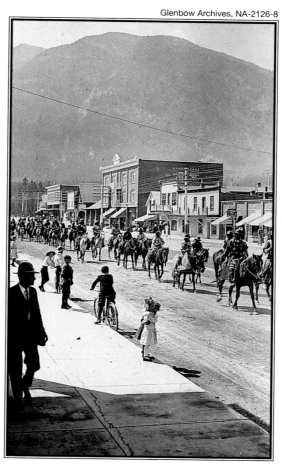

Indian parade on Banff Avenue, Banff. Circa 1915. (Facing page) Mount Temple from The Saddle with a Miss Priest in the foreground, July 6, 1905.

Tourists and the Playground of Canada" and extols its offerings of "Natural Grandeur and Personal Comfort." World-famous mountaineer Edward Whymper is quoted to the effect that "the Canadian Rockies are equivalent to fifty or sixty Switzerlands rolled into one."

The free-spending travellers came via CPR steamships and sleeping cars, stayed in CPR hotels, ate in CPR restaurants, hired horses and carriages from CPR outfitters, and climbed mountains with the help of the railway's imported Swiss guides. Later in the century's first decade, the trains also ferried in carloads of day-trippers from Calgary each summer. Families, church groups and others would ride out to enjoy swims and picnics. Some stayed in hotels or camped, but most returned to the city in the evening. As many as 2,000 a week would visit the area in this manner — the beginning of the enduring love affair between Calgarians and the park.

Banff was essentially an adjunct of the railway, from the time of the park's initial designation in 1885 until well after the Banff Coach Road opened up automobile traffic from Calgary in

---

Clear mountain air may have effected more cures than hot smelly water, but whatever their reason, people felt better, and some stayed for weeks or even months.

1911.[2] It was CPR general manager William Cornelius Van Horne, after all, who originally urged the dominion government to protect the "million-dollar" hot springs. Van Horne was also quick to grasp the commercial value of the mountain vistas. "Since we can't export the scenery," goes his famous maxim, "we'll have to import the tourists."

The Bow Valley in 1900 bore little resemblance to the verdant corridor of later decades. The forests all along the valley had been devastated by repeated fires, caused mainly by careless camping and sparks from steam locomotives. A boisterous coal mining community existed just outside the Banff townsite. There was logging along the Spray and Bow valleys. The ban on hunting was

[1] When it was established in 1887, two years after the government set aside the initial park reserve at Banff, Rocky Mountains National Park became the world's third national park, joining Yellowstone National Park in the United States (1872) and Royal National Park in Australia (1879). The precedent that intrigued the CPR and Ottawa, however, was the commercial success of the Arkansas Hot Springs Reserve, created by the US federal government in 1832.

[2] A ban on automobiles was imposed in 1905 after the September 1904 visit of a four-ton Napier touring car carrying the family of Boston banker Charles J. Glidden. For nearly half of its transcontinental voyage, including the Banff section, the auto's wheels were replaced by steel flanges so it could operate on railway tracks. After completion of the road in 1911 motorists demanded access, and the ban was finally lifted in June 1915.

The Cave and Basin swimming pool, Banff, at the turn of the century. Van Horne urged the government to protect these 'million dollar' springs.

not enforced until the first park wardens were appointed in 1909.

The task of reconciling commerce and conservation fell on the unlikely shoulders of a former Calgary coal merchant, Howard Douglas, selected by the Liberal federal government in 1897 as the park's second superintendent. But Douglas too recognized the Rockies as a national treasure. In his 1902 report to Ottawa he was already quoting directly (without attribution) from American conservationist John Muir:

> All the mountains are still rich in wildness and by means of good roads are being brought nearer civilization every year; the wildest health and pleasure grounds are made accessible and available to many a lover of wildness who without them would never see it.

Douglas set up the warden service and led the campaign to save the nearly extinct buffalo. Largely through his efforts, the area of Rocky Mountains National Park was enormously increased. "Forest parks" were established at Waterton, Jasper and Elk Island.

Perhaps because of the much-publicized "closing of the American frontier," it was a time when no less a figure than the US president, Theodore Roosevelt, celebrated the physical and spiritual benefits of the great outdoors. Adventure, exploration and "preservation" were in vogue among the well-to-do around the world. If such noble and healthy impulses also brought profit to the CPR, so much the better. Indeed, the railway was a valuable ally for Howard Douglas as he sought appropriations from far-away Ottawa.

These same physical and spiritual benefits, of course, had long since drawn the Indians into the Rockies, whose major valleys provided hunting grounds, travel routes and refuge from enemies. Hot springs were favoured meeting places and camps.

Robert Rundle, the frail Methodist missionary for whom the mountain is named, made at least one attempt at climbing. In his diary he speaks of his prayers.

By the time Europeans arrived, Stoney Indians lived in the Bow Valley and along the nearby foothills and mountains, while Kootenays came over the Continental Divide from valleys in what would later be called the BC Interior each year to hunt buffalo on the plains. The Banff hot springs provided a peace ground where the two tribes met to trade and gamble.

Trader and explorer David Thompson visited the Bow Valley as early as 1801, but not the springs. Through the first half of the 19th century, the ferocity of plains tribes like the Blackfoot kept most traders and travellers away from the southern Alberta mountains. The missionaries were not deterred, however, and among them was the Rev. Robert Rundle, for whom the imposing mountain towering over Banff is named. Rundle, a Methodist, made several trips deep into Blackfoot country in the 1840s; in 1844 he went beyond the first fringes of the Rockies. A frail man, he nonetheless made at least one attempt at climbing, although not on the mountain that bears his name. His journal for Nov. 9, 1844, includes this vivid account:

> I became quite ill thro' fatigue...but was in good spirits when climbing, until I was very high up. I made two attempts to get up an elevation but could not succeed. Rocks very steep — felt very weak, so weak that at last I was near fainting whilst passing over a projecting ledge of rock. What a moment of anxiety. I have some recollection of calling to the Almighty

The new Sanitarium building contains in the neighbourhood of 150 rooms, fifty of which are fitted up with baths, closets, etc., all steam heated and furnished with electric light...The dining room, rotunda, and ladies' waiting room are each furnished with a cosy-looking Old English fireplace.

– from an advertisement in the Calgary Herald for the Banff Sanitarium, Aug. 25, 1906.

to assist me and praised be His name, my prayer was heard...I was very weak from want of food, having left without breakfast, and began to feel afraid...ever and anon too I heard the moving stones which terrified me. How hard, too, to pass along the steep sloping sides sloping away to fearful descent. At length, however, I reached the bottom.

Farther north, Jasper House was built by the North-West Company on Brule Lake in 1813.[3] The Athabasca and Yellowhead passes had early been established as fur trade routes to the west coast, a circumstance that played a part in the later blossoming of tourism and mountaineering. David Douglas, the botanist who gave his name to the Douglas fir, was accompanying a Hudson's Bay Company brigade in May 1827 in order to gather botanical specimens. He left his party to make a solo climb of 9,183-foot Mount Brown above Athabasca Pass — Canada's first recorded major climb. Douglas was no surveyor, however, and in his widely circulated journals mistakenly estimated Mount Brown's elevation as 16,000 feet above sea level.

After the railway reached the mountains, climbers and explorers spent years searching in vain for a peak of such proportions, loftier than the tallest peak in the Alps and 1,500 feet higher than Mount Elbert in Colorado, high point of the American Rockies. "We had been humbugged," wrote Toronto geologist A.P. Coleman, after he succeeded in finding and climbing the rather modest Mount Brown in 1893. Mountaineer John Norman Collie, investigating the mystery of fellow Scot Douglas's mistake in 1898, decided that it was based on a map provided to Douglas by that Englishman David Thompson.

Another influential early account concerned the travels of a young British aristocrat, Viscount Milton, and his doctor, Walter Cheadle. The pair barely survived their three-month trip from Edmonton to Kamloops in 1863, but on the way they caught sight of imposing Mount Robson, the real giant of the Canadian Rockies, in the Yellowhead Pass just west of the Continental Divide.

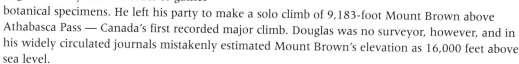

Philip Stanley Abbot untied his safety rope near the summit of Mount Lefroy, lost his footing, and fell 1,500 feet. It was the first recorded death in North American mountaineering.

The North-West Passage by Land, the story of their journey, was immensely popular in England; five editions sold out in eight months. Although Mount Robson would not be successfully climbed until 1913, their description of its cloud-bound mass provided an additional lure for climbers:

On every side the snowy heads of mighty hills crowded round, whilst, immediately behind us, a giant among giants, rose Robson's Peak. This magnificent mountain is of conical form, glacier-clothed, and rugged. When we first caught sight of it, a shroud of mist partially enveloped the summit, but this presently rolled away, and we saw its upper portion dimmed by a necklace of light feathery clouds, beyond which its pointed apex of ice, glittering in the morning sun, shot up far into the blue heaven above, to a height of probably 10,000 to 15,000 feet. It was a glorious sight, and one which the Shushwaps of the Cache assured us had rarely been seen by human eyes, the summit being generally hidden by clouds.[4]

One reason there was so little early exploration of the Rockies was that snow and ice clogged

Banff Springs Hotel in 1904 by Cleveland Rockwell. Its 250 rooms starting at $3.50 a night helped make Banff a Mecca for the jet-setters of the steam age.

[3] Jasper House was apparently named after Jasper Hawes, an early North-West Company clerk at the remote outpost. Banff was the Scottish birthplace of two CPR directors. Perhaps the least likely park name is Waterton, for English naturalist and explorer Charles Waterton, who never visited Canada. Meteorologist Thomas Blakiston bestowed his name on Waterton Lakes when he saw them during a side-trip from the Palliser expedition in the late 1850s.

[4] The origin of the name for 12,972-foot Mount Robson, once known as Robson's Peak, is obscure. It is usually explained as a corruption of the surname of Colin Robertson, a Hudson's Bay Company trader in the 1820s. The native name was Yuh-hai-has-hun, the mountain of the spiral road, but the upward-angling ledges do not reach the summit. In 1909 the Rev. George Kinney of Edmonton and novice guide Donald "Curly" Phillips got within a few hundred feet of Robson's summit before they were turned back by weather and fatigue. On their return, Kinney claimed to have made the first ascent, but Phillips later recanted. The first ascent is credited to guide Conrad Kain and Alpine Club members W.W. Foster and A.H. MacCarthy in 1913.

Dr. R.G. Brett (in 1896), who did a remarkable job marketing the supposed health benefit of the springs, and accommodating tourists in his sanitarium and his two hotels.

many valleys and passes until about 1870. The Athabasca Glacier, for example, once completely covered the route later followed by the Icefields Parkway. Then the latest "little ice age," known as the Cavell Advance, ended and the glaciers began to recede. The 1870s saw a series of key developments. The first surveyors reached the Rockies. In 1875 a CPR surveyor, Henry MacLeod, made the first recorded sighting of Maligne Lake, the scenic gem of Jasper Park. In the same year, two American cowboys happened upon the Banff hot springs, built a cabin and spent the winter there. John "Kootenai" Brown (Vol. 1, p. 44) settled at Waterton Lakes in 1879.

The pivotal event was the arrival of the railway. The CPR track crews got as far as Laggan, as Lake Louise station was then known, by the winter of 1883. That was when Van Horne first visited the Banff area and made the initial proposal for a resort. The federal Department of the Interior agreed to survey a park reserve. Meanwhile, three railway workers staked a claim to the lower hot springs and sold baths to railway workers, surveyors and prospectors.

Toronto geologist Coleman made his first visit to the Rockies in 1884 and ascended the imposing turrets of Castle Mountain. Former railway worker Tom Wilson, credited with discovering Lake Louise and Emerald Lake, set up the first outfitting business to provide horses, guides and gear for tourists. Wilson prospered through the following decades.

In November 1885 the dominion government set aside a small park reservation around the springs. At this point, Ottawa seemed more impressed with the medicinal properties of the waters

---

While the Banff Springs was being built, Van Horne discovered that the kitchens overlooked the rivers and view while the rooms faced the forests. Plans were hastily revised.

---

than with the mountain scenery. As Sir John A. Macdonald, the Conservative prime minister, remarked: "These springs will recuperate the patient and recoup the treasury."

A public commission the following year settled the various claims to ownership of the springs for a few thousand dollars, and the government designated additional reserves that would become Yoho and Glacier national parks in British Columbia. With financial assistance from the CPR, Dr. Brett built the Brett Sanitarium in downtown Banff, and the Grandview Villa at the Upper Hot Springs.

The CPR then commissioned famous architect Bruce Price to design the 250-room Banff Springs Hotel at the confluence of the Bow and Spray rivers. While construction was under way in 1887, Van Horne was horrified to discover that the kitchens overlooked the rivers, while the rooms faced the forests. The plans were hastily revised so the paying guests would get the scenic view. In June 1887 legislation officially created the national park. George Stewart, the first superintendent, a surveyor, laid out the town plan for Banff, built roads and bridges, and oversaw construction of the Cave and Basin baths. He also imposed the park's first hunting and fishing regulations, although there were few means of enforcing them.

Preventing forest fires became a priority after devastating fires swept through the Bow Valley in 1889, threatening the townsite itself. Stewart ordered the clearing of firebreaks around buildings, roads and rail lines, and began the first of many campaigns to educate visitors about fire hazards. That year also saw the first of the "Indian Days" celebrations. The Stoneys were invited to perform dances and display horsemanship as entertainment for trainloads of passengers stranded because of problems on the line through the mountains.

Most park visitors were content to enjoy the spa atmosphere of Banff, but a few wanted greater adventure. To serve them the CPR built a log chalet at Lake Louise in 1890. It was replaced by a larger wood structure three years later, after fire destroyed the original chalet. The dramatic spires and glaciers of the Lake Louise area drew mountaineers like a magnet.[5] Although surveyors and scientists had ascended some peaks, the first purely recreational climber was Samuel Allen of Philadelphia. On his first visit in 1891, Allen climbed Mount Burgess near Field and Devil's Thumb near Lake Louise.

Returning in 1893 with Yale schoolmate Walter Wilcox, Allen made the first reported sighting of Moraine Lake. In 1894 they came back with three friends (calling themselves the Yale Lake Louise Club) to climb Mount Victoria and Temple Mountain and explore Paradise Valley and the Valley of the Ten Peaks. Another group of American mountaineers, the Appalachian Mountain Club, successfully climbed ice-clad Mount Hector in 1895. They vowed to return for more conquests the following year, with unhappy consequences. In their attempt on Mount Lefroy in 1896, Philip Stanley Abbot untied his safety rope near the summit, lost his footing and fell 1,500 feet to his death. It was the first recorded death in North American mountaineering.

CPR officials, worried that Abbot's death would discourage what was becoming a lucrative tourist trade, imported Swiss mountain guide Peter Sarbach to accompany a second, and successful, attempt on Lefroy in 1897.[6] The summit party on Lefroy included John Norman Collie, the Scottish scientist-adventurer who subsequently played a major role in popularizing the Rockies among the world's climbers. Collie returned a year later to make first ascents of four major peaks (Balfour, Thompson, Diadem, Snow Dome) in the course of which he discovered the snowy mass of the Columbia Icefields.

Among the Swiss guides at Banff in 1899 was Edward Feuz, soon joined by his sons Edward Jr., Ernest and Walter, and their cousin Gottfried. They were the first to settle permanently in the Canadian Rockies, and they left an enduring record. In the next four decades, members of the Feuz family led clients on no fewer than 130 first ascents of mountains in the Rockies and the Selkirks — without a single serious injury. The most prolific was Edward Jr., who guided 78 first-ascent parties from 1903 to 1944. Their typical fee was $5 a day. Also in 1899, Walter Wilcox returned to Moraine Lake, the shimmering jewel near Lake Louise that he had first glimpsed six

A CPR advertisement from the Canadian Alpine Journal, 1911. Numerous Switzerlands.

'When on the trail his daily allowance was a bottle of scotch and ten pints of ale...I never saw him farther from a scotch and soda than the length of his arm.'

years earlier. "No scene has given me an equal impression of inspiring solitude and rugged grandeur," he wrote.

While climbers enjoyed a golden age of exploration in the virgin peaks, a bounty of amateur exploration unequalled since the assaults on the Swiss Alps a half-century earlier, the Banff area also bustled with more earthy commerce. Coal had been discovered at several points along the Bow Valley in the 1880s. The first seams were developed at Anthracite, eight miles east of Banff, and at Canmore. Most of the mines were eventually run by the H.W. McNeil Co. Ltd.

While Canmore attracted families, Anthracite was a rowdy frontier town of mainly single men. In 1904 Anthracite died. The mines were shut down and the town left deserted in favour of better coal prospects at Cascade Mountain, three miles north of Banff. The new town of Bankhead (like Canmore, more of a family town, and dominated by eastern Europeans with an underclass of Chinese) survived until the mines closed in 1922.

With a population as high as 1,500, Bankhead, just over two miles east of the Banff station, outnumbered the permanent residents of Banff. It had sewers, water and light before the resort town, and also four churches and facilities for hockey, skating, baseball and tennis. The mine itself was unusual in that the tunnels ran upward into the coal seams inside Cascade Mountain. In 1905 the Western Canada Cement and Coal Company, headed by Sir Sandford Fleming and backed by the CPR, opened a cement plant at Exshaw (part of the park from 1902 to 1930), using local coal

[5] The sport of mountaineering gained popularity after the first ascent of 15,771-foot Mont Blanc in France in 1786. Swiss mountain guides founded their professional organization in 1821. The period from 1855 to 1865, when most of the major peaks in the Swiss alps were first climbed, is known as the "golden age of mountaineering." Its tragic culmination was the conquest of the Matterhorn in 1865 by Edward Whymper and six companions. They reached the summit, but during their descent four of the party fell to their death.

[6] Peter Sarbach was the first of many Swiss mountaineers to guide amateur climbers in the Rockies, most of them living in a Lake Louise cabin in summer and returning to Europe in winter. Before modern climbing aids like nylon ropes and the widespread use of spiked crampons, the guides played a key safety role. The energetic Swiss also performed the arduous work of chopping steps in the ice during ascents of glaciers and steep snow chutes. Near the summit the guide would customarily step aside to allow the client the honour of first reaching the top.

Trousered women scale the heights

THE ROCKIES AROUND BANFF PROVIDED A FELICITOUS PROVING GROUND FOR FEMALE CLIMBERS, BUT THEY WERE NOT A NEW PHENOMENON

Women began climbing mountains soon after men. A Miss Parminter climbed *Le Buet* in the Savoy Alps in 1799, just thirteen years after the generally accepted beginning of male mountaineering. In the middle of the 19th century, Lucy Walker of Liverpool participated in 98 expeditions, including ascents of the Eiger and the Matterhorn. By the time recreational exploration reached the Rockies, women were frequently expedition members, some even leaders.

The Banff pioneers were two women from Philadelphia, Mary Vaux and Mary Schaffer (the future Mary Schaffer Warren), who came to Lake Louise in the summer of 1889. The former worked with her brothers in a fascinating amateur science project, measuring the movement of glaciers, while the latter was later famous for her photography and route-finding in the Athabasca Valley south of Jasper.

Lucy Walker reportedly climbed in dresses and preferred a diet of cake and champagne. Other women climbers devised elaborate drawstrings in their hems to keep out ice and snow. By the end of the Victorian era, however, it was becoming common for women to wear trousers in the mountains. In an article entitled "Camping in the Rockies," in the inaugural 1907 edition of *Canadian Alpine Journal*, Mary Vaux offered practical advice for mountaineers:

> To begin with, a good tent is required, plenty of warm blankets, and a canvas sheet to spread under and over the blankets on the bough-bed, to prevent dampness from above and below; then, a small pillow is a great luxury, and takes but little room in the pack.
>
> Of course, it is presupposed that the women of the party wear rational clothes: knickerbockers, a flannel shirt-waist, and knotted kerchief at the neck, stout boots, with hobnails, laced to the knee, or arranged for puttees, woollen stockings, a felt hat with moderate brim, and a sweater or short coat, to complete the outfit.
>
> A short coat, opened well behind, to allow it to part over the horse's back, and which may be fastened to the

The Challenge of the Mountains

Cover of a CPR promotional brochure, 1909.

saddle, is very necessary in a region where storms must be expected frequently. Each person should be provided with a canvas bag, which can be securely buttoned, wherein to place the necessary toilet articles.

> An extra pair of light shoes, a short skirt to wear in camp and a golf cape with hood, add greatly to the comfort of the camper; also a good-sized piece of mosquito netting, to keep off intruding bulldogs, if you wish to rest in the tent in the heat of the mid-day sun; while a hot water bottle and a box of mustard may be tucked in with a few simple medicines in case of emergency. On two occasions I would have given a great deal for a mustard plaster.

The Alpine Club represented a broad spectrum of naturalists and adventurers until 1928 when the Canadian National Parks Association was formed, after which the Alpine Club focused more narrowly on climbing. Mary Schaffer, leading a party of six to Maligne Lake near Jasper in 1908, later described the joy she felt exploring the unspoiled wilderness by means of a raft they named *HMS Chaba* (Chaba being the Stoney name for the lake):

> With lunch over, we wandered about to drink it all in. How pure and undefiled it was! We searched for some sign that others had been there — not a teepee pole, not a charred stick, not even tracks of game, just masses of flowers, the lap-lap of the waters on the shore, the occasional reverberating roar of an avalanche, and our own voices, stilled by a nameless Presence.

Mrs. Schaffer admitted, on this one occasion, violating her rule about leaving campsites as pristine as they were found; her group carved their initials in a tree trunk. She said her only regret was that Mary Vaux was not with them for the historic occasion. In her honour, they named one of the peaks by the lake Mount Mary Vaux. — *R.B.*

The alpinist Edward Whymper and his supplies. A prodigious thirst and stamina.

and locally quarried limestone. Logging continued in the Bow and Spray river valleys until 1906. Most of the timber was cut in winter with two-man cross-cut saws, hauled by horses to the rivers, and floated downstream to Calgary in drives during spring high water.

In the absence of motor vehicles, hundreds of horses were required for transportation, and much of the open land in the Bow Valley was used for hay and grazing. Several dairies were established to provide milk for Banff, Bankhead, Canmore and Lake Louise, one of them operated by John Brewster, who came out from Ontario in 1887. Brewster's sons, Bill and Jim, explored the surrounding mountains with a Stoney youth named William Twin and soon were guiding tourists on fishing and hunting expeditions.

In 1900 Bill and Jim Brewster used dairy profits to set up their own guide and outfitting business, in competition with Tom Wilson. The CPR sent the enterprising brothers to a sportsmen's show at Madison Square Garden in New York in 1902 to promote tourism in the Rockies. When the CPR decided to unload its own outfitting operations, the Brewsters bought the Banff concession and built an empire that continued into the automobile age.[7]

Another notable figure in the business community was Norman K. Luxton, son of the founder of the *Manitoba Free Press*, who reached Banff after adventures that included crossing the Pacific in a thirty-foot dugout canoe. In 1902 Luxton began publishing the town's first enduring newspaper, the *Crag and Canyon*. Luxton married Georgia McDougall, first white child born in the territory that would become Alberta. He maintained close relations with the Stoney Indians, organized Indian Days as an annual event, and established the Luxton Museum of the Plains Indian. He also built the resort's first year-round hotel, the King Edward, and actively backed Howard Douglas's later efforts to save the plains buffalo herds.

As early as 1898, Douglas had been urging enlargement of Rocky Mountains National Park. With the backing of Calgary politicians A.E. Cross and Arthur L. Sifton, who would become premier in 1910 (see Sect. 6, ch. 2), a bill passed Parliament in 1902 that increased its area tenfold, encompassing the Lake Louise area and the source watersheds of the Bow, Red Deer, Kananaskis and Spray rivers. (In 1911 the park was reduced again by half because of the difficulty of enforcing hunting, fishing, logging and mining regulations, and further reduced in 1930 when Crown land and resources were transferred to provincial control.)

After the Banff Springs Hotel had to turn away 5,000 potential guests in 1902, the CPR responded by twinning the original wing, doubling occupancy to 500. In 1900 two timbered wings had been added to the Lake Louise chalet, to provide accommodation for 200. A hydro dam on Louise Creek supplied the hotel with power. CPR publicists upgraded their efforts to match the expanded facilities. "Little Switzerland" of the 1880s became "Fifty Switzerlands in One" by 1910.

One bright idea was to sponsor three visits to the Rockies by Edward Whymper, "Conqueror of the Matterhorn." It had been more than three decades since Whymper's famous exploits in the

[7]At the peak of the horse era, the Brewster inventory included three hotel omnibuses, twelve tally-ho coaches, nineteen three-seat carriages, twenty surreys, eighteen single rigs and numerous wagons, as well as 146 driving horses. Jim Brewster, who bought out his brother's interest in 1909, introduced the first motor vehicles in the tourist trade in 1915. The Brewster transportation business was acquired by Greyhound of Canada in the 1960s but continued to use the Brewster name.

A group of tourists having breakfast in a tent in Banff in 1903. The road would arrive in 1911.

Swiss Alps, but he was still able to get up mountains in his sixties. He was also a phenomenal drinker with an irascible temper, who had great difficulty keeping guides and outfitters. Moreover, the CPR was disappointed at how little he wrote on their behalf.

There was plenty of wilderness to attract explorers and climbers who could spend weeks in the back country with entourages of guides and pack horses. From Mount Assiniboine to Jasper, they continued to find delightful vistas. A favourite in the first decade of the century was Lake O'Hara, over the Continental Divide from Lake Louise. James Outram described O'Hara as "the fairest of mountain lakelet tarns."

For tourists arriving at Banff station, however, the wilderness was marred by burned-over and logged-over forests, mining activity, and a notable shortage of wildlife. Fires, hard winters and over-hunting had severely depleted the animal population. The last recorded sighting of a native wood bison in the Banff area was in 1858, and elk had almost disappeared as well. One of Douglas's first moves as superintendent was to set

Bringing the buffalo herds back to life

WITH THE PLAINS BISON VIRTUALLY EXTERMINATED, IT WAS DECIDED TO FIND THE STRAGGLERS A HOME. ALBERTA HAD LOTS OF ROOM

The buffalo is perfectly adapted to the interior regions of North America. Its metabolism is marvellously efficient at obtaining nutrition from sparse grass and shrubs, and its great head serves as a shovel to reach forage beneath deep winter snows. Unfortunately, the muscular and ill-tempered animal is not easily domesticated.

An estimated fifty million buffalo once ranged the western plains, but in Canada the guns and horses of natives and Metis, and the loss of habitat, rendered the plains buffalo nearly extinct by the 1870s. Meanwhile the closely related wood buffalo, once common in the Rockies, was virtually wiped out there by hunting, disease and hard winters. The last reported sighting was in the Pipestone Valley, north of Lake Louise, in 1858.

Herds of wood buffalo survived in the boreal forest of northern Alberta, however, and they were protected by a game reserve established in 1906; this large area at the northeast corner of the province became Wood Buffalo National Park in 1922. But at the turn of the century there were only a few herds of plains buffalo remaining, in private sanctuaries like that of Donald Smith, Lord Strathcona, in Manitoba, and public preserves like the buffalo paddock at Banff. As few as 800 plains buffalo were believed to exist in North America.

Some of the cowboys who rounded up the buffalo in Montana, 1908. The artist Charles Russell is in the back row, far right.

Montana ranchers C.A. Allard and Michel Pablo acquired ten buffalo from a local Indian named Walking Coyote in 1883, and 26 more from Nebraska in 1893. After Allard died in 1896 his widow and Pablo maintained the herd, which grew to more than 700 by 1907.

aside a paddock so visitors could observe wildlife.

The first specimens were a small herd of elk, soon joined by two buffalo cows purchased in Texas by a Toronto benefactor. The redoubtable Donald Smith, Lord Strathcona, donated thirteen plains buffalo. Thus until 1908 the Banff herd was ruled by a huge bull captured near Fort Garry in 1872, reputedly the largest in North America, and known as Sir Donald. Other additions included mountain lions, red foxes and mountain sheep. In 1901 Douglas got into hot water when he was caught sponsoring "moose rustling" in Ontario to obtain more animals for the collection.

Stuffed and mounted specimens of wildlife were displayed at the park museum, established in 1895 and moved to its permanent site in 1903. From 1896 to 1945 the museum was tended by meteorologist, curator and hiker Norman Sanson. Every week, winter and summer, Sanson climbed Sulphur Mountain to check the instruments in his observatory. In 1907 a zoo and aviary were established

Open CPR observation car going through the Rockies at the turn of the century. 'Ecosystem preservation' was on its way.

In 1905, threatened by loss of grazing privileges on the Flathead Reservation (about 65 miles [104 km] southwest of Glacier National Park in Montana), Pablo went to Washington and offered to sell the herd to the government. President Theodore Roosevelt favoured the purchase, but Congress refused to make the necessary appropriation. Pablo then approached Alexander Ayotte, Canadian immigration agent at Missoula, who passed the offer to Howard Douglas, superintendent of Rocky Mountains National Park.

"One day Howard Douglas blew into my office," Banff businessman and publisher Norman Luxton recalled, "and asked me if I wanted to buy a thousand head of buffalo.[a] For a second I thought he was having a joke in his usual dry way, then I saw he meant every word." Luxton liked Douglas's proposal. He wanted to bring back the buffalo for three reasons: conservation, tourist attraction, and a possible source of food for Indians.

So Luxton travelled to Winnipeg for two days of meetings with the Interior minister, Frank Oliver, who agreed to authorize negotiations with Pablo. On behalf of the government, Douglas negotiated a price of $245 a head "f.o.b. Edmonton," a shrewd provision that put the burden of capture and shipment in the Americans' hands.

Between 1907 and 1912 Pablo employed as many as eighty cowboys for roundups in Montana, eventually capturing 708 buffalo. Luxton, Douglas, Ayotte and a *Manitoba Free Press* writer went to Montana to watch the first. The buffalo were driven across forty miles of prairie and then corralled and loaded — a particularly arduous task.

Most of them had to be roped and dragged into the rail cars, which were specially reinforced so they could contain the unruly animals. "One bull went straight through the car," Luxton wrote. "He just took the side out as if it had not been there. Another bull broke his legs — well, the Indians had a feast out of that."

The animals' intended home, a 197-square-mile area near Wainwright, had not yet been fenced when the first 250 American buffalo arrived in 1907. They were sent instead to 16-square-mile Elk Island "deer park and game preserve," which was enclosed with a twelve-foot-high wire fence, and so were another 100 head shipped later.

In 1909 most of the Elk Island buffalo were shipped to Wainwright and herded down a long, fenced lane to their new home, which they eventually shared with elk, deer, yaks and cattalo (cow-buffalo crosses). In the 1920s, when the herd began to exceed the park's capacity, some were shipped north to Wood Buffalo National Park.

Buffalo National Park at Wainwright was a popular tourist stop until 1940, when the government converted it to an army training ground. Most of the buffalo herd, then numbering nearly 5,000, was slaughtered for meat and hides. But 48 of the Pablo herd eluded the roundup at Elk Island in 1909. They became the basis for a continuing herd in the sanctuary, which was made a national park in 1911. — *R.B.*

[a] Norman Luxton, publisher of the Banff *Crag and Canyon*, described the buffalo purchase in a manuscript written in 1912. The report was published in 1975 as an appendix to the history of Banff National Park by his daughter, Eleanor Luxton.

adjacent to the museum, where animals and birds were displayed until 1937.

Depletion of the natural wildlife continued, however. Bill Brewster was named part-time game warden in 1901, and the North-West Mounted Police detachment was also supposed to enforce the hunting ban, but there were few arrests for poaching. For one thing, it was almost impossible to determine whether or not game had been taken legally outside park boundaries. Besides, Edwardians had some curious ideas about animals. Elk, moose, buffalo and sheep were "good" creatures which should be protected, but there was no restriction on hunting "bad" predators. These included cougars, bears, wolves, lynx, wolverines, coyotes and hawks.

It was only in 1909 that permanent wardens were appointed to enforce wildlife regulations and watch for fires. Banff's first chief warden, Howard Sibbald, summed up their task: "Protect the park." He recruited colourful characters such as Wild Bill Peyto to range over the vast reaches of the park. As Sid Marty writes:

> The first wardens were hired for their ability to ride and pack horses, handle an axe, travel on snowshoes, shoot straight and generally take care of themselves...They were an independent and self-sufficient bunch, these oldtimers, and not averse to talking to their horses.

In 1908 Rocky Mountains Park and the park reserves (including Waterton, Jasper, Elk Island and the Wainwright buffalo reserve) were transferred to the Department of Forestry. Douglas was promoted to overall command as commissioner, although he kept his office in Banff until 1910 when he moved to Edmonton to be closer to the development of Jasper Park.

Under the care of Kootenai Brown, the Waterton reserve gradually became a popular holiday spot for residents of southern Alberta. Waterton too had suffered from commercial depredation, including a brief but quite spectacular oil boom between 1902 and 1907. The black sticky substance oozing from the banks of Cameron Creek, which flows from Cameron Lake into Upper Waterton, had long been noted — and used. In the 1880s, nearby rancher William Aldridge used gunny sacks to soak it up and squeeze it into barrels, selling it for a dollar a gallon. In 1901, however, a pole-tool drill rig was imported (with great difficulty) from Petrolia, Ontario, and within a year brought in a well, that flowed 300 barrels a day of high-quality crude. Oil City sprouted immediately and several rival companies began busily drilling. But they never duplicated that first well, probably because that first well had been salted. The boom was a fraud.

Logging was Waterton's chief industry, and the 100-foot steamship *Gertrude* went into service on Waterton Lakes in July 1907. She carried passengers, horses and lumber, and towed log booms on the lake. In 1918, no longer serviceable, the *Gertrude* was scuttled in a bay that was then named Steamboat Bay (later Emerald Bay), where she was preserved in forty feet of ice cold water and would become a popular attraction for skindivers half a century later.

Conservationists maintained a steady pressure, however. Elk Island was the first large federally controlled area to be enclosed as a big-game sanctuary. After three years of petitions from territorial game warden W.H. Cooper and Edmonton area residents, the Department of the Interior agreed in 1906 to fence the area. It became a sanctuary for moose, deer and buffalo as well as elk. Elk Island also served between 1907 and 1909 as temporary home for 325 buffalo purchased from the United States, until the Wainwright reserve was fenced (see sidebar).

Although the Grand Trunk Pacific did not reach Jasper until 1911, the government and railway recognized earlier that the area offered many of the same inducements — hot springs, spectacular scenery, mountaineering opportunities — as Banff a quarter-century before. Jasper Forest Park was established in 1907. Howard Douglas visited Jasper for a preliminary inspection in 1909; surveyors arrived the following year. Lewis Swift and his family were the only permanent residents then in that part of the Athabasca Valley, but climbers, explorers, naturalists and adventurers had begun making their way north from Field and Lake Louise.

One of the more notable explorations was led by Mary Schaffer, a Quaker widow from

Endowed with the smallest possible amount of instinct, the little he has seems adapted rather for getting him into difficulties than out of them. If not alarmed at the sight or smell of a foe, he will stand stupidly gazing at his companions in their death-throes until the whole herd is shot down.
– *A "Col. Dodge," described as a "noted authority" on buffalo, quoted in the* **Banff Crag and Canyon, June 1, 1907.**

To determine whether or not the park is becoming more travelled and fulfilling gradually the mission for which it was created, namely as a health and pleasure resort for the benefit and enjoyment of the people, the following comparison of the totals is made from the records for the last five years: 1897, 5,087; 1898, 5,537; 1899, 7,387; 1900, for ten months, 6,533; 1901, 8,156.
– *from the report by Howard Douglas, superintendent of Rocky Mountains Park of Canada (later renamed Banff National Park), to Clifford Sifton minister of the Interior, July 31, 1901.*

Philadelphia, and her friend Mary "Mollie" Adams. Known to the Stoneys as Yahe-Weha (Mountain Woman), Mrs. Schaffer followed an Indian map to locate Maligne Lake in 1908. The group built a raft to get around the lake, and were rewarded with "the finest view any of us had ever beheld in the Rockies." Mary Schaffer later married her guide from that trip, Billy Warren, and settled permanently in Banff. She recounts her travels in *Old Indian Trails of the Canadian Rockies*, republished in 1980 as *A Hunter of Peace* (see sidebar).

As the decade ended, Howard Douglas was developing conservationist ideas that would find expression in the Parks Act of 1911. The outlines of the national park system in Alberta had been drawn, although it would take decades more before modern ideas of "ecosystem preservation" would fully evolve. The suggestion of "Coney Island" development at Banff (a possibly tongue-in-cheek proposal by Bob Edwards of the Calgary *Eye Opener*) met indignant opposition from, among others, the Alpine Club.

About to arrive was one final element: skiing. A Norwegian guest at the Brett Sanitarium had sent a pair of skis to George Paris in 1894, knowing he enjoyed snowshoeing. Paris took off from the Upper Hot Springs, fell and broke a ski, and went back to snowshoeing. In 1910, however, guide Conrad Kain brought some along from his home in Austria, built a small jump on Tunnel Mountain and began cross-country skiing. The sport became really popular only after the first Banff Winter Carnival, writes Eleanor Luxton. The carnival was organized by her father in 1917. But Kain had introduced the factor that would turn the mountain parks into truly year-round resorts.

Curling at Banff in 1906. Four years later another winter sport appeared. It was called 'skiing.'

Hauling grain to the Three Hills elevator, early 1900s. The market seemed as undependable as the weather.

Crushed by costs, the farmer declares war on the tariff

WHEN THE GRAIN PRODUCER AND WESTERN MANUFACTURER LOOKED SOUTH AT THEIR AMERICAN COUNTERPARTS, THEIR CURIOSITY TURNED TO FURY

The guileless farmer does not know the tariff is a blessing
And hastes his hapless plight to show, this disbelief impressing.
The guileless farmer man should go and take a course at college
Where he might stock his think tank up with economic knowledge.

He has no chance, it seems, to learn; he really is too busy.
His ignorance gives much concern and makes great statesmen dizzy.
He should be told by someone who has studied up the question
That with no tariff there would be terrific trade congestion.
— Anonymous poet, *Toronto Star,* December 1905.

by VIRGINIA BYFIELD

However sympathetic to his problems, Alberta's "guileless farmer" of the first decade did not consider his plight an apt subject for hilarity. Already the decisions that determined his fate were made by corporate presidents in Toronto or Montreal, grain brokers in Winnipeg, or politicians in Ottawa. Looking south, he saw American farmers getting more for their wheat (usually) and paying much less for machinery and supplies (always). This first puzzled, then irked, then infuriated him.

The grain grower in the north-west had endured drought, fire, blizzard and backbreaking toil. Now he found himself beset by a seemingly inescapable economic factor. The market for wheat and other grains appeared as undependable as the weather upon which successful production depended, while the cost of transportation and supplies was altogether dependably high. One didn't have to be an economist to understand that perhaps tariffs were a part of the problem.

Other primary industries in the West, chiefly meat, timber and coal, found themselves in much the same bind. They too needed international markets, and machinery and supplies at reasonable prices, meaning American prices. But that route was barred. Under John A. Macdonald's National Policy, invoked by his Conservative government in 1879, tariffs forced the West to fill its need for manufactured goods from central Canada, then pay to ship the goods across the continent. Once the tariff was added to the price of American manufactured goods, they cost more than the Canadian ones. Meanwhile, high freight rates on any factory-made products attempting to move from west to east prevented them from competing in the Ontario market.

There were other snags. Canada's railways couldn't keep up with the producers. Thus in July 1902 the *Calgary Herald*, predicting a bumper wheat crop, foresaw trouble: "Last year the rolling stock of the CPR proved utterly inadequate...There are still many hundreds of thousands of bushels of last year's grain in the country...and every possibility of elevators being blocked owing to the inadequacy of the equipment of the railway company." The struggling farmer must pay his implement and supply bills, observed the *Edmonton Journal*, and when he can't get his grain to market ends up borrowing and paying interest to the banks, and storage fees to the elevators. "The farmers," it concluded, "are therefore practically at the mercy of the railway company."

In 1902, the car shortage hit the coal industry. The Lethbridge mine was practically closed, reported the *Sentinel* in Frank. The Frank mine could produce 30,000 tons a month but could ship only 16,000. Lumberyards at Blairmore, Cranbrook and Moyie were blocked with sawn lumber. The *Calgary Herald* said the Canadian Pacific needed 35,000 boxcars that year. It had 29,000, but was having more built as fast as possible. Another *Herald* item would not assuage resentment: CPR net profits for the twelve months ending June 30, 1902 were $14 million; it was paying out $7.6 million in dividends, or 11.78% on the capital.

Westerners soon decided their only hope was to pressure government, and the government that counted was the one in Ottawa. The cry went up for reciprocity with the United States, by which they meant no tariffs either way at the border, or at a minimum much lower ones. Leading the campaign against protection were the grain farmers whose numbers and whose need were the greatest. Theirs was a marginal industry, in prosperous times modestly profitable, in recessionary times hopeless, and both Europe and North America had been in general depression from about 1873 to 1896.

That slump had shelved the Ottawa plan for a lucrative commercial empire in the West, but the world recovery revived it. Perhaps the vast sums expended on the CPR could be recovered.

Cartoon in the Grain Grower's Guide *depicting the farmer's hapless position in relation to the real powers. Pressure was put on Ottawa.*

The great potential of the West was being stifled, or so westerners tended to believe, by ignorant, incompetent, self-serving central Canadian interests.

Western farm production totalled $53.8 million in 1901, a Toronto *News* article reported, while $71 million was predicted for 1902. This would bring general prosperity everywhere, said the paper, and the banks "which handle all this additional wealth, will greatly increase their volume of business and their lending resources...All classes of industrial securities and bank stocks will increase in value. Capital for investment in new industries will be available from the enormously increased holdings of the banks..."

Central Canada was not inclined to share this wealth with Americans. Nationalism of the

"No truck nor trade with Yankees" variety was strong in Ontario. Between 1867 and 1891 the Tories won four elections on a high tariff platform. The Liberals were philosophically a *laissez-faire* party. They contended that Canadian prosperity depended on a new reciprocity treaty with the

Both Laurier and Borden made preliminary western tours in the spring of 1910. Everywhere their trains stopped, grain growers besieged them with demands for 'the necessities of life.'

Clifford Sifton depicted as the Little Dutch Boy. Prairie farmers found his position on reciprocity wrong-headed.

United States, to replace the one that was signed in 1854 and abrogated by the Americans in 1866. But Wilfrid Laurier managed to lead the Liberals to power in 1896 only by assuring eastern business interests that protection would be continued.

The great political enigma was, as usual, the West's most influential federal politician, Clifford Sifton. As a Liberal MLA in Manitoba in 1890 he had supported a resolution urging the federal Liberal party "to take such steps as may be necessary in order to facilitate the bringing about of unrestricted reciprocity in trade between the Dominion of Canada and the United States of America." But in 1898 he was declaring himself in letters to Sir Wilfrid as entirely

Glenbow Archives, NA-2784-20

UFA members marching to the Legislature, 1909. Later they moved in.

THE EMERGING ECONOMY

From rat pelts to wishing books

The exploding population pushed Alberta's retail sector to new heights of competition and sophistication

by CAROL DEAN

Rapid population growth and the rise of towns and cities presented enterprising westerners in the century's first decade with scores of new ways to make a living, from cigar production to swimsuit manufacture. Retailing bloomed in particular. There were specialty shops, travelling "drummers," catalogue sales, even some newfangled department stores. (Just overgrown general stores, sneered the scoffers.) And while all these novelties appeared, the West's first industry was far from defunct. In fact, the fur trade had become a hotbed of competition.

The chief threat to the long domination of the Hudson's Bay Company came from Revillon Frères, a European fur retailer that established a major depot in Edmonton.[a] Revillon's initial purpose was supply — to secure Canadian fur directly, escaping what it considered inflated HBC prices. The HBC had other rivals. Trader John A. McDougall and his partner Richard Secord remained active. Freelancers like Colin Fraser, who in 1910 alone bought 30,000 muskrat skins on the lower Athabasca and Slave, roamed the north country.[b]

Unsurprisingly the fur trade attracted the Americans. They read that an estimated half-million dollars' worth of pelts went through Edmonton in 1905. The city's warehouses were "enough to make the average woman's mouth water," wrote the *Washington Star*. The *Star*'s correspondent had sent "a photograph of a $35,000 lot which could be put into an ordinary bedroom." "Millions in the Fur Trade," headlined the *Calgary Herald* in 1906.

All this enthusiastic publicity created major problems in the North. Eager American hunters soon experimented in a faster way to bag animals — poison rather than traps. A Fort McMurray trader brought word in 1907 that a party of Americans had spread poison in the Mackenzie region. They caught nothing and left empty-handed, the animals presumably having crawled into the undergrowth to die. But then sled dogs found and ate the poison. Result: no fur, no dogs, and widespread destitution. Supplies and medical help were sent north. The Royal North-West Mounted Police made enough arrests in 1908 to end the practice, and the trade recovered.

Meanwhile the HBC became acutely aware that the arrival of settlers created a major opportunity. In Calgary, the Bay's original 1891 sandstone building was expanded, renovated and restructured. A block-long, three-storey brick HBC store opened in Edmonton in 1905, complete with fancy mirrors and an elevator. Revillon Frères and McDougall & Secord were only months behind with "departmentalized" retail outlets.

Provincial Archives of Alberta, B-10018

Colin Fraser sorting furs in Edmonton, 1900. He alone bought 30,000 muskrat skins on the lower Athabasca and Slave.

[a]Revillon Frères, a Parisian fur business begun by Victor Revillon in the early 1800s, had become by the turn of the century one of the world's largest fur wholesalers, retailers and manufacturers. In 1904 it started Revillon Brothers Ltd. to buy Canadian fur at the source. Theodore Revillon, 26, arrived in Edmonton thoroughly schooled in his father's plants to know the quality and market value of pelts.

[b]Traders could lose their shirts. Colin Fraser, for example, paid 46 cents apiece for his 30,000 muskrat pelts, expecting to get 85 cents at Edmonton — the 1909 price. The 1910 "rat" catch was good, however, and the price had dropped to 35 cents. But the *Edmonton Journal* reported that Fraser's cargo of more luxurious furs — lynx, marten, mink, beaver, sable and black and silver fox — saved him from ruin.

The HBC's attempt at an Alberta retail facelift was not considered adequate by its London board, however. Director Leonard Cunliffe took the unprecedented step of visiting Canada. Accompanying him was Richard Burbidge, who had built a small London grocery store called Harrods into the world's biggest department store.

They considered the HBC's retail outlets "pitiful," writes

potatoes for a local grocer. Within two months Jenkins and a friend had borrowed money to buy the store, renaming it Jenkins & Cornfoot Grocers.

In Edmonton Abe Cristall, owner of Cristall Palace General Store, switched to men's clothing. Continuing his pun on London's famous glass exhibition hall, he called it Cristall Palace Men's Clothing Store. Within days his main

A Bowden dry goods merchant in the early 1900s. Smaller retailers did quite well.

Peter Newman in *Merchant Princes*, and its administration incapable of capitalizing on the prairie boom. "The few stores that had been opened were so badly stocked and so poorly operated that they were turning over their merchandise only once every twelve to 48 months and their accounting techniques were a century out of date."

Smaller Alberta retailers certainly didn't seem threatened by the HBC. Stores, both rural and urban, became social centres, a kind of club where customers exchanged gossip, and argued business and politics, around a pot bellied stove — sometimes even buying something.

Scores of new ones were opened by ardent entrepreneurs. Prince Edward Island farmer Henry Marshall Jenkins was typical. He came to Calgary in 1909, and began by picking over

competitor, William Diamond, had his own campaign going: "Why trade with a Cristall when you can trade with a Diamond?"

Behind the retailers were wholesalers, distributors and local manufacturers. A list of forty prominent Calgary entrepreneurs before 1914 shows more than half in either one or all of these three categories. Small industries proliferated. Among the many: creameries, cheese manufacturers, food processors, soap factories, tanneries, leather products, even prefabricated houses.

All it took was ideas, talent and energy (and usually some money). A.E. Cross's Calgary Brewing and Malting Company, for instance, spun off a soft-drink company, Calgary Beverage. Edmonton's thirst for soft drinks was supplied by J.J.

McLaughlin Co. Ltd. In the Burnt Lake area near Red Deer, Thomas Burgess Millar built three cheese factories. A small cottage industry developed at Banff to make swimsuits for tourists bathing in the hot springs. They were sold at Norman Luxton's Sign of the Goat Curio Shop for fifty cents each.

Governments tried to help, with direct grants, tax concessions, cheap land, and expense-paid promotional tours. One example: A Calgary company got a $10,000 city grant to produce cigars, and in 1900 the first Alberta Special cigar made its appearance. Despite encouraging civic reports on its progress, however, the Alberta Special quietly died within two years.

Calgary council may have made a mistake with the producer, however, not the product. In 1903 the Edmonton Cigar Factory began manufacturing La Palma and La Consequentia cigars. In 1908 it was producing 80,000 a month, and exporting cigars to British Columbia.

Just about every village had a blacksmith and a general store. The latter tried to stock everything people needed from honey to hosiery to harnesses. Rural merchandising inevitably involved considerable credit, and also barter. It is difficult to leave a friend and neighbour in need when the shelves are stocked.

In the Wetaskiwin area one year, many cash-poor settlers cut and hauled willow posts to trade at the general store for food. The stacks of posts got bigger and bigger while the store's shelves got barer and barer. Owner John West began to run low on money. Finally he persuaded the Alberta and Revelstoke Lumber Company to buy sixteen carloads of fenceposts.

Another familiar rural figure was the travelling salesman. In *West of Yesterday*, George Shepherd describes the technique of one man who sold Home Comfort Stoves. He would drive into the yard, and literally throw the stove off the back of his wagon. Then he'd jump up and down on the oven door and hit the stove lids with a hammer — all to show how well built it was, and worth the $85 price. Furthermore, it was right on the doorstep. No waiting for delivery.

Then too there was the famous Eaton's catalogue, some-

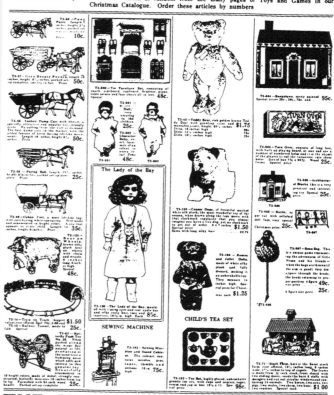

Hudson's Bay Company catalogue, Christmas, 1911. Its retail outlets were pitiful until London sent a fixer.

negotiable, depending on city prices, transportation charges and the bargaining skills of the storekeeper, the catalogue was invaluable. For townspeople it offered a shopping alternative, and gave them a price comparison for local offerings.

Catalogue customers had to pay cash, of course, and delivery might take as long as two months. But Eaton's guaranteed customer satisfaction or money refunded — another startling innovation which, competitors had predicted, would bankrupt

An estimated half-million dollars' worth of pelts went through Edmonton in 1905. The city's warehouses were 'enough to make the average woman's mouth water.'

times called the homesteader's bible or by children the wishing book, which reached the prairies by 1900. More than anything else, it evidenced the profound revolution taking place in retailing. Every catalogue item had a fixed price, and prices that couldn't be changed were still a rarity in the cash-poor, barter-dependent West.

For rural dwellers, reliant on the stock in their local general store or what it could order for them, sight unseen, cost

the store. And if the order was over a certain amount, Eaton's paid the freight.

As homesteaders vividly remembered, the catalogue began a second career in the privy. Truly a useful publication — and in one celebrated case it saved a life. A bride who had to rush her injured husband to a doctor did not know how to harness the horse. So she simply followed the detailed drawings in the Eaton's catalogue. Her husband lived.

against free exchange of flour, wheat, coal and lumber, writes John W. Dafoe, editor of Sifton's *Manitoba Free Press* and his first biographer.[1]

Why the change? Sifton made no bones about it. "I am not like some people we both know — I can learn," he told an interviewer in 1904. He had come to disagree with his party's policy. He did not trust the Americans to stick to a long-term agreement. They had cancelled once already, and Canada had now adapted its production and business to an "independent, self-sufficient policy." Besides, the tariff benefited western industries: "Our interest is to have the first-class wheat of our West milled in Winnipeg or Rat Portage [later Kenora, Ont.], instead of Minneapolis." Transport would get cheaper "as soon as we get our waterways improved to the utmost, and our almost dead-level first-class National Transcontinental Railway built."

Sifton also believed free trade with the United States could not co-exist with the preferential trade treatment Britain had granted Canada. "We are fixed now to deal with Europe, and especial-

How the West was lost – by Bell Canada
ALBERTANS DIDN'T TAKE KINDLY TO THE TELEPHONIC AMBITIONS OF THE ONTARIO COMPANY AND ITS UNPLEASANT MR. SISE

Courtesy of Bell Canada Telephone Historical Collection

For the Bell Telephone Company of Canada in 1890, the great trick was to get the right man in the right place at the right time. As far as Albertans were concerned, Charles Fleetford Sise was the wrong man in the wrong place at the wrong time. This more than anything else, says historian Tony Cashman in *Singing Wires*, set the course of telephone development in Alberta for the entire 20th century.[a]

Bell Canada, named for telephone inventor Alexander Graham Bell, got a charter in 1880 to spread the new technology (known as telephony) from the Atlantic to the Rockies. Why Charles Fleetford Sise, its vice-president and later president, was considered the right man to do the job never did become clear to western Canadians.

Sise was blunt, high-handed, and autocratic. He had captained clipper ships, run Union blockades in the Civil War, and served as secretary to Confederate president Jefferson Davis. He had also, unhappily for him,

Charles Fleetford Sise. Rubbed Alberta the wrong way.

Conflict began early. In 1883, an Edmonton committee applied to Bell for telephone service. Bell offered to put in a few phones but no exchange — in effect, one enormous party line — at a phenomenal price. The city was too small for an exchange and likely to stay that way, said a Bell letter. Furious Edmontonians acted on their own. Alex Taylor, operator for the Dominion Telegraph Company that connected Edmonton with Winnipeg, persuaded his superiors to run a telephone line to St. Albert. The first call was made in January 1885 from Taylor's Edmonton office to W.F. McKenny's store at St. Albert, using two English-made telephones of Spanish mahogany. Calls cost fifteen cents; McKenny got 25 per cent. When he found the chore a nuisance, the St. Albert Mission took over.

Two years later the system had seven subscribers and two

Sise was blunt, high-handed and autocratic. He had captained clipper ships and run Union blockades in the Civil War. He knew nothing about telephony and even less about the West.

---

introduced fire insurance to Chicago shortly before much of the city burned down. Like most people, he knew nothing about telephony. But as soon became plain, he knew even less about western Canadians, who rapidly found two faults with Bell Canada: everything it said, and everything it did.

lines. Legend has it that a vagrant once refused to leave Taylor's store, so Taylor crossed the road to Fort Edmonton and used the phone there to call his own. From the strange machine came a loud voice: "This is God speaking. Get the hell out of that building." The vagrant fled.

ly with Great Britain. There is an unlimited market there for pretty well everything we raise." Moreover, selling western wheat in the States would give no more than the odd seasonal advantage, since the world price was set in Liverpool in any event. In short, Sifton had come round to the Tory tariff position, a shift that would soon have dire political consequences for Laurier.

Prairie grain farmers passionately disagreed with Sifton. They believed, with much justification, that they were at the mercy of *de facto* monopolies: the CPR, the grain companies, eastern manufacturers, and the eastern banks. American alternatives would automatically provide some salubrious competition. The Canadian Manufacturers' Association was conspiring with the Tory party to push for double the tariff on imported cotton items, Frank Oliver's Liberal *Edmonton Bulletin* charged in 1904 — so the Dominion government would make more on the duty, and Canadian manufacturers could hike their prices to match and keep the extra profit. In 1905 the paper quoted an Edmontonian as complaining about the 25% duty on stoves and the 35% duty on implements like

[1] Unlike his boss, *Manitoba Free Press* editor John W. Dafoe favoured reciprocity. When the crunch came in early 1911, writes D.J. Hall in his two-volume Sifton biography, Sifton summoned editor Dafoe to Ottawa, where they argued steadily for nearly a week. In the end, Hall says, they had to "agree to disagree." Dafoe went back to Winnipeg to support reciprocity in the columns of the *Free Press*, while Sifton who owned the *Free Press* campaigned hard to defeat it.

On Nov. 1, 1887, Taylor spoke for fifteen minutes to Battleford, 306 miles (490 km) away, using telephones connected to the telegraph wires. The voices were muffled but

Sclater was too busy cronying with his *Herald* pals in the exchange office, Cashman writes, so Sise fired him. He then persuaded Walker to do the job. But Walker wouldn't dun

---

The first call was made in January 1885 from Taylor's Edmonton office to a store in St. Albert using two English-made telephones of Spanish mahogany. Calls cost fifteen cents.

---

audible. In 1892 he installed a fourteen-line switchboard with Jenny Lauder, aged fourteen, as operator.[b] By 1901 his Edmonton and District Telephone Company was operating 24 hours a day and spreading into rural areas.

Similar local initiatives were occurring across the West, while Charles Fleetford Sise, a.k.a. Bell Canada, looked on disapprovingly from the East. What about Bell's charter? What about its monopoly? But no matter what he did, Sise found, people protested. If he offered service, as in Edmonton, he was accused of ruthless extortion. If he didn't, he was accused of arrogant indifference.

In Calgary, lumberman and ex-Mountie James Walker (Vol. 1 ch. 1) connected his office to his lumber mill, two miles away, by home-made telephone in August 1885. Then he added a switchboard and a twelve-phone system, the wires dangling from ten-foot poles, or lying on the ground, or looped over rooftops. But Calgary was booming, and persuaded Sise to bring in Bell.

All went well at first. Business phones were $40 a year, private $35. Forty-foot poles were erected on Stephen Avenue, and Jack Sclater, a sometime *Herald* illustrator, hired as manager. But

delinquent subscribers. So Sise himself came to Calgary and fired Walker. He found Bell had three employees, about fifty grumbling customers, thirty unpaid accounts, and daytime service only. On a 35% commission he hired Charles Watson, who ran the light plant, assuring Calgarians things would get better. They did, but not much.

At Banff meanwhile, a fast-talking salesman sold some telephones to the hotels and anthracite mine, then disappeared without connecting them. Dominion Telegraph took over in 1888 and service improved. In 1894 the Mormons connected Lethbridge and the NWMP border district to the Cardston and Macleod detachments. Morinville

Provincial Archives of Alberta, A-11685

Telephone crew in Stettler, 1909. Towns and the province were putting up lines so fast, Bell became alarmed.

[a] Tony Cashman is regarded as Alberta's telephone historian. His other books on the subject include *The Telephone Man* and *An Historical Sequence: Morinville and the Telephone 1895-1910.* Another reference work is Margaret Stinson's *The Wired City, A History of the Telephone in Edmonton.*

[b] Jenny would later become the wife of W.A. Griesbach, the Boer War veteran and historian, mayor, MP and senator. She and her five siblings had a mischievous turn. They once spread Limburger cheese on the porch of the sheriff's house before an elegant party. The guests tramped the reeking cheese through the house, many of them deploring the unknown pranksters the next day in telephone calls that Jenny monitored.

spades and forks. And even at inflated prices, the *Lethbridge Herald* charged, western wholesalers often couldn't get "a supply of staple lines of goods." Tariff or no tariff, it proclaimed, "unless Ontario wakens up, the trade of this country will inevitably turn to the United States."

Farmers tried to beat the system by forming co-ops, of which the most notable was the Grain Growers' Grain Company Ltd. in 1906. After a fierce fight and radical restructuring, it was admitted to the Winnipeg Grain Exchange two years later, and would survive as United Grain Growers' Ltd. in Manitoba and Alberta. In addition the farmers kept forming activist groups, heavily influenced by American farm organizations: the Grange (1870s); the Farmers' Union of Manitoba (1880s); the

---

The Conservative member for High River said that a coal train had sat eight days on a siding. Local settlers had finally helped themselves, at gunpoint.

---

and Strathcona were added to the Edmonton system. Macleod brought in a private service. In 1896 the Stair Ranch produced another innovation: a telephone line that connected the ranch to the nearest town via a barbed wire fence. It worked, except when the line got wet.[c]

Bell was active too, however, rebuilding its Lethbridge system (originally installed in 1891) with special wire to withstand high winds, and linking it to Stirling, Raymond and Magrath. A line from Edmonton to Calgary was promised. As Calgary service improved, however, the *Herald* ungratefully demanded that the company pay taxes, and the *Albertan* raked Sise personally for providing "too little too late."

subscriber Edmonton telephone system for $25,000. Sise offered half. The town, about to become a city, offered $17,000. Taylor accepted. The new city's Bylaw No. 3 created Edmonton Telephones, which would survive for the century.

In the meantime, the newly created provincial legislature came down hard on Bell, empowering municipalities to establish telephone systems and promising a provincial long-distance network to connect them.[d] Public Works Minister William Cushing[e] announced construction of provincial

Phone exchange operators at Edmonton Telephone Building, 1910.

Barbed wire telephone lines would spread all over agricultural Alberta. One paper ran an article on how telephones reduced insanity among farm women by alleviating their loneliness.

Medicine Hat told Bell it planned a co-op system. Sise began installing Bell equipment anyway. He did the same in Wetaskiwin, which planned a private operation. In Red Deer the confrontation between town and Bell bordered on war. Ignoring a municipal deal with locally owned Western General Electric, Bell started stringing wire. WGE began to construct an exchange building. Bell kept on stringing wire, and opened service at $30 a year for business phones, $20 for homes. WGE undercut the Bell prices. Soon the town had two hostile systems with one thing in common: public outrage over the service.

Sise chose this moment to announce he was again asking the territorial legislature to confirm Bell's federal monopoly. The unwary member who had agreed to sponsor this resolution the first time had suffered such abuse that he voted against it himself. The second attempt fared no better. Few members of the Legislature liked either Bell or Sise, it appeared. Even when crucial systems worked properly, like the line over the portage on the Slave River at Fort Smith, Bell and Sise got no credit whatever for providing them.

By 1904 Alex Taylor was ill, and willing to sell his 400-

long-distance lines between centres Bell had been avoiding: Calgary to Banff, Edmonton to Lloydminster, Lethbridge to Crowsnest Pass. Sise protested. Bell had expansion plans too, he said — lines from both Wetaskiwin and Lacombe, for instance. Cushing promptly added them to the government schedule.

Both Bell and the province fell to work furiously that winter, 1906-07, which happened to be the worst in Alberta's history. Crews seemed to be stringing wire everywhere. The government began the Calgary-Banff line. Bell began a line south from Calgary, another southeast from Edmonton. The newspapers lamented and deplored Bell, now unkindly referred to as "The Octopus." Sise was merely faking an interest, they said. Sise was responding only to pressure, they said. If the government withdrew, Bell would do nothing,

---

Territorial Grain Growers' Association of Assiniboia (1901); the Manitoba Grain Growers' Association (1903). Alberta formed a provincial branch of the TGGA by 1905, which merged with a rival association, the Alberta Society of Equity, to form the United Farmers of Alberta in 1909. Combining with Ontario farm groups in the Canadian Council of Agriculture in 1909, western growers figured, would surely give them some political clout. Agriculture, after all, was still the nation's biggest industry.

Meanwhile the railways caught up with production, at least for a while. In late October 1905 the *Edmonton Journal* reported that they had moved to market a total of 22,467,000 bushels of wheat, nearly triple the previous year — 16,377,000 bushels on the CPR and over 6,000,000 on the Canadian Northern. There had been so much solid ground for complaint in previous years, the paper commented, "that it is a real pleasure to be able to say...that both railroads have done nobly in the swift handling of the wheat crop of 1905."

they said. Alberta Provincial Telephones, as it became known, was the only dependable hope. Spurred by such support, Alberta's politicians spent more on phones in the province's first three years than they spent on roads.

Now Sise changed tactics. Rather than confrontation, he would try conciliation. Who knows? It might work. It didn't.

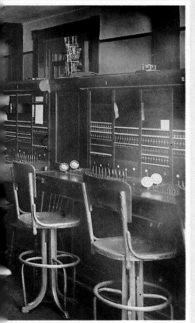
Provincial Archives of Alberta, B-1482

He delegated William Scott, former newspaper editor and twenty-year Bell man, to talk to Cushing. Tell him, said Sise, that no government has ever succeeded in the phone business. Tell him Bell has only the interests of Alberta at heart. Tell him Bell merely wants to spare Alberta the agonies of failure. Cushing was not persuaded. Well then, said Scott, why not divide the province into two non-competing sections (with Bell taking the south)? No sale.

So much for conciliation. Sise went back to confrontation. On Feb. 5, 1907, he served notice on Edmonton city council that Bell would build an Edmonton exchange. The Rutherford government regarded this as an act of war. On Feb. 14, St. Valentine's Day, it announced "A Valentine to the People of Alberta" — more lines, new exchanges, and finally, cheap phones for all Alberta farmers. Historian Cashman has another name for it: "The St. Valentine's Day Massacre of the Bell Telephone Company."

The next move was foreseeable. The Alberta government offered to buy out Bell. Bell refused and an even greater frenzy of telephone construction ensued. That summer government crews put up 544 miles of line, and installed or rebuilt fourteen exchanges. Bell meanwhile strung 100 miles and

added a new Calgary exchange with a new transmission system. The government offered to buy local systems anywhere in the province. The provincial treasury sank $262,262 into telephones in that season alone, more than a quarter of the total budget for the whole North-West Territories two years earlier.

Bell made offers too, but no one was interested. The company's credibility was gone. By now Western General Electric had more than 200 subscribers in Red Deer; Bell had ten. In October Bell finished its Macleod-Lethbridge line. Now calls could actually be made between Edmonton and Lethbridge, for $1.50 in daytime, half that at night. But three days later, no one had tried. Telegrams were quicker and cheaper.

The next year, 1908, a Manitoba announcement heavily influenced Alberta. Premier Rodmond Roblin disclosed that his government was buying out Bell for $3.4 million. How much should Alberta offer? Cushing got four estimates, ranging from $490,000 to $525,000. Bell wanted $750,000. The compromise price was $675,000.

This necessitated a pivotal decision for Alberta — to go into debt for the first time. To pay for the Bell system and finance its own vast expansion plans, the province floated a $2-million bond issue. Once acquired, the habit would grow.

And eight years later Charles Fleetford Sise would retire at age 80 as Bell Canada's president. By then he had firmly rooted his company in Ontario and Quebec. But in the prairie provinces Bell Canada had created such animosity that for the rest of the century telephones would remain a public utility.

— *C.D.*

[c] Barbed-wire telephone lines would spread all over agricultural Alberta in the next fifteen years, linking farm to farm. One newspaper ran an article on how telephones were reducing the incidence of insanity among farm women by alleviating their loneliness.

[d] Alberta became the first government or state on the continent to build and run its own telephone system.

[e] William Cushing, described by Bob Edwards in the *Eye Opener* as "an icy manufacturer of window sashes" and a man who "spent too much time at the opening of new culverts," was a Calgary lumber-goods manufacturer. Manitoba paid a consultant $6,000 for advice on how to start its system — Cushing did it for $13.15. He brought William Moore, manager of Red Deer's Western General Electric, to Edmonton, picked his brain at a hotel, and paid his expenses.

Brick ovens and death-defying log-rollers

THE PROVINCE'S CONSTRUCTION BOOM LAUNCHED TWO INDUSTRIES — ONE WOULD STAY, ONE WOULDN'T

Eau Claire lumber crew, Bow River, Kananaskis area.

Alberta's turn-of-the-century boom, like all other booms, created a bonanza in the building trades, an insatiable demand for construction materials, and what looked like two promising new industries: brickmaking and cement production. Of the two, only cement would outlast the century as an important economic factor. But the biggest demand of all was for lumber. Buildings, railways, telegraph and telephone poles, board sidewalks — all relied on Alberta-grown poplar, spruce and tamarack, and imported BC fir, pine and cedar.

Much of it came from already existing mills: Calgary's Eau Claire Lumber Company and Bow River Mills; Richard Ottewell's mill at Clover Bar; John Walter's lumber company in Strathcona; and the D.R. Fraser and Richard Hardisty sawmills in Edmonton. But as the railways forged ahead they created scores of towns, many of which could boast a sawmill.

Lumbering's most dramatic aspect, of course, was the spring drives that brought the logs down flooding rivers to the sawmills. For their hazardous occupation, writes one-time river driver Roy Devore in an *Alberta Historical Review* article, the men wore heavy mackinaw shirt and trousers, woollen underwear, several pairs of wool socks, and heavy boots with sharpened caulks screwed into the soles. The caulks bit into the

wood as the rivermen leaped from log to log, using peavies or pikepoles to keep the "float" moving.

Too often logs at the front of the float would jam, and the whole river channel would suddenly clog with tangled, twisting timber, white water roaring through the gaps. Dynamite was one solution. Raw manpower was another, less damaging to the product but terribly dangerous. The most skilled men would try to dislodge the foremost logs, then leap for shore as the mass broke loose. One second's hesitation, one misstep on the churning logs meant death. "No river driver was really safe," writes Devore, "until 6 p.m. and quitting time."

There were other dangers. During Eau Claire Lumber's first drive a boat failed to pull out above the Kananaskis Falls and was swept over its series of cataracts. It survived two of the cataracts, but splintered after the third and overturned in the boiling torrent. Three men made it to shore, six perished.

In June 1907 disaster struck on the North Saskatchewan River run. Snow had been exceptionally deep in the mountains that winter. When the mountain ice broke in mid-June the river rose nine feet within hours. The torrent smashed drive boats and dumped men among the now uncontrollable logs as they careered downriver. Still out of control, they swept into Edmonton and smashed through the booms intended to trap them at the mills. Twelve men were killed. Most of the winter cut was gone. Eventually 500,000 board feet was recovered at Battleford and sold there.[a]

The day before he joined his first drive on the upper Red Deer River, Devore recalls, a young Scot had been caught in the logs and drowned, and rare was the day when a river driver didn't fall in and get soaked. But the wet, sweat and dangers of the day's work gave way to lighthearted high-jinks. Log rolling (or burling) was a practised sport, in which two men on the same log would each try to spin the other off.

Devore describes one championship contest between a

Sandstone Company was manufacturing 45,000 bricks daily. In Edmonton, Humberstone Brick and Coal had been firing bricks for fine houses with coal from Humberstone's Grierson Hill mine since 1881. (William Humberstone himself lived in a $250 log house measuring about eighteen feet by 22 feet.) Between 1904 and 1909 there were three brickmaking plants in the Crowsnest Pass, but bricks from Medicine Hat and Redcliff were recognized as the best.

The industry's potential seemed limitless. A government program offered twenty-acre lots for $5 to experienced brickmakers willing to start companies on these properties. Wirecutting of bricks produced varied shapes and sizes. The

---

One second's hesitation, one misstep on the churning logs meant death. 'No river driver was really safe,' writes Devore, 'until six p.m. and quitting time.'

Michigan riverman and a northern Ontario halfbreed, who kept the log rolling for three-quarters of an hour until the half-breed finally caught his opponent off balance. He can see it still, he writes, "the gestures and banter of partisan supporters, the open-mouthed delegation of farmers who lined the riverbank, the water flying upward from that spinning log, and the two dancing, evenly matched figures atop it."

The sawmills were notable for a form of conservation. (It was called "thrift" then.) Nothing was wasted. All sawdust and trimmings fuelled the mill's boilers, or were sold as fuel or insulation. Fire frequently threatened the mills, however; a stray spark could demolish them. Fire was even more of a hazard among the timber stands, where logging crews could find themselves inexplicably surrounded by flames. They suspected nearby farmers trying to clear land (who in turn accused careless loggers) but nothing was ever proved.

Accidents notwithstanding, lumber production was impressive. In 1900 the Edmonton Lumber Company was producing 20,000 board feet a day. D.R. Fraser could turn out 50,000 board feet, and its 1908 production totalled five million, at $1 a thousand for common grades. One small Stettler sawmill took in $1,300 in a single day in 1905.

William Cushing, Public Works minister in the Rutherford government, made his fortune in what a later generation would call a value-added industry. Two hundred employees manufactured name brand XCLR doors and window sashes in his ten-acre east Calgary plant. Despite all efforts, lumber suppliers rarely managed to keep up with demand, however. Calgary alone needed over forty million board feet in 1908, and employed 200 carpenters. Others came and left again. The reason: no housing — they didn't like living in tents. Reason for the housing shortage: too little lumber, too few carpenters.

Brick was more expensive, but was used with increasing frequency for public and commercial buildings, and substantial houses. Even in Calgary, where sandstone remained the first choice of the affluent, the Crandell Pressed Brick and

Toronto-built Berg Machine could turn out 20,000 quick-drying bricks in a ten-hour day, marked with the maker's name.[b] By 1912 there were 42 plants in operation and a further forty being promoted.

However the end came soon. About a third of the government-inspired companies failed to mine the stipulated $100 worth of clay a year. By 1914, the boom over, half of Alberta's 69 plants had closed, and only two would last to the 1990s: Edmonton's J.B. Little & Sons and Medicine Hat's I-XL Industries.[c]

Alberta's other promising construction material, however, would prove more durable. First rate cement needs limestone in quantity, and at Lac des Arcs near Exshaw, 57 miles (92 km) west of Calgary, the CPR's Western Canada Cement and Coal Company had access to a whole mountain of it, graded as North America's finest quality. By 1910 the plant, covering seven acres, was running night and day, using six kilns, each seven by six by eighty feet. Its product, especially admired for its pale hue, would remain popular throughout the century.

— *C.D.*

[a]The 1907 disaster prompted the D.R. Fraser mill to make larger and longer booms of Douglas fir imported from British Columbia. These timbers, sometimes ten feet or more in diameter and up to seventy feet long, were held together and to the docks by extra-heavy chains. They cost nearly $3,000, but D.R. Fraser never lost another boom.

[b]Brick prices ranged from $8 to $20 a thousand. Less than a century later, when the buildings were demolished, the same bricks were sold for up to $350 a thousand. The price differential over that period for "clinkers," over-fired bricks from the bottom layer in the kiln, is more startling. Clinkers were sold as seconds, given away or discarded; in Edmonton, Holy Trinity Church and some 150 houses were built of clinkers, as were a few houses in Medicine Hat and Red Deer and one in Calgary. By 1990 clinkers sold for as much as $2,500 a thousand.

[c]The brickmaking operation started by Ben McCord of Medicine Hat in 1885 originally produced only enough bricks to build the schoolhouse, a warehouse and one residence. But it survived, thanks to the area's high quality clay and abundance of cheap, efficient, natural gas for firing the bricks. In the coming century it would change ownership five times, but in the 1990s, as I-XL Industries Ltd., it would still be operating.

Interior of Burns meat packing plant, Calgary.

By 1907, however, they were not seen as quite so noble. The rough winter that year caused such a severe domestic coal shortage that the Alberta Legislature unanimously endorsed a motion by Malcolm McKenzie (Liberal-Macleod) to appoint an investigating commission. Whether the CPR was to blame he did not know, but he wanted to find out. Conservative Albert J. Robertson (High River) said that in his constituency a coal train had sat eight days on a siding. Local settlers had finally helped themselves, at gunpoint. John R. Boyle (Liberal-Sturgeon) suspected a shortage of railcars, not just weather. There hadn't lately been enough cars for grain either, he observed. And that August, according to newspaper reports, Crowsnest coal mines were still working at half speed, for lack of CPR cars.

The great potential of the West was being stifled, or so westerners tended to believe, by ignorant, incompetent, self-serving central Canadian interests. The *Edmonton Journal* quoted Dr. D.B. Dowling of the Geological Survey of Canada as saying that the country's known coal resources "would supply the needs of the whole civilized world for the next 170 years" and there was much more not yet located. The *Bulletin* calculated that a total of 171 million acres was suitable for cultivation in the north-west, and only five million acres being farmed. Why should all this potential be neglected to protect Canadian railroads and eastern industries?

The crunch came after 1909, when the price of wheat headed downward again, while the cost of transportation and manufactured goods kept rising (along with land values and farmer indebtedness). Protectionist sentiment in the United States was waning at that time. The Payne-Aldrich bill had revised US tariffs upwards, which created a backlash from consumers of Canadian pulp and other raw materials. In 1910 tariff negotiations were resumed.

Sir Wilfrid Laurier moreover was planning to call an election in 1911. Both he and Tory leader Robert Borden made preliminary western tours in the spring of 1910. Everywhere their trains stopped, grain growers besieged them with demands for tariff reductions on farm machinery and supplies and "the necessities of life." Sir Wilfrid was sympathetic.[2] Borden was not. The coal interests got a word in too. Newsmen accompanying a Liberal campaign tour in September, the *Lethbridge Herald* reported, visited the Alberta Railway and Irrigation Company mines. Supply was unlimited, the manager told them, but markets were a problem with coal selling for $3.85 a ton at the mine but eight dollars in Montana. With reciprocity and lower freight rates, business would treble.

That December, just to drive home the point, a delegation of 800 farmers from Ontario and the West converged upon Ottawa. The protective tariff made food more costly for everyone, they argued. It favoured a privileged few at the expense of most of the nation. And it favoured central Canada to the detriment of other regions. The cabinet received them politely. They addressed the House of Commons. No one made any promises.

But in January 1911 the United States offered a completely unexpected deal, which would entirely eliminate the tariff on most agricultural products including grain, live animals, timber and pulpwood, and lower the rates on many processed products and a few manufactured ones. But most Canadian manufacturers (including agricultural implements) would still be protected. The proposal was to adopt these new schedules by concurrent legislation in both countries. Congress would never ratify it, said the nonplussed pro-protectionists. But Congress immediately did ratify it. Still, Laurier thought it would easily pass in Parliament; it seemed just the thing to make everybody at least moderately happy.

He was probably right, too — until Clifford Sifton swung into action. Even a good trade agreement with the United States would be bad for Canada, Sifton insisted. Economic integration would inevitably lead to the "usual ultimate end of political union." The Liberals had no mandate to accept the American proposal, he charged in a major Commons speech; the last three elections had clearly approved the existing fiscal policy. The British market would be lost. Ontario and Quebec would have to remove their bans on exporting pulpwood. The Americans would build no more Canadian branch plants. Canadian millers, fruit growers and meat packers could never stand against US competition. American interests would take over the entire cattle industry of the West: "I cannot tell you how I feel about that great country being made the backyard for the city of Chicago." There would be no end to accommodation — soon there would be pressure to include agricultural implements as well.

If only Canadian farmers would be patient, Sifton said, improved transportation would lower wheat shipment costs by six cents a bushel, secondary industry would proliferate country-wide and Canadian ports would prosper, because "we have finally, definitely won our independence." Sifton organized a revolt of prominent Grits representing among other things, Massey-Harris, the Canadian Northern Railway, the Canadian Bankers' Association, the Steel Company of Canada, the Northern Trusts Company and influential newspapers. He made a deal with Borden, and resigned with regret from his Brandon constituency. And he masterminded an anti-reciprocity campaign that blanketed the country. The Montreal Board of Trade and nine Ontario boards all swung into action. Dafoe quotes Sir William Van Horne, late of the CPR, as declaring his determination to "bust the damned thing."

Delegations of millers, meat packers and fruit growers also made themselves heard, not excluding some western ones. Tariff questions are never simple; the West had its protectionists too, especially in the towns. "The free trader who tries to persuade the people of Edmonton and Strathcona that they can never hope to build up big manufacturing cities will have his trouble for his pains," commented the *Edmonton Journal*. "They know that they have all the natural advantages in their favour and they have enterprise enough to make the most of those advantages if adequate protection for home industries is assured."

The farm organizations both west and east fought back hard, with rallies, study groups, vitriolic rhetoric and endless recitation of prices just across the border. On this note of crisis and bitter controversy Canada would go to the polls in 1911, and the outcome would set the pattern for Canadian politics in the next decade.

[2]Historian W.L. Morton in his *The Progressive Party in Canada* (University of Toronto Press, 1950) quotes a memorable 1894 Winnipeg speech by Laurier on the subject of tariffs. "I denounce the policy of protection as bondage — yea, bondage," he declaimed, "and I refer to bondage in the same manner in which American slavery was bondage." This was music to western ears, but the future prime minister had to tone down that sort of rhetoric — and the philosophy it represented — to get his Liberals elected two years later.

Glenbow Archives, NA-22-1

United Farmers & Equity Association of Alberta. This committee represented the AFA and the Society of Equity and was responsible for the amalgamation of the two groups into the United Farmers of Alberta, January, 1909.

Pat Burns, Calgary's baron of beef

THE ILLITERATE MEAT-PACKER WITH A COW IN HIS BACKYARD SET THE TONE FOR THE ROUGH-HEWN TYCOONERY TO COME

In 1910 when Pat Burns was competing to supply beef along the construction railway routes through the Yellowhead Pass, an English reporter was amazed at the man's audacity:

> He drove a herd of 600 prime cattle over the trail from Quesnel to Hazelton — a matter of 420 miles. About three miles below the latter point on the Skeena River he established a slaughterhouse where the animals were corralled and killed. The dressed carcasses were distributed among the cold storage establishments specially provided down the river. That drive was a remarkable one. The losses en route were only three and the cattle arrived in such prime condition that Pat Burns signed a contract right away for the driving of no less than 5,000 cattle over the same trail during the year 1911, just to supply the railway with fresh meat.

Small wonder that twenty years later Burns was a multi-millionaire, feted by the politicians, business leaders, ranchers and assorted others who jammed the Palliser Hotel banquet hall on July 6, 1931, to celebrate his 75th birthday and share a 3,000-pound birthday cake. Although they may not have realized it, they were also commemorating the transformation of the West from rough frontier to settled society, and the people who made it so. Burns, who came west almost penniless in the 1870s, was now a multi-millionaire philanthropist, dean of Alberta cattlemen and, thanks to fellow Calgarian R.B. Bennett, newly a senator. In a sense he typified a whole generation that "made good."

Whether his personal life was as rewarding as his business career is a matter of some doubt, but Burns is widely described as blunt, gregarious, good-humoured, humble, hard-working, astonishingly generous and — above all — tough and resourceful. Born Patrick O'Bryne to a family of Irish Catholic immigrants, he spent most of his childhood on a rocky Ontario homestead north of Oshawa. "It was the School of Necessity from which the Byrne children graduated with distinction," writes his biographer, Grant MacEwan.[a] Young Burns dug potatoes, worked on neighbouring farms, logged, and clerked in a store.

He dreamt of going west to roam the free range as a cowboy, and a job dragging logs for a timber company opened the

way in 1878. The cash-short logging company paid him off with two oxen, worth $70 live. So Burns slaughtered his first cattle and sold the meat for $140. Then he set out for Winnipeg with one of his brothers, where he worked on a rail gang and took a homestead near Minnedosa.

He spent as much time hauling goods as he did farming his quarter-section. One winter he hauled hay from Minnedosa, which had a surplus, to Brandon, which had a shortage. He bought several ox teams, borrowed sleighs, and built hay racks. He sold the hay for a good price at Brandon, sold the racks for

Glenbow Archives, NA-1149-1

Glenbow Archives, NA-2047-1

(L) Patrick Burns, 1927. (R) P. Burns & Co. advertisement, Calgary City Directory, 1911.

firewood, sold all but one team, then stacked the sleighs atop each other and hauled them home. He netted several hundred dollars.

Burns's first big break came in 1886, when friend and earlier Ontario associate William Mackenzie got him a contract to supply beef for work gangs building a railroad from Quebec to New Brunswick.[b] Bigger contracts followed, on the Regina-Prince Albert and Calgary-Edmonton lines. In Calgary in the early 1890s he set up his first slaughterhouse, a ramshackle wooden building on the Bow River that burned down two years later. Burns rebuilt and expanded. Business boomed. By 1898 he was slaughtering 150 head a week, and in 1899 bought his 9,000-acre Bow Valley Ranch.

Lack of schooling never hampered his shrewd and innovative business dealings. He supplied the roaring Kootenay mining towns, shipping cattle by train to Revelstoke and by barge down the Columbia River. He opened butcher shops in towns like Kaslo, Silverton and Sandon. He made the first risky cattle shipments into the Klondike, selling beef there for a dollar a pound.

He also anticipated the feedlot system. Most ranchers fattened cattle in summer, sold the beef stock in fall (glutting the market and depressing prices), and let the rest fend for themselves over winter. Burns produced hay and systematically fed his cattle. Marketable in winter, they fetched much better prices.

1901 he married Eileen Ellis, the sheltered product of a ranching family from Penticton, BC, after a four-year courtship. It wasn't destined to be a lasting match. He was 45, short, plump, illiterate and Catholic; she was 27, tall, slim, educated and Protestant. Moreover his business dealings scarcely left him time to minister to his wife. Burns built a magnificent $40,000 sandstone mansion for Eileen in 1901 — one of his few personal extravagances — and they had a son, Patrick Michael, in 1906, but she eventually left him and moved to California. There, it was rumoured, she revived a love affair with a former boyfriend. Later, ailing, she moved to Victoria where Burns, reportedly without recrimination, continued to support her until her death from cancer in 1923.

Burns is widely described as blunt, gregarious, good-humoured, humble, hard-working, and above all tough and resourceful. His family life wasn't as rosy.

Moreover, he pursued what economists now call vertical integration: controlling almost every step of an industrial process from raw resource to finished product. He coordinated ranches, farms, dairies, slaughterhouses, tanneries, creameries, and scores of retail outlets. And although he never bought a railroad, he kept a sharp eye on shipping.

Well known and well liked around Calgary for his instant generosity to hundreds of causes and individuals, he was also resented by many smaller farmers and stockmen. After he bought out his only real local competitor, William Roper Hull, Burns was accused of monopolistic practice, and of price-fixing in collusion with Winnipeg cattle exporter T.G. Gordon of Gordon, Ironside & Fares. Under pressure, the Alberta and Manitoba governments held an investigation in 1907.

Burns lost his characteristic good humour. "There never has been a combine in cattle in Canada in the existence of the country," he testified, as reported by the *Calgary Herald*. "I have never had no understanding with no outfit in America." On pricing: "I could give the Commission a list of the people whom I have overpaid...Men like Ironsides and myself are necessary to the country. Without us the country could not eat." Employees and associates testified on his behalf. In mid-investigation the St. Mary's Club, of which he was a benefactor, put on a Burns tribute attended by 150 business leaders. The commission fully exonerated him.

During and after the First World War, Burns kept getting richer. He built refrigerated abattoirs in Calgary, Edmonton, Vancouver, Regina, Winnipeg and Seattle. He had offices in London, Liverpool and Yokohama. He opened 65 creameries and cheese factories and set up eighteen wholesale fruit houses in western Canada, while at the same time expanding his ranching operation and diversifying into oil and mining.

But his family life, of which only sketchy facts are known, appears sad and lonely by contrast. His sister died when he was still young; so did the brother with whom he travelled west. In

Concluding that his son — less than robust and somewhat over-pampered — was not suitable to take over his meat-packing interests, Burns sold them to Dominion Securities Corporation Ltd. (for $15 million) in 1928. Only just 30, Patrick Michael died five months before his father from an apparent heart attack in bed at the Burns house.

Burns retained his beloved ranches and added more, for a total of thirteen including the fabled Bar U and Walrond. His public persona was that of a kind man, giving handsomely to many of the local causes, but also something of a hick. His mansion was opulent enough. But the packing plant czar kept a dairy cow in the back yard. As historian Paul Voisey notes: "Calgary's elite was forever revealing signs of their humble origins. What guardian of old family wealth in Montreal's Westmount would keep a milk cow in the city? Pat Burns kept one in Calgary."

Debilitated by stroke and diabetes, Pat Burns, 80, died in his mansion in the early hours of Feb. 24, 1937. An RCMP guard of honour and another from the Calgary Regiment (whose honorary colonel he had been) accompanied his coffin to St. Mary's Cathedral and a funeral attended by hundreds. The eulogy must have summed the general sentiment: "His passing seems to us to mark the end of a great epoch. Coming, he found little, but he has made this a better place for us to live in. Whatever his hand found to do, he did it with all his might."　— *G.K.*

[a]Pat Burns' family dropped the "O" from "O'Bryne" and switched the "r" and "y" and a sloppy clerk on a riverboat later changed the spelling again. But Burns used the older form on his marriage certificate and other legal documents. As for his birth date, some sources list it as 1854, and the most commonly accepted is 1856, the year inscribed on his gravestone. But according to biographer Grant MacEwan, his mother recorded her son's birth in her prayer book as July 6, 1855.

[b]Pat Burns' friendship with railroader William Mackenzie was to strike a serious snag. Mackenzie invested in Burns' meat-packing operations. Burns considered it a loan, Mackenzie an equity investment. The long-running dispute was finally settled by re-incorporating the entire enterprise as P. Burns and Company Ltd. and giving Mackenzie a one-third interest.

Section Five

LIFE IN A NEW PROVINCE

Chapters by Virginia Byfield, Stephani Keer, Brian Hutchinson,
George Oake, Calvin Demmon, Mary Frances Doucedame & Vicky Maclean

E.F.HAGELL

Bringing in the Thin Ones
by writer, painter and range rider Edward Frederick Hagell
Glenbow Archives, HE-56.31.1

Laying the foundation stone of the Anglican pro-Cathedral, Calgary, Sept. 1904. By the turn of the century the mainline denominations were firmly established.

In the shadow of mortal danger, God was never very far away

IT TOOK A SPECIAL KIND OF GUMPTION TO BE A PIONEER. THE MEN AND WOMEN WHO BROUGHT RELIGION WERE CUT FROM THE SAME CLOTH

by VIRGINIA BYFIELD

The settlers who streamed into Alberta in the first decade of the 20th century were, like all other human beings before and after them, altogether aware that life itself is the ultimate mystery, that their time on this earth was limited, and that they were supposed to use it to some purpose. But far more than their descendants, they were constantly reminded of life's uncertainties. Famine, disease, destitution, homelessness, injury and death were immediate possibilities. Stories of people found starving or mortally stricken were uncomfortably commonplace. In such circumstances men and women find their thoughts turning with little persuasion to God.

Christianity, whether Protestant, Catholic or Orthodox, was to be found at the heart of nearly every small new community from its beginning. Sometimes indeed a church representative was the organizer of the enterprise, and some of the missionaries were there before the settlers. Among the Christian denominations, Roman Catholics and Methodists were first on the scene in what would become southern Alberta, Catholics and Anglicans in the North (see sidebar). Their primary mission was to convert the Indians and, in the case of the French priests, to look after the spiritual welfare of their inter-married relatives, the Metis.

Thus the Oblates of Mary Immaculate, the renowned mission order, had an establishment at Lac Ste. Anne in 1844 and at Lac la Biche in 1853. The famous Fr. Albert Lacombe began his work at St. Albert in 1861, travelling south into the Blackfoot country in 1865 (Vol. 1, p. 74). When the first North-West Mounted Police detachment reached the site of Calgary in 1875, to build a post there, they found two Oblates running Our Lady of Peace Mission from a log cabin on the Elbow River.

Alberta's first resident Methodist missionary was the Rev. Robert Rundle at Fort Edmonton between 1840 and 1848. But Rev. Henry Steinhauer, the Ojibwa convert who founded a great Alberta family, was at Lac la Biche in 1855 and began a mission at Whitefish Lake, ninety miles (145 km) northeast of Edmonton, in 1858. The Rev. George McDougall and his son and successor John were building their mission at Morley, west of Calgary.

By 1900, however, the mainline denominations were well established in the cities and towns, and building in brick as fast as they could. In November 1905, for instance, the *Edmonton Journal* reported the grand opening of First Baptist Church, built to seat 600. In 1893 the Baptist community had consisted of "some eighteen souls." Moreover, the *Journal* noted, the Anglicans had nearly trebled the capacity of All Saints' Church that year, the Methodists and "German Baptists" had opened churches in the city's east end, and the Presbyterians had one under construction in the north.

Outside the towns, however, it was a different story. In the comparatively settled southern half of the province, a new generation of pioneer church-builders was opening a new era, but the evidence of it was thinly scattered. In the view of some oldtimers, of course, things were getting positively soft. Missionaries today have many advantages, Rev. John McDougall told a *Calgary Herald* interviewer in 1903, after an extensive tour of outlying areas. (McDougall retired in Calgary in 1906.) Whitefish Lake now had bi-monthly mail, he noted, and was a mere forty miles from a telegraph station. True, his wagon had broken a spring, and a buggy he tried next had collapsed completely and had to be abandoned. But compared with the old days that was minor.

It was also typical, and rural clergymen perforce travelled a great deal among the far-flung farms and settlements. The Rev. R.E. Finlay, a Methodist, came to Old Vegreville (four miles southwest of Vegreville's later site on the Canadian Northern Railway) in July 1901 when the wild roses

---

The only substantial non-Christian religion among the settlers was Judaism and its numbers were small. There were twelve in 1891 and 242 in 1901.

---

were blooming. Old Vegreville consisted of a log livery barn, he recalled in an article for *Vegreville in Review,* a store with a leaking sod roof and nothing else. Edmonton was ninety miles away by wandering trail, with creeks to ford. "There was an almost unbelievable amount of water everywhere," he writes. "Beaver Lake was as large as the Sea of Galilee then," and Amisk Creek at its southeast end was forty feet wide and ten feet deep at the centre. Until it was bridged he used to carry his saddle across on a makeshift raft, then coax his horse over on a long tether.

Finlay found plenty to do besides preach and offer religious instruction.[1] He also drew up wills, extracted teeth, milked cows when homesteaders were sick, and helped a woman get in a load of hay when her husband was away and fodder had run short. He made a notable hit one day with a farmer whose binder was malfunctioning; it was refusing to knot the sheaves. Finlay, a farmer's son himself, adjusted the knotter and all was well.

Finlay was not the only minister who found farming know-how important. The Rev. John Brown, a Presbyterian, was assigned in 1907 to Strathmore, where the people were kind but there was no church, no congregation, no money, and nowhere to house his wife and small daughter. After trying cooperative makeshifts for two years he decided he must do something else to support his family, and pursue his ministerial vocation on the side. So with church permission John and Violet Brown, now with an infant son as well, went homesteading in the Red Deer River country upstream from Drumheller.

In her memoir *Over the Red Deer: Life of a Homestead Missionary*, Violet Brown recalls driving the wagon up and down their first field, the children asleep at her feet, while her husband broadcast seed by hand from the back of it. It was a hard life and sometimes a hungry one, but after a while they developed several little congregations. Years later, Mrs. Brown writes, she was told of seven other ordained Presbyterian ministers who were also living on homesteads and carrying on their work.[2] It helped the church through a hard time, when clergy grants were too small to live on and

[1] In July 1902, the Rev. R.E. Finlay made a pastoral call at the Merton Cole homestead. "You'd better not come in," Mrs. Cole told him. "Myrtle has something I'm afraid of." So he looked at seven-year-old Myrtle through the window, guessed that she had smallpox, and sent word out to Fort Saskatchewan. "This was the beginning of fifty cases of smallpox," he writes, "but only one death resulted."

[2] Even more Presbyterian missionaries might have been forced to homestead but for the efforts of a man known in the church as "the great superintendent." The Rev. James Robertson of Knox Church, Winnipeg, launched his Church and Manse Building Fund, using ferocious moral suasion on eastern Presbyterian businessmen to supply it, after his first tours of the North-West. Robertson's biographer Ralph Connor describes how in one sod-roofed shack he had been puzzled to see the children ranged down the middle "like soldiers on parade." Then he saw why — the only dry place in the shack was under the wide beam that formed its ridgepole.

A Sunday school picnic near Airdrie, 1908. A new generation of pioneer church builders was opening up a new era.

you couldn't pass the collection plate in rural Alberta because people had no money to give.

Elizabeth B. Mitchell, a perceptive Englishwoman who published her impressions of the prairie religious scene in 1915 (*In Western Canada Before the War*), faults the Anglicans for stubborn adherence to English attitudes. They were often referred to in Alberta as "the English Church." But that being said, she adds, "I saw the Church of England in her glory on the prairie...the glory of Holy Poverty, not of an 'established social position.' "Here she's referring to rural Anglican priests," each with a district as big as an English diocese."

Anglican students would be sent out in summer to batch in "shacks," each tending three little congregations about ten miles apart. The resident priest looked after these young men, teaching them how to care for their horses, keep their shacks decent, find their way around, be helpful to settlers who put them up for the night and — above all — "to remember that on the prairie each of them is just 'a preacher'." In winter, the students were back at college, but the resident was alone in his gigantic district "with perpetual driving in western weather, with the prospect of any sort of queer quarters for a night's rest, and sleeping-bag and outfit of tools to fall back on in case of accidents."[3]

Finlay found plenty to do besides preach. He drew up wills, extracted teeth, milked cows and helped a woman get in a load of hay when her husband was away.

After he had taken supper, for he was hungry, and tired after a long day's journey, we all knelt by Olive's bedroom, and the archdeacon anointed her and prayed God would bless the means used for Olive's recovery. I shall always remember that night. About 2 o'clock in the morning, there was a change for the better... Olive's recovery is only one of the many experiences we had of answer to prayer. Again and again in those mission days, we have proved that true saying "Man's extremity is God's opportunity."

- an account of a daughter's deliverance from measles, contained in Experiences of a Missionary's Wife, by Mrs. Jessie Holmes, who came to Lesser Slave Lake (later named Grouard) from England in 1902.

The Roman Catholics were still very much a presence, of course. North and east of the homesteading Browns, for example, Fr. Hippolyte Beillevaire, a parish priest and professor from the Loire Valley in France, had been toiling for three decades, a saga described in *Battle River Country*. The little French priest began ministering to the Metis at the Laboucane Settlement, a trading post on the Battle River, in 1882. They cut logs along the river banks and on the day after the Feast of All Saints began to build a chapel chinked with moss. Bishop Vital Grandin consecrated the church in the spring of 1884 as St. Thomas Duhamel, giving the same name to the settlement as well.[4]

A diminutive figure in full white beard and hiked-up cassock, Fr. Beillevaire travelled his prairie parish on horseback, by dogsled and, when spring floods raised the river level, by canoe, west to Wetaskiwin and Hobbema, south to Buffalo Lake, north and east to Hay Lakes, Camrose, Beaverhill Lake, Tofield and even the "Settlement Hongrois" at Vegreville.

When the James Ross family moved into the Metis district in 1907, Beillevaire persuaded Mrs. Ross to play the organ for the Catholic church as well as the Presbyterian. He also managed to convert the Rosses to card-playing, of which he was very fond. He watched the Grand Trunk Pacific crews build their enormous bridge across the Battle in 1910 (see story Sect. 3, ch. 4), and New Duhamel boom beside it. He credited his continued good health to his T&B plug tobacco which he also used for weather forecasts. (When the plug got damp, rain was imminent.) In 1935, when the community staged a grand *fête* for his 87th birthday, Fr. Beillevaire was still celebrating the mass daily, although he had shrunk to barely four feet high and often singed his beard with the candle taper. He died in 1937.

For Protestant ministers who were relative newcomers, improvisation was the key. The Rev. J.H. Matthews, a Methodist, was appointed in 1907 to the Pine Creek Mission, the area southeast of Red Deer River and north of Huxley. In a 1971 letter from his retirement home in Derbyshire, printed in *Buried Treasures* by the Elnora History Committee, the 88-year-old clergyman described

LIFE IN A NEW PROVINCE

his life in Alberta. He and William Edwards cut poplar poles to build a room for him onto the Edwards house at Elnora. Meanwhile he established six "preaching places" at various ranches and at the Trenville schoolhouse.

There were certain minor drawbacks. On one occasion a calf burst through the door in the midst of the service. On another a dog fight broke out in the yard during his sermon. The fight ceased abruptly, however, when rancher Ed Ash nailed the combatants with a well-aimed stick of firewood. At the schoolhouse, a parishioner deputed to bring the communion bread found she had forgotten it. Young Louis Greenwood rode to the nearest home only to find its owners absent. He got in through a window, found a loaf, brought it back and cut off pieces with his jackknife, returning the rest of the loaf after the service. "Those early days were truly great," writes the veteran clergyman, "and the Greenwood boys were as fine as they come."

When no minister was available, the settlers improvised. "From 1897 to about 1899, Pa used to hold a Sunday School class with us children on a Sunday afternoon, although Mr. Coleman [a neighbour] used to give us scriptural instruction for several years in the winter evenings, along with school studies," writes John Niddrie in *Derbytown Echoes* of his boyhood on a homestead in the Sundre area. "Today I can quote many of the Golden texts he assigned us nearly three generations ago." Later a Methodist or Presbyterian minister would drive out about twice a month to preach to several families at the Niddrie home, after which most of the congregation stayed for a substantial Sunday dinner.

Cooperation among Protestant denominations was another keynote. In the Fishburn district, southeast of Pincher Creek, services were held at various settlers' homes and at the schoolhouse by Methodist, Presbyterian and Baptist clergy. Some drove out from Macleod by horse and buggy; some were students doing a summer stint at what the Methodists called Kootenai Mission. The faithful of all three denominations got together in 1905 to raise a church, with the men contributing labour while the women supplied meals. On dedication Sunday they put on a great feast in the church, then cleared away the tables for an evening service. The first hymn, participants recall in *Prairie Grass to Mountain Pass* was "The Church's One Foundation." The text for the sermon: "They built a house unto the Lord" (I Kings 8).

Similarly, Presbyterians built churches at Leduc and Clearwater, four miles to the northeast, about 1898. But within a few years, writes C.H. Stout in *From Frontier Days*, "a form of church union had been organized between the Baptist, Methodist and Presbyterian congregations." Much the same was happening everywhere. In *Chatter Chips from Beaver Creek Dam* Florence Hatherly Paice remembers the first church at Castor, sixty miles (96 km) east of Red Deer. Built of sod, it served "Anglicans, Methodists, Presbyterians and anyone else who wanted to use it." One day, she adds, "a fat pig waddled into church," delighting the children as it brushed their bare feet. "Sometimes there would be a dog fight, which provided added entertainment."

Even Catholics had to learn coexistence. "Roman Catholicism has two chief elements, French-Canadian and Irish-American," writes Elizabeth Mitchell. "I fancy there are sometimes rubs between them." She was quite right. Until well after 1910 Alberta's Catholic bishops were francophone Oblates. Virtually all the priests they brought in, whether from Quebec or France, were French-speaking too; most incoming Catholic settlers were not. Otherwise they did their best to accommodate the newcomers (mostly Irish), and also their Eastern Rite brethren from Slavic Europe, the Uniate Catholics (see sidebar).

In 1908 Father Albert Lacombe, by now 81, left his retirement hermitage at Pincher Creek to go to Edmonton. First he addressed the Galicians at their church on Namao Avenue. Then he delivered sermons at the Church of the Immaculate Conception both in French and in what the newspapers described as "his own picturesque English." He recalled the time fifty years earlier "when my feet knew every trail leading out from this hill," and he appealed for more consideration for the Metis. "You newcomers who...spread over the lands like streams dividing, you do not know what we who came first owed to the charity and goodness of these half-breeds..." But there must be limits to coexistence. Presumably with Protestants in mind, he urged his hearers not to endanger their faith, and that of their children, by making mixed marriages.

They all seem to have got on pretty well, however. *Vegreville in Review* describes that community's early "Frenchtown." This was the northeast section where Poulins, Dubucs, Nadeaus,

The Rev. R.E. Finlay. When he arrived, Vegreville was a livery barn and a leaky store and nothing else.

[3]From northern Alberta to the Arctic was the Anglican Diocese of Athabasca, where Bishop William C. Bompas had begun his work in the Peace River country in 1867. The rest of the province was the Diocese of Calgary. In 1903 the *Canadian Churchman* reported 26 priests at work in this vast area, six entirely supported by their congregations and the rest subsidized by eastern mission funds.

[4]Bishop Grandin named the Duhamel settlement for Archbishop Joseph-Thomas Duhamel of Ottawa, likely hoping for helpful patronage. The church got a bell out of it, when the bishop visited the mission at St. Albert in 1892 and was reminded of his namesake on the Battle River. It called the faithful to prayer and rang to warn of prairie fires. In 1961 a new church was built in the hamlet of New Duhamel, two miles east, and the old church, its logs covered with spruce siding, became the charge of the Duhamel Historical Society.

(Above) Fr. Albert Lacombe in 1909. He urged listeners not to endanger their faith. (Below) the dauntless Fr. Hippolyte Beillevaire.

Dumonts and other French-speaking families were settled around their church, school, convent and hospital, but families with names like Stanton, Maloney and Stuparek lived there too. "The [Christmas] Midnight Mass in old St. Martin's Church was the highlight of the Frenchtown winter. Catholics and their Protestant friends crowded into the draughty old building for an uplifting service which featured Latin Mass sung by a talented mixture of Sisters, Dubucs and others."[5]

But Alberta's new religious multiformity by no means ended with Uniate Catholics. The *Edmonton Journal* reported with awe in 1905 that a church census in the city had turned up 37 different "religions" and many of them were "almost unknown in Canada." Most of these were denominational or national variations of Christianity, or what some would see as Christian heresies. Among them: the German Baptist Church of North America; Mennonites from Manitoba, Ontario and Russia; Church of Jesus Christ of Latter-day Saints, i.e. Mormons (see sidebar); Seventh-Day Adventists; the Swedish Evangelical Covenant; Church of the Brethren; Plymouth Brethren; Church of Christ; Christian Scientists; Christadelphians; and Jehovah's Witnesses (then called Russellites).

A few Seventh-Day Adventists, for instance, most noted for their insistence upon a Saturday sabbath, had been immigrating from the United States, and in 1908 a delegation from North Dakota bought 10,000 acres in the Rosebud district northeast of Calgary. The *Edmonton Bulletin* reported that they planned to settle several hundred people there, mostly successful farmers of German origin. An Edmonton Adventist, who observed that he used to be the only one around, was asked how the recently passed Lord's Day Act would affect the newcomers, since it strictly forbade commercial work on Sunday. They would just have to do as he did, he replied: not work on either Saturday or Sunday.

The only substantial non-Christian religion represented among the settlers was Judaism, and its numbers were very small — twelve in 1891 and 242 in 1901, says Stuart Rosenberg in *The Jewish Community in Canada*. Jacob Lion Diamond, who made his way west to Calgary in 1888 and went into the liquor business, may have been the first Jew to settle permanently in Alberta. His brother William followed in 1892, setting up as a tailor.

In 1894 Jacob Diamond managed to assemble a congregation for the High Holy Days communal prayers: himself and William, two other Calgary residents, two from Edmonton, one from Lacombe and five itinerant pedlars. When numbers finally increased enough to build a synagogue in Calgary in 1911, it was called Beth Jacob in his honour. William Diamond moved to Edmonton (where Abe Cristall had opened a general store in 1894) and went into retail clothing. He was central to the founding of Beth Israel Congregation (then called Edmonton Hebrew); Talmud Torah, launched in 1907, became a model for western Hebrew schools.[6]

One Christian offshoot that almost missed Alberta was the Doukhobors, the "Spirit Wrestlers," who came to Canada with the aid of Count Leo Tolstoy and English and American Quakers. They liked the look of a block of twelve townships east of Edmonton,

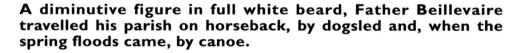

A diminutive figure in full white beard, Father Beillevaire travelled his parish on horseback, by dogsled and, when the spring floods came, by canoe.

but influential Liberal politician Frank Oliver and his *Edmonton Bulletin* raised such an outcry that in 1899 the 7,000 Doukhobors were settled in Saskatchewan instead.[7]

Their relationship with government remained uneasy, to say the least, in anything that touched on their religious views, like oath-taking, statistics, land-holding and education. But what ultimately lost them their Saskatchewan land in 1907 was the fact that Frank Oliver, the Interior minister, refused to interpret the homestead rules as Clifford Sifton, his predecessor, had done. So the Doukhobor colonies moved to the Kootenay country of British Columbia, whence a few hundred migrated east again in 1916 to establish villages around Lundbreck and Cowley in the Pincher Creek area.

It was another religious group, a small and ephemeral one called "the Dreamers," that caused a great stir in 1908 in the Josephburg district southeast of Medicine Hat, supplying

Churches great and small (from top): turn-of-the-century sod church near Castor; Duhamel church; Calgary First Baptist Church, 1906.

many columns of copy to the *Medicine Hat News*.[8] Settler John S. Lehr and his family woke at 1 a.m. on Sunday, April 12, to find their house was on fire. They barely escaped with their lives; Lehr accused his Dreamer neighbours of setting the fire. The heads of the nine Dreamer families were arrested. Testimony at their trial established that Lehr, who had quarrelled with some of them, had received strange and threatening letters from the head of their sect, one Jacob Merkel Sr., who was known as "God Jacob," back in Java, South Dakota.

All the people involved in the case were ethnic Germans from southern Russia who had reached southern Alberta by way of the Dakotas, and members of the *Gemeinde Gottes* (roughly, "People of God"). This was an offshoot of the Millerite or Adventist movement, which preached the imminent second coming of Christ and that Saturday was the proper sabbath, but the Dreamers were an offshoot of the offshoot. At their long Saturday meetings they allegedly recounted and interpreted their dreams; if anyone dreamed ill of a neighbour they believed they must inflict vengeance. Lehr was an Adventist (his middle S stood for "Sabbather") but not a Dreamer.

He testified that one of the accused told him all non-Dreamers must be destroyed as Babel was destroyed. Another, whose mother had previously been fined $20 for shooting at the Lehr children, had threatened to kill Lehr if ever he found him alone, and Lehr's dog had recently been poisoned. Former Dreamers, who said they had left the sect in fear of its murderous demands, confirmed Lehr's testimony. They said letters from "God Jacob," ordering the destruction of people who had sued or otherwise bothered Dreamers, were also read at the

[5] One year the Midnight Mass at Frenchtown was uplifted in a sense, so the story goes, when a full bottle of whiskey dropped from "heaven" (i.e. the choir loft) into the possession of two surprised but grateful recipients below. Its owner had draped his coat over the choir rail, "forgetting that his Christmas cheer was in one pocket."

[6] In this same decade, in 1904, Harry Veiner was born in the then-District of Assiniboia. After two unsuccessful attempts to gain a seat in the provincial Legislature, he was to run for mayor of Medicine Hat in 1951. Although Medicine Hat contained only twenty Jewish families, Harry Veiner won — and he won seven more consecutive terms as well, while building a reputation as the province's most colourful mayor.

[7] Although the Doukhobors proved to be good farmers in Saskatchewan, trouble soon erupted, due in large part to the extremist activities of a minority group, the radical Sons of Freedom sect. In August 1905 the *Edmonton Bulletin* rather smugly informed Edmontonians what they had missed. Several dozen demonstrating Sons adherents had stripped off their clothes outside Yorkton, burned them and begun a march into town. "It appears that a young girl of eighteen or twenty refused to remove her clothing," the *Bulletin* correspondent wrote, "and was stripped by the older women."

[8] The Josephburg where the alleged Dreamer crimes occurred in 1908 was not the community of that name twelve miles northeast of Edmonton, but a predecessor. Immigrants from the villages Brigidau and Josefsberg in Galicia settled south of Medicine Hat from 1888 to 1890, say Eric and Patricia Holmgren in *Over 2,000 Place Names of Alberta*, naming their new home for the latter. But two years of drought drove the Galicians north by 1891, where they founded another Josephburg. The Dreamer families, who had mostly Germanic names, had likely moved to southern Russia in the period of Catherine the Great, whence they migrated to the United States. They had arrived in Alberta from the Dakotas.

The magnificent men of the distant perimeters

The Oblates of Mary Immaculate spearheaded a tough army of superpriests that took on the North and won

As the great tide of immigration challenged the Christian churches in the southerly prairie, a different and much more dangerous task lay upon them in the North. Here the price could be counted not only in hard work and deprivation but also in perilous journeys and lives lost.

While Methodist and Presbyterian missionaries from time to time made an appearance, the churches that dominated the northern missions were the Roman Catholic and Anglican, and towering over them all was one of the most amazing companies of men ever to appear in western Canadian history. They were as intrepid as the fur traders, as tough as the Mounties and as thoroughly disciplined. They were an order of Catholic priests and lay brothers who carried after their names the letters OMI, the Oblates of Mary Immaculate.

Yet working beside them, and sometimes ahead of them, were two orders of nuns — the Sisters of Charity of Montreal, better known as the famed Grey Nuns, and the Sisters of Providence — who staffed the schools and mission hospitals that the Oblates made possible in the North.

Significant, too, was the fact that the man whom one admirer called "as great an Oblate as any" was not an Oblate at all, or a Roman Catholic either. He was William Carpenter Bompas, first Anglican bishop of Athabasca. His hazardous travels in both summer and winter through thousands of miles of northern Alberta and Arctic wilderness won him the admiration of the natives, towards whose interest the whole northern endeavour of both churches was directed.

The key to the northern missionary endeavour lay on a bleak, windswept point near the western extreme of Lake Athabasca, where the crucial battle in the great inter-company war of the fur trade had been fought out nearly half a century earlier (Vol. 1, Sect. 3, ch. 2). This was Fort Chipewyan, now in northern Alberta, which gave access westward to the Peace River and therefore to the Indians of British Columbia's far northern interior; southwestward to the Athabasca River and therefore to the Yellowhead and Athabasca passes through the

Rockies; eastward to the Fond du Lac River and Wollaston and Reindeer Lakes, the latter in what would become northern Manitoba; and northward to the Slave River, Great Slave Lake, the Mackenzie River, Great Bear Lake and the entire western Arctic.

The first missionary to reach the Fort Chipewyan area was a Methodist, Robert T. Rundle, who visited the Hudson's Bay Company fort there in 1841 and whose diary foreshadows the kind of hardship that was to come. Here he is on a winter night on Lesser Slave Lake, March 2, 1842:

Bishop Emile Grouard later in life. He translated the Indian and Eskimo dialects, established schools and left his name on a town.

What a gloomy prospect was before us; our own provisions almost exhausted and none at all for the dogs. Went ashore at Big Point, rested the dogs and supped. Started again at nine o'clock, intending to travel all night as our circumstances were desperate. After proceeding about two hours, the wind shifted and snow fell heavily. Heavens clouded, very cold, wind NW, the cold compelled me to get out of my cariole; and what a dreadful prospect I beheld beggars description...It was so dreadful that at last our guide made for the shore; which we providentially reached at a place where we found some dry willows to make a fire.

The following day:

Dogs starving and eating the ends of the sledges. At dusk we started again. Terribly cold at night, and the men were so fatigued they were falling asleep on the ice, and Mr. MacD. was afraid we would freeze to death. The dogs held out better than we expected; my toes were almost frozen, and I was compelled to get out and walk, though I had no snowshoes.

His party found a cabin and food, and survived. But

Rundle's whole effort in the North could not be followed up because the Methodist manpower was not available. Six years later, however, another clergyman arrived at Chipewyan in the person of Fr. Alexandre-Antonin Tache. Behind his name were the letters OMI, and he was the forerunner of an army.

The Oblates, organized in France in 1816, had been called to Canada in 1847 and assigned to establish the North-West missions. Fr. Jean Thibault (Vol. 1, p. 74) was the first to arrive in the Edmonton area in 1842. Many came from the French gentry, had no experience of physical hardship, and discovered themselves in an unforgiving wilderness doing work that demanded endless travel over raging rivers, or in fly-infested swamps, or through blizzards, hailstorms, or days of rain, in country where settlements were spaced by hundreds of miles. Some perished, some were retired exhausted, many lived to ripe old age, never leaving the lands and the peoples to whom

Bishop Faraud then puts his co-adjutor bishop, Isadore Clut, in charge of the new barges, with a crew of experienced voyageurs for the downstream journey to Chipewyan. With him are two new priests from France, two prospective lay brothers, a Grey Nuns postulant called Marie Marguerite, and a little orphan girl to be raised by the sisters at Fort Chip. At the head of the Grand Rapids, the voyageurs take one look at the rapids and quit, walking back to Lac la Biche. Marie Marguerite meanwhile has become gravely ill. Bishop Clut, leaving her and the child in the care of a priest, strikes overland with the rest of the party to Fort McMurray, which is half-way to Fort Chip. He takes three weeks to round up another crew and they return upriver to the barges.

The ailing Marie Marguerite, now much worse, is carried over the portage as the boats are worked through the Grand Rapids. The other big rapids from there to Fort McMurray

---

Father Grouard became a byword as he braved hunger, danger and every form of hardship. Upon his death the town of Lesser Slave Lake was renamed for him.

---

they had devoted their lives.

Their names — Lacombe, Grouard, Faraud, Clut, Tissier — have become part of the folk history of northern Alberta, but their stories survive in the registers of the Oblate Order: Fr. Felix Marchand, murdered at Frog Lake; Fr. Leo Fafard, murdered at Frog Lake; Fr. Benedict Bremond, drowned in the rapids of the Slave; Fr. Joseph Brohan, drowned in the rapids of the Slave; Bro. Alexis Reynard, vanished on a journey between missions. So runs the record, which carries too the stories of those who survived and lived to tell of it. For example:

Christmas 1869 — Bishop Henri Faraud, having established the Grey Nuns at Fort Providence, where Great Slave Lake flows into the Mackenzie River, discovers he must head back to his headquarters at Lac la Biche in the future Alberta because the Hudson's Bay Company can no longer handle freight for his missions. He therefore dog-teams across the ice of Great Slave Lake, ascends the Slave River to Chipewyan, crosses frozen Lake Athabasca to the Athabasca River which he skirts on its upstream course past the frightful Grand Rapids to La Biche River, then ascends to Lac la Biche and his mission. He has now covered about 1,300 miles and has been travelling for nine weeks.

A carpenter himself, he organizes the construction of special scows to take church supplies from Lac la Biche back down the Athabasca, through the 100 miles of rapids between La Biche River and Fort McMurray. Freight scows have never been able to negotiate the perilous middle Athabasca before. At the same time, he dispatches fourteen Metis drivers under a lay brother to head overland and get the supplies at Fort Carlton on the North Saskatchewan. The drivers come down with smallpox and only six survive the journey, but the goods are delivered.

bring further terrors, then the rest of the trip is completed over the calm waters between McMurray and Fort Chipewyan. The nun is carried ashore and dies a few days later at the mission.

Since Clut has shown that freight scows can manage the Grand Rapids, the following year the church organizes a regular freight service from Lac La Biche downstream. However, a scow carrying only passengers had made the trip three years before. The passengers were a group of Grey Nuns, who had already sustained a two-month overland trip to Lac la Biche and now faced the rigours of the Athabasca. The women, waist-deep in the water, had to help the voyageurs manoeuvre the boats through the roaring cascades. These women would found the first hospitals in the North.

Schools and hospitals appeared as the missions were established, and the church's freighting problems grew. By the turn of the century, it had built two steamboats: one, called the *St. Charles*, on the Peace River, the other, the *St. Joseph*, on the Athabasca and upper Slave. By 1910 its schools and hospitals were staffed by scores of lay brothers and nuns, its missions by more than 100 priests, all with the letters OMI after their names.

Senior among them was a little man with a flowing white beard whose name was to become a byword in the North for 69 years as he braved every form of hardship, hunger and danger, criss-crossing the territory in summer and winter. This was Fr. Emile Grouard, made bishop in 1890 and archbishop in 1930, a year before his death at the age of 91. He translated the Indian and Eskimo dialects, published books in their languages, and established and supervised schools and missions throughout the entire northland. Upon his death the town of Lesser Slave Lake was renamed Grouard.

Only the Anglicans attempted to match such an onslaught. Although their numbers were fewer, their efforts were rewarded with remarkable success. The stories of Bompas, their founding northern bishop, were preserved chiefly in folklore. His own journal is too laconic for story-telling. An example: "I have nearly frozen and nearly drowned this winter already." No detail is provided. However, the distances he travelled equalled those of most Oblates. Like them, he had at least once been forced to eat his own moccasins to survive, and like them he established an extraordinary number of churches.

The Anglican effort in the far North began in 1858, eleven years after the Oblates started at Chipewyan. But the Anglican initiative began at Fort Simpson, where the Liard River flows into the Mackenzie. There the church under HBC auspices stationed a series of missionaries over the next seven years, the fourth being Bompas. He soon was made bishop and other men were sent to help him. They spread southward, establishing missions as they came. In 1876, the Rev. Alfred C. Garrioch opened a church at Fort Vermilion on the Peace River and an Anglican school for native children was started by Mr. and Mrs. E.J. Lawrence. A brother of the teacher, Henry Lawrence, took up farming near Fort Vermilion, proving that grain could be grown in latitudes only slightly south of Greenland. Henry's son, Sheridan, would be known to future Albertans as the Grand Old Man of the Peace River country.

Provincial Archives of Alberta, A-3325

Bishop W.C. Bompas. Like many, he was forced to eat his moccasins to survive.

ministering to, claiming as well their daughter.

But the story of the Anglican mission in the North was probably best told by a woman identified as Jessie Holmes, who came with her husband, an Anglican priest, from comfortable southern England to the Peace River missions in 1902. Her recollections, set forth in the Spring 1964 edition of the *Alberta Historical Review,* describe graphically what happens when a well-bred Englishwoman meets the harsh reality of the Canadian North — leaving the railhead at Edmonton on the back of a wagon in a downpour; horses waist deep in the mudholes of the Athabasca Trail; nearly swept downstream as they ford the swollen Vermilion River because the bridge has been washed out; unable to sleep on the floor of an abandoned shack because things keep brushing her face (they turn out to be mice); almost drowned in a canoe crossing Lesser Slave Lake; learning to cook bear steaks, moose meat, deer cutlets, ducks, geese, saskatoon pie and a dozen other exotic foods until she became superb at it; washing and scrubbing, ironing and sewing for fifty Indian boys and girls at the school at Lesser Slave Lake; fighting measles and whooping cough with every device known to primitive medicine and (praise God!) actually winning because only one child in the school was lost and her own child, though very near death, was saved (she is sure) by a miracle; and finally realizing after many years that this strange and forbidding land is now her own.

Such were the missions to the North, for which before

Bompas' own journal is too laconic for story-telling. 'I have nearly frozen and nearly drowned this winter already,' he writes. No detail is provided.

While the Anglican experience lacked the spectacular elements that so distinguish the Catholic Oblates, it nevertheless bespoke an undeniable integrity of faith. The missionary Garrioch moved from Fort Vermilion to Dunvegan, where he and his wife, Alice, watched in helpless agony while measles and whooping cough in a single season wiped out nearly the entire Beaver Indian band they were

the end of the century some churches would find themselves apologizing. But that would occur in another era, when technology had cloaked nature's ferocity, and when the heroic age of the churches had vanished with the past or had been lost in a fog of new theologies.

— *V.B.*

meetings. They had included W.E. Martin, the magistrate at Irvine (referred to as "Satan's judge") and Martin had indeed gone missing.

The prisoners, who seemed to have defective memories on many points, denied everything. They read only the Bible and sang hymns. They never mentioned dreams except ones like Jacob's in the Bible, and had not set fire to Lehr's house. They had no idea why they were known as Dreamers — that was not their name. After two weeks the prosecution gave up and withdrew the charges, although one man was immediately re-arrested, convicted of perjury and sentenced to two years in jail. There was so much conflicting evidence, observed RNWMP Captain William Parker, who presided, that others too had come close to perjury charges. He bound over the remaining eight accused to keep the peace.[9]

Notwithstanding the alleged proclivities of the Dreamers, the Protestant immigration brought

One of the Methodist preachers called dancing dissipation. 'Why? Because it is at night, in a hot unhealthy room, when people ought to be asleep. It has killed many young people.'

with it a strong sense of morality, private and public, and of service. The Lord's Day Act, prohibiting "trade" on Sunday, was the result of persistent lobbying of Parliament by churches and the Lord's Day Alliance on behalf of what had been known in Britain as the "working class," many of whom were being required to work seven days a week. Until the act clarified the law, Sunday work was prohibited by local legislation, often difficult to enforce. Thus William Brennan of the Alberta Hotel barber shop was accused in 1904 of "shaving Mr. Curry, the Eighth Avenue druggist," on Sunday, Oct. 16. The trial was hampered because of another case currently before the Supreme Court of Canada. Other charges continued to be laid. In 1905, when the townsite lots at Stettler had been auctioned and seven lumber yards could scarcely keep up with the demand for building material, the local Mountie arrested carpenters for working on Sunday.

The Lord's Day Act finally came into force March 1, 1907. In April the newspapers reported "a sensation among the Puritanical section" of the Strathcona City Council over an application to make baths available on Sunday at the Strathcona House. Supplying baths to the public was in the nature of trade, councillors objected, and baths on Sunday were not necessary. The mayor and other councillors were more sympathetic, however, and they sent the request on to a committee. What finally happened to it, the newspapers did not report.

Elizabeth Mitchell notes the energetic activities of another puritanical group, the Woman's Christian Temperance Union and is puzzled because she sees "so little visible drunkenness" in most towns. "The use of strong liquors is not, as at home, intimately associated with the social life of the majority of the population, but a detached and not too respectable habit." Possibly the reformers were already having an effect. The clergy from 1900 to 1910 inveighed against drink and other "social evils" with increasing stridency, and Prohibition came in during the next decade (see ch. 10).

An indignant 1905 sermon at McDougall Methodist in Edmonton, reported in detail by newspapers both there and in Calgary, was typical. The Rev. C.M. Huestis described how two innocent young men had been skinned at poker by an unscrupulous local hotelkeeper. "There is another hotel in this city," he continued, "which though bearing a fine sounding name is nothing less than a dive. Whiskey is not the worst thing that you find there. Everyone who knows could tell you stories of midnight revels held there that are not pleasant. That hotel will ask for a renewal of its licence on Tuesday." Another McDougall speaker warned a packed and attentive audience of the evils of dancing. Some people call dancing a relaxing diversion, he said, but "I call it a dissipation. Why? Because it is at night, in a hot unhealthy room when people ought to be asleep. It has killed many young people, who have gone to a dance and caught cold which later developed into pneumonia."

One mighty crusader against social evil was the Rev. Charles McKillop, renowned in Lethbridge in the 1890s as "the fighting parson" or "the devil dodger," who waged steady war on liquor, gambling and prostitution. McKillop, who had trained as a boxer and worked in Ontario and Quebec logging camps, had very persuasive ways. His friend John D. Higinbotham, the

[9] "We have a detachment in the Dreamer settlement and have had constant day and night patrols," wrote RNWMP Superintendent J.O. Wilson in his 1908 report. "Although we were unable to connect these people with the burning of Lehr's house, their arrest has had a good effect." Magistrate Martin turned up alive after all, having apparently disappeared for reasons of his own, under cover of the Dreamer threats. Things gradually settled down around Josephburg, and the Dreamers seem to have adopted more usual Adventist ways.

William Jennings Bryan. He came to Calgary in 1909 and preached the gospel of the YMCA.

This is the last time you are allowed to torture God, you bloodhound. For many years you have lived on my goods and now you want to destroy God. We will see whose word will come true, God's word or the Devil's word, you dog. You have no share on my earth or anything that therein is, for she belongs to the Lord.
- *example of the type of letter sent by "God Jacob," leader of the Dreamers cult near Medicine Hat, to neighbours in 1908.*

pharmacist, recounts one notable McKillop encounter in his memoir, *When the West Was Young*. McKillop was making a ministerial call on a new family, although he had been warned by a neighbour that they were "dreadful people" who would kill him. He found the householder nailing down flooring with the back of a broadaxe. "Get to hell out of here," the man roared. "What business have you preachers to come around here when you think the menfolk are away at their work?"

"None of your vile insinuations, or I'll give you a lesson you will not soon forget," retorted McKillop. "Put down that axe...Now get up and sit on that chair." Assessing the hefty minister, the bemused man obeyed. Then McKillop noticed a girl peering round the doorway. "Is that your daughter?" Yes, the man allowed, it was his daughter Rosie. "Come in, Rosie, and sit beside your father," McKillop invited. "We're going to have worship." This they proceeded to do, and the family also began attending Knox Presbyterian Church.[10]

McKillop and other ministers also made memorable appearances before the city council, urging action to shut down the Lethbridge red-light district and rescue the "soiled doves" who worked there (Vol. 1, p. 43). That "social evil" kept right on, however. In July 1910 the *Lethbridge Herald* reported "a men's mass meeting" of the Temperance and Moral Reform League at the Baptist Church. The pastor, A.J. Prosser, had accompanied the police to the "segregated district" and found it contained "at least five houses of ill-fame with thirty inmates." Although the mayor had promised no more building would be allowed there, one house was a recent addition. Furthermore, a resident had told Prosser that their best customers were "the married men of this city and not the unmarried ones."

Some $1,500 in fines had been levied for illegal sale of liquor in these houses, he noted. Why no other arrests? The league must apply further pressure on council and police. The street leading to the district should be brilliantly lighted. No new prostitutes should be allowed into town. The houses of ill-fame should be raided, both the women and their customers arrested, and upon conviction their names should be published.

Such ministerial strictures were not taken in good part by everyone. Bob Edwards of the *Eye Opener* indignantly informed his readers in June 1902 that the new young Presbyterian minister at High River, C.D. Campbell, had been trying to reform *him*. The *Eye Opener* was "unfit to be admitted to a decent home," Campbell had told Edwards. It should be elevating and uplifting the community. ("Lead, kindly *Eye Opener*, amid th' encircling booze," was the editor's acerbic comment.) Unless the paper changed its moral tone, the minister threatened, "there would be war."

It didn't, and there was — with Edwards tearing strips off Campbell in column after column. Busybody, mischief-maker and meddler were some of the appellations he applied, along with suitable adjectives such as tactless, offensive, conceited and arrogant. Campbell had also presumed to lecture the local magistrate on his duties, Edwards claimed. He had berated a popular polo player for playing on Sunday. He had accused the High River liveryman of charging him an "exorbitant" fee, although actually, as a parson, he'd been given a special price. He had told leading citizen Jerry Boyce, a divorced man, that he had no business speaking to a single lady on the street, and the town would be better off without him.

"How Dr. Herdman, superintendent of the Western Presbyterian Diocese, ever came to send such a fresh sample to a place like High River, where freshness is the last thing tolerated, will always remain a mystery to this community," Edwards commented. "We may now look for Campbell to assume a martyr-like air and get off spiels about fighting sin in High River, but he may take it straight from us that being a good able-bodied sinner is decidedly preferable to being a damned fool."

But with most western citizens in the century's first decade, their clergy wielded a great deal of moral clout. Elizabeth Mitchell felt that Sunday church-going in the cities was more strictly practised than in England or Scotland. And the clerics got credit for good works of other kinds, notably hospitals and individual help and handouts. Generally speaking, says observer Mitchell, "anyone could be set on his feet by a meal or two...only the sick needed more."

For temporary help people often applied directly to priests and ministers who, poor as they usually were themselves, managed to take care of most emergencies or find someone who could. The Grey Nuns were leaders in care of the sick, founding Edmonton's first hospital in 1896, Holy Cross Hospital in Calgary in 1892, and additionally supplying their nursing skills wherever they seemed needed. When smallpox struck in Calgary, for example, the sisters improvised an isolation ward in tents on Nose Hill. The Methodists, too, carried on strongly in the medical missionary tradition.

Also on the scene was the Salvation Army, with its no-nonsense message and its practical help for the socially and economically lost. The Army began work in Calgary in 1887, says W.E. Mann in *Sect, Cult and Church in Alberta*, and enlisted 24 soldiers in the first month. By 1909 it had spread to several towns and had enrolled a thousand Alberta supporters. On a somewhat higher social level, the Young Men's Christian Association and its female counterpart the YWCA, were very important in the cities. As Mrs. Mitchell notes, they provided "pleasant company as well as shelter" for the hundreds of young men and women who were pouring in.

In 1908 Edmonton's YMCA, operating entirely on public subscription and with the Protestant clergy much involved, opened a three-storey building that housed "social" rooms, classrooms and a lunchroom. In the classrooms subjects like bookkeeping, shorthand and languages were taught. There was sleeping accommodation for fifty, and a gymnasium and swimming pool. When noted American politician and evangelist William Jennings Bryan came by in 1909 on a western lecture tour, Calgary took the opportunity to launch a $50,000 campaign to complete its YMCA building, including overnight accommodation for forty. "Civilization is the harmonious development of body, mind and soul," Bryan told his audience. "The YMCA, of which I have been a member since my young manhood, is a mark of civilization."[11]

Despite all the religious devotion and effort, however, some thoughtful westerners were wondering how well "civilization" really was doing in the early 20th century. In the world beyond their borders, scepticism was gripping the intelligentsia and "modernism" taking hold of the Christian churches. The city clergy noticed that young men, distracted either by urban temptations or seduced by godless philosophies, were absent from their congregations. "Dean Farrar and other clergymen are raising a loud wail over desertion of the churches particularly by young men," observed the *Calgary Herald* in 1902. But what, the editor wondered, was the remedy? The churches were trying to make themselves "centres of social reunion," but such expedients could go only so far: "There is no use in thinking that anything can recall the truants or arrest the exodus but the restoration of belief."

Such foreboding seemed ill founded then. Cities right across the West, for example, lionized Bryan in 1909. In Edmonton, Calgary and Lethbridge crowds of admirers met the Great Commoner at the railway station. Several hundred bought tickets for a YMCA luncheon. Thousands gave him standing ovations at his evening speech, entitled "The Prince of Peace." What's more, intellectuals and opinion makers were well represented. Lieutenant-Governor

'Civilization is the harmonious development of body, mind and soul,' said Bryan. 'The YMCA is a mark of civilization.'

George Bulyea gave a reception for Mr. and Mrs. Bryan. University of Alberta president Henry M. Tory moved the vote of thanks at his Edmonton speech.

Many Albertans doubtless agreed with Bryan's political views on "the tariff, the trusts and the plutocracy," but it was his evangelical Christian views that won their hearts, as the *Calgary Herald* reported in a detailed account. Bryan too was concerned about the future. "It has even been suggested that advanced thought has disproved the belief there is a God," he observed, and he had prepared his lecture — in the hope of "shaming young men who scoff."

Not for another five decades, however, would "men who scoff" gain significant ascendancy in Alberta.

[10] The Rev. Charles McKillop of Lethbridge did not normally make his converts with his fists, but he certainly enjoyed fighting. When he was 57 he added ju-jitsu to his repertoire, says Jacques Hamilton in *Our Alberta Heritage*. That enabled him to throw the town's gigantic waterman, Charlie Hyssop, twice in a friendly bout in 1907, much to Hyssop's distress. But that was McKillop's last fight. He died a few months later.

[11] William Jennings Bryan (1860-1925), Nebraska newspaper owner and populist politician, was elected to Congress in 1890 but thrice defeated as Democratic candidate for the US presidency (1896, 1900, 1908). He then became a popular lecturer, and his 1909 tour of the West on behalf of the YMCA was a resounding success. Many prairie audiences doubtless sympathized with Bryan's radical agrarian politics, but on this tour he wasn't talking politics, but straight Christian evangelism. "I will still be in the church a long time after I am no longer in politics," he told them.

279

Transforming wild country into the perfect garden

THE RANCHERS JOINED PROTESTANT MAINLINERS IN OPPOSING MORMONISM BUT WITH THE FIRST IRRIGATION CANAL, THE MOOD BEGAN TO CHANGE

The immigration of Mormons into southern Alberta remained a hot issue after 1900. They would never fit in, their detractors maintained. With them, they said, the Mormons were undoubtedly bringing, albeit secretly, their commitment to polygamous marriage, a threat to Canadian family structure. Moreover, contended leaders of the dominant Protestant churches, they would always be Mormons first and Canadians second, in mindless thrall to the hierarchy of the Church of Jesus Christ of Latter-day Saints. True, the families that settled the Cardston district in 1887 and the few that followed had proven to be hard workers and excellent farmers. However, declared Professor T.B. Kilpatrick of Knox College, at a Toronto Presbyterian church in 1907, "it is not enough to say they grow good crops...Do they grow good Canadians?"

LDS immigration had powerful defenders, however. One was the dominion government, anxious to populate the arid southern plains. And as time went on the Saints gained some non-powerful defenders too: other settlers, who found them excellent neighbours, and even the newspapers. Said the *Calgary Herald* in 1901: "The whole of southern Alberta contiguous to the boundary line is given over to them, and they have transformed a wild country into a perfect garden."

But the ruckus had slowed Mormon settlement. Anxiety about polygamy increased in 1888 when the Cardston settlers asked Ottawa for permission to bring to Canada the plural wives they had left behind. They were refused. Instead, fearful of importing a practice that had caused so much trouble in Utah (Vol. 1, p. 242), parliament raised the Criminal Code penalty for "unlawful cohabitation" from two years to five in 1890. That year the LDS president issued a manifesto stating he would encourage members to enter into no new marriages that were contrary to the "law of the land." Nevertheless, writes Jessie L. Embry in the historical anthology entitled *The Mormon Presence in Canada*, polygamous marriages were secretly performed by Canadian church officials for the next fourteen years.

Brigham Y. Card in the same anthology contends that polygamy was not the real problem. The US anti-polygamy campaign masked a federal effort to bring the LDS "commonwealth" under control, he writes. Similar factors were present

in Canada. The church wanted to get blocks of land, for example, both to keep its people together and to enable irrigation schemes to begin. Ranchers, anticipating limitation of their grazing lands, objected. So did many other citizens, mistrustful of the Saints' apparent ability to act as a group, and also of such a substantial American presence.

The efforts of the Cardston settlers in the 1890s to incorporate a joint stock company, to provide gristmills, sawmills and irrigation, caused public meetings in Lethbridge, Macleod and Pincher Creek, and a petition to government not to allow the Mormons to become more of a "corporate, political and religious unit" than they already were. With the help of Macleod

A group of Magrath Mormons picnicking. Reports of polygamy were somewhat overstated.

lawyer (and later territorial premier) Frederick Haultain, however, and the influence of C.A. Magrath who represented the Galt interests, the Saints got their company.

The first major irrigation project, a fifty-mile canal running southeast from Kimball on the St. Mary River, was the turning point that established Mormon credibility. The Galts had the necessary political clout, Magrath managed to raise British capital and in 1897 the contractor became the LDS church. The Mormons had plenty of experience with irrigation farming in Utah's Great Basin, and with small Alberta efforts of their own. Cardston founder Charles Ora Card was regarded as an expert. Besides, they could supply the labour.

So the sub-contractors on the job were would-be Mormon settlers who responded to a church campaign in Utah and

Idaho. Half their pay was in money, half in land. When church leaders felt the canal still wasn't getting on fast enough, says historian Howard Palmer in *Land of the Second Chance*, they augmented the volunteer system with "calls" (i.e. direct assignments) issued to selected families. Mormon immigration picked up enormously. When Magrath and the church completed their canal in 1900 there were some 3,000 Mormon settlers in southern Alberta. They kept right on coming until 1908, when most of the land was taken up. They soon began organizing more irrigation projects, but they also got into ranching and a variety of other businesses.

moving in. Although years of drought caused serious hardship, eventually another irrigation system would be installed and three towns founded. C.A. Magrath, by now first mayor of Lethbridge, encouraged Raymond interests to put up a flour mill there, the Ellison Milling and Elevator Company. Several hundred Saints moved into town. A string of supply elevators was added later.

Despite these accomplishments (or possibly because of them), some hostility persisted. Palmer blames the Presbyterian and Methodist churches, dominant in southern Alberta, for keeping it alive. The Presbyterians sent missionaries among

---

The rumour that her father had 24 wives was a yarn. 'You know, Jessie, he never had more than fourteen at any time.'

The town of Raymond had, to borrow some slang from a future era, a sugar daddy. Jesse Knight, wealthy Utah mine owner, sent his two sons north early in 1901 to check on ranching possibilities, and bought 30,000 acres northeast of Magrath. But when he came up himself that spring he saw sugar beet country there, not ranchland. He immediately bought thousands more acres, arranged for irrigation, and contracted to build a $500,000 beet sugar factory — thus inaugurating the Alberta sugar industry.

Within weeks the Knights had brought in men and eighty teams of horses to start ploughing. The townsite of Raymond was laid out, named for Jesse Knight's older son. Mormon immigrants poured in, encountering many of the usual hazards. Hannah Gibb and her five children, for example, arrived in a blizzard Sept. 5 and, as a local history recounts, "that night her cow had twin calves and both froze to death." Mrs. Gibb became "Grandma Gibb," the community's premier mid-wife, who "delivered hundreds of babies and never lost a case."

Raymond, its town charter forbidding liquor, gambling and houses of ill fame, soon had running water (piped from a stream two miles away), church, school, stores, flour mill, electricity (1907) and an opera house (1909). Leading citizen Raymond Knight brought in heavy work horses from England, loaning or selling them to Mormon farmers. A cowboy himself, he is credited by local lore with organizing Alberta's first stampede and also the two-horse race — the riders standing with one foot on each of two galloping horses. Although leading citizens were important, however, they were probably no more important than ordinary Mormon settlers who made a new life and a new land. Elizabeth Munn, daughter of the first family at Raymond, summed it up years later: "I married Alphonzo L. McMullin Sept. 27, 1904, and we have lived here ever since and have done what we could to build up the community."

In 1906 Alberta Stake president E.J. Wood bought for the church a huge Cochrane Ranch holding, some 200 square miles, between the Belly and Waterton Rivers; settlers began

the Saints to convert them to more orthodox beliefs, which was fair enough; the LDS church was a notable evangelizer itself.[a] Less legitimate and most unChristian were efforts to manipulate the law to thwart and limit them, as when a Lethbridge women's group tried to prohibit them from buying land within ten miles of the city. So were the campaigns of denunciation carried on by both denominations through their national papers, pamphlets and public pronouncements.

Thus Prof. Kilpatrick's 1907 speech, in which he also described Mormon settlement as "the greatest grief in Alberta." It caused an indignant reaction in Alberta, where the *Calgary Albertan* and *Lethbridge Herald* published several columns of local endorsements. H.A. Donovan, an Anglican and "brother-in-law of the Very Rev. Archdeacon of Shrewsbury," said he'd lived among Mormons for twenty years and was of the opinion that "take them all around, they are the best settlers in Alberta." Another Anglican noted they celebrated Dominion Day "in hearty regal style," and in his opinion were "Britons first and Mormons after."

The newspapers gave the last word to Alberta Stake president Wood. In a long letter he emphasized his people's desire to live in peace and respect with their neighbours, and their determination to be loyal Canadian citizens and British subjects. His own father, he noted, was a Crimean War veteran. As for Prof. Kilpatrick's question whether they grew good Canadians, "I would say yes, and in a much larger geometrical ratio than many of our neighbours do. There is no 'race suicide' where the people live their religion. Cardston's population numbers some 1,200, of whom more than one-third are under eight years of age." — *V.B.*

[a]Although Presbyterian missionaries seem to have made few converts, they were amiably received. The Rev. Gavin Hamilton was sent in 1897 to preach in Cardston, where he and his wife, Jessie, became good friends of the Card family and other leading Saints. An anecdote credited to Mrs. Hamilton in *Prairie Grass and Mountain Pass*, however, must be apocryphal. A Cardston friend supposedly confided in Mrs. Hamilton there was a nasty story going around that her father had twenty-four wives at once. Never mind, replied Jessie Hamilton, "it's just a yarn." Indeed it was, said the friend: "You know, Jessie, he never had more than fourteen at any time."

The McKay School, Edmonton, 1908. The change from ignorance to knowledge was as much a revolution as that from wilderness to farmland.

An army of young women brought education to Alberta

BOOKS WERE SCARCE, PAY UNCERTAIN, PARENTS SOMETIMES HOSTILE, AND HOUSING OFTEN HIDEOUS, BUT THE SCHOOLS FASHIONED A SOCIETY

by VIRGINIA BYFIELD

It was partly the promise of the vast unknown, teacher Pamela Appleby recalled many years later — the idea of venturing forth alone into Canada's great north-west. And maybe too it was the horse — something she had always wanted — that lured her from her ordered classroom in London, England, to a frontier teaching job that was often thrilling and sometimes, frankly, hideous.

Miss Appleby found herself on a slow train from Calgary to Morrin, a branchline whistle stop 60 miles (96 km) to the northeast, to be the new teacher at Hillsgreen School. Where, she wondered, would she be living? She soon found out: at the home of the school board secretary-treasurer — where she had to share a bed with one of his daughters (a very fat girl).

At school she faced a roomful of pupils, aged five to sixteen. Some had books, many did not. It seemed there was nothing anyone could do about that. Never mind, said she, she would somehow provide lessons. But could the trustees get her something, some handiwork perhaps, to keep the little beginners busy while she was teaching their older brothers and sisters? Certainly not, was the answer: "We don't want any fancy stuff here." And there was the matter of her salary; the trustees had meant to talk to her about that. Unfortunately, they could afford to pay her only a fraction of it. Times, explained the secretary-treasurer, were hard.

The unhappy teacher therefore spent the last fifty dollars of her savings on a little mare called Bessie, to fulfil her longtime dream and gain needed transport. This enraged her landlord, the secretary-treasurer. How dare she? He had scarcely pasture enough for his own animals.

So this was the Canadian West? Homesick and heartsick, Miss Appleby would often go out to the pasture, wrap her arms around Bessie's neck, and weep into the mare's mane.

Pamela Appleby's story, recounted years later to Alberta education historian John C. Charyk (*Syrup Pails and Gopher Tails: Memories of the One-Room School*) was far from unique in the century's first decade.[1] Hundreds of young women like her — along with a much smaller male contingent — were fanning out across the southern half of the province as the effective shock troops of two revolutions: the change from wilderness to settlement, and the change from ignorance to knowledge.

The latter was no less of a revolution than the former. Although the notion of "universal education" or "common schools" was barely fifty years old anywhere, most western settlers were determined to get their children educated. Since the 1880s settlers had been putting together little frame or log buildings on a few donated acres, equipping them as best they could, and hiring a teacher.

Catholic and Protestant missionaries had been running schools in the north-west for forty years before that. A free public school was built in Edmonton in 1881, for about fifty pupils of all ages and hues, and financed by private subscription for three years. But education wasn't keeping pace with settlement. By 1884, says education historian John W. Chalmers in *Schools of the Foothills Province*, the Territorial Council had received petitions for the establishment of 65 schools but had no legislative framework to accommodate them.

Premier Frederick Haultain, who regarded "common schools" as a top priority, right up there with roads and bridges, was entirely sympathetic. The territorial council passed "an Ordinance Providing for the Organization of Schools in the North-West Territories," enabling school districts to be registered, and their trustees to set and collect a local school tax. The territorial government, despite its chronic shortage of money, would provide grants of $250 to $350 per teacher, and $2 for every child who attended at least 100 days a year. It set up a Board of Education with two sections, Protestant and Catholic, each controlling curriculum, teacher appointments and inspection of its own schools. Appropriate clergymen served as inspectors, reporting to their own section of the board.[2]

But the percentage of Protestants in the territories was steadily increasing; they distrusted the

Pioneer teacher Pamela Appleby. One of the education shock troops.

[1] In most rural schools pioneering conditions (or at least semi-pioneering) would prevail for decades to come. Former teacher Blanche Coultis of Brooks, for example, described for historian John C. Charyk the teacherage at Brown SD (near Pollockville in the remote eastern Alberta drylands) where she and her sister lived as late as 1935-36: an uninsulated one-room shack "covered with rubberoid" and heated by a big wood-burning range. This kept them warm if they sat with their feet in the oven; it also once set fire to the wall. From a well half a mile away they lugged water that "had a bad odour and left a red sediment in the pail."

[2] Notable among the 19th century territorial school inspectors was the Rev. D.G. McQueen, appointed in 1887 for Edmonton area Protestant schools. Presbyterian McQueen campaigned for better buildings and teetotal teachers and trustees. E.A. Corbett in *McQueen of Edmonton* quotes an 1889 letter of his: "I may go to the meeting and if I do I will make it pretty hot for M___ ___ and a saloon-keeper who disgraces the Board by his presence among the members." M___ ___ was the teacher, Major Stiff, who did indeed get fired. But the saloonkeeper was hotelman Donald Ross, who got a school named after him, in fact an entire downtown district of Edmonton, Rossdale.

Snapshot of Pamela Appleby with her horse and students. Her roomful of pupils were aged five to sixteen. Some even had books.

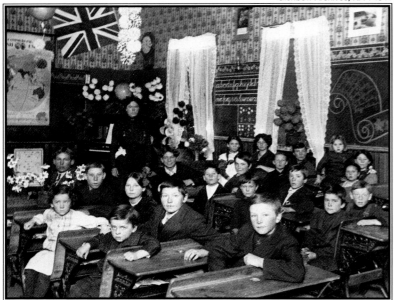

Interior of Harvey SD 1597, Vulcan. With a teacher identified only as Miss Boler in the background. Non-denominational education was considered the ideal.

influence of the Catholic church in education, and they were disproportionately influential. They could hardly oust one church from education, however, without ousting them all. Thus the Protestants chose a public school system under strictly secular authority, doubtless assuming it would remain sufficiently Protestant anyhow. In 1893 the elected Territorial Assembly (successor to the Territorial Council) replaced the two-section Board of Education with a Council of Public Instruction, functioning under new regulations.

Religious teaching was allowed in the last half-hour of the day and French (grudgingly) as a language of instruction (see sidebar story). But the Council of Public Instruction was to control teacher training and qualifications, textbooks, examinations and inspection for all schools. The council actually met as a whole only once, however, in 1893. Haultain, who was both premier and education minister, was constituted a quorum of one for its executive committee.

Haultain was an Anglican and a firm believer in non-denominational education. He hired David J. Goggin, an Orangeman and 33rd-degree Mason, as territorial superintendent of education, including teacher training and examinations. Goggin assembled a staff of university-trained, non-clergy school inspectors (seven of them by 1902), stumped the territories holding two-day "teachers' institutes" and making public speeches. He became very popular. In 1897 a sorehead

Where would she be living? She soon found out: at the home of the secretary-treasurer where she was to share a bed with one of his daughters — a fat girl.

assembly resolution to reduce his $3,000 salary (more than the premier got) to $2,500 was rejected out of hand. Goggin dominated education in the north-west, says Chalmers, until he resigned in 1902, citing "personal and financial" reasons.

Meanwhile a final territorial ordinance in 1901 replaced the Council of Public Instruction with a Department of Education, accelerated the centralizing and secularizing process, and further restricted Catholic schools. Four years later this question of whether separate schools would be allowed when the provinces of Alberta and Saskatchewan were carved out of the North-West Territories — and if so, on what terms — became a national issue, the most contentious that Sir Wilfrid Laurier's Liberal government had to face. In the end, however, the Alberta Act made no essential change. The basic 1901 framework would endure for the rest of the century (see Sect. I, ch. 2).

Because of these efforts, by the time Alberta became a province in 1905 there were 562 schools within its new borders, 1,210 teachers, and more than 34,000 pupils. Hundreds more schools would be added by 1910.[3] And if most of them were something less than pedagogical palaces, the pupils and their parents thought themselves lucky to have a school at all. They were right; it represented quite an achievement. Any three rate-payers could form a committee and petition to form a school district in an area not exceeding five miles in any direction — if the area contained at least eight school-age children. In the countryside, which was where well over half the children were, that was the first hurdle. One rural committee in 1889, possessing only seven prospective pupils, added the name of a youthful new bride. She had no intention whatever of attending school, but the authorities needn't know that. Anyhow, another homesteader with two youngsters soon moved in.

The committee had to get agreement on a site and put the project to a ratepayer vote. Opposition and misunderstandings abounded. "I cannot see why I should be compelled to give any

Whereas the cost of living has very materially increased during the past two years, we find that our present salary is not adequate to meet the increased expenditure. In view of this and as wages have advanced in all other lines of work, we would ask the trustees for an increase of ten dollars a month to our present salaries. During the past years we have endeavoured to give faithful service and believe that the trustees have appreciated our efforts, and will recognize the justice of our request.
- Letter from eight Edmonton teachers requesting a raise, Jan. 20, 1904.

LIFE IN A NEW PROVINCE

land to build the school house," says a 1903 letter to education commissioner W.J. Miller, reprinted in the account of Cheadle-Carseland District *Trails to the Bow*, "...I know you cannot compel me to give it...Hoping this will not make enemies of us, I remain yours respectfully, Mrs. J. Belwer." Mrs. Belwer was correct, of course, but there may have been some neighbourhood pressure.

Bachelor homesteaders, possessed of no children and reluctant to pay school tax of ten cents an acre or so, were a particular concern to school committees, but community spirit usually prevailed. In an *Alberta Historical Review* article, Mrs. M.I. McKenzie describes how her father organized a school district southeast of Innisfail in 1902. Although the deciding vote lay with a bachelor, in the event he did the right thing. In fact, she says, Millner School was actually named after another member of "the bachelor fraternity" who helped to build it.

Then there was the school's name, another delicate matter. The committee would try to get local approval; the government authorities would pick one and attach a number. The result was always informative, Charyk observes, one way or another. Netherby SD 2348, north of Hanna, for example, was named for the English birthplace of several settlers; Springbank for a Calgary brook; Big Rock for the Okotoks erratic boulder; Gumbo, at Twining, for the prairie mud; Princess and Patricia, in southeastern Alberta, for royalty; Lundberg, near Cereal, for the Lund and Berg families; Priddis for the High River settler who donated the site; Aberdeen, near Innisfail, for the governor-general; Bingo, near Coronation, for a dog who happened to be around; University, near Sibbald, because that was as close as any of the local kids might get to one. Settlers near Cayley in 1904 argued so long over the location of their school that the authorities eventually warned them the next official visit would be their "last chance." By then they had managed to agree on a site, so they quickly chose their name: Last Chance.

Territorial Superintendent David J. Goggin. He was an Orangeman and a Mason hired by Haultain to get the system in place.

[3]Alberta's first premier, Alexander Cameron Rutherford, was also convinced that "education is the basis of intelligent citizenship and...the foundation of all good government." Almost as soon as he arrived in the West in 1895, to become the second lawyer in Strathcona, he ran for school board and served nine years.

TAX NOTICE

School District of *Hill Crest* No. *1096* N.W.T.

To *Mr. J. Morrill*

Dinton P.O.

You are hereby notified that you are assessed on the Assessment Roll of the above named School District for the year 190*5* for *640* acres of land the taxes on which at the rate of *5* cents per acre, amount to $ *32* *⁰⁰* and you are further notified that the arrears of taxes due by you to the said District amount to $ and you are required to pay the same forthwith.

Dinton this *aprile* 190*5*

John Lafwaff
Treasurer or Secretary-Treasurer.

Residence of Secretary Treasurer.

Section *8* Tp. *20* Rge. *26* m. *4*

P.O. *Dinton*

School tax notice for Hill Crest School District, 1905. Some bachelors objected to the levy.

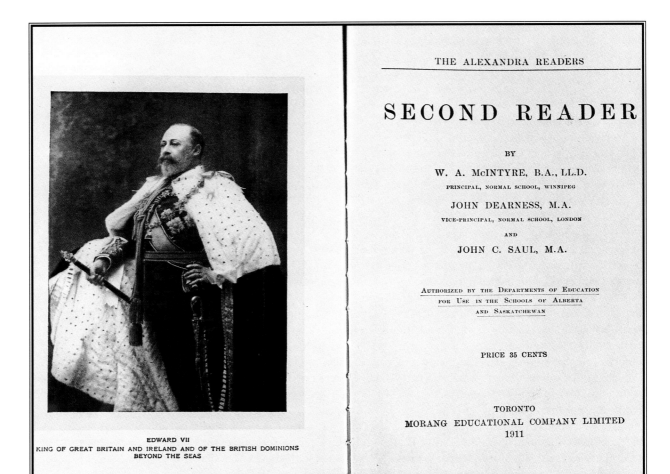

THE ALEXANDRA READERS

SECOND READER

BY

W. A. McINTYRE, B.A., LL.D.
PRINCIPAL, NORMAL SCHOOL, WINNIPEG

JOHN DEARNESS, M.A.
VICE-PRINCIPAL, NORMAL SCHOOL, LONDON

AND

JOHN C. SAUL, M.A.

AUTHORIZED BY THE DEPARTMENTS OF EDUCATION
FOR USE IN THE SCHOOLS OF ALBERTA
AND SASKATCHEWAN

PRICE 35 CENTS

TORONTO
MORANG EDUCATIONAL COMPANY LIMITED
1911

EDWARD VII
KING OF GREAT BRITAIN AND IRELAND AND OF THE BRITISH DOMINIONS
BEYOND THE SEAS

Opening pages of the ubiquitous Alexandra reader. Tales of heroic British adventure, poems from Tennyson and Browning.

Every school shall be provided with the prescribed school register, a globe, ball frames, dictionary, map of the world, map of North America, map of Canada, map of Alberta, a suitable supply of blackboard brushes and crayons, a thermometer, a clock, broom, pail and cup, washbasins and towels, and one or two chairs in addition to the teacher's.
- school essentials listed by the Alberta Department of Education, 1906.

Finally came the building itself, almost always log or frame. Sullivan Lake SD, near Coronation, considered a sod school but found that sod construction had no appeal on the debenture market. So they bought $540 worth of lumber and hired a carpenter to supervise volunteer builders. Other districts asked for tenders. Lauderdale SD in the Castor area, for instance, accepted a construction bid in 1906 of $844 for the building and $63 to paint it white with pea-green trim.

So many eccentric designs kept emerging that the Department of Education began providing blueprints for a standard schoolhouse measuring about twenty feet by thirty feet. Inside the door two sections were partitioned off for cloakrooms (boys' and girls'), with shelves for a pail of water, washbasin and the children's lunch buckets (lard pails were favoured). Next came a pot-bellied stove, fuelled with wood or coal, from which pipes strung beneath the high ceiling theoretically helped spread heat around the single classroom.

The department also provided plans for privies, of which there had to be two — one for boys, one for girls. However meticulously these were built, of course, in summer they were a rich source of insect and other life, and in winter an exercise in acute discomfort. From time to time small children got stuck in the "hole," or were locked in the outhouse, accidentally or deliberately. And in

The school district names were always informative. Gumbo, at Twining, was named for the prairie mud. Bingo, near Coronation, for a dog who happened to be around.

Buffalo Trails and Tales Evelyn Goddard Lagerquist recalls the momentous day at Gilt Edge (near Wainwright) when the boys trapped their elderly female teacher therein "by pulling a lasso rope around it. The poor old soul, it was so dreadful the way we behaved."

Some schools had wells, and some wells were satisfactory. But the first one at Millner, as Innisfail historian Mrs. McKenzie remembered it, was cribbed with spruce; the water consequently tasted so foul that only the horses would drink it. Other schools relied on a nearby stream or slough. Georgina Thomson, who went to school just north of Nanton at Porcupine SD in 1906, recalls in *Crocus & Meadowlark Country* how popular the water-fetching job was in fine weather. It always took a long time; the spring was a quarter-mile away. Besides, there were wildflowers to be picked, gophers to be chased or snared, and mud to play in. Failing any nearby source, water was lugged to the school in cream cans.

Since horses were the main transport, aside from feet, there was usually a school barn to shelter them, along with assorted schoolboy activities of a nefarious nature: playing cards, smoking, talking about sex, and conducting fights out of sight of the teacher. Cleaning out the barn was not a favourite job and the residue of manure would get pretty deep. Charyk tells of one enterprising schoolboy in Namao SD, north of Edmonton, who decided to do the job with blasting caps. He blew off the stable roof; most of the manure remained.

Inside the schoolhouse, the pupils sat at rows of home-made benches; later came factory-made desks, single or double, equipped with inkwells. Beyond these was a low dais with a desk for the teacher, and behind it a blackboard. There might be a clock on the wall, and likely a Union Jack or Canada's Red Ensign, and a portrait of King Edward VII. There might be a wall map or two, and maybe a globe. There might be a harmonium, which came in handy when the school was used, as country

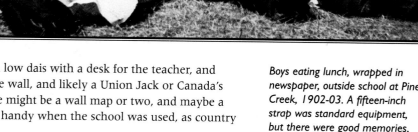

Boys eating lunch, wrapped in newspaper, outside school at Pine Creek, 1902-03. A fifteen-inch strap was standard equipment, but there were good memories, too, like baseball, story-telling and 'pom-pom-pullaway.'

There was usually a barn near the school that sheltered the horses, along with such nefarious schoolboy activities as playing cards, smoking, conducting fights and talking about sex.

ones habitually were, for church services or community festivities.

Not all rural trustees were as mean as Miss Appleby's, but times often *were* hard. Teachers typically had to board in homes that were far from congenial, or live alone in virtual shacks called teacherages — which could be worse. They had to cope single-handed with as many as fifty pupils between the statutory ages of five and sixteen, whose intellects and attitudes varied just as widely, who in some districts could speak not a word of English, and who might not have been in school for several years if ever. But they adapted. "I was eleven years old before I went to school," Harry Buxton of Three Hills reminisces in *As the Years Go By*, "but Mother tutored us at home so when I finally did get to school I took two grades at a time till I caught up."

The initial daily challenge for teacher and pupils alike was simply to get to the school over several miles of rough roads, trails or fields, through summer bugs and winter snow and other natural hazards. The teacher at St. Paul, for instance, lived across a creek from his school. When the bridge washed out one rainy season he borrowed a pig trough from an adjacent farm, and managed to pole himself back and forth for a week. In the early days, writes John Charyk (in *Little White Schoolhouse*), the prairie grass was so thick and deep that children would reach school drenched from dew. Winter naturally posed the worst hazards, and getting home again could be chancy if a blizzard blew up.[4]

Winter also afforded the most extreme discomfort. Somebody — the teacher or a capable pupil — had to start the stove. "I would walk through the deep snow (a mile and a half) very early to

[4]Rural schools often began by operating only from June to September, for one or both of two reasons. Winter weather brought extremely difficult access and heating problems. Besides, paying a teacher for only ten weeks or so was a great deal easier on the ratepayers.

The attempt to rid the ethnics of their ethnicity

THE CHALLENGE WAS TO TEACH THE UKRAINIANS, ROMANIANS, GERMANS, SLAVS, CHINESE, AND THE REST HOW TO SPEAK ENGLISH AND PAY TAXES

In areas of the North-West Territories settled by non-English-speaking groups, teachers faced all the usual pioneering hazards and another big one: language. For example, when a middle-aged teacher, identified as "W. Whillens from Camrose," arrived at Shandro School District near Vegreville in April 1907, he was faced with the job of registering 39 young Ruthenians (we'd now say Ukrainians), aged seven to thirteen, who spoke no English at all. The same was true, of course, of most of the parents who anxiously turned over their offspring to this foreign institution. So Whillens began his first class by having the children, one by one, call out their names. Then he produced a set of pictures and held up one of a

Pupils at the Boian Marea Romanian school north-east of Willingdon in 1910.

horse. "Keen," one pupil volunteered, giving the Ruthenian word. "Horse," said the teacher. "Horse," responded all the children. And so on with pictures of a cow, sheep, man, woman, boy, girl.

From there Whillens moved on to easily demonstrable verbs like "come," "run" and "carry" until finally his multi-aged class was ready to tackle the alphabet. He introduced songs and games, which the children greatly enjoyed, and soon was telling or reading stories to them. When school ended in August, writes Anna Navalkowski in a 1970 article in the *Alberta Historical Review*, Whillens had them divided into Class A, B and C. The Class A pupils could read the First Reader, write simple sentences, and handle simple arithmetic.

Teachers noticed one notable advantage in the ethnic communities, however. Usually the children had been strictly ordered by their parents to listen and learn, and seemed to do their best to obey. Even the older boys were not so inclined to defiance and unseemly pranks, although they tended to drop out as soon as they were old enough to be really useful farm workers. Five years later a few Shandro pupils had managed to reach Standard V (Grade 8), however, and wrote the

departmental examinations at Vegreville.

As settlers poured into Alberta throughout the decade, a whole variety of language pockets developed. Historian John W. Chalmers quotes a 1906 inspector's report: "One half of the rural districts in this inspectorate are in foreign settlements, the nationalities of which are French, German, Norwegian, Swedish and Galician [Galicia was a subdivision of Ukraine at the time]." The most extensive, however, were those established in east-central Alberta by immigrants from Poland, Ukraine, Bosnia, Herzogovina and Bulgaria (all of whom Albertans indiscriminately dubbed "Galician," variously spelled).

Their pressing need, of course, was to learn English. Chinese immigrants in Calgary were having a particularly rough time. Thomas Underwood, proprietor of Diamond Coal and mayor in 1902 and 1903, donated land for a Christian mission that also taught some English classes. Calgary's Germans and Austro-Hungarians, clustered in Germantown (Riverside) on the north flats of the Bow, seem to have fared better. After a 1909 Empire Day visit by Lieutenant-Governor George Bulyea to the local public school, the *Herald* printed one youngster's enthusiastic composition: "We go up and shake hand and tell our names and we are proud...We like to see this big Sir Bulyay again."

In Vegreville the Presbyterian Church opened a night school for Galicians, aged twelve and upward, moving it to Edmonton in 1907. The *Bulletin* reported that classes would be held in Rudyk's Hall on Kinistino Avenue, and that "the project has been enthusiastically taken up by leading Galician residents." Two years later the Reading Camp Association, the organization later known as Frontier College, began work in Alberta among the Grand Trunk-Pacific and Canadian Pacific railway gangs.

The college students who spent their holidays as Reading

Camp instructors were expected to wield pick and shovel along with the men, six days a week and ten hours a day, for the usual wages. They did their teaching in a tent or boxcar in their spare time. Instruction was offered in all sorts of subjects — reading, letter-writing, history, geography and more — but English was a hot item. Instructor D.R. Patterson reported that of his 28 students at Namaka in southern Alberta, eighteen were Poles, three French, two Norwegian, one German and only four English-speaking. English was the most popular subject, arithmetic second.[a]

The public schools, the government felt, must be the means of melting all these disparate ethnicities into a coherent and workable society. It would prove no easy job. On the plus side was the fact that most immigrant parents wanted their children to learn English. On the minus side were the hardships, suspicions and anxieties of these communities and, among the Ukrainians, a nationalist movement that soon set up in active opposition.

When Nikon Shandro and his brothers called a ratepayers' meeting to organize a school, fellow homesteaders immediately protested.[b] Taxation, they forcibly argued, was one of the

by indistinct articulation. Some of them could scarcely make themselves understood in either written or spoken English."

At Vladymir, Kolomea and Lwiw schools the trustees refused outright, so Supervisor Fletcher promptly took over as "official trustee" and made the switch himself. The trustees complained to the department, which got them nowhere. They caved in. Bukovina School north of Vegreville was tougher. When Fletcher replaced that teacher "about twenty ratepayers assembled on the school grounds...in no very pleasant mood. They shook their fists at the teacher and myself and the language they used was unparliamentary to say the least." One of the ex-trustees went into the school and dismissed the children.

That man was summoned before the Fort Saskatchewan police inspector and fined five dollars and costs, but the rebellion continued. The dissidents set up a rival school nearby, all the pupils went there, and Fletcher discovered that the deposed board treasurer was collecting taxes to pay the Ruthenian teacher. "I warned five of the belligerents to pay their taxes to me within ten days or I would recover the same by distraint of chattels." They did not, so he seized a horse from each. The following year, when the department-appoint-

Whillens had the children call out their names. Then he produced a set of pictures and held up one of a horse. 'Keen,' one pupil volunteered, giving the Ukrainian word.

reasons they had left Ukraine. Ah yes, replied the Education Department representative, but if children between seven and fourteen did not attend school, their parents could be punished. The motion passed, taxes were set at $6 a quarter-section, and the settlers built a log school and hired teacher Whillens for four months at $60 a month.

Things seem to have gone smoothly at Shandro School. Its next teacher was Sam Holmes (later killed in action in the First World War), fondly remembered for coaching his young Ruthenians in baseball and football. They made balls of rags tightly bound with twine and carved bats from saplings until the trustees were persuaded to supply sports equipment, and they played against nearby Bukovina and Manawan Schools.

At best it was an exceedingly lonely experience for a teacher. At worst, as Chalmers recounts in his article "Strangers in Our Midst" (*Alberta Historical Review*), it could be outright warfare. Robert Fletcher, the department's "supervisor of schools among foreigners," became aware in 1913 that nationalist agitators (from Manitoba and Saskatchewan, he thought) were trying to take over the Ruthenian schools. He immediately visited the trustees at Oleskow, Podola, Molodia, Zawale, Spring Creek and Stanislawow schools and "persuaded them to dismiss the unqualified Ruthenian in each case and engage a qualified teacher," although some of them were pretty reluctant.

"The majority of these young men had a very indifferent education," wrote Fletcher. "Their written English was faulty in idiomatic expression, while their speech was characterized

ed teacher returned to Bukovina, "he was assaulted by two men, two women and two grown boys." The woman identified as ringleader was sentenced to a $200 fine or a month in jail.

Tough tactics, but the department's determination paid off. In 1914 Fletcher was able to report that the elected Ruthenian/Ukrainian trustees were back in charge and performing their duties "quite smoothly." A few years later the first Ukrainians qualified as teachers. When Chalmers, himself an educator, attended high school graduation exercises in a Ukrainian community in 1960, he noted that "when the school staff marched into the hall, the entire audience rose in tribute. By that year every teacher was Ukrainian in descent, and many were graduates of that same high school." And by that time also, of course, the once marginalized group was represented in every other facet of provincial life: business, medicine, the law, politics — the lot.   — *V.B.*

[a]The Reading Camp Association was launched in 1899 by Alfred Fitzpatrick, a Presbyterian minister from Nova Scotia who preached in northern Ontario lumber camps and decided the men needed education as well as religion. Fitzpatrick was part of the social gospel movement that blossomed in the early 20th century, says Marjorie Z. Robinson in a 1981 *Alberta Historical Review* article. "All educational work is more or less religious," he declared, and devoted his life to the Reading Association.

[b]Shandro School could hardly have been named anything else. Organizer Nikon Shandro, who could read and write Ukrainian, was its first board chairman. It stood on five acres of Sidor Shandro's farm. And Andrew Shandro, who spoke English and would serve as a Liberal MLA from 1913 to 1921, acted as liaison with the Edmonton educational authorities and the board's first secretary-treasurer.

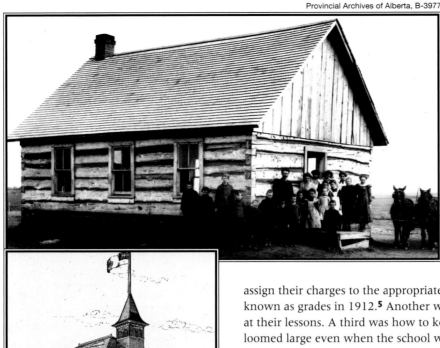

The Bloomfield School, 1905, and design for a prefabricated rural school from a British Columbia timber company, 1904. Most schools were not pedagogical palaces.

light the fire," writes Evelyn Lagerquist. "We would all sit around the stove with all our coats and rubbers on. For that I got the big sum of $1.25 a month." It was also necessary to thaw the ink, which froze overnight. Even after the stove got going, on coldest days pupils near it would be blazing hot, while those farther away worked in coats and mittens. Reminiscences constantly mention the accumulated aroma of those old schoolrooms: wood or coal smoke; the camphor oil or goose grease with which solicitous mothers anointed their offspring against catching cold; boots and mittens drying (or burning) on the stove rail; the residue of pre-school barn chores.

One major problem for teachers was to assign their charges to the appropriate "standards," the term used for what became known as grades in 1912.[5] Another was to keep five or six groups simultaneously busy at their lessons. A third was how to keep order, in class and out. These problems loomed large even when the school was quite small. "If three of my ten scholars were drowned and another hanged, the school would cease to worry me," Paul Wallace, a despondent neophyte at Youngstown, wrote to his family in Ontario, "but providence and the law refuse to aid me."

The first four standards were supposed to have textbooks called "readers," but these were often in very short supply, as Pamela Appleby discovered, despite the efforts after 1905 of Premier Alexander Rutherford. Like his territorial predecessor Haultain, Rutherford took on the education portfolio himself, and in 1907 introduced a tax of $1.25 an acre on land outside existing school districts to raise more money. (A secondary aim was to remove some of the advantage in *not* building a school.) The next year there was $14,000 in the provincial budget for readers up to Standard IV. Moreover, said the premier, this series had won a gold medal in international competition and was "the best...to be found in the Dominion of Canada, and probably on the continent of America."[6]

This "Alexandra Readers" series had five books. There was a primer to begin the teaching of reading. In the *First Book* were simple poems and familiar stories like "The Little Red Hen" and "The Boy Who Cried Wolf" which, not incidentally, also carried a basic moral message. The second, third and fourth books went on to longer stories, adventure, heroic episodes in British and Canadian history, short biographies of famous people, and selections from poets like Longfellow, Browning and Tennyson. Pupils got to know those books from cover to cover, and memorized some of the poems. (This was a demand that boys tended to resent at the time; but as grown men, many would see the beauty and meaning of some verse they had never forgotten.)

Besides the readers there were copybooks in which youngsters practised penmanship by copying sample words and sentences. But assignments for many subjects — arithmetic, spelling, grammar, geography, history — had to be laboriously written out by the teacher on the blackboard. For Standard V there would be, with luck, textbooks; Georgina Thomson refers to "my old enemy *Hill's Lessons in Geometry.*" But Porcupine SD possessed not a single reference book except a dictionary, she notes, and that was typical. Premier Rutherford also helped remedy this after 1908, by instituting a small annual library grant.

Beginners generally used slates, on which they wrote with special slate pencils creating a nerve-torturing screech. For wiping off the slates they had a rag and bottle of water (very handy as well for dampening the seat of a neighbour who happened not to be in it at the moment). Older pupils had five-cent scribblers, in which they wrote with pencils at first. In the higher standards they used detachable-nib pens, with much spillage of ink and use of blotters (from which excellent spitballs could also be made).

Another piece of requisite equipment was a long wooden pointer, an instrument of varied uses. "The teacher started chasing me with her pointer," a Pincher Creek oldtimer reminisces in *Prairie Grass to Mountain Pass,* "and Holly Bruneau...reached out and grabbed her and just sat there with her on his lap. He was about seventeen years old and a real tough guy." In *Fort Macleod: Our Colorful Past* J.H. Mitchell recalls an incident with an opposite outcome, when teacher Billy Day broke his pointer over "a big lad" who defied him, then "went on with his teaching while whittling a fine rock-elm replacement...out of the chastened lad's hockey stick." (But it should be noted that no woman teacher is ever known to have been dumped in the creek by large and irate schoolboys, a fate that befell one male.)

There was of course always a leather strap two or so inches wide by fifteen long, usually discreetly tucked away in the teacher's desk. One early teacher is said to have thrown it in the stove the day he arrived, telling the pupils

Edmonton Public Schools

Edmonton's first superintendent of public schools, James McCaig. Accused of drinking, swearing and kissing a teacher.

they'd better not misbehave or their punishment would be so horrible they'd wish for the strap back. But most teachers used it regularly, and some doubtless overused it. One Cliff Tunney is immortalized in *The Winds of Change* (Edgerton and District Historical Society) as holding "the record for having the most straps in one day. He would have had more but the teacher was exhausted."

But there were many happy times in the little schoolhouses. Their students remember the spelling and geography "bees," checker matches and blackboard games when it was too cold to go out at recess, and sing-alongs and story reading on Friday afternoons. They remember the summer baseball games, when everybody played, and children's games like "pom-pom-pullaway" and "anty-I-over." They especially remember the Christmas concerts, a community highlight, on which they and their teachers worked so hard.

Forever looming in the near distance was the school inspector, whose function it was to show up at least once a year and pronounce judgement upon school, teacher and pupils. They were more than mere departmental agents, says historian Chalmers; locally, the inspector *was* the department. He tried to arrive without warning and observe from the back of the room. (Trustees and pupils and other teachers would usually warn the victim if they could, however.) Inspectorial assessments could be quietly devastating, such as, "It is to be regretted that Miss X does not possess

'If three of my ten scholars were drowned and another hanged, the school would cease to worry me, but providence and the law refuse to come to my aid.'

the elements of governance to a greater degree."

In country schools the inspector also examined the pupils in reading, spelling, composition, arithmetic, geography, history and science, summarily promoting or demoting them. He looked over the building and equipment. He went over the financial records of rural school boards, and if necessary took over for a time as "official trustee" to straighten things out. He checked on attendance, which determined the size of the government grant and which was chronically low. Country kids, for reasons both valid and invalid, were at school less than half the time.[7] But the overall territorial average in 1898 was only 52% according to Superintendent Goggin's report — and it improved only slightly in the ten years. Even town kids averaged two days absent weekly. In

[5]Before 1900 Alberta schools were divided into eight standards all told, which could be further subdivided. Standards I to V were approximately equivalent to Grades 1 to 8, which constituted a good, ordinary, "elementary" education. Standard V was colloquially known as "fifth class leaving" since that's what most pupils did. Standards VI to VIII were secondary school, and much less available.

[6]When critics complained that Alberta's big contract for new school readers should not go to an out-of-province firm (the Morang company in Toronto), Premier Rutherford issued a challenge. If any Albertan could produce anything as good, the job would be his at a bonus. There were no takers. In June 1908 deputy minister D.S. McKenzie wrote to the premier, on holiday in Banff, "Our first car of readers is unloaded and the second car will likely arrive this week." The *Alexandra Readers* would be fixtures in Alberta schools for the next 25 years.

[7]Rural school trustees found two of their responsibilities particularly repugnant — collecting delinquent taxes and nailing young truants. No matter how the school inspectors pressed them, they were most reluctant to seize a neighbour's buggy or cow for unpaid school tax. Tackling him about the School Attendance Act (which applied to girls aged eight to thirteen) was nearly as tough. Urban trustees were spared this latter unpleasantness. Town policemen were usually expected to round up early hookey-players; after 1900 truant officers were appointed. Robert L. Barker, who did the job for both Calgary systems from 1905 to 1935 while the law became increasingly stringent, would serve 410 warning notices on parents by 1917, and take 65 cases to police court.

Central School (later renamed James Short School), Calgary, 1900.

Edmonton in 1895 Inspector J.A. Calder noted with disapproval the absence on inspection day of seven of the eighteen pupils in one classroom.

What kind of brave or desperate individual tackled the job of country school teacher for $40 or $50 a month? All kinds. A third-class teaching certificate required only Standard V and a four-month Normal School course.[8] Standard VII and Normal School earned a second-class certificate, Standard VIII and Normal School a first-class one. In any case, half of Alberta teachers held "provisional certificates." A high percentage of early western teachers came from Britain and eastern Canada, where the pay was lower; very young local women accounted for most of the rest. College students, working their way toward a degree in medicine, law or theology, taught four-month summer terms, or took off a whole year from their studies. But other men, and women, went into teaching as a profession.

One such was Milton Ezra LaZerte, an honours graduate in mathematics and physics from the University of Toronto. He got his first job at the town of Hardisty in east-central Alberta in 1910 (salary $900), where he found conditions little better than strictly rural ones. The school board had arranged for him to eat at the town restaurant and sleep in a room above it; the food was bad, the room worse. LaZerte rebelled. All right, said the trustees, they'd fix something up. What they fixed up, LaZerte told interviewer D.M. Myrehaug in 1972, was a room behind the fire hall, if he would man one of town's two fire trucks. He accepted, but didn't stay long in Hardisty. The next year he was hired as principal of the new Alexandra High School in Medicine Hat, which ranked as a genuine city.

By 1900 the gap between city and country schools was appreciably widening. Towns and cities continued to have their own educational trials and triumphs, of course, but on an increasingly larger scale. By 1909 a *Calgary Herald* article was listing "an array of buildings for school purposes: brick and stone buildings containing from four to ten classrooms," in Medicine Hat, Macleod, Lethbridge, Vegreville, Strathcona, Edmonton, Olds, Didsbury, Red Deer, Lacombe, Wetaskiwin and Calgary.

They too had started small. The Calgary Protestant Public School Board made shift from 1885 to 1897 with a variety of temporary classrooms that included the second floor of the old town hall, just over the police cells.[9] Then the trustees floated an $8,000 loan to build brick Central School (four classrooms) at First Street West and Fourth Avenue. In the '90s they doubled its size and built two more schools: East Ward (a one-room frame building) and South Ward (two-room stone). In January 1900 the Calgary school district had 670 students and listed assets (real estate, buildings, equipment) worth $19,100. The 1899 revenue was $8,000 in local taxes and $5,600 from the North-West Territories government (of which $1,900 had not yet been paid).

By January 1900, says Robert M. Stamp in his history of the Calgary public schools, *School Days: A Century of Memories*, the trustees in an emergency meeting had to authorize more temporary classrooms: the Alberta Hotel sample rooms. The overcrowded condition of the public schools, the *Herald* declared, "is becoming so serious as to call for immediate attention...One lady has had to look after a class of 61 pupils in a room with a seating capacity of 57...Calgary is about to become the capital of the new province of Alberta, and the question of school attendance will have to be attended to at once..."

Calgary was not about to become the capital, however, and in every respect its northern rival was catching up. Edmonton's population in 1901 was 2,626 to Calgary's 4,091; in 1906 the Edmonton total was 11,167, not counting 2,921 in Strathcona across the river, to Calgary's 11,967 (Calgary challenged these figures. See Sect. I, ch. 4). Edmonton's first one-room school, on McKay Avenue, had had two more rooms added and was renting adjacent space by 1894. That year the ratepayers voted to borrow $5,000 to build College Avenue School, a handsome four-room brick structure.

More and more children kept appearing, so in 1903 Edmonton added a real showpiece, high on the riverbank at Queen's Avenue (99th Street) and Isabella Street (104th Avenue). The *Bulletin* described Queen's Avenue School as "modified Romanesque." It had no fewer than five classrooms on the first floor, five on the second, a fine assembly hall on the third, a principal's office and a staff room in the 62-foot tower that distinguished its northwest corner. In 1905 a third brick school, with eight classrooms, was built on the McKay Avenue site of the original frame public school. In

---

By the time Alberta became a province in 1905 there were 562 schools within its new borders, 1,210 teachers, and more than 34,000 pupils.

1908 came Alex Taylor School on Jasper Avenue. In 1909 Norwood School replaced two temporary structures on the city's northern outskirts — after trustees succeeded in ridding the area of a pig corral and a house of ill repute.

Across the North Saskatchewan River, the Strathcona public school board had put up a brick showpiece of its own in 1902, for 150 pupils and a staff of seven: Grandin, later known as Old King Edward. Bigger still was Duggan Street School, built in 1906 and renamed Queen Alexandra in 1910 (the Queen sent an autographed photograph). In 1908 the first 45 students of the new University of Alberta were housed in its third-storey assembly hall (see sidebar story), and founding president Henry Marshall Tory worked there behind a door labelled "Office of the President." Queen Alexandra School cherished this door, and presented it to the U of A on the university's fiftieth anniversary.

The *Edmonton Bulletin* account of the school board annual report for 1909 ("a booklet of eight pages of very presentable appearance" that accounted for every penny disbursed) noted that school enrolment seemed to be doubling every three years. The building committee was recommending twelve rooms for future schools. Debenture indebtedness was now close to half a million dollars, but the 1909 revenue had surpassed $87,000. Edmonton and Strathcona, which would

[8]Why their teacher should be a graduate of something called a Normal School was a puzzle to some children — and parents too. Could it have been necessary perhaps to correct some *abnormality*? The source of this curious term for a teachers' college was the *Ecole Normale Supérieure*, established in Paris in 1794 to be a model (or norm) for other teacher training schools. They generally offered two years beyond the secondary level, and were intended chiefly for elementary school teachers. By the 1960s they had all been absorbed into education faculties with longer lasting programs.

[9]Calgary schoolchildren did not necessarily regard proximity to the jail as a bad thing. Pupil Eddie Lucas (as quoted in *School Days: A Century of Memories* by Robert M. Stamp) recalled how at recess "we innocent children would gather round the barred window," shrieking taunts at old Mother Fulham, the woman who used to drive around town collecting swill for her pigs, drinking copiously, and frequently getting hauled to jail. "Her roaring profanity would have we boys jumping up and down in wild glee." The girls, he said, merely giggled behind their hands.

Edmonton school picnic, 1903. One way or the other, Alberta was being educated.

That noise in the attic? A university's birth

POWERED BY TWO DYNAMOS, THE U OF A WENT FROM LOW-RENT TO ROMANESQUE
IN SCARCELY THE TIME IT TOOK TO RAISE TAXES

"On a day in June 1908, the president of a university not yet in being, in a province which I had never heard of, in a country which I had never visited, came to Harvard and offered me the professorship of English. The offer sounded like midsummer madness."

So wrote, many years later, the Virginian E. K. Broadus, one of the first four professors recruited by the indefatigable Henry Marshall Tory to staff his about-to-be-born University of Alberta. When Broadus got to Strathcona that fall, he found Tory and his other three professors "ensconced in the attic of a small brick public school building...veritable *philosophes sous les toits*" (attic philosophers).

The building was Queen Alexandra School. The U of A's first 45 students (including seven young women) were about to arrive. The following January staff and students moved to the second floor of the new and bigger Strathcona Collegiate Institute. By the fall of 1911 they were in their own building, Athabasca Hall, on a 528-acre river lot campus on Strathcona's western edge, and work had begun on Assiniboia Hall. And by 1913-14, its sixth year, Tory had expanded enrolment to 433 students in four faculties (arts and sciences, applied science, medicine and law) and the staff to 28, not counting the law faculty.

Henry Marshall Tory always was a man in a hurry. But then, so was Premier Alexander C. Rutherford, who laid the groundwork and persuaded Tory, a McGill mathematics professor, to set it all in motion. Rutherford pushed through the act to establish a provincial university, non-denominational and co-educational, in his first legislative session in the spring of 1906. He also instituted a general school tax and dedicated twenty percent of it for the university. And he quietly decided to locate it in Strathcona, however Calgarians might howl when they found out (Sect. 1, ch. 4).

An obvious next step was to ask the dominion government for a land grant to endow Alberta's university, but that got a fast brush-off from Ottawa in March 1907.

Rutherford forged on anyhow. Less than two months after receiving Sir Wilfrid's refusal he had his government buy the site he had chosen, River Lot 5. Meanwhile he and Tory had been conferring for

several years, while Tory was establishing a McGill affiliate in Vancouver, a two-year program called the McGill University College of British Columbia.[a] In early 1907, says Walter H. Johns in *A History of the University of Alberta 1908-1969*, Rutherford met Tory at the Windsor Hotel in Montreal and made him a definite offer of the presidency, effective January 1908.

Tory accepted, and promptly came to Alberta to tour the province, looking for supporters and for students. He found both, writes Walter Johns (himself U of A president from 1959 to 1969). He also met considerable opposition in Calgary, however, where one "outstanding citizen" was actually canvassing schools to deter students from attending. Next came a convocation to elect a chancellor and five senate members (the

Edmonton Archives, EA-10-2769

First class of U of A students, 1908-09. (Above) Henry Marshall Tory, 1908.

government had the right to appoint ten more). The word went out that any graduate of a Canadian or British university who registered and paid a two dollar fee could attend and vote. Registrations totalled 354; convocation was held March 18. The new senate agreed with President Tory that the U of A would accept graduates of Standard VII (Grade 11), would have one faculty (arts and science), and would hire professors of undoubted excellence on five-year renewable contracts at a salary of $2,500.

A major reason for all the hurry was a determination to "keep free from the taint of denominationalism," as Tory expressed it in a 1906 letter to Rutherford. Not that he meant to cast any aspersion "upon denominations as religious institutions," he added. "I am speaking merely of them as educational institutions." Tory himself was an ordained Methodist minister, but he had resigned in 1906, possibly because his work in British Columbia had been opposed and obstructed by graduates of denominational colleges there and also by Victoria College, the Methodist college at the University of Toronto.

The universities of eastern Canada were without exception

He and Rutherford wanted a clear field with no interference from clergy, they agreed. And they got it. True, Alberta College South was duly built on campus in 1910, but functioned mainly as a residence. It was joined by Robertson College which, after the Methodist, Congregationalist and some Presbyterian Churches amalgamated in 1925 to form the United Church, became St. Stephen's College. The university credited its courses in Old and New Testament, and sometimes approved its instructors to teach regular university courses. The same was true when the Christian Brothers were authorized to open St. Joseph's College in 1927. Their approved courses were Christian apologetics and Catholic philosophy. But there was never any doubt who was running things: President Tory and Rutherford, now chancellor.

Not that the two really intended to abandon Christianity. The U of A motto, *Quaecumque vera* (Whatsoever things are true) was chosen at the president's behest by classics professor William H. Alexander from St. Paul's epistle to the Philippians. Alexander also composed a grace for the formal evening meals in the Athabasca Hall dining room: *Fac, Deus noster, ut hoc cibo*

Prof. Alexander's wife Marion, enthralled with the golden poplar leaves against the dark evergreens in 1908, suggested green and gold as the university colours.

---

coalitions of religious colleges; the colleges came first. In Manitoba as well, two church-affiliated colleges preceded the formation of the University of Manitoba. D.R. Babcock in *A Gentleman of Strathcona: Alexander Cameron Rutherford* quotes Rutherford on this point: "My reason for insistence on immediate action was that I had in mind the bickerings which had occurred in Ontario and Manitoba when their universities were projected, and wished to avoid the mistake of having various religious sects erect their own colleges."

Unless they were quickly forestalled, Tory warned, "there will be half a dozen small colleges scattered all over this province, claiming university powers." Several colleges had indeed appeared already. Western Canada College, backed by the Presbyterian church and headed by the Rev. Archibald Oswald MacRae, had opened in Calgary in 1903. The Presbyterians were also planning Robertson College on Whyte Avenue in Edmonton. Edmonton's Alberta College, backed by the Methodists, with Reverend J.H. Riddell of Wesley College, Winnipeg, as principal, was incorporated in 1904. Besides commercial and music courses, it offered two years of undergraduate work and was arranging affiliation with McGill. At first, relations between Riddell, Rutherford and Tory were so amiable that the premier offered "any and all denominational colleges a site of ten acres on the university grounds." Soon, however, Tory was clearly having sober second thoughts. In regard to Riddell, he wrote Rutherford, "We do not want to tie ourselves up in any way that would affect our future relations with the Department of Education."

refecti, quaecumque vera constantius sequamur, secundum Jesu Christi Spiritum (Grant, our God, that refreshed with this food we may more steadily follow whatsoever things are true in the spirit of Jesus Christ).

The growing numbers of students threw themselves energetically into their studies, and all sorts of extracurricular activities as well: *The Gateway* (1910); literary, philosophical and dramatic societies; glee club and mathematical club; dances and *conversaziones* (promenading to music while engaging in conversation); the YWCA and YMCA; and every possible kind of sports club. W.H. Alexander's wife Marion, enthralled with the golden poplar leaves against the dark evergreens in that fall of 1908, suggested green and gold as the university colours. The Johnstone Walker store was able to match the colours and everyone approved, including the senate. The accepted symbolism of colours made these especially appropriate, the senators commented: green for joyous hope, gold for the shining light of knowledge.

— V.B.

[a]Besides launching the University of British Columbia and the University of Alberta, and serving as U of A president until 1928, the amazing Henry Marshall Tory also created the precursor of the Alberta Research Council and organized the "Khaki University" for Canadian soldiers in England. Between 1928 and 1935 he piloted the National Research Council through Depression years when no one else saw any hope for it. And in 1942, at age 77, he became the principal founder of Carleton University in Ottawa, which he served unpaid as president and lecturer until he died in 1947.

amalgamate in 1912, were to add a dozen "permanent" schools between 1911 and 1920, and a variety of temporary ones.

A new question arose. How could Alberta produce good teachers, or support the university its premiers wanted, without more high school classes? The territorial government had instituted bonus grants in 1883 for any school that would add classes above Standard V; some responded. Even in one-room country schools clever teachers and pupils often managed Standard VI. Georgina Thomson describes in an *Alberta Historical Review* article how Porcupine teacher R.J. Johnston prepared her and two classmates for the Standard VI examinations in 1907. "He specialized in mathematics, bookkeeping and grammar, but let us go into a huddle by ourselves and struggle with the literature, geography and history. We all passed." But after that Georgina had to go to Calgary to school.

Although city trustees complained that the extra high school funding never really equalled the expense, they tried to squeeze in the last two standards. The space pressure from below was so great, however, that by 1900 it was clear separate secondary schools would have to be provided, even though high school students were never more than 4% of the school population up to 1910.

The Calgary public board responded by joining three little one-storey frame buildings near the city hall (and the livery stable and dog pound) in 1903 and installing four high school teachers. They called it City Hall School; the students called it Sleepy Hollow. The sandstone Central High School opened in 1908 and was enlarged in 1910. In the north, Strathcona Collegiate Institute opened in 1909.[10] Edmonton used College Avenue school as a high school from 1903 until 1911, when Edmonton High (renamed Victoria in 1913) was completed.

School boards were also much concerned with high school curriculum. Edmonton's first fulltime district superintendent, James McCaig, noted in 1906 that two-thirds of high school students were girls. To make secondary education more immediately relevant, especially for boys, McCaig pressured for more vocational training.[11] After 1907 manual training (woodwork, some metalwork) and domestic science (cooking, sewing) were added, in Edmonton and elsewhere, and commercial courses a little later. Academic courses were expanding as well. Chemistry became a two-year course and physics three. Mathematics and history were continued into Standard VIII.

Each June students above Standard IV wrote departmental examinations, papers sent out from Edmonton in sealed packages and administered on the same date all across the province, then returned to the capital to be marked. This made early summer an anxious time as youngsters waited for their marks to arrive by mail. "Over the summer holidays I tried to forget about the exams," writes Georgina Thomson of her Standard V experience. "One August day, however, we saw a horseman coming from the south at a good speed, and it turned out to be Annie on Nellie...She kept waving a paper in her hand and shouting 'We passed! We both passed!' The Broomfields lived fairly near Stavely and got their mail oftener than we did." (Newspapers also published the departmental results in detail, where there were newspapers.)

The provincial Department of Education was also beginning to concern itself with physical training. In the little rural schools, as Don Benedict recalled many years later in *Hand Hills Heritage*, everybody who could swing a bat or stand in goal got involved in sports at noon hour and recess. The bigger city schools with their playgrounds and gymnasiums required more organization. They had exercises with Indian clubs and, for older boys, interschool team games. For boys, cadet training became a big component of physical education. "Teach Them How to Shoot," headlined the *Edmonton Journal* in a 1907 report on a "Proposal to Give all High School and Normal School Students Courses in Physical Culture." By 1914 every Alberta high school would have a cadet corps, a development supported by trustees because the dominion Department of Militia provided uniforms, rifles, ammunition and targets.

Finding satisfactory teachers, and keeping them for more than a few years, however, remained a major problem. Most women teachers left to get married; many young men went on into law or the clergy or business. Commenting on rural salaries in 1907, Inspector P.H. Thibaudeau observed that any young man who would be long content with them must lack "one or all of the three Gs: Go, Grit and Gumption." The provincial average was $600 and the top salary, for a city principal, was $1,500.

A class in the school at Horse Hills, early 1900s. The teacher is identified as a `Mr. Piquette.'

As for the supply, Chalmers says that before 1893 only 55 teachers were trained in the territories; all the rest were imports. By 1902 Goggin had managed to get more than 800 trained in the NWT to what he considered increasingly high standards, and 2,155 interim certificates were issued to locally trained teachers in Alberta between 1905 and 1914. But even so, in that same period 3,245 interim certificates went to "imports" trained elsewhere.

Normal Schools were the main government answer to the supply problem. The Calgary Normal School, Alberta's first, opened in January 1906 with an enrolment of eight young men and eighteen young women. (The actual ratio of women to men teachers in the field, however, was more like four to one.) Male candidates had to be at least eighteen years old and females sixteen, but some in the initial class were older and had previous teaching experience. The school motto: *Juvare Optamus* (We want to help).

After their four-month course Normal School students were examined on a daunting array of subjects, from grammar and mathematics to hygiene, manual training, educational psychology and class management. The pass mark on each paper was only 34%, Chalmers notes, but certification required a 50% average (70% for a first-class certificate). The students also tried their hand at actual teaching in the associated Normal Practice School, which was staffed by the Calgary public school board. (The province paid the board $15,000 for the site, the *Calgary Herald* noted, and 200 children attended the school to give the would-be teachers someone to teach.) A second Normal School would open in Camrose in 1912 and would get its own extensive building in 1914.

One way and another, by 1910 Alberta was being educated. If the process was somewhat traumatic for the teachers who were working this revolution, many of their stories were ultimately happy ones. Such was the case with Pamela Appleby of Hillsgreen School. Even her story ended happily. Riding her little mare Bessie through the magnificent countryside of the Red Deer River became a great joy to her. She loved the country dances that went on until 5 a.m. so the partygoers could travel home in the light of dawn. She moved in with a friendly family that welcomed Bessie too. Two of her pupils began driving her to and from school with their horse and sleigh. A new secretary-treasurer suddenly produced her salary arrears ($300). She bought a fur coat. So well did she learn to organize her disparate classes that the school inspector offered her a job in Calgary. But she didn't take it; instead she married her English fiance, Reginald Harvey, who was teaching near Munson. And that too was entirely typical of the teachers who brought schooling to the West.

[10] Red-brick Strathcona Collegiate had three floors and a basement, with physics and chemistry laboratories on the first floor and, on the third, the now customary auditorium-cum-gymnasium. With just 71 high school students enrolled in 1909, there was plenty of space for the University of Alberta students as well, when they moved over from Queen Alexandra School. Until 1935 Strathcona Collegiate and Victoria High would be the only secondary schools in the region specifically built as such. And both would still be in full use as the 20th century drew near its end.

[11] Despite his impressive credentials (a Toronto BA and MA, a law degree and all sorts of education certificates) and experience (in Ontario, as head of Lethbridge schools for six years, and as a provincial inspector), Superintendent James McCaig came to grief in Edmonton. In 1911 he was accused of using profane and obscene language, and "indulging in intoxicants." One citizen tailed him for a month, recorded every time he entered a bar, and became a star witness before a school board investigation that dragged on to 1913. The board finally exonerated McCaig and even gave him a $500 raise — but he suddenly resigned on October 31, 1913. In December the explanation emerged. "McCaig Kissed Miss Lobb; is Fined $27.35," proclaimed the *Edmonton Capital*. The superintendent pleaded guilty to common assault on the young teacher, Zaida M. Lobb, and retired to his Lethbridge ranch. He died in 1922.

CHAPTER THREE

Provincial Archives of Alberta, E. Brown Collection, B-3776

A private ward at the General Hospital in Edmonton, 1902. Private patients paid between $3 and $7 a day.

Disease stalked the province as the settlers moved in

THE AFFLICTED WERE CONFINED TO 'PEST HOUSES' BUILT ON DUMPS AS FAMILIES FOUGHT BACK TEARS AND BURIED THEIR DEAD BY NIGHT

by STEPHANI KEER

Disease and death stalked the settlers in Alberta during the first decade of the 1900s, knocking unexpectedly at doors, stealing children from parents, and parents from children.

Typhoid, smallpox, diphtheria, tuberculosis, scarlet fever, even measles, cut across all barriers of class and race. There was a terrible democracy to the diseases and most families lost at least one member to "the fourth horseman."

The sense of helplessness was augmented by the awful distance most people had travelled to this new land of dreams, some of them lured here because a dry climate was seen as a solution to chronic health problems. But the harsh winters claimed lives. So did the unremitting physical demands. So did the high incidence of death in childbirth. So even did the home remedies.

By the decade's end, the medical profession was just beginning to respond to the needs of the new communities and was still desperately short of practitioners. Between 1889 and 1905, 36 doctors had taken up residence in Alberta but, notes one observer, "despite these signs of progress, the high evidence of illness and death, without adequate provision for medical care, still persisted."

Oddly, in 1907, an *Edmonton Bulletin* article, in an abortive attempt at humour, advised would-be immigrants that "foreigners are making fortunes" in Alberta because skilled labourers are in short supply. In fact, it said, "the only trade we have enough of is doctors."

It wasn't so. By 1910, Calgary had completely outgrown its medical facilities. Doctors, nurses and hospital beds were all in short supply. From early in the decade, hospitals had begun appearing all over the province, augmenting the ones in the major centres. But by 1910 these, too, were

Isolation hospital Calgary (right) and staff (left), including the Chinese cook Sing Sing, sometime between 1903 and 1907. Death to one was better than death to dozens.

understaffed. The consequences were not pleasant. Too often, people suffering from communicable disease were thrown into "pest houses," not infrequently built on garbage dumps. And sometimes even room in the "pest houses" wasn't available. The stricken were then confined to their homes or put in tents, and the areas were policed so that no one could enter or leave an infected building. That response, heartless as it seemed nine decades later, was not unreasonable at the time. There were no vaccines, and diseases spread with incredible rapidity, even in rural areas. It was either death to one or death to dozens.

Tuberculosis was a major killer. Poor hygiene, urban overcrowding and malnutrition all encouraged its silent outbreak and spread. Native Indians were particularly vulnerable.

Records from the hospital on the Peigan reserve show patient after patient being treated for scrofula, or TB of the lymphatic glands.

There were others. So enormous was the concern about the transfer of smallpox, leprosy, scarlet fever, cholera, typhus, yellow fever, diphtheria and anthrax that the territorial government passed an order-in-council prohibiting the transportation of the bodies of victims of these diseases in the territories. The bodies of the victims of other diseases could be shipped under very stringent regulations, and then only to points within a 24-hour travelling distance, by rail or water, from the place of death.

The regulations went into grisly detail: "The body must be wrapped in a sheet thoroughly saturated with a strong solution of bichloride of mercury, in the proportion of one ounce of bichlo-

The harsh winters claimed lives. So did the unremitting physical demands. So did the high incidence of death during childbirth. So even did the home remedies.

ride of mercury to one gallon of water, and the body so wrapped must be enclosed in an air-tight zinc hermetically sealed casket and all enclosed in a strong, tight wooden box. Or the body must be prepared for shipment by being wrapped in a sheet saturated as aforesaid and placed in a strong coffin or casket and the said coffin or casket enclosed in a hermetically sealed (soldered) zinc, copper or tin case, and all enclosed in a strong outside wooden box of material not less than one and a half inches thick." The box could not be opened under any circumstances.

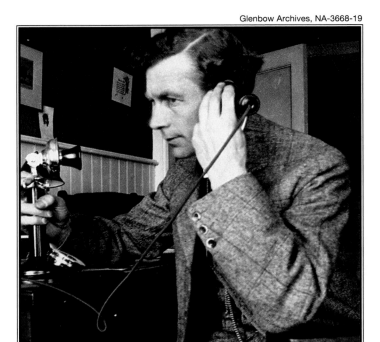

So great was the terror of infection that regular funerals often were discontinued during epidemics. Families would sneak out in the dead of the night, smothering their tears, biting back their cries, to bury a child, often hurrying home to tend to another who would be buried the next night. Friends would not attend. Often, the body was placed in a roughly constructed box and hurriedly thrust into a hastily dug grave, without benefit of clergy or liturgy.

Dorothy Jones, aged 18 months, of the Ponoka district died of scarlet fever and diphtheria, says a local history, "so the authorities insisted that she be buried at night. Her father had the heart-breaking task of driving to the cemetery at Ponoka, after dark, to bury her."

The story was not unusual. J.G. MacGregor in *The Battle River Valley* tells of a couple in the Dried Meat Creek area near Wetaskiwin who lost four of their six children to diphtheria in the 1902 outbreak:

> News of the death flew around the community. And with it flew fear. When Mr. Benson approached his nearest neighbour to lend him a team to haul the caskets of his four children to a burial spot on a hill on his

Dr. Reginald Deane in his Calgary office, around 1910. Doctors were few and far between.

farm, he found the neighbour's door shut in his face.

That day, alone in their bereavement, Benson, his wife and one son fastened straps to each of the four caskets he had hurriedly knocked together and pulled them one at a time up a slope to the freshly dug resting places. There too, all alone, they filled the graves and returned in silent sorrow to their unfinished shack.

Diphtheria held a particular horror for parents of young children. The first sign of this disease was a virulent sore throat, followed by the appearance of white spots in the mouth. A suffocating membrane then developed and, except in instances rare enough to be thought miraculous,

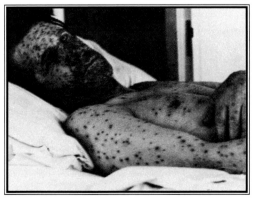

claimed the life of the victim by literally choking him to death, unless a tube was inserted in the trachea to keep the air passage open. Both the surgery and the administration of an antitoxin, effective only in the very early stages, had to be done by a physician.

In 1902, and again in 1906, diphtheria was prevalent enough to be considered epidemic and people were being warned not to share drinking cups, not to come into contact with other people, not to go outside with a sore throat. The 1902 outbreak started in Wetaskiwin and spread east along the trails followed by the new immigrants.

One such immigrant was Conrad Schweer, who headed out from Wetaskiwin with one of his two sons only to be told by a messenger the following morning that the other son was ill. Schweer raced back to Wetaskiwin in time to bury the boy and got back to the place where he had left his other son, only to find that boy had died as well.

Smallpox victim, Edmonton. By 1900 it had reached epidemic proportions, quarantine regulations started to break down.

During the 1906 outbreak, two men who had been quarantined at Frank left their room and boarded the westbound express. A Corporal Askey[1] of the RNWMP wired ahead and the train was held up at Cranbrook. The two men were discovered, immediately quarantined in a tent with the conductor and brakeman, and the whole train was fumigated. The two were eventually tried for breaking quarantine.

All too often, families were afflicted by more than one disease. The Bjorkgren family lost three children in the early 1900s, one to scarlet fever, one to whooping cough and one to diphtheria. One daughter, Elvira, recalled her mother sitting on the bed bathing a two-day-old child while within sight lay her little brother dead but as yet unburied.

There are terse references in articles and books to deaths from other conditions such as appendicitis (which was almost always fatal in the rural areas); from the harsh winter conditions, which annually claimed the lives of people struggling to save their cattle and their livelihood; and from accidents, like the one that took the life of Johnny Weiss.

The little child was riding along on a farm field in the Gooseberry Lake area where ploughing was taking place. He was thrown into the path of the furrow and got his leg cut off. He bled to death before help arrived.

There are also stories of people, like Beau Gaetz and a companion identified only as Brooks, being saved from death. The two prospectors tried to reach the Klondike from the Red Deer area by an overland route. Finding their way blocked by impossible barriers, they were obliged to turn back. As they had provisions and a prospecting outfit, they decided to see what the unexplored country of the North had to offer; for a long time, they made their way through this wilderness where no white man had ventured.

Dr. Deane on his rounds, circa 1906. Horses sometimes foundered in his rush to get to a patient far distant.

The onset of smallpox is usually violent, marked by headache, fever, vomiting, possibly convulsions. The eruptions, in their extreme stages, are particularly disgusting.

At last, they took sick with scurvy and snowblindness. They tied themselves onto their horses and were found, sick and blind, by Indians. The Indians took them to their camp, nursed them back to health and gave them enough provisions to see them back to civilization. They arrived home three years after they had left — long after their families had given them up for dead (ultimately, Beau Gaetz died in an accident — he was hit on the head by a falling tree).

But accidental death was news. Death from pestilence was not. Smallpox was another big killer; the disease that sharply reduced the Indian population in the late 1880s remained a constant threat and, in 1900, reached an epidemic level. A virulent fever was the first sign, followed almost immediately by the pocks themselves, eruptions in the skin that prevented bathing the patient to get the fever down.

The onset of smallpox was usually violent, marked by headache, fever, vomiting, possibly convulsions, and pain in the small of the back. The eruptions start on the third day. In its extreme stages, the disease is particularly disgusting. An early settler who passed through a small Indian settlement at the turn of the century describes one Indian victim: "An old woman crawled through a door, inching along on her elbows, her matted grey hair streaming around her. She moaned again, lifting a sightless face encrusted so thickly with sores running yellow pus that she had no features."

In 1902 at Fernie, BC, just west of the Alberta border in the Crowsnest Pass, seven cases of smallpox were discovered. Two hotels were quarantined and the provincial board of health issued a proclamation declaring the town in a state of quarantine until further notice. Even though the smallpox was said to be of a mild type, it was significant enough to run as the main story in the *Calgary Herald*.

There were concerns in Alberta in 1908 that the province was heading into another smallpox epidemic. "There is no denying that the number of cases of smallpox in [Calgary] are daily on the increase," says the *Edmonton Bulletin* on November 20, "and have reached a stage that is giving some cause for alarm...There have been a number of cases every week and Dr. Macdonald, the city health officer, is being kept busy. At present, the pest house is full and fresh cases are developing every day."

[1] Many of the accounts in this chapter were taken from local histories. The style of the day precluded the use of Christian names. They are therefore lost to us and to history.

Various signs of the times. Small draughty houses and a lack of medical help exacerbated matters.

Though schools and public buildings were being fumigated, quarantine regulations had broken down, said the *Bulletin*. "In one case, the head of the house has been passing backwards and forwards from work without hindrance." People moving from one boarding house to another were suspected of being prime carriers. The report underlines the castelessness of the disease: "[It] is not confining itself to the poorer class or any particular section of the city by any means, but has broken out in some of the best families, where cleanliness is strictly observed."

Maladies later considered controllable were often lethal at the century's turn. MacGregor's *The Battle River Valley* talks of the impact of scarlet fever on one party of immigrants. The group included "the parents of Mrs. E. Clara Losness and their eight children …her uncle Herman Thorson and his little girl, as well as the Bergseths, Larsons and others."

After leaving Camrose, Clara's five-year-old brother became ill. The Bergseth boy also became fretful. A few days later, he, two of Clara's brothers and her baby sister would all be dead.

As they passed Bittern Lake, John Larson's daughter felt feverish and by the time the party reached the site of Camrose, she was so ill with scarlet fever that, while the rest went on, John remained to tend her. Shortly after leaving Camrose, Clara's five-year-old brother

The doctors of yank

PIONEER DENTISTS WERE SHORT ON ANAESTHETIC BUT HANDY WITH PLIERS

Doctors in rural areas often were called on to practise other kinds of medicine. Many had to become dentists, administering rough care as best they could. Dr. Rose, who started practising in Gleichen in 1904, was one of these. A patient recalled his dental ministrations and those of another doctor-cum-dentist unfondly:

"The doctor pulled teeth without cocaine. He pulled my first one in 1908. The tooth broke off and the piece of root was left in to work out of its own accord, which it did after about a year, but the memory did not wear off in a year. Then I got another bad toothache.

"Although I put carbolic acid in the hollow, the pain got me down. I then tried Doctor Toll of Carbon. He got the forceps out of a wrapper and said, 'Sit down in this chair and pull down on the seat.' Once more I had a tooth pulled without anything to deaden the pain…

became ill. Somewhat later, the Bergseth boy also became fretful. A night or so later as they were making camp, John Larson caught up to them to report that he had buried his daughter in Camrose. Next day, while the scarlet fever still raged amongst the younger children, the group reached their homesteads. Before the week was out, Bergseths' boy, two of Clara's younger brothers and her three-month-old sister were all dead.

But few diseases could invoke the terror that arose at the very mention of typhoid — one of the fastest-spreading infections encountered in Alberta in the 1900s. It was almost impossible to guard against contagion because it could be passed on in so many ways: food, water, contact with body waste or by flies.

It gripped its victims quickly, deceptively starting with relatively mild symptoms such as headaches and general lethargy. During the four-week period of the disease, this accelerated into extreme symptoms, including haemorrhaging, high temperatures, delirium and coma. It wasn't unusual for three or four men to be called in to hold down an adult male in the advanced stages of delirium.

Typhoid fever was very much a fact of early Alberta life, with a number of cases reported every year. It reached epidemic levels in 1909. Generally, water was the culprit, as it was in the case of the Rapp family near Lacombe in 1905. They had been given an all-clear from Edmonton on the quality of their drinking water but it was, in fact, unsafe, and the father came down with typhoid. *Wagon Trails to Hard Top*, by the Lacombe History Club, tells the story:

Nurse Nellie Brown in 1896. She began her lengthy career by tending to her dying brothers.

With the house so small and the disease so infectious, he was moved to the hay loft in the barn at Rainforths where two other typhoid victims were being cared for. Here he lay very ill when on Aug. 6 a second son, Anthony, was born. Days later, Mrs. Rapp also developed the fever…Mr. Rapp succumbed to the fever on Aug. 29 (at 40)…He was laid to rest without the presence of his wife and never having seen his infant son.

Mrs. Rapp, seriously ill, wanted so much to die, but with three fatherless children, the struggle for life began despite her bleak future.

When Joe Didsbury hauled teeth out years before, he used painkiller and treated the tooth to a drop of carbolic acid."

Often there were no doctors or dentists and the people relied on someone who happened to have some tools, like John Watkins of Evarts, a community near Sylvan Lake.

When Watkins left Minnesota, his brother gave him two pairs of forceps for pulling teeth. Dozens of people sought his services. He always made them promise that if he started to pull their tooth they had to let him finish, even though they might change their mind during the operation. He then shook hands, asked the patient to open his mouth and got a firm hold on the patient by placing his arm across the victim's shoulder. Painkillers were an unnecessary frill.

Even when there were dentists available, the

A dentist's office in Innisfail, 1904. Anaesthetics were sometimes used.

process was far from comfortable. Dr. Patterson of Cereal was somewhat cavalier in his treatment of patients on occasion, including a woman who needed a decayed tooth pulled at a time Patterson was building a house. He simply put a kitchen chair in the yard, put the woman in the chair and, without any anaesthetic, extracted the tooth.

A travelling dentist made an unrelenting enemy in the Red Deer area when he told a patient to lean up against the wall of a blacksmith shop and open wide, then picked up a three-cornered file from the work bench and pried out the tooth — with the handle.

It's no wonder that Dr. John Smith Stewart, a travelling dentist who covered much of the area south of Calgary, commented that often "the asepsis was very primitive." Stewart's notes and ledgers show that the prices for his services varied widely, from a mere 25 cents to extract a tooth up to $50 for plates and bridgework.

In a diary entry from June 11, 1908, Bessie Dickson of the Neutral Hills area wrote: "Cost to have three teeth pulled and one filled was $3.50. Cost to have two front teeth crowned with gold was $15."

— S.K.

Much the same story recurs in every year of the decade at points all over the province — the essential, life-giving water was killing the people who drank it. Some survived, and even managed to get to hospital, like C.B. Selleck, who had typhoid in January 1906. In *West of the Fifth*, published by the archives committee of the Lac Ste. Anne Historical Society, he recalls:

> Moved to Lac Ste. Anne in late November and lived in Frank McConnell's house. I had typhoid in January and was in General Hospital (Edmonton) for about fifty days as I had a relapse. The rate was $1.50 a day for private room, ninety cents for semi-private and 75 cents public ward.

For people like Selleck, however, the real cost was in the time lost on the farm and homestead. Disease meant no crop, and no crop meant no money.

By October 1908 the *Bulletin* reported that typhoid "has almost reached the epidemic stage" in Edmonton. There were 22 cases at the Misericordia Hospital, eighteen more at the Public Hospital, even more in Strathcona and private nursing facilities. The report, however, said many of these cases came from outside the city and "do not indicate specially unsanitary conditions in the city." The medical health officer, Dr. Tom Whitelaw, had launched an investigation.

By 1909, the fact of a typhoid epidemic was no longer in question anywhere in the province. Lack of refrigeration, contaminated water and the ever-present flies were cited as the causes. The east-central area was hit particularly hard during 1909, with the typhoid scourge exacerbating the woes of farmers already devastated by the great prairie fire of that year, which destroyed countless homes, animals and buildings.

Both problems confronted George Gordon and his father, W.B. Gordon, who arrived at their homestead in Scotfield to find the area had been stripped by the fire. They built a small shack but there was only brackish and stagnant slough water. Mosquitoes were numerous and ravenous. George contracted typhoid and, already delirious, was sent on a 75-mile wagon ride to Castor in the heat of the summer. But there was no hospital in Castor, so he was shipped on a stretcher by freight car to Red Deer, where he spent two months in hospital.

For a variety of reasons, chief among them childbirth (see sidebar), women often predeceased their husbands. This posed a particular problem if there were young children left with the father, who had to be out in the fields for at least ten hours a day. Some widowers were able to find people to care for their children, but the situation of the Pileate family in the Alhambra area was more typical. Family breakup was the only way to provide adequate care. Mabel (Pileate) Peace describes the result: "When I was just a few month old, there was a typhoid fever epidemic and many people died, including my mother, grandmother and Aunt Irene. The three menfolk tried to look after the homestead and me...Eventually, Dad got in contact with the Salvation Army. They found someone

The renowned Dr. F.H. Mewburn and nurses in the Mackenzie River area of the North-West Territories towards the end of his career, in the 1920s. His temper was a source of folklore.

All towels, bed linen, clothing and other materials soiled by the discharge from the patient shall be immersed in a solution of bichloride of mercury of a strength of two drachmas to one gallon of water, or a solution of carbolic acid, eight ounces to one gallon of water, or a solution of chloride of lime, five ounces to one gallon of water, for one hour, and then boiled before being used again.
- *from a City of Edmonton Health Department typhoid fever notice, designed to be hung in the sick-room; about 1910.*

Dr. Harry Mackid, date unknown. He became chief CPR surgeon.

going back to England who would take care of a baby on the trip, so he sent me with them when I was just fourteen months old." She wouldn't see her father again until she was fifteen years old.

It was typhoid fever that led to the lengthy nursing career of Nellie Brown. In 1906, Mary Brown, her daughter Nellie and four young sons, Neil, John, Malcolm and Archie, moved to Stettler from Mount Forest, Ontario. During the first year, Neil and John died within a month of one another of typhoid fever. It was a hard blow. In addition to losing two sons, the family had lost its breadwinners.

It was Nellie who came to the rescue. She had taken some nursing training in the East and set up a hospital in her own home. Later, she ran a hospital for a Dr. Creighton of Stettler, where the first caesarean operation in Alberta was performed. She continued to work in the area and, in 1971, Coronation honoured her for 43 years of continuous service to that town alone.

The profession had countless other heroes, most of them unsung. Some, however, are noted. In *Early Medicine in Alberta* by Heber C. Jamieson, published by the Alberta Medical Association, tribute is paid to Dr. Herman L. McInnes, who served as an Edmonton alderman for nine years,

Ponoka Hospital under construction in 1906. The town name would become synonymous with the psychiatric facility.

Dr. McInnes pioneered medical services in the Edmonton area. Even allowing for hyperbole, accounts of his career leave no doubt he possessed an unfailing fortitude.

Members of the Alberta Medical Council, 1905-10. (L-r, back) Dr. J.D. Lafferty, Calgary; Dr. George Kennedy, Macleod; and Dr. George Macdonald, central Alberta; (front) Dr. Edgar Gower Allan, Edmonton; and Dr. R.G. Brett, Banff.

operated a large and prosperous lumber company, and on top of all this left an astonishing record of painstaking dedication to medicine. A member of the first graduating class of the University of Manitoba medical school, McInnes served in Edmonton from 1886 to 1923, pioneering medical services in the area. Even allowing for hyperbole, the accounts of his medical career leave no doubt he possessed an unfailing fortitude.

It meant "long hours in the saddle on rough and uncertain trails or long treacherous river cutbanks, or by Red River cart, to carry surgical or perhaps obstetrical help to some family half-hidden in the woods or on a distant sunlit hillside where it seemed that there was promise of a fertile soil. But no matter where he went, no matter how sore and weary his body, he carried a sustained cheerfulness which meant much to his ailing clientele. When he died in 1923, not only the profession but the public as a whole felt the loss keenly."

Another such doctor was Frank Hamilton Mewburn, "the Alberta doctor," who arrived in Lethbridge in 1885 and served until his death in 1929. He rapidly gained the trust not only of the townspeople but also of the Bloods in the area. Soon even tribes in the Blackfoot confederacy, although assigned their own white doctors by the Department of Indian Affairs, would take their seriously ill to him for treatment.

But it was in the operating theatre that he created his reputation as one of the West's most volatile characters. Indeed, the only time he was ever known to take an operating-room incident calmly was a day when all the lights in the Galt Hospital in Lethbridge went out during an operation. As the nurses and assistants winced and braced themselves for the inevitable outburst, all they got was the gentle protest that "I can't do the subject justice."

That occasion, however, was the exception. Probably the most famous illustration of Mewburn temper is the one recorded in *When the West Was Young*, by John Higinbotham, who

---

The first meeting of the college saw the adoption of fees. A urine examination would cost between $3 and $10; the first examination for VD between $10 and $30 — payable in advance.

---

writes: "During a mission, at which a number of the Roman Catholic clergy, bishops and priests from various parts of Alberta gathered at Macleod, one of the visiting fathers, who was over 80, was suddenly stricken with a strangulated hernia."

Dr. Mewburn was called in by his associate Dr. G.A. Kennedy and taken to Macleod by the Mounted Police. "He decided to operate at once by local anaesthetic and arranged that one of the bishops should read to the patient and thus divert his mind during the operation. In the midst of the clinic, a fly entered the room and buzzed so close to the operating table that it got on Dr. Mewburn's nerves. His lips began to move convulsively yet he continued with difficulty to work without exploding.

"Finally, as the objectionable intruder persisted in annoying him, he looked at Dr. Kennedy...and said, 'Kennedy, kill that fly or put the bishop out, I don't give a damn which, as I can't hold myself any longer.'" There's no record of which was swatted but there is a record that shows Mewburn never refused an appeal for help and never pressed a person for payment.

He is joined in the history of service by such people at Dr. W.D. Ferris, the president of the Edmonton Medical Society when it was reorganized in 1905 and a member of the school board and the University of Alberta Senate; Dr. Harry Goodsir Mackid of Calgary, who became chief surgeon of the western division of the CPR and, in 1911, president of the Canadian Medical Association; Dr. Thomas Henry Blow who in 1903 became the first specialist in Calgary, limiting his practice to eye, ear, nose and throat concerns; and Dr. Etta Denovan, the first

I was called urgently to rush to a woman in convulsions about forty miles distant. I took my old team and buggy and forced them to the limit to get there. The patient was late in her pregnancy and had had two convulsions...It was in a one-room shack on a hot summer day, and countless mosquitoes came through the cracks in the board walls...I took the pail and dipper to the slough one quarter-mile distant, washed away the green slime on top of the water, filled the pail, and returned to the shack. We stirred up fire enough to boil the water and to bluff at sterilizing the delivery instruments...The woman lived and the baby lived, but I had to shoot one of my old horses because I foundered him on the journey.
- *from the recollections of country doctor G.D. Stanley.*

Provincial Archives of Alberta, A-7633

woman physician in Alberta, who practised in Red Deer with her husband, Dr. H. J. Denovan, until 1903.

Another husband-and-wife team was that of Dr. Alfred Archer and his wife Jessie, a registered nurse, who arrived in Lamont in 1903. Mrs. Archer administered anaesthetic and recalled in memoirs that it was tough "to sell the latest development in health to a community of newcomers newly arrived from rustic environments in eastern Europe."

In one operation, she gave the anaesthetic for a man who had an abscess at the base of his skull. She had a large audience because the man and his relatives agreed to the operation only on the condition that all the relatives could watch. The patient and his family were not in favour of the surgery because they thought the doctor was going to operate on the man's brain. There was a tense silence as Dr. Archer opened the abscess and began deftly to remove the infected matter. But both the Archers nearly lost their professional composure as a large lady relative sighed: "Poor fellow. He never had much brains to start with."

This decade was a foundational one for medicine in Alberta, with the opening of many hospitals, including a home and small hospital in Calgary dedicated to the care of unwed mothers by the Salvation Army; the introduction of such miracles as X-rays in 1908 in Calgary; the establishment of the Victorian Order of Nurses in Calgary and Edmonton in 1909 and the formation of the

The hospital ran well, the budget seemed within reason. Then the rubbing alcohol began to disappear, and in ever-increasing quantities.

public health service.

Before 1905, Alberta, along with the districts of Assiniboia and Saskatchewan, shared in the public health activities of the North-West Territories. On the formation of the province, public health was constituted a branch of the Department of Agriculture. The first Public Health Act of Alberta became law in 1907 and provided for the creation of a provincial board of health, consisting of five members, to which it gave "authority and responsibility in regard to the making and administering of the public health regulations of the province." It also provided for the creation of health districts and a local board of health for each district. The first board of health was appointed later that year and, in 1910, under revised legislation, saw its powers considerably extended.

(L-r) The Galt Hospital in Lethbridge, 1901; Public Hospital, Edmonton, 1909; Holy Cross Hospital, Calgary, 1905. When the lights went out during an operation, Mewburn reacted with uncharacteristic calm.

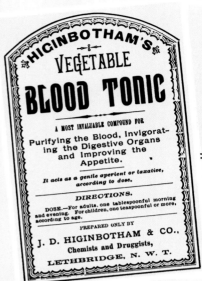

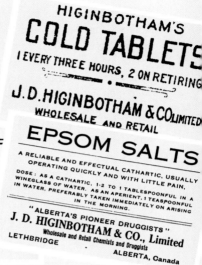

Sweet Spirits Nitre

For Producing Perspiration and Promoting Secretions, Inducing Sleep, Etc.

FOR KINDRED TROUBLES IN HORSES IT IS MUCH ESTEEMED

DOSE—One month, 5 drops; six months, 8 drops; one year, 12 drops; five years, 20 drops; ten years 40 drops; adults, one teaspoonful. Dose for horses two to four teaspoonfuls.

"ALBERTA'S PIONEER DRUGGISTS"
J.D. HIGINBOTHAM & CO. LIMITED
WHOLESALE AND RETAIL
CHEMISTS AND DRUGGISTS
LETHBRIDGE, ALBERTA, CANADA

A selection of advertisements for patent medicines and miracle cures from the first decade of the century. Narcotic or alcoholic ingredients often sold the product.

Stimulating the bowel and clouding the mind

THE PATENT MEDICINE ADS PROMISED A LOT BUT DELIVERED LITTLE MORE THAN A SURREPTITIOUS HIGH OR A DOSE OF WISHFUL THINKING

Patent medicine ads offering cures for pretty well all human discomforts and ailments augmented the financial health of Alberta's first newspapers and appeared on just about every page. Their popularity was in large part because of their ingredients, which included various intoxicants and narcotics, from alcohol to opium. "For many years," wrote Terry Chapman in an article on drug use that appeared in *Alberta History* in 1976, "friendly neighbourhood drug stores turned many housewives and early settlers into drug addicts."

The patent medicines available seemed concerned with three major health issues of the day: purity of the blood; pre-venting "imbalance in the delicate, womanly organs"; and digestion. And these good-for-you things were not sugar-coated. The remedy rarely promised to be pleasant-tasting, but then that wasn't the point.

An ad for Fruit-a-tive is downright blunt. Headlined "Apples, oranges, figs and prunes: the God-given cure for all diseases of bowels, liver, kidneys and skin," it then plunges right into a hard sell:

> Few people seem to realize how important — how absolutely necessary — it is to keep the Bowels, Kidneys

The local boards of health were charged with such things as coping with an outbreak of gastritis among Calgarians, caused by flies landing on exposed meat in shops; and setting up the licensing of milk suppliers after numerous infant deaths in Edmonton from contaminated or unsanitized milk. They also had to cope with complaints like the one from a letter writer to the *Calgary Herald*, who wanted to see a law against "promiscuous spitting" in public.

Responsibility "for the care of the insane" was recognized by the provincial government almost immediately and the act relating to mental disease was passed in 1907. This gave the lieutenant-governor-in-council power to establish mental hospitals. The building of Ponoka Mental Hospital began in 1908 and the first unit was completed in 1911. Before the opening of the Ponoka hospital, patients were sent to Brandon, Man., or held for a short time in general-treatment hospitals. The Ponoka project, said Public Works Minister W.H. Cushing, "is one of the most important matters before the department."

The decade also saw the establishment of the Alberta College of Physicians and Surgeons. On Oct. 18, 1906, the first meeting of the college was held in Calgary. Candidates' exams were

SORE THROAT CURE
Steep one red pepper in one half-pint water. Strain and add a quarter-pint vinegar, one teaspoon each of salt and alum, gargle. If gargle fails, blow flowers of sulphur through a straw into the throat.
- *From* **Homespun Philosophy of Superstition** *by* **Pearl Reuterman.**

and Skin in proper working order. They wonder why they have Sallow Complexions — Indigestion — Headaches — Rheumatism — while all the time their systems are clogged and poisoned with waste tissue and indigestible food which these organs should have removed.

The product being flogged here will naturally do exactly that:

Stimulate and regulate the action of Liver, Bowels, Kidneys and Skin, thus clearing the system of the accumulated waste and poison, purifying the blood, and banishing those distressing troubles that make life miserable.

All of that for just fifty cents a box, or six boxes for $2.50. Of the same ilk is an ad for Dr. Shoop's Restorative, which brings "lasting relief in Stomach, Kidney and Heart troubles." The reader is assured:

No matter how nerves have become impaired, this remedy will rebuild their strength, will restore their vigour. It does no good to treat the ailing organ — the irregular heart, the rebellious stomach, diseased kidneys. They are not to blame. Go back to the nerves that control them — treat the cause — use a remedy that cures through the inside nerves. Sold by Jas. Findlay.

On the same page appears another ad entitled, "A Broad Statement." It declares:

Dr. Leonhardt's Hem-Roid will cure any case of Piles. This statement is made without any qualifications. It is in the form of a tablet. It is the only Pile remedy used internally. It is impossible to cure an established case of Piles with ointments, suppositories, injections or outward appliances. A $1,000 guarantee with every package of Dr. Leonhardt's Hem-Roid.

Price: $1 at all dealers.

Elsewhere in the paper, Paine's Celery Compound promises to ensure freedom "from the infirmities that come with advancing years" and bestows on the aged "a condition of Comfort, Happiness and Peace that No Other Agency Can Give."

Dr. Chase was touting his cure for eczema:

When Baby Millar became a victim of eczema, her parents did everything that could be done to get her cured. Three doctors tried all the means in their power but without success, and then all sorts of remedies were used, with the vain hope that something would bring relief from the disease that seemed to be burning up the living flesh. It was not until Dr. Chase's Ointment was used that relief and cure came. This case is certified to by a prominent Sunday school superintendent of St. Catharines.

Mrs. William Millar, St. Catharines, Ont., writes: 'My daughter, Mary, when six months old contracted eczema and for three years this disease baffled all treatment. Her case was one of the worst that ever came to my notice and she suffered what no pen can ever describe."

Preoccupation with body weight is already an issue. A lengthy advertisement in a 1909 edition of the *Edmonton Journal* urges people to try special diet pills which, with "no help from dieting or exercising," will take off sixteen ounces per day. And breakfast cereals are being pitched as health foods. "Acids," says one advertisement, are now being added to corn flakes as "an aid to digestion."

Finally, a news article in the *Calgary Herald* offers a startling hope that would remain unfulfilled for years to come. A cure for cancer, it says, has been discovered by Dr. Otto Schmidt of Cologne, Germany, who believed he had isolated the parasite that causes this malignancy. — *S.K.*

established and 26 candidates presented themselves for the first licensing examinations. Only 25% was required to pass in chemistry but the college did require 60% in "*materia medica*" and "therapeutics" before it gave the seal of approval to doctors.

This meeting also saw the adoption of the first schedule of fees. At that time, a stethoscopic examination of the chest was something special and a fee of between $5 and $10 was allowed. An examination of a patient's urine was between $3 and $10 and the first examination of a patient with a venereal disease was between $10 and $30 — payable in advance.

This was also the decade that gave rise to nursing schools in the province. In 1905, the first students entered the Edmonton Public Hospital training and in 1906, the Holy Cross Hospital graduated its first three nursing students. The training was rigorous. The students were immediately put onto the ward, working from 7:30 a.m. to 7:30 p.m. Their study time, lectures and exams were taken in their "off" times. Formal nursing schools were established at the Holy Cross and the Edmonton General in 1908. Also that year, the Canadian National Association of Trained Nurses, the forerunner of the Canadian Nurses Association, was formed.

Bob Edwards, in the Calgary *Eye Opener*, championed the nurses, in whose care he frequently found himself when he was in hospital drying out. In 1910, he wrote:

> How would you like to be called upon to sew up a dead man? Cheerful work, we don't think. Yet a gentlewoman of refinement performed this ghastly task but a few weeks ago at the General. Another risked having her brains knocked out by a fellow with the DTs. For this, these nurses are remunerated at the munificent rate of $4 a month. This would be ridiculous were it not so pitiful. They do a good work and earn the blessings of hundreds of patients. Ask any man who has been in the hospital and, although he may be the biggest blackguard on earth, he will call those nurses 'angels'.
>
> The hospital is surely wealthy enough, with private patients paying from $3 to $7 a day. No proper reason can be adduced why the nurses shouldn't get better pay. Four dollars a

A spoonful of sugar helps the tetanus go down
IN MANY ISOLATED HOMESTEADS, THE ONLY DOCTOR WAS MOTHER

Most family medical care fell onto the shoulders of the homesteading wives in early Alberta. Not only did they have the charge of running the house — including cleaning, cooking, baking bread, churning butter, washing clothes on a washboard, weaving, mending, making clothes by hand, looking after the children, preparing the meals — and the garden, and the preserving of berries and fruit and vegetables, but they also worked outside.

They slopped pigs, milked cows, pitched hay, cleaned barns and helped with the harvest. And they had children — under the most extreme circumstances, generally without the assistance of a doctor, nurse or midwife. This accounted for the death of many pioneer wives.

Sometimes, however, the lack of a doctor was fortunate. A doctor in Leduc was believed to be responsible for the death of several patients, as evidenced in this item from *As The Years Go By*, a local history of Three Hills by the Three Hills Rural Community Group:

> While at Leduc, Jack Gibson lost his wife when (his son) was born to a dirty doctor who lost lots of mothers in the area. The people who didn't bother with him saved most of their wives.

The more ubiquitous midwife was often accorded more respect than the rare doctor. After serving in the Spanish-American war in the Philippines and in Cuba and travelling twice around the world, nurse Rachel Deans came to the Brightbank district in 1905 to join her brother. She quickly became indispensable to the community, and was credited with ushering some 150 babies into the world, seldom assisted

Triplets born to the wife of a Dr. Robertson in 1907. He is not otherwise identified. Usually there was a midwife and a 'baby-ketcher' present at the birth.

by a doctor. She never lost a mother and only one baby died.

Sometimes, when possible, midwives worked in twos. The first midwife looked after the mother and the other midwife, or "baby-ketcher," looked after the baby, tied the cord, bathed the child and got it dressed. Frequently, women would help their neighbours with childbirth, adding that to their list of duties. And they nursed their sick children and their husbands, as well as sick neighbours if need be.

Desperation was often the mother of invention for farm wives needing quick home remedies in the absence of doctors. Mrs. Robert Hargreaves of the Little Gap district had a remedy for almost everything. For burns: turpentine or grated raw potatoes. For lice: coal oil, sulphur and lard. For colds: half a teaspoon of ginger tea to one cup of hot water. For diarrhoea: a drop of laudanum in thin flour and water paste or hard-boiled egg in boiled milk for baby, or brandy burned with a red

month will hardly buy seed for a canary. And why cannot they work the nurses four hours on and eight hours off, day and night? Anyhow, the whole thing needs seeing to. Our young ladies studying to be trained nurses…should be treated as fairly as the Galicians who delve in the street sewers, if not in pecuniary reward, at least in length of working hours.

Despite the many medical advances in the 1900s, however, rural care was often given by a nurse or a doctor, working alone for long hours, trying to meet the diverse and growing needs of the community. Many of these people, like Dr. C.H. Lawford, were appointed by the church. Dr. Lawford, a doctor and ordained Methodist minister, was sent as "missionary to the Galicians," with headquarters at the old Fort Victoria mission, northeast of Edmonton, which was established by George McDougall — "the scene of much tragedy at the time of the smallpox."

Because the Indians recognized the virulence of the disease, they often deserted those who

hot nail. As a liniment: one cup of vinegar, one cup of turpentine and one egg white, shaken till creamy, good for man or beast. For coughs: large onion, cut up and covered with water, boiled, the water then strained and mixed with an equal amount of honey.

The Duhamel district also had its list of sure-cure home remedies, most of them just as practical. For example, the best way to treat an area penetrated by a rusty nail is to dissolve

hide behind a door. When the barley has finished popping, your sty has also popped."

Liberal doses of home-made liquor, highly illegal, were used to treat toothaches, even when there were dentists available. The alcohol was held in the mouth for a few minutes and then swallowed. Imaginary toothaches were not uncommon.

When a person had an epileptic seizure, his shirt was removed from his body and wrapped around a stone. This was

Bad cuts were stuffed with flour. A good dose of pepper treated a stomach ache. Puffballs were used to pack into open wounds. Sulphur was used for a sore throat.

one teaspoonful of sugar in turpentine and spread over the infected area. It can also be treated by beating the white of one egg and mixing with half a teaspoon of lard, one heaping tablespoon of flour and a drop of Lysol. The best way to treat pneumonia is to rub the chest, feet and hands with a mixture of skunk fat and turpentine.

Chapped hands were soaked in buttermilk and then rubbed dry in a pan of cornmeal. It hurt but it worked. Bad cuts were stuffed with flour and soon the bleeding stopped. A good dose of pepper treated a stomach ache. Puffballs were used to pack into open wounds. Sulphur was used to treat a severe sore throat. You just put it onto a teaspoon and blew it into the open mouth of the sufferer. If he didn't choke, the sore throat was relieved.

As had his ancestors centuries before, Chan Gowan, who homesteaded near Delia, discovered that if he chewed the foxglove plant, he had more energy. Later, doctors would routinely treat people with digitalis, a heart stimulant from the same plant.

But not all the treatments remained within the realm of the natural. In *Memories: Redwater and District*, a local history, the anonymous author makes it clear that many of the remedies were related to witchcraft and superstition. Styes, for example, were treated thus: "Take nine kernels of barley, throw them on a hot stove counting backwards from nine to one as you throw them on. Throw them on quickly and then

then thrown over a building. Wherever it fell, it was buried. By the time the person burying the rock returned, the patient was fully recovered. A child suffering from ongoing nightmares might well be taken to the home of a person, usually a woman, endowed with the powers of magic. The child was put on a table and a flat pan of cold water was placed on its forehead. The person then melted pure beeswax and dripped this into the pan. When the wax solidified, it took the shape of the object or animal that scared the child. A few magic words were chanted and presto! No more fears.

But the standby physician in every household was mother. In his family summary for *Battle River Country*, Hill Quist of the Verdun district acknowledged the debt owed the women who lived and sacrificed during those pioneer days:

I know those good old days were hard on women. My mother nursed us through the usual childhood ailments, one of which was a very bad type of scarlet fever that nearly caused the end of me. They never had a doctor in all their years on the homestead (which they left in 1903), but made liberal use of simple home remedies. My father often brushed our sore throats with a feather which had been soaked in kerosene. These remedies, plus mother's prayers and her faith in the Great Physician brought us through, but not without much worry and much loss of sleep.

— *S.K.*

had it, leaving them to die and fleeing to save their own lives. They also had to contend with the changing lifestyle that came to them with the development of the prairies.

In *The Prairie Hub,* author J.J. Martin recalls working on the Blackfoot reserve in June, 1910, cooking for the agent who was doing a cattle count in the Cluny, Gleichen and Stobart areas, as well as around the Buffalo Hills and Bassano. He speaks of a decision by Indian superintendent J.A. Markle to plough the land for crops, even though it was best suited for pasturing cattle and ponies. But he went further:

> He had houses constructed with cottage roofs and a fireplace to take the place, as near as possible, of the Indian teepees. The fireplace, with its big flue, was to have about the same effect as the open flap of the old teepees, but when the Indians got set up in their houses, they plugged up the fireplace and set up a stove.
>
> In 1910, there were many of the Indians suffering from tuberculosis, many being walking skeletons. They were living in small log houses along the river, as many as fifteen in one small building, without a window in it. In the prairie days, when the Blackfeet ranged at large, they were healthy, living on fresh camping sites and in the well ventilated teepees. Before the smallpox outbreak in 1870, their numbers were said to be 10,000. In 1910, there were only 750...
>
> In the buffalo days, they had new skin teepees each year, walled up inside by a second one. They could live the year around in them as the sanitation of a campsite was taken care of by nature when the Indians moved to a clean, new camping ground.
>
> White man's food did not agree with the Indian digestive system. Scones made from white flour and fried in beef tallow were the cause of much digestive trouble, many being acute cases of dyspepsia...A sudden change to a new way of living was the downfall of the Indians' health. They had lived on meat, herbs, berries and roots in their natural nomad way of life and change came about too hurriedly.

The doctors treating the natives were often stumped by the attitude of their patients. Despite the best medical advice, Indians suffering from TB would take sweat baths and then plunge into the icy river. And always, the doctors contended with the medicine men of the tribes. Martin looks at the annual meeting of the three Blackfoot bands that came together once a year, in late June, under the headship of Chief Crowfoot.

At this month-long meeting, men and women and medicine practitioners practised new arts to cure the sick and ailing by their magic, conjuring and witchcraft as well as how to appease the ghost of death by the drum beat's rhythm of death; and to smoke the sacred pipe and shake the rattle over the sick. Braves were made, old vows fulfilled and new ones made. The medicine men had practised their cure by magic for many generations, and they looked upon white doctors, who were appointed by the government to call upon their sick patients, as intruders upon their age-old monopoly.

Crowfoot had 27 medicine men attending him as he lay dying in his teepee, near where he is buried. Dr. Henry George was engaged by the government to attend to the chief, but his assistance was refused by Crowfoot, who passed on, a victim of lung trouble. In the pulsate beat of the ghost drum and the sacred power of magic and witchcraft, he passed away to eternal rest and was buried half inside of the Catholic cemetery and halfway out, his feet firmly on pagan soil. (Other sources say Crowfoot accepted George's treatment.)

The medicine men were far from quacks, however, and most were skilled in setting bones, adjusting dislocated joints, tying severed arteries and using tourniquets. Some were also priests and prophets who prayed for the souls of the dead and told the future.

Some of the services of the doctors and nurses were accepted by the Indians, however. Missionary nurses frequently ran orphanages, such as the McDonald Orphanage at Morley, and rarely were able to give up their profession, even when they married and had families of their own, because the demand was so great and there was no one to take their places.

But not quite all the doctors, or those who claimed the title, were paragons of virtue. Medicine produced some zany characters in the province's first years, and Edmonton seemed to have more than its share of them. One of the most famous is Dr. Sullivan (his first name has not survived),

Variola (va-ri'-o-lah) Smallpox, a contagious infectious disease ushered in with severe febrile symptoms, which, in the course of two or three days, are followed by a papular eruption spreading over all parts of the body. During the succeeding two weeks the eruption passes through the stage of vesicles and pustules, the latter going on to the formation of crusts. The falling off of the crusts leaves a pitted appearance of the skin (pockmarks). The period of incubation is about thirteen days.
- from the **Student's Medical Dictionary, 1900.**

who was hired to run an isolation hospital, specializing largely in tuberculosis, the silent but widespread killer of the era. By 1905, when the hospital was built, the smallpox epidemic of 1900 had died down, diphtheria was present but not rampant, and the deadly typhoid fever of 1909 hadn't made its appearance.

Dr. Sullivan was hired by the directors to run the new isolation hospital, built, some felt symbolically, on the city dump. He had been spending the summer as a railway labourer, said Dr. Sullivan, but would now like to return to the practice of medicine. The directors believed him and hired him without further checking.

At first, he seemed satisfactory. The hospital ran well, the budget seemed within reason, the patients were not asked if they had any complaints. Then the rubbing alcohol began to disappear, in ever-increasing quantities. Soon, a nurse established beyond doubt that it was disappearing into Dr. Sullivan. Shortly, "Dr." Sullivan himself disappeared, back to his real profession, a labourer on the railway.

Another Edmonton health official who did a disappearing act was an alderman of 1907. Dr. Turnan really was a doctor and since the city had no medical health officer, he volunteered to act in that capacity. And he did an excellent job, until he heard measles had broken out among the "ladies" of the Norwood district, then on the northern city limits and known for its bars and prostitutes.

The doctor got a health warrant to search out cases of measles which, he warned, could creep into the main city via the unsuspecting customers of the "ladies" and start an epidemic.

He found, however, no evidence of measles, but lingered nonetheless for most of the day in one of the bars. By evening, when he was riding home, his judgement was less than sober and he caused a major scandal by banging on doors of houses along the road, waving his warrant and demanding to check upright and righteous housewives for measles. He left town shortly after that.

Operating room, General Hospital, Calgary, 1908. (Left) Julia Murphy, operating room supervisor, giving anaesthetic.

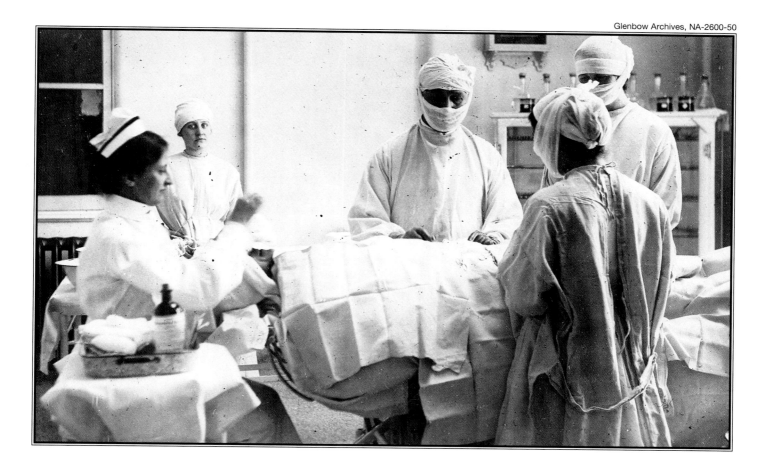

CHAPTER FOUR

High or low, rustic or urban, culture was invariably vigorous

CONCERT HALLS AND DANCE HALLS DOTTED THE EMERGING PROVINCE, BUT BY 1900 THE NEFARIOUS MOTION PICTURE HAD ALREADY ARRIVED

Glenbow Archives, NA-1709-23

An audience is assembled to watch a movie at the Innisfail Opera House in 1910.

by STEPHANI KEER

Between televisions, video cassette recorders, and compact disk players, Alberta's arts, culture and entertainment by the end of the 20th century had become a mainly indoors, personal, sedentary and pre-canned affair. Such was not the case, however, in the century's first decade. Almost all entertainment then was live, and came in a surprisingly large, vigorous and imaginative assortment: travelling opera and play companies, "magic lantern" shows, local "literary societies," acrobatics and, of course, athletics.

Such home entertainment as existed went mainly to the well off. A few, for instance, could afford the Berliner-Victor Gram-O-Phone and enjoy "a concert as you could never hear in any theatre or concert hall." A 1903 ad in the *Edmonton Bulletin* priced them at between $15 and $45, complete with three records and a five-year guarantee.

Virtually all home entertainment was musical. A *Calgary Herald* ad in 1901 offered "The World's Best Music" — 2,200 pages of musical scores for a mere $27. And it could be played on a piano made in Edmonton at the West's only piano manufacturing plant. The Strauss Piano Company opened in 1904 for "the manufacture of high grade pianos," according to the *Edmonton Bulletin*. With a staff of twenty it could build 400 a year, and held weekly recitals at its downtown showroom.

But as the local histories of Alberta make plain, rural people (and that was most of the population) relied more upon local talent and local diversions, such as weddings. In Ukrainian communities these routinely kept going for three days, and in others at least until dawn. In many areas, newlyweds couldn't escape their friends even after the festivities had officially ended. Local bachelors would "chivaree" the couple by hooting, hollering and banging pots and pans outside their home once the lights had gone out until they were invited inside for something more to eat and drink.

More common than weddings were dances. In Greencourt northwest of Edmonton, for example, there was a dance every month, according to *West of the Fifth*, a chronicle of the Lac Ste. Anne district. Greencourt's dance hall measured forty feet by 120 feet and boasted a maplewood floor. Depending on how busy they were farming or how cold it was, between 300 and 800 people would dance to at least a three-piece band: two violins and an accordion. Families would arrive

Ready for a dance at Thorhild in 1910.

'The figures they saw moved on a big screen stretched across the stage and while these walked and ran at bewildering speed, they were lifelike and exciting.'

from "Sangudo on the east, Whitecourt on the west; from Junkins, Mosside, etc., and dance from 8 p.m. till daylight." Supper was served at midnight and sandwiches, cake and coffee around 4 a.m. The men paid $1, ladies attended at no charge, and there was no drinking. Children came too; when they tired they simply rolled up in blankets in a corner and slept.

West of the Fifth also recounts the establishment of the "Peavine Literary Society," a winter

Ukrainian dancing in the Hilliard-Chipman area early in the century.

amusement. "In spite of the swanky name," writes Eustace Reddish, "these meetings were invariably jolly affairs and it was usually a case of standing room only." The activities included debates, concerts, spelling bees, social evenings, with special emphasis on coffee and cake.

Coronation in eastern Alberta lacked a hall in its early days, so people danced in the larger homes. Couches were moved from the living areas and, when there was a bigger crowd than usual, the beds went out too. These dances as well lasted till daylight, if only because it was impossible to see the homeward trail in the dark. South of Coronation at Cereal dances were held in the local school. The music was free, the women attending brought food, and the charge for the evening was ten cents — for those who could afford it.

The same story is told in the Neutral Hills. "It never seemed to be necessary for the partici-

---

Children came to the all-night dances too. When they tired, they simply rolled up in blankets in a corner and slept.

---

pants to sit for two or three hours sipping alcoholic beverages to get in the right mood and frame of mind to dance," notes the author of *Echoes Along the Ribstone*. "They were ready when they came and still ready when they left." People were familiar with "steps from one to seven, minuets imported from half a dozen foreign countries, polkas, lancers, quadrilles, and waltzes with a dozen different variations." At the indispensable midnight supper break, individuals would perform songs, recitations, jigs, boxing, Indian wrestling, feats of magic or whatever moved them. "Regardless of how silly this may sound," *Echoes* says, "at that time, every item was entertainment supreme."

During the summer, dances often gave way to massive community picnics. In *Green Fields Afar*, by C. and J. Middleton, the authors talk about one such affair in the Carstairs district:

Well over a hundred people attended that picnic and we had an abundance of entertainment. One of the cowboys had brought a couple of bucking horses and several had a try at riding them. An obstacle horse-race was a lively spectacle. Foot races were arranged for the younger fry. A quartet off to one side pitched horseshoes with strained attention and careful measurement after each end. On a platform, a young Englishman named Hepburn sang comic songs and did a nonsense monologue. Mr. Johnson and several others made speeches, without saying anything of importance — an ideal accomplishment before a mixed crowd — and the ball game was exciting...But the greatest interest of all was in getting acquainted with one another. Then came supper on the grass with a boilerful of hot coffee to wash it down.

'I don't think I ever saw a swimming suit. The ladies wore dresses into the water and the men wore overalls and usually something over the top half, too.'

The presence of some form of rodeo usually crops up in accounts of such gatherings, as well as riding for pleasure. In some areas, such as Hand Hills north of Drumheller, the picnics were centred around lakes. Morden Lane in *Hand Hills Heritage*, recalls what it was like:

At the early day picnics at Hand Hills Lake, I don't think I ever saw a swimming suit. The ladies wore dresses [into the water] and the men wore overalls and usually something over the top half, too. The lunches were feasts and there were plenty of lovely shady bowers to set up the tables and plenty of private groves in which to change. I don't believe I have ever seen a nicer bathing beach than the south end of Hand Hills Lake, with its gently sloping clear firm sand, the view, the fresh water smell, and the impression you got that the soda in the water was turning your skin whiter.

Photography from the turn-of-the-century onward became a growing art form. Above, Girl with Violin is from the Ernest Brown Collection at the Provincial Archives. The girl is not identified. The fiddler at left is Phil Weinard, of High River.

Not all entertainment was rustic, however. The papers of that decade carry numerous advertisements from people like Charles LaGourgue, "gold medallist of the Conservatoire de Paris, experienced leader of orchestra, teacher of piano, violincello, clarinette, organ, harmonium, solfeggio (theory, transposition, etc.), harmony, composition, accompaniment." He also delivered free recitals on the "celebrated Mustel Organ," and was available by appointment only, for those interested in this "class of music."

The *Calgary Herald* may have complained on April 2, 1901 that the performance of "Madame Albani and her company of artistes from London, England" was a little too highbrow for the paper's taste, with a program "which ran largely to Italian and other foreign languages," but every seat in the opera house was taken at the high price of $1 to $2 by "a splendid audience, representing all that is best

The Edmonton Operatic Company is ready for a performance of Gilbert and Sullivan's Trial By Jury, *1905.*

How happy I feel when
I roll into bed,
The rattlesnake rattles a
tune at my head,
The little mosquito devoid
of all fear,
Crawls over my face and
into my ear,
The little bed-bug so cheerful and bright,
It keeps me up laughing
two-thirds of the night,
And the small little flea
with tacks in his toes
Crawls up through my
whiskers and tickles my
nose.
*- from a popular prairie
song, author unknown.*

in the musical population of central Alberta." Many in the audience were puzzled by the first presentation, Beethoven's Kreutzer Sonata for the violin and piano, "an exceedingly dreary composition of the most classical order." The audience "listened respectfully, as in duty bound, but the uneducated musical barbarian — who by the way is a numerous and important individual out in this Western country — was wondering all the time when the players were going to get down to business." However, after several similar paragraphs, the tone of the review changes: "The *Herald* is free to admit that every member of Madame Albani's company is an artiste who is worth going many miles to hear." The program, the reviewer admits, as a whole was "immensely enjoyed by nearly everybody."

The Calgary Opera House and Hull's Opera House were the scene of numerous entertainments, including the ambitious programs of the Calgary Operatic Society which, in 1900, was entering its sixth season. In 1900, the society was performing *The Geisha*, to the constant applause of the audience. The *Herald* critic suggested only that a "reasonable average could be struck by the management of the costume department between [Captain Katana's] pantaloons and his sleeves. The military tailor of Japan is evidently long on trousers and short on sleeves, which may be all right on general principles but is rather rough on Captain Katana."

Other typical Calgary Opera House performances, these from 1903, were *Uncle Tom's Cabin* and *Ten Nights in a Bar Room*, with a company of 25 travelling in two special cars. In addition to the acting company, there was a band, a concert orchestra, a pack of genuine bloodhounds, a black quartette and a carload of scenery. The next month, the stage was given over to violinist Paul Szigety, playing his $25,000 Guarnerius. Ticket prices were 75 cents for a reserved seat, fifty cents for general admission adult and 25 cents for children.

Over on the stage of Hull's Opera House in May 1900 was a veritable storehouse of culture. The Casino Comedy Company performed *Mrs. Brown's Troubles*, described as a "roaring comedy farce," and eight big novelty acts, headed by Drakero, the great Philipino contortionist. It was all, the public was assured, "clean and refined." Later that month, Harold Nelson and his company appeared in three Shakespearean plays: *Hamlet, Othello* and *The Taming of the Shrew*.

Edmonton, too, was on the cutting edge of the arts in Alberta in the early 1900s. The

Edmonton Operatic and Dramatic Society was formed in November 1903 and opened with *The Chimes of Normandie*, staged in April 1904 under the direction of Vernon Barford. He was also the organist at All Saints (Anglican) Cathedral, played the piano for dances, and organized music festivals for nearly sixty years in the capital. The fee for honorary society membership was $2.50, and the subscription for active members was $1.

The society's inaugural production was fraught with problems. Shortly into rehearsal, it was discovered the lead tenor was really a baritone, and a replacement had to be found. There was no room for scenery on the bandbox stage of Robertson's Hall along with the fifty members of the company and the twelve musicians. The costumes had been rented from Chicago and when they arrived in Edmonton, a customs official unexpectedly demanded full duty. Only string-pulling by Edmonton MP Frank Oliver could get the duty dropped. On opening night, the tenor fainted at the end of the second act — but he recovered and finished the performance.

Edmonton lagged behind Calgary in the culture department. At the turn of the century it had no permanent theatre company and no real theatre. Touring shows were put on at the huge Thistle Rink on Second Street (102nd) or at Robertson's Hall, a much smaller auditorium on the upper floor of a wholesale warehouse on Jasper Avenue East which burned down in May, 1906. A Minneapolis entrepreneur was ready in the wings, and quickly started work on the Empire Theatre. Essentially a vaudeville house, it was thirty feet by fifty feet, with a colonial front, a level floor, a stage and room for 400.

It also was no great success. But in July of that year, 1906, local entrepreneur Alexander W. Cameron announced the Empire would be tied into a major circuit: "All performers will be first class, direct from the Metropolitan Theatres of the South," trumpeted the *Edmonton Bulletin*. There were to be two shows daily, with seats priced at 10 and 15 cents for matinees and 15 and 25 cents for evenings. The program changed twice a week, and the opening bill July 16 featured "Ali Zada the necromancer," the Merritt Sisters who sang and did contortionist tricks, and Miss Elsie Yates singing songs illustrated by lantern slides.

The Music Festival in the Thistle Arena, Edmonton, 1910.

Photographer Ernest Brown who came to Edmonton in 1904 and whose collection includes the works of an earlier photographer, Charles W. Mathers, is shown with his studio equipment in 1913.

But there is no space to tell how we fed, with a prairie appetite, in the men's quarters, on a meal prepared by an artist; how we raced home at speeds no child could ever hear of and no grown-up should attempt...how great horses hauled the motors up the gravelly bank into the town; how there we met people in their Sunday best walking and driving, and pulled ourselves together and looked virtuous; and how the merry party suddenly and quietly vanished because they thought that their guests might be tired. I can give you no notion of the pure, irresponsible frolic of it; of the almost affectionate kindness, the gay and inventive hospitality that so delicately controlled the whole affair; any more than I can describe a certain quiet half-hour in the dusk just before we left, when the company gathered to say goodbye, while the young couples walked in the street, and the glare of the never-extinguished gas lamps coloured the leaves of the trees a strange green.

It was a woman, speaking out of the shadow, who said what we all felt: "You see, we just love our town." "So do we," I said, and it slid behind us.

- *From* **The Town that Was Born Lucky,** *an essay by Rudyard Kipling about his visit to Medicine Hat on Oct. 13, 1907, which appeared in* **Colliers Weekly on May 18, 1908.**

Edmontonians seem not to have shared Cameron's love of live entertainment. Within two months many of the live performances had been replaced by the new moving picture shows. But Cameron was not discouraged. By September, 1906, he had started work on the Edmonton Opera House, an $8,000 building on Jasper Avenue described in the *Edmonton Journal* as "48 by 150 feet, two storeys high, with a 22- by 48-foot full-size stage large enough to accommodate the largest companies."

It opened on schedule in mid-October, although the facility was far from complete, but found itself facing strong competition from the Thistle Arena which had responded to Cameron's challenge by improving its stage facilities and booking the popular Harold Nelson Stock Company to play for more than a week. The Opera House, however, had also booked favourite players, including Claude Amsden and Hazel Davenport, who had built up a major following in Edmonton at the Thistle Arena, and a company led by a duo named Florence and Johnny Pringle.

Performances were held nightly, with matinees on Thursday and Saturday. Reserved seats cost fifty cents, unreserved 35 cents and children paid 25 cents. Despite the grandness of the building and the name of the structure, the seats were very utilitarian, plain chairs put out in more or less straight rows. The Pringle Company stayed with the Opera House until the end of October and occasionally took its productions into the countryside when a touring show booked in at Cameron's auditorium. For example, the Westminster Abbey Choir appeared Oct. 22, 1906, and the Pringles took *East Lynne* to the new opera house at Fort Saskatchewan.

In November, Cameron installed steam heat in his building and in December he dumped the poorly attended Thursday matinees in favour of roller skating every weekday afternoon, with a rental stock of 150 pairs of roller skates. The roller skating craze was such that the *Calgary Herald* noted that "the elusive little rollers still continue to hold sway in all hearts...Even Anna Held, the famous actress, has introduced a skating chorus in her *Parisian Model*, one scene of which depicts a skating rink, with the entire chorus of forty or more mounted on rollers."

By 1907, Cameron had finished the Opera House with new paint and wallpaper and started construction of the Kevin Theatre, a vaudeville establishment with seating for 450. It was adjacent to the Opera House — and when fire broke out in the Kevin in July, 1907, the Opera House was also seriously damaged.[1]

After the fire, Cameron hired two Calgary businessmen, C.W. Willis and W. Cosgrove, to operate the Edmonton Opera House. They had already leased the Lyric Theatre in Calgary and ran what they called the Western Canada Theatrical Circuit, with houses in Saskatchewan and BC. It didn't work. By mid-1908, Cameron had taken the two to court, claiming they had cost him money. The judge agreed, but suggested the difference in theatre income between the two cities was not attributable to negligence by the operators; it merely reflected the superior cultural sophistication of Calgarians.

In the midst of all this, Cameron built yet another theatre. The 200-seat Lyric opened in August, 1907, under the management of its resident baritone, Hilliard Campbell. It was designed to compete with the planned Orpheum, a much more glamorous house which would rival the Opera House. It took only two months for Cameron to sell the Lyric to the Orpheum owner. He then turned his attention back to the site of the burned-out Kevin, where he developed the Dominion Theatre, making the grand new lobby facilities available to Opera House patrons as well. By 1910, however, Cameron seems to have finally given up and left Edmonton altogether.

The truth was that high-end culture was becoming financially disastrous in Alberta and everywhere. The century of the motion picture had begun. It had first appeared in Alberta in early 1900. C.H. Stout, in *From Frontier Days in Leduc and District*, describes the momentous event:

> One night about 1900, a small crowd sat spellbound in R.T. Telford's new hall on Telford Street as soldiers marched and rode on trains and French dandies flirted on the streets of Paris. The figures they saw moved on a big screen stretched across the stage and while these walked and ran at bewildering speed, they were lifelike and exciting. It was the first motion picture show seen in Leduc and tickets for the one-night stand were fifty cents. Folks talked about the new sensation for days, forgetting the eye and ear strains caused by the flickers and the operating machine.

By 1901, the Hull Opera House in Calgary was in on the craze, bringing in a film of the funeral procession of Queen Victoria, who had died in January. "Don't fail to see it," an ad in the *Calgary Herald* exhorted, "as you will witness with your own eyes the Grand Military Funeral of the Greatest Ruler the World has ever had. The views are taken from Hyde Park and as the long procession passes within a distance of thirty feet of you, King Edward and the German emperor at his side, riding a white horse, are life size and are followed by the nobility of Europe with all the Pomp and Splendor of the Great European Courts." Regular Opera House prices of 75, fifty and 25 cents applied.

It wasn't until 1903 that the first moving picture was shown in Edmonton, but the Edmonton Opera House (a forerunner of the Cameron extravaganza) made up for the delay

Glenbow Archives, NC-39-286

Glenbow Archives, NC-39-2961

¹Fire indeed took its toll of Alberta opera houses. Wetaskiwin's Heric Opera House was destroyed when fire broke out in the ladies' dressing room in June 1903. It was so intense that the touring company performing there lost everything, including their jewellery and other personal property valued at approximately $7,000. In addition to the opera house, several other buildings in the town's centre were damaged or destroyed.

Ella Hart, a nurse, came to Alberta from Chicago in the early 1890s. Her art photographs of children provide one of the best collections depicting Alberta life early in the century. Little Girl Holding Rabbit was from Thelma, Alta. Boy and Dog in the Shade is not identified.

by booking not a solo pianist or organist to accompany the film but an entire orchestra. The ad for the "enormous attraction" boasts of "100,000 Bioscope Animated Pictures of Living Canada, representing a 3,000-mile run through the Domin-ion, including the Sights, March and Progress of the World."

By 1910 motion pictures had invaded rural Alberta. For instance, the Pekin Theatre in Castor was showing four films Friday and Saturday night. Typical fare: *The Curly Head* (comic), *The Mexican's Ward* (dramatic), *The Cowboy and the Schoolma'am* (romantic), and *Women's Rights* (a scream).

In fact, culture of all sorts was as enthusiastically promoted in the smaller centres as in Edmonton and Calgary. Medicine Hat, for example, was a hotbed of performing arts in the early 1900s, with choirs, musicians and locally based theatre companies. The town frequently hosted travelling (and increasingly sophisticated) companies, performing Gilbert and Sullivan operettas as well as more classical and contemporary fare. Performances took place in Colter's Opera House until 1902, when the more soundly constructed community centre opened.

The townspeople themselves were hardly bashful. For example, in 1904, under the direction of W.J. Brotherton, the town's only jeweller, an oratorio featured a choir of 35 voices from all the churches of Medicine Hat. Two months later, a group from St. Barnabas Anglican Church put on an ambitious show in the opera house. Called "An Evening With Dickens," the program consisted of 27 tableaux, songs, choruses and sketches from the works of the British novelist performed by 75 members of the congregation.

In Wetaskiwin, a concerted effort to establish a band started in the fall of 1901 and by January an organization had been formed, with George Mayberry as the bandmaster. In May, 1903, the band went to Calgary to compete in a provincial competition and came home first-place heroes with $100.

Newspaper clippings from the decade show such events as an exhibition by famous skater J.K. McCulloch slated for Calgary in January, 1900. McCulloch had twice won the championship of Canada and the United States as well as the championship of the world once in amateur speed contests, and held international records for three distances. His display, however, was of "fancy" skating, accompanied by the Fire Brigade Band.

In 1903, J.W. Bengough, still remembered as one of the great Canadian political cartoonists, put on a public show in Calgary with a sheet of paper and a few crayons. His caricatures of local bigwigs drew applause from the capacity crowd, already impressed by his ability to recite and sing as well as draw. One of the people lampooned was, according to the *Calgary Herald*, "the business manager of this great daily whose classic features were faithfully reproduced as if in a mirror."

In 1908, a "world-famed" tight-wire performer styling himself Professor Cogan (complete with waist-length beard) stretched his wire across McDougall Avenue (100th Street) in downtown Edmonton and performed his daredevil stunts. He drew a large crowd by challenging "any man in the city to stand heels together on the ground and pull him from the wire by means of a rope while he stands balancing on one foot," and by promising to catch a baseball thrown full force by any man any number of times. (Whether he actually did this was not reported.)

In 1909, "aeronaut" Professor Kohl rose some 1,400 feet above Edmonton in his hot-air balloon and then jumped from the basket with a parachute. He was practising for the upcoming Dominion Fair, where he hoped to jump from 4,000 feet. That same year, Edmontonians were treated to the "artistry" of the French-trained roosters Torcat and Flor D'Aliza at the Empire Hotel. The birds "walk tight wires" and "ride bicycles" and even recreate the Jeffries-Johnson heavyweight championship match.

In addition to such exotica, there was much serious visual art, both free-hand and photographic, to record the passing of the frontier. The decade saw the rise of some excellent artists, including Arthur A. Brooke, the son of an English painter, who homesteaded with two brothers west of Didsbury in 1901. In 1902 he sold a number of his sketches to Copp Clarke & Co. of Toronto, which published them, much to his chagrin, as a series of colour lithographs which he thought detestable. He started on a new series of 47, "Sketches of Ranching Life in Sunny Alberta," which were never published. In 1907, he moved to Salmon Arm, BC, where he continued to draw and paint.

Poetry had not yet died the death the 20th century had in store for it. Stephan G. Stephansson had already added to the rich literary repository of his native Iceland before emigrating to the

Markerville district southwest of Red Deer in 1889. When he arrived penniless in the North-West Territories he eked out a living by fishing, hunting and farming, and, when absolutely necessary, he worked on a CPR survey crew. Despite his poverty, he was active in the community: the first chairman of the Markerville School District and one of the organizers of the Tindastoll Butter and Cheese Manufacturing Company. He continued writing poetry, and much of it reflects his love for Canada and Alberta, including this piece from "Toast to Alberta":

> Here veils of Northern Light are drawn
>   On high as winter closes,
> And hoary dews at summer dawn
>   Adorn the wild red roses.
> Sometimes the swelling clouds of rain
>   Repress the sun's caresses;
> But soon the mountains smile again
>   And shake their icy tresses.

But despite his involvement in the community, he wasn't popular. Many of his views, including his opposition to what he saw as the narrow-mindedness of the churches, antagonized his neighbours, as did his propensity for socializing and neglecting his wife and eight children.

Another homesteader, Georges Bugnet, settled in the Rich Valley area north of Edmonton in 1905 and later became renowned through novels and poetry as Alberta's best author in French. His fourth novel, *La Fôret*, relates the brutal transformation of a young, urban French couple, the Bourgoins, who came to homestead in northern Alberta and were eventually defeated by the land. He may have been a member of *Le Cercle Richelieu*, a literary and dramatic society organized in 1905 by Edmonton francophones to preserve French on the prairies.

But perhaps the most famous of all the writers of that decade was Pauline Johnson, a treaty Mohawk princess whose Indian name was Tekahionwake, even though genetically she was three-quarters white. She travelled across Canada giving recitals anywhere, even in bars (for which, as a status Indian, she could technically have been arrested). She wore a buckskin dress trimmed with ermine and adorned with ancient silver brooches hammered from coins by her own forebears, bear-claw necklace and bracelets of wampum, a red broadcloth blanket, moccasins and an eagle feather in her hair. Her accoutrements also included two human scalps hanging at her belt, one inherited from her great-grandfather Jacob Tekahionwake, who adopted the surname Johnson when he was baptized into the Anglican Church. The origin of the other is shrouded in contradictory legend.

But despite the stage gimmickry, Pauline Johnson evoked in her audiences, whether of the schoolroom, poolroom, barroom or meeting hall, an unabashed delight in their country. Alberta's landscape and people had inspired many of her poems, such as "Calgary of the Plains" and "At Crow's Nest Pass." "The Train Dogs," which follows, was written after Miss Johnson and her partner, Walter McRaye, saw a train of huskies come down Jasper Avenue in Edmonton, dragging a sleighload of fur. The dogs were weary, wiry skeletons, McRaye recalled, and the Indian musher was himself played out. Despite that, the man lavished praise on his panting team. "Good dogs," he called to them, "we beat 'em!"

> Out of the night and the North,
>   Savage of breed and of bone,
> Shaggy and swift comes the yelping band,
>   Freighters of fur from the voiceless land
> That sleeps in the Arctic zone.
>
> Laden with skins from the North,
>   Beaver and bear and racoon,
> Marten and mink from the polar belts,
>   Otter and ermine and sable pelts —
> The spoils of the hunter's moon.

> Out of the night and the North,
>   Sinewy, fearless and fleet,
> Urging the pack through the pathless snow,
>   The Indian driver, calling low,
> Follows with moccasined feet.
>
> Ships of the night and the North,
>   Freighters on prairies and plains,
> Carrying cargoes from field and flood,
>   They scent the trail through their wild red blood,
> The wolfish blood in their veins.

CHAPTER FIVE

Playing to win in a whole new ballgame called Alberta

THE HARDY YOUNG SETTLERS OF A TOUGH NEW PROVINCE BROUGHT A FERVOUR TO THEIR SPORTS THAT WOULD LAST THE CENTURY

Glenbow Archives, NC-6-60851

Billy 'The Fighting Scot' Lauder (left) takes on a minor contender called Truscott in June 1908 in Calgary. After several victories, he announced he was going to BC to 'raise fruit.'

by BRIAN HUTCHINSON

The train that whistled into Calgary that fine spring day in June 1902 carried the usual assortment of rough-edged fortune seekers, one of them a small, wiry easterner known as Kid Macleod. Like thousands of travellers before him, Macleod came west with dreams of striking it rich. But he wasn't a would-be rancher or settler. Macleod was a professional boxer, and Calgary, a tough new city, was in love with prize fighting.

Indeed, Calgarians were fans of almost any kind of physical endeavor, the rougher and rowdier the better. The refined played hard at polo and cricket for King and Empire. But hockey, baseball and lacrosse commanded the multitudes, who frequently turned the matches into brawls, the women sometimes as rambunctious as the men.

American-style professionalism had established itself in Alberta by the turn of the century. Businessmen discovered that large, boisterous audiences — men and women alike — were willing to pay cash to watch their boys thrash any outside challenger. The local team became a means of establishing the local reputation and identity. During the decade the newspapers began featuring full sports pages, hailing the accomplishments of the local crews, complete with statistical tables. Hence assorted characters with talent to sell rolled in on the train, among them Kid Macleod.

Billy Stewart[1] was Calgary's purveyor of professional pugilistics when Kid Macleod checked into the Alberta Hotel. He spread the word that Macleod was looking for a challenger. Coolgardie

Men's gymnastics class, Edmonton. Almost any kind of physical endeavour was welcomed.

Smith, a man nearly twice Macleod's size, accepted the offer. No one had ever heard of Smith, but he claimed to be champion of both British Columbia and South Africa. That seemed good enough for local boxing fans, who quickly adopted him as their hometown hero. Everyone was eager to see the eastern boy get thumped. Stewart scheduled a fight for June 13, at 9 p.m. in Hull's Opera House. Ringside seats for the heavily advertised "Grand Boxing Contest" sold for $1, general admission for 75 cents. Sales were brisk, and the betting ran fiercely in favour of Smith.

The fight amounted to an execution. Macleod battered his clumsy opponent around the ring for seven full rounds, the crowd booing and hissing, some shouting, "Fix! Fix!" Afraid he might incite a riot, the diminutive Macleod stopped punching. In the eighth round, he didn't once lay a glove on Smith's lurching frame. But the outcome was inevitable. Macleod won a unanimous decision and was awarded 75% of the gate. Disgruntled fans filed out of the Opera House, complaining that they had witnessed the worst boxing match in Calgary's history.

A year later, it became obvious that most prize fights were hopelessly corrupt. As C.R. Blackburn notes in his 1974 MA thesis, *The Development of Sports in Alberta,* the outcome was usually fixed and the match seldom lasted more than three rounds. After a particularly malodorous match-up, the *Calgary Herald* complained bitterly that crooked promoters were ruining the sport. "Fake Fight Finishes in a Foul," read one alliterative headline of April 9, 1903, then poetically charged on: "How the Foreign Fistic Fancy Fattens on the Fatuity of the Foolish City Farmers."

When police got wind of the illegal match, they raided the makeshift arena. Cappy Smart, the city's fire chief and a fan of the manly art, was one of the many who escaped through a window.

Prize fighting was technically illegal in the territories, but neither the North-West Mounted Police nor the Calgary police enforced the law. But in 1903 an illegal bout was held in an old barn on the outskirts of Calgary. The police got wind of the "secret" match, however, and raided the makeshift arena. Cappy Smart, the city's fire chief and a rabid boxing fan, was one of many spectators who escaped arrest by jumping through an open window.

[1] A solid, scrappy Scot, Stewart never hesitated to step into the ring whenever a boxer failed to show; however, he wasn't very good. In the fall of 1905, he was forced to battle local boy Jake Fullerton after his opponent backed out. Stewart fought dirtily, hitting Fullerton below the belt and was disqualified in the first round. In 1908, after city council raised licence fees to $100 a year, Stewart relinquished his role as Calgary's foremost boxing promoter.

The Edmonton lacrosse team of 1904, and in action against Strathcona. Assault and battery with lacrosse sticks wasn't unusual.

Prize fighting managed to survive, however, and Calgary retained its reputation as Alberta's pugilistic capital. The *Albertan* noted that the city had become a haven for "all pug-uglies and their camp followers in this part of the country." Most fights were held in smoke-filled basements, which added nothing to the sport's prestige. In order to pass themselves off as "amateurs," prize fighters refused to accept gate receipts. They made their own side-bets instead.

Calgary's most celebrated boxer was young Billy Lauder, the "Fighting Scot." A former Canadian amateur light-heavyweight champ by way of Winnipeg, Lauder showed up in Calgary in 1907, boasting he could beat anyone. This caused considerable excitement. Billy Stewart seized the opportunity and organized a fifteen-round bout between Lauder and Barney Mullins of Edmonton, for May 1907. It was a prize fight, in blatant contravention of the law, but because of Lauder's impressive creden-

McKinnon of Edmonton smashed his lacrosse stick down on Fred Richards' head. He hit him again and again. Later Strathcona supporters captured McKinnon and beat him senseless.

tials, not to mention the fact that some of the city's business leaders planned to attend, police chose to look the other way. Chief Tom English said his men would intervene only if the two fighters clung to each other and refused to box.

Over 1,000 people packed into Sherman's Rink on 17th Avenue and Centre Street South to watch the fight. The match was scheduled for 11 p.m., but was held up when Mullins refused to weigh in. Finally, he stepped on the scales, and turned up well over the 148-pound limit. Mullins was forced to concede 10% of his share of the purse to the house. All bets were off, but the fans were treated to one of the most spirited displays of boxing in the city's history. It went the fifteen-round distance and in the end, the decision went to Lauder.

He remained in Calgary, fighting a succession of weaker opponents. But in February 1908 Harry Lombard came to town. The Chicago boxer had a reputation for lightning-fast reflexes and a heavy right hand. He set up his training camp in the Imperial Hotel, giving the locals a chance to evaluate his talent. Word came back that Lauder had no chance against the well muscled Lombard, and Stewart was told to cancel the fight. Instead, he announced the match would be strictly amateur, the prize a $250 silver cup.

Cappy Smart refereed the bout, after Mayor Cameron gave him the go-ahead. Lombard was clearly the stronger of the two, but Lauder used his head and danced about the ring, avoiding his opponent's punches. Late in the final round, Lombard managed to land a tremendous blow to Lauder's head. The local hero staggered, wheeled, and was about to go down when the bell rang.

The bout ended in a draw. A month later, a rematch was held. This time, the police watched from the back of the hall, ready to interrupt the bout if they saw evidence of money changing hands. Lombard seemed slow and heavy, and Lauder was able to pepper him with body blows. It was not as exciting as the first contest, but Lauder ended up winning.

The pair fought once more, this time for the Canadian Lightweight Championship. Sherman's Rink was packed, and fans were treated to a clean, fast bout. Lauder came out on top once again, and then announced his retirement. "I'm going to BC

(Top) Athabasca Landing junior baseball team. (Left) The Western Canada Baseball League's Edmonton Eskimos, 1910. By the turn of the century, baseball was the most organized sport in the province; in the first decade, it went professional.

to raise fruit," he told his startled admirers, adding that since they started monitoring the fights, there wasn't enough money in it for him. But Lauder ended up buying a ranch outside of Calgary instead, and kept fighting, at least once a month. He kept winning too, until December 1908. That's when Eddie Marino, a tough-as-nails nineteen-year-old from Seattle, knocked the champ through the ropes. Lauder won a rematch three months later, but the decision was tainted by controversy. In the middle of the bout, after an intense flurry of punches from each corner, Cappy Smart stopped the fight and raised Lauder's arm in victory. The fans were outraged by the quick decision; Marino went after Smart but was subdued by his cornermen.

Lauder continued to fight, but the Marino incident left him unpopular. In May 1909 Jim Potts defeated Lauder, knocking the former champ out for the first time in his career. Although he left the ring bruised, beaten, and friendless, Lauder went down a sportsman. "Potts is a good man, and I would rather lose to him than any man I know," he declared. He continued to box well into the next decade, but he never regained his form and usually fought outside of Calgary, where audiences were less hostile.

Billy Lauder's demise was the beginning of the end for big-time boxing in Calgary, at least for a few years. In June 1909 an angry cornerman jumped into the ring and pummeled a referee who had decided against his man. Two months later, Calgary's city council voted to ban "all boxing and sparring events where admission is charged." The city bylaw had teeth that the territorial ordinance lacked. Fearing a mass influx of pugilists, the city council in Edmonton quickly passed an identical measure.[2]

In the meantime, for the incorrigibly bloodthirsty, there was always lacrosse. Adapted from the Indian game, this rough-and-tumble business had become Canada's national sport by the end of the 19th century. Teams were formed across the North-West Territories and in 1907 the Alberta

[2]The city's anti-prize-fighting ardour, however, did not long survive the century's first decade. For a few months, fights continued to be held on the outskirts of Calgary, in tents and barns, the police for the most part turning a blind eye. Noah Brusso, a.k.a. Tommy Burns, a former world champion, moved to Calgary in 1910 and became Alberta's pre-eminent fight promoter. He built a large arena in Manchester, on the outskirts of Calgary. He also sold men's clothing from his shop on what would become the Stephen Avenue Mall.

Amateur Lacrosse Association was established with Lethbridge, Medicine Hat, and High River in a southern division, Calgary, Edmonton and Strathcona in a northern. Blackburn notes that the northern games were especially "tough, bloody, and fight-filled."

The most notorious incident, a midsummer night's brawl, took place at the Agricultural Fairgrounds in Strathcona. It began when Norman Main of the Strathcona Bandmen began push-

Polo ponies and riders at the Edmonton Fair in 1905. Appalled by the incivility of some of the colonial sports, the British imported their own pastimes.

The crowd was raised to a high pitch of excitement over the broad jump. Cardell and Haynes who have won frequently in local contests were strong contenders until near the top as were also Griffiths and the Claresholm jumper. Crealock and Duncan who are both fine clean jumpers proved too many for the rest and fought it out an inch at a time until both had smashed the provincial record, the former winning out at 5 ft. 4 3/4 in. It was a fine exhibition.
– from the Lethbridge Herald report on the Alberta Amateur Athletic Association meet, July 1, 1910.

ing Will Powers of the Edmonton Capitals. Powers shoved back. Main gave Powers a whack with his stick. Finally, they began to trade blows, swinging their sticks at each other wildly. As Main was being dragged from the field by a referee, another fight broke out. McKinnon of Edmonton smashed his wooden lacrosse stick down on Fred Richards' head. Then he hit him again, and again. "Blood poured over his face and coat," reported the *Edmonton Bulletin*.

The game was resumed, but a few minutes later, a number of vengeful Strathcona supporters managed to capture McKinnon at the far end of the field. He was beaten senseless, and Strathcona went on to win the match 5-3.

Barney Mullins, the man who lost the boxing match with Billy Lauder, was in the stands that night. Having retired from boxing, Mullins was looking for a new line of work. He wrote to Edmonton's lacrosse captain and offered his unique abilities to the humiliated squad: "In the light of my successes in this phase of lacrosse (pugilistics), which today seems to be the preponderating nature of the game, I believe my services would be invaluable in aiding the Caps to secure the DeVeber Cup." Mullins' generous offer was turned down. Edmonton stumbled to a last-place finish, while the squad from Calgary won the league championship.

Lacrosse attracted large, unruly crowds, sometimes in excess of 1,200, but it wasn't Alberta's favourite summer game. That distinction belonged to baseball, the most organized sport in Alberta by the turn of the century. Baseball enjoyed phenomenal success on the Canadian prairies, chiefly because of its populist American roots. A British journalist named Derry, passing through the northwest in 1902, commented in the *Sheffield Independent* that aside from the "unexpectedly keen interest and cleverness" of Canadian baseball, he was struck by "the intolerably unsportsmanlike spirit displayed by the players according to English ideas." The visitor was especially worried by the verbal sparring the players engaged in. "When I spoke strongly about this unsportsmanlike method the answer I got was 'Well, this isn't a right spirit, but we borrowed it, with the game, from the States.'"

But baseball fans were generally well behaved. There were often ladies in attendance, and

some ballplayers prided themselves on decorum. In 1903, the Medicine Hat "City" team received a challenge from the "Thirsty Thugs." The Thugs turned out to be a delicate bunch, insisting the Medicine Hat players refrain from smoking cigarettes during the game. The challengers "positively decline to play if any of the City nine wear white shoes," reported the incredulous *Medicine Hat News*. After the Thugs won the match, some speculated their strange demands were meant to throw the local boys off their game.

In 1905, a ball team from Fernie, BC, claimed a $500 prize after beating the hometown favourites from Calgary. The *Herald* wasted no time charging that the umpire, "who was arrested

A horse race at the Edmonton fairgrounds, around 1908. This was considered a respectable activity and betting was fierce.

The hot sunny summer of '07 saw the birth of the Western Canada Baseball League, four pro clubs, players from all over the continent and a cap on each team's payroll of $1,200 a season.

during the late gambling scandal," had accepted a bribe. The newspaper's demands for an official investigation were ignored, but not forgotten.

Buying umpires was common but frowned upon; however, buying players was by all means acceptable. Semi-pro teams were scattered all over the southern half of Alberta. Most clubs had a "ringer" or two, journeymen ball players imported from eastern Canada or the United States. The citizens of Macleod were thrilled to learn their team had lured lefty Sammy Cobean from Toronto. Cobean received a percentage of the team's gate receipts, and an extra $80 at the end of the season. When he wasn't throwing fastballs at opponents, Sammy was signing guests into the Macleod Hotel where he was a clerk.

The summer of 1907 brought warm, sunny weather, thousands of new immigrants, and, even more important, Alberta's first experiment with pro ball. The Western Canada Baseball League had four clubs: the Edmonton Eskimos, the Calgary Bronks, the Lethbridge Coal Barons, and the Medicine Hat Hatters. The teams were affiliated with the National League, and recruited their players from all over North America. Money was scarce, however, so owners decided that each team would limit its payroll to $1,200 a season. Deacon White, proprietor and manager of the

(L) Gwynne area hunters, 1910, (r) 1908 Game Regulations. Wildlife preservation was taken seriously very early on. Stupefying prey with opium was strictly prohibited.

Edmonton Eskimos, organized a minstrel show to raise money for uniforms. And what fine outfits they turned out to be: $30 apiece, made from the best broadcloth, colours cardinal and green, with the letter "E" stitched onto the left side of the shirt.

A.D. Fider's team in Calgary was supposed to arrive in town after spring training in Massachusetts, but the Bronks had a disastrous spring exhibition season. They lost every game by huge margins. Furious, Fider fired everyone on the squad, including the manager. A new team was hastily assembled and shipped home to Calgary, but it turned out worse than the original nine. The Bronks finished last that first year, well behind the championship crew from Medicine Hat. The Hatters trained in Ohio, where they had no trouble attracting enough seasoned Americans willing to relocate to a dusty prairie settlement. The fact none of them had ever heard of Medicine Hat didn't seem to matter.

All four teams frequently drew more than 1,000 fans to their home games, but that wasn't enough to prevent the league from losing money. It suspended operations for a year, and re-appeared in 1909, with new clubs in Winnipeg, Brandon, Regina, and Moose Jaw. This time, the

'The Englishman doesn't bully the Indian. He simply ignores him, and by pursuing life as nearly as possible like the one he would lead in England, he makes the Indian understand it is his country. The Englishman impresses that fact upon the Indian even in his games.'

Calgary Bronks were better prepared and enjoyed a much more successful season. The players were more skilled and their manager, Dinny McGuire, was a fiery motivator who constantly chewed gum. Best of all, Edmonton was lousy.

"Oh, joy!" cried the *Calgary Herald,* after the Bronks kicked off the new season by defeating the hapless Eskimos. "Unconfined, unadulterated, excessive and explosive! Edmonton was beaten yesterday." No thanks to the umpire, Mr. Voss, a "murderer, a cutthroat, and a parricide." The fans at Victoria Park were silent until the eighth inning, when the Bronks took the lead off a two-run triple by Zwicker. Every man, woman and child stood and cheered wildly. The *Herald* noted that "the bleachers were nothing but a tossing, roaring, leaping mass of hysterically shrieking lunatics."

Humiliated, the Eskimos took the first train home, destined to become the league's laughing stock. Later that season, they travelled to Regina to play the Bonecrushers. It was 0-0 in the ninth inning when the umpire, "nearly falling over from inward spasms of laughter," called the game "on account of darkness." The Edmonton players filed out of the ball park and returned to their hotel. The Bonecrushers stayed behind, and when the ump reversed his decision and yelled "Play ball," Regina won the game by default. It was later revealed that the umpire was in fact one of the Bonecrushers' pitchers.[3]

The urban rabble might revel in their violent, unseemly spectator games like baseball, lacrosse, and hockey where the action was almost entirely vicarious, meaning that somebody might get hurt down there. But for the more highly bred, there were other thrills, like the crack of the cricket bat or the thundering hooves of the polo horse. And in the last-mentioned pursuit, the injuries were all first hand.

Many of Alberta's British settlers scorned "native" sports as crassly commercial, brutalitarian, unsportsmanlike and unhealthy. They preferred activities that took them into the countryside, games imported from the old country like polo and cricket. These not only provided at least a tenuous link to distant Britain, but also gave possessors of that new toy, the automobile,

Provincial Archives of Alberta, E. Brown Collection, B-9667

Fishing, like hunting, though totally unorganized, would remain one of Alberta's most all-consuming sports. The photo was taken on Devil's Lake near Banff. The date and fisherman are unknown.

occasion for long country rambles. They must be played, of course, in the British way. Jeering one's opponent was unheard of. Extracting payment for participation was absurd.

During the Dominion Day celebrations at Macleod, for instance, displaced Britons delighted to watch a polo game. Local Indians looked on baffled, according to historian Theodora Reeves in her *Alberta History*:

> The Englishman doesn't bully the Indian. He simply ignores him, and by pursuing life as nearly as possible like the one he would lead in England...he makes the Indian understand it is *his* country. The Englishman impresses that fact upon the Indian even in his games.

The new province provided an ideal landscape for polo, especially the open territory in the south where so many remittance men settled.[4] The "Sons of England" organized tournaments all over the region, and by the turn of the century southern Alberta had become the polo capital of Canada. In 1905, an unknown team from High River won the Canadian championships in Toronto, confounding the so-called experts. "The High River men came from a spot scarcely findable on the Canadian prairies map," complained the Toronto *Globe*. "And they ride ponies as ignorant of pedigrees as their ribs are of the tickle of the curry combs."

Horse racing dominated the list of events at annual summer exhibitions held across the province. By 1910, up to 10,000 spectators would crowd the exhibition grounds in Edmonton and Calgary, where prize money sometimes exceeded $6,000. After the Mounties conducted their splendid Musical Ride, after the Indian pow-wow, after the cake walk and the quarter-mile

[3]Once again, the team from Medicine Hat went on to win the WCBL crown. But the league continued to struggle, both financially and with its wild and unruly reputation. It folded for good in 1915, as Canadians focused their attention on the battlegrounds of Europe.

[4]Tragedy struck Millarville's polo team in 1910, when its best player, Justin Deane-Freeman, was killed after a match near San Diego, California. He was knocked off his horse and hit his head, producing a concussion. Doctors performed an operation to remove the pressure but Deane-Freeman failed to recover and died.

The year Patrick almost made it happen

LONG BEFORE THE OILERS, EDMONTON'S HOCKEY ESKIMOS CAPTURED
THE HEARTS OF A YOUNG TOWN READY TO TAKE ON THE EASTERN GIANTS

The air inside Thistle Rink was thicker with smoke, sweat, and excitement that night than ever it had been in its brief history. It was Dec. 11, 1908, and more than 2,000 hockey fans packed themselves in to watch the Edmonton Eskimos battle their cross-river rivals from the older, smugger Strathcona. It wasn't just another game. If Edmonton won,

Whitcroft knew he couldn't win the coveted trophy with his current cast of local talent. To prove it, he held a brief training camp in the Thistle Rink, open to any journeyman with a pair of skates and a hard shot. When that failed to turn up anything promising, Whitcroft went on an unprecedented buying binge, recruiting five professionals from the East: Hugh

The Thistle Rink, Edmonton, around 1902. The air was thick with smoke and excitement the year they played the Wanderers.

they'd go to Montreal, home of the invincible Montreal Wanderers. If the Eskimos got that far, they might just as well capture the Stanley Cup and bring it west to Edmonton (and wouldn't that show Strathcona!).

No one believed Fred Whitcroft when he said Edmonton would be playing for Lord Stanley's trophy. An easterner, Whitcroft came to Edmonton in 1907 to play for and manage the Eskimos. He turned them into western Canadian champs that year. Then he convinced the city's leading businessmen that a cup challenge would be an excellent way to advertise the three-year-old Alberta capital. All they needed to do was provide money. He would provide the team.

Ross, Bert Lindsay, Harold McNamara, Jack Miller, and the speedy Didier Petrie. He even tried to pry the great Fred (Cyclone) Taylor from Pittsburgh, but his offer was not rich enough for the famous forward. Harold Deeton was the only local boy to make the squad.

Deeton, the team's great hope, would have a chance to demonstrate his skills on that big night at the Thistle. Strathcona was more than beaten by Edmonton. The final score was 21-0, and it might have been doubled if not for an heroic effort from 'Scona's goalie. Still, opined the *Edmonton Bulletin*, the club needed two more weeks of practice to reach its prime. In private, Whitcroft told his friends that the

Eskimos still hadn't enough talent to take on the Wanderers. Something was missing, so he went out and found it.

"Tom Phillips Signed!" proclaimed the headlines, the day after the Strathcona match. "Another valuable addition has been made to the Edmonton team in the person of Phillips, generally regarded as one of the fastest hockey players in the country." It was hard to believe. Phillips was a true champion, winner of two Stanley Cups, the last only a year earlier with

himself off the ice. "It's only a sprain," he cried, but the team's trainer, Bill Crowley, wasn't buying it. McNamara twisted his knee and had to sit out the rest of the series. Petrie was slashed across the face and required stitches. Intimidated, the Eskimos shrank back into their own zone and lost 7-4.

Deeton and Miller were inserted into the lineup the next night and performed brilliantly, scoring five goals between them. The rest of the team dished out elbows and body checks

---

'Women were heard to shriek until their voices resembled those of banshees,' said the *Star*, 'and men were heard to howl as if their manhood were at stake.'

---

the Ottawa Silver Seven. Rumour had it Phillips would receive $400 for every game the Eskimos won, and $300 for each loss. The other players were astounded; they would only receive expense money.

Whitcroft had yet another card to play. Three days after Phillips joined the club, Lester Patrick, former captain of the legendary Wanderers, signed on. This was a stunner. The six-foot Patrick, once regarded as the world's best hockey player, had left the Wanderers to work at his father's lumber mill in Nelson, BC. He was playing for a local amateur club when he received Whitcroft's pleading letter. Old Joe Patrick grudgingly gave his son three weeks' leave, and Lester grabbed the next train for Montreal.[a] There he met his new team, who had made the trip a few days earlier.

The two-game series was held in early January 1909. It was a violent, fast-paced affair. The Eskimos were able to skate with the heavily favoured Wanderers, but they weren't pre-pared for the tough play. They were badly bullied in the first game before a disappointing crowd at the Montreal Arena. Phillips suffered a broken ankle; 45 minutes later he dragged

with reckless abandon, driving the fans to a frenzy. The *Montreal Star* reported that "women were heard to shriek until their voices resembled what one would think the voice of a banshee to be like, and men were heard to howl as if their very manhood were at stake." Edmonton won the match 7-6. But because Montreal finished the series with a 13-11 lead in goals scored, the Wanderers retained the Cup. The battle-scarred Eskimos shook hands and went their separate ways. Edmonton's Stanley Cup dream would not come true for 76 years.

Whitcroft mounted another challenge the next year, in 1910. This time, the Eskimos fought the Ottawa Senators for the Stanley Cup, without Phillips and Patrick. Though Deeton, Miller and Ross did return, Edmonton lost the two-game series, 21-11. However, the Eskimos at least managed to win another western hockey championship.

The great Lester Patrick was in no sense finished with hockey. The following year, 1911, he founded the Pacific Coast Hockey Association with his brother Frank. In 1924, he coached the Victoria Cougars to a Stanley Cup victory over the Montreal Canadiens. In 1927 he sold the entire roster to the American teams of the new National Hockey League. He then coached the New York Rangers for thirteen years, winning another three Stanley Cups. It was in New York that he earned the nickname "the Silver Fox." One of the NHL's four divisions was later named after him.

—*B.H.*

Edmonton Archives, EA-500-214

[a]Lester's father, a millionaire, would not allow his son to receive payment from the Eskimos. When he learned Edmonton paid his son $100 for expenses, he asked Lester how much his trav-el and lodging had cost him. "Sixty-two dollars," replied the younger Patrick. "Then you owe Edmonton $38," said his father. Lester sent the Eskimos a cheque for that amount.

The Edmonton Eskimos hockey team of 1907-08.
(L-r, back row) A.M. Stewart, James A. McKinnon, W. Banford, W. Crowley, Alf Kemp; (second row) 'Hay' Miller, Fred Whitcroft, H. Deeton, Bert Boulton; (front row) 'Shorty' Campbell, Allan Parr, Robert Holly.

scurry,[5] the hour arrived for the "speeding events." The horses came in all shapes and sizes, from mixed-breed polo ponies to imported American thoroughbreds, and ran anything from the half-mile dash to the one-and-a-half-mile hurdle race.

Horse racing was considered a respectable activity, and betting was fierce. As historians Donald Wetherell and Irene Kmet note in their book *Useful Pleasures — the Shaping of Leisure in Alberta 1896-1945*, gambling was usually considered a vice. However, they say, "betting on horses escaped

Both the Thistle Rink in Edmonton and the Sherman Rink in Calgary had ceilings, fifty feet high, supported by wooden trusses. Wire mesh kept the fans from running onto the ice surface.

opprobrium. There seems never to have been any attempt in Alberta to eliminate betting on horses; it was so deeply entrenched in all classes of society that the only feasible way to deal with it was to ensure that it was clean."

This was done with limited success. Local exhibition associations or jockey clubs handled the wagers. The Southern Alberta Turf Association and the Alberta Turf Club were typical. They made arrangements for each meet, set the purses, and enforced the rules. But bookmakers still plied their trade, and were blamed for corrupting the sport by bribing jockeys and track officials to throw races. Near the end of the decade, the pari-mutuel betting system appeared, turning over a certain percentage of all bets to a racetrack's administration. Suddenly, charges of corruption

Chasing the little white ball o'er hill and cow pasture

Where there are Scots and their ilk, will inevitably follow
The ultimate pastime of the self-controlled: Golf

Members of the Edmonton Golf Club, circa 1896. The course was located on the future Legislature grounds.

In 1890, a handful of bored North-West Mounted Police officers gathered behind their wooden barracks in Fort Macleod and played a game never before seen in the territory. Using their bare hands, they dug three small, shallow holes in the hard prairie soil. Then the officers took turns knocking a ball around the scrub with a short, iron-footed club. Therewith, golf had come to Alberta.

The windswept, treeless territory was hardly a golfer's paradise, but there was a strong thirst for the game among the newcomers. By the turn of the century, Edmonton and Calgary boasted active golf clubs, patronized by both men and women, but discreetly reserved for the "well bred." Membership fees ranged from fifty cents to $3, and while courses were initially established on crown land, it cost money to prepare them for play and build clubhouses. And of course, the game required a special psychology. As the *Calgary Herald* noted in 1910, "The Scottish temperament was exactly suited to bear with the physical calm and self-control the hard and distressing buffets encountered in play." Englishmen, naturally, passed the test as well.

Apparel was important. Victorian convention stuffed women into suffocating "golf suits" — stockings, covered by riding breeches and dark woolen skirts; blouses and sweaters topped with Eton jackets or golf capes. Men wore two- or three-piece suits, complete with necktie, causing an unbecoming perspiration on hot summer days.

disappeared. Because the new system offered bettors increased odds of winning, bookies were forced out of business.

Racing was not without danger. On June 19, 1907, for instance, James Ross of Beaver Dam would be trampled to death by the pounding hoofs. No one knew what compelled Ross to step onto the Cochrane racetrack, although some said he was pushed. The thoroughbreds were tightly bunched and approaching the home stretch when Ross stumbled into their path. The first two horses knocked him down, the hoofs of another crushed his skull. He was dragged off the track by several men and given some hasty medical treatment, but Ross died within an hour. When the rest of the spectators learned of his fate, they lost interest in the day's events and straggled, sadly, home. People didn't claim their prize money.

The next summer racing enthusiasts had another occasion to mourn. More than 9,000 spectators gathered at Victoria Park in Calgary to watch the 1908 Dominion Day events. Bets were running high, and the crowd was in a good mood. Suddenly, tragedy struck. A piece of lumber was blown from the grandstand roof and flew into the crowd. One person was killed; several others were badly injured. Then Bill Kerfoot, a former manager and co-owner of the Cochrane Ranche, was killed when the horse he was riding spooked and ran into a cow on the fairgrounds.

The racing season drew to a close in September, when the leaves began to change colour and fall, and the sportsman's attention was drawn to other activities. One didn't have to go far to find exotic game. The Calgary Hunt Club organized day trips into the foothills to track down wolves. Usually they brought home coyotes. Wetherell and Kmet note that while hunting in England was

[5]The quarter-mile scurry and the cake walk are spectator games that have vanished without a trace. They were probably gymkhana events such as children continue to play on school sports days, like the three-legged race. But these events often involved horses. One was the brandy and soda race in which the contestants must saddle their horses, ride over a hurdle to a table on which were tumblers and bottles of soda water, open the soda water and pour the contents into the tumblers, drink it and ride back. Then there was the cigar and umbrella race: saddle pony, light cigar and put up umbrella and mount; first past flag with cigar alight and umbrella up wins. These were described in the *Calgary Herald* in September 1900.

One had to be keen. Early courses featured long, ragged fairways and heart-stopping hazards. The Edmonton Golf Club's original course, the future site of Alberta's legislative grounds, had five holes and ran up and down the steep North Saskatchewan River bank. Golfers approaching the first hole had to play past an old graveyard; the third hole lay on the other side of the Edmonton, Yukon and Pacific Railway tracks as they mounted the riverbank towards the Groat ravine.[a] The course was also intersected by a muddy road.

Things weren't much better in Calgary, where the local nine-hole course buttressed the CPR tracks, just south of downtown. Members of the Calgary Golf Club had to put up

Club in 1897, was elected president the next year, and narrowly lost the club championship in 1899. He moved to Edmonton in 1902, and became a mainstay of the club there. His wife, Alice, also a keen golfer, was known for her famous clubhouse teas and dances. These attracted new "social" members not even remotely interested in golf. Because they were private, golf clubs could remain open on Sundays and even sell liquor.

In 1910, urban expansion forced the Calgary Golf Club to move once again, this time for good. The club bought a 110-acre site several miles farther up the Elbow, near the old homestead that Calgary's first white settler, Sam Livingston,

The Edmonton Golf Club's course had five holes that ran over the tracks and past the graveyard. Calgary's had an electric fence to keep the links cow-free.

with dirt putting greens and wandering livestock.

In 1906, the Calgary club bought a piece of land south of its original course, along the Elbow River. With 57 members, the club had enough money to buy electric fencing to keep the cows out. A year later, the Edmonton Golf Club was forced to make way for the new Legislative Building. It moved a little west up the river valley to a location known as Hudson Bay flat, and built a nine-hole course, occupying much of what would survive most of the century as the Victoria golf course.

The game was promoted in both cities by a portly judge named David Scott. A former crown lawyer who had helped send Louis Riel to the gallows, Scott founded the Calgary Golf

occupied after he moved from the original site of Fort Calgary. In 1911, the 18-hole Calgary Golf and Country Club officially opened, and membership exploded to 250.

The same year, the Edmonton Golf Club moved to a $40,000 parcel of land, eight miles upstream from the city, finding at last a permanent home. Meanwhile, a municipal course was established on the abandoned Hudson Bay flat and soon everyone could enjoy the game, regardless of wealth. As a participant sport, golf soon rivalled curling, that other grim, Scottish pastime.

— *B.H.*

[a]The remnant of the old EY&P, west of 109 Street, by the end of the century had become a bike path.

directly linked to upper-class ownership of land, "in North America the abundance of wildlife and the nature of settlement made hunting available to all."

Except on Sundays, of course. Game and bird hunting was forbidden on the Sabbath. Swivel guns, sunken punts and night lights were also illegal. So was the use of grain soaked in opium or other narcotics intended to stupefy prey. Wildlife preservation was taken seriously very early on. The Alberta Gun Club had been established back in 1889 to regulate hunting and educate against indiscriminate shooting and selling of game. Hawks and crows, known to eat the eggs of more worthy birds, were exempt, and gunned down with abandon. Club rules prohibited mixing dust, grease, oil, or any other substance with shot. Muzzle-loading guns were considered unsafe and banned. A hunter or rifleman was liable to a fine for pointing a gun at anyone.

The club had an influence that bothered some for whom wildlife was at best a nuisance and at worst a curse. In 1907, three members of the provincial legislature lobbied against any form of regulation on grounds that "the protection of large game...was inconsistent with the advance of civilization." It was "the right of every man" to kill big game.

The hunting season lasted only two months before the winter cold swept in and chased everyone indoors. At the turn of the century, that often meant the pool hall or the saloon. In 1900, the *Calgary Herald* fretted that "a first-class gymnasium is needed in Calgary...At present the hotel bars are the principal resorts to which young men can go on long winter evenings." Instead of abolishing the sale of liquor, an impossible task, the *Herald* argued that abolitionists should build a gymnasium for tumbling exercises and the new sport of basketball. After all, Edmonton had one. The Young Men's Institute (later the YMCA) was headquartered in a downtown building, and boasted a small, gloomy gym. Much more popular was its billiards room, far removed from the hoodlum-infested pool halls down the street.

Calgary didn't get its gym for nine more years; in the meantime, it could lay claim to the best indoor curling rink in the province. The Alberta Curling Rink on Northcote Avenue, built in 1889 at a cost of $2,500, boasted two sheets, a viewing area, and a cloak room. Curlers from all over Alberta journeyed to Calgary for its famous cash bonspiels. Warm chinook winds sometimes melted the ice at the height of the season, but the high-spirited parties went on as scheduled.[6]

Edmontonians had curled with iron rocks on the North Saskatchewan River until their first indoor rink opened in the late 1880s. In 1902, a new four-sheet rink was built by businessman Richard Secord at what would become 102 Street and 102 Avenue, behind the King Edward Hotel. Two more rinks were built in Edmonton and another in Strathcona. By the end of the decade, there were almost a thousand curlers in the capital.

But the unparalleled winter sport was hockey. Every schoolyard in every town had a skating rink; some even featured incandescent lamps for evening play. When the first indoor rinks appeared, they were reserved for hockey, since owners knew they could make more money selling tickets for hockey games than letting recreational skaters on the ice. The $13,000 Thistle Rink, attached to Secord's curling venue, seated 1,500 spectators and featured a comfortable waiting room. It resembled the Calgary Auditorium, later known as the Sherman Rink, at 17th Avenue and Centre Street South. Both rinks had ceilings nearly fifty feet high, supported by wooden trusses. There were no bothersome posts to obstruct the spectators' view of the ice. Large windows at either end of the rinks let in valuable natural light. Wire mesh kept fans from running onto the ice surface.[7]

Dozens of hockey leagues appeared in the century's first decade, in all age groups. There were Indian teams and all-female teams, although the ladies played a decidedly friendlier game, and wore their shin pads with striped socks pulled over them, gym bloomers, turtleneck sweaters and toques with big pompoms. The men wore plain woollen uniforms with little protection. A good pair of skates sold for $3.50, and featured thin muleskin uppers that couldn't stop the sting of a hard rubber puck or the stiff whack of a wooden stick.

Fans eagerly paid fifty cents to watch the big teams from the Alberta Amateur Hockey Association. The AAHA organized most senior league play in the province, Calgary being the exception. That city refused to participate in the AAHA's schedule. The given reason was the cost of travel. Edmontonians predictably offered another explanation: that Calgary's senior teams were afraid to appear in Edmonton, where the calibre of play was reportedly much higher.

The AAHA insisted that its members play according to the amateur code and not hire

The players of the first [hockey] team have come to the conclusion that they have a substantial cause for complaint against the public, particularly the male portion of it. At matches they strain and exert themselves to delight an enthusiastic throng, and in return the men and boys are inconsiderate enough to pull out their malodorous cheroots, cigars or cigarettes and proceed to fill the rink with smoke. Thus before the match is over, a thick pall of smoke settles down over the ice, obscuring the play, and making it decidedly uncomfortable for the players.
– *excerpt from a letter from 'A Player,' Edmonton Bulletin, Jan. 28, 1903.*

professionals. But the rules were rarely enforced. Journeyman players were imported from across western Canada to play for these "amateur" clubs. A ringer merely had to live in a new city for ten days before he could play for the home side.

Teams played two thirty-minute halves. Each side consisted of seven players — a goalie, a rover, two cover points, and three forwards. No substitution was allowed, except in the case of accident or injury. There were plenty of those, mostly broken noses and separated shoulders. Few were as serious as the one suffered by Shorty Campbell, a dashing member of the Edmonton Eskimos. Shorty was a tenacious, speedy left wing, with enough ability to make him a prospect for the professional leagues in the East. But an incident in 1907 ended his hopes. The Eskimos were playing their rivals from Strathcona, and Shorty had the puck. There was a collision, and the sharp edge of an opponent's skate blade buried deep in Shorty's leg just above the knee. Doctors briefly considered amputating the limb. It wasn't necessary, but Shorty walked with a limp and never played the game again.

The length of the hockey season was limited by weather. It was not uncommon for players to chase pucks through two inches of water.[8] Electric lighting was feeble, and players often complained about tobacco smoke from the stands so thick they couldn't properly see the ice. Rules changed from one match to the next, and teams frequently swapped players, depending on how many points were needed to be made up in the league standings. Referees were spat at and verbally abused, by players and fans alike.

However, this wild, tough and exuberant game enjoyed a fevered popularity in Alberta that it would never lose throughout the whole century. It required, some said, quick thought, physical dexterity and boundless energy, all qualities which, whatever the disparities between north and south, were rapidly coming to characterize the whole province.

Coleman junior hockey team, 1906-07. Every schoolyard in every town had a skating rink.

[6]In 1911, the new Victoria Curling Club was built in Calgary. With seventeen sheets, it was the largest in North America.

[7]Both these buildings burned. The Thistle was lost in 1914; it was replaced by the much larger Edmonton Stock Pavilion. The Sherman went up the next year in a blaze of unexplained origin; it burned to the ground and was later replaced with an arena in Victoria Park.

[8]When the natural ice melted, the rinks housed roller skating and long-distance running events, as well as exhibitions like horse shows. Artificial ice was not introduced to Canada until 1911.

Opinionated, raucous, ribald, the press became our addiction

ALBERTA'S EARLY NEWSPAPERS WERE BOOZE-FLAVOURED ORGANS OF INVECTIVE, RANCOUR AND FUN — IT WAS ALL TOO GOOD TO LAST

by GEORGE OAKE

"It is almost impossible to properly estimate the far-reaching power and influence of the press in this western country where there are fewer social attractions than in more thickly populated countries to direct the attentions of a farmer from the chief recreation of rural life, namely reading, and where the local paper is probably more widely and carefully read than anywhere else in Canada." So wrote deputy commissioner Charles Walter Christian Peterson of the North-West Territories Department of Agriculture in 1902. It was, if anything, an understatement.

Unlike their bland, Toronto-controlled successors two to three generations later, Alberta's early newspapers were opinionated, raucous and ribald — too much fun not to read. Pioneer newspapermen had an undisguised zest for prodding not only their readers but also any source of institutionalized power. The remote government in Ottawa, or the hated Canadian Pacific Railway with its vast grants of prime farmland, made especially attractive victims.

Of course the early editors spent as much time and space lashing each other as they did those in authority, and here they certainly did not lack for targets. Between 1880 and 1910, according to historian Gloria Strathern, 212 dailies and weeklies were published in Alberta. Most were short-lived, some not surviving past the first hand-written edition, however ravenous the reading public for news.

Historian Hugh Dempsey counted seven papers in 1907 in Calgary alone — two dailies, three

Interior of the Calgary Herald's print shop, about 1907. At that time Calgary had seven papers, all of them lively.

Glenbow Archives, NA-1447-32

weeklies and two monthlies, all owned in a city whose population was then 7,000.

In bygone days reporters, editors and publisher, often one man in the same inkstained suit, were just around the corner, and their readers did not confine their disagreements with them to the pen, as Charles Halpin, the editor-publisher of Banff's *Mountain Echo*, found out. Halpin had a bad habit of stealing cordwood to warm his small office, just off what is today Banff Avenue. One of his more determined critics used this knowledge on a cold night in February 1889 to, quite literally, put some heat on the editor.

The same editor, by then with the *Macleod Gazette*, reminisced about the incident: "Some fiend in human shape loaded (with dynamite) a stick of cordwood that did not belong to the editor, but owing to a strange set of circumstances, the particular cordwood went off in the *Mountain Echo*'s office. Needless to say, the explosion paralyzed the *Mountain Echo*, and caused the paper to suddenly suspend publication. The office burned and left nothing but a skeleton and the old Gordon press. It's not quite accurate to say that nothing was left, for the editor escaped from the wreck and is still at large."

Alberta's designation as a province in 1905 did not tame its frontier editorial passions. In 1908, F.H. Schooley, editor of the *Lacombe Advertiser*, unwarily attended a local council meeting where an alderman demanded a retraction of an article he had written. Schooley firmly refused. The *Edmonton Journal* later described what followed. The fuming politician roared over to the press table, "seizing him about the

(Above) Eye Openers *and prayer books being sold on a street corner in Lethbridge, about 1912. Publishing was a serious affair, but not without its amusements.*

Calgary Eye Opener *newsboy William Tone in 1909. Newspaper jobs weren't well-paying, but offered other compensations.*

339

Southam's J.H. Woods, president Calgary Herald, in 1910. Toronto control — though not the homogeneity of later years — came to Calgary by the end of the century's first decade.

The *Eye Opener* has nothing to retract and nothing to be sorry for in anything that has appeared in its columns since Vol. I, No. I.
- *from the Calgary Eye Opener, Dec. 7, 1907.*

throat and choking him." Schooley survived the assault; whether he ran the retraction was not reported.

Such hazards notwithstanding, it's clear Alberta's newsmen relished their role of conscience to the frontier society, none more so than the renowned Bob Edwards, editor of the Calgary *Eye Opener* (see sidebar). "It is simply impossible to run a paper without an occasional error," lamented Edwards, who described what errors could do in a 1902 article. A reader had arrived in his office with a club. "I've come," he said, "to see why you called me a political jobber in your paper today."

"I regret the error of the printer quite as much as you do," replied Edwards, having opened a little drawer and casually removed a gun, which he studied distractedly.

"Ah, then you didn't mean to call me that," said the visitor.

"No sir, I wrote 'robber' very distinctly," replied Edwards.

An apocryphal story? Probably. Edwards may have written the vignette to discourage his legion of critics. It didn't.

Yet for every famous pioneer newsman like Edwards who left his imprint on the province, scores of editors laboured long, hard and obscurely to scratch out a living by relaying the news to a sparsely populated province. Known as tramp journalists, they were actually itinerant publishers who moved restlessly from town to town in search of opportunities and advertisers who would support their enterprise.

History does not record what ever happened to Frank Corby, who hand-wrote the *Gleichen Echo* and posted it on a bulletin board for the town to read in 1904. A press was hard to come by on the prairies. Before the railroads it had to be brought overland by oxcart, as Frank Oliver brought the press that would publish the *Edmonton Bulletin*. Even by train, transport was too costly for most.

"The typical editor-printer, embarking on his new career as a publisher of a weekly newspaper and community leader," writes Leonard D'Albertanson in *Printed Word*, a history of the Alberta Weekly Newspaper Association, "did so largely by the grace of the printer's supply house, the owner of the property in which the new plant was located, and perhaps of a few backers, who provided the small amount of capital necessary to get the enterprise under way."

He recalls one editor he does not identify who, having failed at farming after seven years of trying, persuaded a printers' supply house in Winnipeg to sell him an entire printing plant on $600 credit, then moved both it and his family into a granary, which became the local publishing house.

Such strapped pioneer publishers were forced to become one-man operations. They gathered

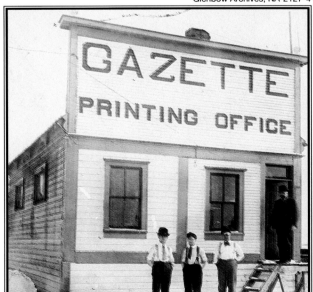

the local news, wrote up telegraph dispatches, hand-set their type, and then, close to exhaustion, ground out the edition on a primitive and rickety press, the most arduous job of all.

Some Alberta newspapers were turned out on Washington presses, an improvement on the old screw-type machine. Each page impression involved rolling out the type bed, inking it with a hand roller, applying a sheet of newsprint to the type bed, then rolling the bed back and providing pressure to produce an imprint with a ponderous hand lever.

Two early joint-publishers eased the effort by using Indians to do the hard work. Charles Dudley Wood and Elias Talbot Saunders, former members of the North-West Mounted Police, rolled off the first edition of the *Macleod Gazette* on July 1, 1882. The printing press had been laboriously transported up the Missouri River to Fort Benton, Montana, then north to Macleod by bull train. They found one thing lacking. Moving the heavy handle back and forth required an engine. John D. Higinbotham in his *When the West was Young* tells how they coped with this. "Twelve Blood Indians, who, stripped to their breech clouts, each took a turn at the handle," he writes, until the

---

'The office burned and left nothing but a skeleton and the old Gordon press. The editor escaped from the wreck, however, and is still at large.'

---

ex-Mounties could acquire an engine.

Some newspapermen, like Wood, prospered.[1] Others had terrible luck. His name is lost to history and he managed to produce only one edition of the *Rocky Mountain Cyclone*, and while humorous in hindsight, his experience illustrated the raw ingenuity of pioneer newsmen who'd let nothing stop the press. The editor of the *Cyclone* had ordered his press and type from the remote East. The press arrived in good condition, but nowhere to be found in any type size were the letters F or K. What to do? Print and be damned, he decided.

"We begin the publication ov the *Cyclone* with some phew diphiculties in the way," he wrote in the lead article of his first and last edition. "The type phounder phrom whom we bought the outphit phor this printing ophice phailed to supply any ephs of cays, and it will be phour or phive weex bephore we can get any...We don't lique the idea ov this variety ov spelling any better than our readers do, but mistax will happen in the best regulated phamilies, and iph the c's, x's and q's hold out we shall ceep the *Cyclone* whirling, aphter a phashion, until the sorts arrive. It's no joque to us; it is a serious aphair."

Publishing certainly was a serious affair, especially for the editors who were chasing down advertisers to make ends meet. Most of the turn-of-the-century Alberta newspapers cost sub-

[1] Wood edited the *Gazette* for 21 years, obtained a law degree and established a legal partnership with Frederick Haultain, later premier of the territories. In 1912 Wood was appointed judge for the judicial district of Weyburn, Sask.

Turn-of-the-century newspaper offices: (l-r) the Olds Gazette, *the* Nanton News, *the* Macleod Gazette, *and* Le Progress *in Morinville. Reporters, editor and publisher were often one man in the same ink-stained suit.*

The 'printer's devil' (errand boy) at the Edmonton Bulletin, 1904. Oxen brought the paper's original press west.

You may laugh at us, & we will not blame you this time, if you do. This issue is not as well printed or as neat as it should be; we had to set, with job-work type, & print with a postal-card press. However we expect our outfit will be here soon, then YOU will sit up and TAKE NOTICE.
- apology contained in a January 1910 issue of the Rocky Mountain Echo.

scribers $1 a year and individual copies were hawked by newsboys for a nickel or a dime because there were no pennies in circulation in Alberta.

The hunger was such that there was even a market for old news. A paper like the *Calgary Herald* might, like a rare wine, be worth more some time after it was published than on the day it came out. *Herald* founder Thomas Braden recalled that his first press run of 500 copies was snapped up by readers in hours. "The price was ten cents per copy," he recounted. "But as there was no change, 25 cents was freely paid, and when the issue was exhausted, fifty cents and $1 were paid for second-hand single copies."

The wretches who worked on salary were rarely well-paid. In one of the few reminiscences of a reporter's lot, C.H. Stout's privately printed book, *Backtrack*, describes "the red-letter day" when

'I regret the error of the printer quite as much as you do,' said Edwards, casually removing a gun from his desk drawer.

he was hired by the *Edmonton Journal* in 1908 at the ten dollars a week a cub could expect for 12-hour days and no job security.

"Finances were very bad at the *Journal* and even the ten dollars a week couldn't be met regularly," he writes. "*Journal* NSF cheques literally flooded the town, despite valiant efforts of accountant Bell...We frequently got $1 from Bell's cash box to buy a dinner, and then skipped the meal, at best only fifteen cents." But Stout, who was born in Illinois before his family moved to Canada, went on to a sterling career with the *Edmonton Bulletin.*

Like Edwards, who came to Alberta from Scotland via Wyoming, many of Alberta's early newsmen were immigrants from afar. A cosmopolitan lot comprised the *Edmonton Journal*'s 1908 newsroom. Stout describes them: "Burly Roy Moss from Seattle was a veteran...Billy DeGraves, an Australian of confident personality and original writing, and Colin Groff, a native Albertan whose father was a member of the *Journal* staff for many years. The managing editor was a man called John Macpherson from Winnipeg and, when news was slim...well, night editor Bill McAdams could be counted on to invent a good yarn to fill the front page."

World news came over commercial wires from Winnipeg in the form of what were called flimsies. The skeletal information in the flimsies was expanded upon locally for the front pages. "One night no flimsies came and local news was slim," Stout recalls. "But Bill reeled off columns about 'Lighting Jerkers Cuss the Northern Lights' and hit the streets with a rattling good front page that delighted waffle counters and coffee shops along Jasper and breakfast tables throughout the town."

If the reporters were inventive, their bosses were a mixed bag, always boomers for the West, and often bigoted: The *Edmonton Journal* on Oct. 21, 1907, approvingly reprinted a *Lethbridge Herald* editorial under the heading: "Cut Them Off." It advised the Alberta government to disenfranchise Japanese and Chinese. "Make these yellow men understand we are not going to allow them to secure any influence in our affairs," it said. Such views were widely shared. But these were insular times. People neither had nor wanted knowledge of a larger world; they had enough trouble protecting the one they knew, so lately emerged from a violent and harsh frontier where those who didn't share and pitch in for the common good met swift consequences. The *Macleod Gazette* drily reported on Oct. 14, 1882: "A man named Bowles was lynched by some cowboys in the Indian Basin. He refused to assist them to fight a prairie fire, and after the boys got it out, they went to the creek where he camped, took him out and hung him."

The offices of the Edmonton Bulletin, *and* Oliver. *The staunch Liberal's slogan was 'Read the Bible and the Bulletin.'*

The cowboy stamped into Braden's office, spurs jangling on the planks, two revolvers and a Bowie knife on his hips. 'I'm the voice of one crying in the wilderness,' he said.

In the same way, ranchers couldn't yet telephone the North-West Mounted Police to deal with thieves, so they dealt with the matter themselves. The *Medicine Hat News* informed its readers on May 28, 1886: "On Saturday night last while Mr. Garteby was camped near the town, two of his horses were driven off in a southerly direction by two Indians. Mr. Garteby's son fired two shots at them and followed them until the trail was lost in darkness." The Gartebys, it was assumed, would recover their own property and seek their own justice.

The Herald Block, Calgary

The Herald Block, Calgary, 1908, and editor Tom Braden. He and Andrews Armour had started in 1883 with a hand press in a tent on the bank of the Elbow.

**I know it ain't so classical
As these big dailies are,
That tell about the prize fights
And the latest movie star,
But just for my enjoyment
There's nothin' I have found
Like the little newspaper
From the old home town.**
- From the poem "Paper from the Old Home Town" which appeared in the Gleichen Call in the early part of the century, date unknown.

The astronomers have discovered a peculiar spot on Saturn and are greatly excited over it. Yet there are plenty of peculiar spots no farther away than Okotoks and Claresholm.
- from the Eye Opener July 18, 1903.

Horses were still causing trouble in the 20th century, as the newspapers routinely reported. Horse-drawn carriage accidents were rampant. The *Lacombe Advertiser* reported in 1907 how a team, spooked by a gunshot, thundered off a bridge carrying five people to their death.

Another carriage collision in Edmonton at what would now be the intersection of 100th Street and Jasper Avenue killed three people and put two in hospital.

While racial tolerance was simply unheard of, women's rights were starting to be heard of — and deplored. The *Edmonton Journal* edified its readers in 1906 about the British votes-for-women campaign: "The rabid female supporters of an extension of the franchise to the fairer sex," said an editorial, "seem determined to render the existence of the British cabinet ministers unbearable, unless their demands for votes are forthwith complied with. What good to their cause they think they do by the creation of hysterical scenes in the lobbies of the House it is impossible to imagine. A perusal of the accounts of these amazing proceedings makes one inclined to thank goodness that the good sense of our Canadian women renders such ambitions inconceivable in this favoured country."

In other words they were, and would remain, the prisoners of the conventional wisdom of their time, whatever that wisdom might be. Yet in one remarkable sense, yesterday's locally based

'The type phounder phrom whom we bought the outphit phor this printing ophice phailed to supply any ephs or cays, and it will be phour or phive weex bephore we can get any.'

publisher maintained a much fiercer independence than his corporate successor. In a young nation, he was almost always a fervent and uncompromising patriot. The word "jingoism" had only lately come into usage, and he would have been proud to have it applied to him.

Thus the *Edmonton Bulletin* fiercely deplored the government's talk of a "commercial union" with the United States, though many in the Liberal party favoured it. It was "naive" to suppose, said the Liberal *Bulletin*, "that the tail could wag the dog" in such an agreement. "If our resources are not being developed as fast as they should be, at least they are still ours, to be developed for our benefit when the time comes."

That editorial doubtless came from the pen of Frank Oliver, the reluctant founder of the *Bulletin*, who launched Alberta's first real newspaper on Dec. 6, 1880 (it would later employ the

LIFE IN A NEW PROVINCE

slogan, "Read the Bible and the Bulletin"). Oliver was born near Brampton, Ont., in 1853. His restless nature took him to Toronto at an early age where he found work in the *Globe*'s composing room. In the early 1870s the young printer ventured to Winnipeg on the then frontier and to the composing room of the *Manitoba Free Press*, later the *Winnipeg Free Press*.[2] But times were bad in the "Gateway to the West," and so in the spring of 1876 Oliver joined an oxcart brigade, creaking its way alongside the lonely telegraph line across the empty prairies to the remote settlement of Fort Edmonton where he set up shop as a trader and storekeeper.

The idea for the *Bulletin* originated with the settlement's telegrapher, Alex Taylor. When interesting news came over the wire Taylor would jot it down in longhand and leave the bulletins on the counter of Frank Oliver's grocery store for the public to read. When Taylor spotted an adver-

---

Southam's financial muscle ensured the survival of the *Herald* and the *Journal* while their competitors, vulnerable to each boom and bust, one by one folded.

---

tisement in the *Manitoba Free Press* that someone in Philadelphia had a $20 printing press for sale he had a brain wave. His friend Oliver had worked on newspapers. Why not persuade Frank to buy the press and set up the territory's first newspaper?

Within weeks a stolid team of oxen was moving the press west. But as luck would have it the Red River cart carrying it tipped over in one of the endless fords of the North Saskatchewan River, dumping all the large type fonts into the water.

When he received the news, Oliver was ready to give up the idea of a newspaper. But not Taylor. He used a large hunting knife to carve the masthead from a wooden ox yoke, and the first four-page *Bulletin*, a mere six inches wide and seven inches deep, hit Edmonton's frozen streets on Dec. 6, 1880.

The little paper thrived and its owner became enamoured of politics. He served in the territorial assembly and later the House of Commons, and was named Prime Minister Sir Wilfrid Laurier's powerful minister of the Interior in 1905. On both sides of the press, he played a key role in making Edmonton capital of Alberta. The paper was run in his absence by like-minded Liberals who kept the home fires burning, according to Oliver's dictates.

"This by no means meant," says newsman Stout in his *Backtrack*, "that Mr. Oliver, when home from Ottawa, didn't shut the door of his dingy little office and at an old desk piled high with books, papers and documents, and always an apple or two, dash off with lead pencil and pile of office copy pads in his truly inimitable style, red-hot editorials that expressed his opinions about public affairs, in a manner that left not a vestige of doubt as to his stand and objective."

From the sepia-tinted pictures of the time Oliver looks gaunt and stern, his handsome face dominated by a huge, full moustache, staring out from history. However, as Stout discovered, he had the same vulnerabilities as other men. When he lost his son, Alan, in the First World War, he tried but failed to disguise his grief. Stout remembers a quivering upper lip under the bristling moustache. Alan was to have taken over the *Bulletin* if he had survived the muddy trenches of France. "Notwithstanding the collapse of his long cherished retirement plans, our aging chief concealed all evidence of his grief, except the donning of a black hat for his walks between the office and his substantial home" overlooking the North Saskatchewan, the river that had consumed the *Bulletin*'s first type. Stout glimpsed the father as distinct from the public man. He was manning the *Bulletin* desk late one night, soon after the tragic telegram arrived. "Mr. Stout," said Oliver. "If you see any reference to Alan in outside papers will you kindly clip them out and save them for me."

Oliver was a complex man who held enormous power, both in government and through the Liberal *Bulletin* which dominated Alberta politics in 1905. But he was also a man of his times, by later standards bigoted. In July of 1905 he told the House of Commons that Ukrainians were so undesirable that other settlers moved out rather than face them as neighbours.

"We did not go out to the North-West simply to produce wheat," he told the Commons. "We went to build up a nation, a civilization, a social system that we could enjoy, be proud of, and transmit to our children, and we resent the idea of having the millstone of the Slav population hung around our necks."

[2]Clifford Sifton, minister of the Interior in the Laurier government, who established western Canada as a Liberal bastion for half a century, secretly acquired ownership of the Conservative *Manitoba Free Press* in 1897. He hired J.W. Dafoe as its editor four years later and it became the Liberal voice of the prairies.

The drunken editor who put all others to shame

BOB EDWARDS' *EYE OPENER* TOOK ON ALL COMERS WITH ITS INIMITABLE BRAND OF WIT, WISDOM AND SLAUGHTERHOUSE EXECRATION

In the golden autumn of 1905, when the province of Alberta was born, Bob Edwards was the best known newspaperman in the West. His *Eye Opener* weekly was the talk not only of Calgary but of distant cities as well. As soon as it began hitting the streets, its circulation took off like a spirited quarterhorse.

Edwards and his sandy moustache could be seen striding purposefully down Stephen Avenue from his rooms in the Cameron Block to the Alberta Hotel, often in quest of an eye-opener at the longest bar in the West. His robust five-foot-seven-inch frame was garbed in grey suit and wing collar, bespeaking a man of substance. Only R.B. Bennett, the Calgary lawyer and future prime minister, was said to be a better dresser.

By 1908 *Eye Opener* circulation topped 18,500, not bad for a one-man operation in a city of barely 10,000. How did a small western weekly of four pages become a national newspaper selling 4,000 copies of each issue in Toronto, 2,600 in Winnipeg and 1,000 in Vancouver, not to mention nearly 1,800 copies hawked to eager travellers on Canadian Pacific trains?

Open any copy of the *Eye Opener* and the explanation lay plain: "Mrs. Alex F. Muggsy, one of our most delightful West End Chatelaines, has notified her friends that her usual Friday musicale is called off for this week. Her husband, Old Man Muggsy, has been entertaining his own friends with a boozical for a change and is in an ugly mood."

While names and locations were changed to protect the guilty, Edwards spared nobody, including the adulterous: "A bouncing ten-pound boy arrived at the home of Mr. and Mrs. P.T. Gilpen of Fifteenth Avenue West last Tuesday. Mr. Gilpen has fired the hired man and engaged a more aged servitor."

Yet the *Eye Opener*'s society column, while a titillation, was a mere sideline in what Edwards termed his "great moral journal." He supported universal suffrage, equal rights for women, and even medicare, at a time when most of his fellow publishers were myopically marching to the beat of distant party drummers in Ottawa.

Edwards at various times published five newspapers in Alberta. In all of them he raged against the Senate as an "impotent relic" that should be abolished or reformed, and demanded minimum-wage laws for workers.

Yet Robert Chambers Edwards was, as the saying went, well born. That event happened in Edinburgh, Scotland, on Sept. 12, 1864. His mother, the daughter of Robert Chambers, co-founder with his brother William of the venerable publishing house of W. & R. Chambers, died within a few weeks of his birth. His father, Alexander Mackenzie Edwards, died four years later on a world cruise, leaving Bob and his brother, Jack, orphans. Two maiden aunts raised the lads, providing them with a classical education at St. Andrews and at the University of Glasgow.

As soon as he could escape his aunts, Bob was off to France, where he started his first publishing venture in Boulogne, a gossipy sheet aimed at wealthy British tourists, known as *The*

Robert C. Edwards, editor of Eye Opener, *and a front page from Sept. 19, 1908. In Alberta, there never was and never has been anything like him.*

Provincial Archives of Alberta, P5238

Traveller. The vapid lifestyle of the rich made him cynical, according to Grant MacEwan in his biography on Edwards, *Eye-Opener Bob: The Story of Bob Edwards*. This doubtless sowed the seeds that would later bloom in the *Eye Opener*'s society column.

The brothers sailed for North America in 1892, arriving at Cheyenne, Wyoming, in the midst of a range war. Better versed in Immanual Kant then Sam Colt, the young men had a rough time. Jack stayed in Wyoming. Bob bounced around, eventually stepping off a train in Winnipeg on his 30th birthday in 1894 with $35 in his pocket and the Kilmarnock edition of Robert Burns' poems. The money was just enough for a further ticket to Sixteenth Siding on the Calgary and Edmonton

Railway, a place soon to be known as Wetaskiwin.

Jack followed and the brothers formed a ranching partnership at nearby Bittern Lake. Soon after, an all-night drinking party left Jack dead. The grieving Bob vowed to change his life. He would do something "useful."

Thus on March 26, 1897, the first issue of the *Wetaskiwin Free Lance* came off the press in Strathcona. Edwards intended to call his four-page weekly "the Wetaskiwin Bottle Works because it would be a corker." He thought better of it, and the *Free Lance* became the first newspaper published between Edmonton and Calgary.

Meanwhile, despite the fate of his brother, Bob Edwards was becoming an inebriate whose binges were legendary. In an attempt to scare Edwards into sobriety, his lifelong friend, innkeeper Jerry Boyce, chained a semi-tamed bear to Edwards' bed in the hotel room where he passed out. The drunken editor staggered in, struck a match to light a bedside candle, and saw the outline of the beast. Believing it to be imaginary, Edwards kicked at the animal as though to order it out of the room. It raked him with its claws. Edwards fled in terror to Boyce's room.

"You'll say it's hallucinations," he gasped, "but honest, Jerry, the hangover beasts are getting damned rough around here. One bit me. Look there. Blood!" Boyce didn't apologize and Edwards didn't quit drinking.

And yet, writes Marie Hamilton, Edwards was not a slob, whatever his weaknesses. "The fact is, Robert Chambers Edwards was a man of culture and literary ability. His sympathy was as wide as the prairie spaces and he knew the pioneers as did no one else. He portrayed the country and its people as they really were, and expressed them on the printed page with letter-perfect fidelity."[a]

Mrs. Hamilton insists that Edwards was not the roisterer popular legend portrays, but kind, shy and very different in person than in print. In his Wetaskiwin days, engaging in his second favourite pastime, walking, Edwards found a small boy peering anxiously into a 20-foot-deep well where his cat had fallen. The editor shinnied down the rope and retrieved the cat. The boy, overjoyed, ran for home, leaving Edwards in the well and unable to climb out. He spent a cold night. Astonished workmen fished him out the following day. Edwards neither wrote nor spoke about his acts of charity, though his friends said they were many.

"He was a reserved and shy little man with an uncontrollable thirst for spirituous liquors which he consumed in lonely bachelor quarters at uncertain intervals," wrote Clarence Stout of the *Edmonton Bulletin* in his autobiography, *Backtrack*.

Edwards set up papers in four more Alberta towns before he headed to Calgary. He had to keep moving because his waggishly sophisticated wit and impish personality did not endear him to its victims in Wetaskiwin, Leduc, Strathcona or High River, especially to the church leaders whom he twitted in print throughout his career. After starting the *Alberta Sun* in Leduc he moved it to Strathcona, suppressing the notion of renaming it "The Strathcolic" because it "would probably produce the equivalent of abdominal pains for pious readers."

From Strathcona he went briefly to Winnipeg, found it dull, and returned to High River where the first *Eye Opener* hit the streets on March 1, 1902. He was soon in the usual hot water with the local clergy and left for Calgary in 1903, after a parting shot at his tormentors: "These small towns are awful. Wetaskiwin threw us down. Leduc threw us down. Strathcona, being dead anyway, shook its shrivelled finger at us. High River is passing us up. Ye Gods! That we should have to live in such places!"

Calgary proved more tolerant, despite his drinking and frequent five- to six-day sojourns in Holy Cross Hospital to dry out. In Calgary his renown became national, but not before an editorial war drove him from the city for two years. It began when one Daniel McGillicuddy rode into Calgary from the East in 1907 and set up a rival paper called the *Calgary Daily News*.

The English-born Ontario newspaperman said his paper would "wear no party collar," but it was clear from the first issue that McGillicuddy favoured Sir Wilfrid Laurier's Liberals and Clifford Sifton, by now resigned from Laurier's cabinet but still the senior Liberal power broker in the West. From the day they met, McGillicuddy and Edwards developed a distaste for one another that exceeded the bounds of journalism. McGillicuddy, former publisher of the *Huron Star* at Goderich, wrote endlessly on Calgary's sins of the flesh and the bottle, while Edwards celebrated Calgary's drinking culture, meanwhile taking well-placed shots at Sifton and Liberal policies.

It was widely rumoured that McGillicuddy had been set up by Sifton to counteract Edwards' growing influence in western Canada. It didn't work. A year after McGillicuddy arrived, the *News* had acquired a circulation of only 3,000 against the *Eye Opener's* 12,000. The frustrated McGillicuddy finally decided on a frontal attack. On Oct. 6, 1908, he wrote a front-page letter to the editor, signed "Nemeses." For the rest of the century it would rank as the most vicious attack on an individual ever

[a]Marie Alvina Hamilton was the wife of *Calgary Herald* editor Zachary Hamilton. Her book, *These Are The Prairies*, largely autobiographical, is among the best in western anecdotal history. It was published in 1948 by the School Aids and Textbook Publishing Company of Regina. She dedicated it to her father and mother who, she said, "when most people are enjoying the quietness and comfort of a well-settled life, embarked on a great adventure in a new and unknown land."

Glenbow Archives, NA-3055-42

published by an Alberta newspaper.

McGillicuddy called the *Eye Opener* a "journalistic hermaphrodite" and demanded that the authorities suppress it. "First I want it to be known," he said, "that Robert C. Edwards is a four-flusher, a tin-horn and a welcher where poker debts are concerned. I intend to show that he is a libeller, a character thief, a coward, a liar, a drunkard, a dope fiend and a degenerate, and I hold the cards to play the game." He promised more letters to prove his case.

Edwards sought advice from his good friend, Paddy Nolan, most famous criminal lawyer in Alberta. The next morning Nolan had McGillicuddy charged with defamatory libel, a criminal offence, and a trial of national interest was soon under way in a packed Calgary courtroom. The jury found McGillicuddy guilty and fined him $100. But for Edwards it was a dubious victory. The six-man jury asked the judge to caution him about the riotous content of his newspaper.

Edwards had an improbable defender. The *Lethbridge News*, which had a reputation for uncommon journalistic restraint, spoke out on Edwards' behalf. "We beg to repeat for the particular information of the old hypocrite who runs the *Calgary News*," it said, "that...if there were more papers and editors in Canada with the independence and fearless-

Edwards' rival Daniel McGillicuddy. The latter called the Eye Opener *a 'journalistic hermaphrodite.'*

Glenbow Archives, NA-2913-4

in the Alberta Hotel, drinking with friends like Paddy Nolan. Conversation in small groups was his forte and more than one *Eye Opener* was entirely written on his table near the bar door which swung open at 7:30 a.m.

And Edwards could still startle Calgary, not the least when in 1917, at 53, the life-long bachelor was married to Kate Penman, a 20-year-old Scotswoman who worked in R.B. Bennett's office. The union was putatively successful.

Then in 1921 Edwards was elected to the Alberta Legislature as an independent. But by now he was noticeably changing. He stayed sober throughout the ensuing session. His health was plainly failing. The *Eye Opener* became more intermittent and on July 29, 1922, published what was to be its last edition.

Edwards was terrified about making his maiden speech in the House, recalls the *Bulletin*'s Stout, but went through with it. "I have always felt the brave words and effort cost him his life. He got out of a sickbed at the Hotel Macdonald, came down to the House with a spirit that wrenched my heart and made me proud...delivered his maiden address (no one protested his reading it, contrary to the rules) and received thunderous applause from all members for its wit and excellence."

One thought gave Edwards satisfaction at the time. His

'Is is not wonderful? Here I am in the legislature and McGillicuddy is in hell — Yours, Bob.'

ness of the *Eye Opener* and Mr. Edwards, and fewer prostituted journalists like the editor of the *Calgary News*, the country would be infinitely better off."

But Edwards was uncharacteristically penitent. In his *Eye Opener* he publicly admitted certain "indiscretions," and to everyone's general astonishment left town to publish the *Eye Opener* in Port Arthur and then Winnipeg. His mission accomplished, McGillicuddy sold the *Daily News* which reappeared on March 26, 1909, as the *Calgary News-Telegram*. Two years later Edwards returned, the *Eye Opener* thrived as never before. Its circulation reached 33,586 in 1912, and excluding Winnipeg dailies it could boast the largest number of readers of any newspaper between Toronto and Vancouver. Edwards loved Calgary, the long days and nights

old foe McGillicuddy, he learned, was dead. "Is it not wonderful?" Edwards wrote to his friend, Zachary Hamilton. "Here am I in the Legislature and McGillicuddy is in hell — Yours, Bob,"

A few months later on Nov. 14, 1922, Bob Edwards died of heart problems complicated by influenza. He was 58. Albertans lost a unique voice that undeniably expressed the rough culture of the province he called home. His puckish humour was as dry as the autumn winds that sweep over the southern plains. He was buried by Kate with some whiskey and his first and last editions of the *Eye Opener* — just in case there was no joy in heaven over a magnificent sinner who wrote, many said, like an angel.

— *G.O.*

BOB EDWARDS' GREATEST HITS

Jan. 27, 1898 — A ridiculous rumour was afloat last week that Mr. Simpson, our MLA (much lamented absentee) was coming up our way on a visit. It beats everything how preposterous rumours of this kind get started. The next thing we hear will be the Prince of Wales coming over to give a *fête champêtre* at the Hobbema Agency.

* * *

Feb. 5, 1898 — We understand that several parties from Leduc are contemplating the journey to the Klondyke in the spring. They ought to get through easily. No experiences can have any terror for men who have lived in Leduc, and no special danger need be apprehended on the trip, unless they take the Leduc string band along.

* * *

Dec. 8, 1898 — Next week will be the anniversary of the birth of the *Wetaskiwin Free Lance*. Congratulatory baskets of flowers can be left at our boarding house. All votive offerings in the shape of bottles had better be taken round to the office, where instructions have been left with "Grassy" as to their disposal. They will be given to the poor.

* * *

April 16, 1901 — The best show of the season was that Ponoka conjuring entertainment last week. The eminent conjurer could make anything disappear he wanted to, especially booze. His gifted manager, Ole Roth, also disappeared with the gate receipts while a performance was in progress. A fashionable throng was present. Mr. and Mrs. Joel Slop were present in a box, or rather a dry goods box, and seemed to enjoy the entertainment. Mrs. Slop was tastefully dressed in fur lined shoes. Mr. Selwyn, her talented father, was becomingly attired in the suit of clothes he had taken from the corpse of the man he murdered last fall, who was known to be a good dresser. Those Ponoka society events are great features up north.

* * *

March 4, 1902 — Mr. W.H. Todd has invested in a ferocious bloodhound. It is one of the most dangerous propositions to bump into after dark that has ever afflicted High River. When you are hungry and want a nice cold bite, go and see Mr. Todd's dog, and he will attend to you.

* * *

Oct. 17, 1903 — There is absolutely no truth in the malicious report that a file of the *Eye Opener* was publicly burned by a common hangman in front of the parliament buildings at Ottawa last month. Parties circulating this report, which is calculated and probably intended to prejudice the moral status of this paper, will be prosecuted.

* * *

June 15, 1907 — We understand — ha ha! — that — haw haw! — R.J. Stuart — ah-yah-haw — ha ha ha! — is going to run — oh oh ha ha — for alderman — ha ha ha ha ha ha! Ha ha ha ha ha ha — ha ha ha ha ha ha ha ha!

* * *

June 13, 1908 — The many friends of Hiram McClusky will learn with pleasure he is now tapered off down to two drinks per hour. Mr. McClusky's iron constitution has stood him in good stead in this, the hour of his affliction.

* * *

June 27, 1908 — Ex-alderman W.G. Hunt, manager for the Massey-Harris Co., and general all-round uplifter of Calgary, has designed a new Canadian flag. The groundwork of his model consists of a Massey-Harris lien note past due, on a field of self-binder *vert*, surrounded by a comulus of compound interest rampant, with a local hotel bar sinister running slantdicular on a wet Sunday. Motto suggested by Sheriff Van Wart, '*Nulla Bona.*'

* * *

Sept. 5, 1908 — The Hon. W.R. Motherwell, minister of something or other in the former Saskatchewan government, on August 13 got the following off his chest: "The *Regina Standard* quotes me as saying, 'I do not take much notice of the *Standard.*' That is true. I do not. But I would rather depend on the *Standard* than on the Calgary *Eye Opener.*" That's all right, old cockie, but try to remember we helped put you where you belong anyway — on the scrap pile.

* * *

May 4, 1912 — Sir Wilfrid Laurier was once on an electioneering tour in Ontario, and, as the elections were bitterly contested, every effort was made to stir up prejudice. One day a Quebec Liberal sent this telegram to Sir Wilfrid: "Report in circulation in this country that your children have not been baptized. Telegraph denial." To this the premier replied, "Sorry to say report is correct. I have no children."

* * *

Sept. 22, 1917 — A correspondent from Olds writes to say that he went into a store there the other day to ask for an *Eye Opener* and was told they did not sell such papers, as it would corrupt the morals of the town. From the fact that one of the Olds ministers of the gospel some three weeks ago eloped with a young lady of that burg, he already having a wife and child in the States, we may be justified in presuming that the morals of Olds need no further corrupting.

* * *

Dec. 18, 1917 — Christmas cooking recipe: Bread Pudding — Gather up all the chunks of bread that have been left over on the plates for the past week and dump them into a bucketful of water. Take a handful of plums and chuck into the mess. Stir with a big spoon and add a little sugar. Dump into a pan and stick in the oven. As soon as it begins to look a trifle less disgusting, take it out and serve as plum pudding.

Oliver had, in 1898, sold the *Bulletin* to a locally owned corporation in which he held a minority position. By 1923, he had severed all ties with it. Oliver died in 1933, but the paper prospered until the 1930s when the Liberals waned as a political force in Alberta. It struggled on, losing readers and advertisers to the Conservative *Edmonton Journal*, and finally its assets were bought by the *Journal*. The *Bulletin* was folded in January 1951.

Two upstarts, the *Calgary Herald* and the *Edmonton Journal* were both started and the *Herald*'s beginnings were as colourful as the *Bulletin*'s. Two Ontario men, Tom Braden, a school teacher from Peterborough, and Andrews Armour, a printer from Barrie, set up a hand-press in a tent on the banks of the Elbow River and the first issue appeared Aug. 31, 1883. Its name alone took up considerable space. It was called the *Calgary Herald, Mining and Ranche Advocate and General Advertiser*.

Mackenzie Bowell, the Belleville compositor and politician who was later the Conservative prime minister of Canada between 1894 and 1896, happened to be passing through town and helped produce the first edition. Several changes of ownership occurred and the *Herald* went daily in 1885, reverting to a twice-weekly operation and then back to a daily before it was sold to the Ontario-based Southam family in 1908.[3]

Braden, a tenderfoot just arrived from Ontario, remembered his first encounter with a strange cowboy who wanted some printing done. The man, encased in buckskin, stamped into Braden's office, spurs jangling on the planks, two revolvers and a Bowie knife on his ample hips. "I'm the voice of one crying in the wilderness," said the cowboy by way of greeting. "Prepare ye the way of the Lord, make his paths straight," he added, and then produced a flask and implored Braden to have a drink. Braden demurred. The flask was placed on Braden's desk, flanked by the two revolvers. "I said have a drink," the cowboy repeated. Though terrified, Braden still refused. The cowboy brightened. "Right, my son," he said, "when sinners entice thee, consent thou not." He then proceeded to order the printing.

In speaking the Conservative cause in Conservative Calgary, the *Herald*'s founders prospered. Three Tories who arrived in 1903 to speak it in Liberal Edmonton did not. Newspapermen John Macpherson, John Cunningham and Arthur Moore came from Portage la Prairie, Man., dedicated to taking on and destroying Oliver's *Bulletin* with their fledgling *Edmonton Journal*. They acquired further financing from local Conservatives, but five years later the *Journal*'s daily circulation still dawdled at about 1,000, and bankruptcy seemed imminent.

W.A. Griesbach of Boer War fame, who would later become a major-general and a Conservative MP (see prologue chapter), wrote to Wilson Southam suggesting the family buy out some of the *Journal*'s shareholders. Charles Bruce in his *News and the Southams* describes what followed. Southam showed the correspondence to a friend and commented: "We are naturally anxious to assist the Conservative party wherever possible, as at present we think they are the party of purity, and we are not averse to getting a bargain in any business proposition if we could raise the funds."

However, it took four more years of dickering before the *Journal* fell into the Southam fold. The reason was its financial uncertainty. J.H. Woods, one of the *Journal*'s major shareholders, warned the Southams in 1909 that the *Journal* would face heavy going "as Edmonton has not any body of Conservatives worth counting on, the town being politically owned by Frank Oliver."

Without the injection of Southam funds the *Edmonton Journal* and *Calgary Herald* might, like so many others, have been footnotes in the history of Alberta journalism. Southam's financial muscle ensured their survival, while their competitors, vulnerable to every boom and bust, folded one by one, leaving the *Journal* and *Herald* without serious competitors until the advent of the *Sun* tabloids seven decades later. And they too, would be controlled from Toronto.

Throughout most of that long drought, Albertans could not read the acidly humorous candour of a Bob Edwards who once described his typical day for curious readers: "We beg to state that he rises every morning contemporaneously with the opening of the bar. After partaking of a jolt, he communes awhile with the bartender and then has another jolt. This makes him a new man, and he has to stand the new man a jolt for luck. After a few more desultory jolts, he goes into the dining room and throws in a little breakfast, not infrequently throwing it up afterwards." So it went before the day ended with "seven or eight nightcaps." Like much else that Edwards wrote the tale had a kernel of truth.

Neither could Albertans relish the undiluted vitriol of a Frank Oliver, blasting everything Tory in the morning and evening *Bulletin*, while the acerbicly Conservative *Calgary Herald* returned the fire just as vehemently in the next day's edition. They were editorialists who preferred the active to the passive voice. Things were not reported to have happened. They happened. Waffle words like "nevertheless" or "notwithstanding" or "in the view of critics" did not inhibit their invective.

In the years to come corporate ownership would absorb even many rural weeklies and heavily sanitize Alberta's press. Technocrats would make the content boringly predictable — the fashion section on Tuesdays, the food on Wednesdays, the used cars on Fridays. By the century's end circulations would be slipping, and still more imported experts would be blaming television, videos, radio and a generation not given to reading anything.

But there may have been another cause. The editors of old had a special sense of time and place. The prairie soil stuck to their boots and was annealed to their souls. If they were sometimes raucous and irresponsible, they were part of Alberta's rich texture. They did not require the endless meetings, the readership surveys, the "focus groups," and the media consultants so indispensable to a latter-day editorial management. To a Frank Oliver or a Tom Braden, it would be like this new mass-produced bread, a homogenized goo. No yeast.

[3]Montreal-born William Southam learned the printing trade in Ontario at the *London Free Press* and with a partner bought the faltering *Hamilton Spectator* in 1877. Thereafter he began buying existing daily newspapers all over the country, with his sons running the business. After acquiring the *Ottawa Citizen*, he bought the *Calgary Herald* and the *Edmonton Journal*. William Southam died in 1932. In 1885 Armour and Braden went on to found the *Medicine Hat News* in a discarded boxcar. The Southam company took over the *News* in 1948.

Group of publishers of Alberta weekly newspapers, 1906.

The frontier wife: she came, she wept and she often won

MAKING A HOMESTEAD A HOME WAS A LIFETIME TASK, MAYBE FUTILE, BUT HER HEROISM BROUGHT FEMALE SUFFRAGE TO THE WEST FIRST

by **VICTORIA MACLEAN**

In buffalo and fur trade days, white men came west mostly for the adventure, the money or the escape. Not so much the young pioneers who invaded the West after 1900. They had come to establish farms, businesses and families. There was, however, a difficulty. There were darn few women.

Alberta, in this sense, was starving. Lax law enforcement allowed a flourishing and ubiquitous trade in prostitution [see sidebar]. But there is more to the male-female bond than occasional sex. Men lacked companionship, and they lacked children. They felt what gold rush poet Robert Service described as "the gnawing hunger of lonely men for a home and all that it means." The settler with a wife had someone for whom to put up a Christmas tree, someone to nag him about gambling and whiskey, someone to chivvy him off to church. Without a wife and

National Council of Women on the steps of the First Presbyterian Church, Edmonton, 1900. Emancipation grew from the harsh prairie soil.

children, he had less incentive to half-kill himself clearing, fencing and breaking the land. Across the West, weary bachelors fell asleep at the table in their lonely shacks and soddies, tinned beans untouched on a cold woodstove.

Homesteading was by its very nature a family enterprise. A pioneer who prospered put it this way to Barry Broadfoot in his anecdotal history *The Pioneer Years 1895-1914*:

> I never actually did get moving until I got myself a wife. Then I didn't have to look after the pigs, the chickens, the milking. And the money we'd get for those things in town, that she did, I could use to hire help and get things done. I rented the first big tractor to come into our valley and you know how? Because my wife was looking after the house and garden and stable part of it, while I was working the land. A single man couldn't do it. They shouldn't have expected him to. The set-up was all wrong, as I see it.

But wrong or not, the western prairie remained notoriously a land of bachelors clear through the decade. Even in the relatively genteel environment of Calgary, it was calculated in 1911 that men outnumbered women three to two. Out in the desolate countryside it was far more extreme.

It was a situation that had always worried those who wanted to see the West settled. In July 1909 the *Lethbridge Herald* added its voice to the many pointing out the economic consequences of male loneliness. "Without the sustaining influence of the fairer sex, the boldest pioneer will weary, then wander; the porcupine will occupy his cabin and the coyote saunter down the trail. Alberta needs women more than men or money." The newspaper urged an organized effort to lure them west. Actually, the CPR and many others had launched recurrent propaganda campaigns making Alberta sound like a cross between a country house in Hampshire and Buffalo Bill Cody's Wild West Show.

Turn-of-the-century eastern newspaper advertisement. Arrival usually brought a rude awakening.

URGENT·!

Thousands of nice girls are wanted in THE CANADIAN WEST.

Over 20,000 Men are sighing for what they cannot get–WIVES ! Shame !

Don't hesitate–COME AT ONCE. If you cannot come, send your sisters.

So great is the demand that anything in skirts stands a chance.

No reasonable offer refused They are all shy but willing. All Prizes ! No Blanks.

Hustle up now Girls and don't miss this chance. Some of you will never get another.

Special Application Card from

Wedding day on the prairies. The photo is of Mr. & Mrs. Ed Hartt, the photo taken by the nurse-photographer Ella Hartt, probably his sister.

European organizations such as churches and orphanages received entreaties, and many responded.[1]

There seems to have been no particular rule as to which kinds of women did best, except that

---

'But oh dear, when I saw what I had landed at! It was dreadful. It was wild country. Not unsafe. But nothing was completed. It was a raw, man's world, not for women.'

---

those who came with their parents or other members of their family were likelier to succeed than those fooled by the highly romanticized recruiting pitches. The luckiest in some respects came with large communities from eastern Europe: from Poland, Romania, Galicia, Russia and Bukovina. They were more accustomed to cold and poverty, and most settled in culturally intact communities.

Many of the east Europeans would later describe the Canadian West not for what it lacked but for what it offered. In compiling *The Last Best West: Women on the Prairie, 1888-1930*, historian Eliane Silverman of the University of Calgary heard why: "We had lived through pogroms...We left Russia in a period of deep famine. We were starving. I was sixteen and looked twelve."

Oppression and privation were not the only motives. Other eastern Europeans came for reasons identical to many of their English, Irish, Dutch, French or American sisters. A Polish woman named Ida Bronowski put it tersely: "I came to join my husband. We married home. I not trust let man go away by himself. I say 'No, if you go, go together.' I hear lots in Poland come from Canada, they talk. Man stay in rooms there, he forget wife and kids. I not trust."

Hester Jane Robinson, who arrived in Calgary in 1905: "The telegram came from my brother Dick, 'Don't come, stay home.' But Mother, my sister Kate, brother Sam and I were packed (with woollen underwear specially purchased) and we left for Canada. I found it a very lonely life..."

When Elizabeth Hanson's husband proposed to leave her at home in Edinburgh until he found a job in Canada, she'd have none of it. She'd heard of men who had left and forgotten about their old-country wives. As she told Professor Silverman, "I wasn't going to be left stranded in the old country with two babies and another on the way. But oh dear, when I saw what I had landed at! It was rather forbidding; it was dreadful. It was a wild country in those days, not unruly, not unsafe, but nothing was completed. It was a raw, man's world, not for

Hulda Swedburg, daughter of Swedish-American settlers, in the family kitchen in the Marchwell district of Saskatchewan in 1906. Note the inevitable coffee pot.

women. At times I was pretty broken-hearted, but it was my own doing. I could have stayed in the old country but I preferred to be with my husband and rough it with him."

British women were among either the best or worst of settlers. Some took to pioneering with the same indomitable spirit that had served the Empire so well in colonial outposts from Rhodesia to Rangoon. They were able to retain the lessons of a "proper" middle-class upbringing while pitching into the raw, robust business of frontier survival. Typical was the Park family in the British ranching area near Cochrane. Daughter Bessie (later MacEwan) and a sister arrived from Scotland without any fear of the cold, because their parents, who had settled earlier, had written that their log cabin

Glenbow Archives, NA-4054-1

Muriel Genevieve McIntosh, 17-year-old daughter of an American immigrant dirt moving contractor, on saddle horse 'Creamo,' with cigarette, liquor bottle and leather chaps, near Strathmore, 1908. She was emphatically not typical.

was "fir-lined" (i.e. panelled inside with lumber) which they took to mean "fur-lined." Nonetheless, the whole family adapted through hard work and ingenuity. Mrs. John Park learned to make sturdy furniture out of apple crates, scrap lumber and barrel staves. Daughter Bessie rose daily at 4 a.m., milked 31 cows, churned butter and sold it at a nearby store. She found pioneer life exhilarating.

There were other Britons like her. In her book *Letters from a Lady Rancher* Monica Hopkins explains how ill prepared she was to pioneer with her Irish-born husband southwest of Priddis. A clergyman's daughter, she had received marital instruction only in "glossing and pressing men's dress shirts." She wrote with cheerful, self-depreciatory humour of learning to keep the woodstove going, rendering lard, churning butter, raising chickens, salting pork, putting in a garden, and helping to brand cattle.[2]

The British, like the rest, kept many of their Old World ways, but unlike the others often felt very superior about it. Canada, after all, belonged to the Empire, not to their coarse American neighbours and not to the Galicians. In the southwest foothills, in the central Alberta parkland,

---

'I never did actually get moving until I got myself a wife. A single man couldn't do it. They shouldn't have expected him to. The set-up was all wrong.'

---

and in pockets elsewhere, the British families strove to put the imperial mark upon the opening province. They played polo and held gala social events, "at-homes," and grand coyote hunts with horses and hounds.[3]

Women faced profound challenges from the moment they began the bone-jarring trip to the homestead. In reality, their destination was often no more than a surveyor's stake in the ground, inscribed with the number of their assigned quarter-section. In the absence of roads, settlers often got lost finding it. Once they did, they had three years to "prove up," meaning to clear and break the stipulated thirty acres.

A typical family arrival is recounted by historian James G. MacGregor in his fine memoir *North-West of Sixteen*, describing that moment in the lives of his father, a 42-year-old veteran of the Scots Guards, and his mother, an apprehensive Englishwoman of 27, with her year-old son in her arms. It was October 1906, and it had taken four days for a hired teamster to bring them over 75 miles of rough trails west of Edmonton to the Pembina valley, where he landed them deep in the

[1]In 1907, thirty young girls were sent from a London orphanage. The youngest, aged seven, was adopted by a Bowden couple and grew up to become Mrs. Gib Hocken, and recorded her recollections in *Candlelight Years*, a local history. In the matter-of-fact tone of the day, she explains that her adoptive parents, a tinsmith and his wife named Fordyce, had produced fourteen children, but only five grew up. Child mortality rates were very high.

[2]Mrs. Hopkins joined virtually all immigrant women in detesting the West's swarming clouds of insects. "The flies are particularly vicious. We get two varieties here and they are perfect brutes. One is called a bulldog and is about the size of a wasp. It takes a chunk of flesh when it bites; the horses go nearly crazy when they know one is flying around them. The other is called a deer fly; it is about the size of a house fly and leaves a poison behind where it has bitten. I always come up in a kind of blister after I have been attacked." And as for mosquitoes, "I have never seen such huge brutes. As a last resort I got a large bran sack, put my legs inside it and tied the top around my waist. With my legs fairly safe, my arms were going like flails all the time."

[3]Britishness was not always admired. Professor Silverman heard this of one woman who refused to Canadianize: "This English lady in the Peace country, she thought she was so superior. She had two little girls, and she was teaching them to speak in the English way, not with this horrible Canadian accent. She wouldn't farm. Her husband [later] bought a hog farm out of Innisfail and went back and forth from the farm to look after things."

Milk follies on a homestead in the Edmonton area. A sense of humour was decidedly therapeutic.

> The Lehmans didn't make money sitting in easy chairs! I myself have done all kinds of farm work, and my girls worked like men to keep the farm going. We were without much money when we came here, eight of us, but inside of four years we had earned 100 head of cattle; then we counted 450 head and we had our homestead patent. We sold out and bought property in the town of Lacombe, paying $18,000, and today $30,000 wouldn't tempt us to sell.
> - Mrs. Charles Lehman, who moved from Saxony to Alberta in 1893, quoted in Home Life of Women in Western Canada *published by the CPR, 1907.*

bush. "'Well, here we are, Mother,' said Dad, with a brave display of optimism. 'Here is the farm.' 'Good Heavens!' was all Mother said." They waved goodbye to the teamster and heard the rattle of his wheels fading into the distance. "'Here we are,' said Dad. 'Farmers.' 'Here we are,' replied Mother, 'cast adrift.' She gazed along the way the teamster had gone, and listened in vain. Then she sat down on a log and cried."

Even when the land already boasted a sod hut, wives remained skeptical. In *Pioneer Tales* A.B. Adshead remembers taking his wife and children to their new home near Olds. "The shades of

Somehow I was never afraid, and used to go outside, the better to hear the coyotes. I still like to hear them howl; they were company when no one else was around.

night were closing in when we neared the farm and my wife nudged me and whispered, 'Where is the house? I don't see any house.' I pointed out the low sod shack, all covered with snow. 'But it's not any bigger than our old pig pen in Ontario,' she said."

Regardless of race or nationality, women came west for a variety of reasons: to teach school, to find husbands, or for sheer adventure. But usually they came with their husbands or their parents — who often turned out to be their only companions. For many of the women who had left the larger centres, as most had, there was one thing they had in common. They were isolated in a wild and unforgiving land. The checkerboard homestead system meant that farms were far apart, and so were all of the comforts of female companionship to which they were accustomed; whether they hailed from a Ukrainian village or the gaslit streets of London or Philadelphia. Now they lived by themselves on a frozen moonscape, their menfolk often away, with nothing to do except work, worry and hope for company.

If men had felt the loneliness keenly before women arrived, for many women it was far

Provincial Archives of Alberta, H-690

worse. In the local history *Prairie Sod and Goldenrod*, Mrs. J. Miller of Crossfield recalled how solitary her little homestead became whenever the men were away hauling fenceposts from the bush or coal from Carbon.

> These trips lasted from three days to a week. It was always quite eerie in the evening with only a small farm light showing across the distant prairie, the coyotes howling and no close neighbours. Somehow I was never afraid, and used to go outside, the better to hear the coyotes. I still like to hear them howl; they were company when no one else was around.[4]

Mrs. MacNeill, a Scotswoman who spent her first seven months with only her husband and brother for company, eagerly made a long journey to her nearest neighbours, only to find that they spoke nothing but German. In the area south of Castor, Benedikte Ausenus didn't see another woman during her first two years on a homestead. On July 21, 1908, the *Edmonton Bulletin* reported the story of a Mrs. Bambrick, the mother of three children, "who is hopelessly insane as the result of the lonely sojourn in the newly opened country." Her husband took her to Edmonton, "where it was decided to send her to the asylum at Brandon."

In the local history *Where the Prairie Meets the Hills*, Elbe Anderson writes, "These grass widows must surely have been the great and unsung heroines of our country." With men so often away

In the winter, garter snakes lived in the roofs of the sod houses, occasionally lowering a reptilian head to savour the heat rising from the cast iron woodstove. Few women felt much nostalgia for soddies.

working for wages, rounding up cattle or hauling supplies, women were sometimes reduced to burning cow dung, and sometimes had no horses at home. "It was not uncommon for the family to be without transportation except for the dog. He might be pressed into service to pull the youngest in a homemade sled. If weather permitted, the whole family thought nothing of a mile or two cavalcade to have afternoon tea with a lonely neighbour lady." There was no other entertainment or distraction: no radios, no telephones, and too little mail.

Unidentified mother and children, Bowden area, early in the century. The need for wives was everywhere voiced; it was a world few women preferred.

[4]Madness induced by loneliness and stress was a constant hazard. Historian Silverman tells of a woman living in a sod house on the open prairie, where no sapling or shrub grew to give form or perspective to the emptiness. Day after day her gaze encountered nothing but snow and sky, and her ear heard only the unending howl of the wind across the plains. The fear began to prey upon her that the wind might not be blowing at all, that the constant banshee wail might be a product of her own tormented thoughts. So she hammered a stake of wood into the ground outside her window, tied a red bandanna to it, and watched it flapping furiously whenever she felt herself losing her grip.

Great Western Garment Co.'s factory in Edmonton early in the century. Soon Alberta women would be leading the charge towards equality.

How To Save Rennet: Take the dark part of the inside of a pig's stomach, cut around it, and peel off, just rinse it up and down two or three times in a dish of cold water, cover a plate with coarse salt, put on alternate layers of rennet and salt. Let lay for a week, then skewer them up in a bunch, and put in a bag with lots of salt and hang up. When you wish to use, put three rennets into a jar with two quarts of water, and steep for a week; add a little more salt. Half a teacupful of this prepared rennet will bring three pails of milk to a hard curd in twenty minutes...Have milk a little warmer than new milk. Be sure not to have it hot.
- Farm and Ranch Review, December 1908

Letters from faraway friends and family were a joyful but infrequent event. Alice Blue, a pioneer in the Queenstown district, wrote that it took two months to get mail: "The Indians would ride out from Gleichen to the Bow River, and swim across with the letters, which would be tied in a handkerchief across their foreheads. For this 'trip' they charged 25 cents." The service was not only cheap but relatively speedy; more commonly homesteaders had to choose between a long journey to a sizable town, or a wait of up to half a year. The Burkholders, near Castor, drove forty miles (65 km) to Stettler. In their first winter near Keephills, the Woodmans picked up their mail at a stopping house four miles away, but it came only twice, delivered by passing loggers.

Many settlers ached with homesickness. Women poured out memories to Eliane Silverman of their mothers' grief: "She cried for days because there was nothing green; when she saw a mustard plant with a little yellow blossom, she picked it and put it on the table." "I remember her crying her heart out all the way out on the train. She brought a piano out here, and she would sit down every night, play 'Home, Sweet Home' and cry." Another confessed, "I missed Norway very much at first. I didn't let anybody see I was crying about it, but I cried many times. I thought if I could pack my things I'd go right back, because it was so far between neighbours."[5]

The pioneer's first house was often a one-roomed shack, with a lean-to for the family horses and milk cow. Although the more prosperous built frame houses with wooden-shingled roofs,

'Here we are,' said Dad. 'Farmers.' 'Here we are,' replied Mother, 'cast adrift.'

poorer families started in one-room log shacks with roofs of sods cut from the soil and lined with tarpaper against the damp. At least one valiant housekeeper followed that with white wallpaper "for cleanliness and good looks." Women waged a constant war against encroaching dust and mud. One pioneer, born in a "soddy," fondly recalled the hard-packed smoothness of their dirt floor, which her mother attacked regularly with a dampened broom.

In spring, soddies grew rather picturesque roof gardens of grasses and wild flowers. When it rained, however, they leaked miserably, and the longer it rained the more they leaked. And with each rainstorm, the roof poles rotted a little more, threatening the occupants with premature burial. In the winter, garter snakes would take up residence in the sods, occasionally lowering a reptilian head to savour the heat rising from the cast iron woodstove. Few women, if any, felt much nostalgia for soddies until long, long after they had moved into something drier and less organic.

Nothing in pioneer days was accomplished easily. The preservation of food was an endless struggle against heat, flies, mice, water, dust and distance. The maintenance of fresh meat in particular was an ongoing challenge. In the summer, chickens were killed and eaten fresh, as was fish. Both were canned in the winter when there was more time. Winter was also the time for salting beef and pork. Around 1900, "beef rings" began to spring up. These were groups of farmers united to supply fresh meat for their own tables; the institution lasted until power and freezers reached the most remote parts of rural Alberta in the '50s. In cash or kind, each member would supply an animal, and one man would be designated to serve as butcher, for a small consideration. Every week, each member of the ring would get "a roast, a boiling piece, and a steak." In a twenty-member ring, using animals dressed at a weight between 400 and 600 pounds, each member received twenty to thirty pounds of fresh meat a week.

The kitchen of an immigrant family whose name went unrecorded, circa 1906. Dark deeds with pigs' stomachs.

But not everyone enjoyed this luxury, and the alternative, home meat-processing, required time, attention and skill. Meat and fish were dried, salted, smoked or "fried out." This was a kitchen version of fur-trade pemmican: fresh pork was sliced, fried dry, packed into crocks and sealed in hot rendered fat. American settlers moving in by wagon often brought a barrel of fried-out pork for the trip and the busy days following arrival.

In the ceaseless search for refrigeration, wells were deployed, holes were dug, ice houses were built, and meat was suspended on tall "gin poles" to keep it in the breeze and away from flies.

Ingredients for tasks like baking could be had close at hand. Cooks rendering lard were advised to seek "the 'leaf fat' that adheres to the ribs and belly of the hog." The recipe for saving rennet, to

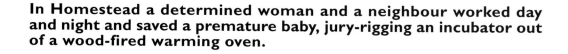

In Homestead a determined woman and a neighbour worked day and night and saved a premature baby, jury-rigging an incubator out of a wood-fired warming oven.

make cheese, began, "Take the dark part of the inside of a pig's stomach..." Egg storage prompted much experimentation. They were commonly packed away in crocks containing salt, oats or bran. The *Farmer's and Housekeeper's Cyclopedia* warned darkly that "eggs taste stale and smell musty when stored in bran, unless they are given a coat of varnish first."

[5]Although Eliane Silverman's is a definitive work, virtually all immigration accounts speak of homesickness. In *Alberta's Pioneers from Eastern Europe* German settler Tova Yedlin recounts, "My father never considered going back, but if my mother had wings she would have flown back. It was really hard for her. She cried more than she ate in those first years."

Pioneer housekeepers had big families and wore out a lot of clothes. It was up to the women to produce not only the clothing but often the soap to wash it (from lard and lye), along with all her other work. Laundering alone was a huge chore, but one undertaken with the usual determination and vigour.[6]

In addition to her workload, a prairie wife often experienced serious problems of supply. In the 1890s and early 1900s, there was a jar shortage that jeopardized the supply of canned meat, fish and vegetables so essential in the winter. But where there's a will there's a way. They collected whiskey bottles, stripped off the labels, and turned them into jars by tying a string soaked in coal oil at the desired point on the bottle and lighting it. The jar-maker then plunged the bottle into cold water and the top portion came off neatly. Lids were made either with paper smeared with egg white or cloth dipped in hot wax. That made one less place for moonshine and one more jar for strawberry jam. Wild raspberries and saskatoons were usually the only available fresh fruit.

Choring and cooking were perhaps the easier parts of the woman's pioneer role. The other half was doctoring the sick and injured, and bearing and raising children. And if the first two were tedious, the latter two could be terrifying. Doctors were few. Around Lethbridge, for example, people described the symptoms to the town pharmacist, who in turn wrote them down and mailed them off to the doctor in Macleod.

Accidents happened frequently. *Hand Hills Heritage* recounts how little Ben Peterson, whose

Mair Polet, wife of a Villeneuve railway engineer and surveyor, with her top-of-the-line kitchen facilities, circa 1906.

LIFE IN A NEW PROVINCE

parents farmed in the district north of Drumheller, had been kicked in the head by a horse and suffered a great gash. His mother stitched the wound, using boiled white linen thread and a darning needle.

In *Farm Women on the Prairie Frontier*, a Ukrainian immigrant named Maria Adamowska recalled, "As I was reaping with the sickle, I cut my finger. The gash was so deep that the finger dangled, just barely held on by the skin. Mother managed to splice it somehow, and the wound healed."

Hazards and adventures abounded. The Henderson family travelled with six children from the BC mines on horseback over the Yellowhead Pass to settle near Strathcona. Mrs. T. Henderson later recalled how she had forded rivers and plodded steep mountain trails with an infant strapped to her bosom and two little ones in her saddle panniards. After 1,000 miles of that, she said, their dirt-floored log cabin with its cozy open hearth seemed like heaven.[7]

The pioneer environment made for level heads and good nerves. Although criminal violence was uncommon, there were few provisions in those days for violent lunatics. The *Calgary Herald* recounted in April 1905 that "a maniac" with an axe had locked a Mrs. Madge and her six children inside their house by nailing the door shut, and had then gone looking for her husband in the fields. Mrs. Madge calmly charged an old muzzle-loader and climbed out an upper window. She found her husband dodging the assailant, gave her husband the weapon and stood back, prepared to assist him with her bare hands if necessary. But the maniac, intimidated, gave up the fight.

It was in the twin matters of sex and childbearing, however, that many women faced their sternest challenges. It was a prudish age, and new brides from "good" families, even farm families, had often learned only Victorian euphemisms about doing their "wifely duty," without finding out until after the ceremony what the duty actually was. Furthermore, these were not unions intended for the furthering of romantic ideals. The primary purpose was economic as often as not. Each farm needed an unpaid workforce, and the more workers the better. For many, if not most, childbearing was an almost annual event.[8]

If affection, or even romantic love, could be had as well, so much the better. But it seems to have been hit and miss, as were most attempts at birth control. Many marriages were arranged, a few were by mail order. The purpose of sex was procreation more than recreation, and broods of a dozen were common. The sexual revolution being preached by American birth control advocate and racial purist Margaret Sanger was far away, contraceptive measures were entirely primitive, and abortion was generally recognized as murder.[9]

For the most part, new life was welcomed with open arms and its survival defended with vigour. In one case at Homestead, a determined woman and her Swedish neighbour worked day and night to save a premature baby, jury-rigging an incubator out of a wood-fired warming oven. They rolled the infant in oil and put him in a "little white casing right up to his neck." Next he went into a shoe box packed with blankets, and from there into the "incubator" for some six weeks. The little fellow was fed with an eye dropper, and eventually thrived. "And by jingo, he's a great big six-foot guy," said the pioneer in concluding her story.

Outside the larger towns, doctors were rarely available. Most women who lived in isolated areas relied on midwives. One pioneer recalls that Ukrainian women used "an older lady. The women would all come to visit you and bring fruit and cookies." In Amber Valley, a black settlement between Edmonton and Lac la Biche, one woman delivered dozens. "She'd stay right in your house until nine days even, and cook and do the wash. Everybody just loved her."

Where possible, the usual practice was to have two midwives in attendance. One came early to organize the household. The other, dubbed the "baby-catcher," attended the actual birth. Midwives had to be able to turn their hand to anything. One story in *Battle River Country* describes how a midwife and her children had arrived to assist at a birth. The woman's husband was away. In the meantime, a prairie fire rolled in. There was no panic as the midwife and her youngsters hitched up the plough and cut a fireguard around the homestead, thus saving it and its occupants.

Childbirth often brought with it the most tragic dramas. In 1910, a pregnant Castor-area woman named Mrs. Wren set out by buggy with her children to have her child in the greater security of Stettler. Twenty-five miles from home she dropped a rein, her horse bolted, the buggy crashed and the passengers were flung to the ground. The men of the household returned from harvest to

[6]In *Farm Women on the Prairie Frontier* Kathleen Strange remembered washday with a verbal shudder: "What a job that always was! Usually, it took me the entire day. In summer, I washed outside; in winter, down in the basement. The boiling sudsy water had to be carried from the stove to wherever my tubs were set. More than once, I burned myself severely, spilling water on unprotected hands and legs."

[7]Not all women were so tolerant of husbands' travel risks, however. In *Wagon Trails to Hardtop* Mrs. A White recalls how her mother Eliza, who had come with Sam White from Kansas in 1900, demanded on a trip back from town that her husband go the long way around a small, shallow lake where the wagon box might float loose. Rather than waste time, Sam and a neighbour put her in a big new washtub and towed her across.

[8]Not typical but certainly illustrative was the family of Russian-German immigrant Gottlieb Wedman of Sprucedale. His three successive marriages produced 23 children.

[9]There was an abortionist in Great Falls, Montana, but that was hard to reach. In February, 1904, the *Lethbridge Herald* reported on its front page that a certain doctor from Calgary had been charged with performing an abortion on a woman from Claresholm. It isn't clear what happened to him.

One of the rare early pictures of prostitutes and their customers, outside a bar in Donald, BC, just over the Rockies, around 1885.

The shady ladies on the edge of town

IN WOMAN-SHORT ALBERTA, BROTHELS OFFERED JOY AND BOOTLEG LIQUOR, BUT OUTRAGE ROSE WHEN THE POLICE BECAME SUSPECTED ACCOMPLICES

It isn't something most histories, especially local histories, like to talk about, but the Last Best West boasted hundreds of brothels. In a land populated disproportionately by young hardworking settlers, cowboys, miners, navvies and policemen, it was to be expected. It was also mostly ignored. In 1909 when the Moral Reform League submitted a petition complaining about prostitution, the Lethbridge city council shrugged its collective shoulders and passed a resolution which said "they cannot suggest any remedy at the present for the state of affairs supposed to exist."

Almost every town had at least one house of ill repute in the early days, and however much incoming preachers and matrons railed against them, they were a stubborn phenomenon that neither police nor judge — often for perfectly dishonourable reasons — were in any hurry to shut down. The newspapers treated what few arrests there were lightly. In 1907 the *Calgary Herald* reported that "Hattie Rodgers and Maud Copeland, two languid ladies of the red slim variety, were fined $25 and costs for keeping a disreputable house. Four ladyettes, Eva Hall, Blanche Palmer, Martha Saunders and C. Thomas, paid $15. They were unable to appear themselves because the hour was very, very early and they were very, very tired. So they sent lawyer Ballachey to plead guilty for them."

For thirty years, the focal point of prostitution in

Lethbridge was "The Point," just west of the downtown area. Two of its leading madams were "Swede"Alice and Carrie "Cowboy Jack" McLean, who were often criticized as much for peddling illegal booze as for marketing their feminine charms. In 1906, Pearl Rogers was arrested at her brothel on Wood Street when she sold bootleg beer to David McLure for fifty cents. McLure was in the bedroom with his boots off when the raid took place and the madam told him, "It's a pity they came before I got the three dollars off you."

The girls might have been illegal, but they were probably clean, judging by the experiences of Jim Gladstone — later Canada's first Indian senator. In 1905 when he was delivering barrels of water in Fort Macleod, the five brothels on the south

---

McLure was in the bedroom with his boots off when the raid took place. The madam thought it a pity; he'd yet to pay.

---

edge of town were surpassed only by the Chinese laundries in the amount of water they used — each about six barrels a week. Gladstone also found the girls to be more than generous tippers come Christmastime.

Brothels, of course, flourished in mining towns such as

Trail, BC. An oldtimer explained to pioneer anecdotalist Barry Broadfoot, "There was this one place run by this Italian woman and there was sort of a lane running by her place. You went down this lane and there was a backhouse there and a clothesline to the house and you gave it three little pulls. Tinkle, tinkle, tinkle, and if there was no answer you stayed out. If two tinkles came back, it meant come on in. No tinkles usually meant that one or two of the town cops were in mama's kitchen drinking her wine and she didn't want any dude barging in, not until she got them out of the way. You can't blame the cops. Even the famous and glorious North-West Mounted Police weren't all that holy."

Calgary's red light district for many years was at Nose Creek, just north of town. By 1906 another group of brothels was operating to the south of the river on Macleod Trail, where, according to the *Calgary Albertan*, "things are going at a tremendous clip."

The reporter described the red light district as a collection of "small wooden cottages with discreet shuttered fronts. Access is ordinarily obtained from the rear. Within, the bare little boarded rooms do not offer much in the way of gilded luxury. A cheap little kerosene lamp supplies the illumination and a decidedly unornamental little round stove the warmth."

Nose Creek still reigned supreme, however. One house there had twelve girls while two others had a total of 25 Japanese women. "In all these houses," said the *Albertan*, "the 'professors' beat out ragtime unhindered and there is quite a procession of vehicles to and fro across the Langevin bridge after dark."

During these years, police and madams often had a much cosier relationship than the moral reformer thought appropriate. Sometimes outrage over police recalcitrance reached a righteous boil. Such was the case in Edmonton in 1909, when the Moral Reform League took the police chief, Major W. Beale, to task. The residents of Norwood claimed "the chief was either incompetent or in collusion with the inmates of the brothels."

Yet as long as there was an over-abundance of young men and a shortage of marriageable women, the brothels continued to flourish. Before the decade was over, readers of Alberta's newspapers were familiar with such euphemisms as "soiled dove," "fallen woman," "white slavery," "segregated areas," and "houses of ill repute."

In Norwood the more things changed, the more they remained the same. By the end of the 20th century residents were still complaining that their community was being used as a haven for hookers. The police, of course, were hard pressed to suggest any remedy for "the state of affairs supposed to exist."

— *V.M.*

Glenbow Archives, NA-3439-2

Two pictures of 'dance hall girls' found among the papers of Edmonton lawyer J.C.F. Bowen, whose clients included prostitutes. He later became lieutenant-governor of Alberta. (Below) houses of ill repute in the Nose Creek district of Calgary, around 1911.

Glenbow Archives, NA-3429-1

Glenbow Archives, NA-673-9

find the horse and shattered buggy in the yard. When they found Mrs. Wren and the children, the woman was unconscious with a broken leg and the baby had been born. Mrs. Wren died after gangrene infected her injured leg, but the baby lived.

Birth brought a similar tragedy to the home of South Peace pioneer Ancel Bezanson, for whom the village on the Smoky River is named. When the health of his wife, Dorothy, failed during her first pregnancy, her father, a doctor, rushed out from Ottawa to attend her. He delivered her of a boy by caesarian section on Christmas Day 1908. She did not recover and died two days later. The Bezanson cattle were wintering many miles away, so there was no milk. Dorothy's sister Lois donned two sheepskin coats, wrapped herself in a lynx robe, tucked the newborn next to her and drove thirty miles by sled through -30 below ice crystals to deliver the infant to a nursing farm-wife named Mrs. Clifford. The boy lived.

But it wasn't just the doctor for whom the prairie wife had to substitute. Sometimes it was the mortician. In *Farm Women on the Prairie Frontier* a pioneer named Clara Middleton recalls women gathering for the ritual preparation of bodies. Although she comments that the women used the opportunity to support and comfort each other, she leaves unsaid the grim reality that this was a job for those with strong muscles and stronger stomachs.[10]

For all its harshness, however, the Great Lone Land offered women a few real satisfactions. Men genuinely valued them. They did not notice that their skin was dried by wind, browned by sun and creased with exertion, and was not, in the fashion of the day, lily white. Beneath the paternalism of traditional culture (European, Asian or Indian, they were all alike in this respect) lay a willingness to listen to what women needed to pacify and civilize the new country.[11] Female suffrage came first to the prairie West, because women in the West too often did a man's job, and did it well.

Tales of this sort are legion in the local histories of Alberta. When Lulu Porter's homestead husband Arthur was invalided with inflammatory rheumatism in the Peace River country, it was not considered all that unusual that she planted and kept a garden when she was pregnant, chored all winter, cut firewood with a dull saw, wallowed in the snow to snare rabbits and walked to the neighbouring farm each day to bring milk to her husband and daughter. Tales of such heroism abounded. Nor did it warrant more than passing comment by the *Medicine Hat News* in 1900 that two girls, aged eleven and thirteen, had trapped two wolves for the ranchers' bounty in 1900. Having only one bullet, they shot the first; the other they roped and dragged to death behind a horse. It was not the kind of country which could allow women a passive and helpless role. Nor did it.

The law, of course, never forgot that they were women, but the double standard cut both ways. It took brawling and assault among men with relative equanimity, but frowned heavily upon wife-beating. The *Edmonton Bulletin* reported in 1904 on the trial of a Mr. Young of Wetaskiwin, charged with cruelty to his wife, who alleged he beat her and tried to set her hair on fire. The courtroom was packed with enraged townfolk, causing the *Bulletin* to comment that had Young not been found guilty, "the populace would doubtless have taken a hand."

Bigamy was another problem women faced in a land so vast and distant from the immigrants' homelands. It was not unheard of for a man to have a wife in both the old

Woman doing laundry, Balzac area, 1905-06.

Glenbow Archives, NA-3731-8

LIFE IN A NEW PROVINCE

and new countries. And given the poor communications, bigamists were unlikely to be caught. However, some of the offenders just seemed to invite discovery, and the penalties were severe; up to seven years. In 1909 the *Lethbridge Herald* reported that a local man had been found to have two wives, one in England, the other in Lethbridge. When his first wife came across an ocean to join her husband, she learned she'd been replaced. Rather than face the wrath of rural justice, the man fled to Scotland with his second wife.

As for polygamy, it was regarded as an abomination. Now that the polygamist plains Indians had been more or less converted to Christianity, Mormons were the only ones suspected of covertly engaging in it. It was partly because of their virulent opposition to this practice that newspapers like the *Macleod Gazette* and the *Calgary Herald* stood so obdurately against the Mormons. The *Herald* huffed that "advocates and practicers of a promiscuous concubinate" weren't welcome in Alberta. The Mormons abandoned the practice early on.

Although sex crimes were rare, they did occur, and were described in the press in the style of the times. The *Edmonton Journal* headed a notorious rape-murder of a young woman in Nanaimo "Is Murdered in Defence of Honour." The *Manitoba Free Press* agreed, saying the victim "had died defending all that is nearest and dearest to womanhood, her honour." More typical, however, was the case of 35-year-old Sam Jones, arrested in 1908 for trying to run off with sixteen-year-old Gertie May Pimm. Jones was released on bail, and young Gertie May was carefully watched. Parental vigilance failed; two months after the arrest the pair successfully eloped.

Sex and marriage, of course, had a funny side on a frontier made up of young people, most of them raised in an age of uncommonly strict propriety and brought to a place of overwhelming practicality. In 1907, after a long and anxious correspondence, an immigrant worker at Frank met his old country mail-order bride at the railway station, according to the *Edmonton Bulletin*. She took one look at him and announced she wouldn't have him. Crestfallen, and out of pocket for her passage and his marriage licence, he arranged for her to marry a friend in exchange for his expenses, and sportingly served as best man. In 1902, the *Calgary Herald* reported the story of a local woman who thought her husband was acting up with their hired girl. She followed him out in the dark to their kitchen one night, a shawl like the hired girl's over her head, and was caught in a passionate embrace. She struck a match triumphantly, only to find she had been seized by the hired man.

On this frontier, as on all others, drunkenness was a problem. For many early Alberta women, the advocacy of temperance and the closing of brothels wasn't prissiness, but a defence of home and family. In western towns and cities, too much scarce family money went to barkeeps, bootleggers and bad women. The wife of a man who availed himself of these frontier fleshpots was left vulnerable to both incurable disease and impoverishment. Historian Paul Voisey devotes an entire chapter of the book *The Best from Alberta History* to the domestic grief that gave rise to the movement for women's suffrage.

Despite isolation, heavy work loads and no vote (or perhaps because of all this), women by 1910 were joining the Woman's Christian Temperance Union in large numbers, demanding that bars be closed, and in fact trying to outlaw liquor altogether. The newspapers of the day abounded with accounts of campaigns to shut down the brothels of Kinistino Avenue (96th St.) in Edmonton and Nose Creek in Calgary. In Big Valley, when the men wouldn't evict prostitutes from town, housewives burned the bawdy house down. By the turn of the decade, the white enamel WCTU pin was almost standard female attire at Protestant church picnics throughout the new province.

Most men responded, as men so often do, by ignoring the demands and hoping they would subside. That was not to be. By 1910 a small army of activists had taken up battle stations across the West. Women like Miss Jean Cullen Reed, a friend of English suffragette Emmeline Pankhurst, was a housekeeper at the Haunted Lakes Ranch near Alix. In the next decade the national movement would launch an explosive offensive, with Alberta women leading the charge.

It is a weird-looking affair; it is a barrel-shaped thing and has two washboards, one above the other, which move in opposite directions and the clothes are supposed to move between them. You notice I say supposed, for that is just what they don't do...Every time we tried to untangle the clothes we scalded our hands and it never struck either of us to turn the heater off. We went on pulling and scalding ourselves and getting madder and madder. I told Billie it was a beastly country where you couldn't even wash your clothes without getting them torn to bits. Billie retaliated by telling me if I had only done what he wanted, put the clothes in the creek, we wouldn't have got our hands scalded.
- *Monica Hopkins in* Letters from a Lady Rancher, *September, 1909.*

[10]Death came earlier for women than men, because of the strain of childbirth and heavy labour. When a younger woman died, her husband was often unable to look after their children. If they were lucky, they could be taken in by neighbouring families. Otherwise they would be sent out to more distant relatives or to orphanages.

[11]Men might have been nominally in charge, but women had minds of their own. As one explained to Professor Silverman about her relationship with her husband, "We never had a scrap of any description. Of course he was the boss, and if he said anything, I didn't dispute him. If I wanted to do it, I did it, and if I didn't, I pleased myself about it. No use arguing with a man if he thinks he's the boss."

Work or travel often spelled death amidst twisted wreckage

TRAIN OR WAGON CRASHES, FLOODS, ELECTROCUTION AND MINE FIRES
WERE AMONG THE CALAMITIES PLAGUING ALBERTA'S FLEDGLING POPULATION

Glenbow Archives, NA-1313-7

The train wreck two miles east of Medicine Hat, July 9, 1908. 'To the ordinary mortal it would seem this awful mortality could be lessened,' said the Calgary Herald.

by CALVIN DEMMON

In May 1902 there arrived in Calgary what the *Herald* described as "A Train of Blood." At Fort William (later part of Thunder Bay) a little boy had fallen off it and been killed. At Dunmore near Medicine Hat, an Italian immigrant fell off and the train ran over him, cutting off both his legs. And as the train approached Calgary, a railway employee named Shaw had his head knocked through a window during a fight and was taken off the train "in pretty badly used-up condition," the *Herald* said, adding that he was arrested for being "whiskey crazy."

Outside of the mines (see Sect. 4, ch. 1), the railway was the favoured playground for death and maiming in the first decade of the century. Scarcely a week went by without a wreck or railway accident of some kind, if not involving a whole train at least a workman. This, of course, had been so in the previous decade (Vol. I, p. 170). But as the Canadian Pacific completed the Crowsnest line, the Canadian Northern and the Grand Trunk Pacific reached across the northern prairie and parkland, and all three spread a network of branch lines throughout the new province, the hazard of railroading became everywhere evident. There were more railway accidents because there were more railways.

Working on the railroad carried with it a significant responsibility. A fully-laden train hurtling down the track was an unstoppable juggernaut, and the slightest miscalculation could bring disaster. In September 1906 a man named McDonald, the night operator at Dunmore, was absent from his post at a crucial moment. That absence allowed a freight train to roll out on the track when another was approaching. The engines collided head-on "with an impact so terrific as to cause the

Lethbridge flood, 1902. One of the houses carried down the swollen Belly River into the Oldman knocked out a bridge.

Rose was scalded and lingered for several days before dying; most of the other crew members were scalded, badly cut or suffered broken bones.

boilers to telescope right up to the piston bar heads and then crumple them up like cardboard toys," the *Medicine Hat News* reported. W.G. Oliver of Cranbrook, who had been riding in the cab with his brother-in-law, engineer William A. Rose, was killed instantly; Rose was scalded and lingered for several days before dying; most of the other members of both crews were scalded or badly cut or suffered broken bones.

Before two years had passed, another collision near Medicine Hat would claim the lives of three crewmen and two passengers under peculiarly similar circumstances. A light locomotive headed east out of the yards collided with the morning passenger train from the west on the track between Dunmore and Medicine Hat. Seven died: four railwaymen and three passengers. An inquest laid a portion of the blame on a Mr. Ritchie, the operator who cleared the light locomotive to leave the Medicine Hat Station. Ritchie had been working twelve hours a day for the previous four days, and had been on duty for twelve hours before the accident; the station was shorthanded because another operator had drowned.

Weather could knock out a train as easily as human error. A coal train ran into deep snow on

An upset buggy at Bow Island, turn of the century. Even on dry land horses could be a bad business.

the track near Frank in January 1907 and was derailed. The fireman jumped and escaped with slight injuries, but Arthur Jardine, the engineer, was pinned under the overturned engine and died.

Editors and reporters alike took to decrying the hazards. In July 1903 the *Edmonton Bulletin,* reporting a freight train wreck a mile and a half south of Lacombe, ended its story with this comment: "People think that the CPR might well expend a few of their surplus thousands on the roadbed of the Calgary and Edmonton Railway." After the death in October 1907 of 22-year-old William Fraser, a CPR brakeman who was smashed to death by a freight train that struck a caboose upon which he was hanging a warning light, the *Lethbridge Herald* inserted into its front page story the observation that "such an accident could not occur without gross carelessness on the part of somebody."

And in December 1908, the *Calgary Herald* noted that in a single month 27 railway employees had been killed and 18 injured in Canada. "The occupation must necessarily be hazardous, but to the ordinary mortal it would seem as though this awful mortality could be lessened," the paper editorialized. "Think of the houses desolated by the death of the 27 railway men...Think of the loss to the nation. Think of those dependent on them for support...There is work for the Canadian Board of Railway Commissioners."

He was in such pain that no one dared pull him out until the doctor arrived. Those who attended during his lengthy ordeal in the thresher said he seemed to have nerves of steel.

For most Albertans, a trip by train was a rare experience. For local purposes the usual means of travel was the horse and the wagon, although by the decade's end the more affluent had taken to automobiles. But horses, being nervous and temperamental, presented hazards of their own, especially between farm and town.

In wagon travel or on horseback, the biggest danger was water because most streams remained unbridged. In summer this might be refreshing, because the streams were low, clean, and thirst-quenching. But in spring they were raging torrents and in winter they were dangerous for their unpredictable ice, yet travellers still had to cross them. Thus, in July 1902, Mr. and Mrs. E. King and their baby were out driving near Millarville, southwest of Calgary, when they came to the Sheep River. King had forded the stream before, so he drove the rig into the water, but when they were nearly across the seat broke and Mrs. King and the infant fell into the icy creek. King plunged in and managed to reach his wife briefly before the current swept them apart again. Finally Mrs. King seized an overhanging branch and held on to it and the baby until her husband brought her to land, but the overchilled baby died of what medicine would later term hypothermia.

The following month, J.L. Ingram and two other horsemen were swimming horses across the South Saskatchewan River, about a mile above Medicine Hat, when Ingram's horse turned over with him and he was carried off by the swift current and drowned.

In the North, where in winter the rivers became sleigh roads, the chief danger lurked at the rapids whose uncertain ice made travel exceedingly risky. A freighter who was carrying Christmas

The men went upstairs. They found the babe dead in a bed. Ferdinand, dead and frozen, lay in the same bed. One of the poor little mites also lay there, and as the men stepped quietly into the room it put an arm around the neck of its dead father and tried to snuggle up for warmth. The poor child's legs were frozen solid nearly to the knees.
- From a newspaper account of the death — from "accidental poisoning," said the coroner — of Edward Ferdinand, his wife and one of their babies, in Edmonton, Jan. 21, 1907.

supplies to the town of Lesser Slave Lake (later Grouard) in December 1905, and who hoped to profit by being the first to reach the town, chanced the ice and hit a thin spot. Two teams of horses and their loads went into the water and he could not save them. When William McCue and his family, settlers from Ontario, arrived in February, they saw a sight that must have made them wonder about their new home: the horses' frozen heads were still sticking up out of the ice.

If the risk of a swollen river was too great, a traveller who wished to continue had no choice but to wait for the waters to recede. One such man, known as Pierre, was travelling southwestward into Edmonton along the Victoria Trail in an oxcart. The trail crossed a number of creeks, but when it came to Sturgeon River, Pierre saw that the river was too deep and turned back, only to find that Sucker Creek had also become impassable. Trapped, he eventually had to kill and eat his

The blaze that blackened east Alberta
A HOMESTEADER'S FEARSOME NIGHTMARE WAS A PRAIRIE FIRE, BUT THE ONE THAT SWEPT THE EAST-CENTRAL PROVINCE IN 1909 WAS THE WORST EVER

Royal Ontario Museum

Paul Kane's A Prairie on Fire Near Edmonton. *The fire of 1909 left millions of acres in one black ruin. The toll in human life could never be counted.*

A homesteader's cabin on the plains might withstand a freezing winter or a scorching summer. It might keep predators away from the children. One thing it could not do. Against a roaring prairie fire, a wooden building sitting alone in a wilderness of dry grass offered no protection at all.

Fire was therefore the most feared of the natural disasters. After a full year in Alberta, anyone still alive and determined to stay knew how to survive a blizzard. Hailstorms could be terrifying, but they were rarely fatal. By clinging to a plank you might float to safety in a flood. But no vehicle existed that could carry a family through a prairie wildfire. It levelled houses, barns, fences, wagons, trees, crops. It killed wildlife and livestock with the same disregard it showed for the lives of settlers and ranchers.

ox. Sucker Creek was later renamed Myrtle Creek, but for a time it was known locally as "Pierre Ate the Ox Creek."

But even on dry land, horses could be a bad business. In February 1900, Lottie Rankin of Calgary, a stenographer, was out for a ride with three friends in a two-seated rig when a wheel struck a large stone and the startled horses bolted. Miss Rankin either jumped or was thrown from her seat, fracturing her skull and dying instantly. In June 1902, rancher J.W. Fearon was killed at High River when the horses pulling his wagon took fright and he was thrown out on his head; in the same month, a 13-year-old boy named Armour was dragged to his death when he became tangled in his horse's rope and it galloped off.

Riding a horse, however, had certain advantages unknown to those who later took to the road

---

In the first decade of this century, Alberta had none of the grid of roads and highways that would one day stop grass fires from fanning across a whole countryside. Furthermore, there was still much unbroken sod. In the late summer and early fall, especially in years when the ground was parched, the prairie became one huge, sprawling fire hazard. Homesteaders learned, either by painful experience or by taking the advice of earlier arrivals, that clearing and maintaining a ploughed fireguard around buildings and haystacks was a chore not to be put off. A fireguard offered protection against the scattered, sporadic fires that blotched the plains every year. Occasionally, though, a fire of such magnitude that it could not be stopped would sweep across the flatlands, leaving in its wake a landscape blackened and dead.

Yet of tens of thousands of grass fires in Alberta history, one stood etched and alone in the memories of east-central Alberta farmers who lived through it. This was the fire of 1909 that would leave as much as five million acres one huge black ruin and a toll in human life whose ultimate numbers no one would ever know.

There had been a forewarning of that fire. It had come in the spring of 1906 when the prairie blazed from Olds to the Red Deer River, fifty miles (eighty km) to the east. This one was apparently touched off by two homesteaders who were, ironically, trying to burn a firebreak to safeguard their property. It spread rapidly, destroying buildings, fences and pastures. It left trapped horses piled dead in corrals whose posts had burned, according to one witness, like giant lighted candles.

But the 1906 fire was only a grim foretaste of the inferno that three years later was to roam, driven on shifting winds, over much of eastern Alberta, creating a black scar that spread over about 15% of the total agricultural acreage in the southern part of the province.[a]

How the great prairie fire of 1909 started is anyone's guess. It may have been touched off by an errant flash of lightning or by a careless homesteader. The plains of east-central Alberta and western Saskatchewan produced a thick blanket of grass and underbrush that was said to be so high that year that horses waded through it as if crossing a shallow sea.

There were, as usual, many small prairie fires during that hot, dry summer, and the homesteaders beat them back with wet gunny sacks. An old ranchers' technique was to shoot a steer; two cowboys would throw loops over front legs and hind and drag the carcass over the flame.

It may have started in just the manner that Dick Imes, who had turned 14 that year, later recalled. In *Shadows of the Neutrals*, Robert J. Roder relates that Imes was out for a horseback ride on a hill above Blood Indian Creek, near the spot where it flows into the Red Deer River about sixty miles (95 km) north of Medicine Hat. From that vantage point, where he had stopped to tighten his cinch, Imes saw Scotty Reid, an employee of the V Bar V Ranch who had camped in a tent alongside the creek, burning fireguards. Imes, who was too far away to help, watched as the fire got away from Reid. Fed and driven by a west wind, it fanned out and spread eastward, soon crossing miles of prairie, burning toward the eastern boundary of Alberta.

By the time it reached the border town of Empress, settlers up and down the Saskatchewan boundary had seen the billowing clouds of smoke and had mobilized every man, woman, child, horse and ox to plough a guard that stretched north for miles. The cleared space was wide and long enough, and their properties were spared.

Glenbow Archives, NA-1502-1

Fighting a prairie fire near Elnora in 1906. Many homesteaders left the blackened prairie for good.

in automobiles. Firmly seated in the saddle of a trusted animal, a rider who might have had one drink too many in town could doze off, secure in the knowledge that the horse would get him home, and a rider who had lost his direction could give the horse its lead in the expectation that the horse knew the way.

Floods were a hazard. In the summer of 1902, a flood devastated the Lethbridge area as the Belly River rose 22 feet above high water mark and families who had settled on the river bottom had to be taken out by boat. Many houses were swept down the river, and a large one being carried along by the fierce current knocked out a wooden bridge. Afterwards, both sides of the riverbank were littered with farm machinery, furniture, wagons, dishes, pictures, pots and pans.

City dwellers were not immune, however, in those days when storm drains were often

---

Stalled at the east, the fire turned westward on a fresh wind, burning so brightly in the night sky that the red horizon could be seen 100 miles (160 km) away. The flames jumped trails and creeks as they blazed to the west. Like the home-

after the main body of the fire had passed.

No precise reckoning of the fire's extent was recorded, nor was the number of dead and injured ever calculated. The total area involved lay between the Red Deer River and Highway

Once again the wind shifted and the fire's energy moved northeast towards Fleet, Coronation and Consort. Children clutched their pets and watched the adults battle the advancing flames.

steaders in Saskatchewan, settlers and ranchers brought ploughs, water barrels, and sacks to beat and starve the fire along a front that stretched north as far as Sullivan Lake, near Castor. Once again the wind shifted, and on the next day the fire's energy moved north and east towards Fleet, Coronation and Consort.

Little children clutched their pets and dolls and watched as the adults battled the advancing flames. Young women made sandwiches and coffee for the char-blackened men along the fire front. Jessie Stewart, a single woman working on a ranch south of Castor, later described the fire as a wild, awesomely beautiful sight.

In the Berry Creek area, it killed a homesteader and burned nearly all the hair from the head of one of his young daughters. Another daughter was so badly burned that she survived only after months in hospital. At Sullivan Lake, a pregnant woman and her daughter were burned to death, while a new bride, confused by the flames, ran the wrong way and was burned and permanently scarred. A man who sheltered his wife and children safely in a slough died when he went back to his house to retrieve something.

Some whose homes lay in the fire's path retreated into their cellars, which they covered with sod, allowing the fire to pass over them. East of Sullivan Lake, a group of homesteaders mounted horses and gathered on a hill where the grass was spotty. When the fire arrived, they whipped the horses at full speed through the flames, coming out safely on the other side.

Horses that ran loose disappeared into the flames and were never seen again. Many other horses, cattle or oxen were found alive but were so grievously burned that they had to be destroyed. Hay and wheat stacks continued burning long

13, the Saskatchewan border and a line west of Highway 36, about five million acres, but not all of it was burned. The area was lightly settled, communications were poor or non-existent, and those who survived were too busy afterwards to sit down and chart the edges of the burned-out area or list the names of those thought to be lost. The flames reportedly burned as far north as Castor and Halkirk, and some said they reached even farther, up to Hardisty or beyond.

Of the antelope and other wildlife that survived, many starved for lack of food. Crops and grass were gone, grazing land was barren, and firewood had vanished. Homesteaders who stayed discovered that buffalo chips, gathered for use in the stove, burned well. But many homesteaders left the blackened prairie for good.

In the Ione area, southwest of Monitor, a rancher named Reed and some of his neighbours had managed to save a strip of grass about six miles wide and ten miles long (ten km by sixteen km), and people came from thirty miles (48 km) away to cut the "prairie wool" and take it home to feed their livestock that winter.

By spring of the following year, new grass appeared and the prairie briefly turned green again, before the short grass wilted under the summer sun. Many who left after the fire returned to their homesteads to begin again, but it was several years before the prairie grasses recovered from the fire's devastation and there was once again enough food and fuel for man and beast.

— C.D.

[a]Federal figures in the 1960s showed Alberta had a farming acreage of 47 million acres. The maximum arable acreage in the Peace River is usually cited as sixteen million. Hence a fire sweeping five million acres would have blackened approximately a sixth of the 31 million in the south.

haphazard at best. In May 1902 a torrential rainstorm flooded rivers and creeks in the Calgary area, washing out bridges, covering railroad tracks, flooding cellars and cutting off traffic between Calgary and Edmonton. The rain continued in June and July; the *Calgary Herald* reported on July 15 that the rivers were "bank full" and the bottom lands deeply covered with water. The Kootenai bridge was out, as were others, and the NWMP buildings west of town had been swept away.

Six years later the *Lethbridge Herald* reported the "Worst Flood in the Country's History," far surpassing the "famous flood of 1902." A 48-hour rainstorm dumped more than two inches of water on the area, filling the Belly River to overflowing, tying up rail service, knocking out telegraph lines, forcing schools to close. A dam at the Knight Sugar factory at Raymond broke, carry-

Suddenly a miner, afire from head to toe, staggered from a burning building. Before he died, he was able to tell what had happened.

ing away a section of railroad track. A train arriving from Macleod "looked like an old mud scow, being completely covered with mud, and the conductor and his crew looked like ditch navvies." At Brocket, the eastbound train stopped on one side of a damaged bridge, the westbound on the other, and they exchanged passengers and baggage and reversed their courses.

Farming brought its own perils. In an attempt to speed up work on the land, farmers made use of machines that could be deadly. Chris Schattsneider, farming in the Ellerslie district, was trying to fix his thresher one afternoon in October 1907 when he slipped and fell feet first into the maw of the machine, which was still running. He was in such pain that no one dared pull him out until Dr. Craig arrived four hours later. Both his feet had to be amputated. Those who attended him during his lengthy ordeal said he was remarkably brave, seeming to have nerves of iron.

Silas Moore, manager of the Alberta Pacific Elevator at Tees, was not as fortunate. On a Wednesday afternoon in January 1910, his brother Paul found his mutilated body in the elevator's machinery, where it had been going around and around for hours.

Mothers of small children on farms were very much aware of the danger posed by water wells, which for children always held a deadly fascination. A three-year-old boy, the child of G.S. Lane who lived near Bronx, sixteen miles southeast of High River, was a typical victim. He was playing in the yard one day when he climbed up on a box to look into the well, and tumbled in.

His mother bravely attempted to rescue him by climbing down into the well on a ladder, but she found that he had struck his head as he fell and was already dead. ·

Electricity was a new and rather fearsome commodity in the early 1900s. Arthur Leggatt nearly lost his life in May 1905 when, as he worked on the roof of a Calgary building, his head grazed a live wire and he was knocked unconscious. He would have fallen from the roof had his arm not caught on a non-electrical wire which saved him until he was rescued, badly burned. Such incidents inspired misconceptions. In November 1906, after the Strathcona coroner's jury ruled that a man's death by electrocution had been caused by faulty insulation, the *Edmonton Journal* ran a front-page story under the headline, "Edmonton's Lights Are Safe." All wiring in the city was always thoroughly inspected by the electrical engineer, Arthur Ormsby, before any connections were made with the current, the newspaper reported reassuringly. But work-

men remained at risk: in August 1910, Robert Jones, an employee of Edmonton's electric department, was killed when he came in contact with a live wire on a street-corner pole and took 2,300 volts through his body.

Coal mining surpassed railroading as a hazardous way to earn a living. Workers in coal mines were in unremitting danger, not only from cave-ins but from fires and from smothering by the carbon dioxide that was a constant menace in their tunnels. Apart from the major disasters (see Sect. IV, ch. 1), the industry steadily logged deaths and injuries. One of the more spectacular was the coal mine fire in an area that now lies near the heart of the city of Edmonton.

The Walter's mine was one of many small mines in the area at the time. It tunnelled beneath Strathcona, near what would become the south end of the High Level Bridge. Late in the evening of June 1907, a fire broke out in the mine, lighting up the night sky and attracting hundreds of onlookers to the hillside. They soon learned that five men were trapped inside it. Suddenly, a miner afire from head to toe staggered from a burning building that enclosed the mine's air shaft. He was carried on a stretcher to a nearby home, then taken to the Strathcona hospital, where he died. Before his death, however, he related what had happened.

The man was foreman George Lamb. He had been summoned by Ed Candler, an engineer for the mine, whose wife had awakened him to tell him the mine was on fire. When Lamb learned what was happening, he rang the alarm and then ran to the mineshaft and descended. Battling through smoke and falling timbers, he succeeded in reaching the bottom, ninety feet down, where he found the five men still alive, huddled together. He tried to persuade them to go up the ladder, but one who did fell back after being overpowered by the smoke. Lamb decided to show them by example that they could make it, and started up the ladder himself. They followed, but one man apparently fell and knocked the others from the ladder as well. Lamb made it out through intense flames, his clothes burned from his body and his flesh charred.

Lamb's sister, Margaret Jane Lamb of Newcastle-on-Tyne, England, received the Edward Medal from the king in March 1908, in recognition of her brother's bravery. Investigators theorized that the fire had started when a candle that was carelessly left burning in the shaft ignited the wood that shored up the walls. Fires had begun in the mine in that manner before. They would begin in that manner again.

Funeral procession after Walter's mine fire in Edmonton, 1907. The flames lit up the night sky and attracted hundreds of onlookers.

Provincial Archives of Alberta, B-1568

The night Turtle Mountain wiped out most of a town

No Alberta disaster was as swift and terrible as the Frank Slide which claimed over 100 lives and was heard 115 miles away

The turn-of-the-century mining town of Frank owed both its short, rambunctious life and its gruesomely spectacular death to Turtle Mountain, a limestone mass that towers 3,000 feet above the valley of the Crowsnest River in the eastern portal of the Crowsnest Pass.

In 1900, Henry Pelletier of Blairmore discovered within Turtle Mountain a massive, vertical coal seam he estimated to be thirty feet (9.1 metres) or more in width. He sold his claim to Samuel W. Gebo, a promoter. Gebo, encouraged by the CPR's ravenous need for coal to fuel its steam engines, enlisted Henry L. Frank, a bearded venture capitalist from Butte, Montana. Operating as the Canadian-American Coal and Coke Co., the pair immediately set to work building a mine — and a brand-new town to go with it — hard up against the mountain's foot.

By 1903, the Frank mine was in full swing. Coal brought out of the mine by horse was loaded into railroad cars on a spur line from the CPR track. Two hundred men were hard at work, most on a day shift and a smaller number on a night crew for maintenance.

At the top of the nearly perpendicular mountain wall, a wedge-shaped section of limestone jutted out over the mine entrance and the flats far below, where a row of seven company-built cottages housed miners and their families. Slightly to the west lay the town proper, a hive of ribald activity whose barrooms were open long after the miners' children had been put to bed.

Brawling and fistfights were commonplace on Dominion Avenue, Frank's main street, and the banker was said to keep four loaded pistols close at hand when he retired to an apartment above his establishment. There were four hotels, two restaurants, a watchmaker, a cigar shop, a drug store, a retail dairy, a laundry and other businesses. The town also offered its 600 inhabitants churches, a two-storey school, a hall for concerts and meetings, a post office and the *Frank Sentinel* once a week.

Frank's boosters called it "the town of the future" and predicted that it would one day rival the American city of Pittsburgh. Those hopes ended abruptly in the dark at 4:10 a.m. on Wednesday, April 29, 1903, when the looming limestone gave way and ninety million tons of rock came roaring down the heavily wooded mountainside, pushing an icy blast of air before it that lifted houses from their foundations and levelled shacks and tents. Chunks of rock struck each other in mid-air, showering sparks; white limestone powder filled the air like a huge, dense, thundercloud as the mass plunged downward.

Scores of inhabitants of the tiny town were killed instantly. Others were spared, though no one could say for sure why death took one and passed another by. Lester Johnson, asleep in one of the company cabins, awoke in the roar to find his pyjamas blown off and a piece of lath driven into his side, through a feather mattress. He survived.

Alex Leitch and his wife, however, were killed instantly, buried in a room of their cabin, as were their four boys. Two of the Leitch girls, Jessie and Rose-Mary, were pinned in a

The town of Frank the day after the slide. In the space of a hundred seconds the rock had blanketed the valley.

double bed by a ceiling joist, but their injuries were minor. A third daughter, an infant named Marion, was thrown from the house, but she reportedly landed safely atop a bale of hay that blew in from the livery stable, half a mile away.

The gargantuan mass of rocks and mud lapped across the valley and continued up the opposite slope for 500 feet before stopping, leaving a sea of limestone as much as 100 feet deep across the valley floor, burying two farmhouses, a bunkhouse, other structures and an unknown number of people under tons of rock. Seven thousand feet of the CPR track through the pass were covered. The town's business section missed the main brunt of the avalanche, but all the buildings and equipment at the mine were scoured from the face of the mountain and the entrance to the mine was blocked, leaving seventeen miners trapped inside. Three men who had been outside the entrance eating their mid-shift meal vanished as if they had never existed.

A railway car at the mine entrance, it was said, was flung two miles across the valley. In Cochrane, 115 miles (185 km) directly north, the noise of the slide sounded like a rifle shot echoing through the hills. George Bond of Ottawa, a guest at the Imperial Hotel in Frank, later described "a violent shaking motion" and "a loud, crashing report, followed by a succession of noises which I can only compare to the continuous bumping noises of freight cars being brought together, with an occasional louder report."

View of Turtle Mountain showing what fell off.

Lethbridge, jumped down from the train and set out across the jumble of rocks, scrambling over chunks as big as boxcars. He reached the other side just in time to flag the train down and save it from ploughing into the limestone wall.

Two houses were on fire, ignited by their coal-burning stoves. Alex Clark's cottage was completely gone, as were his wife and five children; Clark himself was later counted as one of the three men killed outside the mine. Four doors down from the Clark cabin, Lucy Ennis lay pinned under a beam that had broken her collarbone; she had somehow managed to clear the debris from her infant daughter Gladys, saving the baby from suffocation. Under the rubble in a back room of her cabin, rescuers later found Mrs. John Watkins alive; she had

The gargantuan mass of rocks and mud lapped across the valley and continued up the opposite slope for 500 feet before stopping.

A dense white cloud of limedust hung over the town like the smoke from a raging fire.

When the mountain began to fall, a freight engine was working near the mine entrance, picking up coal cars. The engineer, hearing a roar, throttled the engine across a bridge and made it to the other side just before flying rock knocked the bridge from its footings. Brakeman Sid Choquette, aware that the passenger train, the Spokane Flyer, was due in from

been flung into the room from her home next door.

Fifty men, women and children, including several whole families and ten or more foreign miners, who lived on the eastern flat beyond the Clark and Ennis cabins, were irretrievably buried. Another fifty or more men were said to have pitched tents on the valley bottom earlier that week, hoping to find work in town. If so, they perished, but some townsfolk said later that the men might have left before the slide to try their luck in Blairmore. A work crew of about twelve men was buried along the CPR track.

Those who escaped death organized quickly into rescue parties. Bodies of pigs and horses were everywhere, and searchers also found the thigh and leg of a man. The townspeople knew that men had been working in the mine, but

Glenbow Archives, NA-2550-4

The Calgary Herald the day of the slide. The first reports were badly garbled.

they found the entrance completely blocked. Working in shifts, they attempted to clear it. In the meantime, the

5 p.m., thirteen hours after the slide, they broke through to the surface, but they had to dig again to emerge in an area sheltered from rocks that were still falling.

The first reports to the outside world were garbled. A mine explosion was thought to have occurred, or an earthquake, or a volcanic eruption. Choquette, the hero who saved the passenger train, was said to have been driven crazy by the horrible sights he saw. (The story was false; Choquette was fine. He left the CPR, though, to work for the Illinois Central Railroad, retiring in the 1930s.)

Mounties from Pincher Creek, Calgary, Macleod and Lethbridge arrived on a train, along with newspaper correspondents, some of whom contributed to the confusion by filing exaggerated reports and unverified stories.

The deep political instinct for damage control immediately came to the fore. In Ottawa, Alberta Liberal MP Frank Oliver addressed the House on April 30, decrying "the circulation of such unfounded reports, disturbing the public mind, causing anguish to relatives, as well as doubts as to the values of property, [that] are a crime which should be punished." On the mind of Oliver, publisher of the *Edmonton Bulletin*, were perhaps the luridly exaggerated on-the-scene accounts filed by a correspondent for the *Calgary Herald*.

Dr. G.H. Malcolmson of Frank, aided by his nurse, Miss Grassick, cared for the handful of survivors in a makeshift ward in his home; two other physicians who voluntarily arrived by train to help found their services unneeded and returned to their practices in Macleod. Dr. Saul Bonnell, the CPR doctor at Fernie, arrived from the west on a locomotive. He told a friend decades later, "I could see there was nothing a doctor could do."

A substantial chunk of the ledge remained atop the mountain, and teams of men who climbed up to look at it reported seeing enormous fissures.

On May 1, territorial premier Frederick Haultain arrived to assess the situation, and after climbing back and forth over the slide area three times to confer with engineers and town fathers, told the town that E.H. McHenry, the CPR's chief engineer, was firmly convinced that the top of the mountain was still shifting. The townsfolk were moved to Blairmore, as well as to points east on a CPR train that had been sent to carry them to safety; Mounties patrolled the empty town night and

H.L. Frank, the Montana capitalist, died in 1908, having spent his final months in a sanatorium, his nervous system apparently shattered by the knowledge of the tragedy.

seventeen miners who had survived inside realized they would never make it out the shattered, impassable entrance. With their air running out and water from the blocked-up creek and river filling the lower levels of the mine, those who were still able began digging through a narrow coal seam. At

day, however, and no looting was reported.

Haultain returned to Frank on May 10, conferred with McHenry again, received what was more or less an all-clear report, and called a meeting in Blairmore to advise residents that they were free to return to their homes.

But with the mine closed and rocks still falling periodically, there was no rush to go back. On May 24, a group of sightseers who came to see the ruins were frightened out of their wits when 100 pounds of railroad dynamite exploded accidentally; no one was injured.

On May 30, workers finally opened the mine entrance, and inside they found still alive a lone mine horse named Charlie. He had survived by gnawing wood and drinking seepage water. Poor Charlie succumbed before he could be brought out into the daylight, however. One account says he died of fright when his rescuers left him alone again as they raced out to fetch him water and food; according to another account, Charlie died happily after having been supplied with an overabundance of brandy and oats.

By August, a polished piece of limestone from the slide was on display in the window of D.J. Young & Co.'s bookstore in Calgary, "finished just as it was picked up, as square as if cut with a chisel," according to the *Herald*.

In late September a smaller rockslide was reported on the mountainside opposite the town; passengers on a train approaching Frank heard an "appalling" roar and the engineer braked the train and backed it up for several miles. After waiting an hour the train entered Frank and found all the residents waiting in the station to leave; they were taken on to Blairmore and other towns. "Authorities of the town wish to minimize the matter so that Frank will not be affected commercially," the *Herald* said.

That bit of publicity management, and others like it, along with the reopening of the mine, brought life back to Frank. By June 1, 1904, the mine was booming once more, with over 100 men employed therein and the CPR taking its entire output of 350 tons a day, though the *Edmonton Bulletin* reported that huge masses of rock were still falling and "the rumbling and crashing of these in their descent is beginning to bring nervousness on some who were witnesses of the tragedy a year ago."

H.L. Frank, the Montana capitalist, died in 1908, having spent his final months in a private sanatorium, his nervous system apparently shattered by his knowledge of the tragedy. The mine finally ceased operation in 1917, partly because of continued fears that the limestone section overhanging the village would fall, but mostly because competition in the coal industry was fierce and the mine was no longer profitable.

Rumours about the slide persisted for years: the Union Bank had been buried with $500,000 in American silver dollars, said one tale, though the bank stood intact in town for at least eight years after the disaster. "Sole survivors," of whom there were scores, recounted their astonishing first-hand accounts to eager listeners everywhere.

South-east end of town submerged by rock.

In the 1920s, a highway crew working the slide area uncovered a house and a few skeletons, which they buried. Officially, 76 people died in the slide, of whom about twenty were children. No one knows for sure, however, how many men were actually in the construction camp, because its records were obliterated along with its inhabitants. Only twelve bodies were recovered from the whole area. Much of the population of Frank was transient; men known to none but themselves camped on the flats for a few days or weeks before moving on; no doubt some were buried anonymously under the limestone mass, which was estimated to have been 1,300 feet high, 4,000 feet wide and 500 feet thick, and to have spread itself over 3,200 acres.

It still isn't known what caused the collapse. Some theorize that the coal operation weakened the ledge, though others counter that the spring thaw might just as easily have been to blame. Even today, geologists keep an eye on Turtle Mountain and the sensors they have buried within its fissures. Visitors may view an audio-visual slide show about the disaster.

The catastrophe at Frank was the greatest slide in the recorded history of the Rocky Mountains, but it may not have been the first. Indians long before had another name for Turtle Mountain. They called it "the mountain that walked."

— *C.D.*

Caught With the Goods *by Charles Russell. Frontier justice was often ill-informed, but it contained at its heart elements of fair play.*

The not-so-wild Canadian West still knew all about murder

FROM CHEQUE-KITING KILLER ERNEST CASHEL TO MURDERER CHARLES KING AND A MADMAN LOOSE IN A HOSPITAL, MOUNTIES AND HANGMEN WERE BUSY

by CALVIN DEMMON

Alberta from the beginning was more American than the other provinces. American whiskey traders were followed by American cattlemen, then by American settlers. This proximity gave Alberta more of a lawless flavour than its historians generally like to admit — though, thanks to the Mounties (see sidebar) the province was never as wild as the wilder west to the south. Nonetheless there was lots happening to fill the newspaper with lurid crime stories. And when there wasn't, the newspapers made it up anyway.

Courtesy: Hugh Dempsey

The press reported incidents of lawbreaking that ranged from illegal fishing through livestock rustling to murder. In a society where most citizens had recent roots elsewhere, particular emphasis was placed upon the ethnic and cultural affiliations of those charged with crimes. A news story that did not report the name of an assailant or victim would still include the nationality of both if possible. The *Edmonton Bulletin* for Jan. 16, 1903, for instance, relates the case of a shooting ten miles east of Wetaskiwin by referring to the suspect only as "a Galician woman." She shot her husband in the face and the wounded man in turn shot the unnamed Galician man with whom his wife had run off.

Galicians (the term of the day for all Ukrainians) held no monopoly on domestic violence. Anton Walvirch, a Bohemian immigrant who homesteaded just south of Stettler, was left alone to raise a small daughter when his wife died. Within six months he had married again, but on July 2, 1909, Walvirch, who had been drinking, took his rifle and fired a .30-30 bullet into his new wife's chest, leaving the body for his daughter to find when she came home from school.

There was also the case of the Dalmatian woman who was married to an Italian and who was shot and stabbed to death by a Serbian in full view of several witnesses. The dispute involved $61.12 that the Serb had left with the woman while he was a boarder in her home. The *Lethbridge Herald*, after duly noting the nationalities of all the principals, called the 1907 crime "the most horrible tragedy that ever took place around Lethbridge."

In Edmonton, two men were taken to hospital after a June 1908 row in the "foreign colony of Syndicate Avenue" (95th Street) during which Harry Dembicki shot his stepson, Frank Pakarski, with a .25-calibre rifle at close range. What provoked the feud was unclear. "All the parties speak indifferent English and it is difficult to get anything from them," the *Edmonton Journal* explained, adding, "Both men are Poles."

That the earlier arrivals, the English-speaking citizens of Alberta, were both fascinated by and fearful of "foreigners" was clear. None aroused more doubt than the Chinese, referred to in the papers as "Chinamen," "Chinks" or "Celestials" (from the translation of the "heavenly dynasty," alluding to Chinese emperors' descent from gods). But the newspapers clearly reflected a sentiment held by a substantial segment of the English-speaking public. Blaming the Chinese for social problems was common. Calgarians, for example, were disturbed in March 1905 when it became

---

Walvirch, who had been drinking, took his rifle and fired a .30-30 bullet into his new wife's chest, leaving the body for his daughter to find when she came home from school.

---

evident that young boys found it easy to purchase cigarettes despite laws forbidding the sale of tobacco to minors. Some youths were even said to be shortchanging the collection plate on Sunday and using the money to buy cigarettes. Proprietors of downtown tobacco stores vigorously denied their involvement. None of their stores was open on Sunday anyway, they said. The fault, they agreed, lay with the Chinese stores, which, as the *Calgary Herald* readily pointed out, "are open at almost any old time." But the *Herald* found the English-speaking merchants not above suspicion, and editorialized that "those who share the blame owing to vague assertions" should be cleared, meaning presumably the Chinese.

Still, tempers were easily aroused; tales of misdeeds by Chinese were widely circulated and given great credibility. One such report, which later turned out to be untrue, caused a riot in Lethbridge on Christmas Eve 1907. A Chinese waiter was said to have slain a non-Chinese patron with a hammer. Though the rumour was false, a mob of outraged citizens raided the Chinese restaurants on Main Street, overturning tables, breaking counters, smashing windows, and throwing stones at Chinese residents. The *Lethbridge Herald* termed the melee a "race riot" and blamed it on "a Chink with a hammer." Police made few arrests.

Frontier justice was rough and often ill-informed, but it contained at its heart elements of fair play that could not always be discredited. In November 1904 a train from the East arrived in Calgary and passengers who disembarked excitedly related a story about a fight between a white man and a Chinese. The white man's face, those at the station could see, was covered with blood, and Dr. Stewart Mackid was immediately summoned to tend to the man's cuts. There was some discussion of arresting the Chinese, but passengers who had witnessed the altercation said that the white man had been drinking, that it was he who started the quarrel, and that the Chinese had responded only in self-defence. Furthermore, his assailant admitted that the event was his own fault. The Chinese was thereupon allowed to continue on to Vancouver unhampered.

Another isolated occasion of racial harmony occurred in 1905. When Wing Lee of Edmonton filed action in police court against Wong Foo, charging him with stealing $295, the rite of swearing-in was adjusted considerably to accommodate Chinese traditions, at least as officials understood them. In a courtroom filled with Chinese, "a series of hieroglyphics, alleged to have been a Chinese declaration somewhat similar in meaning and intent to the ordinary oath, was inscribed on a slip of paper," the *Bulletin* reported. Next, a rooster's head was cut off, and then the paper was burned. Wing Lee was said to understand that the ceremony cursed him to die in the manner of the rooster if he failed to speak the truth. That seemed convincing enough to the court.

Crime, of course, was in no sense confined to immigrants. Apart from the famed Cashel and King cases (see sidebars), the North-West Mounted Police and local law enforcement had to deal with a dozen other forms of recurrent criminal conduct. Some examples:

BARROOM INCIDENTS

A young cowpuncher named Joseph Gallagher, known as a dangerous man while drinking, lived up to his reputation on July 12, 1904, after the proprietor of the Wilton Hotel in Claresholm refused to sell him whiskey. Gallagher chased the proprietor, Colin Tillotson, through the hotel, throwing chairs at him before Tillotson escaped. Back in the bar, Gallagher helped himself to the whiskey, then went to the livery stable and was just mounting his horse when a RNWMP Corporal called Hartzog tried, unsuccessfully, to arrest him. Gallagher then rode back to the hotel and attempted to lasso Tillotson but the hotelkeeper dodged the rope.

After Gallagher had ridden from town, Hartzog obtained a warrant for his arrest. He found the wanted man in a shack near the town and arrested him without difficulty. The story had a tragic

---

After a Chinese waiter was accused of slaying a white patron with a hammer, a mob raided the restaurants, overturning tables, smashing windows and stoning the Chinese residents.

---

twist. Later that day, Gallagher awoke and was allowed to sit outside. When he asked for a drink of water the policeman obliged. However, Gallagher took the opportunity to grab a revolver and rush out of the building, firing a shot at, and missing, the policeman. Hartzog shot back and hit the cowboy in the left arm. Gallagher was taken to hospital but his arm was so badly shattered it had to be amputated. When he finally appeared in court several months later, the judge thought the young cowboy had suffered enough and let him off with a suspended sentence.

CATTLE RUSTLING

Finding a young, unbranded calf or heifer on a cattle range was a common enough occurrence, and a crooked cowboy could profit from such a discovery. Using a "running iron" — a straight branding iron with which any desired brand could be traced on an animal's hide — a rustler could quickly convert a calf to his own use. Such opportunities were frequently seized when they presented themselves. In December 1900, Inspector J.O. Wilson of the NWMP investigated a charge of rustling filed by George W. Johnson of Horse Creek against two young Cochrane brothers, James and John Hewitt, who were discovered to be holding in a corral a roan calf that Johnson said was his. James Hewitt at first claimed it was the offspring of a blind cow they owned, but John Hewitt finally admitted that he and his brother had taken the calf from a cow that they found dead in Horse Creek. However, there was insufficient evidence to gain a conviction and the case was dismissed.

INDIANS

Trouble on Indian reserves was another problem for the Mounties. They were empowered to investigate, but determining the truth could be difficult.

In November 1907, three people — a bootlegger named Harry White and a Peigan woman and boy — were found slain at Fifteen Mile Lake, near Lethbridge. Several days later the body of New

Robe, the husband of the murdered woman, was found in his home on the Peigan Reserve. The NWMP determined that New Robe had committed suicide and that the shells found near the scene of the Fifteen Mile Lake murder matched those in the gun with which he killed himself. Police surmised that the bootlegger got the woman drunk and was caught in a compromising situation by her jealous husband. The boy had been an innocent witness and was also killed. The victims are buried in the Roman Catholic cemetery in Lethbridge.

RNWMP officers (Cpl. Fred Moses on right) with unidentified prisoners in Pincher Creek, around 1906. There wasn't always the time to wait for the Mounties.

When Edmonton police raided the Boys Own Cigar Store on a Saturday night in 1909, the card players remained calm even as they stared down the muzzles of police revolvers.

Rumours of a fight between two Indian brothers on the Blackfoot Reserve southeast of Calgary, near the Bow River, were abundant in July, 1909. Sun Calf, described in the *Lethbridge Herald* as "the most incorrigible Indian among the Blackfeet," was said to have shot and killed Old Bull, his brother. In another version of the same rumour the weapon was an axe. A staff sergeant called McLeod and his scouts captured Sun Calf in the brush along the river and took him before a justice of the peace, who learned that Old Bull was not dead at all, but was recuperating in the hospital at North Camp. At the preliminary hearing in September, Sun Calf, who attended drunk, was bound over for trial. He broke free from his captors while being escorted back to his cell and ultimately made it to the United States. Not one to settle into a peaceful life, Sun Calf had some trouble with the law in Montana, returned to Canada in 1910, and was promptly arrested, then sentenced to nine months in jail for attempted murder and escaping custody.

EMBEZZLEMENT

Businesses know they have more to fear from their own employees, when it comes to theft, than from outsiders, and the Canadian Pacific was no exception. Actual train robberies were few, but a conductor who habitually pocketed part of the fares he collected from passengers could over a period of time take from the railroad as much money as an armed bandit. In an effort to encourage employee honesty, the CPR used undercover agents they called "spotters," railroad detectives who would ride the lines and watch out for misdeeds on the part of trainmen.

The CPR yards at Calgary were placed under observation by spotters in the summer of 1904,

---

The Wilderness Murder

Was Charles King guilty? There was no body, but there was a lot of incriminating evidence

The newspapers called it "The Wilderness Murder." If it had not been for the keen observational skills of Indians in the Athabasca region, however, the murder might never have been discovered and its perpetrator, Charles King, might never have hanged for it.

King rode into the Moostoos Indian Reserve, near Sucker Creek in the vicinity of Lesser Slave Lake, one day in October, 1904, headed northward with three pack-horses and a dog about which an Indian boy noticed something odd: the dog would not follow the white man. This was remarkable enough that the boy told Chief Moostoos, who remembered it later when another Indian, Joseph Kisanis, told of having seen two white men camping near his tepee at Swan Hill, and of having heard a gunshot on the third night of the men's stay.

Moostoos, who could put two and two together, notified the North-West Mounted Police. Sergeant Anderson arrived with Constable McDonald to investigate. They visited the Swan Hill camp and Anderson ran his fingers through the ashes of the fire. He found pieces of what appeared to be skull bone, along with some gold tooth fillings. In a nearby slough, Moostoos and the two policemen found a pair of boots containing a gold nugget, and other objects including a piece of a broken iron needle that exactly fitted a piece they had found in the ashes of the fire.

The evidence was circumstantial. King was found and under questioning said his partner, whose name was Lyman, had headed off on the Sturgeon Lake Trail. Indian trackers could find no evidence that such was the case, however. King was arrested and taken to Edmonton.

Further investigations revealed that the missing man was Edward Hayward, a miner from British Columbia. He had met

Provincial Archives of Alberta, B-1868

Charles King. The dispute with his partner appeared to be about gold.

King in Nelson, BC, and the two men became partners, leaving Edmonton in August, 1904, after outfitting themselves at the Ross Brothers hardware store with $199.95 worth of hunting and trapping equipment.

At King's trial, which began at Edmonton in February, 1905, 71 witnesses came forward to testify, including Moostoos and numerous other Indians. Most said they had seen King and Hayward together in various locations. King listened intently, never moving from a fixed position, looking each witness right in the eye.

King's lawyer, O.M. Biggar, mounted a spirited defence. How, he demanded, was King to prove that he had not killed a man whose body had never been found? Who was to say that Hayward was not now alive in some remote part of British Columbia, far from telegraph lines and newspapers? He cited cases in which men had been hanged and afterwards found

---

LIFE IN A NEW PROVINCE

and several railwaymen were soon afterwards fired. One CPR employee, a conductor poetically named Alf Fiddler, who was accused of not turning in all fares, was said to be of wide acquaintance in the West and well liked by the trainmen. Not so the spotters, who were despised. "While the officers of the company at Calgary are very popular with the men, the line is drawn at 'spotters,'" the *Calgary Herald* explained. Fiddler's trial brought one of the spotters into the courtroom, where he was himself spotted. The *Herald* reporter, no doubt influenced by the opinions of the railroaders who pointed the man out, described him as though he were a wanted criminal: "A big, heavy-set stranger...of heavy features, very large head, prominent nose and chin, weighs probably 200 pounds, protruding stomach, wears his stiff hat well down over his eyes, and is perhaps forty years of age." Besides observing acts of larceny, spotters were not above engaging in what would in a later day be described as entrapment. Two spotters pretending to be trainmen approached an engine crew in the Calgary yards one night, chatted a while, and offered the engineer and fireman whiskey. The men accepted, but regretted that choice the next day when they were summoned

innocent, and he hinted that Moostoos and some of the other Indians knew more about the case than might be expected of them. King, he said, should be the beneficiary of any uncertainty as to whether Hayward was dead, and if he was dead whether he was murdered, and if murdered, whether King was the guilty party.

The crown prosecutor, C. de W. McDonald, responded that the remains of a body had been found, that the body was that of Edward Hayward, and that King was the only man who could have murdered him. King had told many conflicting stories, all different from what was known to be true, McDonald said. It was ridiculous to think Hayward would go away and leave behind such valuable things as a gold nugget, wrapping it in a boot and tossing it into a slough. The motive for the murder was probably the love of gain, McDonald said; shortly after the murder, King had sold for

Provincial Archives of Alberta, B-1861

Mounties with murder trial witnesses. Seventy-one came forward to testify.

do with it...I know he was alive when I last saw him. If he is dead I hope you will find out who did it. I am sure I never did it."

On Sept. 30, 1905, King was hanged at the police barracks at Fort Saskatchewan. The *Edmonton Journal* of that date described him as a man who left home at age twelve and was

---

In the ashes of the fire Anderson found pieces of what felt like a skull bone, along with some gold fillings. In a slough he found a boot containing a gold nugget.

$200 the outfit he and Hayward had acquired.

The jury returned a guilty verdict against King on March 9, 1905. Before sentence was pronounced, the judge asked if he had anything to say. He paused for some time before replying, "Nothing I know of." He was sentenced to be hanged on May 10.

King's lawyer appealed to the Supreme Court and a new trial was held in June, but after three days King was once again found guilty of murder and sentenced to death. This time, King was more eloquent. "I am not guilty," he said in a low, firm voice. "If the man Hayward is dead, I had nothing to

"intellectually an infant, no finer feelings ever having been stirred and knowing naught of the love of parents, friends or home." He had been a model prisoner during his four months under sentence of death. Before the executioner, the renowned J.R. Radcliffe of Toronto, sprang the trap that caused him to fall in the noose and break his neck, King repeated his claim that he was not a murderer.

"I do not know what you are hanging me for," he said. "I am an innocent man — God knows that I am an innocent man. I have nothing on my mind. I would not have that crime on my mind for killing him." —*C.D.*

before their bosses, who knew all about what had happened. But the accused got off with a reprimand when the fireman explained that he had been ill the night before and merely took the whiskey for his health.

UNEXPLAINED SHOOTINGS

Frank Wright of Ponoka died of a shotgun blast fired by Charles Hall on the evening of May 16, 1905. Hall was arrested on a charge of shooting with intent to kill, but after listening to witnesses and then deliberating for only eight minutes, a jury found that Hall shot Wright accidentally, having mistaken him for a bear.

GAMBLING

When Edmonton police raided the Boys Own Cigar Store at 11 o'clock on a Saturday evening in May 1909, the card players remained calm even though they found themselves staring into the

---

'The assaults upon Mr. Hull's safe,' said the *Herald*, 'were of the most amateurish nature and there are not wanting indications that the thieves were no adepts at the business.'

---

muzzles of police revolvers. One of them placed the cards he had been holding on the table — four aces — and remarked that the officer with the Colt had the only hand that would beat his.

The unfortunate cigar store players — 32 of them were arrested that night and hauled off to the police station for booking — must have been expecting an eventual raid. Cigar stores were an easy target for the police; in March, a number of gambling games in the back of such stores in Edmonton had been shut down. Leaders of the temperance movement had been pushing successfully for the removal of slot machines from stores and a general ban on gambling.

Glenbow Archives, NA-3267-48

A child detention home in Lethbridge, about 1910. The degree and severity of youth crime required the provision of more than just a slap on the wrist.

A similar crackdown took place in Lethbridge, at the behest of the city council. At a meeting in May 1910 the council called on Police Chief J. Gillespie to describe the problem. Gillespie said he viewed gambling as a sort of disease, one that could not entirely be eradicated, but that his policy was to make it as unpleasant as possible for those who made their living at it. His efforts had been quite successful, he said: such gambling as continued to occur was very light except around the CPR's paydays.

BURGLARY AND ROBBERY

Criminals came in two varieties — the amateur and the professional. It was an amateur job of breaking and entering at the Calgary butcher shop of W.R. Hull late one night in February, 1902; the perpetrators were thwarted by Hull's safe, which they tried unsuccessfully to open by prying and whacking it with two meat cleavers they found inside the establishment. They tried again at the Imperial Hotel, where they managed to wrest the cash register outside and get it open, escaping with its contents. The *Herald* deplored their night's work for incompetence. "The assaults upon Mr. Hull's safe," it declared, "were of the most amateurish nature and there are not wanting indications that the thieves were no adepts at the business."

More experienced, though still not skilled enough to actually escape arrest, were three gang members who robbed a Chinese restaurant in Lethbridge in September 1910, removing $23 from the till and running off after knocking the proprietor unconscious. An alert Constable Brown, who noticed blood on the clothing of a man waiting at the depot, arrested him and another whom he later found inside a Belgian restaurant. The Chinese victim identified them both. Chief Gillespie said one of the men was the scout for a gang of safecrackers headed towards Lethbridge from Manitoba.

CRIME ON THE TRAIL

Though Edmonton, Calgary, Lethbridge and other Alberta cities produced a steady stream of unlawful activity, crime was by no means confined to the municipalities. One difference between crime within the bounds of civilization and crime in the wilderness is the manner by which a law-breaker is made to stop. When the nearest Mountie is days away, those at the scene must weigh the consequences and decide whether or not to take the law into their own hands.

That decision was faced early in 1907 by three men who were waiting out the winter in a cabin at the Big Eddy, a turbulent point on the McLeod River near Edson, where the river joins with Sundance Creek. A pack saddler named Hornbeck (in some accounts, Hornback or Hornbach; there is no official police record of the incident), camping along the Sundance, was hard hit by the winter's severity. When the last of his horses perished, he made his way to a small trading post, where he brandished a rifle and drove the owner out. Hornbeck stayed in the store for several days, emerging at intervals to fire his rifle at a downhill cabin occupied by four men, including the unfortunate trading post operator, who had taken refuge there.

The occasional shots fired at their cabin the men could tolerate. What they could not abide was something else Hornbeck started to do. He would step outside the trading post, hold up a sack of flour or beans, and rip the sack open with a knife, dumping its contents onto the snow. For the four men in the cabin, all of whom knew starvation in the wilderness as a deadly possibility, destroying food in the dead of winter was an unforgivable offence. One set out on snowshoes to bring a Mountie from Lac Ste Anne, but the three remaining knew it would be days before he returned, and they reasoned that when he did, the Mountie would kill Hornbeck anyway. The next time Hornbeck stepped out with his gun, they fired three shots and killed him. When the Mountie arrived he arrested the men and took them, with Hornbeck's corpse, to face trial. The three were acquitted on the grounds of self-defence.

MADMEN

In February 1901 a young man named Lott, suffering from a mania that required treatment at the General Hospital in Calgary, walked into the operating room, picked up an amputating knife, and stabbed Dr. R.D. Sanson twice. Dr. Sanson, highly popular in Calgary, was treated by Dr. George A. Ings; Lott was confined in the NWMP barracks.

In January 1909 William Hall, a 19-year-old mental patient at the Alberta Sanatorium, hijacked an unattended Canadian Northern engine at the Edmonton rail yards and crashed it into a beer car. The car was damaged but the beer was saved. "If it weren't for that old car, I'd been going yet," Hall said.

YOUTH CRIME

Adults held no monopoly on lawless acts either, but the question for officials was how to deal with young offenders. In October 1906 the two McPherson boys, who though just ten and twelve years old were already the possessors of lengthy records with the Calgary police, made use of a ventilator to escape from a jail cell where they were being held after one of their escapades. They were recaptured on the Canadian Pacific tracks, where they had gone to catch a freight train out of town. Police were in a quandary what to do about them. Clearly they required more than a slap on the wrist — they had been in court at various times on charges ranging from armed robbery to attempted safecracking. Yet they were thought too young to be held for long periods in jail. The *Albertan* suggested it was time for the provincial government to establish a detention and correction facility for wayward youngsters. Such sentiment was not

Calgary's first hanging. Members of RCMP and prisoner emerging from holding area in basement of court house, on 7th Avenue West.

Glenbow Archives, NA-2854-131

The eventual hanging of Ernest Cashel

THE TALE OF THE SKINNY LITTLE CHEQUE-KITING MURDERER WHO BECAME ALMOST A FOLK HERO TO CALGARIANS IN 1904

Ernest Cashel walked firmly, without shaking, to the scaffold at the rear of the Calgary jail on the morning of Feb. 2, 1904. He looked nothing at all like a famous murderer and escape artist, almost a folk hero, who had been captured just nine days earlier after the greatest manhunt in the history of Alberta. The Rev. George Kerby, his spiritual adviser, said a short prayer before the white cap was placed over Cashel's head and the noose around his neck. Kerby then began reciting the Lord's Prayer. When he reached the words, "Lead us not into," the hangman, a ruddy-faced Englishman named J.R. Radcliffe, sprang the trap. Cashel was allowed to hang motionless for twenty minutes to ensure that he was dead. It was the first hanging in Calgary in twenty years, and it ended the life of one of frontier Alberta's best-known criminals.

A native of Wyoming who had trained as a barber, Cashel was a slim, unimpressive young man when he first appeared in the Ponoka area. But he brought some bad habits with him. While working at Shepard, just south-east of Calgary, he wrote fourteen bad cheques on his employer's account. The Calgary City Police arrested him for forgery, but on Oct. 14, 1902, he escaped, fleeing from an escort by exiting through an open window in the washroom on a train. Then on November 19, D.A. Thomas of Pleasant Valley reported that his brother-in-law, Isaac Rufus Belt, a 60-year-old bachelor, had disappeared from his ranch east of Lacombe.

Corporal Alick Pennycuick of the NWMP was assigned to the case. Pennycuick learned that a young man who gave his name as Elseworth — an alias Cashel favoured — had been a guest at Belt's ranch, and that a pony, a new saddle, clothing, blankets and tools had also disappeared.

Pennycuick tracked Cashel to the Metis settlement at Shaganappi Point, just west of Calgary, where the fugitive had bought some ammunition and clothing under the name of Nick Carter, the fictional detective. The NWMP detachment at Banff searched the area around Canmore, found Cashel,

Cashel under arrest in Calgary, 1903. He led the police on a merry chase.

socks and boots — had washed ashore where Haynes Creek empties into the Red Deer River. It was Belt, and he had a bul-

---

At Christmas, ten days after his hanging date, Cashel sent a taunting note to the Mounties vowing he'd never be taken alive and suggesting they send the executioner home.

---

and took him prisoner. He had been loose for three months.

On May 14, 1903, Cashel was sentenced at Calgary to three years in jail on the forgery charges. Pennycuick, meanwhile, had gathered enough evidence linking Cashel to Belt's disappearance to convince any reasonable man, he believed. But where was the corpse? On July 23 he got the break for which he had been waiting. A man's body — naked except for

let hole in him. Cashel was charged with murder and put on trial October 19. Despite the best efforts of his lawyer, the famed Paddy Nolan, Cashel was convicted of the murder of Isaac Rufus Belt. The jury took just 35 minutes to reach its decision.

While Cashel was awaiting execution with two officers guarding him, his brother John arrived from the US to pay his last respects. He visited the prisoner several times, and on December 10 — five days before the scheduled hanging — John Cashel secretly passed his brother two revolvers. When a guard came to secure Cashel for the night, Cashel pulled the guns, locked three constables in his cell, took the keys and walked out, remarking, "I don't want to shoot you, but I'm in a bad way."

At Christmas, ten days after he was supposed to hang and still very much at large, Cashel sent a taunting note to the Mounties, vowing never to be taken alive and suggesting that they send Radcliffe the executioner back where he came from.

Various sightings of the young desperado were reported during the next few weeks while a manhunt of unprecedented scope was carried out under the direction of Superintendent G.E. Sanders of the NWMP Calgary detachment, who meticulously charted the times and places of robberies attributed to Cashel and deduced that he must be hiding in the Shepard district. Sanders and a party of 32 men searched each house east of Calgary, and then proceeded to the William Pitman ranch, where on the morning of January 24 they found Cashel beneath a trapdoor inside a shack. Cashel fired a

The victim, Isaac Rufus Belt. He was found naked where Haynes Creek meets the Red Deer River.

shot at a constable, and the police beat a retreat, then they decided to burn the building down. After threatening to kill himself, Cashel finally crawled from the smoking cellar and declared, "I am sick of the whole business." He shook hands all round with the search party.

Cashel's brother, John, drew a year in prison. Two residents east of Calgary were arrested and convicted of aiding a fugitive, it having been determined that they had allowed Cashel to live in a haystack for some time before his capture.

Cashel spent the night before his death reading the Bible. He wrote letters to his mother and his brother — "To read them," said the Rev. Mr. Kerby, "would melt a heart of stone." He also wrote a cautionary letter to young men, warning them to shun books containing tales about such ruffians as Diamond Dick, Nick Carter, Buffalo Bill and the James Boys. Those books, he said, had inspired him to his life of crime. He confessed to the murder of Belt shortly before he was hanged.

— *C.D.*

Supt. Gilbert Sanders, 1903. By meticulously charting the time and place of the robberies, he tracked Cashel to his lair.

uncommon. In August 1908 a nine-year-old boy was confined in the Calgary police barracks on a misdemeanour offence until the Rev. W.A. Lewis intervened and arranged to have the boy placed under the care of "a respectable farmer."

PRISON BREAKS

Most adult criminals were not so fortunate as the boy who served his term on a farm. Those whose crimes were severe were sent to the Edmonton Penitentiary, a stark structure whose main cellblock later became a warehouse and whose vegetable garden was to become the site of Clarke Stadium. Some of the penitentiary's residents plotted successful escapes. On July 12, 1909, a black American called Black Jack Johnson and a Moose Jaw thief named J.C. Atkinson were on a work detail, digging a ditch outside the fence. They simply laid down their tools and ran off. Guards who witnessed the escape attempted to shoot, but had forgotten to load their rifles.

Lose the Mounties? Never!

To people of the new province, the benefits of the Mounted Police were self-evident

If there was one territorial perquisite that Albertans at the turn of the century did not want to give up, it was the presence of the North-West Mounted Police. The NWMP[a] were law enforcement on the prairies, their vigilant patrols safeguarding the settlers. In 1896 this devotion of westerners had actually saved the Mounties from extinction.

That year the Laurier Liberals came to power committed to abolishing the force. Its purpose, said Laurier, had been to control the Indians. With the suppression of the North-West Rebellion in 1885 that purpose was now at an end. So loud and vigorous was the alarm in the West, however, that Laurier scrapped the plan and instead the NWMP grew with the population of the territories.

Then as provincehood approached in the new century, the Mounties seemed threatened again because law enforcement was a provincial responsibility. Again those who relied on the Mounties were so alarmed that the federal government continued to operate the force, in effect renting the service to the new provincial governments.

A 1902 editorial in the *Calgary Herald* spoke the view of the whole West: the Mounties' services would be required no matter what form of government, said the *Herald*. One of their most important duties was keeping a close eye on the Indians, and a mere change in bureaucratic structure would not remove that need. The Mounties were, in the *Herald*'s phrase, "the body of men who in the exercise of their duties have contributed more to the opening up and pacific settlement of the West than any other factor." No one could tell how long the Indians would remain peaceful if the Mounties were to withdraw, the *Herald* declared.

Superintendent A.B. Perry was appointed commissioner of the NWMP in 1900, and had immediately begun to modernize the force. He redesigned his men's uniforms, for one thing, swapping the white helmet they once wore for a wide-brimmed Stetson hat, and discarding their white gloves and

The uniform, circa 1904, with stetson. Supt. Perry threw out the white gloves, gauntlets and helmets. Opposite page, mounted in full regalia.

James J. Boulton, Uniforms of the Canadian Mounted Police, Turner-Warwick Publications Inc.

gauntlets.[b] He also reorganized the duty system, assigning men to special patrols that moved across the plains constantly, rather than keeping them at stationary detachments.

A stickler for organization, Perry imposed the rule that every member of the force must file detailed reports on all aspects of his work. The reports would be forwarded through channels to NWMP headquarters in Regina, where they would be filed and cross-indexed. Complained one officer: "Any prisoner in our guardroom for a week will, I can safely say, have 25 sheets of foolscap devoted to him."

But Perry's insistence that his men write down in a formal manner whatever they observed paid off during the manhunts for fugitive Ernest Cashel, especially when Superintendent G.E. Sanders of the Calgary detachment charted Cashel's movements so carefully that he was able to deduce the area where the fugitive was hiding out (see other sidebar).

In 1906, when Captain R. Burton Deane, an outspoken man who had no tolerance for incompetence, was appointed

At first, residents in and around Edmonton were terrified at the thought of such desperados being on the loose. It was clear that the two remained in the vicinity: they stole clothing and food from farmhouses, and an occasional chicken from a henhouse, and on one memorable evening were invited to dinner by a German family unaware of their histories. On another night they stole a pair of trousers from a surveyor's shack on the Mill Creek rail line. When the man awoke and set out bare-legged through the woods, he was nabbed by a posse under the assumption that he was Atkinson. According to Tony Cashman's *Best Edmonton Stories*, the general populace, after hearing such amusing tales about the fugitives, ceased to regard them as a threat. The two men were never recaptured.

A much more violent escape was attempted on March 17, 1910 at Edmonton, when more than 100 prisoners, armed with crude weapons they had fashioned and smuggled into their cells,

to the command of the Calgary post, the division consisted of sixty officers and men, enough to handle crime, but not to settle disputes between individuals. In his 1916 memoirs, Deane reconstructed a conversation he held with a man who sought the Mounties' help in a matter Deane thought should be left to the courts. "I have not a man to give you," Deane recalled saying. "...Sometimes I am puzzled to find a single man for any duty whatever — when the courts are going full blast, and escorts and orderlies have to be found for them, lunatics and convicted prisoners have to be conducted to their respective destinations, horses in the post have to be groomed and fed, even if they are turned into the corral to exercise themselves — do you not realize that if I had not prisoners here the horses would never be groomed at all?"

Deane was responsible for Alberta's only jail for females, which was located, as was his house, on the 35-acre Barrack Reserve, on the south side of the Bow River opposite St. Patrick's Island where the Bow receives the Elbow on the later site of the Fort Calgary Park. Up to 24 women were sometimes held in accommodations meant for twelve at the most. The male side was equally jammed. "On one occasion I had 96 prisoners, all told, in my custody, in premises which were intended to receive only about 55 men, women and lunatics," he wrote.

The 1910 annual report showed that 13,326 prisoners had been taken into custody in all districts during the preceding decade. Villages, railway stations and isolated settlements were increasing so rapidly that the force would have to be doubled to meet all the demands on it, according to the report.

Meanwhile, the Mounties earned a world-wide reputation for "always getting their man."[c] However, sometimes they got the wrong one. A Constable Forbes, on the trail of a man who had

assaulted his family and neighbours, persuaded an ex-Mountie named Firth to accompany him, having learned that the fugitive was travelling with a second man. When Forbes and Firth saw two men riding ahead, they overtook them. Forbes arrested one man, quieting his protests by pushing him into a mudhole and then handcuffing him to a tree. Firth, meanwhile, was trying to pull the second man off a horse. Forbes rushed up and kicked the man's horse out from under him while Firth held the suspect by the throat. Only then did they discover that neither prisoner was the man they wanted.

Filing the written report that Perry required of his men in such circumstances, Forbes added truthfully, "I found I had arrested the wrong man. But he was very peaceful."

— *C.D.*

[a]The force became the RNWMP in 1904 when Edward VII accorded them royal status in recognition for their service in the Boer War. They would become the national Royal Canadian Mounted Police in 1920, upon amalgamation with the Dominion Police, a body responsible for policing parliamentary property in Ottawa.

[b]As early as 1890, the Mounties had wanted a replacement for their helmets and forage caps. They had taken to wearing wide-brimmed felt hats bought in local stores. In 1891 the force experimented with a felt "prairie hat," but it became water-logged in rain. Other official choices were similarly unpopular as the men continued to wear their unofficial headgear, especially the wide-brimmed American cowboy hat made by John B. Stetson. By the time a contingent of NWMP officers attended Queen Victoria's Diamond Jubilee in 1897, the Stetson had been given tacit sanction. It became part of regulation dress in 1903, finding ready sale to the men at $4.25.

[c]This expression, later popularized by Hollywood, was first used (more or less) by the *Fort Benton Record*, Fort Benton, Montana Territories, on April 12, 1977. In speaking admiringly of the Mounted Police, the newspaper said, "...but the MPs are worse than bloodhounds when they scent the track of a smuggler and they fetch their man every time."

RCMP Museum, Regina

prepared to break out of their two-tiered cell block. One of the conspirators, James McQuillan, armed himself with an iron bar and approached John Dharty, a guard, ordering him to stand up against a window. When McQuillan lashed out with the bar, Dharty produced a concealed baton and whacked him twice in the head. The two were soon locked in combat. Things looked bad for Dharty until a Japanese convict working in the kitchen telephoned the deputy warden to report the fight. The deputy arrived with a gun and ushered McQuillan back to his cell. A search of the cellblock produced numerous weapons and revealed the extent of the conspiracy. McQuillan was moved to a punishment cell, where he was shackled to the wall in darkness. The Japanese prisoner was pardoned and discharged.

McQuillan, his sidekicks, and others who failed in their attempts to break out would have found incomprehensible the actions of a prisoner called Monty the Mexican. According to Cashman, Monty made an easy escape from the Edmonton pen, was gone for a few weeks, and then showed up at the prison gates again. Whatever misadventures he suffered during his absence are not recorded, but he told the surprised gatekeepers that he would rather be a prisoner in Edmonton than a free man anywhere else.

Monty the Mexican was the beneficiary of a system that employed police, lawyers, judges and prison guards for one purpose: preserving the peace, safety and justice of the law-abiding citizens of Alberta. Sometimes, those whose job it was to make the system work were overwhelmed. As the province grew, so did reports of crime. There were too many cases to hear, the facilities were inadequate for the purpose, there were too many prisoners to house. It was a problem that would persist throughout the century's first decade and beyond.

In Edmonton in 1904, police court was held in the only available location, the fire hall, and the court's proceedings were sometimes interrupted by the sounding of fire alarms and the hurried entry of the fire team, headed for the hose wagon. In Calgary at decade's end, conditions were not much better. Magistrate Crispin E. Smith discovered the local barracks were so overcrowded that criminals he sent there because they deserved punishment were being turned away at the doors.

An overloaded system was bound to break down occasionally and to produce wrongdoings of its own. Police chiefs seemed particularly prone to excess, and were frequently charged with misuse of power. Edmonton Police Chief J.H. Dean resigned on Feb. 7, 1905, after an investigation by

I am commanded to inform you under Section 70 Chapter 50 revised statutes of Canada that his excellency the Governor-General has thought it fit to order that the law be allowed to take its course in the case of Ernest Cashel sentenced to be executed in Calgary on the fifteenth day of December...
- Telegram sent via the CPR telegraph to the lieutenant-governor of the NWT from Under-Secretary of State Joseph Pope.

the City Council determined that he had stolen $15 from an immigrant. The immigrant, whose English was poor, had asked the chief for help in counting his money, but the evidence showed that the chief palmed a portion of it while counting it.

In Calgary in January 1908, the local Citizens League filed a list of charges against Police Chief Tom English, alleging, among other things, that he knew of and consented to the presence of bawdy houses within the city limits, that he allowed merchants to sell liquor without licences, that he compromised criminal prosecutions, that he tolerated gambling, and that he insulted citizens in public.

Scandal erupted in Edmonton in January 1909 when it was alleged that local justices of the peace were making illegal judgements in questionable cases. If an accused person was found guilty of a crime, the Criminal Code sometimes called for imprisonment rather than a fine.

JPs were said to be levying fines anyway. Justice of the Peace T.H. Wilson explained that in one case he was not sure that a man charged with stealing $15 in the Jasper Avenue Penny Arcade was guilty. He fined the man therefore, he said, because he could not have put him in jail with a clear conscience. He added his belief that if he had sent the man to jail, the sentence would have been appealed and reversed, an outcome that he would apparently have considered unjust.

The *Edmonton Journal* called Mr. Wilson's explanation "remarkable" and noted that the magistrate was allowed to keep for himself fines levied in such cases, but that if a case went up to a higher court he received no remuneration at all.

Through it all that undefinable social phenomenon called "respect for law and order" gradually took deep root in Alberta, however polyglot its population. By the decade's end, people awakened to the fact that the frontier had disappeared. Something vaguely thought of as civility had taken its place. The milder wild West would become milder still.

Edmonton Penitentiary, about 1911. More than 100 prisoners armed with crude weapons had tried to escape.

Provincial Archives of Alberta, A-5264

The bar of the Alberta Hotel, Edmonton, 1905. A distinct aroma of tobacco cud, stale beer, smoke and manure.

A drunk and disorderly province on the rocky road to prohibition

AS THE BARS AND BOOZE COMPANIES DID A RECORD BUSINESS, THE PREACHERS AND THE PROTO-FEMINISTS RALLIED THEIR FORCES FOR A SHOWDOWN

by MARY FRANCES DOUCEDAME

Technically speaking Alberta did not have saloons. They were customarily called bars, and they began the 20th century as an ignominious refuge from boredom, loneliness and work. They were despised by some, tolerated by most, revered by a few, and sporadically attacked by the clergy. However, by the end of the century's first decade this had changed. By now they had become the prime target of a well organized temperance movement, whose leaders sought nothing less than their total annihilation. And as the laws tightened down upon them, with total prohibition a step away, no one sprang to their rescue.

(Below) cartoon from Bob Edwards' Eye Opener of Sept. 22, 1906, uncharacteristically decrying the effects of booze; (left) a Woman's Christian Temperance Union group from Regina, 1908.

OUR LEADING INDUSTRY

Raw Material.

Product.

Finished Product.

The boldest editorials of the day merely opposed prohibition as unenforceable, not undesirable, while the loyal patrons sheepishly shrugged. What could you say in defence of these places anyway?

They were hardly what you could call elegant — one large room, devoid of tables, chairs or even coat hooks, the bar running almost its full length, the customers in line along it, as one preacher noted, "like pigs at a trough." There were two railings, one below to uphold the foot, the other a handrail to uphold everything else, lest it fall. Which it often did.

Beneath the lower rail lay a weighted cuspidor. The spittoon had been abolished. It tended to topple, spilling its contents onto the floor, especially when a game of kick-the-spittoon got underway, much resented by the porter who had to clean it up. In some Calgary bars, doubtless obsessed with hygiene, or those in certain lumber or mining camps, a trough with flowing water ran under the foot railing to carry away the spittle to a sewer. One such was 100 feet long, its owners noted proudly.

In the quest for sanitation, however, even the cuspidors failed, though conscientious hoteliers often provided several. As the evening wore on, aim deteriorated. People missed. Floors were a collage of old stains. And the distinct aroma of tobacco cud was added to an atmosphere otherwise composed of stale beer and smoke — along with manure, horse sweat, maybe abattoir odour, or machine oil, or printers' ink, depending on the pursuits of the clientele.

Of course, the better places had extras — a towel or two beneath the handrail perhaps, or, as in the bar at the Edmonton Hotel, a touch of the exotic, potted palms with the hunting trophies along the big mirrored wall behind. Less pretentious places might settle for girlie calendars and booze ads, and a sign declaring, "Positively no credit."

The charm and romance of all this escaped the comprehension of the Temperance and Moral Reform League or the zealous ladies of the Woman's Christian Temperance

---

The bars were hardly elegant: one large room, no furniture except for the bar itself with the customers lined up 'like pigs at a trough.'

Union. To them the bar was, frankly, loathsome. Booze was the prime source of most evil and the bar was the prime source of most booze. Within it, they did not see camaraderie and companionship, merely the families left penniless after payday, the job accidents, the beaten wives, the neglected children. Government welfare didn't exist. Only the churches might help the impoverished. To the preachers and the first feminists, therefore, the solution was glaringly plain: stop the drinking.

But the roots of the drinking habit ran deep and the war upon it had been distinguished by no particular success. Man had been fermenting fruit into alcohol for 6,000 years. In Canada, the first temperance meeting was held for the Indians in 1648. The first temperance society was founded in Nova Scotia in 1828. The first prohibition law was passed by New Brunswick in 1855 and soon

---

To the preachers and the first feminists the solution was glaringly plain: stop the drinking.

---

repealed. But it inspired others. Why advocate temperance, which meant moderate drinking? Why not prohibition which meant no drinking at all — or so it was supposed. But gradually alcohol's detractors ceased to be known either as temperance advocates or prohibitionists. They were, simply, "the drys." Their foes — if you could find any to speak out on the subject — were "the wets."

Booze arrived in the West long before anybody had heard of either drys or wets. Fur traders and buffalo hunters, far from wives and family, were unlikely to find satisfactory leisure in a good book. For them, liquor was not a problem but a solution. Few histories have better depicted drink-

Tales from the Demon Drink File
In the pre-prohibition days there were stories of intoxication and crapulence to turn the wettest dry — not that they did

Tales of alcohol-related tragedy and accident that increasingly appeared in Alberta newspapers during the century's first decade fuelled the cause of the drys. Here are some examples:

In 1904, a citizen of Gleichen wandered out of a bar and decided he needed a little rest. His mangled body was found by a railway engineer who heard groaning beneath his train. The man had gone to sleep on the main line of the CPR, and the train had stopped on top of him. Whether he survived was not reported.

* * *

In February 1905, Joseph Gesudion, 32, a Morinville wagon teamster recently arrived from Montreal, drove a load of freight into Edmonton, then crossed the river to Strathcona to see a hockey game. After the game he stopped for a few at a bar, then with six other teamsters and their sleighs tackled the wintry trail back to Morinville. Gesudion's team was last in line. He never arrived. The others found his body two hours later, frozen stiff where he'd fallen. Reported the *Edmonton Bulletin*: "The supposition is that when the unfortunate man fell from his load he lay in a stupefied condition until he perished."

* * *

In December 1907, Iwan Palcak and Dmytro Macabarski were returning home from a Liberal meeting in Wostok, fifty miles (eighty km) northeast of Edmonton, when their team bolted. Macabarski broke his arm; Palcak was killed, skewered

Glenbow Archives, NA-1130-15

Cowboys Alex McKay (with Bible) and Ed Townend drinking it up at Cochrane in the early 1900s. Did alcohol cure or cause depression?

Interior of a Calgary liquor store, Sept. 30, 1907.

through the mouth and neck by the tongue of the upset wagon. He left a wife and seven small children. The Liberal candidate had, as was usual, provided four kegs of beer at the local hotel for the audience. "Most drank too much," reported the *Edmonton Journal*. The supposition was clear: drunk driving spooked the horses.

* * *

At Wetaskiwin the same year, the proprietor of the King Edward Hotel and one of his permanent guests were enjoying

Carstairs. The newspapers first assumed he had drowned because he had been drinking heavily. Later friends said he had been "very despondent at times, and often spoke of suicide."

* * *

In January 1905 W.A. Bryan of Cardston locked himself in his room at the Imperial Hotel in Calgary, wrote his wife a last letter, and took a mixture of strychnine and beer, then regretted it and shouted for help. People managed to break into the

The settler from near Red Deer was discovered to have been consuming three gallons of whiskey a week. The police concluded he drank himself to death.

a Sunday morning eye opener. Suddenly they clutched their stomachs and became extremely ill. Explanation: someone had "carelessly left close to hand" a ginger beer bottle filled with window cleaner, a solution of wood alcohol and ammonia. They suffered severe internal burns and narrowly escaped death.

* * *

The *Calgary Herald* disclosed in December 1906 that a settler near Red Deer had been found dead in his home. He was discovered to have been consuming three gallons of whiskey a week. The police concluded he drank himself to death.

* * *

Alcohol was often blamed for suicides, though a later age would learn to ask whether the victim was depressed because he drank, or was drinking because he was depressed. Thus:

In May 1905 the body of Edward Forrester, a Boer War veteran, turned up in the "slough past the buttes" near

room and a doctor was summoned. But Bryan died within thirteen minutes of drinking the poison.

* * *

George Duggan, a trapper and round-up cook in the Rosebud district, bagged about fifty coyotes a month, using strychnine in a liver bait. He kept a small vial of the poison in his pocket, and he used to say, "just in case of need when tired of life." In 1909, after a two-week bender on one of his twice-yearly visits to Gleichen, the need came. Drinking with a buddy, he slipped some strychnine into his own beer. At that point the friend, unaware of what Duggan had done, took exception to something he said and told him to go to hell. "I'll be there in a few minutes," replied Duggan, then stiffened with pain and fell on the floor. A doctor from a drugstore next door came promptly. "What did you take?" he asked Duggan. "None of your damned business," said the trapper, and died moments later. —*M.F.D.*

Setting a poor example

SIR JOHN A, TO NAME BUT ONE, HARDLY SHRANK FROM THE BOTTLE

Barring a few teetotallers, most politicians were game for a drink. Campaigns were lubricated with liquor and the standard political gift was a case of whiskey.

The drinking reputation of Prime Minister Sir John A. Macdonald was widely known, though few people knew the horrible details. After the fall of his government in 1873, the prime minister of Canada was seen reeling around the corridors of parliament for several weeks. He sometimes appeared publicly when he was "indisposed," as the saying went, but if anything booze sharpened his wit.

According to one tale, he sat rocking back and forth on a platform, seemingly both drunk and asleep, while his opponent, Liberal leader George Brown, a militant teetotaller, decried from the same platform the failures of the Macdonald government. When it came his turn to speak, Macdonald suddenly awakened and stood up. Then, before the horrified crowd, the prime minister of Canada threw up.

Even in those days it would have finished the career of a lesser man. But Macdonald, with great care pulling out a handkerchief and wiping his face and clothing, the crowd all the while aghast and silent, finally spoke. "Ladies and

---

Macdonald suddenly awakened and rose to his feet. Then, before the horrified crowd, the prime minister of Canada threw up.

---

gentlemen," he said, "I'm terribly sorry this has happened. [Pause] But I have to tell you..." Here, he wheeled towards Brown, now sitting contemptuously behind him, "...that every time this fellow speaks, it has the same effect upon me." The crowd roared. The day was saved.

On another occasion he declared: "I know enough of the feeling of this meeting to know that you would rather have John A. drunk than George Brown sober." Pierre Berton in his *National Dream* recalls another legend. Advised to speak to his colleague, D'Arcy McGee, about McGee's drinking problem, Macdonald told him: "Look here, McGee, this government can't afford two drunkards and you've got to stop."

Although he certainly didn't have Macdonald's reputation, Sir Wilfrid Laurier took a drink, and Premier Rodmond Roblin who defeated a prohibition movement in Manitoba eloquently defended drinking as "the manifestation of the social and the intellectual qualities of a man as

contra-distinguished from the ordinary brute creature." Prohibition, he said, would be absolutely impossible without exterminating the race, "and therefore I refuse to acknowledge the desirability of any such action."

F.W.G. Haultain, premier of the North-West Territories from 1891 to 1905, began his legal career defending accused whiskey traders and horse thieves at Macleod. He himself regularly joined in bull sessions with cattlemen, newsmen and remittance men at the Macleod Hotel where whiskey flowed freely.

In 1905 Calgary alderman Jack Clark was beaten up in a saloon. Clark had been loudly vindicating his vote on a recent council motion, but with such insulting language and disorderly conduct that "the gentleman to whom he referred" gave him a "severe thrashing," the *Edmonton Bulletin* reported. Afterwards he "quieted down and was taken home to remove the blood from his battered countenance."

—*M.F.D.*

Sir John A. Macdonald. 'I'm terribly sorry this has happened,' he said. Then came the zinger.

ing on the prairies, or anywhere else for that matter, than James H. Gray's 1972 publication, *Booze*. The Calgary historian describes Winnipeg, gateway to the frontier, as a "turbulent, rowdy, bawdy town," which, with a population of only 100 in 1870, already boasted five hotels, all of them "heavy on booze and light on rooms." Sated patrons customarily slept off their stupor on the floor.[1]

One of these institutions, "Browse's Hotel," was respectable enough for the local clergy to accommodate Miss Bella McLean when she arrived as a Methodist missionary. The floors of the hotel, she wrote, were "carpeted with native mud, black as coal." All hotels were likely carpeted in mud, especially after a rain or spring thaw, observes Gray.

With the coming of the Canadian Pacific, drinking increased. The navvies were known for a prodigious thirst. So were the running crews. So were the management. Michael Haney, construction boss on the CPR Section 15, couldn't recall a single engineer, contractor or traveller who wasn't a hard drinker. Though prohibition supposedly reigned in the construction sites, almost every transaction was consummated with a glass. With the construction crews came a boom, so men drank. When the crews moved on, a depression set in, so the men drank again. Then in Manitoba towns booze went on sale in grocery stores. The custom grew that the purchaser bought a bottle and passed it around, so the problem spread through residential neighbourhoods.

Throughout the West, men of God railed against drunkenness, and their sermons were often reprinted in the newspapers. It soon so obsessed many of them that they could preach an hour-long sermon about "drink" and never mention God or the Bible. The allure of liquor seemed to baffle them. Baptist minister A.A. Cameron once polled Saturday night drinkers in Winnipeg. "Why spend your time in a bar drinking?" he asked. Came the repeated replies: "Where else is there to go? What else is there to do?"

And if there was little to do in Winnipeg, there was even less in the tiny settlements of the North-West Territories where an ostensible prohibition on the sale of alcohol and the North-West Mounted Police failed to staunch the flow. Under the NWT Act of 1875, liquor could be ordered legally from the East. These "legal" bottles were continually refilled with rotgut bought from American bootleggers who crossed the border in the dead of night at places like Whisky Gap, near Milk River.

In the 1870s it came as raw alcohol, stored in five-gallon drums hanging on either side of a packhorse. Once in Canada, it was watered down. Tobacco, brown sugar and bluestone were added for flavour and colour. One entrepreneur discovered that coffin varnish with hot water and a little sugar was "a real toddy when you had nothing better." So he shipped quantities of coffin varnish into Canada via bull team from Fort Benton until a suspicious Mountie at Macleod inquired of the trainmaster, "In what locality are so many people passing away that constant importations of coffin varnish are a necessity?"

The year after the CPR arrived in Calgary, the Rev. J.W. Dyke of the Methodist Church so

WCTU membership card of Louise McKinney, future Alberta MLA and WCTU president.

One entrepreneur discovered that coffin varnish with hot water and a little sugar was 'a real toddy when you had nothing better.'

raged against illicit liquor that his sermon filled two columns of the *Herald*. No doubt it was this that helped prompt NWMP Colonel William Herchmer to mount a series of raids on hotels and private homes, imposing stiff fines. But not all Calgarians took this positively, and as the colonel walked home one night he was beaten senseless by citizens unappreciative of his efforts.

[1] Gray identifies Winnipeg's first five hotels as the CPR, a three-storey brick structure near the Fort Garry Gate; the American, dubbed "the Dutchman's," near what would become Portage and Main; the Royal near Water Street; and Browse's and O'Lone's, near the Red River docks. Proprietor Bob O'Lone died in a brawl in his own hotel.

Letter received from a Wetaskiwin liquor merchant in response to a postcard from a Red Deer bar requesting a price list, June 4, 1900.

He never suspected a thing, and I then boldly kept right on giving it regularly, as I had discovered something that set every nerve in my body tingling with hope and happiness that I could see a bright future spread out before me — a peaceful happy home, a share in the good things of life, and an attentive loving husband, comforts and everything dear to a woman's heart; for my husband had told me that whiskey was vile stuff and he was taking a dislike to it. - Advertising testimonial from woman who had used 'Tasteless Samaria Prescription' in her husband's coffee to great success, Calgary Herald, Jan. 16, 1904.

Thus in December Mayor George Murdoch called a meeting of the town's 450 residents. Did they want the law enforced or didn't they? The answer: No, not that way. They petitioned the territorial council. The NWMP's liquor control power should be curtailed. No more searches without warrants. No more pocketing half the fine money. No more acting as prosecutor, judge and jury. The council granted only the last demand, appointing a stipendiary magistrate. He turned out to be worse than the Mounties, jailing a local editor and a councillor and firing the "wet" town council (Vol. I, p. 258).

The NWT liquor law was softened by degrees. In 1887 the sale of 4% beer was allowed and whiskey permits made easier to obtain. Liquor imports promptly increased sevenfold. Four years later prohibition was repealed entirely. The bars arrived and inspectors were appointed to monitor them. The Mounties backed off liquor control. The inspectors acted only on complaint. Drunkenness surged.

The preferred drink in the West was whiskey. There was a ritual. When ordering a drink, custom required you also treat a friend. The two drinks cost 25 cents. The bartender set out a bottle and two small tumblers. You poured just enough to cover the bottom of the glasses. Then you both tossed it back in one gulp. "Treating" increased consumption but at least made for companionship. "Rolling the bones" (i.e., dice) made for fights. The "bones," explains J.J. Martin in *The Prairie Hub*, were made of ivory and kept in a cylindrical box of tanned cowhide behind the bar. Coin-tossing games were also popular. Drinks were often the stake, with sometimes the barman and the house included in a round.

The air was usually blue with smoke. Cigarette smokers rolled their own cigarettes with Zig-Zag wheat straw papers and Bull Durham tobacco, carried in a pouch with a drawstring. Some stalwarts smoked dried alfalfa leaves. A favourite chaw was Macdonald's West-over plug that also did for pipes.

Drinking was also allowed in licensed restaurants (not more than two licences issued per town of 3,000), in the dining cars of trains and in clubs. When the government debated stopping the sale of liquor in clubs, one legislator argued that at least the clubs avoided "the disgusting conditions of the bars."

Farmers in town to shop filled the bars on Saturdays but most were judicious drinkers. They lived from crop to crop on credit and banks considered drunks bad risks. After the bar closed some would go to the all-night dances. Admission was typically 75 cents for men, ladies free, possibly because of the chronic shortage of girls. Cowboys made far better customers. Their twice-yearly trip to town was a prolonged vacation that included a visit to the barber, the brothel and one long drunk.

A bartender must not refuse a drink to a man sober enough to stand. As one bartender put it, a man was drunk only when he "was down on his back reaching upwards for the floor." He would then be led or carried to the door and shoved or hurled out to the standard plank catwalk in front of the hotel. Beyond it was the mud in which he might awaken some hours later. In winter some towns contracted with a livery stable to sweep the alleys for drunks after midnight, paying for the service out of the fines levied on those found "drunk in a public place." One Regina policeman performed this duty with a wheelbarrow. Nevertheless tragedies were recurrent (see sidebar).

Railway workers sustained their reputation for roistering. Edith Clark in her *Trails of Tail Creek Country* tells of the night when a big dance was planned at Lamerton. Some of the 200-man track-laying crew, building the Grand Trunk Pacific line through the town, got drunk before the dance began, and resolved to "take Lamerton apart" and move it to Mirror, two and a half miles down the line. The men of the town formed a posse, rounded up the railway workers, and locked them in the creamery cooler until morning. The dance was postponed indefinitely.[2]

Such brawls did not often end without bloodshed. A CPR work gang, on leave in Cochrane, irked a drunk rancher named Hewitt who picked a fight with the whole gang. His brother dragged him back into the hotel. Then he slipped outside again. Another fight ensued. His brother and friends found him under some thirty navvies, one of them holding a pistol. In the continuing scuffle the pistol went off harmlessly, but Hewitt was found with a knife embedded in his spine and another rancher was taken to hospital with a ripped-open liver.

The whole work gang was taken to court the next day and all pleaded their innocence. The *Calgary Herald* sarcastically commented:

> They are a pretty tough-looking gang of innocents. Some had their heads in bandages, some had cuts, one had a battered face, but none of the men were in the fight or heard any firearms discharged. They were all either in a store or carrying water to the car. One knife with bloodstains on it had been used to cut onions. Something like drawing blood from a turnip.

The case was adjourned. Its eventual outcome was not reported.[3]

Upon all this the drys looked with increasing horror. Many traced the trouble to the waves of immigration descending upon the West. At the Manitoba WCTU convention in 1905 one of the resolutions ended: "In Canada are wanted neither the morals nor the ideals which exist among the debased populations of Europe." Added the *Moose Jaw Times* piously: "Among the Canadians there are many who do not drink at all. Among the French there are very few who do not drink. Among the Germans and half-breeds there are absolutely none at all."

As the decade unfolded, the newspapers began attributing almost all crime and tragedy to alcohol. The words "Booze Blamed" began many headlines. "Drink Caused Crime," proclaimed the *Edmonton Bulletin* in July 1906, the reporter assuming that what else could have caused a man to kill his wife. In Alberta between 1906 and 1910 drunkenness convictions accounted invariably for a third of all crimes. Bootlegging accounted for more. The Alberta government made 1,305 prosecutions in Calgary and Edmonton alone in 1907, at a cost of $25,000 to the taxpayer.

Newspaperman Bob Edwards of *Eye Opener* fame (see Chapter 6, this section) regarded these proceedings with the mixed emotions of an alcoholic. On the one hand he hated the drys for getting so self-righteous. On the other he hated the brewers and distillers for getting so rich, and for the chaos they indirectly inflicted on families. However, in the next decade he would take sides, and become one of the more astonishing converts to the temperance cause, and would one day vote for prohibition.

In the meantime, with some justification, he seemed to take personally the profits made on alcohol. In a January 1905 edition, he complained of the markup on a barrel of beer — $1.80 to brew it, $12 to the hotel, $20 to the customer. The brewers offered to cut their price if the hoteliers would pass on the savings. The hoteliers wouldn't. Beer was fifteen cents a glass, 25 cents for two, and that was that.

[2]Lamerton was about 35 miles (56 km) northeast of Red Deer. It once had a population of about 150, and was incorporated as a village. It disappeared from the map in 1915, when its buildings were moved to nearby Mirror, where the rail line had gone. The drunken mob's plan was not so preposterous as it sounds. Entire towns, built in expectation of a railway's arrival, were often moved when railway surveyors took a line in an unexpected direction.

[3]Appearing in court was not a sobering prospect for some hardened drinkers, as a 1909 article in the *Edmonton Bulletin* would indicate:
Attorney: Are you under the influence of liquor now?
Witness: No, sir.
Attorney: Did you have a drink before breakfast?
Witness: Just one.
Attorney: Have you had any since?
Witness: No. Have you?
It was a few moments before order was restored.

Calgary Brewing and Malting Company delivery trucks, 1907. By mid-decade, declared Bob Edwards, the company was `milking the city' of $50,000 a year.

Glenbow Archives, NB-28-25

"Try and assuage your thirst in Calgary on ten cents," grumbled Edwards. "It is an actual fact that ten cents won't buy a drink of ANY KIND in this town, except during the summer when the soda fountains are running." Small towns were cheaper. In Castor in 1909, Carl Stettler was selling whiskey at his new hotel for ten cents a shot or $1.25 for 26 ounces.

Edwards spoke wistfully of what he regarded as more civilized societies. In England and the US men spoke of

The Edmonton Brewing and Malting Company, 1900. Laurier's reluctance to legislate prohibition, some suggested, was influenced by big liquor interests.

"chasing the can" or "rushing the growler." A thirsty work crew would send a lad to fetch a bucket of beer for ten cents. "Imagination pales," he wrote, "before the idea of a working man in Calgary trying to rush the growler. It would take his whole day's pay to get the can filled."

According to Edwards, the Calgary Brewing & Malting Company took $50,000 a year out of the city in the middle of the decade (in 1902 it had declared an annual 276,840 gallons to Inland Revenue). In 1903, the Strathcona and Edmonton Breweries and Malting Companies put two new brands on the market within two months of each other, both claiming to "excel" the Calgary brand, while Lethbridge Brewing made Alberta Pride.

The brewers, altogether sensitive to the rising tide of the prohibition movement, tried a new tack in marketing. Beer was suddenly discovered to be good for you. In a February 1909 ad in the *Lethbridge Herald* the local brewery assured readers: "Your Doctor Advises Beer," then went on to extol this "food and a tonic. A trifle of alcohol — an aid to digestion."

Other breweries spread the same good news. "Ask Your Doctor about Schlitz Beer..." ran another ad, this one in the *Calgary Herald*. "Tell him that Schlitz beer is aged for months before it is marketed — aged in glass enamelled steel tanks. He will say that it cannot cause biliousness. Tell him that every bottle is pasteurized after it is sealed. He will say that such beer must be germless." Schlitz, "the beer that made Milwaukee famous," was imported by the Calgary Wine & Spirit Company on Eighth Avenue and pushed with a dash of snobbery: "Common beer is sometimes substituted for Schlitz," the ad warned. "To avoid being imposed upon, see that the cork or crown is branded."[4]

The newspapers echoed the theme. A July 1905 article in the *Edmonton Journal* went into lengthy, unsubstantiated detail about when drink ceased to be food and started to be poison (more than a few ounces a day). In a 1909 sermon at Knox Presbyterian in Calgary, the Rev. J.A. Clark insisted that scientists had "torn to tatters" this old theory — most recently, he said, at an international conference on alcoholism in London made up of commissioners of 25 governments.

Then there were the "cures" for alcoholism. Frantic wives were often taken in by them. The Samaria Remedy Company offered to send its product by mail order from Toronto. Its ad in the *Herald* in 1904 is presented as a news article and gives an unnamed woman's testimonial. It had cured her husband and saved her family. She had sneaked it into his coffee at every meal, as instructed. All correspondence, the ad promised, would be "sacredly confidential."

The belief that alcoholism was a disease, with God and total abstinence the only cure,

The results of our commission saw that beer is par excellence the nutritive alcoholic beverage ...When a man drinks good beer he drinks and eats at the same time, just as when he eats a bowl of soup.
- *an excerpt from 'a recent British government medical commission' report quoted in a letter to the editor of the* **Edmonton Journal** *from E. Chamberlain, April 20, 1910.*

RED CROSS GIN

assists digestion.

appeared sixty years before Alcoholics Anonymous came into being and espoused it. It was the main conclusion of the book, *Strong Drink; and the Curse and the Cure* (subtitled, *What Shall we do to be Saved From the Demon Drink?*), written by Timothy Shay Arthur, which came out in 1877 in the US. "The first half of *Strong Drink* is a novel about the fall and redemption of a variety of drunkards," observes historian Gray. "It reads like a serialized transcript of a beginner's-night confessional at an AA meeting." He regards Arthur as a leading influence in the temperance movement.

Assorted beer and liquor labels. Companies were not above concocting medical endorsements in these days before substantial government regulation.

The Rev. C.M. Heustis launched a tirade against drunkenness. He had been shocked to see two young girls from good families drunk. This was the way 'a girl loses the bloom of her nature.'

This began in the West when exasperated Manitobans voted prohibition in, shortly after the thirsty territories had legislated it out. But prohibition in Manitoba would require enabling federal legislation. Instead of providing it, Prime Minister Sir Wilfrid Laurier in 1898 called a national plebiscite on prohibition. Though women were not yet allowed to vote, it nevertheless passed everywhere but in Quebec. The drys were jubilant. Then Laurier, his eye on his own province, refused to enact it. The turnout at the polls had been only 25 per cent, he said. That was not enough.[5]

Laurier's reluctance to legislate was predictable. Politicians, even dry ones, were not ready to write prohibition into law. They argued that it would be impossible to enforce, and that in the fierce prairie climate hotels were a necessity and room rents alone couldn't sustain them. Others saw less noble motives, notably the huge revenues alcohol brought the government, to say nothing of the politicians' own penchant for drink.

The *Eye Opener*'s Edwards had another theory:

> The greatest single power at an election is the hotel element and every practical politician knows it. They can make or break a government at their own sweet will. The church crowd may not believe this, because they don't want to believe it. It is the case just the same, and our strait-laced friends may as well look facts straight in the face. Even in England every government during the last fifty years that has attempted to monkey with the liquor traffic has been thrown out of power (ostensibly over some other question, of course), the trick being turned by the disgruntled publicans and their mighty host of customers. It would, you know, be most undignified for a British government to acknowledge that it had been fanned out by a bunch of boozers.

[4]Many Scotch whiskeys were already on the market and would remain for the century: John Dewar's, Buchanan's Black and White, Dawson's Extra Special, Haig & Haig's Three Stars, Old Smuggler, were all advertised in 1905 Alberta newspapers. Among Canadian whiskeys, Seagram's and Hiram Walker's Canadian Club were already leading the field.

[5]The Tory *Calgary Herald* put this refusal down to more Laurier "hypocrisy," and cited the case of Sydney Arthur Fisher, Laurier's minister of Agriculture. He's an admirable teetotaller, said the *Herald*, yet very liberal — indeed liberal enough to have sent down a whole case of Canadian whiskey to a government convention at last year's Wolverhampton exhibition. "But when his liberalism touched his pocket he was shy, and turned the account in to his department and it was paid by the public."

(Clockwise from top) women at a WCTU convention in Calgary, 1911; two examples of pledge cards. The cards were pocketbook size and were carried as a constant reminder.

TOUCH NOT. TASTE NOT.

PLEDGE.

I hereby promise, by the help of God, to abstain from the use of all intoxicating liquors, including wine, beer, and cider, as a beverage.

HANDLE NOT.

TASTE NOT. TOUCH NOT.

Look not thou upon the wine when it is red, when it giveth its color in the cup.

At the last it biteth like a serpent and stingeth like an adder.

PLEDGE

I Solemnly Promise, by the help of God, to abstain from the use of all Intoxicating Liquors and Tobacco.

HANDLE NOT.

I am a prohibitionist. What I propose to prohibit is the reckless use of water. Its effect on health, habits and moral character of the community is disastrous. Look at the interminable series of typhoid cases with which our hospitals are filled from month to month, people dying who never died before, young men and maidens who have not reached the middle arch of life passing away down to a watery grave...If men would only confine themselves to a good stiff rasping old whiskey like Old Cobra, Calgary would be happier and better today. Any germ that can live after a gulp of Black Cobra has struck it, must be a Corker.

- Bob Edwards, writing in the jocular personage of Albert Buzzard-Cholomondeley, English remittance man, Calgary Eye Opener, March 17, 1904

Events in Canada seemed to sustain this scepticism. After the Laurier refusal, Manitoba Tories moved quickly to capitalize on the dry backlash. Then in opposition, they persuaded the wet Rodmond P. Roblin to vacate the party's leadership in favour of Winnipeg lawyer Hugh John Macdonald, Sir John's son, whose "sympathies were as dry as Roblin's were wet." In the 1899 election, Macdonald swept the province, pledged to act on the prohibitionist will. "If we broke our pledge, we should be as guilty of a criminal act as the man who robbed another's house," he declared, "for we should have robbed the people of their votes." In 1900 he introduced a bill closing all bars and outlawing the sale of alcohol except by prescription. It allowed for private importation by permit to be consumed in homes only, a loophole required by the constitution.

But before the bill took effect, Macdonald resigned to contest a federal seat, which he lost. Roblin replaced him. The bill was overturned in the courts, Roblin called another plebiscite in 1902 and the wets won. The drys charged fraud — no voters' lists, irregularities at every poll, twice as many votes cast in St. Boniface as there were citizens. No matter. Manitobans went right on drinking and elected Roblin's government three times more.

Similarly in Saskatchewan, the drys demanded Liberal premier Walter Scott call a prohibition plebiscite. He said he would, but the drys must outnumber the wets by 50,000 before he'd enact it. They knew they couldn't achieve this, so they resorted to the old Canada Temperance Act of 1878, which allowed individual towns to vote themselves dry. In a massive campaign they lined up enough petitioners in about 100 towns to force a vote. But municipal officials balked. Petitions were lost. Key town officers were always unable to sign things at key times. Votes were held in only forty towns, and then the lawyers successfully challenged the outcome of these. In the end, most all of Saskatchewan stayed wet.

At first, dry fervour seemed to wane the farther west you travelled. In the 1898 plebiscite, Manitoba went dry four to one, the North-West Territories two to one, the District of Alberta four to three. But then in 1907 things began to happen. The Rev. W.G.W. Fortune organized the Temperance and Moral Reform League of Alberta. His first target: the closing hours of the bars and the custom of treating. He was not without support. There had been temperance meetings at Alberta churches as early as 1903. The Rev. C.M. Heustis at the McDougall Methodist Church in

They always got their dram — or frequently anyway

BEHIND THE SCARLET TUNIC SOMETIMES LURKED A PRODIGIOUS THIRST

The North-West Mounted Police so effectively enforced the law of the territories they won powerful public support that would endure for a century. In the enforcement of the liquor laws, however, they singularly failed. Not only were they unable to coerce the public into compliance, they from time to time failed to control the drinking habits of their own members.

In 1886, H Troop at Lethbridge got its back pay and went on a prolonged collective binge that terrorized the town. At Fort Macleod two drunk Mounties held up a visitor from Saskatoon on the main street, relieved him of his wallet, and returned to the hotel to carry on drinking. In February 1886 the *Macleod Gazette* complained of yet another incident of drunks firing off guns in the streets. "This time it was some policeman...This blazing away with a pistol whenever a man gets drunk, whether it be a policeman or a civilian, is getting monotonous and must be put down with a high hand."

The Mounties were supposed to spill the seized booze onto the ground. There were dark suspicions of underground containers at their posts to capture the spills. Moreover, incentives to spur more diligent enforcement often backfired. Constables were offered a "moiety" (from the French word *moitié* or "half") for a successful arrest. Half the fine went to the arresting officer. Since it could double a man's monthly pay the police were suspected of inventing evidence to collect spending money.

"The sympathy of many of the settlers are against us in this matter," lamented Commissioner William Herchmer in his 1887 report. "Liquor is run into the country in every conceivable manner, in barrels of sugar, salt and as ginger ale, and even in neatly constructed imitation eggs, and respectable people, who otherwise are honest, will resort to every device to evade the liquor laws." Complained Superintendent J.H. McIllree of the Calgary detachment in 1888: "My men, endeavouring to do their duty, are made a laughing stock."

Two decades later, the bars had been legalized, but policing problems remained. The *Lethbridge Herald* reported in March 1906 that Corporal Kimbry in charge of the Crowsnest Pass detachment donned plain clothes and took a freight to Coleman. Here he charged the local hotel for serving liquor on Sunday and fined the drinkers $5 each. The Coleman Hotel's lawyer later won an acquittal for his client, and preferred charges against the corporal. Witnesses testified that after his one-man raid he'd moved on to an unlicensed "disorderly house," had a few drinks himself, and laid no charges. The corporal was suspended pending a military trial.

—M.F.D.

A turn-of-the-century North-West Police canteen. The Mounties were supposed to spill the booze they seized on the ground — that was the theory, anyway.

Seven carcasses of dressed hogs containing contraband liquor believed bound for the working rail crews. Seized near Jasper about 1910.

BEETROOT WINE
Scrape and slice thinly five medium beets; boil till tender in one gallon water; strain and make liquid up to gallon with boiling water; add three pounds of sugar; pinch cayenne pepper; boil ten minutes; strain; cool to lukewarm; add one yeast cake. Keep in warm place ten days to ferment. Strain and bottle. Ready in a few days, better kept longer.
- *Pioneer recipe from the early 1900s.*

Edmonton had launched a tirade against drunkenness in a sermon in May 1905. Reported the *Calgary Herald*: "He spoke for an hour and used names freely." The minister had been shocked to see two young girls drunk ("not common girls, they belonged to the best families"). Such was the way, he warned, that "a girl loses the bloom of her nature."

At Calgary's Central Methodist Church, the Rev. W.J. Kerby charged in a sermon, likewise reprinted in the *Herald*, that some of the city's hotel proprietors were doping their liquor and then picking their customer's pockets. He told a tale of a woman with small children forced onto the street because her husband drank. She was looking for a place to put the children while she went to work. On the drink question, only one side or the other could be right, he declared. People must decide.

As field secretary for the Temperance and Moral Reform League, Fortune took to the warpath. He scoured the province, reporting liquor infractions by bars to the Attorney-General and getting them "stamped out." In January, 1908, he and a league delegation met with the cabinet demanding local option in the province by majority vote and a bar closing time of 7 p.m. Later that year at the league's convention, he called for a province-wide plebiscite and predicted that 75% of the people would vote to suppress the liquor traffic.

The Woman's Christian Temperance Union meanwhile endorsed the league's motions and worked to dry up Alberta through local option, although their ultimate goal was prohibition. One of their tools was the traditional signing of abstinence pledge cards, which the reformed drinker was to carry around with him. The ladies themselves signed these cards. The "poison" may never have passed their lips anyway, but this was at least an affidavit that it never would. At their 1907 convention for Saskatchewan and Alberta, held in Edmonton, they came out against alcoholic medicine and liquored candies and they called for better enforcement of the Lord's Day Act. Their number included some women who would make history nationally in the next decade—like the redoubtable Nellie McClung, and Louise McKinney, a Claresholm school teacher who headed the WCTU in Alberta and Saskatchewan for 20 years and was elected to the Legislature in 1917.

The surly Edwards in the meantime called the prohibitionists "impractical cranks" who weren't taken seriously and were "the greatest obstacle in the way of temperance." Other editors criticized the drys less candidly. In a March 1902 editorial, the *Calgary Herald*'s managing director, J.J. Young, observed that moderates were afraid to express themselves on prohibition, a movement he called "entirely one of sentiment with expediency left out of the question...It is not so very long ago since it was a crime to bring liquor into the territories; yet a thousand Mounted Policemen could not stop the traffic...In the event of [prohibition] being enacted every young man became a criminal in the eyes of the law as soon as he bought a drink, that anyone who desired liquor must frequent all sorts of shady resorts and mix with the off-scourings of the country to obtain it."

The *Lethbridge Herald* was similarly scornful. On Dec. 6, 1905, an editorial called "this idea of a bunch of radicals asking the government to close the bars in Alberta and have the booze sold under the management of the provincial authorities [is] the rankest rot ever put in this country." It went on to describe how temperance had failed in various American states.

Undeterred, the prairie reformers came together at a big rally in Winnipeg in November 1907 that was remarkable for two reasons. First, all churches, not just the Protestant ones, sent a representative, including Unitarians and Catholics. There were also some trade unionists. Indeed, the Catholic church had seen a need for temperance in the New World as early as the 17th century when the Jesuits called for a halt to the brandy trade with the Indians.

Louise McKinney, a Claresholm school teacher who headed the WCTU and was elected to the Legislature in 1917.

However, the ecumenical harmony of the 1907 conference was short-lived. "The militant Orangemen who led the...movement backed not an inch away from their traditionally militant anti-Catholic stance," writes Gray. Nor could novelist and temperance evangelist Nellie McClung resist taking potshots at Catholics every time she spoke. So the ostracized Catholics cooled to the cause.

The lasting effect of the big conference was the brilliant campaign slogan that it launched. It said simply: "Banish the Bar." And by now prohibition was winning converts outside the churches. No more was it just an idea of teetotallers and the religious activists. It was luring the temperate drinkers to its fold. Its new slogan didn't say drinking was bad, only bars. And who would want to come publicly to the defence of the notorious bar?

By 1910 the drys had gained enough ground in Alberta to seriously concern the hoteliers and their loyal patrons. A 1907 law had already doubled the licence fee to $400 for hotels serving populations of 10,000 or more. In 1908, licences were limited to one per 500 population. Bars had to be closed at 10 p.m. instead of 11:30, and the drys pressed on for a 7 p.m. closing. In 1910 drinking in clubs was banned.

The drinkers seemed to take the laws passively. A man interviewed by the *Edmonton Bulletin* when the 10:00 closing went into effect said only that going home earlier would probably make him feel and work better the next day. He noted that the hoteliers were contradicting themselves, saying people would still drink as much and complaining the government was ruining their business. "The hotel men must anticipate a real reduction in business or why should they mind as they do?" he asked.

But the drys saw the new closing law only as a preliminary victory. They were going for the jugular. And the hotel men knew what they were after. It was more than just "Ban the Bar." It was total prohibition.

Running a scow through the rapids, second portage, Slave River early 1900's.
Provincial Archives of Alberta, B-3017

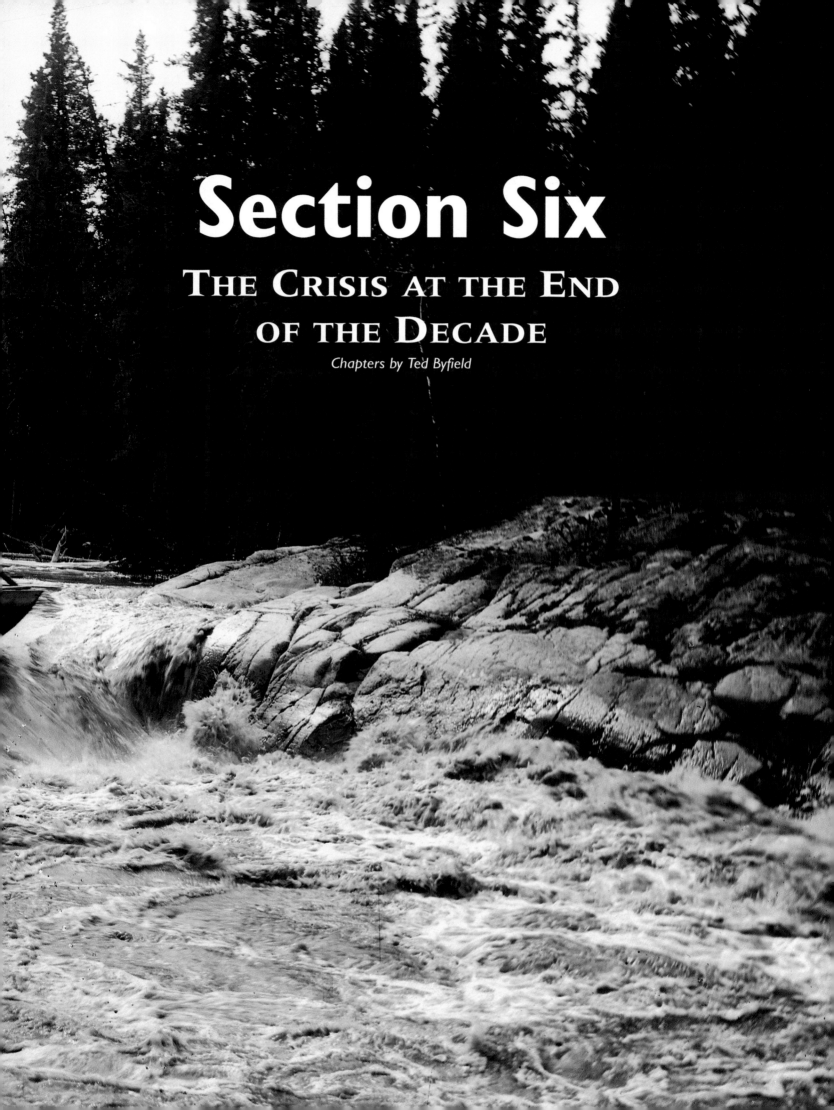

Section Six

THE CRISIS AT THE END OF THE DECADE

Chapters by Ted Byfield

ALEXANDER RUTHERFORD

Born: Feb. 2, 1857, near Osgoode, south of Ottawa

Died: June 11, 1941, in Edmonton

Career Apex: First premier of Alberta, 1905-1910

Major Accomplishment: He ensured Edmonton's place as the permanent capital and facilitated the building of the University of Alberta in Strathcona.

Quotation: 'I appeal to you for the elimination of selfish and partisan considerations. I appeal to you, not as Liberals or Conservatives, but as Albertans. The province must stand before the party.'

A vast northern territory comes as Alberta's bonanza

THE ENORMOUS PEACE RIVER COUNTRY AND THE GATEWAY TO THE ARCTIC
MESMERIZED THE POLITICIANS AND LED TO RUTHERFORD'S FALL

The province of Alberta which suddenly appeared on the map of Canada on September 1, 1905, carried a delightful surprise for the residents of the old territorial District of Alberta. It covered more than double the area most people had expected. Its border had been moved east to the 110th degree of longitude, taking an 80-mile-wide strip off the former districts of Saskatchewan and Assiniboia, a strip that included Medicine Hat. But, much more spectacularly, the topmost boundary had been extended northward by five degrees of latitude, 345 miles (550 km), to take in most of the vast District of Athabasca, an almost wholly unpopulated land that the territorial negotiators had neither expected nor asked for. It has never become clear why the federal government bestowed so much territory on Alberta (less administrative cost is one theory). But at the time no one was arguing. This surprising bonus had great implications for both the politics and the economics of the new province.

For one, it brought into Alberta much of the fabled Peace River prairie, sixteen million acres of what many said was prime grain land, which sprawled from the fur-trading post of Hudson's Hope beyond Fort St. John in the British Columbia interior 300 miles east (480 km) to the vicinity of Lesser Slave Lake. A long arm of it stretched north in the Peace River valley to the post of Fort Vermilion, near the 59th parallel of latitude — the one that passes about 100 miles (160 km) south of the southern tip of Greenland. Here grain was already being grown successfully for local consumption.

Alberta's new northland would embrace more still. It would take in the mysterious tar sands of the lower Athabasca Valley, and it would include on its northern boundary the strategic Slave River, beyond whose twelve miles of rapids it was possible in summer for fur-traders, missionaries and a slowly growing number of tourists to travel by steamboat to Great Slave Lake, the Mackenzie River, Great Bear Lake and the Arctic Ocean. Politically, the Edmonton-oriented Rutherford government saw immediately that it changed the position of the capital. No longer need Edmonton be described as situated on the "northern fringe" of settlement. It could now be portrayed as the centre of the province and the gateway to the whole western Arctic. Here was

No longer would Edmonton be described as situated on the 'northern fringe.' It could now be portrayed as the centre of the province and Gateway to the Arctic.

material for the sort of vision that so captivated the public imagination in those days; the sort of vision Sir John A. displayed with the CPR, or Teddy Roosevelt with the Panama Canal. And in the entire 20th century Alberta would never again have a man so desperately wanting to be a visionary as its first premier, Alexander Cameron Rutherford.

Laurier had chosen him premier because he looked like a manageable man, and the federal government regarded both Alberta and Saskatchewan as subsidiaries. After all, Ottawa had created them. Ottawa had established their fiscal basis. Ottawa had appointed their first premiers. Ottawa had chosen their interim capitals and, through careful gerrymandering in the case of Alberta, had assured they would become permanent capitals. Finally, the federal Liberal organization had helped assure the election of their first governments. Rutherford, as premier, was expected to protect Ottawa's interest in Alberta. He could run the show locally, but had to consult Ottawa on any major moves. Though Rutherford had not been the top choice for the job (see Sect. I, ch. 4) he seemed dependable enough. He could be controlled.

This was a mistake. Rutherford was 47 when he became premier, and his view of the premier's function plainly differed from Laurier's. Rutherford wasn't going to be a lieutenant, but a general in his own right. He saw Alberta not as the creature of Ottawa but as another Ontario in the making, with just as promising a future, and just as independent a role within Confederation. Since Alberta needed a university, for example, he passed the legislation and asked Laurier for federal funding. Laurier's refusal was chilly: "The provinces of Alberta and Saskatchewan are now more wealthy than the Dominion Government." Undeterred, Rutherford found the property and funded it through the provincial treasury (see Sect. 5, ch. 2). The premier saw no reason why he couldn't

'Every man's friend who never locked his door'

A LUCKY STRIKE GAVE TWELVE-FOOT DAVIS
THE WHEREWITHAL FOR A SMALL TRADING POST EMPIRE

At 101st Street and 102nd Avenue in the centre of the town of Peace River stands the twelve-foot statue of the man they call Twelve-Foot Davis. Not too many understand, however, why this entirely historical individual is cherished in the folklore of Alberta's North. It was not the dimensions of his physical frame, but the length and breadth of his charity that put Henry Fuller Davis on that pedestal.

Davis, who was actually not much more than five feet tall, was born in Vermont around 1820, came west for the California gold rush, then north in the Cariboo rush into BC where his native Yankee shrewdness won him his nickname. Noting that two claims near Barkerville were both proving good producers, Davis checked the registry office and discovered that the surveys left an unclaimed twelve-foot strip between them. He registered the strip to his own name, and made a handsome profit on it. Thereafter he was Twelve-Foot Davis.

But he noticed also that selling goods to miners and trappers promised a more dependable income than claim-staking. So he crossed into the Peace country and set up a chain of trading posts, actually little cabins, as far down the river as Fort Vermilion.

Thereafter he would haul goods overland from British Columbia and travel up and down the river by scow, holding sales at each of the cabins. Though physically diminutive, he had enormous strength and would regularly haul a 200-pound load over the mountains, double what his men carried. In between his visits he left the cabins unlocked and supplied with wood, a free resting place for weary or endangered travellers.

Davis lived much of the year at Dunvegan where his generosity endeared him to natives, settlers and missionaries. He was also celebrated as a cook, a trade he'd learned as a boy. Davis's pumpkin pies were the talk of the North.

Blind and crippled in old age, he died and was buried at Lesser Slave Lake in 1900. Ten years later trader Jim Cornwall had his bones transferred to a grave at Peace River overlooking the sweep of his beloved Peace valley. Beneath his statue in Peace River an inscription reads: "He was every man's friend, and never locked his cabin door."   — T.B.

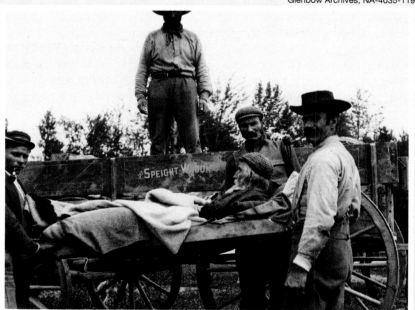

Twelve-Foot Davis in his last years. Renowned for generosity and for those pumpkin pies.

apply the same sort of take-charge approach to the North. Unfortunately for Rutherford, management of the North would prove tougher than building a couple of Romanesque academic buildings in Strathcona.

The problem posed by this rich new acquisition was one of accessibility. The Slave, which rolls north off the top of the Alberta map, is like the trunk of a tree, drawing its waters from three great branches. One is the Peace River, which flows 900 miles from the mountains of northern BC, draining a 120,000-square-mile watershed, 73,500 square miles of it in Alberta. The second is the

When wet, the Athabasca Trail was a 100-mile horror of mud, treacherous fords, washed-out bridges and broken axles. After that, things got worse.

Athabasca, which comes in from the Rockies in the vicinity of Jasper. The third is Lake Athabasca and the Fond du Lac River, flowing from the east into the Slave from northern Saskatchewan and northern Manitoba.

Two of these, the Peace and the Athabasca, lie mostly within Alberta, but the connections between them were poor. One route from the Athabasca to the Peace involved going back to the trunk and up the other branch — that is, descending the Athabasca to the Slave and then going up the Peace. The other involved ascending a tributary of the Athabasca called the Lesser Slave River, crossing to the western extremity of Lesser Slave Lake, then trekking over a 95-mile portage to what was known as Peace River Crossing.

Moreover, this whole Slave-Peace-Athabasca basin was isolated from the North Saskatchewan Valley, where settlers were now streaming in, by a land barrier 100 to 200 miles wide, much of it muskeg. By 1905 the chief route across this barrier was the Athabasca Trail, connecting the North Saskatchewan at Edmonton with Athabasca Landing. In dry weather it was reasonably passable.

Tracking barges up the Athabasca below Grand Rapids in 1901. A painful work, said one passenger, exhausting, expensive and dangerous.

Rev. White is a very fussy, nervous old gentleman who is quite alarmed at his own recklessness in getting into such an expedition. Low has roughed it in the North for years, knows the rivers, etc. and knows there is no danger. He has a comical streak in him, and delights in working on the fears of the poor clergyman. He is steering and with a very dramatic air will say, "I don't know whether I can make this corner or not," and paddle away furiously, when if he sat back and let her drift no harm could possibly happen. It is very funny.
- William C. McKillican diary, June 13, 1908.

Stuck on the Athabasca Trail, early 1900s. What was needed, thought Rutherford, was a northern railroad connecting Edmonton to the riverboat system.

In wet it was a 100-mile (160-km) horror of mud, treacherous fords, four-foot-deep potholes, washed-out bridges, and broken axles. Once across it, the Peace-bound traveller had a choice. He could either go upstream to the Lesser Slave route with its 95-mile portage, which was bad. Or he could take the other downstream route to the Slave and up the Peace, which was worse — worse because it meant running the rapids of the middle Athabasca, including the notorious Grand which regularly wrecked freight scows and cost lives. To Rutherford the solution to all this was embraced in a single word: railroads.

This normally rather stiff, stodgy (and thoroughly decent) man was enthralled by the stories and promise of the North, in particular the Peace River area, most of it only recently ceded by treaty. The District of Athabasca had remained Indian territory until 1899 when the tribes were persuaded to sign Treaty No. 8 (see Sect. 3, ch. 3). By then the Mounties were able to make regular patrols through it. At the end of the century's first decade, the total white population of the Peace area still fell short of 2,000, most of them survivors either of the fur trade or the Klondike gold rush. The area's original settlement, the century-old fur trade centre of Dunvegan, was about to disappear because measles and whooping cough had driven away the local Indians who had kept it going. Only the factor's house and a few teepees remained. Both the Catholic mission and the Anglican church had been abandoned, though the name Dunvegan still seemed to cast a mystical charm in the south.[1]

However, other centres were growing up. Sixty miles (95 km) to the south, near the Wapiti River, the newly established settlement of Bear Creek was growing up. Upon it the local populace would soon bestow the more elegant (i.e. French) name of Grande Prairie.[2] Fifteen miles (25 km) west of Bear Creek at beautiful Saskatoon Lake a major settlement was under way (nothing

---

Laurier had chosen Rutherford because he looked like a manageable man, and the federal government regarded the new provinces as subsidiaries. Ottawa had created them.

---

substantial would endure). Downriver from Dunvegan another substantial community was appearing at Peace River Crossing, where the trail arrived from Lesser Slave Lake. It was already being called Peace River Town and by 1909 had 240 white inhabitants. Across the river from the town and running upstream was the church colonization scheme known as the Shaftesbury Settlement.

The whole Peace region captured the imagination of the Canadian and American media, which recurrently sent special correspondents to travel its steamboat and wagon-road transportation system (see sidebar), and describe its endlessly rolling and virtually unoccupied farmlands. The *Montreal Herald* in a 1907 piece called it "the Dreamland of Canada" and soliloquized on the mysterious peacefulness and tranquility that the great river conveyed as it slipped, broad and silent, through its enormous valley.[3]

Whether the Peace country could support a grain or ranching industry had been a matter of controversy involving, curiously, the conflicting views of two scientists who were father and son. The eminent naturalist John Macoun[4] in the report of the Geological Survey of Canada for 1873

The first legislature on the steps of McKay Avenue School, May 9, 1906. Rifts and resentments were starting to develop.

had unreservedly recommended the Peace as a grain producing area:

> The prairie vegetation is almost identical with that of Edmonton, except for a few eastern species. This being so, can we not, with justice, say that what they raise at Edmonton can likewise be raised on the plains bordering the Peace River? Although summer frosts are not unknown at Dunvegan, they do little if any harm...I know that many doubts will be cast on the truthfulness of this statement, but from a careful perusal of many published tables of the climatology of the district in question and my own observations, I can come to no other conclusion than this, that the day is not far distant when the most sceptical will believe even more than I now assert.

Among the "most sceptical" was Macoun's son, James, sent to the Peace region by the Geological Survey of Canada in 1903. His findings were the precise reverse:

> I have been forced to the conclusion that, notwithstanding the luxuriant growth that is to be seen almost everywhere, the upper Peace River country to which so many eyes are now turned will never be a country in which wheat can be grown successfully. That grain will mature occasionally there is no doubt, but that it will ever become the staple product of any considerable area I do not believe.[5]

The whole Peace region captured the imagination of the Canadian and American media, which recurrently sent special correspondents to travel its steamboat and wagon-road routes.

Two developments in 1907 decided the issue for the government, however. One was the report of a special Senate committee. It exhaustively examined the evidence and found conclusively that grain crops were being produced not only in the relative summer warmth of the valley floor but on the rolling prairie lands above it. "There is in the Peace River section of the country,"

[1] Though Dunvegan by then scarcely existed, turn-of-the-century Alberta railway promoters named a projected line to the Peace area the Edmonton Dunvegan and British Columbia Railway. In the decade 1910-20, the line would actually be built, setting off a fire sale of "urban" lots in downtown Dunvegan, which by then consisted of abandoned buildings and a graveyard. The Dunvegan Bridge, built at the site in 1957 to carry Alberta Highway 2 across the Peace River, preserved the name.

[2] Topographically the Peace River region is divided by the river itself. The big agricultural area south of the river is the Grande Prairie. The area north of the river in Alberta divides into the Fairview and Berwyn prairies, lying roughly between a point twenty miles west of Peace River town to a few miles east of Dunvegan, a strip about forty miles long by ten to twenty miles wide. A belt of poorer ground separates this strip from the Clear Hills Prairie to the north. The Battle River Prairie lies northwest of the Clear Hills Prairie. Another fertile prairie, not designated by name, begins in the vicinity of Hines Creek, northwest of Fairview, and extends to the BC border. Beyond the BC border lie the Pouce Coupe and Rolla prairies, as well as the Rose Prairie north of Fort St. John.

[3] The great river received its name *Unchaga* or "peace" after the Crees and the Beavers signed a treaty around the year 1780 at Peace Point, about sixty miles (95 km) upstream from its junction with the Slave.

[4] It was the same John Macoun who ferociously advocated settlement in the Palliser Triangle (Vol. I, p. 236), a recommendation that has been a matter of controversy ever since.

[5] John Macoun maintained until his death the feasibility of export grain production in the Peace region, indeed lived to see it happen. When told that his son's report refuted his own, the elder Macoun replied: "James was always the cautious sort."

A scow being lowered down the Vermilion Chutes on the Peace River, date unknown. A passenger experiencing this on the Athabasca's Grand Rapids called it 'a nightmare.'

The *Northern Light* is the boat that plies on the remainder of the Little River, and on Lesser Slave Lake. It is smaller than the *Midnight Sun*, and has only one deck. It is a sidewheeler; the *Midnight Sun* is a sternwheeler. There are no berths or staterooms, the passengers stow themselves away among the freight or sleep on the roof.
- from the diary of Peace country traveller and agriculturalist William C. McKillican, June 1, 1908.

said the committee's report, "as much good agricultural land fit for settlement as there is settled in Manitoba, Saskatchewan and Alberta today..."

The other development was the publication of an illustrated booklet called *The Peace River Trail*, by A.M. Bezanson, a Peace River settler and the first great promoter of the region's potential. Bezanson declared he was not interested in selling land but settling on it, and was writing to persuade others to settle on it as well. He besought his readers to:

Imagine a West with no hostile Indians, no sun-scorched desert of burning sands, no alkaline plains devoid of vegetation, no lurking dangers of any kind to trap the unwary traveller: but a West of broad prairies and timbered hills, where both water and feed for horses can always be found in abundance, and where the traveller can make his bed upon the ground, whenever fancy may dictate, with no fear of his rest being disturbed by intruder in any form. Imagine a West with trading posts being established near the most fertile sections, connected either by great natural waterways or good roads, so the settler need experience no difficulty in getting supplies, and where, if he be willing to work, he may by trapping in the winter make enough money to keep him in supplies for the year...

So level is the country, and so free from natural disadvantages, that our party of eleven, with two freight wagons, two buckboards, and three saddle horses, made 220 miles very easily in seven and a half days...Between these two points we saw only one house, and that belonging to an Indian, and nowhere on this road was there a visible sign of a wagon ever having travelled it before.

Bezanson's booklet became a sensation and sold 5,000 copies. One who almost certainly read it was Premier Rutherford, though he had no need of visionary inspiration. He had plenty of his own. As a fulfiller of visions, however, Rutherford lacked an indispensable ingredient. He thought clearly, but was careless of detail. He was the kind of lawyer who "develops business for the firm," letting others slog at the bookwork. The hard head in his cabinet belonged to his minister of public works, William Henry Cushing, who was 53 when he joined the government, a Calgary lumber goods manufacturer who had to suffer in silence the outrage of Calgary Liberals over the government's pro-Edmonton decisions.

Privately Cushing smarted over them too, and a deep rift began to develop between him and the senior Edmonton minister in the cabinet. This was Charles Wilson Cross, a 36-year-old lawyer who served as attorney-general and provided much of the government's political sagacity. These three — Rutherford, Cushing and Cross — formed the cabinet's inner ring. Outside the ring looking in was the deputy speaker, John Robert Boyle, another Edmonton lawyer, a year older than Cross, who also disliked and distrusted Cross[6] and who considered himself cabinet material unfairly excluded from power. The tireless premier, meanwhile, was provincial treasurer and minister of education as well.

In the Legislature's first term, things could hardly have gone better for Rutherford. The Tories were in utter disarray. Their leader, R.B. Bennett, had no seat in the House and resigned after the

THE CRISIS AT THE END OF THE DECADE

1905 election. He continued to serve as Canadian Pacific counsel in Calgary, growing richer through lucrative business deals put together by his friend Max Aitken, the future Lord Beaverbrook.[7] Bennett still took a fitful interest in provincial affairs, however, enough to keep his name before the public. Dr. R.G. Brett of Banff, long a member of the territorial legislature, took over but his leadership was nominal.

The Tory *Calgary Herald* softened its virulent anti-Liberal deprecations. The *Edmonton Journal* continued on the attack, chiding Rutherford's "machine politics," and deploring Ottawa's refusal to give Alberta control of its resources. But none of this criticism stuck. When a vacancy came up in the constituency of Vermilion in 1906, the government won the by-election by acclamation. Even the acid Bob Edwards of the *Eye Opener* extended Rutherford a hand. He wrote to the premier on March 20, 1907:

Albert J. Robertson, opposition leader in Alberta's first legislature. Hopelessly outnumbered, he simply gave up, leaving Rutherford free to dream up his ill-fated scheme of a northern railway.

> Permit me to congratulate you on the splendid work accomplished by your government during the session just closed. Your wisdom in protecting the treasury from the bold onslaughts of that fake immigration association and your kindness to the Alpine Club have gained for you the solid friendship of my little rag — if that friendship is worth anything.

When Rutherford left for Britain in May, to attend the Imperial Conference on Education, the Strathcona Board of Trade held a banquet for him at which both Conservatives and Liberals paid him tribute. (W.H. Cushing, noted the *Edmonton Bulletin*, sent his regrets.) In the federal election of 1908, the Laurier government lost ground. The Liberals' standing in the House was reduced to 133 from 139. In Alberta, however, which now had seven Commons seats, the Liberals remained strong, taking four of them. In the election of 1904, they had won only two of the then four seats in the District of Alberta.

Meanwhile the two-man Tory opposition in the Legislature became a one-man opposition when Cornelius Hiebert, the Mennonite MLA for Rosebud, began sitting as an Independent. (He would run as an Independent in the 1909 election and be defeated by a Liberal.) The remaining Tory, Albert J. Robertson from High River, could do little against such a phalanx and didn't try. Hence when Rutherford stumbled, the Tories could not take advantage of it.

The stumble came through the combination of two Rutherford visions: railroads and the North. Legislatively his government had, except in two respects, behaved prudently and predictably. The House between 1906 and 1909 passed some seventy bills, many of them housekeeping measures. The university was established, school districts were reorganized, a workmen's compensation program was set up, and an eight-hour day was legislated for coal miners. The number of provincial constituencies was increased from the original 25 to 41.

There had been some jolly moments, such as the arrival in Edmonton of 'Allie' Brick, member for Peace River, who brought along his two pet moose. And some proud ones, as when excavations began for the new Legislative Building in 1907 (see Sect. 2, ch. 1). In the meantime, for their third session, in 1908, the legislators moved out of the McKay School and into temporary quarters in the new Terrace Building at Seventh Street (107th) and Calgary Avenue (96th).[8]

The first unusual sphere of activity had been telephones. Cushing, in a bitter war with the Bell company, had established a provincial system that would become Alberta Government Telephones (see Sect. 4, ch. 4). The second area was the Rutherford railway program, a massive incursion by the province into the railway industry, effectively as banker or loan guarantor, envisioning at least two major lines into the North through the forest and muskeg barrier that separated the North Saskatchewan from the Athabasca. This program was Rutherford's pre-election package for the 1909 vote.

Like much else about the railway industry of that time, the Rutherford program would later

[6] The probable origins of Boyle's antipathy to Cross were explained in an article in *Alberta History*. In 1905 both Boyle and Cross sought the provincial Liberal nomination in Edmonton constituency. Cross was constituency president. The Edmonton seat in the territorial legislature was vacant at the time, but the vacancy was ignored because that body was about to pass out of existence. Cross had himself named territorial candidate, and then, when the province came into being on September 1, he had the constituency executive meet and declare the territorial candidate as the provincial candidate. Thus he effectively shut out Boyle. Subsequently Boyle ran in Sturgeon and won, but never again trusted Cross. The article was written by Helen Boyd, Boyle's daughter.

[7] Bennett and Aitken masterminded three big corporate amalgamations; those that resulted in Calgary Power (later TransAlta Utilities), Canada Cement (later Lafarge Canada) and Pacific Elevators (later absorbed by Federal Grain, later still, the Alberta Wheat Pool).

[8] The original Terrace Building, a three-storey red brick structure built in 1906 beside Fort Edmonton, was demolished in 1959 and replaced by a new Terrace Building in 1961.

The complex steamboat system that united the North

BEFORE THE RAILWAY THE GRUELLING ATHABASCA TRAIL LED TO A LAND
WHERE RAPIDS ROARED AND RAIN MIGHT BE YOUR BED COMPANION

Long before the provincially guaranteed branch line railways first connected Alberta's northland with the rest of the province in 1912, northern Albertans had established a reliable system of transportation that extended to the shores of the Arctic Ocean. It depended at worst on wagon roads and on huge crews dragging scows through rapids. But at best it depended on a species of vessel that made its appearance in the North in the year 1883, the paddlewheeled steamboat.

By 1910 paddlewheelers and one propeller-driven craft were operating on more than 4,000 miles (6,435 km) of lakes and rivers of the northern province and western Arctic. But the only access to this entire network was an old wagon road that ran from Edmonton to Athabasca Landing (now simply Athabasca), known as the Athabasca Trail, a fragment of which remains as Edmonton's Fort Road.

In one form or another, the trail was used by the HBC for the last half of the 19th century. For a few miles, it followed the old Victoria Trail, which skirted the north bank of the North Saskatchewan to the Methodist mission at Victoria near the future Pakan. But when the Athabasca-bound traveller reached the crossing of the Sturgeon, about four miles north of Fort Saskatchewan, he turned off on a branch trail northward for Athabasca Landing. (In 1887, the Hudson's Bay Company made a shortcut that took the trail from northeast Edmonton directly to the elbow of the Sturgeon near a community called Battenburg.)

In one of the first of the twenty books he produced on the history of Alberta, *The Land of Twelve-Foot Davis* (1952), historian James G. MacGregor takes his readers over the Athabasca Trail, which he had obviously traced himself, much of it probably on foot. He describes the HBC's efforts to keep to the high ground as much as possible, and out of mudholes. He tells of the trail's stopping places — like the one kept by "the Widow LeClair" at beautiful Lily Lake, and Joe Patry's place at what later became Waugh, and Cap Gullion's at

Halfway Lake, and Lewis's stopping place which would become Lewiston which in turn would become Perryvale.[a] The trail followed the Tawatinaw River to Billy Smith's place just outside Athabasca Landing. Smith himself made fourteen 200-mile round trips in the winter of 1905-06, says MacGregor, each of them taking about a week.

By 1910, Athabasca Landing was a bustling town of warehouses, river docks, shipbuilders, a sawmill, Catholic and Anglican missions, pool rooms, boarding houses, a Royal North-West Mounted Police post and the Grand Union Hotel. It had quickly recovered from the flood that swamped most of it in 1904. Here many of the river boatmen made their homes, and here too the traveller encountered James K. Cornwall's Northern Transportation Company, one of the three operators

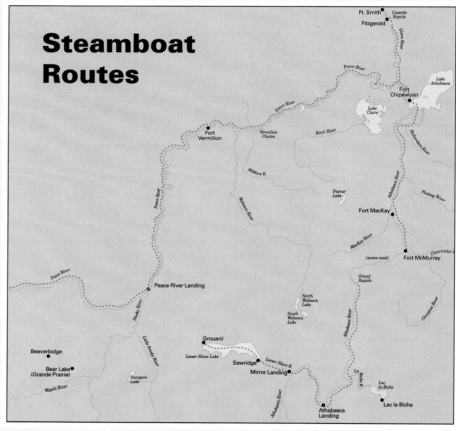

Steamboat Routes

of the northern steamboat system, the other two being the HBC and the Oblate Order.

Cornwall, probably the best known of all northerners, had risen to prominence with the country, and would continue to do so. Born in Brantford, Ontario, he had worked as a seaman on the Great Lakes and Atlantic, as a navvy in the construction of the Canadian Pacific's Crowsnest line, and come north to work the river boats before the turn of the century. The potential of the Peace country fascinated him and he became its most effective promoter, known far and wide as Peace River Jim. In partnership with Fletcher Bredin in 1898 he started a trading business in the Peace country in competition with the HBC. In 1903, Revillon Frères, the Parisian furrier that invaded the HBC empire, bought Cornwall and Bredin out. Then, acquiring a third partner, J.H. Woods, they formed Northern Transportation.

In 1910 Cornwall organized and paid for a tour of the whole Peace country by a party of journalists from influential American and Canadian newspapers and magazines. It was a stupendous success and fanned the flames of international interest in the region. However, there were two views in the North about Cornwall, one that he was out for the Peace country and the other that he was out for Cornwall. The former was by far the more widely held.[b]

The Athabasca was one of the four great rivers of the North that steamboats could use. Of the four the Mackenzie was navigable for its entire 2,635-mile (4,240-km) length, from Fort Providence at its source to its mouth on the Beaufort Sea. The other three each had an impassable barrier.

The Athabasca was navigable from Jasper to the Grand Rapids, 165 miles (265 km) downstream from the Landing. In the 87 miles (140 km) between the Grand and the mouth of the Clearwater at Fort McMurray, it plunges a total of 400 feet and could be negotiat-

Into this marshland from the southwest pours the Peace. It, too, has its barrier. It is easily navigable 175 miles upstream (280 km) to Vermilion Chutes, a violent rapids impassable for steamboats. However, above the Chutes the Peace was easily managed for the entire 525 miles (845 km) upstream to Hudson's Hope in northern BC.

The great marsh at the mouth of the Peace and Athabasca is drained northward by the Slave, but this river too is blocked ninety miles (145 km) downstream at what was once called Smith's Landing, later Grahame's landing and would ultimately be known as Fitzgerald. The town sits almost exactly on the

The steamboat Grahame on the Athabasca, 1901. The craft were manufactured on the riverbank.

northern boundary of the province. Beyond Fitzgerald for sixteen miles the Slave thunders through five rapids to Fort

---

The Grahame could make it upstream the 110 miles from Fort Chipewyan to Fort McMurray in thirty hours. This was considered astounding. It used to take a week.

---

ed only by special scows. The Grand Rapids stood at the head of this "death strip," and goods were transferred by a little railway built across a one-mile island that bypassed their worst section. For the nearly 100 miles (160 km) between Fort McMurray and the mouth, the Athabasca runs as smooth as a fishpond.

The delta of the Athabasca is a huge marshland that forms the western extremity of Lake Athabasca, and on a rocky promontory on its northern fringe stands Fort Chipewyan.

Smith, named like so many other things for Donald Smith, Lord Strathcona. Below Smith, the Slave was navigable to its mouth on Great Slave Lake which gives access to the Mackenzie, Great Bear River, Great Bear Lake and the Arctic.

This meant that the steamboat system consisted of four segments, separated from one another by rapids over which goods and passengers must be hauled by wagon. Between Fort Smith and the Arctic, the propeller-driven *Wrigley*, ninety feet long and fourteen feet wide, provided summer service all the way to the Arctic. In the segment between Fort McMurray, Grahame's Landing and Vermilion Chutes ran the *Grahame*, the first paddlewheeler in the system that could make it upstream 110 miles from Fort Chipewyan to McMurray in thirty hours. This was considered astounding. The ten or twenty men it took to track one old York boat up the river were lucky to make twenty miles a day. Meanwhile in 1892 the Oblates commissioned another paddlewheeler, the *St. Joseph*, to run the same route as the *Grahame*.

Between Vermilion Chutes and Hudson's Hope plied the *St. Charles*, launched by the Oblate Order in 1903, and the *Peace River*, commissioned by the HBC two years later. Above the Grand Rapids on the Athabasca Jim Cornwall's *Midnight Sun* and the HBC's *Athabasca* did the work. But here there was another river barrier, more problematic than the big rapids because sometimes boats could get through and most times they could not. It was a tributary of the upper Athabasca, the Lesser Slave River, whose unpredictable water levels caused constant trouble.

The source of the Lesser Slave River was the lake of that name, at the western end of which was Lesser Slave Lake settlement, later Grouard. On the lake Cornwall ran another vessel, the sidewheeler *Northern Light*. A 95-mile wagon road connected the lake with Peace River Crossing. Without the Lesser Slave River problem, boats could get from there to Athabasca Landing. At least one, the *Athabasca*, was nearly wrecked in the attempt, though the HBC saved it.

Since the steamboats themselves could not be freighted overland, they had to be manufactured beside the waters they would serve. Their boilers and engines were hauled in by wagon over the Athabasca Trail and transported downstream or up.

Settlers headed for Peace River usually used the upper Athabasca route. That is, they endured the Athabasca Trail, then went upstream to Mirror Landing at the mouth of the Lesser Slave, then trundled overland for sixteen miles to the head of the river, traversed the lake on the *Northern Light*, and took the long wagon road over to Peace River Crossing.

Travellers headed for Great Slave Lake, Mackenzie and the Arctic took the *Midnight Sun* or the *Athabasca* down to the Grand Rapids, then faced the terrors of scow travel between there and Fort McMurray. Elizabeth Taylor, who made the trip in 1892, kept an interesting record of it. She watched the men loading freight on the *Athabasca* at the Landing: tobacco put up in 65-pound canvas packages; "Old Honesty" oysters from Mobile, Alabama, packed securely in wooden boxes; sugar by the keg; blankets from England by the bale; greasy sacks of bacon; wooden cases of peaches.

All were stowed with an eye to maximum use of available space. Her cabin was furnished with a bed and hay tick mattress and nothing else. No sooner was she in bed than water fell on her face, then began sprinkling the whole cabin because the deckhead leaked. She spent the night sitting up. At the Grand Rapids she was transferred to a scow. Thereafter things became exciting. She describes several crews grasping lines to lower a single vessel down through a roaring stretch of the river:

Fifteen men behind and five in front were holding it back with ropes, the men on a slippery narrow ledge where it seemed impossible for anyone to stand. It seemed dreadful, like some nightmares I have had, but it was over in a few minutes.

I never tired of watching the men of the brigade. As we approached a stretch of rapids, at a signal from the steersman the great oars would be put in place and with shouts the men would bend to their work — rising to their feet at every stroke, hair flying, spray dashing from the long blades — and the boat would be sent down the current at a speed that outstripped that of the rapids and placed the boat under the control of the steersman. Then when we reached a quieter place the oars would be shipped, and the men would stretch out comfortably on the pieces, smoking. I listened in vain for any of the old voyageur songs — not one was to be heard.

Usually the scows were scrapped for lumber when they reached Fort McMurray, a practice that provided a scow-building industry for Athabasca Landing where up to a hundred new ones were built each year. But some goods such as fur must make the return trip upstream. This meant dragging the flat-bottomed vessels through the current, a painful, exhausting, expensive and dangerous job. The scows were tracked from a shore line, the men trudging up the bank while a steersman and bowsman aboard guided the vessel around obstructions.

The upstream trip took as much as three weeks and things often went wrong. MacGregor tells how once in 1913 it took the crews of a whole flotilla, eighty men on a single tracking line, to work each scow up through a particularly bad stretch of the river. Miss Taylor was a passenger on the upstream trip three months later. She recalls:

Six men in harness drew the boat along, a stout leather band passing around the chest and being attached to the main line. The latter was about 200 feet long and the boat was drawn along in the stream at quite a distance from the shore. The motion was delightful and in good weather nothing can be pleasanter than this way of travelling. The only sound was the low whistling of Baptiste at the helm with his occasional word to Jules at the prow...

(Yet) it seemed unkind to feel so comfortable when the men in harness were toiling so hard to pull the craft along. And painful work it was, climbing over the rocks, plunging into the water to the waist, scrambling over fallen trees, sometimes climbing over the sloping hillside high above the rapids, and sometimes forced by the power of the waters to give up foot after foot of ground.[c]

There were other routes into the North, though never as functional or dependable. The fur traders originally had come in from the East, ascending the Churchill River through the future northern Saskatchewan to its headwaters on Lac la Loche, crossing the 13-mile Methy portage, and descending the Clearwater to the Athabasca at Fort McMurray below the rapids. But this was feasible only for canoes.

Later the HBC opened a winter road between Fort Edmonton and Fort Assiniboine, on the Athabasca below what would become Whitecourt, and above the Lesser Slave River. But the long overland stretch was impractical for freight hauling, and impossible in summer.

The Oblates developed a trail between the North Saskatchewan and their mission at Lac la Biche. But the outlet of that lake to the Athabasca is above the Grand, so the worst problem remained. At one point the Oblates tried cutting a trail between Lac la Biche and Fort McMurray, the future route of the Alberta and Great Waterways Railway, but the bush and muskeg defeated them.

Not until 1911 was a direct overland route to the Peace River district punched through. After the Grand Trunk Pacific reached Edson, the provincial government in 1910 surveyed a trail from there to Sturgeon Lake, where it connected with an older road that ran west across to Grande Prairie. Known as the Edson Trail, it was corduroyed by the province, whose crews also bridged the rivers. At the end of the decade it became the main thoroughfare into the Peace until the railways arrived. The horror stories the Peace settlers would tell about it would make the Athabasca Trail seem like a superhighway. But the major movement of settlers into the Peace must be told in a later volume. By 1910 it had barely begun.

The railways instantly rendered the great trails obsolete. The Canadian Northern reached Athabasca Landing in 1912, the Edmonton, Dunvegan and British Columbia (later to become part of the Northern Alberta Railways) reached Peace River Crossing in 1916, and the Alberta and Great Waterways Railway finally got to the junction of the Clearwater and the Athabasca in 1919. The tough scowmen of the Athabasca vanished forever. There was no economic reason for civilization to exist on the dangerous section of the river between the Grand Rapids and Fort McMurray, except for oil explorers who came before the century (Vol. 1, p. 250) and would appear from time to time throughout it.

Otherwise the middle Athabasca returned to the pristine state in which the white man had found it. Thereafter it would make headlines only when canoeists attempted its rapids and drowned; something they did with considerable regularity throughout the century. The bodies of many were never recovered.   — *T.B.*

Athabasca Land Co. advertisement for Gateway Heights, Athabasca Landing, 1911. It was not until that year that a direct overland trail to Peace country was pushed through.

[a]Stopping places were the truck stops of the turn of the century, hostels along trails, sometimes scarcely defined. They were frequently a homesteader's dwelling. Guests brought their own blankets, paid only for their meals. The Rev. R.E. Finlay, the first Christian minister to settle in the Vegreville area, wrote of the nearby Dennis Stopping Place, "In case of rain, [guests] were allowed to come into the house and make a bed on the floor; otherwise they were expected to make a bed outside in a horse stall or granary or alongside a hay or straw stack, or under the vehicle in which they travelled...It was a common thing for Dennis Stopping Place to have twelve or fifteen men, who had stopped overnight, on the premises for breakfast. Mrs. Dennis, on short notice, could provide for all with porridge, eggs, griddle cakes and strong coffee, the main items of the bill of fare."

[b]Cornwall ran for the Peace River seat in the Legislature in 1905 and was defeated by Thomas Allan "Allie" Brick. He took the Liberal nomination and was elected in 1909. As the next chapter relates, he figured centrally in the Alberta and Great Waterways Railway promotion whose fiscal side destroyed the Rutherford government.

[c]Another woman who travelled on the Athabasca, Agnes Deans Cameron, kept a copy of a cook's dinner menu on an upstream scow. Monday: dried caribou and rice. Tuesday: salt fish and prunes. Wednesday: mess-pork and dried peaches. Thursday: salt horse and macaroni. Friday: sow-belly and bannock. Saturday: fish and beans. Sunday: repeat. The menu would change, of course, if the crew chanced to encounter a moose or a deer.

seem close to insane. Ernest Watkins in his informative political history entitled *The Golden Province*, published for Alberta's 75th anniversary in 1980, sets forth some of these absurdities. In the wild optimism of the first decade, railways seemed a winner from every viewpoint. The farmers wanted them because the closer their farm to the elevator, the less the cost in delivering their grain. The politicians liked them because they won the farm vote. The railroad contractors liked them because they couldn't lose; they made their money building the line, not operating it. The investors liked them because railway bonds were guaranteed by governments. The governments liked them because they assumed that the boom would go on forever, that the railways would all therefore be profitable, and that the guarantees would never be called. But, as the governments were soon to learn, booms do not last forever, few railways would be profitable, and the guarantees would very definitely be called.

Provincial Archives of Alberta, E. Brown Collection, B-2970

(347) TOWING TRADERS BOATS DOWN SLAVE RIVE PHOTO BY G.H. MATHERS. EDMONTON, ALTA.

Rutherford announced his new railway policy in November 1908 in a series of press interviews. A provincial Department of Railways was being established, he said, and he would be its minister (his third portfolio in addition to the premiership). Railways were needed all over the province and the government would guarantee the bonds of any company that could itself raise 35% of the capital cost of the line. It must put up 10% of that in cash before government bond guarantees would become effective.

In the interviews, Rutherford produced what amounted to an election slogan: "The great need of this province is for railways." But, he said, "men will not build railways in a new country without some government assistance. They will demand that their bonds be guaranteed." Then he aimed one at Laurier: "We have been asking the federal government to extend this help, and we will continue to do so. But if they will not help us, then we will do it ourselves. The railways must be built."

When the first Legislature met for its last session in January 1909, its schedule demonstrated what all this meant. The Grand Trunk Pacific planned construction of 491 miles of branch lines in Alberta and the province would guarantee the bonds at $13,000 a mile. The Canadian Northern planned 920 miles of branch lines and the same guarantee would apply. A railway incorporated in 1906, the Alberta North Western planned to build from Edmonton to Athabasca Landing to Lesser Slave Lake to Peace River Crossing. If the capitalization could be found, this would qualify for bond guarantees next year. The Canadian Northern opened such a line in 1912, but only as far as Athabasca Landing.

Finally came the crowning project of them all. Work would begin immediately on what would be called the Alberta and Great Waterways Railway, to run 350 miles from Edmonton to Lac la Biche and Fort McMurray where the Clearwater River flows into the Athabasca.[9] This was the southern terminus of the whole Mackenzie waterways system and would make Edmonton the "Gateway to the Arctic." The line would be guaranteed at $16,000 a mile. All these bills flowed through the legislature with little debate. Lieutenant-Governor George Bulyea gave royal assent on February 25 and Rutherford called an election for March 22, 1909, with the railroad program the central plank in his platform.

The campaign was much the same one-sided effort that had characterized the election of 1905. Rutherford had actually opened it on the last day of the session with a spirited attack on Senator James Lougheed who, he said, was "the real power behind the [Tory] throne" in Alberta. "He has been roving about Alberta for the last two or three weeks," said Rutherford, "trying to drum up some opposition to the government of Alberta when he should be attending to his duties as a senator at Ottawa." If Lougheed wanted to oppose his government, said the premier, he should resign his Senate seat and take the leadership of the provincial Conservative Party.

As it happened, nobody wanted that job. Bennett had decisively rejected the Tory leadership, and agreed to run in Calgary, now a two-seat constituency, but only on the condition he not be party leader. M.S. McCarthy, the Calgary MP, had also turned it down, as had William A. Griesbach, the former mayor of Edmonton. So the Tories went into the campaign under their ineffectual house leader A.J. Robertson. They let eight seats go to the Liberals by acclamation, and in four more the candidates ran as "Independent Conservatives."

The Liberals opened their campaign at Edmonton with a huge rally in support of Cross and Rutherford, which began with the crowd singing, "We're all pals together." Little heed was paid the fact that one of the "pals" was absent, namely Cushing, this time "unavoidably detained" in Calgary. Rutherford went to Calgary to speak on Cushing's behalf, pointing out that many of the new railway branch lines would be built in the south; the war between south and north could now be considered over. It was not. Bennett in a rousing speech on the election's eve declared that a vote for Cushing was a vote for Edmonton. The speech doubtless succeeded, for Bennett was one of two Tories elected. The other was George Hoadley in Okotoks.

The result province-wide was another massive Liberal landslide. The Liberals took 35 seats, and gained two more in the deferred elections in Peace River and Athabasca. The socialists elected Charles M. O'Brien in Rocky Mountain (see Sect. 4, ch. 1). This with the Red Deer Independent and the two Tories completed the House. Rutherford was now the undisputed master of the province. But the cracks in his party were widening, and fourteen months later his political career was to lie in ruins.

The morals of this north country are rather shocking to one who has been accustomed to a high standard. There are practically no white women in the country and the native women are entirely devoid of honour. The men are as bad or worse. What the white men are may be seen from the fact that there are practically no pureblooded Indians in the country.
- Ibid, June 13, 1908.

(340) RAPIDS ON SLAVE RIVER AT THE 3 RD PORTAGE   PHOTO BY C.W.MATHERS EDMONTON,ALTA.

Third portage on the Slave River rapids, 1901. The paddlewheelers from Fort McMurray had to discharge their cargoes above this point at Grahame's Landing, later Fitzgerald.

Courtesy: Speaker of the Legislature of Alberta.

ARTHUR LEWIS SIFTON

Born: Oct. 26, 1858, at St. Johns, Canada West

Died: Jan. 21, 1921, in Ottawa

Career Apex: Second premier of Alberta, 1910-1917

Major Accomplishment: He held together the Liberal party, badly split in the previous
administration. When premier he gained the franchise for women.

Quotation: 'The only thing I have to announce is that I have nothing to announce.'

In fifteen terrible weeks Rutherford met destruction

WITH ONE LETHAL DISCLOSURE AFTER ANOTHER ON THE A&GW CONTRACT
BENNETT AND THE REBEL LIBERALS HUNTED DOWN HIS ATTORNEY-GENERAL

For Alexander Cameron Rutherford, the summer of 1909 could scarcely have been improved upon. The province was faring well. Though a shortage of investment capital had slowed growth in 1907, the downturn had proved brief and the pace of progress was now increasing. He had won another resounding election victory. In September he turned the sod for the new University of Alberta Arts Building,[1] and two days later saw the cornerstone laid for the new Legislature.

His personal affairs were equally propitious. His son Cecil was enrolled in the U of A (albeit reluctantly; he would have preferred McGill). His daughter was at a private school in Toronto. His considerable real estate investments included the "Rutherford Block" on Whyte Avenue, farm property in the future Bonnie Doon and a summer cottage at Banff. In May he had bought a 1.3-acre piece of Laurent Garneau's farm next to the university site, for a magnificent two-storey home to be designed in the Strathcona office of the British architectural firm of Wilson & Herrald.[2] Work on it was about to begin.

The new railway program was off to a fine start. The biggest single project was the Alberta and Great Waterways Railway, the A&GW as it was popularly known. Behind it were two brothers named Clarke from Kansas City, Missouri — bankers, Rutherford was given to understand, with Canadian associates in Winnipeg. Their chief executive, William Rockwell Clarke[3], announced in September the railroad would reach Fort McMurray in three years.

The A&GW was discussed regularly at cabinet. Public Works Minister Cushing raised some objection to the $20,000-per-mile guarantee on the bonds, but did not pursue it. In November the $7,400,000 issue was taken up by the J. Pierpont Morgan people in New York and sold, some said at a premium, in London. It should have. The interest rate was 5%, a full percentage point above other issues, and the guarantee was $7,000 higher. But this after all was a "colonization road." Bigger risk. In November the first sod was turned sixteen miles (25 km) north of Edmonton, 300 men were employed grading the right of way near Gibbons, surveying began near Lac la

Provincial Archives of Alberta, A-2720

*Attorney-General Cross:
He was the central target.*

A sketch of banker Clarke, made from a news photo, 1910.

[1] Although work began immediately, the Arts Building triumph was to prove as ephemeral as Rutherford's political success. When his government fell the following spring, construction was stopped. A new Arts Building was started in 1913 and the original foundation swept away.

[2] This, of course, was to become Rutherford House, restored by the Alberta government in 1971 and opened in 1974 as a museum and cultural centre.

[3] The Clarke brothers were the sons of a Kansas City banker who played a key role in American western railroad development, a wild era of phoney stock promotions, politicking, political connivance, amazing engineering accomplishment and graft. The *Edmonton Bulletin* had extravagantly interviewed William R. Clarke after the A&GW bill passed the Legislature in 1909. "The passage of this act is epochal," said the *Bulletin* exuberantly, the writer not realizing how prophetic his observation would prove. Clarke in the interview waxed eloquent on the potential of the North. However, noted the reporter, "the man wouldn't talk much about himself." The Clarke family fortune vanished, like many others, in the crash of 1929.

Biche, Clarke announced that 200 miles (320 km) would be built the following year, and a contract was let locally to supply ties. Meanwhile, all the paperwork was being handled by Rutherford's No.1 lieutenant, Attorney-General Charles Wilson Cross, and his department. Cross was the exceedingly popular senior member for Edmonton whose landslide victory in March had surpassed even Rutherford's in Strathcona.

In October 1909, Rutherford expanded the cabinet slightly. DeVeber, minister without portfolio, had gone to the Senate in 1906. Finlay, the minister of Agriculture, had retired. He named Duncan Marshall, a farmer and owner of the newspaper in Olds, to Agriculture, and two more as ministers without portfolio: William Buchanan, publisher of the *Lethbridge Herald*, who would probably head up a new department, Municipalities; and Prosper Lessard, an Edmonton wholesale merchant who sat for the constituency of Pakan.

With the new year, 1910, came a slightly discordant note. The Tory press carried criticisms of the work on the A&GW, alleging that the rail was light, and laid on spruce ties over mud. The word "graft" was being bandied about. A letter to the *Bulletin*, signed by one James Smith, said the contract for ties was a farce. Like everything else, they were being supplied by something called the Canada West Construction Company. Its address: Winnipeg. This raised eyebrows. If railway and contractor were the same, the latter could cheat the former undiscovered. If the railway spent too much on construction and failed, the government must

Works Minister Cushing:
It began with rumours he'd quit.

take over and make good on the bonds. However nothing suggested a tie-up between the Clarkes and Canada West Construction except that both had a Winnipeg connection.

As Rutherford prepared for the session, however, no such dark thoughts appear to have concerned him. He was "an apolitical politician," says Douglas R. Babcock in his biography, *A Gentleman of Strathcona*. He now had an enormous caucus and was aware of no friction in it. True, Cushing of Calgary still resented the university decision, and perhaps was annoyed by a loss of control over railways by his cherished Public Works Department, and was irritated by Rutherford's inattention to detail.[4] But this surely was not a serious difficulty.

Over the weekend Rutherford's calm was shattered, as he discovered what a less sanguine premier would have known for months.

Others might find things suspicious where Rutherford did not. For instance, he knew that Jim Cornwall, the new member for Peace River, had long had an interest in a company that had a federal charter for a railway to Fort McMurray but was unable to get a provincial guarantee on the bonds. Now one had been given to Clarke. Why wasn't Cornwall resentful? He even seemed keen on the A&GW. Doubtless it was his enthusiasm for the North. The possibility that Cornwall had become Clarke's partner did not dawn on Rutherford. Why, even Attorney-General Cross seemed mightily concerned for the A&GW project. That must be his enthusiasm for Edmonton, of course.

FEBRUARY CIRCULATION.

The total circulation of The Journal (Morning and Evening) for February was 108,758 copies, being a total daily average of 4,321 copies, of which 3,888 copies were circulated in the city daily.

Evening Journal

Vol. 7, No. 57.

EDMONTON, ALBERTA, WEDNESDAY, MARCH 9, 1910

FORECAST.

ALBERTA — Fair and comparatively mild today and Thursday.

EIGHT PAGES

W. A. BUCHANAN FOLLOWS ATTORNEY-GENERAL
CUSHING POSITIVELY REPUDIATES THE STATEMENT THAT HE WILL GO BACK
PREMIER RUTHERFORD SAYS "I HAVE NOTHING TO SAY"

As January unfolded came further worrisome press stories, reporting rumours of Cushing's resignation. Cushing denied them, but obliquely: "I have not yet heard any intimation I am not wanted in the cabinet." But Cushing had said nothing directly, so how could such rumours be taken seriously? Finally, the opposition now had a spokesman of unparalleled competence in R.B. Bennett, something it hadn't possessed in the first session. But Bennett led a group of two against a government caucus of 37. So apart from eloquent talk, what harm could he do?

In this blissful confidence, Rutherford entered Legislature Hall, the temporary chamber behind the Terrace Building, on Thursday, Feb. 10, 1910. "What is promised to be an uneventful session of the Legislature opened today," wrote the *Edmonton Bulletin* (in what could stand for the whole century as one of Alberta journalism's most celebrated misapprehensions). Rutherford listened serenely while Lieutenant-

The ensuing three months revealed that intrigue and skulduggery had been encircling him for at least a year.

Governor Bulyea read the throne speech, and then placidly heard Bennett read off a series of predictable questions on the Waterways contract.

The following afternoon, Friday, came the first real shock. John R. Boyle, the Edmonton lawyer and Liberal member for Sturgeon, was on his feet with more questions on the A&GW, and a demand for production of documents. While they were reasonable enough, they sounded like opposition questions. The House adjourned until Tuesday, while the Tory *Journal* observed that Boyle's questions "will serve to clear the Waterways contract from charges of graft which have hovered around it from the start." Then the editorial added ominously: "Bennett and Boyle say, 'Wait till Tuesday.'"

Over the weekend Rutherford's calm was shattered, as he discovered what a less sanguine premier would have known for months. Much of his caucus was in full revolt, and clearly in contact with the Tory press. "Rumours of Strife in Liberal Party — Minister of Public Works Rumoured to Have Resigned," headlined the *Journal* on Monday. The accompanying story said that sixteen members had lined up with "the insurgents," the term that would henceforth be used to describe them. Cushing had been asked whether he intended to quit and had replied: "I never like to fore-

Provincial Archives of Alberta, A-1424

Peace River's Cornwall: He was Clarke's secret partner.

Glenbow Archives, NA-1351-2

Tory leader Bennett: 'We've been made a laughing stock,' he declared.

[4]Several days before the bombshell session of 1910 opened, Cushing, his senior minister in the south, wrote testily to Rutherford: "I enclose another letter regarding payment of the school site in Calgary. It is now four years since you sent me to Calgary to make this purchase. Is it possible to have this amount paid at once?" This concerned the site for the provincial normal school which the province had acquired from the Calgary School Board.

Deputy A-G Woods:
He drew up the contract.

cast my intentions." It was the first of a hundred blows Rutherford would suffer as the ensuing three months revealed that a widening orbit of intrigue and downright skulduggery had been encircling him for at least a year. Indeed, he had been living in a dream, which now rapidly resolved into a nightmare.

The target, apart from himself, was plainly Attorney-General Cross, whom Boyle detested. Cross's deputy, Sydney B. Woods, had handled the Waterways contract and the bond issue. But the leader of the insurgents must surely be Cushing, who had missed the opening two days of the sitting because he was ostensibly laid up in his room at the King Edward Hotel with a cold.[5] Instead, Rutherford now discovered, he had been holding caucus meetings there with the insurgents. Rutherford spent the weekend trying to talk Cushing around without success. On Monday Cushing handed in a written resignation and cleared his personal belongings out of his office. His resignation was announced in the *Journal* Tuesday. When the House sat that afternoon, the galleries were jammed and people even waited outside. "The proceedings were of the tamest variety," reported the *Bulletin*, not quite accurately. The first collision had occurred.

Boyle's questions were answered. The directors of the A&GW were Clarke, William Bain and G.D. Minty, the latter both of Winnipeg. The requisite $50,000 paid-up capital of the A&GW had indeed been posted by the company's principals at the Merchants Bank in Edmonton. The $7,400,000 proceedings from the bond issue were on deposit as follows: $6 million with the Royal Bank, $1 million with the Dominion, $400,000 with the Union. It was drawing interest at 3 1/2%. (The company must pay 5% to the bondholders.)

Boyle now spoke, undisguised, as an opposition member. Were the rumours of the Cushing resignation true, he asked? He noted the newspaper reports and the empty seat. Rutherford, still hoping to reconcile Cushing, replied: "I do not credit all newspaper reports. I have no intimation to make regarding a resignation in the cabinet."

"Are we to understand," snapped Boyle, "that the premier does not consider that the House is entitled to this information?" "The prime minister has stated," replied Rutherford (using the then-acceptable title of a provincial premier), "that he has no communication to make to the House."

That night, reported the *Journal*, the insurgents were closeted at the King Edward until midnight. The following day, Thursday, Cushing appeared in the House and sat as a private member; Rutherford announced his departure from the cabinet, and tabled the resignation letter and his

reply. Cushing said he did not agree with the terms of the Waterways contract, and knew nothing of them until the details had been tabled in the House. He told Rutherford: "You have utterly failed to protect the interests of the people." In his reply Rutherford said that Cushing had attended every one of several cabinet meetings at which the terms had been discussed. Cushing said he hoped to make a further statement Monday.

Then came more trouble. Boyle declared that vital documents were missing from the material supplied the House on the contracts. Cross, whose department kept most of it, said he knew of nothing relevant that had not been produced. Meanwhile the war continued in the press. The *Calgary Herald* chided the *Edmonton Bulletin* for not commenting on the story. The Edmonton paper replied: "The *Bulletin* is inclined to an old-fashioned and perhaps now unpopular notion that a newspaper should wait till it knows what it is talking about before offering an opinion on it." It doubted the *Herald* would understand such an inhibition, however.

When the House returned after the weekend, hundreds waited outside the Terrace Building to hear first what was going on inside, the gallery being packed. Boyle promptly escalated the conflict. He served notice of a motion to cancel the Waterways contract and have a government commission take over the railway. His motion gave reasons: a line to Fort McMurray needed to be only 230 miles, not the 350 provided for in the contract, so the project was grotesquely over-capitalized. The government had made no estimate of its own on the job, in fact a government engineer had not been appointed to inspect it until that month. The construction specifications were inadequate. The guarantee was exorbitant. This was a

Sturgeon's Boyle:
He teamed up with the Tories.

Cushing told Rutherford: 'You have utterly failed to protect the interests of the people.'

motion of non-confidence. If it passed, Rutherford was out. At the same time, Boyle and Bennett castigated the government for "stripping the files" of the Attorney-General's Department. Documents were missing, they insisted.

Cushing still declined to speak. He would do so during debate on the Boyle motion, he said. This was set to begin on Thursday, the 24th. "The air has been charged with rumour," fumed the Liberal *Bulletin,* "and the public led to expect a cyclone of unknown proportions...Gossips who write and gossips who talk have been wagging their busy pens and tongues." The *Calgary News* deplored "the hysterical speculation fostered by the *Albertan* and the *Herald.*"

Cushing led off the debate Thursday. He declared that he had attended only one cabinet meeting at which the contract had been discussed, had warned Rutherford that he trusted neither Clarke nor Clarke's engineer, J.A.L. Waddell, on the estimates, and was shocked to discover jurisdiction over railways being taken away from his department. Then, dramatically, he offered to post a $500,000 bond guaranteeing that he himself would build the line at $16,000 a mile on a proper standard, or $12,000 on the present Clarke standard. "The issue is not a sectarian one and is not a question of north against south," he declared.

Rutherford in reply saw more to the revolt than mere opposition to a contract. "There is a nest of traitors in the Liberal ranks," he declared. "If it had not been for our railway policy Cushing would not have been elected. His statement that he can build the road for $16,000 is a big bluff. We have our engineer's estimate that the road will cost $29,135 per mile."

The insurgents shouted at Rutherford: "Call his bluff! Call his bluff!" And Boyle angrily described the A&GW contract as "the most careless, slipshod arrangement ever made by any government." He added: "If, because I disagree with this railway policy, I am a traitor, then I prefer to be one." Roared E.H. Riley, Liberal member for Gleichen and a close friend of Cushing's: "I say to the premier, 'Will you call his bluff?' An effort has been made to stampede this House

[5]The King Edward, an ornate four-storey brick structure with corner-suite balconies topped by a sort of bell-tower roof, had been opened in 1906 at First Street (101st) and Athabasca Avenue (102nd). It would survive until it burned in 1978, much of this time one of Edmonton's more fashionable hotels. It was replaced by the Manulife Building which opened in 1983.

An Edmonton Journal *cartoonist reacts to the disappearance of the A&GW directors, April 14, 1910.*

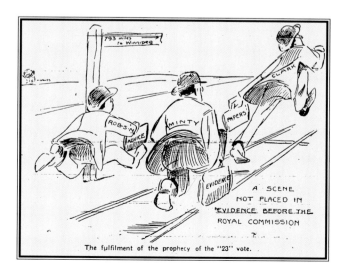

Edmonton's McDougall:
He voted against his own motion.

on the grounds that it is an effort of the south to prevent the development of the North. I say to the premier: 'Dare to be a Daniel and tear up this agreement.'" He thereupon ripped a copy of it in two before the awestruck galleries.

Until the end of the month the debate continued in this vein, the House for the first time sitting late, often till midnight, and Rutherford rousing further suspicions by refusing the press access to the tabled documents. "Premier's Secrecy Futile and Absurd," headlined an editorial in the *Journal,* which informed the premier: "Alberta boasts some of the cleverest reporters in the Dominion of Canada if not in America." They would find out what was in the documents anyway, just as they had found out about Cushing's resignation. In the meantime, "it leaves room for the impression the government has something to hide."

By March 5 the government had offered an amendment to the Boyle motion that effectively whitewashed the issue. It was seconded by John A. McDougall, the long-time merchant, former mayor and now junior member for Edmonton. But on that date the event occurred that the public had been waiting for. R.B. Bennett, arriving after the weekend by special train from Calgary and attired in characteristic elegance, spoke to the amendment. It was a performance such as the Alberta House had never before seen. It went on for one hour before the supper break and four hours after, an exhibition of oratorical grandeur that even the *Bulletin* felt constrained to admire.

Bennett made specific charges. He said that Clarke had sold the bonds to Morgans at par, and Morgans had sold them at a 10% premium, so that there was a $740,000 profit, about $200,000 to $300,000 of which was returned to Clarke as a "rake-off." There would be other rake-offs. The Canada West Construction Company which was to build the over-priced road was "nothing more nor less than a subsidiary of the Alberta and Great Waterways Railway." Its

Cushing sat with folded hands, a look of approbation blended with a sort of admiring pride on his face...

president was Bertrand R. Clarke, brother of William R. "Large financial interests," said Bennett, had attempted to bribe him to keep quiet about this whole matter.

He listed documents missing from the official files — correspondence with Morgans, for instance. "These papers are not here. Where are they? If we cannot have the documents, then at least give us the sacred ashes!"

Among papers that *were* there, he produced the working copy of the original act. Clauses appearing in all the other railway contracts had been struck out in the case of the A&GW. A requirement for provincially chartered railways that at least two directors live in the province had been eliminated. Another, which would have opened the company's books to public inspection, carried the notation: "Objected to. See C.W.C." And who acted for the A&GW Railway? Oliver Mowat Biggar, a partner in the attorney-general's former law firm.[6] In another amendment the bond guarantee on siding construction was doubled to $40,000, although sidings could usually be built for half the cost of the line beside them.

The Bennett assault undoubtedly distressed the Rutherford caucus. "During the entire speech, the treasury benches were uneasy," said the *Journal,* "and the nervous alarm among the government supporters, as to who would be next to be singled out for the terrific rain of invective, was noticeable."

Reported the *Herald*:

Scathing, denunciating, simple and plain, the words of Bennett poured forth upon the government benches, having no effect on the attorney-general, except to make him take more notes, having no effect appreciably on the pleasant mask of the premier, though doubtless the shafts went deeper and deeper until they rankled. The stoicism showed by the government was scarcely less admirable than the masterly oration of the Calgary speaker. Cushing sat with folded hands, a look of approbation blended with a sort of admiring pride on his face, for this speaker was from his home city. Boyle leaned forward across the desk

Dear Mr. Rutherford:
No doubt the events of the last few months have been more or less unpleasant to you, but I write as one friend to another to assure you that all those who know you have the same regard for you today as before your troubles commenced. There is no cloud upon your personal honour, and, after all, that is what is important.
With best wishes,
Yours faithfully,
J.P. Whitney
Premier of Ontario
June 7, 1910
—From the Rutherford Papers, Provincial Archives of Alberta.

THE CALGARY DAILY HERALD

TWENTY-SEVENTH YEAR, No. 7712.   CALGARY, ALBERTA, WEDNESDAY, MARCH 9, 1910   FAIR AND VERY MILD   10 PAGES

C.W. CROSS RETIRES

and drank in the words, his inscrutable smile coming now and again at some particularly pointed remark.

One member was moved decisively by the Bennett speech. McDougall, who had seconded the government's amendment, pronounced himself persuaded, and declared he would vote with the insurgents and against his own amendment.

Bennett ended his speech with a whole new issue. He charged that one Hopkins, an emissary for Cross just then sitting outside the bar of the House, had informed the Automatic Telephone Company in Calgary before last year's election that the provincial system would buy a $93,000 automatic exchange for Calgary if the company donated $12,000 to Cross's election campaign. Cross leapt to his feet, vehemently denying it. Bennett turned to Cushing. Was this not true, he demanded. "Substantially true," replied Cushing. Bennett accepted the attorney-general's denial, but then called for an investigation of Hopkins' activities. He had not, it was noted, withdrawn the charge.

The Bennett speech gravely shook the government ranks, and as the debate proceeded throughout the following week, Rutherford strove hard to hold his caucus together. Everything he tried made matters worse. He proposed a special commission to supervise the A&GW's work, consisting of himself as Railways minister, the provincial railways engineer appointed in February, and the deputy minister of Public Works. The last, John Stock, a Cushing appointee, promptly announced he would not serve.

Then Rutherford went to Cushing, offering him his old portfolio back in a cabinet that did not include Cross. Cushing turned him down, and on March 9 the biggest bombshell of all burst. Cross resigned. He was unwilling, he said, to serve in a cabinet that included Cushing. He did not know that Cushing wouldn't serve in it either. Then Buchanan quit, denouncing the A&GW contract and declaring he would vote with the insurgents. Deputy attorney-general Woods quit, and Rutherford refused to accept his resignation. When the House met on March 10 Rutherford was alone on the front bench with Marshall and Lessard. Meanwhile Cross announced that he was returning to the law firm of Short, Cross & Biggar — which would become Short, Cross, Biggar & Woods with the expected addition of the former deputy attorney-general.

The newspapers began writing Rutherford's political

6 The Edmonton lawyer, Oliver Mowat Biggar, was a grandson of Sir Oliver Mowat, a Father of Confederation and premier of Ontario from 1872 to 1896. He was also a nephew of William Hodgins Biggar, general counsel for the Grand Trunk Pacific, for whom the town of Biggar, Saskatchewan, is named.

Calgary Daily Herald *cartoon of May 27, 1910 depicts Rutherford abed and Clarke reaching for the Provincial Guarantee.*

SAFEGUARDING THE PROVINCE!

obituary. "Government Will Probably Admit Defeat at This Afternoon's Session of the House," headlined the *Journal,* and in the accompanying story it announced the new "insurgent" cabinet: Cushing as premier and Public Works minister, Boyle as attorney-general, Riley and McDougall as ministers without portfolio, Dr. David Warnock, a veterinarian of Pincher Creek, as minister of Agriculture, and George P. Smith of Camrose as minister of Education. The Liberal caucus had met the previous evening, reported the *Journal.* Rutherford had made a proposal under which he could remain in office, but the caucus had rejected him. Rutherford would resign today.

This time America's greatest reporters proved wrong. If Rutherford couldn't hold a majority, neither could Cushing. So Rutherford adopted another expedient. He would remain in office and try to weather the motion of confidence. If he did, he would put a money supply bill through so the government could carry on, and then appoint a royal commission to examine the whole Waterways question. On March 11 he returned to the House. Beside him on the front bench was Cross, now back in the government. Several days later the insurgents were defeated 20-17, the two Tories and one independent voting with fourteen insurgent Liberals.[7]

Lethbridge's Buchanan:
He joined the insurgents.

Thereafter Rutherford easily gained passage of his supply bill and named as a commission three judges of the Supreme Court — D.L. Scott, Horace Harvey and N.D. Beck — to find out if any member of the Legislature or government had an "interest" in the Waterways Railway contract. The opposition press objected. This meant the commission would not concern itself with the merits of the contract, merely with the possibility of collusion. The resolution was passed, however, and the House adjourned until May 26 to see what the judges would discover.

That was on March 19, 1910, and the judges met as a commission ten days later in Legislature Hall. Before them were the assembled luminaries of Alberta politics: the premier, along with his counsel, P.J. "Paddy" Nolan, the celebrated Calgary lawyer; the attorney-general with his former law partner Oliver Biggar as counsel; Peace River's Jim Cornwall with a Regina lawyer, Norman Mackenzie; and (the judges doubtless shuddered to see) Calgary lawyer R.B. Bennett representing, as he said, "sixteen members of the Legislature commonly known as the insurgents." Beside Bennett was Edmonton lawyer E.E. Parlee, also for the insurgents. Finally there was a Winnipeg

Justices Harvey, Scott and Beck:
They didn't say, 'Not guilty,' but
rather, 'Not proven.'

lawyer, Hugh A. Robson[8], representing the Alberta and Great Waterways Railway and its president, William R. Clarke.

The preliminaries over, Robson addressed the commission. "An insinuation has been rather broadly spread," he declared, doubtless looking directly at the press table, "that Mr. Clarke, the president of the railway company whom I represent, would not be here. Now I wish to take the opportunity of stating, in order that it may be as fairly stated as the other report was, that is entirely uninformed, and that Mr. Clarke will be here to testify in proper time."

Documents were then piled before the commissioners representing, they were assured, everything in the government's possession that pertained to the A&GW contract. The commission adjourned until April 14 to give time to read it all. When they reassembled on that date to begin public hearings, however, Calgary lawyer William L. Walsh, who was serving as one of two com-

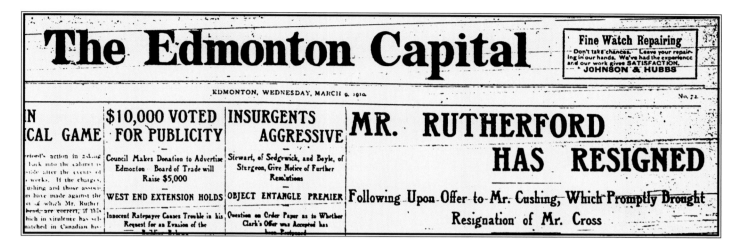

The Edmonton Capital

Fine Watch Repairing
Don't take chances. Leave your repairing in our hands. We've had the experience and our work gives SATISFACTION.
JOHNSON & HUBBS

EDMONTON, WEDNESDAY, MARCH 9, 1910.

No. 72.

IN CAL GAME

$10,000 VOTED FOR PUBLICITY

Council Makes Donation to Advertise Edmonton — Board of Trade will Raise $5,000

WEST END EXTENSION HOLDS

Innocent Ratepayer Causes Trouble in his Request for an Evasion of the

INSURGENTS AGGRESSIVE

Stewart, of Sedgewick, and Boyle, of Sturgeon, Give Notice of Further Resolutions

OBJECT ENTANGLE PREMIER

Question on Order Paper as to Whether Clark's Offer was Accepted has

MR. RUTHERFORD HAS RESIGNED

Following Upon Offer to Mr. Cushing, Which Promptly Brought Resignation of Mr. Cross

mission counsels, made the announcement that finally doomed the Rutherford government. That at any rate is the conclusion of Lewis G. Thomas in his history of the Alberta Liberal Party.[9]

That morning, said Walsh, a letter had been delivered to him announcing that Clarke would not be appearing before the commission. His counsel, Winnipeg lawyer Robson, had likewise withdrawn and left the province, thereby putting himself beyond the subpoena of the Alberta court. An A&GW director, George Minty, a Winnipeg lawyer, had agreed to testify, but only on condition the commission go to Manitoba to hear him. The commission was later told that Clarke was on his way to the hearings when he abruptly left the train at Swift Current, after learning he would be subject to questioning by Bennett as counsel for the insurgents. Bennett, as a CPR lawyer, knew far more about the industry than any of the judges or the other lawyers. "In view of these developments which have only arisen in the last half hour," said Walsh, "my learned friend, Mr. Johnstone, and I are nonplussed." (The other commission counsel was L.M. Johnstone of Lethbridge.)

Bennett sprang to his feet. "The continuance of this investigation will be nothing more than a farce," he declared. He said that both Minty and Robson had been in the city as late as nine o'clock the previous night and should have been subpoenaed. "In a Winnipeg court we will have no power to compel evidence. It means this commission is to be a laughing stock of a few bounders who live entirely outside of the province...Here is a company whose head office is in this province, incorporated by this Legislature, three of whose directors are outside of its jurisdiction and decline to come here to give evidence, and the secretary is sick."

All of which seemed patently true. There remained those whom the commission could examine, however, and in the course of the next nine weeks it took 3,226 pages of typewritten evidence. It heard Minty in Winnipeg. It asked the Missouri courts to honour its subpoena there, but was

Glenbow Archives, NA-1147-1

Counsel Johnstone: 'What checks had been made on Clarke, Mr. Premier?'

[7]Charles M. O'Brien, the socialist member for Rocky Mountain, after lecturing the House at length on the deplorable waywardness of unscrupulous capitalism, voted with the government.

[8]Hugh Amos Robson was a distinguished counsel in the West. Former assistant attorney-general in the territorial government, he was named to the Manitoba Court of King's Bench at the height of the Waterways controversy, and later became a member of the Manitoba Public Utilities Commission and in 1929 a member of the Manitoba Court of Appeal.

[9]L.G. Thomas's *The Liberal Party in Alberta: A History of Politics in the Province of Alberta 1905-1921* was by the 1990s the only published account of the fall of the Rutherford government. Douglas R. Babcock's biography of Rutherford, *A Gentleman of Strathcona*, merely touches on it. A 1990 University of Alberta master's thesis by Jay Stewart Heard, entitled "The Alberta and Great Waterways Dispute," goes into more detail on the evidence taken by the commission than anything else undertaken. Thomas bypasses the commission's evidence. It is, in other words, a little-examined area of Alberta history.

turned down. The information it gathered left the Rutherford government unsalvageable. The following are some of its discoveries:

• William R. Clarke had in effect put no money into the A&GW Railway. His supposed "paid-up capital" of $50,000 had been achieved by opening an account at the Merchants Bank in Edmonton, overdrawing it by $50,000, paying the money to the railway so that it showed as paid in, presenting the railway with a $50,000 bill for his fees as promoter and drawing the money out again, then using the $50,000 received for the fee to retire the overdraft.

• Clarke's engineer, Waddell, had two estimates on the cost of the Waterways railway — one for $17,000 a mile (with one variable opinion that reduced this to as low as $6,000 a mile) which he provided to Clarke, and another for $26,000 a mile which Clarke provided to the government.

• The maximum commission that the Morgan company could have taken on the bond sale was 3%. Therefore of the 10% premium paid for the Alberta-guaranteed A&GW bonds, at least 7% or $518,000 was left over and available for what Bennett had called Clarke's "rake-off." There was no evidence Clarke had taken such a rake-off, but Clarke couldn't be examined.

• It so happened that Clarke formed the Canada West Construction Company with a cash capitalization of $500,000 at the same time this money would have become available.

• Clarke was in active partnership with J.K. Cornwall from 1907 onward, and had a contract to buy a controlling interest in Cornwall's Northern Transportation Company. However, this occurred before Cornwall became an MLA in the 1909 election.

• Though he was Cornwall's intimate friend and had been his solicitor, Attorney-General Cross swore before the commission that he had no knowledge of the business arrangement between Cornwall and Clarke.

• In A&GW correspondence, repeated references were made to Clarke's "friend" in the Alberta government. Minty identified the "friend" as the attorney-general.

• The commission discovered in the Edmonton telegraph office copies of some sixty telegrams between Attorney-General Cross, Minty and Clarke, and also between Minty and deputy attorney-general Woods. None of these had been filed with the commission.

• At the time the bonds were turned over to Morgans in New York, Attorney-General Cross

Glenbow Archives,
NA-1296-1

Counsel Walsh:
'We have been left nonplussed,' he said.

The premier, he intimated, was the tool in the hands of the attorney-general, and the attorney-general was the man behind, the man that was engineering the deal.
– From the Edmonton Journal of March 6, 1910, reporting on the speech by R.B. Bennett in the Legislature on the Waterways railway contract.

A.L. Sifton, brother of the great Clifford, close-mouthed, not brilliant but shrewd, and known unaffectionately as 'Little Arthur.'

was believed by his office to be holidaying in Hawaii. Actually he was in New York with Cornwall. Cornwall and Clarke said their presence in New York was mere coincidence.

• Preparations for Cross's visit to New York, however, were made by Clarke and Minty.

• Cross's private secretary, along with one of Clarke's employees, went to the Legislature Hall close to midnight March 8, the eve of Cross's brief resignation from the Rutherford cabinet, took fifteen to twenty boxes of Cross's personal files from the attorney-general's office, and brought them in two wagons to the private secretary's home. The commission never did question Cross about this. The judges may have assumed the incident was connected with Cross's resignation.

None of this, however, constituted direct evidence that a member of the Legislature or government had an "interest" in Clarke's enterprises, apart from Cornwall who had acquired his interest before he became an MLA. (There was no such thing as disclosure rules in those days.) In testimony before the commission, nothing more was conceded. Examples:

The examination of the attorney-general on why Clarke referred to him as "friend":

Commission counsel Walsh: Minty in his evidence tells us you are the party referred to as "your friend." Can you state what warrant Minty had in referring to you in these words?

Cross: I cannot. Of course, I assume a great many people refer to me as being their friend. Sometimes I am their friend and sometimes I am not.

Walsh: Was there any particular reason as far as you are aware why your name should not have been spelled right out in the letter? It is not a long name.

Cross: No reason at all.

Walsh: It [a Minty letter to Clarke] spells out "Cornwall" which is a longer name…"Cornwall and your friend."

Cross: No reason as far as I am concerned.

Walsh: I suppose there hadn't been any arrangement between you and Minty and Clarke that reference to you should be made in this mysterious manner?

Cross: Absolutely none. I wish he had referred to me by my own name.

On how Cross could possibly not have known his close friend Cornwall had a business relationship with Clarke:

Walsh: There is no doubt in the world Cornwall was personally interested in seeing this go through.

Cross: There is no doubt about that.

Walsh: There is no doubt you and he were on terms of great intimacy, personal and professional, in December 1908.

Cross: Yes, but I want to say this to you, that I never discussed with Cornwall or with any of my friends matters of government policy or matters that took place in cabinet meetings. I have never been that way. I don't talk to any of my friends along lines of that character.

On Cross's meeting with Clarke in New York at the time the bonds were sold:

Cross: I met him in the hotel — at least he came to see me — in the Waldorf.

Walsh: Was the meeting with Mr. Clarke prearranged or accidental?

Cross: It wasn't prearranged as far as I was concerned. At least, he may have been following my movements. I don't know.

Walsh: Well, was there any reason why any meeting should take place between you and him then, so far as the railway was concerned?

Glenbow Archives, NA-1514-4

Premier Rutherford in 1910: In a few short weeks, his dream was shattered.

Cross: No. Absolutely none.

Walsh: Well, we have here, Mr. Cross, a telegram...

Cross: Except this — that I would have been very anxious to have the railway built. If I could have seen him, I would certainly have urged upon him the necessity of getting busy with his road.

Walsh: (Reading the telegram, discovered in the telegraph office, from Minty to Clarke) Minty says, 'Friend has already started east.' Minty has testified this meant Cross.

Cross: He didn't know that from me.

Later the attorney-general was cross-examined by Bennett on why he had not filed the telegrams with the commission:

Cross: I think you will notice that some of them were written by a clerk in my office, to whom I may have telephoned, or I may have sent the telegram without keeping a copy.

Bennett: Those telegrams would hardly have been sent without your authority.

Cross: I'm not suggesting that for a moment.

Bennett: A very considerable number of them were sent to you. Can you say why these should not be in the files of the government?

Cross: I assume none of them were important so far as the province is concerned.

Bennett: They all refer to a public matter.

Cross: Yes and to a private member of the Legislature urging on Mr. Clarke to build the railway.

Bennett: You sent them as a private member, not as attorney-general?

Cross: I sent them as member for Edmonton...That is the best explanation I can give you.

Bennett: But it had escaped your mind. You had forgotten you received them.

Cross: I had forgotten them.

Bennett: Just a passing circumstance in your life.

Cross: I'm telling you, Mr. Bennett, I didn't remember them. If you don't believe it, I don't care.

Bennett: (later concluding) To make it perfectly clear, you have no interest, and know of no interest, being held for you or on your behalf, for any person or persons in connection with Mr. Clarke's enterprise or any of them?

Cross: I absolutely have no interest of any kind.

Rutherford himself was questioned on how much checking he had done on Clarke before committing the province to a $7,400,000 deal with him:

Commission counsel Johnstone: Did you have any better idea who he was than you did at first (i.e. at their first meeting)?

Rutherford: Oh yes, there were letters from banking people.

Johnstone: These are the letters no doubt which appear in Mr. Cross's file?

Rutherford: I presume so. They were from financial institutions.

Johnstone: You have no recollection of ever having seen any other documents referring to Mr. Clarke's standing than these?

Rutherford: No, we have not.

Johnstone: Are these all you had seen at that time?

Rutherford: Mr. Clarke himself, I remember, had a letter from some bank, some financial institution in Kansas City, referring to his standing.

Johnstone: From the bank in Kansas City?

Rutherford: In Kansas City.

Johnstone: And these are all the credentials that you ever saw concerning Mr. Clarke? All that you have seen?

Rutherford: Yes.

Long before the commission's hearings ended in July, events at the political level reached a crisis. The House had adjourned until May 26. Whatever was to happen to Rutherford must be decided before then. But decided by whom? By the Rutherford loyalists? By the insurgents? By the party as a whole meeting in convention? There was an answer to this question, unthinkable to provincial politicians of a later day, but not then: Obviously the decision must be made in Ottawa. Laurier assigned the problem to his three chief Alberta lieutenants: Frank Oliver, George Bulyea and Senator Peter Talbot, the same three who had chosen Rutherford to begin with.

That Rutherford must go was certain, but who would replace him? Oliver was out for three reasons. First, he didn't want it. Second, since he had been so long in Ottawa, he had little personal following left even in Edmonton. Finally, he was viewed by the loyalists as the implicit foe of Cross and the behind-the-scenes sponsor of the Cushing-Boyle revolt. Talbot was also disadvantaged. He didn't want it either, and was probably unacceptable to both groups in the Legislature.

What about Cushing? But he was now doubly disqualified. First, the whole Rutherford wing of the party would never have him. Second, his performance before the Waterways commission had been disastrous for him. It seemed conclusive that he had indeed attended the meetings he denied attending and consented by silence to the contract he was attacking.

It came down therefore to a single candidate — the enigmatic individual who had once served as Haultain's senior lieutenant and had become chief justice of Alberta when Haultain refused the job — Arthur Lewis Sifton, older brother of the great Clifford, tough, close-mouthed, not brilliant but distinctly shrewd, and known (but only behind his back and not affectionately) as Little Arthur. That Little Arthur should be unenthusiastic about stepping into such a rats' nest seemed understandable and it took Bulyea from March 9 until May

Lieutenant-Governor Bulyea: He couldn't sleep the whole night.

Lessard nonchalantly watered the lawn hour after hour to allay suspicion. By nine in the evening, a deal was made.

17 to persuade him. But that was only part of the problem. Sifton must be accepted by the two warring factions, neither of whom wanted him because he would probably form a cabinet that excluded anyone prominent on either side.

The task of breaking the news to both sides fell to Talbot, who was president of the Alberta Liberal Association. He met some of the insurgents in Buchanan's room at the Yale Hotel, and simply told them Sifton was the new leader. There was an uproar. G.P. Smith, a Camrose school principal slated for the education ministry in the Cushing government, was especially wrath. "I have delivered the message," said Talbot and he left. Cushing, meanwhile, was sitting expectantly beside the telephone at the King Edward (an *Edmonton Journal* reporter spied on him through the door transom) waiting for Bulyea to call. The phone did not ring.

On May 2 a secret caucus of both groups finally gave a tentative approval, but the Rutherford forces soon backed away from it. When Sifton arrived in Edmonton on Tuesday, May 24, two days before the House was to meet, there was still no agreement. Bulyea later told Saskatchewan Premier Walter Scott that he was beside himself with worry. On Wednesday the press simply announced without confirmation that Sifton would become premier. But it was far from certain. With the House slated to meet the following afternoon, Rutherford people came and went by ones and twos at the home of Rutherford minister Prosper E. Lessard on Fifth Street (105th), while Lessard nonchalantly watered the lawn hour after hour to allay suspicion. Finally by nine o'clock in the evening, a deal was made. The Rutherford group would accept Sifton provided Cross stayed in the government. This was communicated to Sifton, who turned the deal down. He didn't want Cross under any circumstances.

It was now about 2 a.m., thirteen hours to go, and Rutherford still had not resigned. Bulyea told Scott he couldn't sleep the whole of that night. He saw Rutherford in the morning. What was said between them no one has ever reported. But by 11 a.m., he had Rutherford's resignation. Bulyea wrote Scott: "This has been an awful mess and an awful bunch to handle. I confess I do not want to go through the same again."

Rutherford loyalist Prosper Lessard: The parties came and went all day.

When the House met, Rutherford was in the premier's place and Cross in his accustomed seat beside him, yet something was different. Rutherford, said the *Lethbridge Herald,* "looked pale and worn, and as he entered the House alone and took his seat he made a rather pitiful figure. He had been proud of his position as prime minister of Alberta. The rapid dissolution of his following was a severe blow to him."

The House first formally passed a message of condolence to the Royal Family on the death on May 6 of King Edward VII. That accomplished, and with the members still on their feet, the lieutenant-governor suddenly appeared, dressed not in his accustomed uniform of office, but in a tweed suit with a bowler hat. Said Bulyea: "I have to announce to you that the resignation of Premier Rutherford was placed in my hands this morning and has been accepted by me, and I have called upon the Hon. A.L. Sifton to form a government, and he has assumed that responsibility and has been sworn in as president of the executive council. It is my will that Premier Sifton shall submit the personnel of his cabinet and his policy to the members of this Legislative Assembly for ratification at an early date, due notice of which will be given you. In the meantime it is my will that the meeting of the Legislative Assembly be prorogued, and I do declare it formally prorogued." He then wished them a happy summer, and left. No doubt for a few seconds the members stared at each other in seeming disbelief. Suddenly the whole row was over. Bennett and the *Journal* called the act unconstitutional, but what could be done about it?

The following evening, in one of the more extraordinary exhibitions in Alberta politics, a huge number of Edmontonians — the estimates ran to "thousands" — paraded behind two bands down Jasper Avenue to the Windsor Hotel. They bore a big banner that read: "Cross for Attorney-General." They were determined their man should get into the Sifton cabinet.

Speeches followed from the Windsor's balcony — by ex-premier Rutherford, Paddy Nolan and Cross himself, who vowed that he would serve Sifton as he had Rutherford. He then introduced to the crowd "the girl whom I love," Mrs. Cross, and to a resounding three cheers and the screech of bagpipes, the meeting broke up. The point had been to pressure Sifton into accepting Cross, of course, which he did not do. Indeed in the cabinet he announced the following Monday, as was foreseen, none of the principals of the Waterways fight was included.

In the meantime, Sifton did not call the House until November, giving him six months to clean up the mess. When the House assembled, the commission report was finally made public. Mr. Justice Harvey and Mr. Justice Scott found that no member of the government or the Legislature had an "interest" in the A&GW contract except Cornwall, whose activities they did not criticize. But they deplored the contract itself as ill-conceived and a terrible deal for the province. Mr. Justice Beck dissented only in observing that his two fellow judges had exculpated Cushing. He had concluded that Cushing was as much to blame for the contract as his two fellow ministers. It was noteworthy, and the Tory press pointed out, that the judges did not pronounce the principals in the affair as "not guilty," merely that the case against them was "not proven."

As Arthur Sifton left the building after observing the sitting from the Legislature gallery, a reporter asked him for an announcement on his cabinet. "The only thing I have to announce," he replied coldly, "is that I have nothing to announce until Monday." This was in sharp contrast to the affable Rutherford. It was very plain that in the next decade Alberta would have a very different premier. But then, Alberta would also have a very different decade.

Index

policy, 179; Peigan, 171, 175; Peigan reserve, 179; ranching, 171, 174; restrictive legislation, 170, 171; Sarcee, 171; schools, 172, 173, 174, 175; Slaveys, 169; Stoneys, 171, 179; treaties, 169, 170; Woods Cree, 196

Industry (see Economics and Industry)

Innisfail, 75

J

James Short School, 120

Jeffers, Allan M., 94

Johnson, Pauline, 323

K

Kerby, Rev. George, 386, 387

King Edward Hotel, 426, 427, 435

King, Charles, 382-383

Kirby, Rev. W.J., 386, 387, 404

King, William L.M., 213, 214, 215-216

Klondike, 169, 301

Kootenay Plains, 179

L

Lacombe, Father Albert, 50, 161, 268, 271, 272

Lacombe (town), 47, 56, 160, 182, 185, 272, 344

Lake Athabasca, 274

Lake Louise, 242, 245, 246, 248

Laurier, Sir Wilfrid, 30, 34, 37, 39, 40-49, 53-57, 59, 60, 61, 63, 65, 72, 74, 103, 104, 108, 109, 111, 112, 184, 215, 284, 345, 409, 410, 412, 415, 420, 435

LaZerte, M.E., 292

Leduc, 65, 198

Lessard, Prosper, 435

Lesser Slave Lake, 109, 275, 411, 412, 418

Lethbridge, 181, 185, 187, 191, 233, 251

Lethbridge Herald, 72, 158, 185, 187, 188, 213, 214, 215, 216, 222, 232, 243, 253, 343, 353, 365, 379, 403, 424, 436

Lloyd, Rev. G.E., 59, 162, 163, 164

Lloydminster, 113, 137

Lougheed, Senator James, 47, 78, 120, 191, 193, 421

Lumbering industry, 245, 260, 261

Luxton, Norman K., 245, 247

Lyric Theatre, 220, 321

M

Macdonald, Sir John A., 16, 396

MacEwan, Grant, 30, 31, 68, 121, 125

MacGregor, James G., 355

Mackintosh, C.H., 30, 68

Mackintosh, Marion St. Clair, 29, 30, 31, 33, 36, 43, 51, 61, 68, 69

Mackenzie, William, 56, 103, 104, 105, 107, 108, 111, 113, 115, 117

Mackid, Dr. Harry G., 304, 305

MacLean, Dr. James D., 99

MacLeod, Malcolm H., 106, 107

Macleod Gazette, 78, 339, 341, 365

Macleod (town) 31, 63

Macoun, James, 412, 413

Manitoba Act, 411

Mann, Donald, 56, 103, 104, 107, 108, 111, 113, 115, 117

Mannville, 160

May, Mayor Gus, 90, 91, 92

McCaig, James, 296

McCarthy, Maitland S., 75, 77, 78

McCauley, Matt, 85

McClung, Nellie, 404

McDougall, John A., 90, 92, 94, 95, 97, 100, 428, 429, 430

McDougall, Rev. John., 269

McInnes, Dr. Herman L., 305

McKay School, 82, 83

McLeod River, 116

Meat Packing Industry, 264, 265

Medical facilities: 298-307; hospitals, 307-308; Ponoka Mental Hospital, 308; rural care, 307, 311, 312

Medicine Hat (town), 47, 59, 74, 105, 181, 185, 187, 191, 218, 233, 320, 367

Medicine Hat News, 33, 85

Mewburn, Dr. F.H., 304, 305, 306

Midwifery, 245, 361

Minto, Lord, 167

Moore, John T., 72, 75

Motherwell, William R., 37, 213

Mulock, William, 42, 55

N

Nanton, 208

News and newspaper: 338-351; circulation, 338-339; costs, 342; editors and publishers, 339, 340, 341, 342, 343, 346-348, 351; flimsies, 343

Nolan, Paddy, 386, 430, 436

Nordegg, Martin, 137

North Saskatchewan River, 100, 113

North-West Mounted Police (also Royal North-West Mounted Police), 15, 18, 64, 81, 141, 154, 155, 157, 208, 211, 212, 227, 230, 248, 266, 277, 300, 325, 343, 388, 403

Norwood School, 99

Nursing: 309-311; association, 309; training, 309; wages, 310

O

O'Brien, Charles M., 217, 222, 223

Oblates of Mary Immaculate, 268, 269, 274, 275

Old Scona High School, 99

Olds (town), 160, 166

Olds, The Battle of, 187

Oliver, Frank, 32, 38, 43, 44, 46, 48, 50, 51, 59-62, 66, 70-78, 83, 115, 131, 215, 272, 343, 344, 345, 351

P

Parks & Tourism: 238-249; access roads, 239, 246, 248; Banff Hot Springs, 238, 239, 240, 242; Elk Island, 240, 247, 248; guiding, 243, 245; history, 239, 240, 241, 242; industry, 242, 243, 245, 246, 248; Jasper Resort, 242, 244, 248; Lake Louise, 242, 243, 245, 246; mountain climbing, 241, 242, 243, 244, 245, 246; paddocks, 246, 247; parks facilities, 239, 242, 243, 245; Rocky Mountains National Park, 238, 240, 245, 248; Waterton Lakes, 240, 242, 248; women in, 244, 248-249

Peace River (town), 412

Peace River, 409, 413

Peace River Crossing, 411

Peace River Country: 408-420; grain growing, 413; railways, 415, 420, 421; steamboats, 416-419; stopping houses, 419

Pedley, Frank, 170, 179

Pinkham, Bishop W. Cyprian, 172, 173

Ponoka, 182

Prince, Peter, 121, 126

Prostitution (see also Crime and Frontier Women): 313, 352; brothels, 362-363

Public Works Health Act, 307

Q

Queen Alexandra School, 293

Queen's Hotel, 115

R

Racism and bigotry (also look under Advertising, Indians), 127, 128, 145, 146, 147, 148, 149, 150, 210, 272, 343, 379, 380

Railways: 102-117, 180-191; builders, 103-109, 111-117, 184; construction, 105, 109, 113, 115, 116, 183, 184;